# THE GREEK TRAGEDIES

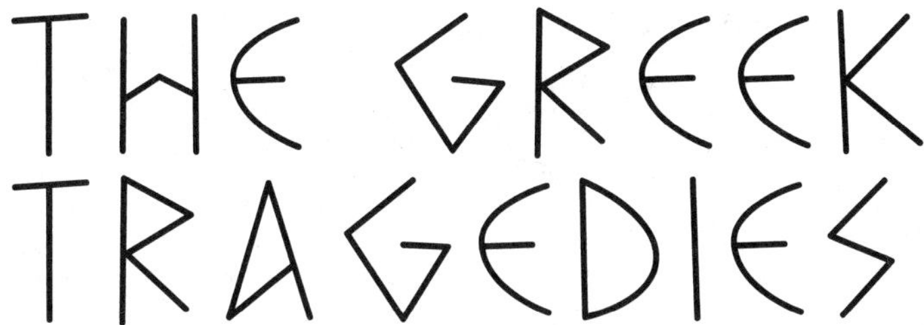

# THE GREEK TRAGEDIES

## Seventeen Plays by Aeschylus, Sophocles & Euripides

Edited by David Grene & Richmond Lattimore

With introductions and notes by
Mark Griffith & Glenn W. Most

*The University of Chicago Press* CHICAGO AND LONDON

The University of Chicago Press, Chicago 60637
The University of Chicago Press, Ltd., London

Published 2025
Printed in the United States of America

34 33 32 31 30 29 28 27 26 25     1 2 3 4 5

ISBN-13: 978-0-226-84469-5 (paper)
ISBN-13: 978-0-226-84468-8 (ebook)
DOI: https://doi.org/10.7208/chicago/9780226844688.001.0001

This volume brings together selected plays from *Aeschylus I* and *II*, *Sophocles I* and *II*, and *Euripides I–III* and *V*, edited by David Grene and Richmond Lattimore, third edition edited by Mark Griffith and Glenn W. Most, published 2013 by the University of Chicago Press.

Library of Congress Control Number: 2025013227

⊗ This paper meets the requirements of ANSI/NISO Z39.48-1992 (Permanence of Paper).

Authorized Representative for EU General Product Safety Regulation (GPSR) queries: **Easy Access System Europe**—Mustamäe tee 50, 10621 Tallinn, Estonia, gpsr.requests@easproject.com
Any other queries: https://press.uchicago.edu/press/contact.html

# CONTENTS

# HOW THE PLAYS WERE ORIGINALLY STAGED

Nearly all the plays composed by Aeschylus, Sophocles, and Euripides were first performed in the Theater of Dionysus at Athens, as part of the annual festival and competition in drama. This was not only a literary and musical event, but also an important religious and political ceremony for the Athenian community. Each year three tragedians were selected to compete, with each of them presenting four plays per day, a "tetralogy" of three tragedies and one satyr-play. The satyr-play was a type of drama similar to tragedy in being based on heroic myth and employing many of the same stylistic features, but distinguished by having a chorus of half-human, half-horse followers of Dionysus—sileni or satyrs—and by always ending happily. Extant examples of this genre are Euripides' *The Cyclops* (in *Euripides*, vol. 5) and Sophocles' *The Trackers* (partially preserved: in *Sophocles*, vol. 2).

The three competing tragedians were ranked by a panel of citizens functioning as amateur judges, and the winner received an honorific prize. Records of these competitions were maintained, allowing Aristotle and others later to compile lists of the dates when each of Aeschylus', Sophocles', and Euripides' plays were first performed and whether they placed first, second, or third in the competition (unfortunately we no longer possess the complete lists).

The tragedians competed on equal terms: each had at his disposal three actors (only two in Aeschylus' and in Euripides' earliest plays) who would often have to switch between roles as each play progressed, plus other nonspeaking actors to play attendants and other subsidiary characters; a chorus of twelve (in Aeschylus' time) or fifteen (for most of the careers of Sophocles and Euripides), who would sing and dance formal songs and whose Chorus Leader would engage in dialogue with the characters or offer comment on the action; and a pipe-player, to accompany the sung portions of the play.

All the performers were men, and the actors and chorus members all wore masks. The association of masks with other Dionysian rituals may have affected their use in the theater; but masks had certain practical advantages as well—for example, making it easy to play female characters and to change quickly between roles. In general, the use of masks also meant that ancient acting techniques must have been rather different from what we are used to seeing in the modern theater. Acting in a mask requires a more frontal and presentational style of performance toward the audience than is usual with unmasked, "realistic" acting; a masked actor must communicate far more by voice and stylized bodily gesture than by facial expression, and the gradual development of a character in the course of a play could hardly be indicated by changes in his or her mask. Unfortunately, however, we know almost nothing about the acting techniques of the Athenian theater. But we do know that the chorus members were all Athenian amateurs, and so were the actors up until the later part of the fifth century, by which point a prize for the best actor had been instituted in the tragic competition, and the art of acting (which of course included solo singing and dancing) was becoming increasingly professionalized.

The tragedian himself not only wrote the words for his play but also composed the music and choreography and directed the productions. It was said that Aeschylus also acted in his plays but that Sophocles chose not to, except early in his career, because his voice was too weak. Euripides is reported to have had a collaborator who specialized in musical composition. The costs for each playwright's production were shared between an individual wealthy citizen, as a kind of "super-tax" requirement, and the city.

The Theater of Dionysus itself during most of the fifth century BCE probably consisted of a large rectangular or trapezoidal dance floor, backed by a one-story wooden building (the *skênê*), with a large central door that opened onto the dance floor. (Some scholars have argued that two doors were used, but the evidence is thin.) Between the *skênê* and the dance floor there may have been a narrow stage on which the characters acted and which communicated easily with the dance floor. For any particular play, the *skênê* might represent a palace, a house, a temple, or a cave, for example; the interior of this "building" was generally invisible to the audience, with all the action staged in front of it. Sophocles is said to have been the first to use painted scenery; this must have been fairly simple and easy to remove, as every play had a different setting. Playwrights did not include stage directions in their texts. Instead, a play's setting was indicated explicitly by the speaking characters.

All the plays were performed in the open air and in daylight. Spectators sat on wooden seats in rows, probably arranged in rectangular blocks along the curving slope of the Acropolis. (The stone semicircular remains of the Theater of Dionysus that are visible today in Athens belong to a later era.) Seating capacity seems to have been four to six thousand—thus a mass audience, but not quite on the scale of the theaters that came to be built during the fourth century BCE and later at Epidaurus, Ephesus, and many other locations all over the Mediterranean.

Alongside the *skênê*, on each side, there were passages through which actors could enter and exit. The acting area included the dance floor, the doorway, and the area immediately in front of the *skênê*. Occasionally an actor appeared on the roof or above it, as if flying. He was actually hanging from a crane (*mêchanê*: hence *deus ex machina*, "a god from the machine"). The *skênê* was also occasionally opened up—the mechanical details are uncertain—in order to show the audience what was concealed within (usually dead bodies). Announcements of entrances and exits, like the setting, were made by the characters. Although the medieval manuscripts of the surviving plays do not provide explicit stage directions, it is usually possible to infer from the words or from the context whether a particular entrance or exit is being made through a door (into the *skênê*) or by one of the side entrances. In later antiquity, there may have been a rule that one side entrance always led to the city center, the other to the countryside or harbor. Whether such a rule was ever observed in the fifth century is uncertain.

# I.

# AESCHYLUS

# INTRODUCTION TO AESCHYLUS

Aeschylus was born sometime in the 520s BCE into an aristocratic family based in Eleusis, twelve miles to the west of central Athens. So he was a teenager when the ruling monarchical family of the Pisistratids was expelled and the first democracy at Athens was created (510–508). As well as becoming the greatest tragic playwright of his generation, Aeschylus fought against the Persians at Marathon (490), where his brother was killed, and in the sea battle at Salamis (480). He began producing plays in the 490s, won his first victory in 484, and continued writing tragedies until shortly before his death in 455. The epitaph that was written on Aeschylus' tomb (in Gela, Sicily)—allegedly composed by him and his family—mentions his service at Marathon against the Persians, but says nothing about his achievement as a playwright.

The titles of over ninety plays by Aeschylus are recorded, though only six survive that can be attributed to him with certainty (scholars are divided about the authenticity of the *Prometheus Bound* that is transmitted under his name). On several occasions he composed his plays for the annual competition to be a continuous and coherent sequence, with the three tragedies forming almost a single—very extended—three-act play, as we find with the *Oresteia*. (The fourth play of the sequence was of course a satyr-drama, usually connected thematically to the three preceding tragedies; see p. 1 above.) Unfortunately, we do not possess more than one play from any of Aeschylus' other trilogies; and we possess only small fragments from any of his satyr-plays. Some of Aeschylus' rivals likewise produced connected trilogies:

but some did not, preferring to compose three quite separate tragedies on different themes; and sometimes Aeschylus did this too, as in the case of the plays produced with his *Persians* (472). It is striking that Sophocles, who began his playwriting career in 468 BCE and for over a decade was competing against Aeschylus, seems never to have adopted the "connected" trilogy format at all; nor subsequently did Euripides.

Tragedy and satyr-drama were already well established in Athens by the late sixth century, and when Aeschylus began to produce plays he was competing against several famous rivals, most notably Phrynichus, Choerilus, and Pratinas. Almost nothing of their work survives, so it is impossible to gauge to what point the art of tragedy had advanced before Aeschylus. Some scholars have regarded him as being effectively the "creator" of Greek tragedy, but it is clear that his predecessors and rivals were highly regarded, especially for their music and choral song, and the fact that he seems to us to be such a powerful innovator may be due in part to the loss of his rivals' works. In any case, Aeschylus undoubtedly played a major role in developing tragedy to its pinnacle of dramatic sophistication and moral power, and he established himself as by far the most popular and influential of all the tragedians before Sophocles, winning thirteen first prizes in the years between 484 and 458.

Aeschylus' unique tragic style is especially remarkable for its extensive and intensive use of the chorus: some of the choral songs extend for over 150 lines each, and the variety of meters and complexity of structure and lyric registers are astonishing. His style too is bold and unconventional, with extensive use of metaphor and imagery. Aeschylus was credited by some with introducing the second speaking actor, and possibly also (late in his career) the third (though some ancient critics credited this to the young Sophocles). Another innovative move of his was to cast the chorus as leading characters in certain plays (for example, *The Suppliant Maidens* and *The Eumenides*). He also seems to have been among the first to have taken dramatic advantage of the *skênê* building: the *Oresteia* is the first surviving drama to contain scenes that require three speaking actors on stage simultaneously; and the positioning of the Watchman on the roof in *Agamemnon*, and the frequent references throughout the trilogy to the "door" and to entrances in and out of the "house" or "temple," are unprecedented in earlier plays.

Aeschylus is said to have visited Sicily at some point during the 470s as the guest of Hieron, ruler of Syracuse and Acragas, and to have composed and presented plays there. But he appears to have been resident in Athens for most of the rest of his life, producing plays about Achilles and Patroclus, about Pentheus and Dionysus, about Niobe, about Ajax, Philoctetes, and the death of Hector (all themes popular also with later tragedians), and others too, in addition to those trilogies of which parts or all survive to the present: *The Seven against Thebes* (467), *The Suppliant Maidens* (probably 463), and his masterwork, the *Oresteia* (458). The date, and even the authenticity, of the Prometheus trilogy (of which *Prometheus Bound* survives complete, as well as several fragments of *Prometheus Unbound*) are very uncertain: these issues are discussed further in the introduction to that play. Within a year of producing the *Oresteia*, Aeschylus left Athens for another visit to Sicily, and died there in 456 or 455.

We know nothing about the personality or lifestyle of Aeschylus, though we do know that one of his sons, Euaion, was a renowned beauty, as well as being a playwright and actor of distinction. The other son, Euphorion, was also a very successful tragedian, and the family continued to flourish in the world of Athenian theater throughout the fifth and fourth centuries. Aristotle and other ancient sources report that Aeschylus was an initiate of the Eleusinian Mysteries in honor of the goddesses Demeter and Persephone, and that he was once prosecuted for revealing secret aspects of the Eleusinian Mysteries in one of his plays—but was acquitted. Scholars both ancient and modern, while viewing such stories with some degree of skepticism (since ancient "biographies" of poets tend to be wildly fanciful and unreliable), have generally agreed that Aeschylus' plays consistently display a serious and challenging engagement with religious matters, though they disagree as to whether specifically Eleusinian and eschatological elements can be identified.

After his death, Aeschylus' reputation continued to flourish. His sons doubtless helped to keep his plays in the public eye; and an ancient tradition (perhaps not trustworthy) states that the Athenians passed a special decree allowing Aeschylus' plays to be revived at the annual festival, an honor granted to no other deceased playwright. One way or another, some of his plays clearly did continue to be performed and to be read, at least by the highly educated, since allusions and parodies are frequently found in the plays of Euripides and Aristophanes. When Aristophanes came to write the *Frogs*, shortly after the death of Euripides in 405, he presented the clash between old and new tragedy as a contest between Aeschylus and Euripides. In the quotations and parodies that abound in that comedy, Aeschylus' style is consistently represented as being "grandiloquent," high-flown to the point of obscurity or bombast, and geared to maintaining the dignity and solemnity of the tragic genre, as against Euripides' modernizing tendencies and introduction of more everyday issues, unpoetic language, and low characters.

During the fourth century, Aeschylus' plays, along with those of Sophocles and Euripides but no other Athenian tragedians, were acknowledged as classics and as being especially worthy of being preserved and performed—though it seems that by this date there was little concern for keeping whole trilogies together (plays instead were catalogued alphabetically), and also a diminishing interest in satyr-plays. A more or less complete collection of Aeschylus' plays was made in Alexandria during the third century BCE, and even though Aeschylus' plays were generally regarded as being less accessible and enjoyable than Sophocles' and especially Euripides'—because of Aeschylus' more archaic language, large amounts of choral lyric, and limited opportunities for actors and rhetoricians to exploit the argumentative and ethical dimensions of the characters' speeches—all three tragedians were read in both Greek and Roman schools throughout antiquity.

Scores of fragments from Aeschylus' plays, mostly quite short, are found in quotations by other authors and in anthologies from the period between the third century BCE and the fourth century CE; but they are far fewer and less extensive than the fragments of Sophocles or (especially) Euripides; and the same is true of papyrus finds. So while Aeschylus remained a classic both in the schools and among later practitioners of the dramatic art (including Naevius, Ennius, Accius, Pacuvius, and Seneca in Rome), familiarity with his work at first hand seems to have become increasingly limited, even in the schools. Some of his plays certainly were much better known than others, and the selection of seven plays that we possess was probably made in the second century CE: from that point on, the other plays ceased to be copied and thus eventually were lost to posterity. At Byzantium (Constantinople, today Istanbul), three plays in particular were most widely copied, the triad consisting of *Prometheus Bound*, *The Seven against Thebes*, and *The Persians*. The other four plays fell into almost complete neglect, and two of them (*The Suppliant Maidens* and *The Libation Bearers*) are preserved in only one manuscript copy. It is sobering to realize that without this one manuscript, we would not possess the complete *Oresteia* trilogy.

Aeschylus' reputation in the modern era has rested almost entirely on the seven plays that survive in our medieval manuscripts. During the Renaissance and Enlightenment periods, his plays were still relatively little read and seldom performed. Things changed when German and British Romantic poets and intellectuals of the eighteenth and nineteenth centuries began to pay more attention to archaic Greek literature and to aspects of Hellenic culture that had for long been regarded as "primitive" or crude. Aeschylus became the object of increasing admiration and study, for his arresting and large-scale religious questioning, his powerful presentation of moral and political problems, his musical and ritualistic energy, and his sheer linguistic exuberance and density. Since the nineteenth century, indeed, his plays have been regarded as the foundation stones of Western drama. The *Oresteia* has always been by far the most widely read and often staged, though *Prometheus Bound* has also been influential with progressives and revolutionaries of various hues. Aeschylus' reputation continued to grow throughout the twentieth century, especially because of his challenging representation of gender conflict and sociopolitical crisis; his plays have been more widely read and staged, decade by decade, and nowadays he stands unchallenged as the true "father of Greek tragedy."

# THE PERSIANS

*Translated by* SETH BENARDETE

# THE PERSIANS: INTRODUCTION

### *The Play: Date and Composition*

Aeschylus' *Persians* is the earliest surviving Greek tragedy. It was first performed in 472 BCE, as part of a tetralogy made up of plays on quite different themes. We know the titles of the other three plays, though the plays themselves have been lost except for fragments: *Phineus*, *Glaucus of Potniae*, and the satyr-drama *Prometheus Fire-Kindler*. All three were on mythological subjects, and it appears they had little in common. So in this particular year Aeschylus followed the pattern that was more usual with other tragedians, including Sophocles and Euripides, of composing four quite separate plays as his entry into the competition, rather than a tightly connected tetralogy like the *Oresteia*. The production won first prize.

We are informed by ancient sources that the play was performed at least once in Sicily, a year or two after its first performance in Athens, at the request of the ruler of Syracuse, Hieron. We do not know whether Aeschylus rewrote the play for this performance or adapted it to take into account the Sicilians' victory over Eastern invaders (the Carthaginians), which occurred on almost the same date as the Athenian victory over the Persians at Salamis; and, if so, which version we possess today.

### *The Story*

The idea of basing a tragic drama on a recent historical event, rather than on traditional myth, may seem surprising to modern readers; but it was apparently not so unusual in the early decades of tragic competition in Athens. In fact Aeschylus' celebrated predecessor and rival, Phrynichus, had previously produced a tragedy, *The Phoenician Women*, on exactly this same theme; and an ancient scholar quotes the first line of Phrynichus' play to demonstrate that Aeschylus' whole play was heavily dependent on it.

The momentous events of 480–479 BCE were of course well known to all Greeks; and the Athenians had played a central role in them. King Xerxes of Persia had led an enormous invading force of troops and ships into Greece. Athens had been evacuated and occupied by the invading forces, but in an amazing reversal, Athenian ships had crushingly defeated the Persian navy and thereby ruined the Persian strategy of a combined land and sea operation to take over the rest of the mainland. Xerxes himself had watched the crucial sea battle off the island of Salamis, just a few miles from the city of Athens. Afterward, a considerable contingent of the Persian forces, including Xerxes, returned home, leaving a large army to continue the campaign on land. The next spring (479) this army was in turn resoundingly defeated by Greek forces led by the Spartans, at the battle of Plataea. Thus the Persians had for a second time in a decade been repelled (the first time had been Darius' much smaller assault, defeated by Athenian infantry at Marathon in 490), and the independence of Athens and other Greek city states had been preserved.

These events immediately acquired a status in the Greek national consciousness comparable to the capture of Troy, or the exploits of Theseus and Heracles—eminently suitable material for tragic drama. At the same time, it would hardly be appropriate for a living Greek man to be made the central focus of a tragedy: instead, Aeschylus followed the example of Phrynichus and set his play in the Persian court, with the main focus on the royal family. Nonetheless, this tragedy concentrating on the disastrous turnaround of the Persian king's fortunes was obviously at the same time a celebration of Athenian success in particular and of Greek discipline and values in general.

The action of Aeschylus' play takes place in front of the tomb of King Darius at the palace in Sousa, Persia's capital city. The chorus of Persian elders (a body of senior advisers to the royal family) begins by anxiously discussing the status of the expedition that left to invade Greece several months earlier, led by King Xerxes himself. Then the queen (not named in the play, though we know from Herodotus and from Persian documents that this is Atossa, widow of Darius and mother of Xerxes) arrives to talk with them, and tells them of an ominous dream she has had. A messenger arrives, announcing the catastrophic defeat at Salamis and narrating in detail the loss of Persian lives and ships, including the painful and costly march of retreat through northern Greece. The queen and chorus are devastated, but also relieved to learn that Xerxes is safe and returning home, though his clothing is in shreds (from mourning) and his spirit broken. The chorus, at the queen's suggestion, now conjures up the dead spirit of King Darius, Xerxes' father, from his tomb. Darius expresses disapproval and disappointment at his son's failure, and goes on to predict the impending defeat at Plataea. After Darius' ghost returns to the underworld, and the queen also departs to prepare to greet her son, Xerxes himself arrives, and the final scene consists of a long lyric lament, sung in antiphonal exchange between the chorus and their king.

Aeschylus' play is the earliest extant account of the events of the Persian Wars: the much more extensive and detailed narrative of Herodotus in his *Histories* was not composed until some forty years later. But the play was never intended to accuratcly represent historical reality. Although it has plenty of oriental coloring (costumes, exotic wailing and dancing, self-abasement of the chorus in the presence of royalty), for the most part the Persians speak like Greeks and observe largely Greek customs and religion. The resounding lists of foreign names are colorful but not very authentic. The scale of the massacre of Persian troops on land that is described as the culmination of the slaughter at Salamis (lines 441–71) seems to be greatly exaggerated. The references to Darius' unblemished military record are somewhat fanciful, and Xerxes' entry on foot in the final scene, with torn clothing and minimal retinue, suggests a degree of catastrophe and humiliation far removed from the actual Persian experience.

Instead of historical authenticity, Aeschylus sought and achieved brilliant dramatic impact, especially through such striking effects as the queen's dream, the apparition of the ghost of old king Darius, the pathos of Persian loss and bewilderment, and the elaborate incantations and lamentations of the chorus.

After Aeschylus' *Persians*, we do not hear of any further stagings of tragedies depicting recent historical events in the fifth-century Athenian theater. Certainly neither Sophocles nor Euripides ever wrote such a play. We do not know why this change of fashion occurred. By contrast, in the Roman theater, historical dramas constituted a flourishing genre, with *Octavia* (attributed, wrongly, to Seneca) a sole surviving example.

*Transmission and Reception*

Beyond the play's reperformance in Sicily, *The Persians* continued to be well known in Athens throughout the fifth century, and Herodotus must have known the play, though he makes little obvious use of Aeschylus' particular themes or language. At the end of the century, the exotic flavor of Aeschylus' music and choreography in the play is mentioned approvingly in Aristophanes' *Frogs*, and the innovative musician and poet Timotheus drew extensively from it in his own *Persians* (of which a substantial fragment survives on papyrus). In the Hellenistic period, the Jewish playwright Ezekiel likewise adapted episodes from Aeschylus' play for his *Exodus* (*Exagogê*). But for the most part, it was Herodotus' account of Xerxes' invasion and the Persian royal court that was best known and most influential for later writers and composers.

In general, Aeschylus' plays were much less widely read in ancient schools or for pleasure than the plays of Sophocles or (especially) Euripides. Most of them gradually ceased to be copied and faded into oblivion. When the time came to make a selected edition of seven Aeschylean plays (at some point in the Roman period, perhaps for school use), *The Persians* was included, doubtless because of its ever-topical subject matter—the defeat of an Eastern threat and the humiliation of an overly ambitious ruler. The play survived into the Byzantine and Renaissance eras and, along with *The Seven against Thebes* and *Prometheus Bound*, made its way into the triad of Aeschylean plays that were copied frequently from the twelfth to the fifteenth century. As a result, some of the manuscripts of the play contain quite extensive marginal comments (scholia).

Since the Renaissance, plays and operas loosely based on *The Persians* have been fairly common, though Herodotus and the late antique *Alexander Romance* have generally been much more influential. A number of operas titled *Xerxes* were composed during the seventeenth and eighteenth centuries: most bear little resemblance to Aeschylus' play. Much closer to Aeschylus' tragic vision are T. Maurice's *Fall of the Mogul* (1806) and Percy Bysshe Shelley's *Hellas* (1821), written during the period when Greece was fighting for independence against the Ottoman Empire.

Since the 1920s *The Persians* has been performed in all parts of the world. Often the political allegory has been overt, with Xerxes suggesting a Nazi or Soviet or domestic dictator, or implying a warning to the contemporary US as an overreaching imperialist power. Sometimes "Eastern" music and performance style has been incorporated in imaginative ways. Notable productions include those of Dimitri Rondiris for the Greek National Theater (1939, 1958, 1967), Karolos Koun with the Theatro Technis (1965–67), Mattias Braun (1960s), the Berliner Ensemble (1961, 1972, 1983), Peter Sellars (1993), and Ellen McLaughlin (1995).

Both in adapting and in interpreting this tragedy, theater practitioners and critics have been divided as to whether Aeschylus was aiming to flatter the Athenians by celebrating their military and cultural superiority over the luxurious, feminized "other" of the East, or was sympathetically exploring the disastrous effects on any community of an unnecessary war caused by an impetuous and overly ambitious leader. The truth is doubtless that he was doing both.

# THE PERSIANS

*Characters* CHORUS of Persian elders
QUEEN of Persia (Atossa), widow of Darius, and mother of Xerxes
PERSIAN MESSENGER
GHOST OF DARIUS
XERXES, king of Persia

*Scene: The palace of Xerxes at Sousa; in the foreground the tomb of Darius.*

*(Enter Chorus from the side.)*

CHORUS [*chanting*]
*Of the Persians gone*
*to the land of Greece*
*here are the trusted:*
*as protectors of treasure*
*and of golden thrones.*
*We were chosen by Xerxes—*
*emperor and king,*
*son of Darius—*
*in accord with age,*
*guards of the country.*
*For the king's return*
*with his many-manned troops*
*doom is the feeling*
*in my heart convulsed,*
*as it faces the future.*

*For all Asia is gone,*
*its strength and its youth:*
*and the women lament for their men.°*
*To the city of Persians*
*neither herald nor horseman returns.*
*And some have left Agbatana*
*and some Sousa and*
*ancient Cissa,*
*both on horse and on ship*
*and on foot displaying*
*legions of battle:*
*Artaphrenes, Megabates,*
*Astaspes, Amistres,*
*leaders of Persians, kings*
*who are slaves of the greatest of kings,*
*guarding the legions they rush,*
*both as bowman and knight,*
*with their temper resolved,*
*fearful in aspect,*
*dreadful in battle;*
*and exultant in horses*
*Artembares, and Masistres,*
*and the brave archer Imaeus,*
*and Pharandakas,*
*and the driver of horses*
*Sousthenes.*
*And others were sent*
*by the nourishing Nile:*
*Egyptian-born Sousiscanes,*
*Pegastagon, great Arsames*
*ruler of sacred Memphis;*
*and Ariomardus*
*governing ancient Thebes;*
*and those who dwelling by marshes*
*are rowers of ships,*
*skillful and countless.*

*And the Lydians soft*
*who inhabit the coast*
*follow commanders and kings:*
*Metrogathes and brave Arcteus,*
*and golden Sardis sent*
*many charioteers,*
*with horses by twos and by threes,*
*fearful the sight to behold.*
*And the neighbors of Tmolus—*
*they threaten to yoke*
*in servitude Hellas;*
*and the Mysian lancers,*
*Tharybis, Mardon,*
*anvils of battle;*
*and golden Babylon*
*pours forth her crowds—*
*borne by their ships—*
*who in drawing the bow*
*rely on their boldness.*
*And the tribes from all Asia*
*who carry the saber*
*follow beneath the*
*awesome parade of their king.*
*Thus of the Persian land*
*of her men the flower is gone,*
*nursed by the earth, and all Asia*
*laments, consumed by longing;*
*and parents and wives*
*counting the days*
*tremble at lengthening time.*

[*singing*]

STROPHE A

*The destroyer of cities now,*
*that kingly army, has gone*
*over the strait to the land*

*on linen-bound pontoons;*
*tightly was clamped the Way*
*of Helle, Athamas' daughter,*
*as the neck of the sea was yoked.*

ANTISTROPHE A

*And the furious leader drives*
*the herd of populous Asia,*
*wonderful over the earth.*
*And admirals stern and rough*
*marshals of men he trusts:*
*gold his descent from Perseus,*
*he is the equal of god.*

STROPHE B

*In his eyes lazuli flashing*
*like a snake's murderous glances,*
*with his mariners, warriors, many,*
*and his Syrian chariot driving,*
*hard on the glorious spearmen*
*the archer Ares he leads.*

ANTISTROPHE B

*To the great torrent of heroes*
*there is none worthily equal,*
*who resist, by defenses secured,*
*the unconquerable billows of ocean:*
*Persians are never defeated,*
*the people tempered and brave.*

STROPHE C

*For divine fate has long prevailed,*°
*enjoining Persians to wage wars*
*which destroy towers and ramparts,*
*along with glad tumult of horsemen,*
*and cities overthrown.*

ANTISTROPHE C

*Later, when the vast ocean was foaming,*

*whitened by the boisterous winds,*
*they learned, trusting to cables*
*and to pontoons which convey men,*
*to cross the sacred sea.*

EPODE

*Deceitful deception of god—*
*what mortal man shall avoid it?*
*With nimbleness, deftness, and speed*
*whose leaping foot shall escape it?*
*Benign and coaxing at first*
*it leads us astray into nets which*
*no mortal is able to slip,*
*whose doom we never can flee.*

STROPHE D

*Thus clothed in black my heart is torn,*
*fearful for those Persian arms:*
*lest the city hear, alas!*
*that reft of men is Sousa;*

ANTISTROPHE D

*and lest the city of Cissa shall,*
*with crowds of women crying,*
*sing antiphonal, alas!*
*and rend their garb of mourning.*

STROPHE E

*All the horse and infantry,*
*like a swarm of bees have gone*
*with the captain of the host,*
*who joined the headlands of either land,*
*crossing the yoke of the sea.*

ANTISTROPHE E

*Beds with longing fill with tears,*
*Persian wives in softness weep*
*each her bold warrior husband*
*dispatched with gentle love and grief,*

*as they're left alone in the yoke.*

[*chanting again*]
*But come, Persians,*
*let us in this ancient palace sit,*
*and deep and wisely found our thoughts:*
*How does King Xerxes fare, Darius' son?*
*How fare his people? Has arrows' hail*
*or strength of spear conquered?*
*But look, she comes,*
*a light whose splendor equals the eyes of gods,*
*the mother of our king: I kneel.*
*Now all must address and salute her.*

(*Enter the Queen from the palace, with attendants.*)

CHORUS LEADER [*now speaking*]
O most majestic Queen of Persians, in ample folds adorned,
hail, aged mother of Xerxes! Consort of Darius, hail!
Consort of the god of Persians, mother of a god you are,
unless the fortune of our army brings us now a change.

QUEEN
Leaving my gold-clad palace, marriage chamber
of Darius and of myself,
his queen, I've come. Care quite grates my heart;
I fear, my friends, though not fearful for myself,
lest great wealth's gallop trip prosperity—
exalted by Darius and some god—
in its own dust. But, unexpectedly,
that dread has doubled: sums of cowardly
wealth do court contempt, and indigence
quenches ambition's flame, even if there's strength.
Though wealth we have unstinted, yet I fear
for my precious eye, Xerxes, whose presence here
I count the palace's eye. So things stand thus.
Advise my reason, Persians, old sureties:
all my gains with your counsel lie.

CHORUS LEADER

O Queen of Persia, be assured that never
twice do you have to tell us word or deed
which our willing strength can guide; for we
are loyal, whom you call your counselors.

QUEEN

With frequent, constant, and nocturnal dreams
I have lived, ever since my son, gathering
his army, departed, his will to pillage Greece;
but never a more vivid presence came
than yesternight's.
Into my vision it seemed two women came,
one decked out in Persian robes, the other
in Dorian, both of them flawless and impressive,
excelling in beauty any who live today.
Sisters they were, and inheriting their father's land,
one received Greece, the other Asia to dwell.
Then strife arises between them, or so I dreamed;
and my son, observing this, tries to check
and soothe them; he yokes them to a chariot,
bridles their necks: and one, so arrayed, towers
proud, her mouth obedient to reins;
but the other stamps, annoyed, and rends apart
her trappings with her hands; unbridled, seizes
the chariot and snaps its yoke in two.
My son falls; his father, Darius, pitying,
stands by his side—but at his sight Xerxes
tears his robes. Thus in the night these visions
I dreamed: but when, arisen, I touched the springs'
fair-flowing waters, approached the altar, wishing
to offer sacrifice religiously
to guardian deities, whose rites these are,
then to Phoebus' hearth I saw an eagle fleeing.
Dumb in dread I stood: a falcon swooped
upon him, its wings in flight, its claws plucked

at his head: he did no more than cower, hare-like.
Those were my terrors to see, and yours to hear.
My son, should he succeed, would be admired;
but if he fails, Persia cannot hold him
to account. Whichever comes, safe returned, sovereign
he shall still rule.

CHORUS LEADER

Queen mother, excessive fear
or confidence we do not wish to give you.
If your dreams were ominous, approach
the gods with supplications; pray that these
be unfulfilled, and blessings be fulfilled
for you, your son, your city, and your friends.
Next you must pour libations to the Earth
and the dead; and beg Darius, of whom you dreamed,
to send those blessings from the nether world
to light, for you and for your son; and to hide
in darkness evils contrary, retained
within the earth. Propitious be your prayers.
We, prophetic in our spirit, kindly,
counsel you thus: and we judge that all will prosper.

QUEEN

Ah, loyally have the first expounders answered
my dreams; and may these blessings ripen
for my son and for our house as well!
All, as you enjoin, I'll sacrifice
to the gods and friends below, as soon as I
return to the house. But one thing more I wish
to know, my friends: where is Athens said to be?

CHORUS LEADER

Far from here, toward the dying flames of sun.

QUEEN

Yet still my son yearned to track it down?

CHORUS LEADER

Then all Hellas would be subject to the king.

QUEEN

So rich in numbers are they?

CHORUS LEADER

So great a host
as dealt to Persians many miseries.

QUEEN

Are bow-plucked shafts their main armament?°

CHORUS LEADER

No; spears wielded close and panoply of shields.

QUEEN

What else besides? Have they sufficing wealth?

CHORUS LEADER

Their earth is veined with silver treasuries.

QUEEN

Who commands them? Who is shepherd of their host?

CHORUS LEADER

They are slaves to none, nor are they subject.

QUEEN

But how could they withstand a foreign foe?

CHORUS LEADER

Enough to vanquish Darius' noble host.

QUEEN

We mothers dread to calculate.

CHORUS LEADER

But soon you'll know all: a Persian runner comes,
bearing some fresh report of good or ill.

*(Enter Persian Messenger from the side.)*

MESSENGER

O cities of Asia, O Persian land,
and wealth's great anchorage!
How at a single stroke prosperity's
corrupted, and the flower of Persia falls
and is gone. Alas! the first messenger of woe,
he must disclose entire what befell:
Persians, all the barbarian host is gone.

CHORUS [*singing in this interchange with the Messenger, who speaks in reply*]

STROPHE A

*O woe! woeful evil,*
*novel and hostile.*
*Alas! Persians weep*
*hearing this woe,*
*unexpected.*

MESSENGER

How all has been destroyed, and I behold
the unexpected light of my return!

CHORUS

ANTISTROPHE A

*Oh, long seems our aged*
*life to us elders,*
*alas! hearing woe*
*Unexpected.*

MESSENGER

And since I was witness, not merely subject to rumor,
I can indicate what sorrows came.

CHORUS

STROPHE B

*Woe upon woe, in vain*
*the crowd of missiles, massed,*
*came from Asia to Greece.*

MESSENGER

The lifeless rotting corpses glut the shore
and adjacent fields of Salamis.

CHORUS

ANTISTROPHE B

*Woe upon woe, of friends*
*the sea-dyed corpses whirl*
*vagrant on craggy shores.*

MESSENGER

The bow protected none, but all the host,
defeated in the naval charge, was lost.

CHORUS

STROPHE C

*Raise a mournful, doleful cry*
*for Persians wretched:*
*all they made, all woe.*
*Alas! the host destroyed.*

MESSENGER

O most hateful name of Salamis!
O woe! how I groan recalling Athens.

CHORUS

ANTISTROPHE C

*Athens hateful to her foes.*
*Recall how many*
*Persian women are widowed,*
*and mothers have lost their sons.*

QUEEN

Long am I silent, alas! struck down
by disasters exceeding speech and question.
Yet humans must perforce endure misfortunes
that are sent by the gods. Speak, disclose entire
what befell, quietly, though you grieve.

Who did not die? For whom of the captains
shall we lament? Whose sceptered death drained his ranks
manless?

MESSENGER

Xerxes himself lives to behold the light.

QUEEN

O for my palace you spoke a greater light,
and after blackest night a whiter day!

MESSENGER

But Artembares, captain of ten thousand
horse, was dashed against Silenia's
rugged shore; and satrap Dadakes,
spear-struck, did lightly tumble from his ship;
and native-born Tenagon, the bravest
Bactrian, still haunts sea-buffeted
Ajax' isle; and Lilaeus, Arsames,
and Argestes, conquered near the island
where doves do thrive, now butt their heads on the rocks;
and the neighbors of Egyptian Nile-waters,
Adeues, Arcteus, and, third, shielded
Pharnouchus, from a single ship
were drowned; and Matallus, satrap of Chrysa,
dying, leader of a thousand horse,
changed to richest red his thickset flowing
beard, and dipped his skin in crimson dyes;
and Magian Arabus and Bactrian
Artabes, all aliens in a savage
country, perished; Amphistreus, who wielded
the much-belaboring spear, and Amistres,
brave Ariomardus, all made Sardis weep;
and Mysian Seisames, Tharybis,
commander of five times fifty ships,
his race Lyrnaean, handsome to look upon
(his fortune was not so), dead he lies;
Syennesis too, the leader of Cilicians,

who taxed the enemy with toil above all others,
has died, nobly. So many of the rulers I
recall, but of the many woes, report
but few.

QUEEN

Alas! I hear the greatest
of misfortunes, shame of Persians, and shrill
lament. But tell me, returning to your tale,
what was the total number of Greek ships,
that thought themselves a match for Persian arms
in naval combat?

MESSENGER

Had numbers counted,
the barbarian warships surely would have won;
the Greeks but numbered thirty tens, and ten
apart from these a chosen squadron formed.
But Xerxes led—and this I know full well—
a thousand, of which seven and two hundred
ranked supreme in swiftness. The count stood so.
Seemed we unequal to you? Some deity destroyed
our host, and weighting down the balance swung
the beam of fortune. The gods saved the city
of the goddess Pallas.

QUEEN

What? Athens still
stands unsacked?

MESSENGER

As long as there are men
the city stands secure.

QUEEN

What was the beginning
of disaster? Tell me. Who began?
The Greeks? My son—exultant in his numbers?

MESSENGER

Either an avenger or a wicked
god, my Lady (whence it came I know not)
began the whole disaster. From Athenian
ranks a Greek approached, addressing Xerxes
thus: "When the gloom of blackest night
will fall, the Greeks will not remain, but leap
to their rowing benches, and each by secret course
will seek to save his life." And he your son,
upon hearing this, in ignorance of the Greek
man's guile and the jealousy of gods,
harangued his captains publicly: "As soon
as sunlit rays no longer burn the earth
and darkness sweeps the quarters of the sky,
rank the swarm of ships in three flotillas:
have them guard the entrances, the straits' sea-pound;
and girdle others round Ajax' island.
And if the Greeks escape their evil doom,
contriving secret flight, all your heads
will roll. I warrant it." So he spoke
in confident pride: of the god-given future
he knew nothing. So, having eaten, they set
themselves in order, each heart obedient,
and each sailor looped the thong about his oar.
When the glare of sunlight died, and night
came on, every rower was at his oar,
and each marine took up his proper weapons.
Rank encouraged rank, and longboats sailed
to the stations each had been assigned.
All night the captains kept the fleet awake;
and night ran on. Yet no Greek army set
secret sail: and when the steeds of day,
white and luminous, began to cross
the sky, a song-like, happy tumult sounded
from the Greeks, and island rocks returned
the high-pitched echo. Fear fell among us,

deceived in hope; for they (and not as if to flee)
chanted a solemn paean, and to battle
rushed with fervent boldness: trumpets flared,
setting every Greek aflame. At once
concordant strokes of oars in roaring eddies
slapped the waters' depths: soon we saw
them all: first the right wing led in order,
next advanced the whole armada.
A great concerted cry we heard: "O Greek
sons, advance! Free your fathers' land,
free your sons, your wives, the sanctuaries
of paternal gods, the sepulchers
of ancestors. Now the contest's drawn:
all is at stake!" A babel of Persian tongues
rose to meet it: no longer would the action
loiter. Warships struck their brazen beaks
together: it was a Greek ship that began
the charge, as a Phoenician vessel's stern
was smashed; then others drove against each other.
At first the floods of Persians held the line,
but when the narrows choked them, they could not help
each other, but smitten by each others' prows,
they shattered their oars entirely on the bronze.
The Greek warships, calculating, dashed
round and encircled us; ships showed their bellies:
no longer could we see the water, charged
with ships' wrecks and with the blood of men.
Corpses glutted beaches and the rocks.
Every warship urged its own escape
in anarchic rout. And meanwhile the enemy
with broken bits of oars and splintered wreckage
were clubbing and spiking our men in the water
like tunny or some other catch of fish.
Moans, shrieks, and cries of lamentation
possessed the open sea, until the black
eye of evening, closing, hushed them. The sum

of troubles, even if I should rehearse them
for ten days, I could not exhaust. Rest
assured: never in a single day
so great a number died.

QUEEN

Alas! a sea of troubles breaks in waves
upon the Persians and barbarian tribes.

MESSENGER

But what we've told would scarcely balance woes
untold: misfortune came upon them, which
swung the beam to weigh them double these.

QUEEN

But what greater hatred could fortune show?
What misfortune came upon the soldiers,
to tilt the scale of troubles even further?

MESSENGER

All those Persians who were in nature's prime,
excellent in soul and nobly bred to grandeur,
always first in trust, met their death
in infamy, dishonor, and in ugliness.

QUEEN

Oh, wretched am I, alas! What catastrophe
destroyed them?

MESSENGER

There is an island fronting Salamis,
small, scarce an anchorage for ships,
where the dancer Pan rejoices on the shore;
there Xerxes sent those men to kill
any shipwrecked enemies who sought the island
as a refuge (for easily, he thought,
the Greek army would be overcome);
he also bid them rescue friends. He judged
the future badly. For when god gave the Greeks

the glory of sea victory, that same day,
now armed in bronze, they leaped ashore, and drew
the circle tight around the island. Thus
surrounded, our men had nowhere they could turn.
Many rattled to the ground, whom stones
had felled, and others killed by arrows, shot
from bowstring; and then in a final rush
the Greeks came at them, hacking, mangling their limbs,
until the life of every single one
was gone.
Xerxes wailed, beholding the lowest depths
of woe. Seated on a hill that near
the sea looked over all his host, he ripped
his robes and poured out piercing lamentation;
then dispatched his regiments on land: they fled
orderless. Now you may lament their fate
added to the others' summed before.

QUEEN

O hateful deity! how you deceived
the Persians! Bitter was the vengeance
which my son at famous Athens found:
she could not sate her appetite with those
whom Marathon had made the Persians lose.
For these my son, exacting as requital
punishment (or so he thought),
called on himself so numerous
a train of woes. Tell me, what ships escaped?
Where are they now? Can you clearly tell?

MESSENGER

The captains of the remaining ships set sail
before the wind, fleeing in disorder;
but the land army perished in Boeotia:
some in want of water, racked with thirst,
while others, gasping emptily on air,
crossed to Phocis, Locria, the Malian

Gulf, where Spercheian waters kindly drench
the plain; and thence Achaea and Thessaly
received us, starving: it was there most died
in hunger and in thirst: both we felt.
To Magnesia and Macedonia we came,
the River Axius, the reedy marsh
of Bolbe, the mountain Pangaeon,
and Thrace. There in the night a god
roused winter out of season, and froze solid
the stream of holy Strymon: all who had
believed the gods were naught now sang their prayers,
making obeisance both to Earth and Sky.
When the army finished its many invocations
to the gods, it started crossing over the ice.
And whoever set out before the sun god's rays
spread and scattered in the sky, this man
was safe. But soon the brilliant orb of sun,
its rays aflame, melted the river's midst;
one man fell on the next; happy he whose breath
of life was cut short quickest! The survivors
did make their way—but painfully—through Thrace
and have arrived at last to hearth and home,
few out of many. Thus the city of Persians
may lament, regretting the loss of dearest youth.
Truthful I have been, but omit many
of the woes a god has hurled against the Persians.

*(Exit Messenger to the side.)*

CHORUS LEADER

O deity so full of toil and trouble!
How heavily you leaped upon all Persia!

QUEEN

Ah! woe is me, the army all destroyed.
O bright night's spectacle of dreams,
how clearly you foresaw my miseries,

and you, my counselors, how poorly you have judged.
But yet, as you have counseled thus,
first to the gods I'll offer prayer; and then
to Earth and the dead I'll come to offer gifts
from the house, a rich libation. I know I pray
for what is done and gone, but a brighter
fortune, in time to come, may there yet be.
And you, worthy of trust, exchange worthy counsel;
my son, should he return before my own
return, comfort and escort him home:
I worry that to woes he'll add more woe.

*(Exit Queen into the palace.)*

CHORUS [*chanting*]

*O Zeus, King, you destroyed*
*the multitudinous, proud*
*host of the Persian men;*
*and the cities of Sousa*
*and of Agbatana*
*you've buried in darkness of grief.*
*Many with delicate hands*
*rending their veils,*
*drenching their breasts,*
*swollen with tears,*
*sharing their woe.*
*The ladies of Persia*
*softly are weeping,*
*desiring each*
*him to behold*
*wedded but lately;*
*forsaking their couches,*
*soft with their coverlets,*
*the joy of their youth,*
*now they lament their sorrows,*
*insatiate, full of woe.*
*And I recite the mourning song,*

*doom of the gone,*
*woe upon woe.*

[*singing*]

STROPHE A

*Now all Asia*
*desolate, void,*
*sighs lament:*
*Xerxes led,*
*alas,*
*Xerxes lost,*
*O woe,*
*Xerxes heedless all discharged*
*with ocean argosies.*
*Why was Darius so long without harm,*
*archery's captain of citizens,*
*loved lord of Sousa?*

ANTISTROPHE A

*Armies, navies*
*lazuli-eyed,*
*linen-winged*
*warships carried,*
*alas,*
*warships destroyed,*
*O woe,*
*warships smashed with their rams driven by Greek hands.*
*Scarcely escaped was the leader alone*
*(so we have heard) in the Thracian*
*plains, wintry paths.*

STROPHE B

*They of the first death,*
*alas,*
*left by necessity,*
*woe,*
*round by Cychraean shores,*
*Oh,*

*moan in your anguish,*
*cry to the heavens your grief,*
*Oh,*
*wail long-weeping*
*mournful cries.*

ANTISTROPHE B

*Torn in the sea-swirl,*
*alas,*
*mangled by voiceless*
*woe,*
*fish of the unstained sea.*
*Oh,*
*houses deprived grieve,*
*childless, to heavens their loss.*
*Oh,*
*elders mourning,*
*hear all woe.*

STROPHE C

*They throughout the Asian land*
*no more will Persian laws obey,*
*no more the lordly tribute pay*
*exacted by compulsion;*
*nor falling faceward to the earth*
*will they make obeisance now:*
*lost is the kingly power.*

ANTISTROPHE C

*Nay, no longer is the tongue*
*kept in check, but loose are men*
*when loosened is the yoke of power,*
*to shout aloud their liberty.*
*And Ajax' island, soaked with blood*
*its earth, and washed round by the sea,*
*holds the remains of Persia.*

*(Enter the Queen from the palace, carrying offerings.)*

QUEEN

My friends, if one's experienced in troubles,
one knows that, when a flood of evil comes,
we tend to fear for everything; but when
a god provides an easy voyage, we think
that fortune's never-changing wind will blow
forever. So now, to me all things are full of fear
and visions from the gods assail my eyes,
and my ears already ring with cureless songs:
thus consternation terrifies my sense.
Therefore I departed from the palace,
returning here, unaccompanied
by chariots, by pomp and ceremony:
to the father of my son I bring
libations, propitious offerings for the dead;
some sweet white milk taken from a cow
unblemished; glowing honey from the flower-
working bee, with liquid droplets of a maiden
stream are mingled; and this elixir
of an antique vine, whose mother is
the wild field; and golden-green the fruit
of fragrant olive trees, always flourishing
their leafy age; and plaited flowers, children
of the fecund earth. Over these libations,
the honors that I lavish on the gods below,
my friends, recite your hymns and incantations:
summon Darius' great spirit to return.

CHORUS [*chanting*]

*O Queen of the Persians,*
*honored lady,*
*to the dark chambers*
*libations pour;*
*while we with our songs*
*will request from the gods,*
*who conduct the dead souls*

*from the world below,*
*to be kindly and help.*
*You sacred divinities*
*dwelling below,*
*Earth and Hermes*
*and King of the Shades,*
*conduct his spirit*
*back up to the light*
*from the world of the dead!*
*He alone of all mortals*
*might know some remedy,*
*and show us the end of our troubles.*

[*singing*]

STROPHE A

*Does he hear, the blessed king*
*equal to god,*
*as I pronounce now*
*resonant chantings,*
*barbarous, mournful,*
*clear and diverse?*
*Miserable sorrows I shall cry out.*
*Below does he hearken?*

ANTISTROPHE A

*Earth and the other gods,*
*leaders of the dead,*
*let him arise thence,*
*glorious spirit, god of the Persians,*
*Sousa his mother;*
*send up the man whom,*
*never surpassed,*
*the Persian land buried.*

STROPHE B

*Loved is the man, loved his tomb*
*hiding his loving ways.*

*Aedoneus, spirit conductor,*
*may Aedoneus release him*
*and send to us King Darius. Ah!*

ANTISTROPHE B

*Never by war wasted his men,*
*never in foolish ruin.*
*Called a god in wisdom*
*by Persians, and god-wise he was,*
*ruling his people well. Ah!*

STROPHE C

*Pashah, ancient pashah,*
*appear on the height of your tomb,*
*raise your saffron-dyed slipper,*
*reveal the peak of your royal crown.*
*Come to us, Father Darius, Oh!*

ANTISTROPHE C

*Hear the recent sorrows,*
*O master of masters, appear!*
*A deadly gloom hovers around us;*
*all the youth has perished now.*
*Come to us, Father Darius, Oh!*

EPODE

*Ah! Ah!*
*O much-lamented by your friends in death,*
*my lord, my lord, what does this mean,°*
*this twofold failure?*
*All the ships of this land*
*with triple banks of oars*
*are gone, gone.*

*(The Ghost of Darius appears.)*

DARIUS

O faithful followers, companions
of my youth! O Persian counselors!

What burden's burdening the city, and why
is the earth groaning and beaten, all furrowed up
by fingernails? Anxious, I saw my wife
beside my tomb, and graciously received
her offerings; and you lament now, standing
at my tomb, with cries for resurrection
calling piteously. Ascent is not so easy.
The chthonic deities more readily
receive than give; but I, a potentate
among them, came. Be quick, that I be un-
reproached for being late. What recent woe
weighs now so heavily upon the Persians?

CHORUS [*singing*]

STROPHE

*I feel awe to behold you,*
*I feel awe to address you,*
*whom I feared in time past.*

DARIUS

Since I have risen obeying your lamentations
don't lengthen your account, but speak succinctly,
recounting everything. So lay aside
your reverence toward me.

CHORUS [*singing*]

ANTISTROPHE

*I tremble to please you;*
*I tremble to tell you*
*what is hard to tell friends.*

DARIUS *(To the Chorus.)*

Well, since this ancient fear obstructs your sense,

*(Turning now to the Queen.)*

you, aged consort of my marriage,
noble Queen, cease weeping and tell me clearly.
All human beings suffer human troubles;

and many woes arise, some from the sea,
and others from the land, to those who live
a longer span of life.

QUEEN

O King, who in your happy fate exceeded
mortal happiness! For while you still
beheld the light of sun, you spent your life
in enviable happiness, like god's;
and now I envy you your dying too,
before you had to see this depth of woe.
Everything, Darius, you will hear
succinctly: all of Persia is destroyed.

DARIUS

How? A lightning bolt of hunger? Civil
strife within the city?

QUEEN

No, but all
the host's destroyed at Athens.

DARIUS

Who among
my sons was leader of the troops? Tell me.

QUEEN

Furious Xerxes, who drained the country manless.

DARIUS

By foot or warship was his vain attempt?

QUEEN

By both: a double front of doubled hosts.

DARIUS

But how did so great an army cross the water?

QUEEN

Devices yoked the Strait of Helle and made
a pathway.

DARIUS

He accomplished that? To close
the mighty Bosphorus?

QUEEN

So it was; some god
laid hold of him.

DARIUS

Ah, yes! a great divinity
must have deceived his sense.

QUEEN

And one can see
the evil end he brought about.

DARIUS

So what befell
them all, so that you thus lament?

QUEEN

The navy,
destroyed, destroyed the troops on land as well.

DARIUS

Complete destruction by the spear for all?

QUEEN

Yes, Sousa groans for emptiness of men.

DARIUS

Ah! The goodly host and brave defenders!

QUEEN

All the Bactrians destroyed, no youth remains.°

DARIUS

Oh! What youth of allies has he ruined!

QUEEN

Xerxes alone, with just a few they say . . .

DARIUS
Ended how? Any hope of his survival?

QUEEN
. . . safely came to the bridge that joined the lands.

DARIUS
Saved, and reached our continent? Is this true?

QUEEN
Yes, a clear report without dispute.

DARIUS
Ah, that prophecy was quick to act!
Zeus hurled against my son its fulfillment,
while I had been praying that many years would pass
before the gods would make an end; but when
a man is young and eager, god joins in.
So now a fountain of troubles has been found
for all those that I care for; and my son
is the one who has discovered it, in ignorance.
He hoped, in youthful confidence, to check
the sacred waters of the Hellespont
by chains, as if it were a slave. He smoothed
the army's way, yoking the Bosphorus
with hammered shackles. Mortal though he was,
in folly he thought to master all the gods,
including Poseidon. Wasn't his mind diseased?
So now I fear the wealth I labored so
to acquire will fall the prey of conquerors.

QUEEN
From wicked men advising thus, young Xerxes
eagerly learned; they said you acquired great wealth
by warfare, while he, in cowardice, played
the warrior at home, and multiplied
by nothing his ancestral wealth. Thus often
these wicked men reproached him. So he planned
this warlike expedition against Greece.

DARIUS

So his deed is done, great and unforgettable!
Never had anyone before made this city
Sousa so empty and so desolate,
since Zeus, our lord, bestowed that honor:
one man to wield the scepter of authority
over all of Asia, rich in flocks.
First was Medus leader of our people;
next his son fulfilled the office well,
whose reason was the helmsman to his spirit;°
third was Cyrus, fortunate, whose rule
brought peace to all he cared for: he acquired
the Lydian people and the Phrygians too,
and marched his might against all of Ionia:
no god resented him, for he was wise;
and fourth to rule the land was Cyrus' son,
while fifth was Mardus, the one who shamed his country
and ancestral throne; but worthy Artaphrenes
(aided by guile) and his noble friends
whose task this was, slew him in his palace,
and I was with them too. I drew the lot
to rule the empire; and I often led
a mighty host, but never did I cast
so great a woe upon my city. Xerxes,
my son, as young in age as sense, ignored
all my instructions. Know this well, my comrades
like in age to me: of all who've held
these powers, none has caused such sufferings.

CHORUS LEADER

To what end, my lord Darius, do you press
these words of yours? How could we, the Persian people,
fare the best in future?

DARIUS

If you lead
no expedition to the land of Greece,

not even if the Median force be greater;
for the Greek soil itself is their own ally.

CHORUS LEADER
What do you mean by that, "their own ally"?

DARIUS
Their land starves to death excessive numbers.

CHORUS LEADER
But, be sure, we'll raise a well-equipped
and chosen army.

DARIUS
But even they, who now
remain in Greece, shall find no safe return.

CHORUS LEADER
What? Shall not all the Persian host return
across the Strait of Helle?

DARIUS
Few of many,
if the oracles of gods are credited:
as we gaze at what has passed, there are no half-measures
in the outcome of the prophecies—either all
or none come true. In which case, he has left,
behind in Greece, trusting his empty hopes,
chosen numbers of his host, now stationed
where Asopus floods the plain and gives rich nurture
for Boeotian crops; there they'll suffer soon
the lowest depths of woe, as final payment
for insolent acts and godless arrogance.
Invading Greece, they felt no awe or reverence;
they did not hesitate to plunder images
of gods and put their temples to the torch;
altars were no more, and statues of divinities
were uprooted and torn right off their bases
in utter confusion. Thus having acted wickedly

they now no less are suffering in return;
and other woes the future holds in store.
For still the fount of evils is not quenched.
It wells up, and overflows: so great will be
the sacrificial cake of clotted gore
made at Plataea by the Dorian spear.
And corpses, piled up like sand, shall witness
mute, even to generations to come,
before the eyes of men, that never, being
mortal, ought we to cast our thoughts too high.
Insolence, once blossoming, will bear
its fruit, a tasseled field of doom, from which
a deadly harvest must be reaped, all tears.
Behold the punishment of these! Remember
Greece and Athens! Lest anyone disdain
his present fortune, lusting after more,
and end up squandering great prosperity.
Zeus is the chastener of overboastful
minds, a grievous corrector. Therefore advise
my son, admonished by reason, to be wise
and cease his overboastful temper from
sinning against the gods. And you, aged
mother of Xerxes, go to the palace;
gather up rich and brilliant clothes, and go
to meet your son; for he, in grief, has rent
his embroidered robes to shreds. Gently soothe
him with your words: to yours alone he'll listen.
Now I shall descend to the darkness below.
Elder counselors, farewell, and though
in time of troubles, give your hearts each day
some pleasure: wealth can't benefit the dead.

*(Exit the Ghost of Darius.)*

CHORUS LEADER

Ah, many the woes upon us and the woes
still to come have grieved me hearing them.

QUEEN

O god! How many sorrows move against me!
But one torment bites me deepest of all,
to hear how such dishonor holds my son's
body and its robes. So I shall go
to gather proper clothing, and try to meet
him as he comes. When evils fall on those
we dearly love, never shall we betray them.

*(Exit the Queen into the palace.)*

CHORUS *[singing]*

STROPHE A

*Oh! What a great and a good way of life was ours,*
*civilly ordered, as long as the aged*
*ruler of all,*
*sure and unconquerable king,*
*equal to god,*
*Darius ruled the land.*

ANTISTROPHE A

*Glorious arms we displayed, and the bulwarks of custom*
*all they did guide.° And returning from battle*
*grief had we none,*
*victors, unburdened of all,*
*happy and glad,*
*to home again we came.*

STROPHE B

*For many the cities he sacked never crossing the Halys,*
*nor leaving his hearth to rush forth.*
*At the mouth of the River Strymon,*
*near Thracian places,*
*the islands of Achelous,*

ANTISTROPHE B

*the cities beyond the Aegean, surrounded by towers,*
*obeyed him our lord, and who round*
*the broad Strait of Helle were dwelling,*

*and recessed Propontis,*
*and the gateway of Pontus*

STROPHE C

*and the islands along the headland washed by the sea*
*lying close to shore:*
*Lesbos and Chios and Samos the olive-planted,*
*Paros and Naxos and Mykonos,*
*and Tenos the neighbor of Andros.*

ANTISTROPHE C

*And the islands in the midst of the sea he ruled:*
*Ikaros and Lemnos,*
*Rhodos and Knidos and cities of lovely Cyprus,*
*Paphos and Soli and Salamis,*
*whose mother city's cause of all these sorrows.*

EPODE

*Thus the wealthy and populous cities of Greeks,*
*the Ionian province, he ruled;*
*and the strength of his helmeted men*
*was unwearied, with innumerable allies.*
*But now all too clearly we bear god-given reversals*
*in war, overcome by these blows from the sea.*

*(Enter Xerxes alone, from the side.)*

XERXES [*chanting*]
*Oh, oh, what misery! Hateful my fate,*
*how unexpected,*
*how savagely swooped the deity*
*on Persia's people! What will befall me?*
*My limbs give way as I see these aged citizens.*
*Zeus! Would that death had covered me too*
*with the Persians gone!*

CHORUS [*chanting*]
*Oh alas, king, for the brave host,*
*and the great honor of Persian rule,*

*for the ranks of men whom a god has slain.*

[*singing*]
*Nations wail their native sons,°*
*who by Xerxes were killed*
*and now cram Hades;*
*many heroes, Persia's bloom,*
*archers, thick array of men,*
*myriads have perished.*
*Oh, oh, king of noble strength,*
*cruelly, cruelly Asia has to kneel.*

XERXES [*singing until the end of the play in a lyric interchange with the Chorus, which sings in reply*]

STROPHE A

*Here am I, ah, most lamentable:*
*to my native and ancestral land*
*I've become nothing but evil.*

CHORUS

*Loudly shall I send, to greet your return,°*
*an evil-omened shout, an evil-practiced cry:*
*a weeping wail I shall sing,*
*the wail of a Mariandynian mourner.*

XERXES

ANTISTROPHE A

*Send a wail of evil sound*
*lamenting and grievous; now*
*this god again has changed for me.*

CHORUS

*Mourning wail all-weeping shall I send,*
*in honor of the people's sufferings and sea-struck toils:°*
*again a wailing filled with tears I'll cry.*

XERXES

STROPHE B

*Ionian Ares triumphed,*

*protector of their ships,*
*their partisan in war,*
*reaping gloomy flats of sea*
*and demon-haunted shores.*

CHORUS

*Oh, oh!*
*Lament and learn it all.*
*Where are the others?*
*Where is your retinue, your comrades*
*like Pharandakas,*
*Sousas, Pelagon, and Agabatas,*
*Dotamas, Psammis, Sousiscanes*
*who went from Agbatana?—*

XERXES

ANTISTROPHE B

*I left them dead there;*
*they fell from the Tyrian ships on the shore of Salamis,*
*and so were gone, their corpses*
*pounding stubborn shores.*

CHORUS

*Oh, oh! But where is Pharnouchus*
*and brave Ariomardus?*
*Where is lord Seualces,*
*Or noble-born Lilaeus,*
*Memphis, Tharybis, and Masistres,*
*Artembares and Hystaechmes?*
*All these I ask you about.*

XERXES

STROPHE C

*Oh oh, woe!*
*All of them, after gazing*
*on ancient, hateful Athens,*
*at one stroke, ah, ah, wretchedly*
*gasp out their lives on the shore.*

CHORUS

*Did you leave that Persian there too,*
*your trusted universal eye*
*who made his count by myriads,°*
*Batanochus' favorite son . . .*
*. . . of Seisames, of Megabates,°*
*great Parthus and Oebares you left behind?*
*O woe, O woe, O miseries!*
*You tell of woes on woes for the Persians.*

XERXES

ANTISTROPHE C

*Oh oh, woe!*
*The magic wheel of longing*
*for my friends you turn, you tell me*
*hateful sorrows. Within my body*
*my heart cries, cries out.*

CHORUS

*And for others still we are longing:*
*the leader of ten thousand men*
*of Mardia, Xanthes, and Anchares,*
*and Diaixis and Arsames,*
*masters of horsemen;*
*and Dadakes and Lythimnas,*
*and Tolmus insatiable in battle.*
*I am shocked to see about the moving tents*
*none of these now following.*

XERXES

STROPHE D

*Gone are the hunters of the pack.*

CHORUS

*Gone, alas, nameless.*

XERXES

*Oh oh, woe.*

CHORUS

*Woe, O gods*
*who brought these unexpected miseries!*
*How fiercely gleams the eye of doom.*

XERXES

ANTISTROPHE D

*Struck from our success by woes . . .°*

CHORUS

*We've been struck by new . . .*

XERXES

*. . . by new agonies.*

CHORUS

*Woe, ah!*
*We met the Ionian sailors without success:*
*how luckless was the Persians' war.*

XERXES

STROPHE E

*Ah, I am struck, appalled that I lost such an army.*

CHORUS

*What is not lost, you curse of the Persians?*

XERXES

*Look at the remnants of my power.*

CHORUS

*I see, I see.*

XERXES

*And this receptacle . . .*

CHORUS

*What is this that is saved?*

XERXES

*. . . my treasure of arrows.*

CHORUS

*How few from so many!*

XERXES

*We are deprived of protectors.*

CHORUS

*The Greeks stand firm in combat.*

XERXES

ANTISTROPHE E

*Alas, too firm! I saw an unexpected misery.*

CHORUS

*You mean the crowd of ships, routed and broken?*

XERXES

*I tore my garments at this calamity.*

CHORUS

*Ah, O woe!*

XERXES

*And even more than woe.*

CHORUS

*Double and triple the woe.*

XERXES

*Painful to us, but to enemies joy.*

CHORUS

*And cut short was our power.*

XERXES

*I am stripped of escorts.*

CHORUS

*Sea-dooms stripped us of our friends.*

XERXES

STROPHE F

*Weep, wet your cheeks for the pain, and come homeward.*

CHORUS

*Ah, ah, misery.*

XERXES

*Cry out antiphonal to me.*

CHORUS

*A woesome gift in response to woe.*

XERXES

*Raising a cry, join together our songs.*

XERXES AND CHORUS

*O woe, woe, woe upon woe.*

CHORUS

*Hearing this calamity,*
*Oh! I am pierced.*

XERXES

ANTISTROPHE F

*Sweep, sweep, sweep with the oar, and groan for my sake.*

CHORUS

*Ah, ah! Pain, pain!*

XERXES

*Cry out antiphonal to me.*

CHORUS

*My duty is here, O master, lord.*

XERXES

*Lift up your voice in lamenting now.*

XERXES AND CHORUS

*O woe, woe, woe upon woe.*

CHORUS

*Black with bruises again the blows are mixed,*
*Oh, with the groans.*

XERXES

STROPHE G

*Beat your breast too and cry Mysian laments.*

CHORUS

*Pain, pain.*

XERXES

*Tear the whitened hair of your beard.*

CHORUS

*With clenched hand, grimly mourning.*

XERXES

*Shriek a piercing cry.*

CHORUS

*And so I shall.*

XERXES

ANTISTROPHE G

*Tear the folds of your garments with strength of hand.*

CHORUS

*Pain, pain.*

XERXES

*Pluck your hair and voice your pity for the army.*

CHORUS

*With clenched hand, grimly mourning.*

XERXES

*Drench your eyes.*

CHORUS

*Yes, so I weep.*

XERXES

EPODE

*Cry out antiphonal to me.*

CHORUS

*Oh, O woe.*

XERXES

*Go wailing to your homes.*

CHORUS

*O woe, ah!*

XERXES

*Cries of woe throughout the city.*

CHORUS

*Yes, cries of woe indeed.*

XERXES

*Softly stepping, moan in grief.*

CHORUS

*O Persian land in hardness stepped.*°

XERXES

*Oh, oh, by triple banks of oars . . .*

CHORUS

*Oh, oh, . . . our ships were destroyed by theirs.*

CHORUS

*We shall escort you*
*with mournful lament.*

*(Exit all.)*

# PROMETHEUS BOUND

*Translated by* DAVID GRENE

# PROMETHEUS BOUND: INTRODUCTION

*The Play: Date and Composition*

Almost nothing is known about the date or ancient performance history of *Prometheus Bound*. The play has survived to the modern era among the manuscripts of Aeschylus' plays, and until recently most scholars took for granted that it was indeed composed by him, as part of a connected trilogy. (The surviving fragments of this probable trilogy appear in *Aeschylus*, vol. 1, pp. 217–21; and see pp. 68–70 below for further discussion.) Some have argued that *Prometheus Bound* was a relatively early work, on the basis of its dramaturgy and style. But others have regarded it as among Aeschylus' latest compositions (which would place it in the 460s or early 450s BCE), and have compared it to the *Oresteia* for its bold trilogic worldview and religious scope.

In many respects the play is unlike any of the other six Aeschylean dramas that survive complete: the small amount and simple style of the choral lyrics, the use of actor's monody, and various other structural and stylistic features have led many scholars to conclude that Aeschylus was not in fact its author at all, or that he left the play incomplete and it was finished by members of his family. Whoever its author(s), the play and trilogy were presumably first performed at the Great Dionysian Festival in Athens, though a few scholars have suggested Sicily instead as a possible venue.

*The Myth*

In preindustrial societies all over the world, myths have recounted the acquisition by human beings of the divine spark of fire through a theft from the gods, usually performed by a bird or animal, sometimes by a man or even one of the gods themselves. For the Greeks, it was the pre-Olympian god Prometheus who was generally credited with this theft.

In several accounts (though this is not mentioned in our play), Prometheus was also the creator of human beings, molding them out of clay; and he was supposed to have been the father of Deucalion and Pyrrha, the two human beings who survived the great flood and repopulated the world. So Prometheus' role as a god uniquely connected and devoted to human beings seems to have been integral to his mythical personality. The etymology of his name contributed further to this: the Greeks interpreted the name Pro-metheus—probably correctly—as meaning "forethinker," whether in the sense of "thinking in advance" or "thinking on behalf of others." In cult, however, Prometheus seems to have been more specifically celebrated as a god of technology, especially of pottery, and especially in Athens, where an annual festival was held in his honor and he was worshipped in conjunction with Hephaestus and Athena.

Previous to the fifth century BCE, by far the most important literary accounts that survive of Prometheus and his interactions with Zeus and the Olympian gods come from Hesiod's two famous poems. In the *Theogony*, Prometheus tricks Zeus over the distribution of sacrificial meat between gods and humans. In retaliation, Zeus withholds (or "hides") fire from mortals, whereupon Prometheus steals and gives it to them. As punishment he is chained to a pillar and an eagle is sent to eat his liver, day after day, for centuries to come. The text seems to suggest that Heracles will eventually deliver him (with Zeus' permission) from his punishment. In the *Works and Days*, the emphasis is more on another consequence of Prometheus' repeated defiance of Zeus: the creation by Zeus and the other Olympian gods of Pandora, the first woman, as a bane of mankind. Hesiod does not state in either version why Prometheus tries to help humans in the first place: it just seems to be taken for granted. Both poems emphasize the deceptiveness of Prometheus and the greater wisdom and power of Zeus.

Doubtless other stories about Prometheus existed in abundance before Aeschylus: but none of them have survived in the literary record, though visual representations of several Promethean scenes are common from the archaic period onward. Aeschylus himself composed a satyr-drama, *Prometheus Fire-Kindler* (*Prometheus Pyrkaeus*), which was performed together with his tragedy *The Persians* in 472 BCE. Several papyrus fragments of this satyr-play survive, and a number of fifth-century red-figure vase paintings seem also to have been influenced by it, as they show satyrs dancing enthusiastically around the fire-wielding Prometheus.

Those, then, were the traditional mythical elements that our author was working with. In *Prometheus Bound*, the outline of the story differs little from Hesiod's, but its trajectory and significance have been much modified, almost inverted. Zeus is here described as a youthful and impetuous tyrant, and Prometheus' theft of fire seems to have been motivated, as he explains in the play, by an unwillingness to allow Zeus to exterminate the whole human race. Another significant alteration is Prometheus' parentage: whereas in Hesiod, Prometheus is son of a Titan (Iapetus) and thus Zeus' cousin, in *Prometheus Bound* he is himself of that older generation of Titans (hence Zeus' uncle), and his mother is the supremely august Earth-Themis—an unusual merging of these two closely related figures into one. Furthermore Prometheus in this play has prophetic powers (apparently an invention of Aeschylus), and these are vital to the drama and its sequel: for Prometheus alone knows of a destiny concerning the sea nymph Thetis, that if she has a son he will be mightier than his father. This secret becomes a crucial bargaining chip for Prometheus in his prolonged confrontation with Zeus, who lacks this prophetic knowledge. (The audience of the play is aware that the eventual outcome of the story will in fact be that the gods arrange for Thetis to marry the human Peleus instead—and their son will be the mighty Achilles. Presumably this outcome was revealed in the course of the rest of the trilogy, now lost.)

Apart from these stories about Prometheus that Athenian theatergoers would know in advance, and the particular associations that the god of pottery, technology, and crafts might have for them, they would also be familiar with the many stories of Heracles' labors and his killing of the eagle that was tormenting Prometheus. So the audience would not be surprised to find Heracles playing a major role later in the trilogy. But the author of *Prometheus Bound* has added to the mix of his play (and trilogy) a further mythological ingredient that was surely unexpected: the story of Io, the young maiden from Argos whom Zeus persistently harassed and eventually impregnated. In our play, the arrival of this tormented young woman, now half transformed into a cow and pursued by a buzzing, biting gadfly, comes as a complete surprise to both Prometheus and the audience. Io's lengthy explanation of her recent sufferings, and Prometheus' predictions to her of her future travels and eventual conception, introduce an intensely human and musical-choreographic element into a play that is otherwise dominated by divine characters and lengthy narratives; and Io's miseries, caused by the crude appetite of the new, young ruler of the gods, make an effective complement to the sufferings of the older and defiant Titan.

We do not know how the original audience responded to this play, whether they were inspired or appalled by Prometheus' defiance and the shrill accusations he levels against Zeus and his regime. His final words of indignation as the windstorm and earthquake begin to engulf him at the end of the play are exciting and disturbing. How will things end? The audience's reactions must have been shaped by the way the rest of the trilogy went: and to this we must now turn.

### *The Prometheus Trilogy*

Our surviving play, *Prometheus Bound*, was almost certainly part of a connected trilogy of tragedies, of which the next play in sequence was titled *Prometheus Unbound* (*Prometheus Lyomenos*; more literally translated, *Prometheus Being Released*). The title of the third play is less certain. Probably it was *Prometheus Firebringer* or *Firecarrier* (*Prometheus Pyrphoros*), since a play of this title is mentioned in an ancient list of Aeschylus' dramas. Although *Prometheus Unbound* does not survive as a complete text in any medieval manuscript, more than a dozen ancient quotations or citations from the play are known, some of them quite substantial, and as a result we have a fairly good idea of the plot and characters. For *Prometheus Firecarrier*, however, the evidence is much slimmer. And we have no idea what the title or subject was of the satyr-play that completed the tetralogy.

The most likely sequence and contents for the trilogy seem to be the following:

1. *Prometheus Firecarrier:* Prometheus steals fire from the gods and gives it to humankind. He is sentenced by Zeus to an eternity of punishment.
2. *Prometheus Bound* (our surviving play).
3. *Prometheus Unbound:* Prometheus is still chained at the beginning of the play. A chorus of Titans arrives, newly released from Tartarus by Zeus. Prometheus describes to them his miseries. Then he is perhaps visited by his mother, Earth (Gê, or Gaia), who, like Ocean in *Prometheus Bound*, tries to persuade him to be reconciled with Zeus and offers to intercede on his behalf. Heracles then enters, on his way to retrieve the Apples of the Hesperides (one of his twelve labors). Prometheus tells him about his future travels and labors; Heracles shoots the eagle that has been eating Prometheus' liver. At some point Prometheus reveals the name of Thetis, who is being (or is about to be) pursued sexually by Zeus and who (Prometheus explains) is destined to bear a son mightier than his father. Grateful for this information, Zeus approves Prometheus' release, either by Heracles or by one of the gods (perhaps Hephaestus, or Athena, or Hermes). The play and trilogy end with the institution in Athens and elsewhere of a celebratory festival and torch race, the Prometheia, and with

an explanation of why humans wear wreaths (as a token of Prometheus' former bondage).

Some scholars, however, have argued for a different sequence and reconstruction:

1. *Prometheus Bound* (our surviving play).
2. *Prometheus Unbound:* As above, except that the play ends with the release of Prometheus, and the final phase of celebrations is not included.
3. *Prometheus Firecarrier:* The festival and torch race of the Prometheia are introduced, and human beings celebrate the gift of political wisdom newly granted by Zeus (and Prometheus?).

The main objection to the first reconstruction is that *Prometheus Bound* includes extensive accounts of Prometheus' gifts to humankind, described as if for the first time. The main objection to the second reconstruction is that the contents of the third play seem rather thin, perhaps insufficient to sustain much dramatic tension and interest. Given the almost complete loss of that play, however, we must reconcile ourselves to never knowing exactly how the trilogy was organized.

### *Transmission and Reception*

Apart from a couple of allusions in Old Comedy of the 420s BCE to scenes from the *Prometheus* trilogy, there is little evidence that these plays were widely read or performed in antiquity. The figure of Prometheus continued to be employed extensively, of course, in mythological and philosophical contexts throughout antiquity and the medieval period, but usually as the personification of "forethought" and "providence"; he was no longer presented as a fierce opponent of Zeus and the Olympian gods, nor in connection with Io.

In general, after the fourth century BCE, Aeschylus' plays were much less widely read or performed than those of Sophocles or (especially) Euripides. Many of them gradually ceased to be copied and thus faded into oblivion. But all three plays of the Prometheus trilogy appear to have been catalogued among the ninety-plus dramas attributed to Aeschylus in the Alexandrian library (third century BCE), and *Prometheus Unbound* in particular was well enough known that authors such as Cicero, Strabo, Plutarch, and Arrian could quote from it extensively. When a selected edition of seven Aeschylean plays was made at some point in the Roman period, perhaps for school use, *Prometheus Bound* was included, but not *Prometheus Unbound*—for reasons unknown to us.

The play thus survived into the Byzantine and Renaissance eras, and was included (along with *The Persians* and *The Seven against Thebes*) in the triad of plays that were copied extensively during the twelfth-fifteenth centuries. Several of the manuscripts of the play contain copious marginal comments (scholia), a few of which date back to the classical period and tell us something of what took place in the other plays of the trilogy. A few lines and phrases from *Prometheus Bound* also show up in the Byzantine cento *The Passion of Christ* (*Christos Paschôn*). But for the most part, during the early modern period the play seems to have been seldom read. "Promethean fire" was generally regarded as a symbol for the intellectual and progressive capacity of human beings, but not for any kind of defiance of the supreme deity.

With the eighteenth-century Enlightenment, this began to change, and *Prometheus Bound* emerged as a favorite inspiration for radical and antireligious authors and artists. Voltaire included in his opera *Pandora* (1740) scenes of rebellion by Prometheus and other gods against Jupiter; and the young Johann Wolfgang von Goethe wrote the first two acts of a drama (1772–74), opening with the words "I refuse!," which he never completed but adapted instead into a lyric poem, *Prometheus* (1775). By the end of the eighteenth century, scholars had collected and studied the fragments of the rest of the trilogy, and were speculating about the overall story line: in 1802 Johann Gottfried Herder composed an ambitious *Prometheus Unbound*, parts of which were later set to music by Franz Liszt (1850). Percy Bysshe Shelley developed further the notion of a Prometheus-inspired rebellion against established divine authority in his own *Prometheus Unbound* (1820). Later in the nineteenth century, both Friedrich Nietzsche and Karl Marx likewise deployed the image of the Aeschylean Prometheus as a symbol for their respective notions of human artistic and political potential, and since then numerous adaptations have carried the trend forward and into the twenty-first century.

During this time, the play has been frequently performed, in original or adapted form, often provoking bold approaches to the staging and to various possibilities for overt or implied political commentary. Performances of note include the spectacular 1927 production of the play in Modern Greek at Delphi, designed and directed by Angelos Sikelianos and Eva Palmer (parts of which were captured on film and can be viewed on video); the Greek National Theater production directed by Alexis Solomos (1976–77); the Theatro Technis production directed by Karolos Koun (1983–84); and Richard Schechner's adaptation *The Prometheus Project* (New York, 1985). A number of science-fiction novels and films have also been based, however loosely, on elements of the Prometheus story, beginning with Mary Wollstonecraft Shelley's *Frankenstein; or, The Modern Prometheus* (1816); and Tony Harrison's provocative film *Prometheus* (1998) adapted our play to address the uses and abuses of technology in modern Europe. Operas based partly on it include Gabriel Fauré's *Prométhée* (1900, revised 1914–17; with libretto by Jean Lorrain and Ferdinand Hérold), Carl Orff's *Prometheus* (Munich 1968), and Luigi Nono's *Prometeo* (1984, with libretto by Massimo Cacciari).

Overall, whoever wrote it, *Prometheus Bound* stands out as one of the most famous and starkly impressive monuments of Greek drama. Its images of suffering and resistance, and the ideas that it raises of cosmic turmoil and potential overthrow of the established order, continue to challenge and inspire artists and thinkers all over the world.

# PROMETHEUS BOUND

*Characters* MIGHT, a henchman of Zeus
VIOLENCE (nonspeaking character)
HEPHAESTUS
PROMETHEUS
CHORUS of daughters of Ocean
OCEAN
IO, daughter of Inachus, the king of Argos
HERMES

*Scene: A bare and desolate crag in the Caucasus.*

*(Enter Might and Violence, followed by Hephaestus carrying blacksmith's tools.)*

MIGHT

This is the world's limit that we've come to;
the Scythian country, an unpeopled desert.
It's your job now, Hephaestus, to carry out
the commands the Father laid on you, to nail
this malefactor to the high craggy rocks
in fetters unbreakable of adamantine chain.
For it was your flower, the brilliance of fire
that enables all the arts, your flower he stole
and gave to humankind; this is the sin
for which he must pay the gods the penalty—
so that he may learn to accept the sovereignty
of Zeus and quit his human-loving ways.

HEPHAESTUS

Might and Violence, with you the command of Zeus
has found fulfilment; for you there is nothing
still left to tackle. But, for myself, I have not
the heart to bind a god who's my own kin
violently here on this wintry cliff.
Yet it's utterly required for me to have the heart
to do just that, for it is no light matter
to neglect or disrespect the Father's words.
High-contriving Prometheus, son of Themis,
the goddess of straight counsel, this is not
of your will nor of mine; yet I shall nail you
to this crag in bonds of indissoluble bronze,
far from men. Here you shall neither hear
the voice nor see the form of any mortal.
You'll be grilled by the sun's bright fire and change the fair
bloom of your skin; then you'll be glad when night
comes with her mantle of stars and hides the sun's
light; but then the sun will scatter the frost
again at dawn. The pain of your present torture
will be there always to wear you down; for he
that can relieve it has not yet been born.
Such is the reward you reap for loving humans.
For you, a god, feared not the anger of gods,
but gave honor to mortals beyond what was just.
So in return, you'll guard this loveless rock—
standing, sleepless, never bending the knee:
many a groan and many a lamentation
you'll utter, but they will not help you; no,
the mind of Zeus is hard to soften with prayer,
and every ruler's harsh whose rule is new.

MIGHT

Come, why are you holding back? Why are you pitying—
in vain? Why is it that you do not hate a god

whom the gods hate most of all? Why don't you hate him,
since it was your honor that he betrayed to men?

HEPHAESTUS

Kinship has strange power, and our life together.

MIGHT

Yes. But to turn deaf ears to the Father's words—
how can that be? Do you not fear that more?

HEPHAESTUS

You are always pitiless, always full of ruthlessness.

MIGHT

There is no point singing dirges over him.
Don't labor uselessly at what doesn't help at all.

HEPHAESTUS

O handicraft of mine—that I deeply hate!

MIGHT

Why do you hate it? To speak simply, your craft
is in no way to blame for his present troubles.

HEPHAESTUS

Yet I wish this craft were allotted to someone else!

MIGHT

Everything has its burdens, except ruling
over the gods. For only Zeus is free.

HEPHAESTUS

I know—I can see that here! And I have no answer.

MIGHT

Hurry then. Throw the chain around him, so
the Father may not see you being slow.

HEPHAESTUS

There are the fetters, there: you can see them.

MIGHT

Put them on his hands; now with the hammer, strike
with all your strength; nail him to the rock.

HEPHAESTUS

It is being done now. I am not idling at my work.

MIGHT

Hammer it more; put in the wedge; leave nothing
loose. He's clever at finding a way out
even from hopeless difficulties.

HEPHAESTUS

Look now, his arm is fixed immovably.

MIGHT

Nail the other fast, that he may learn, for all
his cleverness, that he's not as smart as Zeus.

HEPHAESTUS

No one, save Prometheus, can justly blame me.

MIGHT

Drive the obstinate jaw of the adamantine wedge
right through his breast; drive it hard.

HEPHAESTUS

Ah, Prometheus, I groan for your sufferings.

MIGHT

Are you pitying again, and groaning for Zeus' enemies?
Have a care, lest some day you may be pitying yourself.

HEPHAESTUS

You see a sight that hurts the eye to see it.

MIGHT

I see that he is getting what he deserves.
Now cast the chest bands firmly around his sides.

HEPHAESTUS

I am forced to do this; do not keep urging me.

MIGHT

Yes, I will urge you, and hound you on as well.
Get below now, and hoop his legs in strongly.

HEPHAESTUS

There now, the task is done. It's not taken long.

MIGHT

Hammer the piercing fetters with all your power,
for the overseer of our work is harsh.

HEPHAESTUS

Your looks and the refrain of your tongue are alike.

MIGHT

You can be softhearted. But do not blame
my stubbornness and harshness of temper.

HEPHAESTUS

Let us go. He has the harness on his limbs.

*(Exit Hephaestus to the side.)*

MIGHT *(To Prometheus.)*

So now, play the insolent; now, plunder
the privileges of the gods and give them
to creatures of a day. What kind of help
can mortals offer to save you from these sufferings?
The gods misname you when they call you Forethought:
it's you yourself who need Forethought, by which
to extricate yourself from this contrivance.

*(Might and Violence depart to the side. Prometheus is left alone.)*

PROMETHEUS

Bright sky, springs of the rivers, swift-winged winds,
numberless laughter of the sea's waves, Earth,
mother of all, and all-seeing circle of the sun:
I call upon you all to see what I,
a god, suffer at the hands of gods.

[*chanting*]

*See with what kind of tortures*
*worn down I shall wrestle ten thousand*
*years of time—such are*
*the shameful shackles that he,*
*the new commander of the Blessed Ones,*
*has devised against me.*
*Ah, ah!*
*I groan for the present sorrow,*
*I groan for the sorrow to come.*
*When shall the time come*
*to ordain a limit to my sufferings?*

[*speaking*]
But what am I saying? I have foreknowledge of
all that shall be; it's clearly known to me,
and none of these pains shall come as a surprise.
So must I bear, as lightly as I can,
the destiny that fate has given me;
for I know well that against necessity,
in all its strength, no one can fight and win.
I cannot speak about my fortune, cannot
hold my tongue either. It was mortals, humans,
to whom I gave great privileges, and
for that was yoked in this unyielding harness.
I hunted out the secret spring of fire
that filled the fennel stalk, which when revealed
became the teacher of each craft to men,
a great resource. This is the crime committed
for which I stand convicted, and I pay
nailed in my chains under the open sky.

[*singing*]
*Ah! Ah!*
*What sound, what unseen smell approaches me,*
*god-sent, or mortal, or mingled?*
*Has someone come to earth's end*

*to look on my sufferings,*
*or wishing something else?*

[*chanting*]
*You see me a wretched god in chains,*
*the enemy of Zeus, hated of all*
*the gods that enter Zeus's halls,*
*because of my excessive love for mortals.*
*Ah, ah! What is that? The rustle*
*of birds' wings near? The air whispers*
*with the gentle strokes of wings.*
*Everything that comes toward me*
*is occasion for fear.*

(*The Chorus enters.*)°

CHORUS [*singing while Prometheus chants in response*]

STROPHE A

*Fear not: this is a company of friends*
*that comes to your mountain with swift*
*rivalry of wings.*
*Scarcely had we persuaded our father's*
*mind, and the quick-bearing winds*
*speeded us hither. The sound*
*of stroke of iron rang through our cavern*
*in its depths, and it shook from us*
*shamefaced modesty; unsandaled*
*we have hastened on our chariot of wings.*

PROMETHEUS

*Ah, children of teeming Tethys*
*and of him who encircles all*
*the world with unsleeping stream,*
*father Ocean:*
*look, see with what chains*
*I am nailed on the craggy heights*
*of this ravine to keep a watch*
*that none would envy.*

CHORUS

ANTISTROPHE A

*I see, Prometheus, and a mist of fear and tears*
*assails my eyes as I see your body*
*wasting away on these cliffs*
*in adamantine bonds of bitter shame.*
*For new are the steersmen that rule Olympus,*
*and new are the customs by which Zeus rules,*
*customs that have no justice to them,*
*but what was great before he brings to nothingness.*

PROMETHEUS

*I wish that he had hurled me*
*underneath the earth and underneath*
*the House of Hades, host to the dead—*
*yes, down to limitless Tartarus,*
*yes, though he bound me cruelly*
*in chains unbreakable,*
*so neither god nor any other being*
*might have found joy in gloating over me.*
*Now as I hang, the plaything of the winds,*
*my enemies can laugh at what I suffer.*

CHORUS

STROPHE B

*Who of the gods is so hard of heart*
*that he finds joy in this?*
*Who is there that does not feel*
*sorrow answering your pain—*
*save only Zeus? For he malignantly,*
*always cherishing a mind*
*that does not bend, has subdued the breed*
*of Ouranos, nor shall he cease*
*until either he satisfies his heart*
*or someone take the power from him—power that's hard to take!—*
*by some device of subtlety.*

PROMETHEUS

*Yes, there will come a day*
*when he will need me, me that now*
*am tortured in bonds and fetters—*
*he will need me then,*
*this president of the Blessed Ones—*
*to show him the new plot whereby he can be*
*despoiled of his throne and his power.*
*Then not with honeyed tongues*
*of persuasion will he enchant me;*
*he will not cow me with his threats*
*to tell him what I know,*
*until he frees me from my cruel chains*
*and pays me recompense for what I suffer.*

CHORUS

ANTISTROPHE B

*You are stout of heart, unyielding*
*to the bitterness of pain.*
*You are free of tongue, too free.*
*But piercing fear has disturbed my mind;*
*your misfortunes frighten me.*
*Where and when is it fated*
*to see you reach the term, to see you reach*
*the harbor free of trouble at the last?*
*A disposition none can touch, a heart*
*that no persuasions soften—these are his,*
*the son of Cronus.*

PROMETHEUS

*I know that he's savage, his justice*
*a thing he keeps by his own standard;*
*yet that will of his shall melt*
*to softness in due course,*
*when he is broken in the way I know;*
*and though his temper now*

*is oak-hard, it will be softened:*
*eagerly he'll come to meet*
*my eagerness, to join*
*in amity and union with me—*
*one day he will come.*

CHORUS LEADER [*speaking*]

Reveal it all to us: tell us the story
of what the charge was on which Zeus caught you
and punished you so cruelly with such dishonor.
Tell us, if telling will not injure you.

PROMETHEUS [*speaking*]

To speak of this is bitterness. To keep silent
bitter no less; and every way is misery.
When first the gods began their angry quarrel,
and god matched god in growing faction, some
eager to drive old Cronus from his throne
so Zeus might rule—the fools!—others again
eager that Zeus should never be their king,
I then with the best counsel tried to win
the Titans, sons of Ouranos and Earth,
but failed. They would have none of crafty schemes
and in their savage arrogance of spirit
thought they would lord it easily by force.
But she that was my mother, Themis, Earth—
she is but one although her names are many—
had prophesied to me how it would be,
just as it was determined, and she said,
"Not by strength nor overmastering force
must victory be decided, but the conquest
must be by guile." This is what I told them,
but they wouldn't even consider it at all.
Then with those things before me it seemed best
to take my mother and join Zeus's side,
and he was just as willing as we were;
thanks to my plans the dark receptacle

of Tartarus conceals the ancient Cronus,
him and his allies. These were the services
I rendered to this tyrant and these pains
the payment he has given me in return.
This is a sickness rooted and inherent
in the nature of a tyranny:
that the one who holds it doesn't trust his friends.
But you have asked on what particular
charge he now tortures me: this I will tell you.
As soon as he ascended to the throne
that was his father's, straightway he assigned
to the several gods their several privileges
and portioned out the power; but to the unhappy
breed of mankind he gave no heed, intending
to blot the race out and create a new one.
No one opposed these plans save I: I dared.
I rescued men from shattering destruction
that would have carried them to Hades' house
and therefore I am tortured on this rock,
a bitterness to suffer, and piteous
to see. I gave priority to mortals
in pity, but found none of it for myself.
Instead I'm being disciplined like this,
pitilessly, a spectacle that brings
shame and dishonor to the name of Zeus.

CHORUS LEADER

Iron-minded and made of stone would be indeed,
Prometheus, anyone who did not sympathize
with your sufferings. I would not have chosen
to see them, and now I see, my heart is pained.

PROMETHEUS

Yes, to my friends I am pitiable to see.

CHORUS LEADER

Did you perhaps go further than you have told us?

PROMETHEUS

I caused mortals to cease foreseeing death.

CHORUS LEADER

What cure did you provide against that sickness?

PROMETHEUS

I placed in them blind hopes.

CHORUS LEADER

That was indeed
a great benefaction that you gave to mortals.

PROMETHEUS

Besides this, I also gave them fire.

CHORUS LEADER

And do creatures of a day now possess bright fire?

PROMETHEUS

Yes, and from it they shall learn many crafts.

CHORUS LEADER

Then these are the charges on which—

PROMETHEUS

Zeus tortures me and gives me no respite.

CHORUS LEADER

Is there no limit set to end your pain?

PROMETHEUS

None save when it will seem good to Zeus.

CHORUS LEADER

How will it ever seem good to him? What hope
is there? Do you not see how you have erred?
It is not pleasant for me to say you've erred,
and for you it is a pain to hear. But let us speak
no more of this; instead, look for some means
of deliverance and release from your torment.

PROMETHEUS

It is an easy thing for one whose foot
is on the outside of calamity
to give advice and to rebuke the sufferer.
I knew all this, and all that I did wrong
I did on purpose; I shall not deny it.
In helping mortals I brought pain on myself;
but yet I did not think that with such tortures
as these I should be withered on these cliffs,
up high, alone, on this deserted hillside.
    But do not sorrow for my present suffering;
alight on earth and hear what is to come
so you may know it all, right to the end.
I beg you, alight and join your sorrow with mine:
misfortune wanders everywhere, and settles
now upon one and now upon another.

CHORUS [*chanting*]

*Willing our ears,*
*that hear you cry to us, Prometheus.*
*Now with light foot I'll leave*
*the rushing car and sky,*
*the holy path of birds,*
*and approach the rugged earth:*
*I long to hear the story*
*of your troubles to the end.*

*(The Chorus exits.° Enter Ocean, riding on a winged sea monster.)*

OCEAN [*chanting*]

*I come to my destination*
*completing a long journey,*
*to visit you, Prometheus.*
*I direct my swift-winged bird*
*with the mind alone, no bridle.*
*In my heart I share the pain*
*for your misfortunes; you know that.*

*I think that it is kinship*
*that makes me feel them so.*
*Besides, apart from kinship,*
*there's no one that I hold*
*in higher estimation than you.*
*This you soon shall know for sure*
*and know beside that in me*
*there is no mere word-kindness;*
*tell me how I can help you,*
*and you will never say*
*that you have any friend*
*more loyal to you than Ocean.*

PROMETHEUS

What do I see? Have you, too, come to stare
in wonder at this great display, my torture?
How did you have the courage to come here
to this land, mother of iron, leaving the stream
called after you and the rock-roofed, self-established
caverns? Was it to feast your eyes upon
the spectacle of my suffering and join
in pity for my pain? Now look and see
the sight, this friend of Zeus, that helped set up
his monarchy, and see what agonies
twist me, by his instructions!

OCEAN [*now speaking*]

Yes, I see,
Prometheus, and I want, indeed I do,
to advise you for the best, for all your cleverness.
Know yourself and reform your ways to new ways,
for new is he that rules among the gods.
But if you throw about such angry words,
words that are whetted swords, soon Zeus will hear you,
even though his seat aloft is far removed,
and then your present multitude of pains
will seem like child's play. My poor friend, give up

this angry mood of yours and look for ways
of freeing yourself from these troubles. Maybe
what I say seems to you both old and commonplace;
but this is what you pay, Prometheus, for
that tongue of yours which talked so high and haughty:
you are not yet humble; still you do not yield
to your misfortunes, and you wish, indeed,
to add some more to them; now, if you follow
me as your teacher, you will not rear and kick
against the rider's whip, seeing that our king,
ruling alone, is harsh and sends accounts
to no one's audit for the deeds he does.
Now I will go and try if I can free you,
so you be quiet; do not talk so much.
Since your mind is so subtle, don't you know
that a thoughtless tongue is subject to correction?

PROMETHEUS

I envy you, that you stand so clear of blame,
yet shared and dared in everything with me!
Now let me be, and do not get involved.
Do what you will, you'll never persuade him!
He is not easily won over: look,
take care you are not harmed for your journey here.

OCEAN

By nature you're much better at advising
others than yourself. I take my cue
from deeds, not words. Do not restrain me now
when I am eager to go to Zeus. I'm sure,
I'm sure that he will grant this favor to me,
to free you from these torments you have now.

PROMETHEUS

I thank you and will never cease; for eagerness
is not what you are wanting in. Don't trouble,
for you will trouble to no purpose, and no help

to me—even if you really do want to trouble.
No, rest yourself, keep out of the way;
just because I'm unlucky I would not,
for that, have everyone else be unlucky too.
No, for my heart is sore already when
I think about my brothers' fortunes—Atlas,
who stands to westward of the world, supporting
the pillar of earth and heaven on his shoulders,
a load beyond all bearing; also Typhon,
the earthborn dweller in that Cilician cave,
whom I saw and pitied, a hundred-headed monster,
dreadful, yet conquered and brought low by force.°
Once against all the gods he stood, opposed,
hissing out terror from his grim jaws; his eyes
flashed gorgon-glaring lightning as he thought
to smash the sovereign tyranny of Zeus.
But down upon him came the unsleeping bolt
of Zeus, the lightning-breathing flame, onrushing,
which hurled him from his high aspiring boasts.
Struck to the heart, his strength was blasted dead
and burnt to ashes; now a sprawling mass
useless he lies, hard by the narrow seaway
pressed down beneath the roots of Aetna. High
above him on the mountain peak the smith
Hephaestus works at the anvil. Yet one day
there shall burst out rivers of fire, devouring
with savage jaws the fertile, level plains
of Sicily with their fair fruits; such wrath
boiling with weapons of fire-breathing surf,
an unapproachable torrent, shall Typhon vomit,
though Zeus's lightning's left him but a cinder.
But all of this you know: you don't need me
to be your teacher; reassure yourself
as you know how—this cup I shall drain myself
until the high mind of Zeus shall cease from anger.

OCEAN

So do you not know, Prometheus, that words
are healers of a temper that is sick?

PROMETHEUS

Yes, if one tries at just the right moment
to soften the heart, and doesn't violently
seek to reduce the anger that's still swelling.

OCEAN

Tell me, what danger do you see for me
in loyalty to you, and courage therein?

PROMETHEUS

I see just useless effort—and silly good nature.

OCEAN

Allow me then to be sick of this sickness, since
it's profitable, if one's wise, to seem foolish.

PROMETHEUS

This shall seem to be *my* fault, more than yours.

OCEAN

Clearly your words send me home again.

PROMETHEUS

Yes, lest your grieving for me bring you enemies.

OCEAN

The one who newly sits on the all-powerful throne?

PROMETHEUS

Yes, his is a heart you should beware of vexing.

OCEAN

Your own misfortune's my teacher, Prometheus.

PROMETHEUS

Off with you, then! Begone—keep your present mind.

OCEAN

These words fall on very responsive ears.
Already my four-legged bird is pawing the air,
the level track of heaven, with his wings,
and he'll gladly bend the knee in his own stable.

*(Exit Ocean. The Chorus reenters from the side.)*°

CHORUS [*singing*]

STROPHE A

*I cry aloud, Prometheus, and lament your bitter fate,*
*my tender eyes are trickling tears,*
*their fountains wet my cheek.*
*With these cruel things done by his own private laws,*
*Zeus the tyrant shows his haughtiness*
*of temper toward the gods that were of old.*

ANTISTROPHE A

*Now all the earth has cried aloud, lamenting:*
*they lament what was magnificent of old,*
*in sorrow for your fall and for your brethren's fall.*°
*All the mortals who in holy Asia hold*
*their stablished habitation, all lament*
*in sympathy for your most grievous woes,*

STROPHE B

*and the dwellers in the land of Colchis,*
*maidens, fearless in the fight,*
*and the host of Scythia, living*
*round the lake Maeotis, living*
*on the edges of the world,*

ANTISTROPHE B

*and Arabia's flower of warriors*
*and the craggy fortress keepers*
*near Caucasian mountains, fighters*
*terrible, crying for battle,*
*brandishing sharp-pointed spears.*

STROPHE C

*Only one other of the Titans have I seen*
*before this day, in torture and in bonds*
*unbreakable, god though he was,*
*Atlas, whose strength and might*
*were surpassing; now he bends his back*
*and groans beneath the load of earth and heaven.°*

ANTISTROPHE C

*The wave cries out as it breaks into surf;*
*the depth cries out, lamenting you; the dark*
*Hades, the hollow underneath the world,*
*sullenly groans below; the springs*
*of sacred flowing rivers all lament*
*the pain and pity of your suffering.*

PROMETHEUS

Don't think I'm silent out of pride or stubbornness:
in self-awareness my heart is gnawed away
to see myself insulted as I am.
Yet who was it but I who distributed
their honors to these new gods? I'll say no more
of this; you know it all; but hear what troubles
there were among mortals, how I found them mindless
but made them intelligent and masters of their minds.
I'll tell you this, not blaming human beings,
but to explain the goodwill of my gifts.
For humans in the beginning had eyes but saw
to no purpose; they had ears but did not hear.
Like the shapes of dreams they dragged through their long lives
and muddled everything haphazardly.
They did not know how to build brick houses
to face the sun; nor how to work in wood.
They lived beneath the earth like swarming ants,
in sunless caves. For them there was no secure
token for telling winter or flowering spring,

nor summer with its crops; and all they did
they did without intelligent calculation
until I showed them the rising of the stars,
and the settings, hard to observe. And I invented
numbers for them, preeminent among all skills.
and the combining of written letters as a means
of remembering all things, the Muses' mother,
skilled in craft. It was I who first yoked beasts
to be slaves in harness and under pack saddles,°
as substitutes for humans in hard tasks;
and I harnessed to the carriage obedient horses,
the crowning pride of wealth and luxury.
It was I and none other who discovered ships,
sail-winged wagons that bear men over the sea.
Such—to my misery—were the devices which
I discovered for mortals, but I have no clever means
to rid myself of my own present affliction.

CHORUS LEADER

You have suffered terribly. Bewildered in your mind
you are astray, and like a bad doctor who
has fallen sick, you have lost heart not finding
by what drugs your own illness might be cured.

PROMETHEUS

If you hear the rest you will marvel even more
at the crafts and the resources I contrived.
Greatest was this: when one of mankind fell sick
there was no defense for him—neither healing food
nor drink nor unguent; for lack of cures they wasted,
until I showed them the blending of mild remedies
with which they drive away all kinds of sickness.
The many ways of prophecy I charted;
I was the first to judge what out of dreams
came truly real; and for mankind I gave meaning
to ominous cries, hard of interpretation,

and to the significance of road encounters.
The flight of hook-taloned birds I analyzed,
which of them were in nature propitious
and which unlucky; what habits each species has,
what are their hates and loves and affiliations.
Also I taught of the smoothness of the entrails
and what color the bile should have to please the gods,
and the dappled symmetry of the liver lobe.
It was I who burned the thigh bones wrapped in fat
and the long shank bone; I set mortals on the road
to the murky craft of divination, making
the flaming signs, once dim, now clear to see.
So much for these things. Then beneath the earth
those hidden blessings, copper, iron, silver,
and gold—who can claim to have discovered them before me?
No one, I am sure, who wants to speak to the purpose.
In one short sentence understand it all:
all human arts come from Prometheus.

CHORUS LEADER

Well, don't help mortals beyond due occasion
while careless of yourself in your own troubles.
I am of good hope that you, freed of these bonds,
will one day be no less in power than Zeus.

PROMETHEUS

Not yet has fate that brings all things to pass
determined this. First I must be tormented
by ten thousand pangs and agonies, as I am now,
before I can escape my chains.
Craft is far weaker than necessity.

CHORUS LEADER

Who then is the steersman of necessity?

PROMETHEUS

The three-formed Fates and the remembering Furies.

CHORUS LEADER
And is Zeus, then, weaker than these?

PROMETHEUS
Yes,
for he too cannot escape what is fated.

CHORUS LEADER
But what is fated for Zeus save eternal rule?

PROMETHEUS
You cannot know that yet; do not entreat me.

CHORUS LEADER
This must be some solemn secret that you're hiding.

PROMETHEUS
Think of some other story; this one's not seasonable
to utter, it must be wholly hidden.
For only by so keeping it can I
escape my shameful bonds and agonies.

CHORUS [*singing*]

STROPHE A

*May Zeus never, Zeus that controls*
*the whole universe, oppose*
*his power against my mind;*
*may I never be lazy*
*or slow to give my worship at*
*the sacrificial feasts*
*when the bulls are killed beside*
*the quenchless stream of father Ocean;*
*may I never sin in word;*
*may these precepts still abide*
*in my mind nor melt away.*

ANTISTROPHE A

*It is a sweet thing to draw out*

*a long, long life in cheerful hopes,*
*and feed the spirit in the bright*
*benignity of happiness;*
*but I shudder when I see you*
*wasted with ten thousand pains,°*
*all because you did not tremble*
*at the name of Zeus: your mind*
*was yours, not his, and at its bidding*
*you regarded mortal beings*
*too high, Prometheus.*

STROPHE B

*Kindness that can't be requited—tell me, where*
*is the help in that, my friend? What support*
*in creatures of a day? You did not see*
*the feebleness that draws its breath in gasps,*
*a dreamlike feebleness by which the race*
*of humans is held in bondage, a blind prisoner.*
*So the plans of mortals shall never*
*surpass the ordered law of Zeus.*

ANTISTROPHE B

*This I have learned while I looked on your fortunes,*
*these deadly pains of yours, Prometheus.*
*A dirge for you came to my lips, so different*
*from the other song I sang to crown your marriage,*
*in honor of the bath and of the bed,*
*upon the day you won her with your gifts°*
*to be your wife—my sister, Hesione,*
*and so you brought her home to share your bed.*

*(Enter Io from the side, with horns like an ox on her head.)*

IO [*chanting*]
*What land is this? What race of men?*
*Who is it I see here being tortured*
*in rocky bondage? What is the crime*

*he's paying for? Tell me, to what part*
*of the world have my wanderings brought me?*

[*singing*]
*O, O, O,*
*there it is again, there again—it stings me,*
*the gadfly, the ghost of earthborn Argus;*
*keep it away, keep it away!*
*I'm frightened when I see the shape of Argus,*
*Argus the herdsman with ten thousand eyes.*
*He stalks me with his crafty eyes; he died,*
*but the earth didn't hide him; still he comes*
*even from the depths of the underworld to hunt me:*
*he drives me starving by the sands of the sea.*

STROPHE A

*The loud reed pipes, glued with wax,*
*drone their sleep-giving melody:*
*O, O, O!*
*Where am I brought by my far-wandering wanderings?*
*Son of Cronus, what fault, what fault*
*did you find in me that you should yoke me*
*to a harness of misery like this, O, O,*
*that you should torture me so to madness*
*driven in fear of the gadfly?*
*Burn me with fire; hide me in earth; cast me away*
*to monsters of the deep for food; but do not*
*begrudge me the granting of this prayer, King.*
*Enough have my much-wandering wanderings*
*exercised me; I cannot find*
*a way to escape my troubles.*
*Do you hear the voice of the cow-horned girl?*

PROMETHEUS [*speaking*]
Surely I hear the voice of the gadfly-haunted
daughter of Inachus, who fired with love
the heart of Zeus and now through Hera's hate
is violently driven on courses overlong.

IO [*still singing*]

ANTISTROPHE A

*How is it you speak my father's name?*
*Tell me, who are you? Who are you? Oh*
*who are you that so exactly accosts me by name?*
*You have spoken of the disease that the gods have sent to me*
*which wastes me away, pricking with goads,*
*so that I am moving always*
*tortured and hungry, wild bounding.*
*Quick-sped I come,*
*a victim of Hera's jealous plots.*
*Who has been so wretched, O, O,*
*before me, as to suffer as I do?*
*But declare to me clearly*
*what I have still to suffer, what would avail*
*against my sickness, what drug would cure it.*
*Tell me, if you know:*
*tell me, declare it to this unlucky, wandering girl.*

PROMETHEUS

I shall tell you clearly all that you would know,
weaving no riddles, but simply, in plain words,
as it is just to open one's lips to friends.
You see Prometheus, giver of fire to men.

IO [*now speaking*]

You that have shown yourself a shared blessing
to all mankind, unhappy Prometheus,
for what are you being punished in this way?

PROMETHEUS

I have just now ceased from telling my mournful tale.

IO

Then will you grant me this favor?

PROMETHEUS

Say what it is
you are requesting; you will learn it all.

IO

Tell who it was that nailed you to the cliff.

PROMETHEUS

The plan was Zeus', but it was Hephaestus' hand.

IO

What was the offense for which this is the punishment?

PROMETHEUS

It's enough that I have told you clearly so far.

IO

In addition, then, indicate to me what date
will be the limit of my wanderings.

PROMETHEUS

Better for you not to know this than to know it.

IO

Don't hide from me what I am due to suffer.

PROMETHEUS

It's not that I begrudge you this favor that you ask.

IO

Why then delay to tell me everything?

PROMETHEUS

No grudging, but I hesitate to break your spirit.

IO

Do not have more thought for me than I want myself.

PROMETHEUS

Since you're so eager, I must speak; hear me.

CHORUS LEADER

Not yet. Give to me, too, a share of pleasure.
First let us question her about her sickness,
and let her tell us of her ruinous fortunes.
Then she can learn from you her sufferings to come.

PROMETHEUS

It is your task, Io, to gratify these spirits,
who are moreover your father's sisters. For
wailing and lamenting one's ill fortune,
when one will win a tear from those who listen,
is well worthwhile.

IO

I know not how I should distrust you; clearly
you will hear all you want to know from me.
Yet I'm ashamed to speak about that storm,
god-sent, that ruin of my beauty, and
how it came upon me. There were constant
night visions that kept haunting me and coming
into my maiden chamber and exhorting
with winning words, "O maiden greatly blessed,
why are you still a virgin, you who might
make marriage with the greatest? Zeus is stricken
with desire for you; he's afire to try the act
of love with you; do not disdain the bed
of Zeus. Go, child, to Lerna's grassy meadow,
to where your father's flocks and cattle stand
so that Zeus's eye may cease from longing for you."
With such dreams I was cruelly beset
night after night until I took the courage
to tell my father of my nightly dreams.
He sent to Pytho many an embassy
and to Dodona seeking to discover
what deed or word of his might please the gods;
but those he sent came back with riddling oracles
dark and beyond the power of understanding.
At last the word came clear to Inachus
charging him plainly that he cast me out
of home and country, drive me out unsupervised
to wander to the limits of the world;
if he should not obey, the oracle said,

the fire-faced thunderbolt would come from Zeus
and wipe out his whole race. These were the oracles
of Loxias, and Inachus obeyed them.
He drove me out and shut his doors against me
with tears on both our parts, but Zeus's bridle
compelled him to do this against his will.
Immediately my form and mind were changed
and all distorted; as you see, with horns,
pricked on by the sharp-biting gadfly, leaping
in frenzied jumps I ran beside the river
of Cerchnea, good to drink, and Lerna's spring.
The earth-born herdsman Argus followed me
whose fierceness knew no limits, and he spied
after my tracks with all his hundred eyes.
Then an unlooked-for doom, descending suddenly,
took him from life; I, driven by the gadfly,
that god-sent scourge, am driven always onward
from one land to another. That is my story.
If you can tell me what remains for me,
tell me, and do not out of pity try
to soothe me with kindly lies; there is no sickness
more shameful in my view than made-up words.

CHORUS [*singing*]

*Hold! Keep away! Alas!*
*never did I think that such strange*
*words would come to my ears;*
*never did I think such intolerable*
*sufferings, an offense to the eye,*
*shameful and frightening, so*
*would chill my soul with a double-edged point.*
*Ah, ah, what a fate!*
*I shudder when I look on Io's fortune.*

PROMETHEUS

You groan already; you are full of fear too soon:
wait till you hear besides what's still to come.

CHORUS LEADER

Speak, tell us to the end. For the sick it is sweet to know
beforehand clearly the pain that still remains.

PROMETHEUS

The first request you made of me you gained
lightly: from her you wished to hear the story
of what she suffered. Now hear what still remains,
what sufferings this girl must yet endure
from Hera. Do you listen, child of Inachus,
hear and lay up my words within your heart
so you may know the limits of your journey.
First turn to the sun's rising and walk on
over the fields no plough has broken; then
you will come to the nomad Scythians, who live
in wicker houses built on well-wheeled wagons,
aloft; they are armed with bows that strike from far.
Do not draw near them; rather let your feet
skirt the rocky coast where the waves moan,
and pass through their country; on your left there live
the Chalybes who work with iron: these
you must beware of; for they are not gentle,
not people whom a stranger dare approach.
Then you will come to the River Insolence
that well deserves its name, but do not cross it—
it is not a stream that can be easily forded—
until you come to Caucasus itself,
the highest of mountains, where the river's strength
gushes from its summit. So you must
cross its peaks, the neighbors of the stars,
and take the road southward until you reach
the man-hating Amazons, who one day
shall live around Thermodon in Themiscyra
where Salmydessus stands, that rocky cape,
hostile to sailors, stepmother of ships.
The Amazons will set you on your way

and gladly; you will reach Cimmeria,
the isthmus, at the narrows of the lake.
Leave this with a bold heart and then traverse
the channel of Maeotis, and hereafter
for all time men shall talk about your crossing,
and they shall call the place for you Cow's-Ford.
Leave Europe's mainland then, and enter Asia.

*(To the Chorus.)*

Do you not think the tyrant of the gods
is equally brutal in all the things he does?
He is a god, yet sought to lie in love
with this girl who's mortal, and on her he's brought
this curse of wanderings. Bitter indeed, poor girl,
you've found this suitor for your favors. Yet
you still must think of all that I have told you
as only the prelude.

IO

Oh, oh!

PROMETHEUS

Again, you are crying and lamenting: what
will you do when you hear of the evils yet to come?

CHORUS LEADER

Is there more suffering to come that you must tell her?

PROMETHEUS

A wintry sea of agony and ruin.

IO

What good is life to me then? Why do I not throw
myself at once from this rough crag, to strike
the ground and find release from all my troubles?
It would be better to die once for all
than suffer all one's days.

PROMETHEUS

You'd find it hard to bear these trials of mine,
since for me death is not decreed at all.
Death would be indeed release from pain;
but for me there is no limit of suffering set
till Zeus shall fall from power.

IO

And is that possible?
You mean that Zeus' rule might one day fall?

PROMETHEUS

You would be glad, I think, to see that outcome.

IO

Of course, since it's from Zeus I suffer so.

PROMETHEUS

Then know that this is truly how things are.°

IO

Who will despoil him of his sovereign scepter?

PROMETHEUS

His own light-witted decisions will undo him.

IO

How? Tell me, if there is no harm to telling.

PROMETHEUS

He'll make a marriage that one day he'll regret.

IO

With god or mortal? Tell me, if it may be told.

PROMETHEUS

Why ask what marriage? That is not to be spoken.

IO

Is it from his wife that he shall lose his throne?

PROMETHEUS
Yes, she'll bear him a son mightier than his father.

IO
And has he no escape from this downfall?

PROMETHEUS
None, save myself—if I'm freed from my chains.

IO
But who is there to free you, against Zeus's will?

PROMETHEUS
It has to be one of your own descendants.

IO
What, shall a child of mine free you from torment?

PROMETHEUS
Yes, in the thirteenth generation to come.

IO
No longer can I grasp your prophecy.

PROMETHEUS
Then do not seek to learn your own troubles further.

IO
Don't offer me the gift and then withhold it.

PROMETHEUS
I'll give you then just one of the two stories.

IO
Which stories? Say, and let me have the choice.

PROMETHEUS
Yes, I will give that to you: either to tell you
clearly the rest of your troubles, or my deliverer.

CHORUS LEADER
Please, grant her the one and grant me the other favor;
don't disappoint us. Tell her what remains

of her wanderings in the future; and tell us
of your deliverer. That is what I want.

PROMETHEUS

Since you have so much eagerness, I will not
refuse to tell you all that you have asked me.
First to you, Io, I shall tell the tale
of your sad wanderings, rich in groans—inscribe
the story in the tablets of your mind.
When you shall cross the channel that divides
Europe from Asia, turn to the rising sun,
and cross the sun-scorched plains, that waveless sea,°
until you arrive into the Gorgon land
and the flat stretches of Cisthene's country.
There live the ancient maids, children of Phorcys:
three swan-formed hags, with but one common eye,
single-toothed monsters, such as nowhere else
the sun's rays look on nor the moon by night.
Near are their winged sisters, the three Gorgons,
with snakes to bind their hair up, mortal-hating—
no mortal that looks on them shall still draw breath—
this is the garrison I tell you of.
Hear, too, of yet another gruesome sight,
the sharp-toothed hounds of Zeus, that have no bark,
the griffins—beware of them!—and the host
of one-eyed Arimaspians, horse-riding,
that live around the waters that flow with gold,
of the River Pluto: do not go near them.
A land far off, a nation of black people,
these you shall come to, men who live hard by
the fountain of the sun where is the river
Aethiops—travel by its banks along
to a cataract where from the Bybline hills
the Nile pours its holy, healthful waters.
This river shall be your guide to the three-cornered
land of Nilotis, and there, by fate's decree,

there, Io, you shall find your distant home,
a colony for you and your descendants.
If anything of this is still obscure
or difficult, ask me again and learn
clearly: I have more leisure than I wish.

CHORUS LEADER

If there is anything further or left over
you have to tell her of her deadly traveling,
tell it. If that is all, grant us in turn
the favor we asked for earlier. You remember?

PROMETHEUS

The limit of her wanderings she now
has heard, complete; but so that she may know
that she has not been listening to no purpose
I shall recount what she endured before
she came to us here: this I give as pledge,
a witness to the good faith of my words.
The great part of the story I omit
and come to the last stage of your wanderings.
When you had come to the Molossian plains
around the steep ridge of Dodona, where
the oracular seat is of Thesprotian Zeus,
the talking oaks, a wonder past belief:
by them full clearly, in no riddling terms,
you were hailed Zeus' glorious wife-to-be.
Does any of this wake sweet memories?
Then, goaded by the gadfly, on you hastened
by the shoreline path to the great Gulf of Rhea.
But then in backward course, as if storm-driven,
you had to reverse your tracks; in time to come
that inlet of the sea shall bear your name
and shall be called Ionian, a memorial
to all men of your journeying; these are proofs
for you, of how my mind sees something farther
than what is visible.

*(To the Chorus.)*

For what is left,
to you and to her this I shall say in common,
taking up again the track of my old tale.
There is a city, on the furthest edge of land,
Canobus, near the mouth and issuing point
of the Nile: it's there that Zeus shall restore your mind,°
touching you with a hand that brings no fear,
and through that touch alone shall come your healing.
You shall bear Epaphus, dark of skin, his name
recalling Zeus's touch and his begetting.
This Epaphus shall reap the fruit of all
the land that is watered by the broad-flowing Nile.
From him five generations, and again
to Argos they shall come, against their will,
in number fifty, women, fleeing from
a marriage with their cousins; but these cousins,
their hearts with lust aflutter, just like hawks
barely outdistanced by fleeing doves, will come
hunting a marriage that's not theirs to hunt;
the gods shall grudge the men these women's bodies,
and the Pelasgian earth shall welcome them°
in death, for death shall claim them in a fight
where women strike in the dark, a murderous vigil.
Each wife shall rob her husband of his life
dipping in blood her two-edged sword; even so
may Cypris come, too, upon my enemies.
But one of these girls, softened by love's charms,
will spare her bedfellow, her purpose blunted;
and she shall make her choice—to bear the name
of coward and not murderer, and she
shall bear in Argos a family of kings.
To tell this clearly needs a longer story,
but from her seed shall spring a man renowned
for archery, and he shall set me free.

Such was the prophecy which ancient Themis
my Titan mother opened up to me;
but how and by what means it shall come true
would take too long to tell, and if you heard,
the knowledge would not profit you.

IO [*chanting*]

*Eleleu, eleleu!*
*It grabs me again, the twitching spasm,*
*the mind-destroying madness, burning me up,*
*as the gadfly's sting pricks like fire;°*
*my heart in its fear knocks on my breast.*
*There's a dazing whirl in my eyes as I run*
*out of my course driven by the wild winds*
*of maddening frenzy; my tongue ungoverned*
*babbles, the words in a thick muddy flow*
*crash into the waves of hateful ruin*
*without aim or sense.*

(*Exit Io to the side.*)

CHORUS [*singing*]

STROPHE A

*A wise man indeed he was*
*that first in judgment weighed this word*
*and gave it tongue: the best by far*
*it is to marry in one's rank and station;*
*let no one working with his hands aspire*
*to marriage with those lifted high in pride*
*because of wealth or ancestral glory.*

ANTISTROPHE A

*Never, never may you see me,*
*O you Fates, drawing close°*
*to the bed of Zeus, to share it as his partner,*
*nor ever may I be joined with a god for my wooer.*
*I feel dread when I see Io, hating her husband,*
*her virginity ravaged, in bitter wandering*
*because of Hera's fierce wrath.*

EPODE

*But when a match has equal partners*
*then I fear not; may the eye*
*inescapable of the mighty gods*
*not look on me with desire.*
*That is a fight that none can fight, a fruitful*
*source of fruitlessness. I would not*
*know what I could do; I cannot see*
*how I would escape the plans of Zeus.*

PROMETHEUS

Yet shall this Zeus, for all his arrogance,
be humble yet: such is the match he plans,
a union that shall drive him from his power
and from his throne, out of the sight of all.
So shall at last the final consummation
be brought about of father Cronus' curse
which he, driven from his ancient throne, invoked
against the son deposing him; no one
of all the gods save I alone can tell
a way for him to avoid such troubles: I
do know this, and how. So let him confidently
sit on his throne and trust his heavenly thunder
and brandish in his hand his fiery bolt;
nothing shall all of this avail against
a humiliating and intolerable fall.
Such is the wrestler that Zeus is setting up
against himself, a monster hard to fight.
This enemy shall find a fire to best
the lightning bolt, a thunderclap to excel
the thunderclap of Zeus; and he shall shatter
Poseidon's trident, with quakes on sea and land.
So, in his crashing fall shall Zeus discover
how far apart are rule and slavery.

CHORUS LEADER

What you want for Zeus is what you're stating as fact.

PROMETHEUS

They are my wishes, yet what shall come to pass.

CHORUS LEADER

So should we expect someone to conquer Zeus?

PROMETHEUS

Yes; Zeus will suffer worse than I do now.

CHORUS LEADER

Have you no fear of uttering such words?

PROMETHEUS

Why should I fear, since death is not my fate?

CHORUS LEADER

But he might give you pain still worse than this.

PROMETHEUS

Then let him do so; all this I expect.

CHORUS LEADER

Wise are the worshippers of Necessity.

PROMETHEUS

Worship, pray; flatter whatever king
is king today; but I care less than nothing
for Zeus. Let him do just as he likes;
let him be king for his short time: he won't
be king of the gods for long.
But look, here comes
the footman of Zeus, that fetch-and-carry messenger
of the new king. Certainly he has come here
with news for us.

*(Enter Hermes from the side.)*

HERMES

You, subtle spirit, you
bitter and overbitter, you that sinned
against the immortals, giving honor to

the creatures of a day, you thief of fire:
the Father has commanded you to say
what marriage of his is this you brag about
that shall drive him from power—and declare it
in detail and no riddles. You, Prometheus,
don't cause me a double journey; you can see
that Zeus is not softhearted in such matters.

PROMETHEUS

Your speech is pompous sounding, full of pride,
as fits the lackey of the gods. You are young
and young your rule, and you think the citadel
in which you live is free from sorrow. From it
have I not seen two previous tyrants fall?
The third, who now is king, I shall see too
fall, of the three most suddenly, most dishonored.
Do you think that I will cower before these gods,
—so new—and tremble? I am far from that.
Hurry away, back on the road you came.
You shall learn nothing that you ask of me.

HERMES

By previous obstinacy just like this
you've brought yourself to these your present torments.

PROMETHEUS

Be sure of this: when I measure my misfortune
against your slavery, I would not change.

HERMES

It is better, I suppose, to be a slave
to this rock, than Zeus's trusted messenger!

PROMETHEUS

. . . . . . . . . . . . . . . . . .
Thus should one insult the insolent!°

HERMES

You seem to revel in your present state.

PROMETHEUS

Revel? I wish my enemies reveled so—
and you are one that I surely count among them.

HERMES

Oh, you would blame me too for your calamity?

PROMETHEUS

In a single word, I hate all of the gods
that unjustly returned me ill for good.

HERMES

Your words declare you mad, and mad indeed.

PROMETHEUS

Yes, if it's madness to detest my enemies.

HERMES

No one could bear you if you were successful.

PROMETHEUS

Alas!

HERMES

Alas? Zeus does not know that phrase.

PROMETHEUS

But time in its aging course teaches all things.

HERMES

Yet you have not yet learned a wise discretion.

PROMETHEUS

True: or I wouldn't be speaking to a servant.

HERMES

It seems you will not grant the Father's wish.

PROMETHEUS

I should be glad, indeed, to requite his kindness!

HERMES

You mock me like a child!

PROMETHEUS

And are you not
a child, and sillier than a child, to think
that I should tell you anything? There's not
a torture or device of any kind
which Zeus can use to make me speak these things,
till these atrocious shackles have been loosed.
So let him hurl his smoky lightning flame,
and throw into turmoil all things in the world,
with white-winged snowflakes and deep bellowing
thunder beneath the earth: he shall not bend me
by all of this to tell him who is fated
to drive him from his tyranny.

HERMES

Think, here and now, if this seems to your interest.

PROMETHEUS

I have already thought—and laid my plans.

HERMES

Bring your proud heart to recognize discretion—
O foolish spirit—in the face of ruin.

PROMETHEUS

You're annoying me pointlessly, as if you were
advising the waves. Let it not cross your mind
that any fear of Zeus will make me turn
womanish-minded, or that I shall entreat
the one I hate so greatly, with prayerful hands,
to loose me from my chains: I am far from that.

HERMES

I have said too much already—so I think—
and said it all in vain: you are not softened;
your purpose is not dented by my prayers.
You're like a colt new-broken, with the bit
clenched in its teeth, fighting against the reins,
and bolting. You are far too bold and confident

in your weak cleverness. For obstinacy
standing alone is the weakest of all things
in one whose mind is not possessed by wisdom.
Think what a storm, what triple wave of ruin
will rise against you, if you will not hear me,
and there's no escape for you. First this rough crag
with thunder and the lightning bolt the Father
shall split in pieces, and shall hide your body
wrapped in a rocky clasp within its depth;
a vast extent of time you must fulfill
before you see the light again, returning.
Then Zeus's winged hound, the blood-red eagle,
shall butcher tatters of your flesh, a feaster
coming unbidden, every day: your liver
bloodied to blackness will be his repast.
And of this pain do not expect an end
until some god shall show himself successor
to take your tortures for himself, agreeing
to go down to lightless Hades and the shadows
of Tartarus' depths. Bear all this in mind
and so determine. This is no feigned boast
but all too surely spoken. The mouth of Zeus
does not know how to lie, but every word
he brings to fulfilment. Look, you, and reflect
and never think that obstinacy is better
than wise counsel.

CHORUS LEADER

Hermes seems to us
to speak not altogether out of season.
He bids you quit your obstinacy and seek
a wise good counsel. Listen to him. Shame
it were for one so wise to fall in error.

PROMETHEUS [*chanting*]

*Before he told it I knew this message,*
*and there is no disgrace in suffering*

*at an enemy's hand, when the hate is mutual.*
*So, let the curling tendril of fire*
*from the lightning bolt be sent against me;*
*let the air be stirred with thunderclaps,*
*winds with their blasts convulse the world;*
*let earth be shaken to her foundations,*
*roots and all, by the blasts of the storm;*
*let the waves of the sea confuse the paths*
*of heavenly stars in a fierce torrent;*
*this body of mine, let him hurl it to hell,*
*to the blackness of Tartarus, with harsh eddies*
*of fierce necessity! But he shall never*
*bring me to death.*

HERMES [*chanting*]
*Such words are a madman's, a lunatic's plan:*
*every note's out of tune in his boastful song;*
*his mind is deranged.*
*But you now, at least,*
*you, who are so sympathetic with his troubles,*
*get away from this place, quickly go elsewhere,*
*lest the hard and deafening roar of the thunder*
*destroy your wits.*

CHORUS [*chanting*]
*No, say something else*
*different from this: give me other advice*
*that might persuade me; this word of yours*
*was intolerable, that you lured me with.*
*How can you tell us to act like cowards?*
*I want to endure along with him*
*what we must endure.*
*I have learned to hate all traitors; no*
*disease do I spit on more than treachery.*

HERMES [*chanting*]
*Well, remember my warning before it happens:*
*when you are overtaken by ruin don't then*

*blame fortune—don't say that it was Zeus*
*that brought you to calamity*
*quite unforeseen. Do not do this,*
*but blame yourselves; for now you know*
*what you are doing, so neither suddenly*
*nor secretly your own lack of good sense*
*will have tangled you all in the net of ruin,*
*past all hope of rescue.*

(*Exit Hermes to the side. Sounds of thunder and lightning are heard.*)°

PROMETHEUS [*chanting*]
*Now it's words no longer: now in truth*
*the earth is staggered; in its depths the thunder*
*bellows and roars, the fiery tendrils*
*of the lightning-flash blaze out, and clouds*
*carry the dust along in whirls.*
*All the winds' blasts*
*dance in a fury one against the other*
*in violent confusion: sky and sea*
*are one, all mingled together.*
*Such is the storm*
*that comes against me plainly from Zeus*
*to work its terrors. O holy Mother,*
*O sky that circling brings light to all,*
*you see how unjustly I suffer!*

(*Exit.*)

# THE ORESTEIA

*Translated by* RICHMOND LATTIMORE

AGAMEMNON

THE LIBATION BEARERS

THE EUMENIDES

# THE ORESTEIA: INTRODUCTION

*The Plays: Date and Composition*

Aeschylus' most famous and perennially successful masterpiece, the tetralogy of plays comprising *Agamemnon*, *The Libation Bearers* (in Greek, *Choephoroi*), *The Eumenides*, and the satyr-drama *Proteus*, won first prize in the Athenian tragedy competition of 458 BCE. The three tragedies are the only connected trilogy to have survived from antiquity. We do not know when the title *Oresteia* for the whole group was first assigned, but we find *The Libation Bearers* being referred to individually as "The Oresteia" in Aristophanes' *Frogs*. The three tragedies later came to be listed separately (in alphabetical order) among the plays of Aeschylus, and seem most often to have been read separately too. We cannot tell how often the whole trilogy was performed after its initial production; but some ancient readers certainly knew the sequence of plays, and it cannot be mere accident that these three tragedies were included among the seven that were preserved in our medieval manuscript tradition.

*The Myth*

The sequence of calamities and grisly deeds of vengeance within the family of Tantalus was a common subject of poetic narratives and dramas in antiquity; likewise the saga of tales about the Trojan War and its aftermath. Aeschylus wove together several elements from both of these traditions to make his complex yet tightly connected tetralogy. The most important are the following.

Tantalus' son Pelops had two sons, Atreus and Thyestes. They squabbled about the inheritance and throne. In pursuit of his ambitions, Thyestes seduced Atreus' wife, but Atreus got his revenge by pretending to seek reconciliation, inviting his brother to dinner, and there serving him his own (Thyestes') children to eat, chopped into pieces and cooked in a stew. When Thyestes realized what had happened he pronounced a curse on Atreus and all his descendants.

After some years had passed, Atreus' two sons, Agamemnon and Menelaus, became the kings of Mycenae/Argos and Sparta, respectively—though sometimes they are described in the *Oresteia* as being still a united pair, "the Atreidae," both of them apparently residing in the "House of Atreus." They were married to the two daughters of King Tyndareus of Sparta, Clytaemestra (sometimes spelled Clytemnestra) and Helen.

Meanwhile, Thyestes' one surviving son, Aegisthus (cousin of Agamemnon and Menelaus), was growing up separately, planning vengeance for Atreus' crime against his father.

When the Trojan prince Paris/Alexander, son of King Priam, visited Menelaus and eloped with his wife, Helen, Agamemnon organized a huge Panhellenic expedition to recapture her and punish Paris, Priam, and the whole city of Troy. The expedition assembled at Aulis (on the east coast of mainland Greece), but before it could sail for Troy a favorable wind had to be obtained—which could only be brought about, apparently, through the sacrifice of Iphigeneia (also spelled Iphigenia), the eldest daughter of Agamemnon and Clytaemestra. (In most versions of the myth, the goddess Artemis actually saves Iphigenia at the last moment and substitutes a deer instead, though everyone present still believes the girl has been killed. In the *Oresteia*, such a rescue is neither directly indicated nor explicitly excluded.)

While Agamemnon is away fighting for ten years at Troy, Clytaemestra, bitterly resentful of his killing of their daughter, forms an adulterous relationship with Aegisthus, who is still planning to avenge his father and brothers for Atreus' crime. Together they plot Agamemnon's death. When Agamemnon returns victorious from Troy, bringing with him vast war-spoils and a new Trojan slave concubine, Cassandra, daughter of King

Priam, Clytaemestra welcomes him and lures him into the palace, where, with Aegisthus' help, she kills him and Cassandra. They take control of Argos/Mycenae and become rulers—what the Greeks would call "tyrants," or nonhereditary kings. So ends the first play, *Agamemnon*.

Several years later, Orestes, the son of Agamemnon and Clytaemestra, who as a child was not present at the killing of his father and has grown up in Phocis (near Delphi) as the ward of Strophius and his son Pylades, consults with the god Apollo at Delphi and is told that he must seek vengeance for his father's murder. He returns to Argos, accompanied by Pylades, is reunited with his sister Electra, and successfully carries out his long-awaited revenge, killing Aegisthus and Clytaemestra and thus regaining his kingdom and inheritance. At this point, the avenging spirits, or curses, of his mother (in Greek, *Erinyes*) begin to hound him, and he flees in a state of acute mental disturbance. Here ends the second play, *The Libation Bearers*.

Orestes goes to Delphi for purification of the matricidal blood, and Apollo continues to protect him against the Furies. But they persist in pursuing and tormenting him, and eventually some kind of resolution has to be found. In Aeschylus' version, this takes place in Athens when a trial is held before the Court of the Areopagus, with Athena herself presiding.

The Areopagus Council was a venerable Athenian institution, composed of former archons—high-ranking elected officials. In the years just before the first production of the *Oresteia*, amid bitter civic dissension, new reforms had been enacted by the democracy, removing many of the council's powers but leaving it with its traditional responsibility for homicide trials. The idea of having the Argive hero Orestes come to Athens and be prosecuted in front of the Areopagus Court may or may not be Aeschylus' own invention: scholars disagree. In the trial, the Furies are the prosecutors, Apollo the defense counsel. As the result of an evenly split vote, Orestes is acquitted, and Athena, through her great patience and tact, manages to persuade the Furies not to punish the city of Athens for its leniency toward a matricide but to accept instead a position of honor for themselves within the city: they are to become the "august goddesses" who will live in the caves below the Acropolis and will protect the city in the future from all kinds of ills. Thus *The Eumenides*—and the trilogy—comes to an end. (Alas, we know little about how the fourth play proceeded, the satyr-drama *Proteus*; but see *Aeschylus*, vol. 2, pp. 165–66.)

Most of the elements in this saga were already familiar to Aeschylus' Athenian audience. Homer's *Odyssey* was especially important for the pointed parallels and contrasts drawn between Orestes and Telemachus, Aegisthus and the suitors, Clytaemestra and Penelope—though the actual matricide is not explicitly mentioned, and no ugly consequences for Orestes' vengeance seem even to be implied. Important too was the epic poem from the Trojan Cycle titled *Returns* (*Nostoi*), ascribed to Homer; but this is now lost and we do not know how it treated Agamemnon's death and Orestes' vengeance. Many other poetic and visual treatments were in circulation, including perhaps Pindar's eleventh Pythian ode (scholars disagree whether that poem was composed before or after the *Oresteia*). Vase paintings and sculptures of the sixth and early fifth centuries tend to focus on the killing of Aegisthus, not of Clytaemestra, and thus give the vengeance a complexion very different from Aeschylus'. The most influential "source" for Aeschylus seems to have been Stesichorus' choral lyric poetry (from sixth-century Sicily), which appears to have dwelt quite vividly on the troubling issues of matricide, including descriptions of Clytaemestra dreaming about a snake, a prominent Nurse character, and vengeful Furies pursuing Orestes so that Apollo has to intervene. Surviving fragments of Stesichorus' poems on this theme also show that, like Aeschylus in *The Libation Bearers*, he included a recognition scene between Orestes and Electra involving a lock of hair.

Whether other Athenian playwrights before Aeschylus had handled this story we do not know. Probably. But it is likely he was the first to draw together so many strands of the Agamemnon-Clytaemestra-Aegisthus-Helen-Orestes-Electra-Furies story into a trilogy, together with such a rich assortment of events and personalities from the Trojan War; and likely too that it was his innovation to have Orestes come to Athens and be tried before the Areopagus council, with Apollo, the Furies, and Athena all in court together. The masterstroke of a chorus composed of Furies is likely also to have been new, and surprising.

*Transmission and Reception*

The *Oresteia* was immediately very successful and influential. Numerous other Athenian playwrights revisited parts of this story, often alluding more or less openly to Aeschylus' treatment, and sometimes deliberately, even flamboyantly, diverging from his version of the events. Among surviving plays, Euripides' *Electra, Iphigenia among the Taurians, Orestes,* and *Iphigenia at Aulis* all owe obvious debts to the *Oresteia*, as does Sophocles' *Electra*. Athenian red-figure vase painters, and in due course south Italian painters as well, were likewise familiar with the trilogy: especially popular were scenes depicting the death of Cassandra; the meeting at Agamemnon's tomb of Orestes and Pylades, wearing travelers' clothes, with Electra and her jug of libations; and the pursuit of Orestes by the Furies and Apollo's protection of him at Delphi. In later years, depictions of the madness of Orestes became a common feature too, though these were generally based more on Euripides' versions than on Aeschylus'.

In later Greek and Roman literature and art, all these themes continued to be well known and frequently adapted. But it is generally hard to identify particular debts to the *Oresteia* rather than to the *Electra* plays of Sophocles and Euripides, both of which were very popular, or to Euripides' enormously successful *Orestes*. Roman playwrights under the Republic (Ennius, Pacuvius, Accius) all composed plays on parts of this story, though these do not survive; and Seneca's *Thyestes* and *Agamemnon*, composed in the first century CE, both became extremely influential on Elizabethan English dramatists as well as on neoclassical French and Italian writers and painters.

While it is impossible to assess how often the *Oresteia* or individual plays from it were performed in the centuries between Aeschylus' death and the Renaissance, these were certainly among the better known of Aeschylus' dramas, and were included in the Greek and Roman school curriculum, though it looks as if awareness of the satyr-play, *Proteus*, faded out of the picture relatively early. In later antiquity, the selection of seven Aeschylean tragedies (perhaps for school use) included all three parts of the *Oresteia*, which might indicate that the trilogy was still recognized as a unity. These seven plays survived—barely—to form our medieval manuscript tradition of Aeschylus; but by the tenth century copyists had apparently ceased to pay attention to the trilogic connections, and *The Libation Bearers* in particular fell out of general circulation. Only a single manuscript (the famous Mediceus, which ended up in the library of Lorenzo Medici in Florence) preserves this play; and even in this the opening lines are lost.

Since the nineteenth century, the almost cosmic scale of the *Oresteia*, its ritualistic and religious qualities, its progressive moral and political "message" focusing on the transition from family vendetta to legal process, and its sheer poetic, dramatic, and visual brilliance have ensured that it is frequently performed (sometimes *Agamemnon* alone, but often all three plays) and constantly adapted by modern writers and visual artists. Indeed, it is universally regarded not only by historians of theater but also by philosophers, political theorists, and literary critics as one of the greatest masterpieces of Western culture. The German operatic composer Richard Wagner's notion of a *Gesamtkunstwerk* ("total work of theater art"), as well as his deployment of recurrent *leitmotivs*, drew heavily from his reading of the *Oresteia* and its dense systems of verbal and visual imagery. More recently, the stark and pervasive gender politics of the trilogy have also provoked continuing attention and discussion.

Translators, playwrights, and adapters who have tackled all or part of the *Oresteia* include Robert Browning (1877); Robinson Jeffers, *The Tower beyond Tragedy* (1924, revised 1950); Eugene O'Neill, *Mourning Becomes Electra* (1931); Jean-Paul Sartre, *Les Mouches* [*The Flies*] (1943); Tony Harrison (1981). Particularly distinguished modern stage productions of the trilogy, entire or adapted, include those by Max Reinhardt (1911), Martha Graham (*Clytemnestra*, 1958), Tyrone Guthrie (1967), Karolos Koun with the Theatro Technis (Epidaurus, 1980), Peter Stein (Berlin, 1980), the National Theater of Great Britain (1981, translated by Tony Harrison; directed by Peter Hall), Ariane Mnouchkine with Le Théâtre du Soleil (*Les Atrides*, 1991, translated by Hélène Cixous), and Yael Farber (*Molora*, South Africa, 2011).

# AGAMEMNON

*Characters* WATCHMAN
CHORUS of Argive Elders
CLYTAEMESTRA, wife of Agamemnon
HERALD
AGAMEMNON, son of Atreus and king of Argos
CASSANDRA, daughter of King Priam of Troy
AEGISTHUS, cousin of Agamemnon

*Scene: Argos, in front of the palace of King Agamemnon. The Watchman is posted on the roof.*

WATCHMAN

I ask the gods some respite from the weariness
of this watchtime measured by years I lie awake
elbowed upon the Atreidae's roof dogwise to mark
the grand processionals of all the stars of night
burdened with winter and again with heat for men,
dynasties in their shining blazoned on the air,
these stars, upon their wane and when the rest arise.
I wait; to read the meaning in that beacon light,
a blaze of fire to carry out of Troy the rumor
and outcry of its capture; to such end a lady's
male strength of heart in its high confidence ordains.
Now as this bed stricken with night and drenched with dew
I keep, nor ever with kind dreams for company—
since fear in sleep's place stands forever at my head
against strong closure of my eyes, or any rest—

I mince such medicine against sleep failed: I sing,
only to weep again the pity of this house
no longer, as once, administered in the grand way.
Now let there be again redemption from distress,
the flare burning from the blackness in good augury.

*(A light shows in the distance.)*

Oh hail, blaze of the darkness, harbinger of day's
shining, and of processionals and dance and songs
of multitudes in Argos for this day of thanks.
Ho there, ho!
I cry the news aloud to Agamemnon's queen,
that she may rise up from her bed of state with speed
to raise the rumor of gladness welcoming this beacon,
and singing rise, if truly the citadel of Ilium
has fallen, as the shining of this flare proclaims.
I also, I, will make my choral prelude, since
my lord's dice cast aright are counted as my own,
and mine the tripled sixes of this torchlit throw.
May it only happen. May my king come home, and I
take up within this hand the hand I love. The rest
I leave to silence; for an ox stands huge upon
my tongue. The house itself, could it take voice, might speak
aloud and plain. I speak to those who understand,
but if they fail, I have forgotten everything.

*(Exit. Enter the Chorus from the side.)*

CHORUS [*chanting*]
*Ten years since the great contestants*
*of Priam's right,*
*Menelaus and Agamemnon, my lord,*
*twin throned, twin sceptered, in twofold power*
*of kings from god, the Atreidae,*
*put forth from this shore*
*the thousand ships of the Argives,*
*the strength and the armies.*

*Their cry of war went shrill from the heart,*
*as eagles stricken in agony*
*for young perished, high from the nest*
*eddy and circle*
*to bend and sweep of the wings' stroke,*
*lost far below*
*the fledglings, the nest, and the tendance.*
*Yet someone hears in the air, a god,*
*Apollo, Pan, or Zeus, the high*
*thin wail of these sky-guests, and drives*
*late to its mark*
*the Fury upon the transgressors.*

*So drives Zeus, the great god of guests,*
*the Atreidae against Alexander:*
*for one woman's promiscuous sake*
*the struggling masses, legs tired,*
*knees grinding in dust,*
*spears broken in the onset.*
*Danaans and Trojans*
*they have it alike. It goes as it goes*
*now. The end will be destiny.*
*You cannot burn flesh or pour unguents,*
*not innocent cool tears,°*
*that will soften the gods' stiff anger.*
*But we, dishonored, old in our bones,*
*cast off even then from the gathering horde,*
*stay here, to prop up*
*on staves the strength of a baby.*
*Since the young vigor that urges*
*inward to the heart*
*is frail as age, no warcraft yet perfect,*
*while beyond age, leaf*
*withered, man goes three-footed*
*no stronger than a child is,*
*a dream that falters in daylight.°*

*But you, lady,*
*daughter of Tyndareus, Clytaemestra, our queen:*
*What is there to be done? What new thing have you heard?*
*In persuasion of what*
*report do you order such sacrifice?*
*To all the gods of the city,*
*the high and the deep spirits,*
*to them of the sky and the marketplaces,*
*the altars blaze with oblations.*
*The staggered flame goes sky-high*
*one place, then another,*
*drugged by the simple soft*
*persuasion of sacred unguents,*
*the deep-stored oil of the kings.*
*Of these things what can be told*
*openly, speak.*
*Be healer to this perplexity*
*that grows now into darkness of thought,*
*while again sweet hope shining from the flames*
*beats back the pitiless pondering*
*of sorrow that eats my heart.*

[*singing*]

STROPHE A

*I have mastery yet to proclaim the wonder at the wayside*
*given to kings. Still by god's grace there surges within me*
*singing magic*
*grown to my life and power,*
*how the wild bird portent*
*hurled forth the Achaeans'*
*twin-stemmed power single-hearted,*
*lords of the youth of Hellas,*
*with spear and hand of strength*
*to the land of Teucrus.*
*Kings of birds to the kings of the ships,*

*one black, one blazed with silver,*
*clear seen by the royal house*
*on the right, the spear hand,*
*they alighted, watched by all*
*tore a hare, ripe, bursting with young unborn yet,*
*stayed from her last fleet running.*
*Sing sorrow, sorrow: but good win out in the end.*

ANTISTROPHE A

*Then the grave seer of the host saw through to the hearts divided,*
*knew the fighting sons of Atreus feeding on the hare*
*with the host, their people.*
*Seeing beyond, he spoke:*
*"With time, this foray*
*shall stalk the city of Priam;*
*and under the walls, Fate shall spoil*
*in violence the rich herds of the people.*
*Only let no doom of the gods darken*
*upon this huge iron forged to curb Troy—*
*from inward. Artemis the undefiled*
*is angered with pity*
*at the flying hounds of her father*
*eating the unborn young in the hare and the shivering mother.*
*She is sick at the eagles' feasting.*
*Sing sorrow, sorrow: but good win out in the end.*

EPODE

*Lovely she is and kind*
*to the tender young of ravening lions.*
*For sucklings of all the savage*
*beasts that lurk in the lonely places she has sympathy.*
*She demands meaning° for these appearances*
*good, yet not without evil.*
*Healer Apollo, I pray you*
*let her not with crosswinds*
*bind the ships of the Danaans*

*to time-long anchorage*
*forcing a second sacrifice unholy, untasted,*
*working bitterness in the blood and fearing no man.*
*For the terror returns like sickness to lurk in the house;*
*the secret anger remembers the child that shall be avenged."*
*Such, with great good things beside, rang out in the voice of*
*Calchas,*
*these fatal signs from the birds by the way to the house of the*
*princes,*
*wherewith in sympathy*
*sing sorrow, sorrow: but good win out in the end.*

STROPHE B

*Zeus: whatever he may be, if this name*
*pleases him in invocation,*
*thus I call upon him.*
*I have pondered everything*
*yet I cannot find a way,*
*only Zeus, to cast this dead weight of ignorance*
*finally from out my brain.*

ANTISTROPHE B

*He who in time long ago was great,*
*throbbing with gigantic strength,*
*shall be as if he never were, unspoken.*
*He who followed him has found*
*his master, and is gone.*
*Cry aloud without fear the victory of Zeus;*
*you will not have failed the truth.*

STROPHE C

*Zeus, who guided men to think,*
*who has laid it down that wisdom*
*comes alone through suffering.*
*Still there drips in sleep against the heart*
*grief of memory; against*

*our will temperance comes.*
*From the gods who sit in grandeur*
*grace is somehow violent.*

ANTISTROPHE C

*On that day the elder king*
*of the Achaean ships, not faulting*
*any prophet's word,*
*shifted with the crosswinds of fortune,*
*when no ship sailed, no pail was full,*
*and the Achaean people sulked*
*along the shore at Aulis facing*
*Chalcis, where tides ebb and surge:*

STROPHE D

*and winds blew from the Strymon, bearing*
*sick idleness, ships tied fast, and hunger,*
*distraction of the mind, carelessness*
*for hull and cable;*
*with time's length bent to double measure*
*by delay crumbled the flower and pride*
*of Argos. Then against the bitter wind*
*the seer's voice clashed out*
*another medicine*
*more hateful yet, and spoke of Artemis, so that the kings*
*dashed their staves to the ground and could not hold their tears.*

ANTISTROPHE D

*The elder lord spoke aloud before them:*
*"My fate is angry if I disobey these,*
*but angry if I slaughter*
*this child, the beauty of my house,*
*with maiden bloodshed staining*
*these father's hands beside the altar.*
*What of these things goes now without disaster?*
*How shall I fail my ships*

*and lose my faith of battle?*
*To urge the wind-changing sacrifice of maiden's blood*
*angrily, for the wrath is great—it is right.° May all be well yet."*

STROPHE E

*But when he put on necessity's yoke*
*he changed, and from the heart the breath came bitter*
*and sacrilegious, utterly infidel,*
*to warp a will now to be stopped at nothing.*
*The sickening in men's minds, mad,*
*reckless in first cruelty brings daring. He endured then*
*to sacrifice his daughter*
*in support of war waged for a woman,*
*first offering for the ships' sake.*

ANTISTROPHE E

*Her supplications and her cries of father*
*were nothing, nor the child's lamentation*
*to kings passioned for battle.*
*The father prayed, called to his men to lift her*
*with strength of hand swept in her robes aloft*
*and prone above the altar, as you might lift*
*a goat for sacrifice—with a guard*
*against the lips' sweet edge, to check*
*the curse cried on the house of Atreus*
*by force and a bit's speechless power.*

STROPHE F

*Pouring then to the ground her saffron mantle*
*she struck the sacrificers with*
*the eyes' arrows of pity,*
*lovely as in a painted scene, and striving*
*to speak—as many times*
*at the kind festive table of her father*
*she had sung, and in the clear voice of a stainless maiden*
*with love had graced the song*
*of worship when the third cup was poured.*

ANTISTROPHE F

*What happened next I saw not, neither speak it.*
*The crafts of Calchas fail not of outcome.*
*Justice tilts her scale so that those only*
*learn who suffer; and the future*
*you shall know when it has come; before then, forget it.*
*It is grief too soon given.*
*All will come clear in the next dawn's sunlight.*
*Let good fortune follow these things as*
*the one who is here desires,*
*our Apian land's single-hearted protector.°*

*(Enter Clytaemestra.)*

CHORUS LEADER

I have come in reverence, Clytaemestra, of your power.
For when the man is gone and the throne void, his right
falls to the prince's lady, and honor must be given.
Is it some grace—or otherwise—that you have heard
to make you sacrifice at messages of good hope?
I should be glad to hear, but must not blame your silence.

CLYTAEMESTRA

As it was said of old, may the dawn child be born
to be an angel of blessing from the kindly night.
You shall know joy beyond all you ever hoped to hear.
The men of Argos have taken Priam's citadel.

CHORUS LEADER

What have you said? Your words escaped my doubting mind.

CLYTAEMESTRA

The Achaeans are in Troy. Is that not clear enough?

CHORUS LEADER

This slow delight steals over me to bring forth tears.

CLYTAEMESTRA

Yes, for your eyes betray the loyal heart within.

CHORUS LEADER

Yet how can I be certain? Is there some evidence?

CLYTAEMESTRA

There is, there must be; unless a god has lied to me.

CHORUS LEADER

Is it dream visions, easy to believe, you credit?

CLYTAEMESTRA

I accept nothing from a brain that is dull with sleep.

CHORUS LEADER

The charm, then, of some rumor, that made rich your hope?

CLYTAEMESTRA

Am I some young girl, that you find my thoughts so silly?

CHORUS LEADER

How long, then, is it since the citadel was stormed?

CLYTAEMESTRA

It was the night, the mother of this dawn I hailed.

CHORUS LEADER

What kind of messenger could come in speed like this?

CLYTAEMESTRA

Hephaestus, who cast forth the shining blaze from Ida.
And beacon after beacon picking up the flare
carried it here; Ida to the Hermaean horn
of Lemnos, where it shone above the isle, and next
the sheer rock face of Zeus on Athos caught it up;
and plunging skyward to arch the shoulders of the sea
the strength of the running flare in exultation,°
pine timbers flaming into gold, like the sunrise,
brought the bright message to Macistus' sentinel cliffs,
who, never slow nor in the carelessness of sleep
caught up, sent on his relay in the courier chain,
and far across Euripus' streams the beacon flare

carried to signal watchmen on Messapion.
These took it again in turn, and heaping high a pile
of silvery brush flamed it to throw the message on.
And the flare sickened never, but grown stronger yet
outleapt the river valley of Asopus like
the very moon for shining, to Cithaeron's scaur
to waken the next station of the flaming post.
These watchers, not contemptuous of the far-thrown blaze,
kindled another beacon vaster than commanded.
The light leaned high above Gorgopis' staring marsh,
and striking Aegyplanctus' mountaintop, drove on
yet one more relay, lest the flare die down in speed.
Kindled once more with stintless heaping force, they send
the beard of flame to hugeness, passing far beyond
the promontory that gazes on the Saronic strait
and flaming far, until it plunged at last to strike
the steep rock of Arachnus near at hand, our watchtower.
And thence there fell upon this house of Atreus' sons
the flare whose fathers mount to the Idaean beacon.
These are the changes on my torchlight messengers,
one from another running out the laps assigned.
The first and the last sprinters have the victory.
By such proof and such symbol I announce to you
my lord at Troy has sent his messengers to me.

CHORUS LEADER

The gods, lady, shall have my prayers and thanks straightway.
And yet to hear your story till all wonder fades
would be my wish, could you but tell it once again.

CLYTAEMESTRA

The Achaeans have got Troy, upon this very day.
I think the city echoes with a clash of cries.
Pour vinegar and oil into the selfsame bowl,
you could not say they mix in friendship, but fight on.
Thus variant sound the voices of the conquerors
and conquered, from the opposition of their fates.

Trojans are stooping now to gather in their arms
their dead, husbands and brothers; children lean to clasp
the aged who begot them, crying upon the death
of those most dear, from lips that never will be free.
The Achaeans have their midnight work after the fighting
that sets them down to feed on all the city has,
ravenous, headlong, by no rank and file assigned,
but as each man has drawn his shaken lot by chance.
And in the Trojan houses that their spears have taken
they settle now, free of the open sky, the frosts
and dampness of the evening; without sentinels set
they sleep the sleep of happiness the whole night through.
And if they reverence the gods who hold the city
and all the holy temples of the captured land,
they, the despoilers, might not be despoiled in turn.
Let not their passion overwhelm them; let no lust
seize on these men to violate what they must not.
The run to safety and home is yet to make; they must turn
the post, and run the backstretch of the double course.
Yet, though the host come home without offence to high
gods, even so the anger of these slaughtered men
may never sleep. Oh, let there be no fresh wrong done!
Such are the thoughts you hear from me, a woman merely.
Yet may the best win through, that none may fail to see.
Of all good things to wish this is my dearest choice.

CHORUS LEADER

My lady, you speak graciously like a prudent man.
I have listened to the proofs of your tale, and I believe,
and go to make my glad thanksgivings to the gods.
This pleasure is not unworthy of the grief that gave it.

*(Exit Clytaemestra into the palace.)*

[*chanting*]
*O Zeus our lord and Night beloved,*
*bestower of power and beauty,*

*you slung above the bastions of Troy*
*the binding net, that none, neither great*
*nor young, might outleap*
*the gigantic toils*
*of enslavement and final disaster.*
*I gaze in awe on Zeus of the guests*
*who wrung from Alexander such payment.*
*He bent the bow with slow care, that neither*
*the shaft might hurdle the stars, nor fall*
*spent to the earth, short driven.*

[*singing*]

STROPHE A

*They have the stroke of Zeus to tell of.*
*This thing is clear and you may trace it.*
*He acted as he had decreed. A man thought*
*the gods deigned not to punish mortals*
*who trampled down the delicacy of things*
*inviolable. That man was wicked.*
*The curse on great daring*
*shines clear; it wrings atonement*
*from those high hearts that drive to evil,*
*from houses blossoming to pride*
*and peril. Let there be*
*wealth without tears; enough for*
*the wise man who will ask no further.*
*There is not any armor*
*in riches against perdition*
*for him who kicks the high altar*
*of Justice down to the darkness.*

ANTISTROPHE A

*Persuasion the persistent overwhelms him,*
*she, strong daughter of designing Ruin.*
*And every medicine is vain; the sin*
*smolders not, but burns to evil beauty.*
*As worthless bronze rubbed*

*at the touchstone relapses*
*to blackness and grime, so this man*
*tested shows vain*
*as a child that strives to catch the bird flying*
*and wins shame that shall bring down his city.*
*No god will hear such a man's entreaty,*
*but whoever turns to these ways*
*they strike him down in his wickedness.*
*This was Paris: he came*
*to the house of the sons of Atreus,*
*stole the woman away, and shamed*
*the guest's right of the board shared.*

STROPHE B

*She left among her people the stir and clamor*
*of shields and of spearheads,*
*the ships to sail and the armor.*
*She took to Ilium her dowry, death.*
*She stepped forth lightly between the gates*
*daring beyond all daring. And the prophets*
*about the great house wept aloud and spoke:*
*"Alas, alas for the house and for the champions,*
*alas for the bed signed with their love together.*
*Here now is silence, scorned, unreproachful.*
*The agony of his loss is clear before us.*
*Longing for her who lies beyond the sea*
*he shall see a phantom queen in his household.*
*Her images in their beauty*
*are bitterness to her lord now*
*where in the emptiness of eyes*
*all passion has faded."*

ANTISTROPHE B

*Shining in dreams the sorrowful*
*memories pass; they bring him*
*vain delight only.*
*It is vain, to dream and to see splendors,*

*and the image slipping from the arms' embrace*
*escapes, not to return again,*
*on wings drifting down the ways of sleep.*
*Such have the sorrows been in the house by the hearthside;*
*such have there been, and yet there are worse than these.*
*In all Hellas, for those who swarmed to the war,*
*the heartbreaking misery*
*shows in the house of each.*
*Many are they who are touched at the heart by these things.*
*Those they sent forth they knew;*
*now, in place of the young men*
*urns and ashes are carried home*
*to the houses of the fighters.*

STROPHE C

*The god of war, money changer of dead bodies,*
*held the balance of his spear in the fighting,*
*and from the corpse-fires at Ilium*
*sent to their dearest the dust*
*heavy and bitter with tears shed*
*packing smooth the urns with*
*ashes that once were men.*
*They praise them through their tears, how this man*
*knew well the craft of battle, how another*
*went down splendid in the slaughter:*
*and all for someone else's woman.*
*Thus they mutter in secrecy,*
*and the slow anger creeps below their grief*
*at Atreus' sons and their quarrels.*
*There by the walls of Ilium*
*the young men in their beauty keep*
*graves deep in the alien soil*
*they hated and they conquered.*

ANTISTROPHE C

*The citizens speak: their voice is deep with hatred.*
*The curse of the people must be paid for.*

*There lurks for me in the hooded night*
*terror of what may be told me.*
*The gods fail not to note*
*those who have killed many.*
*The black Furies, stalking the man*
*fortunate but without justice,*
*wrench back again the set of his life*
*and drop him to darkness. There among*
*the ciphers there is no more comfort*
*in power. And the vaunt of high glory*
*is bitterness; for god's thunderbolts*
*crash on the towering houses.°*
*Let me attain no envied wealth;*
*let me not plunder cities,*
*neither be captured in turn, and face*
*life in the power of another.*

EPODE

*From the beacon's bright message*
*the swift rumor runs*
*through the city. If this be real*
*who knows? Perhaps the gods have sent some lie to us.*
*—Who of us is so childish or so short of wit*
*that by the beacon's messages*
*his heart flamed must sink down again*
*when the tale changes in the end?*
*—It is like a woman indeed*
*to take the rapture before the fact has shown for true.*
*Women believe too easily, are too quick to shift*
*from ground to ground; and swift indeed*
*the rumor voiced by a woman dies again.*

CHORUS LEADER

Now we° shall understand these torches and their shining,
the beacons, and the interchange of flame and flame.
They may be real; yet bright and dreamwise ecstasy
in light's appearance might have charmed our hearts awry.

I see a herald coming from the beach, his brows
shaded with sprigs of olive; and upon his feet
the dust, dry sister of the mud, makes plain to me
that he will find a voice, not merely kindle flame
from mountain timber, and make signals from the smoke,
but tell us outright, whether to be happy, or—
but I shrink back from naming the alternative.
That which appeared was good; may yet more good be given.

And any man who prays that different things befall
the city, may he reap the crime of his own heart.

*(Enter the Herald from the side.)*

HERALD

Soil of my fathers, Argive earth I tread upon,
in daylight of the tenth year I have come back to you.
All my hopes broke but one, and this I have at last.
I never could have dared to dream that I might die
in Argos, and be buried in this beloved soil.
Hail to the Argive land and to its sunlight; hail
to its high sovereign, Zeus, and to the Pythian king.
May you no longer shower your arrows on our heads.
Beside Scamandrus you were grim; be satisfied
and turn to savior now and healer of our hurts,
my lord Apollo. Gods of the marketplace assembled,
I greet you all, and my own patron deity
Hermes, beloved herald, in whose right all heralds
are sacred; and you heroes that sent forth the host,
propitiously take back all that the spear has left.
O great hall of the kings and house beloved; seats
of sanctity; divinities that face the sun:
if ever before, look now with kind and glowing eyes
to greet our king in state after so long a time.
He comes, Lord Agamemnon, bearing light in gloom
to you, and to all that are assembled here.
Salute him with good favor, as he well deserves,
the man who has wrecked Ilium with the spade of Zeus

vindictive, whereby all their plain has been laid waste.
Gone are their altars; the sacred places of the gods
are gone, and scattered all the seed within the ground.
With such a yoke as this gripped to the neck of Troy
he comes, the king, Atreus' elder son, a man
fortunate to be honored far above all men
alive; not Paris nor the city tied to him
can boast he did more than was done him in return.
Guilty of rape and theft, condemned, he lost the prize
captured, and broke to sheer destruction all the house
of his fathers, with the very ground whereon it stood.
Twice over the sons of Priam have atoned their sins.

CHORUS LEADER

Hail and be glad, herald of the Achaean host.

HERALD

I am happy; I no longer ask the gods for death.

CHORUS LEADER

Did passion for your country so strip bare your heart?

HERALD

So that the tears broke in my eyes, for happiness.

CHORUS LEADER

You were taken with that sickness, then, that brings delight.

HERALD

How? I cannot deal with such words until I understand.

CHORUS LEADER

Struck with desire of those who loved as much again.

HERALD

You mean our country longed for us, as we for home?

CHORUS LEADER

So that I sighed, out of the darkness of my heart.

HERALD

Whence came this black thought to afflict the mind with fear?

CHORUS LEADER

Long since it was my silence kept disaster off.

HERALD

But how? There were some you feared when the kings went away?

CHORUS LEADER

So much that as you said now, even death were grace.

HERALD

Well: the end has been good. And in the length of time
part of our fortune you could say held favorable,
but part we cursed again. And who, except the gods,
can live time through forever without any pain?
Were I to tell you of the hard work done, the nights
exposed, the cramped sea-quarters, the foul beds—what part
of day's disposal did we not cry out loud?
Ashore, the horror stayed with us and grew. We lay
against the ramparts of our enemies, and from
the sky, and from the ground, the meadow dews came out
to soak our clothes and fill our hair with lice. And if
I were to tell of wintertime, when all birds died,
the snows of Ida past endurance she sent down,
or summer heat, when in the lazy noon the sea
fell level and asleep under a windless sky—
but why live such grief over again? That time is gone
for us, and gone for those who died. Never again
need they rise up, nor care again for anything.
Why must a live man count the numbers of the slain,
why grieve at fortune's wrath that fades to break once more?
I call a long farewell to all our unhappiness.
For us, survivors of the Argive armament,
the pleasure wins, pain casts no weight in the opposite scale.
And here, in this sun's shining, we can boast aloud,
whose fame has gone with wings across the land and sea:°
"Upon a time the Argive host took Troy, and on

the houses of the gods who live in Hellas nailed
the spoils, to be the glory of days long ago."
And they who hear such things shall call this city bless'd
and the leaders of the host; and high the grace of god
shall be exalted, that did this. You have the story.

CHORUS LEADER

I must give way; your story shows that I was wrong.
Old men are always young enough to learn, with profit.
But Clytaemestra and her house must hear, above
others, this news that makes luxurious my life.

*(Clytaemestra enters from the palace.)*

CLYTAEMESTRA

I raised my cry of joy, and it was long ago
when the first beacon flare of message came by night
to speak of capture and of Ilium's overthrow.
But there was one who laughed at me, who said: "You trust
in beacons so, and you believe that Troy has fallen?
How like a woman, for the heart to lift so light."
Men spoke like that; they thought I wandered in my wits;
yet I made sacrifice, and in the womanish strain
voice after voice caught up the cry along the city
to echo in the temples of the gods and bless
and still the fragrant flame that melts the sacrifice.

Why should you tell me then the whole long tale at large
when from my lord himself I shall hear all the story?
But now, how best to speed my preparation to
receive my honored lord come home again—what else
is light more sweet for woman to behold than this,
to spread the gates before her husband home from war
and saved by god's hand?—take this message to the king:
Come, and with speed, back to the city that longs for him,
and may he find a wife within his house as true
as on the day he left her, watchdog of the house
gentle to him alone, fierce to his enemies,

and such a woman in all her ways as this, who has
not broken the seal upon her in the length of days.
With no man else have I known delight, nor any shame
of evil speech, more than I know how to temper bronze.

HERALD

A vaunt like this, so loaded as it is with truth,
it well becomes a highborn lady to proclaim.

CHORUS LEADER

Thus has she spoken to you, and well you understand,
words that impress interpreters whose thought is clear.
But tell me, herald; I would learn of Menelaus,
that power beloved in this land. Has he survived
also, and come with you back to his home again?

HERALD

I know no way to lie and make my tale so fair
that friends could reap joy of it for any length of time.

CHORUS LEADER

Is there no means to speak us fair, and yet tell the truth?
It will not hide, when truth and good are torn asunder.

HERALD

He is gone out of the sight of the Achaean host,
vessel and man alike. I speak no falsehood there.

CHORUS LEADER

Was it when he had put out from Ilium in your sight,
or did a storm that struck you both whirl him away?

HERALD

How like a master bowman you have hit the mark
and in your speech cut a long sorrow to brief stature.

CHORUS LEADER

But then the rumor in the host that sailed beside,
was it that he had perished, or might yet be living?

HERALD

No man knows. There is none could tell us that for sure
except the Sun, from whom this earth has life and increase.

CHORUS LEADER

How did this storm, by wrath of the divinities,
strike on our multitude at sea? How did it end?

HERALD

It is not well to stain the blessing of this day
with speech of evil weight. Such gods are honored apart.
And when the messenger of a shaken host, sad faced,
brings to his city news it prayed never to hear,
this scores one wound upon the body of the people;
and that from many houses many men are slain
by the two-lashed whip dear to the war god's hand, this turns
disaster double-bladed, bloodily made two.
The messenger so freighted with a charge of tears
should make his song of triumph at the Furies' door.
But, carrying the fair message of our hopes' salvation,
come home to a glad city's hospitality,
how shall I mix my gracious news with foul, and tell
of the storm on the Achaeans by god's anger sent?
For they, of old the deepest enemies, sea and fire,
made a conspiracy and gave their hand in oath
to blast in ruin our unhappy Argive army.
At night the sea began to rise in waves of death.
Ship against ship the Thracian stormwind shattered us,
and gored and split, our vessels, swept in violence
of storm and whirlwind, beaten by the breaking rain,
drove on in darkness, spun by the wicked shepherd's hand.
But when the sun came up again to light the dawn,
we saw the Aegean Sea blossoming with dead men,
the men of Achaea, and the wreckage of their ships.
For us, and for our ship, some god, no man, by guile
or by entreaty's force prevailing, laid his hand

upon the helm and brought us through with hull unscarred.
Life-giving fortune deigned to take our ship in charge
that neither riding in deep water she took the surf
nor drove to shoal and break upon some rocky shore.
But then, delivered from death at sea, in the pale day,
incredulous of our own luck, we shepherded
in our sad thoughts the fresh disaster of the fleet
so pitifully torn and shaken by the storm.
Now of these others, if there are any left alive
they speak of us as men who perished, must they not?
Even as we, who fear that they are gone. But may
it all come well in the end. For Menelaus: be sure
if any of them come back that he will be the first.
If he is still where some sun's gleam can track him down,
alive and open-eyed, by blessed hand of god
who willed that not yet should his seed be utterly gone,
there is some hope that he will still come home again.
You have heard all; and be sure, you have heard the truth.

*(Exit the Herald to the side.)*

CHORUS [*singing*]

STROPHE A

*Who is he that named you so*
*fatally in every way?*
*Could it be some mind unseen*
*in divination of your destiny*
*shaping to the lips that name*
*for the bride of spears and blood,*
*Helen, a hell on earth? All too truly*
*hell for ships, hell for men and cities,*
*from the bower's soft curtained*
*and secluded luxury she sailed then,*
*driven on the giant west wind,*
*and armored men in their thousands came,*
*huntsmen down the oar blade's fading footprint*

*to struggle in blood with those*
*who by the banks of Simoeis*
*beached their hulls where the leaves break.*

ANTISTROPHE A

*And on Ilium in truth*
*in the likeness of the name*
*the sure purpose of the Wrath drove*
*marriage with death: for the guest board*
*shamed, and Zeus kindly to strangers,*
*the vengeance wrought on those men*
*who graced in too loud voice the bride-song*
*fallen to their lot to sing,*
*the kinsmen and the brothers.*
*And changing its song's measure*
*the ancient city of Priam*
*chants in high strain of lamentation,*
*calling Paris him of the fatal marriage;*
*for it endured its life's end*
*in desolation and tears*
*and the piteous blood of its people.*

STROPHE B

*Once a man fostered in his house*
*a lion cub, from the mother's milk*
*torn, craving the breast given.*
*In the first steps of its young life,*
*mild, it played with children*
*and delighted the old.*
*Caught in the arm's cradle*
*they pampered it like a newborn child,*
*shining-eyed and broken to the hand*
*to stay the stress of its hunger.*

ANTISTROPHE B

*But it grew with time, and the lion*
*in the blood strain came out; it repaid*

*thanks to those who had fostered it*
*in blood and death for the sheep flocks,*
*a grim feast forbidden.*
*The house reeked with blood run,*
*nor could its people beat down the bane,*
*the giant murderer's onslaught.*
*This thing they raised in their house was blessed*
*by god to be priest of destruction.*

### STROPHE C

*And that which first came to the city of Ilium,*
*call it a dream of calm*
*and the wind dying,*
*the loveliness and luxury of much gold,*
*the melting shafts of the eyes' glances,*
*the blossom that breaks the heart with longing.*
*But she turned in midstep of her course to make*
*bitter the consummation,*
*whirling on Priam's people*
*to blight with her touch and nearness.*
*Zeus hospitable sent her,*
*a Vengeance to make brides weep.*

### ANTISTROPHE C

*It was made long since, grown old now among men,*
*this saying: human wealth*
*grown to fullness of stature*
*breeds again nor dies without issue.*
*From high good fortune in the blood*
*blossoms the quenchless agony.*
*But far from others I hold my own*
*mind; only the act of evil*
*breeds others to follow,*
*young sins in its own likeness.*
*Houses clear in their right are given*
*children in all loveliness.*

STROPHE D

*So Outrage aging is made ripe*
*in men's dark actions,*
*ripe with the young Outrage*
*late or soon, when the dawn of destiny*
*comes and birth is given*
*to the spirit none may fight nor beat down,*
*sinful Daring; and in those halls*
*the black-visaged Disasters stamped*
*in the likeness of their fathers.*

ANTISTROPHE D

*But Righteousness still shines out*
*in the smoke of mean houses.*
*Her blessing is on the just man.*
*From high halls starred with gold by reeking hands*
*she turns back*
*with eyes that glance away to the simple in heart,*
*spurning the strength of gold*
*stamped false with flattery.*
*And all things she steers to fulfillment.*

*(Enter Agamemnon from the side in a chariot,*
*with Cassandra beside him.)*

CHORUS [*chanting*]

*Behold, my king: sacker of Troy's citadel,*
*own issue of Atreus.*
*How shall I hail you? How give honor*
*not shooting too high nor yet bending short*
*of this moment's fitness?*
*For many among men are they who set high*
*the show of honor, yet violate justice.*
*If one is distressed, all others are ready*
*to grieve with him: yet the teeth of sorrow*
*come nowhere near to their heart's edge.*
*And in joy likewise they show joy's semblance,*
*and torture the face to the false smile.*

*Yet the good shepherd, who knows his flock,*
*the eyes of men cannot lie to him,*
*who with water of feigned*
*love seem to smile from the true heart.*
*But I: when you marshaled this armament*
*for Helen's sake, I will not hide it,*
*in ugly style you were written in my heart*
*for steering aslant the mind's course*
*to bring home by blood*
*sacrifice and dead men that wild spirit.°*
*But now, in love drawn up from the deep heart,*
*not skimmed at the edge, we hail you.*
*You have won; your labor is made gladness.*
*Ask everyone: you will learn in time*
*which of your citizens have been just*
*in the city's service, which were reckless.*

AGAMEMNON

To Argos first, and to the gods within the land,
I must give due greeting; they have worked with me to bring
me home; they helped me in the vengeance I have wrought
on Priam's city. Not from the lips of men the gods
heard justice, but in one firm cast they laid their votes
within the urn of blood that Ilium must die
and all her people; while above the opposite vase
the hand hovered and there was hope, but no vote fell.
The storm clouds of their ruin live; the ash that dies
upon them gushes still in smoke their pride of wealth.
For all this we must thank the gods with grace of much
high praise and memory, we who fenced within our toils
of wrath the city; and, because one woman strayed,
the beast of Argos broke them, the fierce young within
the horse, the armored people who marked out their leap
against the setting of the Pleiades. A wild
and bloody lion swarmed above the towers of Troy
to glut its hunger lapping at the blood of kings.

This to the gods, a prelude strung to length of words.
But, for the thought you spoke, I heard and I remember
and stand beside you. For I say that it is true.
In few men is it part of nature to respect
a friend's prosperity without begrudging him,
as envy's wicked poison settling to the heart
piles up the pain in one sick with unhappiness,
who, staggered under sufferings that are all his own,
winces again to the vision of a neighbor's bliss.
And I can speak, for I have seen, I know it well,
this mirror of companionship, this shadow's ghost,
all those who seemed my friends in their sincerity.
Just one of them, Odysseus, he who sailed unwilling,
once yoked to me pulled all his weight, nor ever slacked.
Dead though he be or living, I can say it still.

Now in the business of the city and the gods
we must ordain full conclave of all citizens
and take our counsel. We shall see what element
is strong, and plan that it shall keep its virtue still.
But that which must be healed—we shall use medicine,
or burn, or amputate, with kind intention, take
all means at hand that might beat down corruption's pain.
So to the king's house and the home about the hearth
I take my way, with greeting to the gods within
who sent me forth, and who have brought me home once
 more.
My prize was conquest; may it never fail again.

CLYTAEMESTRA

Grave gentlemen of Argolis assembled here,
I take no shame to speak aloud before you all
the love I bear my husband. In the lapse of time
modesty fades; it is human.
 What I tell you now
I learned not from another; this was my own sad life
all the long years this man was gone at Ilium.

It is evil and a thing of terror when a wife
sits in the house forlorn with no man by, and hears
rumors that like a fever die to break again,
and men come in with news of fear, and on their heels
another messenger, with worse news to cry aloud
here in this house. Had Agamemnon taken all
the wounds of which the tale was carried home to me,
he had been cut full of gashes like a fishing net.
If he had died each time that rumor told his death,
he must have been some triple-bodied Geryon
back from the dead with threefold cloak of earth upon
his body, and killed once for every shape assumed.
Because such tales broke out forever on my rest,
many a time they cut me down and freed my throat
from the noose overslung where I had caught it fast.
And therefore is your son, in whom my love and yours
are sealed and pledged, not here to stand with us today,
Orestes. It were right; yet do not be amazed.
Strophius of Phocis, comrade in arms and faithful friend
to you, is keeping him. He spoke to me of peril
on two counts; of your danger under Ilium,
and here, of revolution and the clamorous people
who might cast down the council—since it lies in men's
nature to trample on the fighter already down.
Such my excuse to you, and without subterfuge.

For me: the rippling springs that were my tears have dried
utterly up, nor left one drop within. I keep
the pain upon my eyes where late at night I wept
over the beacons long ago set for your sake,
untended left forever. In the midst of dreams
the whisper that a gnat's thin wings could winnow broke
my sleep apart. I thought I saw you suffer wounds
more than the time that slept with me could ever hold.

Now all my suffering is past; with griefless heart
I hail this man, the watchdog of the fold and hall;

the rope that keeps the ship afloat; the post to grip
groundward the towering roof; a father's single child;
land seen by sailors after all their hope was gone;
splendor of daybreak shining from the night of storm;
the running spring a parched wayfarer strays upon.
Oh, it is sweet to escape from all necessity!

Such is my greeting to him, that he well deserves.
Let none bear malice; for the harm that went before
I took, and it was great.
Now, my beloved one,
step from your chariot; yet let not your foot, my lord,
sacker of Ilium, touch the earth. My maidens there!
Why this delay? Your task has been appointed you,
to strew the ground before his feet with tapestries.
Let there spring up into the house he never hoped
to see, where Justice leads him in, a crimson path.

In all things else, my heart's unsleeping care shall act
with the gods' aid to set aright what fate ordained.

*(Clytaemestra's handmaidens spread a red carpet between the chariot and the door.)*

AGAMEMNON

Daughter of Leda, you who kept my house for me,
there is one way your welcome matched my absence well.
You strained it to great length. Yet properly to praise
me thus belongs by right to other lips, not yours.
And all this—do not try in woman's ways to make
me delicate, nor, as if I were some Asian prince
bow down to earth and with wide mouth cry out to me,
nor cross my path with jealousy by strewing the ground
with robes. Such state befits the gods, and none beside.
I am a mortal, a man; I cannot trample upon
these tinted splendors without fear thrown in my path.
I tell you, as a man, not god, to reverence me.

Discordant is the murmur at such treading down
of lovely things; while god's most lordly gift to man
is decency of mind. Call that man only bless'd
who has in sweet tranquility brought his life to close.
If I could only act as such, my hope is good.

CLYTAEMESTRA

Yet tell me this one thing, and do not cross my will.

AGAMEMNON

My will is mine. I shall not make it soft for you.

CLYTAEMESTRA

Might you in fear have vowed to do such things for god?

AGAMEMNON

Only if the one who advised so knew the full purpose.°

CLYTAEMESTRA

If Priam had won as you have, what would he have done?

AGAMEMNON

I well believe he might have walked on tapestries.

CLYTAEMESTRA

Be not ashamed before the criticism of men.

AGAMEMNON

The people murmur, and their voice is great in strength.

CLYTAEMESTRA

Yet he who goes unenvied shall not be admired.

AGAMEMNON

Surely this lust for conflict is not womanlike?

CLYTAEMESTRA

Yet for the mighty even to give way is grace.

AGAMEMNON

Does such a victory as this mean so much to you?

CLYTAEMESTRA

Oh yield! The power is yours. Freely give way to me.

AGAMEMNON

Since you must have it—here, let someone with all speed
take off these sandals, slaves for my feet to tread upon.
And as I crush these garments stained from the rich sea
let no god's eyes of hatred strike me from afar.
Great the extravagance, and great the shame I feel
to spoil such treasure and such silver's worth of weaving.

So much for all this. Take this stranger girl within
now, and be kind. The conqueror who uses softly
his power is watched benevolently by god from afar,
and this slave's yoke is one no man will wear from choice.
Gift of the host to me, and flower exquisite
from all my many treasures, she attends me here.

Now since my will was bent to listen to you in this
my feet crush crimson as I pass within the hall.

CLYTAEMESTRA

The sea is there, and who shall drain its yield? It breeds
precious as silver, ever of itself renewed,
the purple ooze wherein our garments shall be dipped.
And by god's grace this house keeps full sufficiency
of all. Poverty is a thing beyond its thought.
I could have vowed to trample many splendors down
had such decree been ordained from the oracles
those days when all my study was to bring home your life.
For when the root lives yet the leaves will come again
to fence the house with shade against the Dog Star's heat,
and now you have come home to keep your hearth and
  house,
you bring with you the symbol of our winter's warmth;
and when Zeus ripens the green clusters into wine
there shall be coolness in the house upon those days
because the master ranges his own halls once more.

Zeus, Zeus accomplisher, accomplish these my prayers.
Let your mind bring these things to pass. It is your will.

*(Agamemnon and Clytaemestra enter the palace.*
*Cassandra remains in the chariot.)*

CHORUS [*singing*]

STROPHE A

*Why must this persistent fear*
*beat its wings so ceaselessly*
*and so close against my mantic heart?*
*Why this strain unwanted, unrepaid, thus prophetic?*
*Nor can valor of good hope*
*seated near the chambered depth*
*of the spirit cast it out*
*as dreams of dark fancy; and yet time*
*has buried in the mounding sand*
*the sea cables since that day°*
*when against Ilium*
*the army and the ships put to sea.*

ANTISTROPHE A

*Yet I have seen with these eyes,*
*Agamemnon home again.*
*Still the spirit sings, drawing deep*
*from within this unlyric threnody of the Fury.*
*Hope is gone utterly;*
*the sweet strength is far away.*
*Surely this is not fantasy.*
*Surely it is real, this whirl of drifts*
*that spin the stricken heart.*
*Still I pray; may all this*
*expectation fade as vanity*
*into unfulfillment, and not be.*

STROPHE B

*Yet it is true: the high strength of men*
*knows no content with limitation. Sickness*

*chambered beside it beats at the wall between.*
*Man's fate that sets a true*
*course yet may strike upon*
*the blind and sudden reefs of disaster.°*
*But if before such time, fear*
*throw overboard some precious thing*
*of the cargo, with deliberate cast,*
*not all the house, laboring*
*with weight of ruin, shall go down,*
*nor sink the hull deep within the sea.*
*And great and affluent the gift of Zeus*
*in yield of plowed acres year on year*
*makes void again sick starvation.*

ANTISTROPHE B

*But when the black and mortal blood of man*
*has fallen to the ground before his feet, who then*
*can sing spells to call it back again?*
*Did Zeus not warn us once*
*when he struck to impotence*
*Asclepius, who in truth charmed back the dead men?*
*Had the gods not so ordained*
*that fate should stand against fate*
*to check any man's excess,*
*my heart now would have outrun speech*
*to break forth the water of its grief.*
*But this is so; I murmur deep in darkness*
*sore at heart; my hope is gone now*
*ever again to unwind some crucial good*
*from the flames about my heart.*

*(Enter Clytaemestra from the palace.)*

CLYTAEMESTRA

Cassandra, you may go within the house as well,
since Zeus in no unkindness has ordained that you
must share our lustral water, stand with the great throng

of slaves that flock to the altar of our household god.
Step from this chariot, then, and do not be so proud.
And think—they say that long ago Alcmene's son
was sold in bondage and endured the bread of slaves.
But if constraint of fact forces you to such fate,
be glad indeed for masters ancient in their wealth.
They who have reaped success beyond their dreams of hope
are savage above need and standard toward their slaves.
From us you shall have all you have the right to ask.

CHORUS LEADER

What she has spoken is for you, and clear enough.
Fenced in these fatal nets wherein you find yourself
you should obey her if you can; perhaps you cannot.

CLYTAEMESTRA

Unless she uses speech incomprehensible,
barbarian, wild as the swallow's song, I speak
within her understanding, and she must obey.

CHORUS LEADER

Go with her. What she bids is best in circumstance
that binds you now. Obey, and leave this chariot seat.

CLYTAEMESTRA

I have no leisure to stand outside the house and waste
time on this woman. At the central altarstone
the flocks are standing, ready for the sacrifice
we make to this glad day we never hoped to see.
You: if you are obeying my commands at all, be quick.
But if in ignorance you fail to comprehend,
speak not, but make with your barbarian hand some sign.

CHORUS LEADER

I think this stranger girl needs some interpreter
who understands. She is like some captive animal.

CLYTAEMESTRA

No, she is in the passion of her own wild thoughts.

Leaving her captured city she has come to us
untrained to take the curb, and will not understand
until her rage and strength have foamed away in blood.
I shall throw down no more commands for her contempt.

*(Exit Clytaemestra into the palace.)*

CHORUS LEADER

I, though, shall not be angry, for I pity her.
Come down, poor creature, leave the empty car. Give way
to compulsion and take up the yoke that shall be yours.

*(Cassandra steps down from the chariot.)*

CASSANDRA [*singing throughout the following interchange, while the Chorus Leader speaks in response*]

*Oh shame upon the earth!*
*Apollo, Apollo!*

CHORUS LEADER

You cry on Loxias in agony? He is not
the one who usually has to do with grief.

CASSANDRA

*Oh shame upon the earth!*
*Apollo, Apollo!*

CHORUS LEADER

Now once again in bitter voice she calls upon
this god, who has not part in any lamentation.

CASSANDRA

*Apollo, Apollo!*
*Lord of the ways, my ruin.*
*You have undone me once again, and utterly.*

CHORUS LEADER

I think she will be prophetic of her own disaster.
Even in the slave's heart the gift divine lives on.

CASSANDRA

*Apollo, Apollo!*

*Lord of the ways, my ruin.*
*Where have you led me now at last? What house is this?*

CHORUS LEADER
The house of the Atreidae. If you understand
not that, I can tell you; and so much at least is true.

CASSANDRA
*No, but a house that god hates, guilty within*
*of kindred blood shed, torture of its own,°*
*the shambles for men's butchery, the dripping floor.*

CHORUS LEADER
The stranger is keen-scented like some hound upon
the trail of blood that leads her to discovered death.

CASSANDRA
*Behold there the witnesses to my faith.*
*The small children wail for their own death*
*and the flesh roasted that their father fed upon.*

CHORUS LEADER
We had been told before of this prophetic fame
of yours: we want no prophets in this place at all.

CASSANDRA
*Ah, for shame, what can she purpose now?*
*What is this new and huge*
*stroke of atrocity she plans within the house*
*to beat down the beloved beyond hope of healing?*
*Rescue is far away.*

CHORUS LEADER
I can make nothing of these prophecies. The rest
I understood; the city is full of the sound of them.

CASSANDRA
*So cruel then, that you can do this thing?*
*The husband of your own bed*
*to bathe bright with water—how shall I speak the end?*

*This thing shall be done with speed. The hand gropes now, and the other*
*hand follows in turn.*

CHORUS LEADER

No, I am lost. After the darkness of her speech
I go bewildered in a mist of prophecies.

CASSANDRA

*No, no, see there! What is that thing that shows?*
*Is it some net of death?*
*Or is the trap the woman there, the murderess?*
*Let now the slakeless fury in the race*
*rear up to howl aloud over this monstrous death.*

CHORUS LEADER

Upon what demon in the house do you call, to raise
the cry of triumph? All your speech makes dark my hope.

CHORUS [*singing now and throughout the following interchange with Cassandra, who continues to sing as well*]

*And to the heart below trickles the pale drop*
*as in the hour of death*
*timed to our sunset and the mortal radiance.*
*Ruin is near, and swift.*

CASSANDRA

*See there, see there! Keep from his mate the bull.*
*Caught in the folded web's*
*entanglement she pinions him and with the black horn*
*strikes. And he crumples in the watered bath.*
*Guile, I tell you, and death there in the caldron wrought.*

CHORUS LEADER

I am not proud in skill to guess at prophecies,
yet even I can see the evil in this thing.

CHORUS

*From divination what good ever has come to men?*
*Art, and multiplication of words*

*drifting through tangled evil bring*
*terror to them that hear.*

CASSANDRA
*Alas, alas for the wretchedness of my ill-starred life.*
*This pain flooding the song of sorrow is mine alone.*
*Why have you brought me here in all unhappiness?*
*Why, why? Except to die with him? What else could be?*

CHORUS
*You are possessed of god, inspired at heart*
*to sing your own death*
*song, the wild lyric as*
*in clamor for Itys, Itys over and over again*
*her long life of tears weeping forever grieves*
*the brown nightingale.*

CASSANDRA
*Oh for the nightingale's pure song and a fate like hers.*
*With fashion of beating wings the gods clothed her about*
*and a sweet life they gave her and without lamentation.*
*But mine is the sheer edge of the tearing iron.*

CHORUS
*Whence come, beat upon beat, driven of god,*
*vain passions of tears?*
*Whence your cries, terrified, clashing in horror,*
*in wrought melody and the singing speech?*
*Whence take you the marks to this path of prophecy*
*and speech of terror?*

CASSANDRA
*Oh marriage of Paris, death to the men beloved!*
*Alas, Scamandrus, water my fathers drank.*
*There was a time I too at your springs*
*drank and grew strong. Ah me,*
*for now beside the deadly rivers, Cocytus*
*and Acheron, I must cry out my prophecies.*

CHORUS

*What is this word, too clear, you have uttered now?*
*A child could understand.*
*And deep within goes the stroke of the dripping fang*
*as mortal pain at the trebled song of your agony*
*shivers the heart to hear.*

CASSANDRA

*O sorrow, sorrow of my city dragged to uttermost death.*
*O sacrifices my father made at the wall.*
*Flocks of the pastured sheep slaughtered there.*
*And no use at all*
*to save our city from its pain inflicted now.*
*And I too, with brain ablaze in fever, shall go down.*

CHORUS

*This follows the run of your song.*
*Is it, in cruel force of weight,*
*some divinity kneeling upon you brings*
*the death song of your passionate suffering?*
*I cannot see the end.*

CASSANDRA [*now speaking*]

No longer shall my prophecies like some young girl
new-married glance from under veils, but bright and strong
as winds blow into morning and the sun's uprise
shall wax along the swell like some great wave, to burst
at last upon the shining of this agony.
Now I will tell you plainly and from no cryptic speech;
bear me then witness, running at my heels upon
the scent of these old brutal things done long ago.
There is a choir that sings as one, that shall not again
leave this house ever; the song thereof breaks harsh with
menace.
And drugged to double fury on the wine of men's
blood shed, there lurks forever here a drunken rout
of ingrown vengeful spirits never to be cast forth.

Hanging above the hall they chant their song of hate
and the old sin, and taking up the strain in turn
spit curses on that man who spoiled his brother's bed.
Did I go wide, or hit, like a real archer? Am I
some swindling seer who hawks his lies from door to door?
Upon your oath, bear witness that I know by heart
the legend of ancient wickedness within this house.

CHORUS LEADER [*speaking*]
And how could an oath, though cast in rigid honesty,
do any good? And still we stand amazed at you,
reared in an alien city far beyond the sea;
how can you strike, as if you had been there, the truth?

CASSANDRA
Apollo was the seer who set me to this work.

CHORUS LEADER
Struck with some passion for you, and himself a god?

CASSANDRA
There was a time I blushed to speak about these things.

CHORUS LEADER
True; they who prosper take on airs more delicate.

CASSANDRA
Yes, then; he wrestled with me, and he breathed delight.

CHORUS LEADER
Did you come to the getting of children then, the two of you?

CASSANDRA
I promised that to Loxias, but I broke my word.

CHORUS LEADER
Were you already possessed with the skills of god?

CASSANDRA
Yes; even then I read my city's destinies.

CHORUS LEADER

So Loxias' wrath did you no harm? How could that be?

CASSANDRA

For this my trespass, none believed me ever again.

CHORUS LEADER

But we do; all that you foretell seems true to us.

CASSANDRA

But this is evil, see!
Now once again the pain of grim, true prophecy
shivers my whirling brain in a storm of things foreseen.
Look there, see what is hovering above the house,
so small and young, imaged as in the shadow of dreams,
like children almost, killed by those most dear to them,
and their hands filled with their own flesh, as food to eat.
I see them holding out the inward parts, the vitals,
oh pitiful, that meat their father tasted of . . .
I tell you: There is one that plots vengeance for this,
the strengthless lion rolling in his master's bed,
who keeps, ah me, the house against his lord's return;
my lord too, now that I wear the slave's yoke on my neck.
King of the ships, who tore up Ilium by the roots,
what does he know of this accursed bitch, who licks
his hand, who fawns on him with lifted ears, who like
a secret death shall strike the coward's stroke, nor fail?
No, this is daring when the female shall strike down
the male. What can I call her and be right? What beast
of loathing? Viper double-fanged, or Scylla witch
holed in the rocks and bane of men that range the sea;
smoldering mother of death to breathe relentless hate
on those most dear. How she stood up and howled aloud
and unashamed, as at the breaking point of battle,
in feigned gladness for his salvation from the sea!
What does it matter now if men believe or no?
What is to come will come. And soon you too will stand
beside, to murmur in pity that my words were true.

CHORUS LEADER

Thyestes' feast upon the flesh of his own children
I understand in terror at the thought, and fear
is on me hearing truth and no tale fabricated.
The rest: I heard it, but wander still far from the course.

CASSANDRA

I tell you, you shall look on Agamemnon dead.

CHORUS LEADER

Peace, peace, poor woman; put those bitter lips to sleep.

CASSANDRA

Useless; there is no god of healing in this story.

CHORUS LEADER

Not if it must be; may it somehow fail to come.

CASSANDRA

You pray, yes; but they—they plan to strike, and kill.

CHORUS LEADER

What man is it who moves this beastly thing to be?

CASSANDRA

What man? You did mistake my divination then.

CHORUS LEADER

It may be; I could not follow through the schemer's plan.

CASSANDRA

Yet I know Greek; I think I know it far too well.

CHORUS LEADER

And Pythian oracles are Greek, yet hard to read.

CASSANDRA

Oh, flame and pain that sweeps me once again! My lord,
Apollo, King of Light, the pain, aye me, the pain!
This is the woman-lioness, who goes to bed
with the wolf, when her proud lion ranges far away,

and she will cut me down; as a wife mixing drugs
she wills to shred the virtue of my punishment
into her bowl of wrath as she makes sharp the blade
against her man, death that he brought a mistress home.
Why do I wear these mockeries upon my body,
this staff of prophecy, these garlands at my throat?
At least I will spoil you before I die. Out, down,
break, damn you! This for all that you have done to me.
Make someone else, not me, luxurious in disaster . . .
Lo now, this is Apollo who has stripped me here
of my prophetic robes. He watched me all the time
wearing this glory, mocked by all, my dearest ones
who hated me with all their hearts, so vain, so wrong;
called like some gypsy wandering from door to door
beggar, corrupt, half-starved, and I endured it all.
And now the seer has done with me, his prophetess,
and led me into such a place as this, to die.
Lost are my father's altars, but the block is here
to reek with sacrificial blood, my own. We two
must die, yet die not vengeless by the gods. For there
shall come one to avenge us also, born to slay
his mother, and to wreak death for his father's blood.
Outlaw and wanderer, driven far from his own land,
he will come back to cope these stones of inward hate.
For this is a strong oath and sworn by the high gods,°
that he shall cast them headlong for his father felled.
Why am I then so pitiful? Why must I weep?
Since once I saw the citadel of Ilium
die as it died, and those who broke the city, doomed
by the gods, fare as they have fared accordingly,
I will go through with it. I too will take my fate.
I call as on the gates of death upon these gates
to pray only for this thing, that the stroke be true,
and that with no convulsion, with a rush of blood
in painless death, I may close up these eyes, and rest.

CHORUS LEADER

O woman much enduring and so greatly wise,
you have said much. But if this thing you know be true,
this death that comes upon you, how can you, serene,
walk to the altar like a driven ox of god?

CASSANDRA

Friends, there is no escape for any longer time.

CHORUS LEADER

Yet the last bit of time is to be honored most.

CASSANDRA

The day is here and now; I cannot win by flight.

CHORUS LEADER

Woman, be sure your heart is brave; you can endure much.

CASSANDRA

None but the most unhappy ever hear such praise.

CHORUS LEADER

Yet there is a grace on mortals who so nobly die.

CASSANDRA

Alas for you, father, and for your lordly sons.
Ah!

CHORUS LEADER

What now? What terror whirls you backward from the door?

CASSANDRA

Foul, foul!

CHORUS LEADER

What foulness then, unless some horror in the mind?

CASSANDRA

That room within reeks with blood like a slaughterhouse.

CHORUS LEADER

What then? Only these animals butchered at the hearth.

CASSANDRA

There is a breath about it like an open grave.

CHORUS LEADER

This is no Syrian pride of frankincense you mean.

CASSANDRA

So. I am going in, and mourning as I go
my death and Agamemnon's. Let my life be done.
Ah friends,
truly this is no wild bird fluttering at a bush,
nor vain my speech. Bear witness to me when I die,
when falls for me, a woman slain, another woman,
and when a man dies for this wickedly mated man.
Here in my death I claim this stranger's grace of you.

CHORUS LEADER

Poor wretch, I pity you the fate you see so clear.

CASSANDRA

Yet once more will I speak, and not this time my own
death's threnody. I call upon the Sun in prayer
against that ultimate shining when the avengers strike
these monsters down in blood, that they avenge as well
one simple slave who died, a small thing, lightly killed.
Alas, poor men, their destiny. When all goes well
a shadow will overthrow it. If it be unkind
one stroke of a wet sponge wipes all the picture out;
and that is far the most unhappy thing of all.

*(Exit Cassandra into the palace.)*

CHORUS [*chanting*]

*High fortune is a thing insatiable*
*for mortals. There is no man who shall point*
*his finger to drive it back from the door*
*and speak the words: "Come no longer."*
*Now to this man the blessed ones have given*
*Priam's city to be captured*

*and return in the gods' honor.*
*Must he give blood for generations gone,*
*die for those slain and in death pile up*
*more death to come for the blood shed?*
*What mortal else who hears shall claim*
*he was born immune to the demon of harm?*

AGAMEMNON *(Inside the house.)*

Ah, I am struck a deadly blow and deep within!

CHORUS LEADER

Silence: who cried out that he was stabbed to death within the house?

AGAMEMNON

Ah me, again, they struck again. I am wounded twice.

CHORUS LEADER

How the king cried out aloud to us! I believe the thing is done.
Come, let us put our heads together, try to find some safe way out.

CHORUS *(Each member speaking excitedly in turn.)*

Listen, let me tell you what I think is best to do.
Let the herald call all citizens to rally here.

No, better to burst in upon them now, at once,
and take them with the blood still running from their blades.

I am with this man and I cast my vote to him.
Act now. This is the perilous and instant time.

Anyone can see it, by these first steps they have taken,
they purpose to be tyrants here upon our city.

Yes, for we waste time, while they trample to the ground
deliberation's honor, and their hands sleep not.

I cannot tell which counsel of yours to call my own.
It is the man of action who can plan as well.°

I feel as he does; nor can I see how by words
we shall set the dead man back upon his feet again.

Do you mean, to drag our lives out long, that we must yield
to those shaming the house, and leadership of such as these?

No, we can never endure that; better to be killed.
Death is a softer thing by far than tyranny.

Shall we, by no more proof than that he cried in pain,
be sure, as by divination, that our lord is dead?

Yes, we should know what is true before we speak our mind.
Here is sheer guessing and far different from sure
knowledge.

From all sides the voices multiply to make me choose
this course; to learn first how it stands with Agamemnon.

*(The doors of the palace open, disclosing the bodies of Agamemnon and Cassandra, with Clytaemestra standing over them.)*

CLYTAEMESTRA

Much have I said before to serve necessity,
but I will feel no shame now to unsay it all.
How else could I, arming hate against hateful men
disguised in seeming tenderness, fence high the nets
of ruin beyond overleaping? Thus to me
the conflict born of ancient bitterness is not
a thing new thought upon, but pondered deep in time.
I stand now where I struck him down. The thing is done.
Thus have I wrought, and I will not deny it now.
That he might not escape nor beat aside his death,
as fishermen cast their huge circling nets, I spread
deadly abundance of rich robes, and caught him fast.
I struck him twice. In two great cries of agony
he buckled at the knees and fell. When he was down
I struck him the third blow, in thanks and reverence
to Zeus beneath the ground, the prayed-for Savior of the dead.
Thus he went down, and the life struggled out of him;

and as he died he spattered me with the dark red
and violent driven rain of bitter-savored blood
to make me glad, as plants stand strong amidst the showers
of god in glory at the birthtime of the buds.

These being the facts, elders of Argos assembled here,
be glad, if it be your pleasure; but for me, I glory.
If libations were proper to pour above the slain,
this man deserved, more than deserved, such sacrament.
He filled our cup with evil things unspeakable
and now himself come home has drunk it to the dregs.

CHORUS LEADER

We stand here stunned. How can you speak this way, with mouth
so arrogant, to vaunt above your fallen lord?

CLYTAEMESTRA

You try me out as if I were a woman and vain;
but my heart is not fluttered as I speak before you.
You know it. You can praise or blame me as you wish;
it is all one to me. That man is Agamemnon,
my husband; he is dead; the work of this right hand
that struck in strength of righteousness. And that is that.

CHORUS [*singing*]

STROPHE A

*Woman, what evil thing planted upon the earth*
*or dragged from the running salt sea could you have tasted now*
*to show such brutality and walk in the people's hate?*
*You have cast away, you have cut away. You shall go homeless now,*
*crushed with men's bitterness.*

CLYTAEMESTRA

Now it is I you vote to be cast out from my city
with men's hate heaped and curses roaring in my ears.
Yet look upon this dead man; you did not cross him once
when with no thought more than as if a beast were butchered,

when his ranged pastures swarmed with the deep fleece of
flocks,
he slaughtered at the altar his own child, my pain
grown into love, to charm away the winds of Thrace.
Were you not bound to hunt him then clear of this soil
for the guilt stained upon him? Yet you hear what I
have done, and lo, you are a stern judge. But I say to you:
go on and threaten me, but know that I am ready,
if fairly you can beat me down beneath your hand,
for you to rule; but if the god grant otherwise,
you shall be taught—too late, for sure—to keep your place.

CHORUS [*singing*]

ANTISTROPHE A

*Big are your thoughts, your speech is a clamor of pride.*
*Swung to the red act drives the fury within your brain*
*signed clear in the flecks of blood on your eyes.*
*Yet to come is stroke given for stroke*
*avenging, when you are forlorn of friends.*

CLYTAEMESTRA

Now hear you this, the right behind my sacrament:
By my child's Justice driven to fulfillment, by
her Wrath and Fury, to whom I sacrificed this man,
the hope that walks my chambers is not traced with fear
while yet Aegisthus makes the fire shine in my hearth,
my good friend, now as always, who shall be for us
the shield of our defiance, no weak thing; while he,
this other, is fallen, stained with this woman you behold,
plaything of all the golden girls at Ilium;
and here lies she, the captive of his spear, who saw
wonders, who shared his bed, the wise in revelations
and loving mistress, who yet knew the feel as well
of the men's rowing benches. Their reward is not
unworthy. He lies there; and she who swanlike cried
aloud her lyric dying lamentation, now

lies next to him, his lover, and to me has given
a delicate excitement, spicing my delight.°

CHORUS [*singing*]

STROPHE B

*O that in speed, without pain*
*and the slow bed of sickness,*
*death could come to us now, death that forever*
*carries sleep without ending, now that our lord is down,*
*our shield, kindest of men,*
*who for a woman's grace suffered so much,*
*struck down at last by a woman.*

[*chanting*]
*Alas, Helen, crazed heart*
*for the multitudes, for the thousand lives*
*you killed under Troy's shadow:*
*now as your final memorial,*
*you're adorned in blood never to be washed out.*
*Surely a demon then*
*of Strife walked in the house, men's agony.*

CLYTAEMESTRA [*chanting throughout the following interchange with the Chorus*]

*No, be not so harsh, and don't invoke*
*in prayer death's ending,*
*neither turn all wrath against Helen*
*for men dead, that she alone killed*
*all those Danaan lives, to work*
*the grief that is past all healing.*

CHORUS [*singing*]

ANTISTROPHE B

*Spirit that kneels on this house and on the two*
*strains of the blood of Tantalus,*
*in the hands and hearts of women you steer*
*the strength tearing my heart.*
*Standing above the corpse, obscene*

*as some carrion crow it sings*
*the crippled song and is proud.*°

CLYTAEMESTRA

*Now have you set the speech of your lips*
*straight, calling by name*
*the spirit thrice glutted that lives in this race.*
*From it, deep in the nerve is given*
*the love and the blood drunk, that before*
*the old wound dries, it bleeds again.*

CHORUS [*singing*]

STROPHE C

*Surely it is a huge*
*and angry spirit haunting the house you cry;*
*alas, the bitter story*
*of a doom that shall never be done with;*
*and all through Zeus, Zeus,*
*first cause, prime mover.*
*For what thing without Zeus is done among mortals?*
*What here is without god's blessing?*

[*chanting*]
*O king, my king,*
*how shall I weep for you?*
*What can I say out of my heart of pity?*
*Caught in this spider's web you lie.*
*Your life gasped out in indecent death,*
*struck prone to this shameful bed*
*by your lady's hand of treachery*
*and the stroke twin-edged of the iron.*

CLYTAEMESTRA

*Can you claim I have done this?*
*Speak of me never*
*more as the wife of Agamemnon.*°
*In the image of this corpse's queen*

*the old stark avenger*
*of Atreus for his revel of hate*
*struck down this man,*
*last blood for the slaughtered children.*

CHORUS [*singing*]

ANTISTROPHE C

*What man shall testify*
*your hands are clean of this murder?*
*How? How? Yet from his father's blood*
*might swarm some fiend to assist you.*
*The black ruin that shoulders*
*through the streaming blood of brothers*
*strides at last where he shall win requital*
*for the children who were eaten.*

[*chanting*]
*O king, my king*
*how shall I weep for you?*
*What can I say out of my heart of pity?*
*Caught in this spider's web you lie,*
*your life gasped out in indecent death,*
*struck prone to this shameful bed*
*by your lady's hand of treachery*
*and the stroke twin-edged of the iron.*

CLYTAEMESTRA

*No shame, I think, in the death given*
*this man. And did he not*
*first of all in this house wreak death*
*by treachery?*
*The flower of this man's love and mine,*
*Iphigeneia of the many tears—*
*he dealt with her even as he has suffered now.*°
*So let his speech in Death's house be not loud.*
*With the sword he struck;*
*with the sword he paid for his own act.*

CHORUS [*singing*]

STROPHE D

*My thoughts are swept away and I go bewildered.*
*Where shall I turn the brain's*
*activity in speed when the house is falling?*
*There is fear in the beat of the blood rain breaking*
*wall and tower. The drops come thicker.*
*Still fate grinds on yet more stones the blade*
*for more acts of terror.*

[*chanting*]
*Earth, my earth, why did you not fold me under*
*before ever I saw this man lie dead*
*fenced in by the tub of silver?*
*Who shall bury him? Who shall mourn him?*
*Shall you dare this who have killed*
*your lord? Make lamentation,*
*render the graceless grace to his soul*
*for huge things done in wickedness?*
*Who over this great man's grave shall lay*
*the blessing of tears*
*worked soberly from a true heart?*

CLYTAEMESTRA

*Not for you to speak of such tendance.*
*Through us he fell,*
*by us he died; we shall bury.*
*There will be no tears in this house for him.*
*It must be Iphigeneia*
*his child—who else*
*shall greet her father by the whirling stream*
*and the ferry of tears*
*to close him in her arms and kiss him.*

CHORUS [*singing*]

ANTISTROPHE D

*Here is anger for anger. Between them*
*who shall judge lightly?*

*The spoiler is robbed; he killed, he has paid.*
*The truth stands ever beside god's throne*
*eternal: he who has done shall suffer; that is law.*
*Then who shall tear the curse from their blood?*
*The house is glued to ruin.*

CLYTAEMESTRA

*You see truth in the future*
*at last. Yet I wish*
*to seal my oath with the Spirit*
*in the house: I will endure all things as they stand*
*now, hard though it be. Hereafter*
*let it go forth to make bleed with death*
*and guilt the houses of others.*
*I will take some small*
*measure of our riches, and be content*
*that I swept from these halls*
*the murder, the sin, and the fury.*

*(Enter Aegisthus from the side, with his armed bodyguard.)*

AEGISTHUS

O splendor and triumph of this day of justice!
Now I can say once more that the high gods look down
on mortal crimes to vindicate the right at last,
now that I see this man—sweet sight—before me here
sprawled in the tangling nets of fury, to atone
the calculated evil of his father's hand.
For Atreus, this man's father, King of Argolis—
I tell you the clear story—drove my father forth,
Thyestes, his own brother, who had challenged him
in his king's right—forth from his city and his home.
Yet poor Thyestes came again to supplicate
the hearth, and win some grace. He found a safe portion
nor soiled the doorstone of his fathers with blood spilled.
Not his own blood. But Atreus, this man's godless sire,
angrily hospitable set a feast for him,
in seeming a glad day of fresh meat slain and good

cheer; then served my father his own children's flesh
to feed on. For he carved away the extremities,
hands, feet, and cut the flesh apart, and covered them
served in a dish to my father at his table apart,
who with no thought for the featureless meal before him ate
that ghastly food whose curse works now before your eyes.
But when he knew the terrible thing that he had done,
he spat the dead meat from him with a cry, recoiled
and kicked the table over, pledging with strength his curse:
"Thus crash in ruin all the seed of Pleisthenes."
Out of such acts you see this dead man stricken here,
and it was I, in my right, who wrought this murder, I
third-born to my unhappy father, and with him
driven, a helpless baby in arms, to banishment.
Yet I grew up, and justice brought me home again,
till from afar I laid my hands upon this man,
since it was I who pieced together the deadly plot.
Now I can die in honor again, if die I must,
having seen him caught in the nets of his just punishment.

CHORUS LEADER

Aegisthus, this strong vaunting in distress is vile.
You claim that you deliberately killed the king,
you, and you only, planned the pity of this death.
I tell you then: There shall be no escape, your head
shall face the stones of anger from the people's hands.

AEGISTHUS

So loud from you, stooped to the meanest rowing bench
with the ship's masters lordly on the deck above?
You are old men; well, you shall learn how hard it is,
at your age, to be taught how to behave yourselves.
But there are chains, there is starvation with its pain,
excellent teachers of good manners to old men,
wise surgeons and exemplars. Look! Can you not see it?
Kick not at the goads for fear you hit them, and be hurt.

CHORUS LEADER

So then you, like a woman, waited the war out
here in the house, shaming the master's bed with lust,
and planned against the lord of war this treacherous death?

AEGISTHUS

It is just such words as these will make you cry in pain.
Not yours the lips of Orpheus, no, quite otherwise—
his voice of rapture led all creatures in his train;
you shall be led away, for babyish cries sobbed out
in rage. Once broken, you will be easier to deal with.

CHORUS LEADER

How shall you be lord of the men of Argos, you
who planned the murder of this man, yet could not dare
to act it out and cut him down with your own hand?

AEGISTHUS

No, clearly the deception was the woman's part,
and I was suspect, that had hated him so long.
Still with his money I shall endeavor to control
the citizens. The mutinous man shall feel the yoke
drag at his neck, no oat-fed racehorse running free,
but hunger, grim companion of the dark dungeon
shall see him trudging, broken to the hand at last.

CHORUS LEADER

But why, why then, you coward, could you not have slain
your man yourself? Why must it be his wife who killed,
to curse the country and the gods within the ground?
Oh, can Orestes live, be somewhere in sunlight still?
Shall fate grown gracious ever bring him back again
in strength of hand to overwhelm these murderers?

AEGISTHUS

You shall learn then, since you stick to stubbornness of
mouth and hand.

CHORUS LEADER°

Come on now, my trusty comrades: here is work for you to do.

AEGISTHUS

Come on now! Let every man clap fist upon his ready sword.

CHORUS LEADER

I as well am ready-handed; I am not afraid of death.

AEGISTHUS

Death you said and death it shall be; so I take up the word of fate.

CLYTAEMESTRA

No, my dearest, dearest of all men, we have done enough. No more
violence. Here is a monstrous harvest and a bitter reaping time.
There is pain enough already. Let us not be bloody now.
Honored gentlemen of Argos, go to your homes now and give way°
to the stress of fate and season. We could not do otherwise
than we did. If this is the end of suffering, we can be content
broken as we are by the brute heel of angry destiny.
Thus a woman speaks among you. Shall men deign to understand?

AEGISTHUS

Yes, but think of these foolish lips that blossom° into leering gibes;
think of the taunts they spit against me daring destiny and power,
sober opinion lost in insults hurled against my majesty.

CHORUS LEADER

It was never the Argive way to grovel at a vile man's feet.

AEGISTHUS

I shall not forget this; in the days to come I shall be there.

CHORUS LEADER

Nevermore, if god's guiding hand brings Orestes home again.

AEGISTHUS

Exiles feed on empty dreams of hope. I know it. I was one.

CHORUS LEADER

Have your way, gorge and grow fat, soil justice, while the power is yours.

AEGISTHUS

You shall pay, make no mistake, for this foolishness.

CHORUS LEADER

Crow and strut, brave cockerel by your hen; you have no threats to fear.

CLYTAEMESTRA

Do not heed their empty yappings; come now, dearest, you and I
have the power; we two shall bring good order to our house at least.

*(Exit Aegisthus and Clytaemestra into the palace.)*

# THE LIBATION BEARERS

*Characters*

ORESTES, son of Agamemnon and Clytaemestra
PYLADES, his friend
ELECTRA, his sister
CHORUS of Asian serving-women
A SERVANT (doorkeeper)
CLYTAEMESTRA, queen of Argos; now wife of Aegisthus
THE NURSE, Cilissa
AEGISTHUS, now king of Argos
A FOLLOWER of Aegisthus

*Scene: Argos, in front of the palace.*

*(Enter Orestes and Pylades, from the side.)*

ORESTES

Hermes, lord of the dead, you who watch over the powers
of my fathers, be my savior and stand by my claim.°
Here is my own soil that I walk. I have come home;
and by this mounded gravebank I invoke my father
to hear, to listen.
He met his end in violence through a woman's treacherous tricks . . .
Here is a lock of hair for Inachus, who made
me grow to manhood. Here a strand to mark my grief.
I was not by, my father, to mourn for your death
nor stretched my hand out when they took your corpse away.

*(Enter the Chorus, with Electra, from the other side.)*

But what can this mean that I see, this group that comes
of women veiled in dignities of black? At what
sudden occurrence can I guess? Is this some new
wound struck into our house? I think they bring these urns
to pour, in my father's honor, to appease the powers
below. Can I be right? Surely, I think I see
Electra, my own sister, walk in bitter show
of mourning. Zeus, Zeus, grant me vengeance for my father's
murder. Stand and fight beside me, of your grace.
Pylades, stand we out of their way. So may I learn
the meaning of these women; what their prayer would ask.

*(Orestes and Pylades conceal themselves, to one side.)*

CHORUS [*singing*]

STROPHE A

*I came in haste out of the house*
*to carry libations, hurt by the hard stroke of hands.*
*My cheek shows bright, ripped in the bloody furrows*
*of nails gashing the skin.*
*This is my life: to feed the heart on hard-drawn breath.*
*And in my grief, with splitting weft*
*of ragtorn linen across my heart's*
*brave show of robes*
*came sound of my hands' strokes*
*in sorrows whence smiles are fled.*

ANTISTROPHE A

*Terror, the dream diviner of*
*this house, belled clear, shuddered the skin, blew wrath*
*from sleep, a cry in night's obscure watches,*
*a voice of fear deep in the house,*
*dropping deadweight in women's inner chambers.*
*And they who read the dream meanings*
*and spoke under guarantee of god*
*told how under earth*

*dead men held a grudge still*
*and smoldered at their murderers.*

STROPHE B

*On such grace without grace, evil's turning aside*
*(Earth, Earth, kind mother!)*
*bent, the godless woman*
*sends me forth. But terror*
*is on me for this word let fall.*
*What can wash off the blood once spilled upon the ground?*
*O hearth soaked in sorrow,*
*O wreckage of a fallen house.*
*Sunless and where men fear to walk*
*the mists huddle upon this house*
*where the high lords have perished.*

ANTISTROPHE B

*The pride not to be warred with, fought with, not to be beaten down*
*of old, sounded in all men's*
*ears, in all hearts sounded,*
*has shrunk away. A man*
*goes in fear. High fortune,*
*this in man's eyes is god and more than god is this.*
*But, as a beam balances, so*
*sudden disasters wait, to strike*
*some in the brightness, some in gloom*
*of half dark in their elder time.*
*Desperate night holds others.*

STROPHE C

*Through too much glut of blood drunk by our fostering ground*
*the vengeful gore is caked and hard, will not drain through.*
*The deep-run ruin carries away*
*the man of guilt. Swarming infection boils within.*

ANTISTROPHE C

*For one who assaults the bride's pure bed, there is no cure.*
*All the world's waters running in a single drift*

*may try to wash blood from the hand*
*of the stained man; they only bring new blood guilt on.*

EPODE

*But as for me: gods have forced on my city*
*resisted fate. From our fathers' houses*
*they led us here, to take the lot of slaves.*
*And mine it is to wrench my will, and consent*
*to their commands, right or wrong,*
*to beat down my edged hate.*
*And yet under veils I weep*
*the futile destinies of*
*my lord; and freeze with sorrow in the secret heart.*

ELECTRA

Attendant women, who order our house, since you
are with me in this supplication and escort
me here, be also my advisors in this rite.
What shall I say, as I pour out these outpourings
of sorrow? How say the good word, how make my prayer
to my father? Shall I say I bring it to the man
beloved, from a loving wife, and mean my mother? I
have not the daring to say this, nor know what else
to say, as I pour this liquid on my father's tomb.°
Shall I say this sentence, regular in human use:
"Grant good return to those who send to you these flowers
of honor: gifts to match the—evil they have done."
Or, quiet and dishonored, as my father died
shall I pour out this offering for the ground to drink,
and go, like one who empties garbage out of doors,
and turn my eyes, and throw the vessel far away?
Dear friends, in this deliberation stay with me.
We hold a common hatred in this house. Do not
for fear of any, hide your thought inside your heart.
The day of destiny waits for the free man as well
as for the man enslaved beneath an alien hand.
If you know any better course than mine, tell me.

CHORUS LEADER

In reverence for your father's tomb as if it were
an altar, I will speak my heart's thought, as you ask.

ELECTRA

Tell me then, please, as you respect my father's grave.

CHORUS LEADER

Say words of grace for those of goodwill, as you pour.

ELECTRA

Whom of those closest to me can I call my friend?

CHORUS LEADER

Yourself first; all who hate Aegisthus after that.

ELECTRA

You mean these prayers shall be for you, and for myself?

CHORUS LEADER

You see it now; but it is you whose thought this is.

ELECTRA

Is there some other we should bring in on our side?

CHORUS LEADER

Remember Orestes, though he wanders far away

ELECTRA

That was well spoken; you did well reminding me.

CHORUS LEADER

Remember, too, the murderers, and against them . . .

ELECTRA

What shall I say? Guide and instruct my ignorance.

CHORUS LEADER

Invoke the coming of some man, or more than man.

ELECTRA

To come to judge them, or to give them punishment?

CHORUS LEADER

Say simply: "one to kill them, for the life they took."

ELECTRA

I can ask this, and not be wrong in the gods' eyes?

CHORUS LEADER

Of course, to hurt your enemy when he struck first.

ELECTRA

Almighty herald of the world above, the world
below:° Hermes, lord of the dead, help me; announce
my prayers to the charmed spirits underground, who watch
over my father's house, that they may hear. Tell Earth
herself, who brings all things to birth, who gives them
    strength,
then gathers their big yield into herself at last.
I myself pour these lustral waters to the dead,
and speak, and call upon my father: Pity me;
pity your own Orestes. How shall we be lords
in our house? We have been sold, and go as wanderers
because our mother bought herself, for us, a man,
Aegisthus, he who helped her hand to cut you down.
Now I am what a slave is, and Orestes lives
outcast from his great properties, while they go proud
in the high style and luxury of what you worked
to win. By some good fortune let Orestes come
back home. Such is my prayer, my father. Hear me; hear.
And for myself, grant that I be more temperate
of heart than my mother; that I act with purer hand.
Such are my prayers for us; but for our enemies,
father, I pray that your avenger come, that they
who killed you shall be killed in turn, as they deserve.
Between my prayer for good and prayer for good I set
this prayer for evil; and I speak it against Them.
For us, bring blessings up into the world. Let Earth
and conquering Justice, and all gods beside, give aid.

Such are my prayers; and over them I pour these drink offerings.

*(To the Chorus.)*

Yours the mode now, yours to make these flower with fierce laments, and incantation for the dead.

CHORUS [*singing*]

*Let the tear fall, that clashes as it dies*
*as died our fallen lord;*
*die on this mound that fences good from evil,*
*washing away the death stain accursed*
*of drink offerings shed. Hear me, oh hear, my lord,*
*majesty hear me from your dark heart; oh hear,*
*oh oh!*
*Let one come, in strength*
*of spear, some man at arms who will set free the house*
*holding the Scythian bow backbent in his hands,*
*a mighty god of war spattering arrows*
*or closing to combat, with sword hilted fast to his hand.*

ELECTRA

Father, the earth has drunk my offerings poured to you. But something has happened here, my women. Help me now.

CHORUS LEADER

Speak, if you will. My heart is in a dance of fear.

ELECTRA

Someone has cut a strand of hair and laid it on the tomb.

CHORUS LEADER

What man? Or was it some slim-waisted girl?

ELECTRA

There is a mark, which makes it plain for any to guess.

CHORUS LEADER

Explain, and let your youth instruct my greater age.

ELECTRA

No one could have cut off this strand, except myself.

CHORUS LEADER

Those others, for whom it were proper, are full of hate.

ELECTRA

Yet here it is, and for appearance matches well . . .

CHORUS LEADER

With whose hair? Tell me. This is what I long to know . . .

ELECTRA

With my own hair. It is almost exactly like.

CHORUS LEADER

Can it then be a secret gift from Orestes?

ELECTRA

It seems that it must be nobody's hair but his.

CHORUS LEADER

Did Orestes dare to come back here? How could this be?

ELECTRA

He sent it, this severed strand, to do my father honor.

CHORUS LEADER

It will not stop my tears if you are right. You mean
that he can never again set foot upon this land.

ELECTRA

The bitter wash has surged upon my heart as well.
I am struck through, as by the cross-stab of a sword,
and from my eyes the thirsty and unguarded drops
burst in a storm of tears like winter rain, as I
look on this strand of hair. How could I think some other
man, one of the citizens, could ever be lord of hair like this?
She never could have cut it, she who murdered him
and is my mother, but no mother in her heart
which has assumed god's hate and hates her children. No.

And yet, how can I say in open outright confidence
this is a treasured token from the best beloved
of men to me, Orestes? Does hope fawn on me?
Ah
I wish it had the kind voice of a messenger
so that my mind would not be torn in two, I not
shaken, but it could tell me plain to throw this strand°
away as trash, if it was cut from a hated head,
or like a brother could have mourned with me, and been
a treasured splendor for my father, and his grave.
The gods know, and we call upon the gods; they know
how we are spun in circles like seafarers, in
what storms. But if we are to win, and our ship live,
from one small seed could burgeon an enormous tree.
But see, here is another sign. Footprints are here.
The feet that made them are alike, and look like mine.
There are two sets of footprints: of the man who gave
his hair, and one who shared the road with him. I step
where he has stepped, and heelmarks, and the space between
his heel and toe are like the prints I make. Oh, this
is torment, and my wits are going.

*(Orestes comes forward from his place of concealment.)*

ORESTES

Pray for what is to come, and tell the gods that they
have brought your former prayers to pass. Pray for success.

ELECTRA

Upon what ground? What have I won yet from the gods?

ORESTES

You have come in sight of all you long since prayed to see.

ELECTRA

How do you know what man was subject of my prayer?

ORESTES

I know about Orestes, how he stirred your heart.

ELECTRA

Yes; but how am I given an answer to my prayers?

ORESTES

Look at me. Look for no one closer to you than I.

ELECTRA

Is this some net of treachery you catch me in, stranger?

ORESTES

Then I must be contriving plots against myself.

ELECTRA

It is your pleasure to laugh at my unhappiness.

ORESTES

I only mock my own then, if I laugh at you.

ELECTRA

Are you really Orestes? Can I call you by that name?

ORESTES

You see my actual self and are slow to learn. And yet
you saw this strand of hair I cut in sign of grief
and shuddered with excitement, for you thought you saw
me, and again when you were measuring my tracks.
Now lay the severed strand against where it was cut
and see how well your brother's hair matches my head.°
Look at this piece of weaving, the work of your hand
with its blade strokes and figured design of beasts. No, no,
control yourself, and do not lose your head for joy.
I know those nearest to us hate us bitterly.

ELECTRA

O dearest, treasured darling of my father's house,
hope of the seed of our salvation, wept for, trust
your strength of hand, and win your father's house again.
O bright beloved presence, you bring back four lives
to me. To call you father is constraint of fact,
and all the love I could have borne my mother turns
your way, while she is loathed as she deserves; my love

for a pitilessly slaughtered sister turns to you.
And now you were my steadfast brother after all.
You alone bring me honor; but may Force, and Right,
and Zeus almighty, third with them, be on your side.°

ORESTES

Zeus, Zeus, gaze on all that we try to do. Behold
the orphaned children of the eagle-father, now
that he has died entangled in the twisting coils
of the deadly viper, and the young he left behind
are worn with the wasting of starvation, not full grown
to bring home to their nest the prey as their father did.
I, with my sister, whom I name, Electra here,
stand in your sight, children whose father is lost. We both
are driven in exile from the house that should be ours.
If you destroy these father's fledglings who gave you°
sacrifice and high honor, from what hand like his
shall you be given the sacred feast which is your right?
Destroy the eagle's brood, and you have no more means
to send your signs to mortals for their strong belief;
nor, if the stump rot through on this our royal tree,
shall it sustain your altars on sacrificial days.
Safe keep it: from a little thing you can raise up
a house to grandeur, though it now seem overthrown.

CHORUS

O children, silence! Saviors of your father's house,
be silent, children. Otherwise someone may hear
and for mere love of gossip carry news of all
you do, to those in power, to those I long to see
some day as corpses in the bubbling pitch and flame.

ORESTES

The big strength of Apollo's oracle will not
forsake me. For he charged me to win through this hazard,
with divination of much, and speech articulate,
warning of chill disaster under my warm heart
were I to fail against my father's murderers;

told me to cut them down in their own fashion, turn
to bull-like fury in the loss of my estates.
He said that else I must myself pay penalty
with my own life, and suffer much grim punishment;
spoke of the angers that come out of the ground from those
beneath who turn against men; spoke of sicknesses,
ulcers that ride upon the flesh, and cling, and with
wild teeth eat away the natural tissue, how on this
disease shall grow in turn a leprous fur. He spoke
of other ways again by which the Avengers might
attack, brought to fulfillment from my father's blood.
There's a dark weapon of those dead men underground
all those within my family who fell turn to call
upon me; madness and empty terror in the night
on one who sees clear those visions in the dark:
they tear him loose and shake him until, with all his body
degraded by the collar of bronze, he flees his city.°
And such as he can have no share in the communal bowl
allowed them, no cup filled for friends to drink. The wrath
of the father comes unseen on them to drive them back
from altars. None can take them in nor shelter them.
Dishonored and unloved by all the man must die
at last, shrunken and wasted away in painful death.
  Shall I not trust such oracles as this? Even if
I do not trust them, here is work that must be done.
Here numerous desires converge to drive me on:
the god's urgency and grief for my father, and with these
the loss of my estates wears hard on me; also
the thought that these my citizens, most high renowned
of men, who toppled Troy with hearts of valor, must
go subject to this pair of women; since "his" heart
is really female; or, if not, that soon will show.

CHORUS [*chanting*]
*Almighty Destinies, by the will*
*of Zeus let these things*

*be done, in the turning of Justice.*
*In return for the word of hatred spoken, let hate*
*be a word fulfilled. The spirit of Right*
*cries out aloud and extracts atonement*
*due: blood stroke for the stroke of blood*
*shall be paid. Who acts, shall suffer. So speaks*
*the voice of the age-old wisdom.*

ORESTES° [*singing throughout this lyric interchange with Electra and the Chorus*]

STROPHE A

*Father, O my dread father, what thing*
*can I say, can I accomplish*
*from this far place where I stand, to mark*
*and reach you there in your chamber*
*with light that will match your dark?*
*Yet it is called an action*
*of grace to mourn in style for the house,*
*once great, of the sons of Atreus.*

CHORUS [*singing*]

STROPHE B

*Child, when the fire burns*
*and tears with its teeth at the dead man*
*it cannot wear out the proud spirit.*
*He shows his wrath in the after-*
*days. One dies, and is lamented.*
*Light falls on the man who killed him.*
*He is hunted down by the deathsong*
*for sires slain and for fathers,*
*disturbed, and stern, and avenging.*

ELECTRA [*singing throughout this lyric interchange*]

ANTISTROPHE A

*Hear me, my father; hear in turn*
*all the tears of my sorrows.*
*Two children stand at your tomb to sing*

*the burden of your death chant.*
*Your grave is shelter to suppliants,*
*shelter to the outdriven.*
*What here is good; what escape from grief?*
*Can we outwrestle disaster?*

CHORUS [*chanting*]

*Yet from such as this the god, if he will,*
*can work out strains that are fairer.*
*For dirges chanted over the grave,*
*the winner's song in the royal house;*
*bring home to new arms the beloved.*

ORESTES

STROPHE C

*If only at Ilium,*
*father, and by some Lycian's hands*
*you had gone down at the spear's stroke,*
*you would have left high fame in your house,*
*for your children seen in the streets*
*admiration from all;*
*your tomb would be a deep piled bank of earth*
*founded in a land across the sea,*
*a light burden for your household;*

CHORUS [*singing*]

ANTISTROPHE B

*loved then by those he loved*
*down there beneath the ground*
*who died as heroes, he would have held*
*state, and a lord's majesty,*
*vassal only to those most great,*
*the kings of the underdarkness.*
*For he was king on earth when he lived°*
*over those whose hands held power of life*
*and death, and the staff of authority.*

ELECTRA

ANTISTROPHE C

*No, but not under Troy's*
*ramparts, father, should you have died,*
*nor, with the rest of the spearstruck hordes*
*have found your grave by Scamandrus' crossing.*
*Sooner, his murderers*
*should have been killed, as he was,*
*by those they loved, and have found their death,*
*and people remote from this outrage*
*had heard the distant story.*

CHORUS [*chanting*]

*Child, child, you are dreaming, and dreaming is a light*
*pastime, of fortune more golden than gold*
*or the Blessed Ones north of the North Wind.*
*But the stroke of the twofold lash is pounding*
*close. Helpers are gathering underground*
*for some of us, while the hands of those who rule*
*are unclean, and these are accursed.*
*Power grows on the side of the children.°*

ORESTES

STROPHE D

*This cry has come to my ear*
*like a deep-driven arrow.*
*Zeus, Zeus, send up from below*
*ground the delayed destruction*
*on the cruel heart and the all-daring*
*hand, for the right of our fathers.*

CHORUS [*singing*]

STROPHE E

*May I claim the right to close the deathsong°*
*chanted in glory across*
*the man speared and the woman*
*dying. Why hide what deep within my breast always*

*flitters? Long since against the heart's*
*stem a bitter wind has blown*
*fierce anger and burdened hatred.*

ELECTRA

ANTISTROPHE D

*May Zeus, from all shoulder's strength,*
*pound down his fist upon them,*
*ah, ah! smash their heads.*
*Let the land once more believe.*
*There has been wrong done. I ask for right.*
*Hear me, Earth. Hear me, grandeurs of Darkness.*

CHORUS [*chanting*]
*It is but law that when the red drops have been spilled*
*upon the ground they cry aloud for fresh*
*blood. For the death act calls out on Fury*
*to bring up from those who were slain before*
*new ruin on ruin accomplished.*

ORESTES

STROPHE F

*Hear me, you lordships of the world below.*
*Behold in assembled power, curses come from the dead,*
*behold the last of the sons of Atreus, foundering*
*lost, without future, cast*
*from house and right. O Zeus, where shall we turn?*

CHORUS [*singing throughout the rest of this lyric interchange*]

ANTISTROPHE E

*The heart jumps in me once again*
*to hear this piteous prayer.*
*Disconsolate then was I*
*and now my heart darkens within*
*deep down, to hear you speak it.*
*But when strength came back hope lifted*
*me again, and the sorrow*
*was gone and the light was on me.°*

ELECTRA

ANTISTROPHE F

*Of what thing can we speak, and strike more close,*
*than of the sorrows they who bore us have given?*
*So let her fawn if she likes. It softens not.*
*For we are bloody like the wolf*
*and savage born from the savage mother.*

CHORUS

STROPHE G

*I struck my breast in the stroke-style of the Arian,*
*the Cissian mourning woman,*
*and the hail-beat of the drifting fists was there to see*
*as the rising pace went in a pattern of blows*
*downward and upward until the crashing strokes*
*played on my hammered, my all-stricken head.*

ELECTRA

STROPHE H

*O cruel, cruel*
*all-daring mother, in cruel processional*
*with all his citizens gone,*
*with all sorrow for him forgotten*
*you dared bury your unbewept lord.*

ORESTES

STROPHE J

*O all unworthy of him, what you tell me.*
*Shall she not pay for this dishonor*
*for all the immortals,*
*for all my own hands can do?*
*Let me but take her life and die for it.*

CHORUS

ANTISTROPHE J

*Know then, they hobbled him beneath the armpits,*
*with his own hands. She wrought so, in his burial*
*to make his death a burden*

*beyond your strength to carry.*
*The mutilation of your father. Hear it.*

ELECTRA

ANTISTROPHE G

*You tell of how my father was murdered. Meanwhile I*
*stood apart, dishonored, nothing worth,*
*in the dark corner, as you would kennel a vicious dog,*
*and burst in an outrush of tears, that came that day*
*where smiles would not, and hid the streaming of my grief.*
*Hear such, and carve the letters of it on your heart.*

CHORUS

ANTISTROPHE H

*Let words such as these*
*drip deep in your ears, but on a quiet heart.*
*So far all stands as it stands;*
*what is to come, yourself burn to know.*
*You must be hard, give no ground, to win home.*

ORESTES

STROPHE K

*I speak to you. Be with those you love, my father.*

ELECTRA

*And I, all in my tears, ask with him.*

CHORUS

*We gather into murmurous revolt. Hear*
*us, hear. Come back into the light.*
*Be with us against those we hate.*

ORESTES

ANTISTROPHE K

*War-strength shall collide with war-strength; right with right.*

ELECTRA

*O gods, be just in what you bring to pass.*

CHORUS

*My flesh crawls as I listen to them pray.*
*The day of doom has waited long.*
*They call for it. It may come.*

STROPHE L

*O pain grown into the race*
*and blood-dripping stroke*
*and grinding cry of disaster,*
*moaning and impossible weight to bear.*
*Sickness that fights all remedy.*

ANTISTROPHE L

*Here in the house resides*
*the cure for this, not to be brought*
*from outside, never from others*
*but within themselves, through the raw brutal bloodshed.*
*Here is the song sung to the gods beneath us.*

[*chanting*]
*Hear then, you blessed ones under the ground,*
*and answer these prayers with strength on our side,*
*free gift for your children's conquest.*

ORESTES [*now speaking*]

Father, O King who died no kingly death, I ask
the gift of lordship at your hands, to rule your house.

ELECTRA [*speaking*]

I too, my father, ask of you such grace as this:
to murder Aegisthus with strong hand, and then go free.°

ORESTES

So shall your memory have the feasts that men honor
in custom. Otherwise at the tables when offerings
burn for the earth, you shall be there, but none give heed.

ELECTRA

I too out of my own full dowry then shall bring

libations for my bridal from my father's house.
Of all tombs, yours shall be the lordliest in my eyes.

ORESTES

O Earth, let my father emerge to watch me fight.

ELECTRA

Persephone, grant still the wonder of success.

ORESTES

Think of that bath, father, where you were stripped of life.

ELECTRA

Think of the casting net that they contrived for you.

ORESTES

They caught you like a beast in toils no bronzesmith made.

ELECTRA

Rather, hid you in shrouds that were thought out in shame.

ORESTES

Will you not waken, father, to these reproaches?

ELECTRA

Will you not raise upright that best beloved head?

ORESTES

Send out your Right to battle on the side of those
you love, or give us holds like those they caught you in.
For they threw you. Would you not see them thrown in turn?

ELECTRA

Hear one more cry, father, from me. It is my last.
Your nestlings huddle suppliant at your tomb: look forth
and pity them, female with the male strain alike.

ORESTES°

Do not wipe out this seed of the Pelopidae.
So, though you died, you shall not yet be dead, for when
a man dies, children are the voice of his salvation

afterward. Like corks upon the net, these hold
the drenched and flaxen meshes, and they will not drown.
Hear us, then. Our complaints are for your sake, and if
you honor this our argument, you save yourself.

CHORUS LEADER

None can find fault with the length of this discourse you drew
out, to show honor to a grave and fate unwept
before. The rest is action. Since your heart is set
that way, now you must strike and prove your destiny.

ORESTES

So. But I am not wandering from my strict course
when I ask why she sent these libations, for what cause
she acknowledges, too late, a crime for which there is
no cure. Here was a wretched grace brought to a man°
dead and unfeeling. This I fail to understand.
The offerings are too small for the act done. Pour out
all your possessions to atone one act of blood,
you waste your work, it is all useless, reason says.
Explain me this, for I would learn it, if you know.

CHORUS LEADER

I know, child, I was there. It was the dreams she had.
The godless woman had been shaken in the night
by floating terrors, when she sent these offerings.

ORESTES

Do you know the dream, too? Can you tell it to me right?

CHORUS LEADER

She told me herself. She dreamed she gave birth to a snake.

ORESTES

What is the end of the story then? What is the point?

CHORUS LEADER

She wrapped it warm in clothing as if it were a child.

ORESTES

A little monster. Did it want some kind of food?

CHORUS LEADER
She herself, in the dream, gave it her breast to suck.

ORESTES
How was her nipple not torn by such a beastly thing?

CHORUS LEADER
It was. The creature drew in blood along with the milk.

ORESTES
No vapid dream this. A man is the vision's subject.°

CHORUS LEADER
She woke screaming out of her sleep, shaky with fear,
as torches were kindled all about the house, out of
the blind dark that had been on them, to comfort the queen.
So now she sends these mourning offerings to be poured
and hopes they are medicinal for her disease.

ORESTES
But I pray to the earth and to my father's grave
that this dream is for me and that I will succeed.
See, I divine it, and it coheres all in one piece.
If this snake came out of the same place whence I came,
if she wrapped it in robes, as she wrapped me, and if
its jaws gaped wide around the breast that suckled me,
and if it stained the intimate milk with an outburst
of blood, so that for fright and pain she cried aloud,
it follows then, that as she nursed this hideous thing
of prophecy, she must be cruelly murdered. I
turn snake to kill her. This is what the dream speaks loud.

CHORUS LEADER
I choose you my interpreter to read these dreams.
So may it happen. Now you must rehearse your side
in their parts. For some, this means the parts they must not
play.

ORESTES
Simple to tell them. My sister here must go inside.

I charge her to keep secret what we have agreed,
so that, as they by treachery killed a man of high
degree, by treachery tangled in the self-same net
they too shall die, in the way Loxias has ordained,
my lord Apollo, whose word was never false before.
Disguised as an outlander, for which I have all gear,
I shall go to the outer gates with Pylades
whom you see here. He is hereditary friend
and companion-in-arms of my house. We two shall both
assume
the Parnassian dialect and imitate the way
they talk in Phocis. If none at the door will take us in
kindly, because the house is in a curse of ills,
we shall stay there, till anybody who goes by
the house will wonder why we are shut out, and say:
"Why does Aegisthus keep the suppliant turned away
from his gates, if he is hereabouts and knows of this?"
But if I once cross the doorstone of the outer gates
and find my man seated upon my father's throne,
or if he comes down to confront me, and uplifts
his eyes to mine, then lets them drop again, be sure,
before he can say: "Where does the stranger come from?" I
shall plunge my sword with lightning speed, and drop him
dead.
Our Fury who is never starved for blood shall drink
for the third time a cupful of unwatered blood.
Electra, keep a careful eye on all within
the house, so that our plans will hold together.

*(To the Chorus.)*

You,
women: I charge you, hold your tongues religiously.
Be silent if you must, or speak in the way that will
help us. And now I call upon the god who stands
close, to look on, and guide the actions of my sword.

*(Exit Orestes and Pylades to the side, Electra into the palace.)*

CHORUS [*singing*]

STROPHE A

*Numberless, the earth breeds*
*dangers, and the awful thought of fear.*
*The bending sea's arms swarm*
*with bitter, savage beasts.*
*Torches blossom to burn along*
*the high space between ground and sky.*
*Things fly, and things walk the earth.*
*Remember too*
*the storm and wrath of the whirlwind.*

ANTISTROPHE A

*But who can recount all*
*the high daring in the will*
*of man, and in the stubborn hearts of women*
*the all-adventurous passions*
*that couple with man's overthrow.*
*The female force, the desperate*
*love crams its resisted way*
*on marriage and the dark embrace*
*of brute beasts, of mortal men.*

STROPHE B

*Let him, who goes not on flimsy wings*
*of thought, learn from her.*
*Althaea, Thestius'*
*daughter: who maimed her child, and hard*
*of heart, in deliberate guile*
*set fire to the bloody torch, her own son's*
*age-mate, that from the day he emerged*
*from the mother's womb crying*
*shared the measure of all his life*
*down to the marked death day.*

ANTISTROPHE B

*And in the legends there is one more, a girl*
*of blood, figure of hate*
*who, for the enemy's*
*sake killed one near in blood, seduced by the wrought*
*golden necklace from Crete,*
*wherewith Minos bribed her. She sundered*
*from Nisus his immortal hair*
*as he all unsuspecting*
*breathed in a tranquil sleep. Foul wretch,*
*Hermes of death has got her now.*

STROPHE C

*Since I recall cruelties from quarrels long*
*ago, in vain, and married love turned to bitterness*
*a house would fend far away*
*by curse; the guile, treacheries of the woman's heart*
*against a lord armored in*
*power, a lord his enemies revered,°*
*I prize the hearth not inflamed within the house,*
*the woman's right pushed not into daring.*

ANTISTROPHE C

*Of all foul things told in legend the Lemnian*
*outranks, a vile wizard's charm, detestable*
*so that men name a hideous*
*crime "Lemnian" in memory of that wickedness.*
*When once the gods loathe a breed*
*of men they go outcast and forgotten.*
*No man respects what the gods have turned against.*
*What of these tales I gather has no meaning?*

STROPHE D

*The sword edges near the lungs.*
*It stabs deep, bittersharp,*
*and Right drives it. For that which had no right*

*lies not yet stamped into the ground, although*
*one in sin transgressed Zeus' majesty.*

ANTISTROPHE D

*Right's anvil stands staunch on the ground*
*and the smith, Destiny, hammers out the sword.*
*Delayed in glory, pensive from*
*the murk, Vengeance brings home at last*
*a child, to wipe out the stain of blood shed long ago.*

*(Enter Orestes and Pylades from the side, carrying baggage and dressed as travelers.)*

ORESTES

In there! Inside! Does anyone hear me knocking at
the gate? I will try again. Is anyone at home?
Try a third time. I ask for someone to come from the house,
if Aegisthus lets it welcome friendly visitors.

SERVANT *(Inside.)*

All right, I hear you. Where does the stranger come from,
then?

ORESTES

Announce me to the masters of the house. It is
to them I come, and I have news for them to hear.
And be quick, for the darkening chariot of night
leans to its course; the hour for wayfarers to drop
anchor in some place that entertains all travelers.
Have someone of authority in the house come out,
the lady of the place or, more appropriately,
its lord, for then no delicacy in speaking blurs
the spoken word. A man takes courage and speaks out
to another man, and makes clear everything he means.

*(Enter Clytaemestra from inside the palace.)*

CLYTAEMESTRA

Friends, tell me only what you would have, and it is yours.
We have all comforts that go with a house like ours,

hot baths, and beds to charm away your weariness
with rest, and the regard of honest eyes. But if
you have some higher business, more a matter of state,
that is the men's concern, and I will tell them of it.

ORESTES

I am a Daulian stranger out of Phocis. As
I traveled with my pack and my own following
making for Argos, where my feet are rested now,
I met a man I did not know, nor did he know
me, but he asked what way I took, and told me his.
It was a Phocian, Strophius; for he told me his name
and said: "Friend, since in any case you make for Argos,
remember carefully to tell Orestes' parents
that he is dead; please do not let it slip your mind.
Then, if his people decide to have him brought back home,
or bury him where he went to live, all outlander
forever, carry their requests again to me.
For as it is, the bronze walls of an urn close in
the ashes of a man who has been deeply mourned."
So much I know, no more. But whether I now talk
with those who have authority and concern in this
I do not know. I think his father should be told.

CLYTAEMESTRA

Ah me. You tell us how we are stormed from head to heel.
Oh curse upon our house, bitter antagonist,
how far your eyes range. What was clean out of your way
your archery brings down with a distant deadly shot
to strip unhappy me of all I ever loved.
Even Orestes now! He was so well advised
to keep his foot clear of this swamp of death. But now
set down as traitor the hope that was our healer once
and made us look for a bright revel in our house.

ORESTES

I could have wished, with hosts so prosperous as you,
to have made myself known by some more gracious news

and so been entertained by you. For what is there
more kindly than the feeling between host and guest?
Yet it had been abuse of duty in my heart
had I not given so great a matter to his friends,
being so bound by promise and the stranger's rights.

CLYTAEMESTRA

You shall not find that your reception falls below
your worth, nor be any the less our friend for this.
Some other would have brought the news in any case.
But it is the hour for travelers who all day have trudged
the long road, to be given the rest that they deserve.
Escort this gentleman with his companion and
his men, to where our male friends are made at home.
Look after them, in manner worthy of a house
like ours; you are responsible for their good care.
Meanwhile, we shall communicate these matters to
the masters of the house, and with our numerous friends
deliberate the issues of this fatal news.

*(Exit all but the Chorus, into the palace.)*

CHORUS [*chanting*]

*Handmaidens of this house, who help our cause,*
*how can our lips frame*
*some force that will show for Orestes?*
*O Lady Earth, Earth Queen, who now*
*ride mounded over the lord of ships*
*where the king's corpse lies buried,*
*hear us, help us.*
*Now the time breaks for Persuasion in stealth*
*to go down to the Pit, with Hermes of death°*
*and the dark, to direct*
*trial by the sword's fierce edge.*

CHORUS LEADER

I think our newcomer is at his deadly work;
I see Orestes' old nurse coming forth, in tears.

*(Enter the Nurse, Cilissa, from inside the palace.)*

Now where are you going, Cilissa, through the palace gates,
with sorrow as your hireless fellow wayfarer?

NURSE

The woman who is our mistress told me to make haste
and summon Aegisthus for the strangers, "so that he
can come and hear, as man to man, in more detail
this news that they have brought." She put a sad face on
before the servants, to hide the smile inside her eyes
over this work that has been done so happily
for her—though on this house the misery is now complete
from the plain story that the stranger men have brought.
But as for that Aegisthus, oh, he will be pleased
enough to hear the story. Poor unhappy me,
all my long-standing mixture of misfortunes, hard
burden enough, here in this house of Atreus,
when it befell me made the heart ache in my breast.
But never yet did I have to bear a hurt like this.
I took the other troubles bravely as they came:
but now, darling Orestes! I wore out my life
for him. I took him from his mother, brought him up.
There were times when he screamed at night and woke me from
my rest; I had to do many hard tasks, and now
useless; a baby is like a beast, it does not think
but you have to nurse it, do you not, the way it wants.
For the child still in swaddling clothes cannot tell us
if he is hungry or thirsty, if he needs to make
water. Children's young insides are a law to themselves.
I needed second sight for this, and many a time
I think I missed, and had to wash the baby's clothes.
The nurse and laundrywoman had a combined duty
and that was I. I was skilled in both handicrafts,
and so Orestes' father gave him to my charge.
And now, unhappy, I am told that he is dead

and go to take the story to that man who has
defiled our house; he will be glad to hear such news.

CHORUS LEADER

Did she say he should come back armed in any way?

NURSE

How, armed? Say it again. I do not understand.

CHORUS LEADER

Was he to come with bodyguards, or by himself?

NURSE

She said to bring his followers, the men-at-arms.

CHORUS LEADER

Now, if you hate our master, do not tell him that,
but simply bid him come as quickly as he can
and cheerfully. In that way he will not take fright.
It is the messenger who makes the bent word straight.

NURSE

But are you happy over what I have told you?

CHORUS LEADER

Perhaps: if Zeus might turn our evil wind to good.

NURSE

How so? Orestes, once hope of the house, is gone.

CHORUS LEADER

Not yet. It would be a poor seer who saw it thus.

NURSE

What is this? Have you some news that has not been told?

CHORUS LEADER

Go on and take your message, do as you were bid.
The gods' concerns are what concern only the gods.

NURSE

I will go then and do all this as you have told
me to. May all be for the best. So grant us god.

*(Exit the Nurse to the side.)*

CHORUS [*singing*]

STROPHE A

*Now to my supplication. Zeus,*
*father of Olympian gods,*
*grant that those who struggle hard to see*
*temperate things done in the house win their aim°*
*in full. All that I spoke*
*was spoken in right. Yours, Zeus, to protect.*

MESODE

*Zeus, Zeus, make him who is now*
*in the house stand above those who*
*hate. If you rear him to greatness,*
*double and three times*
*and blithely he will repay you.*

ANTISTROPHE A

*See the colt of this man whom you loved*
*harnessed to the chariot*
*of suffering. Set upon the race he runs*
*sure control. Make us not see him break*
*stride, but clean down the course*
*keep the pace of his striding speed.*

STROPHE B

*You that, deep in the house*
*sway their secret pride of wealth,*
*hear us, gods of sympathy.*
*For things done in time past°*
*wash out the blood in fair-spoken verdict.*
*Let the old murder in*
*the house breed no more.*

MESODE

*And you, who keep, magnificent, the hallowed and huge*
*cavern, O grant that the man's house lift up its head*

*and look on the shining of daylight*
*and liberty with eyes made*
*glad with gazing out from the helm of darkness.*

ANTISTROPHE B

*And with Right may the son*
*of Maia lend his hand, strong to send*
*wind fair for action, if he will.*
*Much else lies secret he may show at need.*
*He speaks the secret word, by*
*night hoods darkness on the eyes*
*nor shows more plainly when the day is there.*

STROPHE C

*Then at last we shall sing*
*for deliverance of the house*
*the woman's song that sets the wind*
*fair, no thin-drawn and grief-*
*struck wail, but this: "The ship sails fair."*
*My way, mine, the advantage piles here, with wreck*
*and ruin far from those I love.*

MESODE

*Be not fear-struck when your turn comes in the action,*
*but with a great cry "Father"*
*when she cries "Child" to you*
*go on through with the innocent murder.*

ANTISTROPHE C

*Yours to raise high within*
*your body the heart of Perseus*
*and for those under the ground you loved*
*and those yet above, to exact*
*what their bitter passion may desire; make*
*bloody ruin of the Gorgon inside the house;°*
*wipe out the man stained with murder.*

*(Enter Aegisthus from the side, alone.)*

AEGISTHUS

It is not without summons that I come, but called
by messenger, with news that there are strangers here
arrived, telling a story that brings no delight:
the death of Orestes. For our house, already bitten
and poisoned, to take this new load upon itself
would be a thing of dripping fear and blood. Yet how
shall I pass upon these rumors? As the living truth?
For messages made out of women's terror leap
high in the upward air and empty die. Do you
know anything of this by which to clear my mind?

CHORUS LEADER

We heard, yes. But go on inside and hear it from
the strangers. Messengers are never quite so sure
as a man's questions answered by the men themselves.

AEGISTHUS

I wish to question, carefully, this messenger
and learn if he himself was by when the man died
or if he heard but some blind rumor and so speaks.
The mind has eyes, not to be easily deceived.

*(Aegisthus goes inside.)*

CHORUS [*chanting*]

*Zeus, Zeus, what shall I say, where make*
*a beginning of prayer for the gods' aid?*
*My will is good*
*but how shall I speak to match my need?*
*The bloody edges of the knives that rip*
*man-flesh are moving to work. It will mean*
*utter and final ruin imposed*
*on Agamemnon's*
*house, or our man will kindle a flame*
*and light of liberty, win the domain*
*and huge treasure again of his fathers.*
*Forlorn challenger, though blessed by god,*

*Orestes must come to grips with two,*
*so wrestle. Yet may he throw them.*

*(A shriek is heard from inside the house.)*

[*singing*]
*Listen, it goes*
*but how? What has been done in the house?*

CHORUS LEADER [*speaking*]
Stand we aside until the work is done, for so
we shall not seem to be accountable in this
foul business. For the fight is done, the issue drawn.

*(Enter a Follower of Aegisthus, running from inside the house.)*

FOLLOWER
O sorrow, all is sorrow for our stricken lord.
Raise up again a triple cry of sorrow, for
Aegisthus lives no longer. Open there, open
quick as you may, and slide back the door bars on the women's
gates. It will take the strength of a young arm, but not
to fight for one who is dead and done for. What use there?
Ho there, ho!
My cry is to the deaf and I babble in vain
at sleepers to no purpose. Clytaemestra, where
is she, does what? Her neck is on the razor's edge
and ripe for lopping, as she did to others before.

*(Enter Clytaemestra.)*

CLYTAEMESTRA
What is this, and why are you shouting in the house?

FOLLOWER
I tell you, the living are being killed by the dead ones.

CLYTAEMESTRA
Ah, so. You speak in riddles, but I read the rhyme.

We have been won with the treachery by which we slew.
Bring me quick, somebody, an axe to kill a man

*(Exit Follower.)*

and we shall see if we can beat him before we
go down—so far gone are we in this wretched fight.

*(Enter Orestes and Pylades from the palace, with swords drawn.)*

ORESTES

You next: the other one in there has had enough.

CLYTAEMESTRA

Beloved, strong Aegisthus, are you dead indeed?

ORESTES

You love your man, then? You shall lie in the same grave
with him, and never be unfaithful even in death.

CLYTAEMESTRA

Hold, my son. Oh take pity, child, before this breast
where many a time, a drowsing baby, you would feed
and with soft gums sucked in the milk that made you strong.

ORESTES

What shall I do, Pylades? Be shamed to kill my mother?

PYLADES

What then becomes thereafter of the oracles
declared by Loxias at Pytho? What of sworn oaths?
Count all men hateful to you rather than the gods.

ORESTES

I judge that you win. Your advice is good.

*(To Clytaemestra.)*

Come here.

My purpose is to kill you over his body.
You thought him bigger than my father while he lived.
Die then and sleep beside him, since he is the man
you love, and he you should have loved got only your hate.

CLYTAEMESTRA

I raised you when you were little. May I grow old with you?

ORESTES

You killed my father. Would you make your home with me?

CLYTAEMESTRA

Destiny had some part in that, my child.

ORESTES

Why then
destiny has worked this death for you as well.

CLYTAEMESTRA

A mother has her curse, child. Are you not afraid?

ORESTES

No. You bore me and threw me away, to a hard life.

CLYTAEMESTRA

I sent you to a friend's house. This was no throwing away.

ORESTES

I was born of a free father. You sold me.

CLYTAEMESTRA

So? Where then is the price that I received for you?

ORESTES

I could say. It would be indecent to tell you.

CLYTAEMESTRA

Or if you do, tell also your father's follies.

ORESTES

Blame him not. He suffered while you were sitting here at home.

CLYTAEMESTRA

It hurts women to be kept from their men, my child.

ORESTES

The man's hard work supports the women who sit at home.

CLYTAEMESTRA

I think, child, that you mean to kill your mother.

ORESTES

No.

It will be you who kill yourself. It will not be I.

CLYTAEMESTRA

Take care. Your mother's curse, like dogs, will drag you down.

ORESTES

How shall I escape my father's curse, if I fail here?

CLYTAEMESTRA

I feel like one who wastes live tears upon a tomb.

ORESTES

Yes, this is death, your wages for my father's fate.

CLYTAEMESTRA

You are the snake I gave birth to, and gave the breast.

ORESTES

Indeed, the terror of those dreams saw things to come
clearly.° You killed, and it was wrong. Now suffer wrong.

*(Orestes and Pylades take Clytaemestra into the palace.)*

CHORUS LEADER

I have sorrow even for this pair in their twofold
downfall. But since Orestes had the hardiness
to end this chain of bloodlettings, here lies our choice,
that the eyes' light in this house shall not utterly die.

CHORUS [*singing*]

STROPHE A

*Justice came at the last to Priam and all his sons*
*and it was heavy and hard,*
*but into the house of Agamemnon returned*
*the double lion, the double assault,*
*and the Pythian-steered exile*

*drove home to the hilt*
*vengeance, moving strongly in guidance sent by the god.*

MESODE

*Raise up the high cry O over our lordships' house*
*won free of distress, free of its fortunes wasted*
*by two stained with murder,*
*free of its mournful luck.*

ANTISTROPHE A

*He came back; his work lay in the secret attack*
*and it was stealthy and hard,*
*but in the fighting his hand was steered by the very daughter*
*of Zeus: Right we call her,*
*mortals who speak of her and name her well. Her wind*
*is fury and death visited upon those she hates.*

STROPHE B

*All that Loxias, who on Parnassus holds*
*the huge, the deep cleft in the ground, shrilled aloud,*
*by guile that is no guile*
*returns now to assault the wrong done and grown old.*
*Divinity keeps, we know not how, strength to resist*
*surrender to the wicked.*
*The power that holds the sky's majesty wins our worship.*

MESODE

*Light is here to behold.*
*The big bit that curbed our house is taken away.*
*Rise up, you halls, arise; for time grown too long*
*you lay tumbled along the ground.*

ANTISTROPHE B

*Time brings all things to pass. Presently time shall cross*
*the outgates of the house after the stain is driven*
*entire from the hearth*
*by ceremonies that wash clean and cast out the furies.*
*The dice of fortune shall be thrown once more, and lie*

*prosperous and smiling*
*up at the new indwellers come to live in the house.*

*(The doors of the house open, to show Orestes standing over the bodies of Clytaemestra and Aegisthus, while attendants display the net-like garment in which Clytaemestra had entangled Agamemnon and which she herself displayed after his murder.)*

ORESTES

Behold the twin tyrannies of our land, these two
who killed my father and who sacked my house. For a time
they sat upon their thrones and kept their pride of state,
and they are lovers still. So may you judge by what
befell them, for as they were pledged their oath abides.
They swore together death for my unhappy sire
and swore to die together. Now they keep their oath.
Behold again, O audience of these evil things,
the engine against my wretched father they devised,
the hands' entanglement, the hobbles for his feet.
Spread it out. Stand around me in a circle and
display this net that caught a man. So shall, not my
father, but that great father who sees all, the Sun,
look on my mother's sacrilegious handiwork
and be a witness for me in my day of trial
how it was in all right that I achieved this death,
my mother's: for of Aegisthus' death I take no count:
he has his seducer's punishment, no more than law.
But she, who plotted this foul death against the man
by whom she carried the weight of children underneath
her belt, burden once loved, shown hard and hateful now,
what does she seem to be? Some water snake, some viper
whose touch is rot even to him who felt no fang
strike, by that brutal and wrong daring in her heart.
And this thing: what shall I call it and be right, in all
eloquence? Trap for an animal or winding sheet
for a dead man? Or bath curtain? Since it is a net,
robe you could call it, to entangle a man's feet.

Some highwayman might own a thing like this, to catch
the wayfarer and rob him of his money and
so make a living. With a treacherous thing like this
he could take many victims and warm his heart within.
May no such partner as she was come to live with me.
Sooner, let god destroy me, with no children born.

CHORUS [*chanting*]
*Ah, but the pitiful work.*
*Dismal the death that was your ending.*
*He is left alive; pain flowers for him.*

ORESTES
Did she do it or did she not? My witness is
this great robe. It was thus she stained Aegisthus' sword.
Dip it and dip it again, the smear of blood conspires
with time to spoil the beauty of this precious thing.
Now I can praise him, now I can stand by to mourn
and speak before this web that killed my father; yet
I grieve for the thing done, the death, and all our race.
I have won; but my victory is polluted, and has no pride.

CHORUS [*chanting*]
*There is no mortal man who shall turn*
*unhurt his life's course to an end not marred.*
*There is trouble here. There is more to come.*

ORESTES
I would have you know, I see not how this thing will end.
I am a charioteer whose course is wrenched outside
the track, for I am beaten, my rebellious senses
bolt with me headlong and the fear against my heart
is ready for the singing and dance of wrath. But while
I hold some grip still on my wits, I say publicly
to my friends: I killed my mother not without some right.
My father's murder stained her, and the gods' disgust.
As for the spells that charmed me to such daring, I
cite above all the seer of Pytho, Loxias. He

declared I could do this and not be charged with wrong,
while if I refused, the punishment I will not speak:
no archery could hit such height of agony.
And look upon me now, how I go armored in
leafed branch and garland on my way to the centerstone
and sanctuary, and Apollo's sacred ground,
the shining of the fabulous fire that never dies,
to escape this blood that is my own. Loxias ordained
that I should turn me to no other shrine than this.
To all men of Argos in time to come I say
they shall be witness, how these evil things were done.
I go, an outcast wanderer from this land, and leave
behind, in life, in death, the name of what I did.

CHORUS LEADER

No, what you did was well done. Do not therefore bind
your mouth to foul speech. Keep no evil on your lips.
You liberated all the Argive city when
you lopped the heads of these two snakes with one clean
stroke.

ORESTES

No!
Women who serve this house, they come like Gorgons, they
wear robes of black, and they are wreathed in a tangle
of snakes. I can no longer stay.

CHORUS LEADER

Orestes, dearest to your father of all men,
what fancies whirl you? Hold, do not give way to fear.

ORESTES

These are no fancies of affliction. They are clear,
and real, and here; the bloodhounds of my mother's hate.

CHORUS LEADER

It is the blood still wet upon your hands, that makes
this shaken turbulence be thrown upon your sense.

ORESTES

Ah, Lord Apollo, how they grow and multiply,
repulsive for the blood drops of their dripping eyes.

CHORUS LEADER

There is one way to make you clean: let Loxias
touch you, and set you free from these disturbances.

ORESTES

You cannot see them, but I see them. I am driven
from this place. I can stay here no longer.

*(Exit, to the side.)*

CHORUS LEADER

Good luck go with you then, and may the god look on
you with favor and guard you in kind circumstance.

CHORUS [*chanting*]

*Here on this house of the kings the third*
*storm has broken, with wind*
*from the inward race, and gone its course.*
*The children were eaten: that was the first*
*affliction, the curse of Thyestes.*
*Next came the royal death, when a man*
*and lord of Achaean armies went down*
*killed in the bath. Third*
*is for the savior. He came. Shall I call*
*it that, or death? Where*
*is the end? Where shall the fury of fate*
*be stilled to sleep, be done with?*

# THE EUMENIDES

*Characters* THE PYTHIAN PRIESTESS OF APOLLO

APOLLO

HERMES (silent character)

ORESTES, son of Agamemnon

GHOST of Clytaemestra

CHORUS of Furies (Eumenides)

ATHENA

JURYMEN (silent)

SECOND CHORUS, women of Athens

*Scene: For the first part of the play (1–234) the scene is Delphi, in front of the sanctuary of Pythian Apollo. The action of the rest of the play (235 to the end) takes place at Athens, on the Acropolis in front of the temple of Athena.*

*(Enter the Pythian Priestess, from the side.)*

PYTHIA

I give first place of honor in my prayer to her
who of the gods first prophesied, the Earth; and next
to Themis, who succeeded to her mother's place
of prophecy; so runs the legend; and in third
succession, given by free consent, not won by force,
another Titan daughter of Earth was seated here.
This was Phoebe. She gave it as a birthday gift
to Phoebus, who is called still after Phoebe's name.
And he, leaving the pond of Delos and the reef,
grounded his ship at the roadstead of Pallas, then

made his way to this land and a Parnassian home.
Deep in respect for his degree Hephaestus' sons
conveyed him here, for these are builders of roads, and
changed
the wilderness to a land that was no wilderness.
He came so, and the people highly honored him,
with Delphus, lord and helmsman of the country. Zeus
made his mind full with godship and prophetic craft
and placed him, fourth in a line of seers, upon this throne.
So, Loxias is the spokesman of his father, Zeus.
These are the gods I set in the proem of my prayer.
But Pallas-before-the-temple has her right in all
I say. I worship the nymphs where the Corycian rock
is hollowed inward, haunt of birds and paced by gods.
Bromius, whom I forget not, sways this place. From here
in divine form he led his Bacchanals in arms
to hunt down Pentheus like a hare in the deathtrap.
I call upon the springs of Pleistus, on the power
of Poseidon, and on final loftiest Zeus,
then go to sit in prophecy on the throne. May all
grant me that this of all my entrances shall be
the best by far. If there are any Hellenes here
let them draw lots, so enter, as the custom is.
My prophecy is only as the god may guide.

*(She enters the temple and almost immediately comes out again, crawling on all fours.)*

Things terrible to tell and for the eyes to see
terrible drove me out again from Loxias' house
so that I have no strength and cannot stand on springing
feet, but run with hands' help and my legs have no speed.
An old woman afraid is nothing: a child, no more.
See, I am on my way to the wreath-hung recess
and on the centerstone I see a man with god's
defilement on him postured in the suppliant's seat

with blood dripping from his hands and from a new-drawn
sword,
holding too a branch that had grown high on an olive
tree, decorously wrapped in a great tuft of wool,
and the fleece shone. So far, at least, I can speak clear.
In front of this man slept a startling company
of women lying all upon the chairs. Or not
women, I think I call them rather Gorgons, only
not Gorgons either, since their shape is not the same.
I saw some creatures painted in a picture once,
who tore the food from Phineus, only these have no
wings, that could be seen; they are black and utterly
repulsive, and they snore with breath that drives one back.
From their eyes drips the foul ooze, and their dress is such
as is not right to wear in the presence of the gods'
statues, nor even in any human house.
I have never seen the tribe that spawned this company
nor know what piece of earth can claim with pride it bore
such brood, and without hurt and tears for labor given.
Now after this the master of the house must take
his own measures: Apollo Loxias, who is very strong
and heals by divination, reads portentous signs,
and so purifies the houses others hold as well.

*(Exit the Pythia. The doors of the temple open and show Orestes surrounded by the sleeping Furies, Apollo and Hermes beside him.)*

APOLLO

I will not give you up. Through to the end standing
your guardian, whether by your side or far away,
I shall not weaken toward your enemies. See now
how I have caught and overpowered these rabid creatures.
The repulsive maidens have been stilled to sleep, those gray
and aged children, they with whom no mortal man,
no god, nor even any beast, will have to do.
It was because of evil they were born, because

they hold the evil darkness of the Pit below
earth, loathed alike by men and by the heavenly gods.
Nevertheless, run from them, never weaken. They
will chase your track as you stride on across the long
land, and your driven feet forever pound the earth,
on across the main water and the circle-washed
cities. Be herdsman to this hard march. Never fail
until you come at last to Pallas' citadel.
Kneel there, and clasp the ancient idol in your arms,
and there we shall find those who will judge this case, and
words
to say that will have magic in their figures. Thus
you will be rid of your afflictions, once for all.
For it was I who made you strike your mother down.

ORESTES

My lord Apollo, you understand what it means to do
no wrong. Learn also what it is not to neglect.
None can mistrust your power to do good, if you will.°

APOLLO

Remember: let not the fear overcome your heart.
Hermes, you are my brother from a single sire.
Look after him, and as you are named the god who guides,
be such in strong fact. He is my suppliant. Shepherd him
with fortunate escort on his journeys among men.
The wanderer has rights which Zeus acknowledges.

*(Exit Apollo into the temple, Orestes guided by Hermes to the side. Enter the Ghost of Clytaemestra.)*

CLYTAEMESTRA

You would sleep, then? And what use are you, if you sleep?
It is because of you I go dishonored thus
among the rest of the dead. Because of those I killed
reproaches among the perished never cease for me
and I am driven in disgrace. I say to you

that I am charged with guilt most grave by these. And yet
I suffered too, horribly, and from those most dear,
yet none among the powers is angered for my sake
that I was slaughtered, and by matricidal hands.
Look at these gashes in my heart, think where they came
from. Eyes illuminate the sleeping brain,
but in the daylight man's future cannot be seen.°
Yet I have given you much to lap up, outpourings
without wine, sober propitiations, sacrificed
in secrecy of night and on a hearth of fire
for you, at an hour given to no other god.
Now I watch all these honors trampled into the ground,
and he is out and gone away like a hunted fawn
so lightly, from the very middle of your nets,
sprung clear, and laughing merrily at you. Hear me.
It is my life depends upon this spoken plea.
Think then, O goddesses beneath the ground. For I,
the dream of Clytaemestra, call upon your name.

*(The Furies stir in their sleep and whimper.)*

CLYTAEMESTRA

Oh, whimper, then, but your man has got away and gone
far. He has friends to help him, who are not like mine.

*(They whimper again.)*

CLYTAEMESTRA

Too much sleep and no pity for my plight. I stand,
his mother, here, killed by Orestes. He is gone.

*(They moan in their sleep.)*

CLYTAEMESTRA

You moan, you sleep. Get on your feet quickly, will you?
What have you yet got done, except to do evil?

*(They moan again.)*

CLYTAEMESTRA

Sleep and fatigue, two masterful conspirators,
have dimmed the deadly anger of the mother-snake.

*(The Chorus start violently, then cry out in their sleep.)*

CHORUS [*singing*]

*Get him, get him, get him, get him! Make sure!*

CLYTAEMESTRA

The beast you are after is a dream, but like the hound
whose thought of hunting has no lapse, you bay him on.
What are you about? Up, let not work's weariness
beat you, nor slacken with sleep so you forget my pain.
Scold your own heart and hurt it, as it well deserves,
for this is discipline's spur upon her own. Let go
upon this man the stormblasts of your bloodshot breath,
wither him in your wind, after him, hunt him down
once more, and shrivel him in your stomach's heat and flame.

*(Exit the Ghost. The Chorus begin to waken and enter from the temple, one by one.)*

CHORUS LEADER

Waken. You are awake, wake her, as I did you.
You dream still? On your feet and kick your sleep aside.
Let us see whether this prelude was in vain.

CHORUS [*singing*]

STROPHE A

*Sisters, we have had wrong done us.*
*When I have undergone so much and all in vain.*
*Suffering, suffering, bitter, oh shame shame,*
*unendurable wrong.*
*The hunted beast has slipped clean from our nets and gone.*
*Sleep defeated me, and I lost my prey.*

ANTISTROPHE A

*Shame, son of Zeus! Robber is all you are.*
*A young god, you have ridden down powers gray with age,*

*honored the suppliant, though a godless man, who hurt*
*the mother who gave him birth.*
*Yourself a god, you stole the matricide away.*
*Where in this act shall any man say there is right?*

STROPHE B

*The accusation came upon me from my dreams,*
*and hit me, as with a goad in the midgrip of his fist*
*the charioteer strikes,*
*but deep, beneath lobe and heart.*
*The public scourger's cutting whip is mine to feel*
*and the weight of pain is big, heavy to bear.*

ANTISTROPHE B

*Such are the actions of the younger gods. These occupy*
*by unconditional force, beyond all right, a throne*
*that runs reeking blood,*
*blood at the feet, blood at the head.*
*The very stone center of earth here in our eyes horrible*
*with blood and curse stands plain to see.*

STROPHE C

*Himself a seer, he has spoiled his secret shrine's*
*hearth with the stain, driven and hallooed the action on.*
*He made man's way cross the place of the ways of god*
*and blighted age-old distributions of power.*

ANTISTROPHE C

*He has wounded me, but he shall not get this man away.*
*Let him hide under the ground, he shall never go free.*
*Cursed suppliant, he shall feel against his head*
*another murderer rising out of the same seed.*

*(Enter Apollo again, from his sanctuary.)*

APOLLO

Get out, I tell you, go and leave this house. Away
in haste, from your presence set the mantic chamber free,
else you may feel the flash and bite of a flying snake

launched from the twisted thong of gold that spans my bow
to make you in your pain spew out the black and foaming
blood of men, vomit the clots sucked from their veins.
This house is no right place for such as you to cling
upon; but where, by judgment given, heads are lopped
and eyes gouged out, throats cut, and by destruction of seed
the potency of boys is ruined,° where mutilation
lives, and stoning, and the long moan of tortured men
spiked underneath the spine and fixed on stakes. Listen
to how the gods spit out the manner of that feast
your appetites prefer. The whole way you look is guide
to what you are—the likes of whom should hole in the cave
of the blood-reeking lion, not wipe off your filth
on others nearby, in this oracular sanctuary.
Out then, you flock of goats without a herdsman, since
no god has such affection as to tend this herd.

CHORUS LEADER

My lord Apollo, it is your turn to listen now.
Your own part in this is more than accessory.
You are the one who did it; all the guilt is yours.

APOLLO

So? How? Continue speaking, until I understand.

CHORUS LEADER

You gave this outlander the word to kill his mother.

APOLLO

The word to exact price for his father. What of that?

CHORUS LEADER

You then dared take him in, fresh from his bloodletting.

APOLLO

Yes, and I told him to take refuge in this house.

CHORUS LEADER

Yet you abuse us, after we escorted him here?

APOLLO

Yes. It was not for you to come near this house.

CHORUS LEADER

And yet we have our duty—to do what we have done.

APOLLO

An office? You? Sound forth your glorious privilege.

CHORUS LEADER

This: to drive matricides out of their houses.

APOLLO

Then
what if it be the woman and she kills her husband?

CHORUS LEADER

Such murder would not be the shedding of kindred blood.

APOLLO

You have made into a thing of no account, no place,
the sworn faith of Zeus and of Hera, lady
of consummations, and Cypris by such argument
is thrown away, outlawed, and yet the sweetest things
in man's life come from her, for married love between
man and woman is bigger than oaths, guarded by right
of nature. If when such kill each other you are slack
so as not to take vengeance nor eye them in wrath,
then I deny your manhunt of Orestes goes
with right. I see that one cause moves you to strong rage
but on the other clearly you are unmoved to act.
Pallas divine shall review the pleadings of this case.

CHORUS LEADER

Nothing will ever make me let that man go free.

APOLLO

Keep after him then, and make more trouble for yourselves.

CHORUS LEADER

Do not try to curtail my privilege by argument.

APOLLO

I would not take your privilege if you gave it me.

CHORUS LEADER

No, for you are called great beside the throne of Zeus
already, but the motherblood drives me, and I go
to win my right upon this man and hunt him down.

APOLLO

But I shall give this suppliant help and rescue, for
if I willingly fail him who turns to me for aid,
his wrath, before gods and men, is a fearful thing.

*(Exit all separately. The scene is now Athens, on the Acropolis in front of the temple and statue of Athena. Enter Orestes from the side. He takes up a suppliant posture at the feet of the statue.)*

ORESTES

My lady Athena, it is at Loxias' behest
I come. So take in of your grace the wanderer
who comes, no suppliant, not unwashed of hand, but one
blunted at last, and worn and battered on the outland
habitations and the journeyings of men.
Crossing the dry land and the sea alike, keeping
the ordinances of Apollo's oracle
I come, goddess, before your statue and your house
to keep watch here and wait the issue of my trial.

*(Enter the Chorus from the side.)*

CHORUS LEADER

So. Here the man has left a clear trail behind; keep on,
keep on, as the unspeaking accuser tells us, by
whose sense, like hounds after a bleeding fawn, we trail
our quarry by the splash and drip of blood. And now
my lungs are blown with abundant and with wearisome
work, mankilling. My range has been the entire extent
of land, and, flown unwinged across the open water,

I am here, and give way to no ship in my pursuit.
Our man has gone to cover somewhere in this place.
The welcome smell of human blood has told me so.

CHORUS [*singing*]

*Look again, look again,*
*search everywhere, let*
*not the matricide*
*steal away and escape.*

(*They see Orestes.*)

*See there! He clings to defense*
*again, his arms winding the immortal goddess'*
*image, so seeks acquittal out of our hands.*
*It shall not be. His mother's blood spilled on the ground*
*cannot come back again.*
*It is all soaked and drained into the ground and gone.*

*You must give back for her blood from the living man*
*red blood of your body to suck, and from your own*
*I could feed, with bitter-swallowed drench,*
*turn your strength limp while yet you live and drag you down*
*where you must pay for the pain of the murdered mother,*
*and watch the rest of the mortals stained with violence*
*against god or guest*
*or hurt parents who were close and dear,*
*each with the pain upon him that his crime deserves.*
*Hades is great, Hades calls men to reckoning*
*there under the ground,*
*sees all, and inscribes it deep in his recording mind.*

ORESTES

I have been beaten and been taught, I understand
the many rules of absolution, where it is right
to speak and where be silent. In this action now
speech has been ordered by my teacher, who is wise.
The stain of blood dulls now and fades upon my hand.

My blot of matricide is being washed away.
When it was fresh still, at the hearth of the god, Phoebus,
it was absolved and driven out by sacrifice
of a pig, and the list were long if I went back to tell
of all I met who were not hurt by being with me.
Time in his aging overtakes all things alike.
Now it is from pure mouth and with good auspices
I call upon Athena, queen of this land, to come
and rescue me. She, without work of her spear, shall win
myself and all my land and all the Argive host
to stand her staunch companion for the rest of time.
Whether now ranging somewhere in the Libyan land
beside her father's crossing and by Triton's run
of waters she sets her foot upright or enshrouded
rescuing there her friends, or on the Phlegraean plain
like some bold man of armies sweeps with eyes the scene,
let her come! She is a god and hears me far away.
So may she set me free from what is at my back.

CHORUS LEADER

Neither Apollo nor Athena's strength can win
you free, save you from going down forgotten, without
knowing where joy lies anywhere inside your heart,
blood drained, chewed dry by the powers of death, a wraith,
  a shell.
You will not speak to answer, spew my challenge away?
You are consecrate to me and fattened for my feast,
and you shall feed me while you live, not cut down first
at the altar. Hear the spell I sing to bind you in.

CHORUS [*chanting*]

*Come then, link we our choral dance.*
*Ours to show forth the power*
*and terror of our music, declare*
*our rights of office, how we conspire*
*to steer men's lives.*
*We hold we are straight and just. If a man*

*can spread his hands and show they are clean,*
*no wrath of ours shall lurk for him.*
*Unscathed he walks through his life time.*
*But one like this man before us, with stained*
*hidden hands, and the guilt upon him,*
*shall find us beside him, as witnesses*
*of the truth, and we show clear in the end*
*to avenge the blood of the murdered.*

[*singing*]

STROPHE A

*Mother, O my mother night, who gave me*
*birth, to be a vengeance on the seeing*
*and the blind, hear me. For Leto's*
*youngling takes my right away,*
*stealing from my clutch the prey*
*that cowers, whose blood would wipe*
*at last the motherblood away.*

REFRAIN A

*Over the beast doomed to the fire*
*this is the chant, scatter of wits,*
*frenzy and fear, hurting the heart,*
*song of the Furies*
*binding brain and blighting blood*
*in its stringless melody.*

ANTISTROPHE A

*This the purpose that all-involving*
*Destiny spun, to be ours and to be shaken*
*never: when mortals assume outrage*
*of their own hand in violence,*
*these we hound, till one goes*
*under earth. Nor does death*
*set them altogether free.*

REFRAIN A

*Over the beast doomed to the fire*

*this is the chant, scatter of wits,*
*frenzy and fear, hurting the heart,*
*song of the Furies*
*binding brain and blighting blood*
*in its stringless melody.*

STROPHE B

*When we were born such lots were assigned for our keeping.*
*So the immortals must hold hands off, nor is there*
*one of them who shall sit at our feasting.*
*In pure white robes I have no interest and no portion.°*

REFRAIN B

*I have chosen overthrow*
*of houses, where the battle god*
*grown within strikes near and dear*
*down. So we swoop upon this man*
*here. He is strong, but we wear him down*
*for the blood that is still wet on him.*

ANTISTROPHE B

*Being eager to save all others from these concerns*
*by our efforts we provide for the gods immunity,°*
*and no appeal comes to them,*
*since Zeus has ruled our blood-dripping company*
*outcast, nor will deal with us.*

REFRAIN B

*I have chosen overthrow*
*of houses, where the battle god*
*grown within strikes near and dear*
*down. So we swoop upon this man*
*here. He is strong, but we wear him down*
*for the blood that is still wet on him.*

STROPHE C

*Men's illusions in their pride under the sky melt*
*down, and are diminished into the ground, gone*

*before the onset of our black robes, and the dancing*
*of our vindictive feet against them.*

REFRAIN C

*For with a long leap from high*
*above and dead drop of weight*
*I bring foot's force crashing down*
*to cut the legs from under even*
*the runner, and spill him to ruin.*

ANTISTROPHE C

*He falls, and does not know in the daze of his folly.*
*Such in the dark of man is the mist of infection*
*that hovers, and moaning rumor tells how his house lies*
*under fog that glooms above.*

REFRAIN C

*For with a long leap from high*
*above, and dead drop of weight,*
*I bring foot's force crashing down*
*to cut the legs from under even*
*the runner, and spill him to ruin.*

STROPHE D

*All holds.° For we are strong and skilled;*
*we have authority; we hold*
*memory of evil; we are stern,*
*nor can men's pleadings bend us. We*
*accomplish our duties, spurned, outcast*
*from gods, standing apart in slime*
*unlit by the sun. Rocky and rough are the paths*
*for those who see and alike for those whose eyes are lost.*

ANTISTROPHE D

*Is there a man who does not fear*
*this, does not shrink to hear*
*how my place has been ordained,*
*granted and given by destiny*

*and the gods, absolute? Privilege*
*primeval yet is mine, nor am I without place*
*though it be underneath the ground*
*and in no sunlight and in darkness that I must stand.*

*(Enter Athena, in full armor.)*

ATHENA

From far away I heard the outcry of your call.
It was beside Scamandrus. I was taking claim
of land, for there the Achaean lords of war and first
fighters gave me large portion of all their spears
had won, the land root and stock to be mine for all
eternity, for the sons of Theseus a choice gift.
From there, sped on my weariless feet, I came, wingless
but in the rush and speed of the aegis fold.° And now
I see upon this land a strange new company
which, though it brings no terror to my eyes, brings still
wonder. Who are you? I address you all alike,
both you, the stranger kneeling at my image here,
and you, who are like no seed ever begotten, not
recognized by the gods as goddesses, nor yet
stamped in the likenesses of any human form.
But no. This is the place of the just. Its rights forbid
to speak evil of another who is without blame.

CHORUS LEADER

Daughter of Zeus, you shall hear all compressed to brief
measure. We are the eternal children of the Night.
Curses they call us in our homes beneath the ground.

ATHENA

I know your race, then, and the names by which you are
called.

CHORUS LEADER

And soon you shall be told of our prerogatives.

ATHENA

I can know them, if someone will give me a clear account.

CHORUS LEADER

We drive from home those who have shed the blood of men.

ATHENA

Where is the place, then, where the killer's flight shall end?

CHORUS LEADER

A place where happiness is nevermore allowed.

ATHENA

Is he one? Do you blast him to this kind of flight?

CHORUS LEADER

Yes. He murdered his mother by deliberate choice.

ATHENA

Not by compulsion, nor fear of someone's wrath?

CHORUS LEADER

Where is the spur to justify man's matricide?

ATHENA

Here are two sides, and only half the argument.

CHORUS LEADER

He is unwilling to give or to accept an oath.

ATHENA

You wish to be called righteous rather than act right.

CHORUS LEADER

No. How so? From the wealth of your wisdom, explain.

ATHENA

I say, wrong must not win merely by oaths.

CHORUS LEADER

Examine him then yourself. Decide it, and be fair.

ATHENA

You would turn over authority in this case to me?

CHORUS LEADER

By all means. We respect your merits and whence they are
derived.°

ATHENA

Your turn, stranger. What will you say in answer? Speak,
tell me your country and your birth, what has befallen
you, then defend yourself against the censure of these;
if it is confidence in the right that makes you sit
guarding this image near my hearth, a supplicant
in the tradition of Ixion, sacrosanct.
Give me an answer which is plain to understand.

ORESTES

Lady Athena, first I will take the great worry
away that lies in these last words you spoke. I am
no supplicant, nor was it because I had a stain
upon my hand that I sat at your image. I
will give you a strong proof that what I say is true.
It is the law that the man of the bloody hand must speak
no word until, by action of an expert purifier,
the slaughter of a young animal has washed his blood away.
Long since, at the homes of others, I have been absolved
thus, both by running waters and by victims slain.
I count this scruple now out of the way. Learn next
with no delay where I am from. I am of Argos
and it is to my honor that you ask the name
of my father, Agamemnon, lord of seafarers,
and your companion when you made the Trojan city
of Ilium no city any more. He died
without honor when he came home. It was my mother
of the dark heart, who entangled him in intricate nets
and cut him down. The bath is witness to his death.
I was an exile in the time before this. I came back

and killed the woman who gave me birth. I don't deny it.
My father was dear, and this was vengeance for his blood.
Apollo shares responsibility for this.
He counterspurred my heart and told me of pains to come
if I should fail to act against the guilty ones.
This is my case. Decide if it be right or wrong.
I am in your hands. Where my fate falls, I shall accept.

ATHENA

The matter is too big for any mortal man
who thinks he can judge it. Nor yet do I have the right
to analyse cases of murder where wrath's edge
is sharp, and all the more since you have come, and clung
a clean and innocent supplicant against my doors.
You bring no harm to my city. I respect your rights.
Yet these, too, have their work. We cannot brush them aside,
and if this action so runs that they fail to win,
the venom of their resolution will return
to infect the soil, and sicken all my land to death.
Here is dilemma. Whether I let them stay or drive
them off, it is a hard course and will hurt. So, since
the burden of the case is here, and rests on me,
I shall select judges of manslaughter, and swear
them in, establish a court into all time to come.
Litigants, call your witnesses, have ready your proofs
as evidence under bond to keep this case secure.
I will pick the finest of my citizens, and come
back. They shall swear to make no judgment that is not
just, and make clear where in this action the truth lies.

*(Exit Athena, to the side.)*

CHORUS [*singing*]

STROPHE A

*Here is overthrow of all*
*established laws,° if the claim*
*of this matricide shall stand*

*good, his crime be sustained.*
*Should this be, every man will find a way*
*to act at his own caprice;*
*over and over again in time*
*to come, parents shall await*
*the deathstroke at their children's hands.*

ANTISTROPHE A

*We are the Angry Ones. But we*
*shall watch no more over works*
*of men, and so act. We shall*
*let loose indiscriminate death.*
*Man shall learn from man's lot, forejudge*
*the evils of his neighbor's case,*
*seek respite and escape from troubles:*
*pathetic prophet who consoles*
*with strengthless cures, in vain.*

STROPHE B

*Nevermore let one who feels*
*the stroke of accident, uplift*
*his voice and make outcry, thus:*
*"Oh Justice!*
*Throned powers of the Furies, help!"*
*Such might be the pitiful cry*
*of some father, of the stricken*
*mother, their appeal. Now*
*the House of Justice has collapsed.*

ANTISTROPHE B

*There are times when fear is good.*
*It must keep its watchful place*
*at the heart's controls. There is*
*advantage*
*in the wisdom won from pain.*
*If the city, if the man*
*rears a heart that nowhere goes*

*in fear, how shall such a one*
*any more respect the right?*

STROPHE C

*Refuse the life of anarchy;*
*refuse the life devoted to*
*one master.*
*The in-between has the power*
*by a god's grant always, though*
*his ordinances vary.*
*I will speak in defense*
*of reason: for the very child*
*of vanity is Violence;*
*but out of health*
*in the heart is born the beloved*
*and the longed-for, prosperity.*

ANTISTROPHE C

*All for all I tell you: show*
*respect for the altar of right.*
*You shall not*
*eye advantage, and kick*
*it over with foot of force.*
*Vengeance will be upon you.*
*The appointed end awaits.*
*Let someone see this and take*
*care, to mother and father,*
*and to the guest*
*in the gates welcomed, give all honor,*
*respecting their position.*

STROPHE D

*The man who does right, free-willed, without constraint*
*shall not lose happiness*
*nor be wiped out with all his generation.*
*But the transgressor, I tell you, the bold man*
*who heaps up confusion of goods unjustly won,*

*at long last and perforce, when his ship toils*
*in the storm must strike his sail*
*midst the wreck of his rigging.*

ANTISTROPHE D

*He calls on those who hear not, caught inside*
*the hard wrestle of water.*
*The divinity laughs at the hot-hearted man,*
*the man who said "never to me," watches him*
*pinned in distress, unable to run free of the wave crests.*
*He had good luck in his life. Now*
*he smashes on the reef of right*
*and drowns, unwept and forgotten.*

*(Athena reenters from the side, guiding eleven citizens chosen as jurors° and attended by a herald.)*

ATHENA

Herald, make proclamation and gather in the host
assembled. Let the stabbing voice of the Etruscan
trumpet, blown to the full with mortal wind, crash out
its high call to all the mustered populace.
For in the filling of this deliberative assembly
it is best for all the city to be silent and learn
the measures I have laid down into the rest of time.
So too these litigants, that their case be fairly tried.

*(Trumpet call. All take their places. Enter Apollo.)*

CHORUS LEADER

My lord Apollo, rule within your own domain.
What in this matter has to do with you? Declare.

APOLLO

I come to testify. This man, by observed law,
came to me as suppliant, took his place by my hearth and hall,
and it was I who cleaned him of the stain of blood.
I have also come to help him win his case. I bear
responsibility for his mother's murder.

(*To Athena.*)

You

who know the rules, initiate the trial. Preside.

ATHENA (*To the Furies.*)

I declare the trial opened. Yours is the first word.
For it must justly be the accuser who speaks first
and opens the case, and makes plain what the action is.

CHORUS LEADER

We are many, but we shall cut it short. You, then,
word against word answer our charges one by one.
Say first, did you kill your mother or did you not?

ORESTES

Yes, I killed her. There shall be no denial of that.

CHORUS LEADER

There are three falls in the match and one has gone to us.

ORESTES

So you say. But you have not even thrown your man.

CHORUS LEADER

So. Then how did you kill her? You are bound to say.

ORESTES

I do. With drawn sword in my hand I cut her throat.

CHORUS LEADER

By whose persuasion and advice did you do this?

ORESTES

By order of this god, here. So he testifies.

CHORUS LEADER

The prophet god guided you into this matricide?

ORESTES

Yes. I have never complained of this. I do not now.

CHORUS LEADER

When sentence seizes you, you will talk a different way.

ORESTES

I have no fear. My father will aid me from the grave.

CHORUS LEADER

Kill your mother, then put trust in a corpse! Trust on.

ORESTES

Yes. She was polluted twice over with disgrace.

CHORUS LEADER

Tell me how, and explain it to the judges here.

ORESTES

She murdered her husband, and thereby my father too.

CHORUS LEADER

Of this stain, death has set her free. But you still live.

ORESTES

While she lived, why did you not descend and drive her out?

CHORUS LEADER

The man she killed was not of blood congenital.

ORESTES

But do I then share with my mother a blood bond?

CHORUS LEADER

Yes, you butcher. How else could she have nursed you in
her womb? Do you forswear your mother's intimate blood?

ORESTES

Yours to bear witness now, Apollo, and expound
the case for me, if I was right to cut her down.
I will not deny I did this thing, because I did
do it. But was the bloodshed right or not? Decide
and answer. As you answer, I shall state my case.

APOLLO

To you, judges, established by Athena in your power,
I shall speak justly. I am a prophet, I shall not
lie. Never, for man, woman, nor city, from my throne
of prophecy have I spoken a word, except
that which Zeus, father of Olympians, might command.
This is justice. Recognize then how great its strength.
I tell you, follow our father's will. For not even
the oath that binds you is more strong than Zeus is strong.

CHORUS LEADER

Then Zeus, as you say, authorized the oracle
to this Orestes, stating he could wreak the death
of his father on his mother, and it would have no force?

APOLLO

It is not the same thing for a noble man to die,
one honored with the king's staff given by the hand of god,
and that by means of a woman, not with the far cast
of fierce arrows, as an Amazon might have done,
but in a way that you shall hear, O Pallas and you
who sit in state to judge this action by your vote.

He had come home from his campaigning. He had done
better than worse, in the eyes of a fair judge. She lay
in wait for him. It was the bath.° When he was at
its edge, she hooded the robe on him, and in the blind
and complex toils tangled her man, and chopped him down.

That is the story of the death of a great man,
revered in all men's sight, lord of the host of ships.
I have called the woman what she was, so that the people
whose duty it is to try this case may be inflamed.

CHORUS LEADER

Zeus, by your story, gives first place to the father's death.
Yet Zeus himself shackled elder Cronus, his own

father. Is this not contradiction? I testify,
judges, that this is being said in your hearing.

APOLLO

You foul animals, from whom the gods turn in disgust,
Zeus could undo shackles, such hurt can be made good,
and there is every kind of way to get out. But once
the dust has drained down all a man's blood, once the man
has died, there is no raising of him up again.
This is a thing for which my father never made
curative spells. All other states, without effort
of hard breath, he can completely rearrange.

CHORUS LEADER

See what it means to force acquittal of this man.
He has spilled his mother's blood upon the ground. Shall he
then be at home in Argos in his father's house?
What altars of the community shall he use? Is there
a brotherhood's lustration that will let him in?

APOLLO

I will tell you, and I will answer correctly. Watch.
The mother is no parent of that which is called
her child, but only nurse of the new-planted seed
that grows. The parent is he who mounts. A stranger she
preserves a stranger's seed, if no god interfere.
I will show you proof of what I have explained. There can
be a father without any mother. There she stands,
the living witness, daughter of Olympian Zeus,
she who was never fostered in the dark of the womb
yet such a child as no goddess could bring to birth.
In all else, Pallas, as I best may understand,
I shall make great your city and its populace.
So I have brought this man to sit beside the hearth
of your house, to be your true friend for the rest of time,
so you shall win him, goddess, to fight by your side,
and among men to come this shall stand a strong bond
that his and your own people's children shall be friends.

ATHENA

Shall I assume that enough has now been said, and tell
the judges to render what they believe a true verdict?

CHORUS LEADER

Every arrow we had has been shot now. We wait
on their decision, to see how the case has gone.

ATHENA

So then. How shall I act correctly in your eyes?

APOLLO

You have heard what you have heard, and as you cast your votes,
good friends, respect in your hearts the oath that you have sworn.

ATHENA

If it please you, men of Attica, hear my decree
now, as you judge this case, the first trial for bloodshed.
For Aegeus' population, this forevermore
shall be the ground where justices deliberate.
Here is the Hill of Ares, here the Amazons
encamped and built their shelters when they came in arms
in rage at Theseus, here they piled their rival towers
to rise, a new city against his city long ago,
and sacrificed for Ares. So this rock is named
from then the Hill of Ares. Here the reverence
of citizens, their fear and kindred do-no-wrong
shall hold by day and in the blessing of night alike
all while the people do not muddy their own laws
with foul infusions. But if bright water you stain
with mud, you nevermore will find it fit to drink.
No anarchy, no rule of a single master. Thus
I advise my citizens to govern and to grace,
and not to cast fear utterly from your city. What
man who fears nothing at all is ever righteous? Such
be your just terrors, and you may deserve and have

salvation for your citadel, your land's defense,
such as is nowhere else found among men, neither
among the Scythians, nor the land that Pelops held.
I establish this tribunal. It shall be untouched
by money making, grave but quick to wrath, watchful
to protect those who sleep, a sentry on the land.
These words I have spun out are for my citizens,
advice into the future. All must stand upright
now, take each man his ballot in his hand, think on
his oath, and make his judgment. For my word is said.

*(One by one, the eleven mortal jurors walk forward to place their voting pebble into an urn: each time, Apollo or the Chorus speaks.)*

CHORUS LEADER

I give you counsel by no means to disregard
this company. We can be a weight to crush your land.

APOLLO

I speak too. I command you to fear, and not
make void the yield of oracles from Zeus and me.

CHORUS LEADER

You honor bloody actions where you have no right.
The oracles you give shall be no longer clean.

APOLLO

My father's purposes are twisted then. For he
was appealed to by Ixion, the first murderer.

CHORUS LEADER

Talk! But for my part, if I do not win the case,
I shall come back to this land and it will feel my weight.

APOLLO

Neither among the elder nor the younger gods
have you consideration. I shall win this suit.

CHORUS LEADER

Such was your action in the house of Pheres. Then
you beguiled the Fates to let mortals go free from death.

APOLLO

Is it not right to help the man who shows respect
and piety, above all when he stands in need?

CHORUS LEADER

You won the ancient goddesses over with wine
and so destroyed the orders of an elder time.

APOLLO

You shall not win the issue of this suit, but shall
be made to void your poison to no enemy's hurt.

CHORUS LEADER

Since you, a young god, would ride down my elder age,
I must stay here and listen to how the trial goes,
being yet uncertain to loose my anger on the state.

ATHENA

It is my task to render final judgment here.
This is a ballot for Orestes I shall cast.
There is no mother anywhere who gave me birth,
and, but for marriage, I am always for the male
with all my heart, and strongly on my father's side.
So, in a case where the wife has killed her husband, lord
of the house, I shall not value her death more highly than his.
And even if the votes are equal, Orestes is the winner.
You of the jurymen who have this duty assigned,
shake out the ballots from the vessels, with all speed.

ORESTES

Phoebus Apollo, what will the decision be?

CHORUS LEADER

Darkness of night, our mother, are you here to watch?

ORESTES

This is the end for me. The noose, or else the light.

CHORUS LEADER

Here our destruction, or our high duties confirmed.

APOLLO

Shake out the votes accurately, Athenian friends.
Be careful as you pick them up. Make no mistake.
In the lapse of judgment great disaster comes. The cast
of a single ballot can restore a house entire.

ATHENA

The man before us has escaped the charge of blood.
The ballots are in equal number for each side.

ORESTES

Pallas Athena, you have kept my house alive.
When I had lost the land of my fathers you gave me
a place to live. Among the Hellenes they shall say:
"A man of Argos lives again in the estates
of his father, all by grace of Pallas Athena, and
Apollo, and with them the all-ordaining god
the Savior"—who remembers my father's death, who looked
upon my mother's advocates, and rescues me.
I shall go home now, but before I go I swear
to this your country and to this your multitude
of people into all the bigness of time to be,
that never man who holds the helm of my state shall come
against your country in the ordered strength of spears,
but though I lie then in my grave, I still shall wreak
helpless bad luck and misadventure upon all
who step across the oath that I have sworn: their ways
disconsolate make, their crossings full of evil
augury, so they shall be sorry that they moved.
But while they keep the upright way, and hold in high
regard the city of Pallas, and align their spears
to fight beside her, I shall be their gracious spirit.

And so farewell, you and your city's populace.
May you outwrestle and overthrow all those who come
against you, to your safety and your spears' success.°

*(Exit Orestes to the side. Exit also Apollo.)*

CHORUS *[singing throughout this interchange with Athena, who speaks in response]*

*Gods of the younger generation, you have ridden down*
*the laws of the elder time, torn them out of my hands.*
*I, disinherited, suffering, heavy with anger*
*shall let loose on the land*
*the vindictive poison*
*dripping deadly out of my heart upon the ground;*
*this from itself shall breed*
*cancer, the leafless, the barren*
*to strike, for the right, their low lands*
*and drag its smear of mortal infection on the ground.*
*What shall I do? Afflicted*
*I am mocked by these people.*
*I have borne what cannot*
*be borne. Great the sorrows and the dishonor upon*
*the sad daughters of Night.*

ATHENA

Listen to me. I would not have you be so grieved.
For you have not been beaten. This was the result
of a fair ballot which ended up even. You were not
dishonored, but the luminous evidence of Zeus
was there, and he who spoke the oracle was he
who ordered Orestes so to act and not be hurt.
Do not be angry any longer with this land
nor bring the bulk of your hatred down on it; do not
render it barren of fruit, nor spill the dripping rain
of death in fierce and jagged lines to eat the seeds.
In complete honesty I promise you a place
of your own, deep hidden underground that is yours by right

where you shall sit on shining chairs beside the hearth
to accept devotions offered by your citizens.

CHORUS

*Gods of the younger generation, you have ridden down*
*the laws of the elder time, torn them out of my hands.*
*I, disinherited, suffering, heavy with anger*
*shall let loose on the land*
*the vindictive poison*
*dripping deadly out of my heart upon the ground;*
*this from itself shall breed*
*cancer, the leafless, the barren*
*to strike, for the right, their low lands*
*and drag its smear of mortal infection on the ground.*
*What shall I do? Afflicted*
*I am mocked by these people.*
*I have borne what cannot*
*be borne. Great the sorrow and the dishonor upon*
*the sad daughters of Night.*

ATHENA

No, not dishonored. You are goddesses. Do not
in too much anger make this place of mortal men
uninhabitable. I have Zeus behind me. Do
we need to speak of that? I am the only god
who knows the keys to where his thunderbolts are locked.
We do not need such, do we? Be reasonable
and do not from a reckless mouth cast on the land
spells that will ruin every thing which might bear fruit.
No. Put to sleep the bitter strength in the black wave
and live with me and share my pride of worship. Here
is a big land, and from it you shall win first fruits
in offerings for children and the marriage rite
for always. Then you will say my argument was good.

CHORUS

*That they could treat me so!*

*I, the mind of the past, to be driven under the ground*
*outcast, like dirt!*
*The wind I breathe is fury and utter hate.*
*Earth, ah, Earth*
*what is this agony that crawls under my ribs?*
*Night, hear me, O Night,*
*mother. They have wiped me out*
*and the hard hands of the gods*
*and their treacheries have taken my old rights away.*

ATHENA

I will bear your angers. You are elder born than I
and in that you are wiser far than I. Yet still
Zeus gave me too intelligence not to be despised.
If you go away into some land of foreigners,
I warn you, you will come to yearn for this country.
Time in forward flood shall ever grow more dignified
for the people of this city. And you, in your place
of eminence beside Erechtheus in his house
shall win from female and from male processionals
more than all lands of men beside could ever give.
Only in this place that I haunt do not inflict
your bloody stimulus to twist the inward hearts
of young men, raging in a fury not of wine,
nor, as if taking the heart from fighting cocks,
engraft among my citizens that spirit of war
that turns their battle fury inward on themselves.
No, let our wars range outward—may they range full fierce
and terrible, for those desiring high renown.
No true fighter I call the bird that fights at home.
Such life I offer you, and it is yours to take.
Do good, receive good, and be honored as the good
are honored. Share our country, the beloved of god.

CHORUS

*That they could treat me so!*
*I, the mind of the past, to be driven under the ground*

*outcast, like dirt!*
*The wind I breathe is fury and utter hate.*
*Earth, ah, Earth*
*what is this agony that crawls under my ribs?*
*Night, hear me, O Night,*
*mother. They have wiped me out*
*and the hard hands of the gods*
*and their treacheries have taken my old rights away.*

ATHENA

I will not weary of telling you all the good things
I offer, so that you can never say that you,
an elder god, were driven unfriended from the land
by me in my youth, and by my mortal citizens.
But if you hold Persuasion has her sacred place
of worship, in the sweet beguilement of my voice,
then you might stay with us. But if you wish to stay
then it would not be justice to inflict your rage
upon this city, your resentment or bad luck
to armies. You can be landholders in this country
if you will, in all justice, with full privilege.

CHORUS LEADER [*speaking*]

Lady Athena, what is this place you say is mine?

ATHENA

A place free of all grief and pain. Take it for yours.

CHORUS LEADER

If I do take it, shall I have some definite powers?

ATHENA

No household shall be prosperous without your will.

CHORUS LEADER

You will do this? You will really let me be so strong?

ATHENA

So we shall straighten the lives of all who worship us.

CHORUS LEADER

You guarantee such honor for the rest of time?

ATHENA

I have no need to promise what I cannot do.

CHORUS LEADER

I think you will have your way with me. My hate is going.

ATHENA

Stay here, then, in this land, and gain others too as friends.

CHORUS LEADER

I will put a spell upon the land. What shall it be?

ATHENA

Something that has no traffic with evil success.
Let it come out of the ground, out of the sea's water,
and from the high air make the waft of gentle gales
wash over the country in full sunlight, and the seed
and stream of the soil's yield and of the grazing beasts
be strong and never fail our people as time goes,
and make the human seed be kept alive. Make more
the issue of those who worship more your ways, for as
the gardener works in love, so love I best of all
the unblighted generation of these upright men.
All such is yours for granting. In the speech and show
and pride of battle, I myself shall not endure
this city's eclipse in the estimation of mankind.

CHORUS [*singing throughout the following interchange with Athena, who chants in response*]

STROPHE A

*I accept this home at Athena's side.*
*I shall not forget the cause*
*of this city, which Zeus all powerful and Ares*
*rule, stronghold of divinities,*
*glory of Hellene gods, their guarded altar.*
*So with forecast of good*

*I sing this prayer for them*
*that the sun's bright magnificence shall break out wave*
*on wave of all the happiness*
*life can give, across their land.*

ATHENA

*Here are my actions. In all goodwill*
*toward these citizens I establish in power*
*these great divinities, difficult to soften.*
*To them is given the handling entire*
*of men's lives. That man*
*who has felt the full weight of their hands°*
*takes the strokes of life, knows not whence, not why,*
*for crimes wreaked in past generations*
*drag him before these powers. Loud his voice*
*but the silent doom*
*hates hard, and breaks him to dust.*

CHORUS

ANTISTROPHE A

*Let there blow no wind that wrecks the trees.*
*I pronounce words of grace.*
*Nor blaze of heat blind the blossoms of grown plants, nor*
*cross the circles of its right*
*place. Let no barren deadly sickness creep and kill.*
*May flocks fatten. Earth be kind*
*to them, with double fold of fruit*
*in time appointed for its yielding. Secret child*
*of Earth, her hidden wealth, bestow*
*blessing and surprise of gods.*

ATHENA

*Strong guard of our city, hear you these*
*and what they portend? Fury is a high queen*
*of strength even among the immortal gods*
*and the undergods, and for humankind*
*they accomplish their work, absolute, clear:*

*for some, singing; for some, life dimmed*
*in tears; theirs the disposition.*

CHORUS

STROPHE B

*Death of manhood cut down*
*before its prime I forbid:*
*girls' grace and glory find*
*men to live life with them.*
*Grant, you who have the power.*
*And O, steering spirits of law,*
*goddesses of Destiny,*
*sisters from my mother, hear;*
*in all houses implicated,*
*in all time heavy of hand*
*on whom your just arrest falls,*
*most august among goddesses.*

ATHENA

*It is my glory to hear how these*
*generosities*
*are given my land. I admire the eyes*
*of Persuasion, who guided the speech of my mouth*
*toward these, when they were reluctant and wild.*
*Zeus, who guides men's speech in councils, was too*
*strong; and my ambition*
*for good wins out in the whole issue.*

CHORUS

ANTISTROPHE B

*This my prayer: civil war*
*fattening on men's ruin shall*
*not thunder in our city. Let*
*not the dry dust that drinks*
*the black blood of citizens*
*through passion for revenge*
*and bloodshed for bloodshed*

*be given our state to prey upon.*
*Let them render grace for grace.*
*Let love be their common will;*
*let them hate with single heart.*
*Much wrong in the world thereby is healed.*

ATHENA

*Are they taking thought to discover that road*
*where speech goes straight?*
*In the fearsome look of the faces of these*
*I see great good for our citizens.*
*While with goodwill you hold in high honor*
*these Kindly Spirits, their will shall be good, as you steer*
*your city, your land*
*on an upright course clear through to the end.*

CHORUS

STROPHE C

*Farewell, farewell. High destiny shall be yours*
*by right. Farewell, citizens*
*seated near the throne of Zeus,*
*beloved by the Maiden he loves,*
*civilized as years go by,*
*sheltered under Athena's wings,*
*revered in her father's sight.*

ATHENA

*Goddesses, farewell. Mine to lead, as these*
*attend us, to where*
*by the sacred light new chambers are given.*
*Go then. Sped by majestic sacrifice*
*from these, plunge beneath the ground. There hold*
*off what might hurt the land; pour in*
*the city's advantage, success in the end.*
*You, children of Cranaus, you who keep*
*the citadel, guide these guests of the state.*

*For good things given,*
*your hearts' desire be for good to return.*

CHORUS

ANTISTROPHE C

*Farewell and again farewell, words spoken twice over,*
*all who by this citadel,*
*mortal men, spirits divine,*
*hold the city of Pallas, grace*
*this my guestship in your land.*
*Life will give you no regrets.*

*(A second Chorus, of women of Attica, begins to enter, from the side.)*

ATHENA [*now speaking*]

Well said. I assent to all the burden of your prayers,
and by the light of flaring torches now attend
your passage to the deep and subterranean hold,
as by us walk those women whose high privilege
it is to guard my image. Flower of all the land
of Theseus, let them issue now, grave companies,
maidens, wives, elder women, in processional.°
In the investiture of purple-stained robes
dignify them, and let the torchlight go before
so that the kindly company of these within
our ground may shine in the future of strong men to come.

*(The first Chorus begin to replace their black robes with reddish-purple ones.)*

SECOND CHORUS [*singing*]

STROPHE A

*Home, home, O high, O aspiring*
*Daughters of Night, aged children, in kindly processional.*
*Bless them, all here, with words of good omen.*

ANTISTROPHE A

*In the primeval dark of earth-hollows*

*held in high veneration with rights sacrificial*
*bless them, all people, with words of good omen.*

STROPHE B

*Wish favor, wish justice for this land,*
*and follow, august goddesses, flushed in the flamesprung*
*torchlight, delighting in your journey.*
*Singing all follow our footsteps.*

ANTISTROPHE B

*There shall be peace forever between these people*
*of Pallas and their guests. Zeus the all-seeing*
*joined with Destiny to confirm it.*
*Singing all follow our footsteps.*

*(Everybody departs, in procession.)*

# II.

# SOPHOCLES

# INTRODUCTION TO SOPHOCLES

Sophocles was born in about 495 BCE, into a wealthy family from the deme of Colonus, close to the city center of Athens. He was thus about thirty years younger than Aeschylus (who died in 455), and about ten or fifteen years older than Euripides (who died just a few months before Sophocles, in 405).

In addition to being the most successful tragedian of his time, Sophocles was active in Athenian public life: he was appointed a treasurer (*hellenotamias*) in 443–42, elected a general (*strategos*) in 441–40 along with Pericles, and perhaps again in the 420s with Nicias; and he was selected to be a special magistrate (*proboulos*) during the emergency administration of 412–11, all of this in marked contrast to the apolitical life of Euripides. There was also an ancient tradition (perhaps apocryphal) that when the cult of the healing god Asclepius was first brought to Athens, it was for a while located in Sophocles' house.

Although we know for certain few details of Sophocles' personal life, he apparently had at least one son, Iophon, by his wife Nicostrate, and another, Ariston, by his mistress Theoris. Ariston's son was in turn named Sophocles, and both Iophon and Sophocles Jr. became successful tragedians. Among his friends were such luminaries as Herodotus, Pericles, and Ion of Chios, and he was said to be sociable and a "good-natured" man. He had a reputation for being something of a flirt and bisexual playboy. Stories that were later told of the octogenarian Sophocles' legal feuds with his sons may have been triggered by his depiction of fierce, lonely, embittered men in his plays (Ajax, Philoctetes,

Teiresias, and especially Oedipus cursing his son in *Oedipus at Colonus*).

Sophocles' career as a dramatist was long, prolific, and immensely successful. His first production in the annual tragedy competition at Athens was in 468 BCE. The plays he entered are not known, but they resulted in a victory over Aeschylus. Sophocles was still composing plays right up to his death in 405 (*Philoctetes*, produced in 409; *Oedipus at Colonus*, produced posthumously in 401).

Ancient sources knew the titles of 120 plays by Sophocles, which should mean thirty groups of four for the annual competition, each comprising three tragedies and a satyr-play. It is recorded that he won eighteen victories (thus even outdoing Aeschylus' thirteen, and far more than Euripides' five), and that he was never ranked lower than second in the competition. Unlike Aeschylus, Sophocles never composed a connected trilogy, that is, a sequence of plays performed together that focused on the same characters or family (like, for example, the *Oresteia*). Unfortunately we do not know what principles he may have used in designing each set of four plays in any given year. All of the seven plays we possess seem to have been performed in different years, and we do not even know the titles of any of the lost plays that accompanied them. As far as we can tell, however, each play was intended to be treated as a separate masterpiece—fully intelligible and self-contained on its own terms.

Any attempt to trace a development in Sophocles' style or worldview during his long career is hampered not only by the loss of all but seven of his plays, but also by the uncertain dating of several of the ones we do have. Sophocles' tragedies rarely contain references to actual current events or issues, and they rarely elicited parodies from Aristophanes (as several of Euripides' did). For only two Sophoclean plays do we possess definite information about their date of production, based on the original fifth-century festival competition records: *Philoctetes* (409) and *Oedipus at Colonus* (405/401). There is good external evidence for dating *Antigone* to 442 or 441, but for the other four plays we have to rely on stylistic—hence subjective—criteria. Most scholars nowadays are inclined to date *Ajax* and *The Women of Trachis* quite early (to the 460s–440s). *Electra* is probably late (perhaps 415–10). The date of *Oedipus the King* is uncertain, though many would like to place it in the early 420s because of its vivid depiction of plague—not a compelling argument.

Sophocles inherited from Aeschylus and the other early tragedians a well-established set of dramatic conventions and formal structures, and he does not appear to have made radical innovations of his own, except perhaps in the musical aspects, since he is credited with being the first Athenian playwright to introduce "Phrygian" and "Lydian" scales into the melodies of his lyrics. (None of this music survives.) Ancient critics disagreed as to whether it was Aeschylus or Sophocles who first employed a third speaking actor—earlier the rule had been that only two were allowed. Aristotle says that Sophocles was first, and that he also introduced scene-painting. In general, however, it was Euripides, along with his younger contemporary Agathon, who were generally regarded as the chief iconoclasts and experimenters in artistic forms and subject matter. Sophocles' gifts lay rather in refining and elaborating the possibilities of the tragic form: tightly constructed plots, more complex dialogue scenes, exploration of extreme emotional states and character contrasts, the subtle interweaving of spoken and musical elements, and an extraordinary richness and fluidity of verbal expression that is often very difficult to capture in English translation. To Aristotle in the fourth century, as to many lovers of drama since, Sophocles' plays appear to represent the pinnacle of what Greek tragedy was capable of achieving, the fulfilment of its very "nature."

After Sophocles died, his plays continued for centuries to be widely read and (presumably) performed all over the Greek-speaking world. A more or less complete collection of his plays was made in Alexandria during the third century BCE, though this no longer exists. Hundreds of fragments from his lost plays are found in quotations by other authors and in anthologies, and while he was never as widely read or imitated as Euripides or Menander (let alone Homer), Sophocles remained a classic both in the ancient schools and among later practitioners of the dramatic arts (including Ennius, Accius, and Pacuvius; Seneca; Corneille and Racine). The seven plays we possess today were probably selected in the second century CE, and from that point gradually the other plays ceased to be copied, and thus eventually were lost to posterity. At Byzantium (Constantinople, now Istanbul), three plays in particular were most widely copied: the "triad" of *Ajax*, *Electra*, and *Oedipus the King*. But the rest were never as close to extinction as the tragedies of Aeschylus, whose difficult style and more old-fashioned dramaturgy made his works less appealing to later readers.

A large papyrus unearthed at Oxyrhynchus (first published in 1912) contains a substantial chunk of the previously lost satyr-play titled *The Trackers* (*Ichneutai*), which is included in translation in this new edition of the Chicago Greek tragedies. Further papyrus finds have continued to add important scraps to our knowledge both of Sophocles' tragedies and of his satyr-dramas. But for the most part, even though we know that, for example, his *Phaedra* was influential and popular throughout antiquity, as were *Polyxena*, *Thyestes*, *Tereus* (about Procne and Philomela), *Inachus* (a satyr-play about Zeus and Io), and numerous other lost plays, Sophocles' reputation in the modern era has rested almost entirely on the seven plays that survive in medieval manuscripts. Of these, *Oedipus the King*, *Antigone*, and *Electra* have always been the most widely read and often staged, but all seven have been central to the discussions of theater historians, philosophers, and theorists of tragedy, and all of them have provoked adaptations, paintings, and translations in abundance, all over the world. Indeed, since the late eighteenth century, for many critics and philosophers it has been Sophocles' plays—along with Shakespeare's—that have been taken to represent the culmination of the genre of tragedy and its capacity to represent human experience and heroic suffering.

# THE THEBAN PLAYS

ANTIGONE

*Translated by* ELIZABETH WYCKOFF

OEDIPUS THE KING

*Translated by* DAVID GRENE

OEDIPUS AT COLONUS

*Translated by* ROBERT FITZGERALD

# THE THEBAN PLAYS: INTRODUCTION

Unlike Aeschylus' *Oresteia* and the trilogy that included his *Seven against Thebes*, the three Sophoclean plays we possess that deal with the family of Oedipus were not written to be performed together. Indeed, they seem to have been composed over several decades. *Antigone* was probably first performed in 442 or 441. The date of *Oedipus the King* is quite uncertain, though often surmised as being in the 420s. *Oedipus at Colonus* was produced posthumously by Sophocles' son in 401. The three plays occasionally disagree with one another in factual details, and in several passages of *Oedipus at Colonus* the hero is found correcting or critiquing ideas that had been propounded in the earlier *Oedipus the King*. Nonetheless, there are many respects in which the three plays speak to one another and convey a consistent portrayal of this family's terrible history, so it makes sense to consider them together in this introduction, even while it must be emphasized again that this is not a "trilogy" in the proper sense of that term.

*The Myth*

The story of the doomed descendants of King Labdacus of Thebes—Laius, Oedipus, and the sons of Oedipus, Eteocles and Polyneices—was extremely well known and often recounted in early Greek literature. The saga rivaled that of the Trojan War in popularity and significance, and various parts of it were narrated in epic poems (including the *Thebais* and the *Oedipodeia*, both now lost) attributed to Homer or one of his successors. It was also taken up in many lyric poems (including one by Stesichorus, of which fragments survive on papyrus). There were, of course, many different versions of the whole story, but the main outlines remain fairly consistent: King Laius and his wife, Jocasta (sometimes she has a different name), are informed by the oracle of Apollo that if she conceives and bears a son, he will grow up to kill his father and marry his mother. They do proceed to have a baby son, however, whom (in Sophocles' version, at least) they leave on a deserted hillside to die. He is rescued by a shepherd, and adopted by King Polybus of Corinth and his wife, Merope. The boy, named Oedipus, grows up believing himself to be Polybus' son and heir.

In due course, Oedipus encounters his real father at a crossroads, though neither recognizes the other. They fight and Oedipus kills Laius. He then comes to Thebes, which is being terrorized by the monstrous Sphinx. Oedipus solves the Sphinx's riddle and is hailed as the new king by the Thebans, which entails marrying the widow of the recently deceased king, Laius—she is, of course, his mother. In Sophocles' version of the story Oedipus and Jocasta have four children: two boys, Polyneices and Eteocles, and two girls, Antigone and Ismene. Eventually, the truth about Oedipus' identity (and the parricide and incest) is discovered.

What happens next varies from version to version. In some, Jocasta commits suicide, in others not. In some Oedipus continues to be the king of Thebes, in others, he either goes into exile or is deposed from the throne but remains in Thebes; in some, he blinds himself. It is not known when this detail of self-blinding was invented: it may have been Sophocles' innovation, though there seem to be hints of it in Aeschylus' (earlier) *Seven against Thebes.*

The ghastly problems continue into the next generation, with Oedipus' two sons quarreling violently about the succession. (In some versions of the story, Oedipus is still alive; in others he has already died.) Again, different versions account differently for this quarrel and its consequences; but in all of them Polyneices goes to live for a while in Argos, marries the daughter of the Argive king, Adrastus, and persuades the Argives to provide him with an army, with the intention of regaining the Theban throne by force. He and six other champions (the "Seven against Thebes") attack the city at its seven gates, while Eteocles organizes its defense. In the battle, the two brothers meet face to face and kill one another. Still, the defenders are victorious and the city is not captured.

Creon, Jocasta's brother and a leading military commander and former advisor to Oedipus, takes over as ruler. He decides to give honorific burial to Eteocles, but denies it to Polyneices (and in most versions, he denies burial also to the Argive dead). A dispute arises over the matter: in some versions (for example, in Euripides' *Suppliant Women*) the Athenians send an army to help the Argives defeat Creon and force the Thebans to surrender the Argive dead for proper burial. Sophocles seems to be innovating in *Antigone* by having only the corpse of Polyneices be the object of dispute, with the dead man's sister, Antigone, being the one who is resisting Creon and demanding the burial.

Where Oedipus was finally laid to rest seems to have been quite open-ended. Other elements in the story too, such as the role of Ismene or the possible intervention of Teiresias at one point or another, were handled quite differently by various authors, as was the issue of Apollo's oracle and its possible significance.

Of the surviving thirty-two Greek tragedies, no fewer than six are based on this Theban saga: apart from these three plays of Sophocles, we have Aeschylus' *Seven against Thebes* and Euripides' *Suppliant Women* and *Phoenician Women*. In addition, we know of numerous lost tragedies that dealt with this myth, including an *Antigone* and an *Oedipus* by Euripides and the two other plays of the Theban trilogy by Aeschylus (*Laius* and *Oedipus*).

## *Antigone*

Sophocles is reported to have won first prize with his production of *Antigone* (probably in 442 or 441 BCE). We do not know the names of the other three plays that he presented that year. The play's considerable success and popularity seem to have influenced other writers and theater-makers profoundly, to the extent that Aeschylus' *Seven against Thebes* (first produced in 467) was extensively revised—some decades after its author's death—to make the final scenes follow the same dramatic course as Sophocles' play.

The idea of building a tragic plot around the bold and defiant resistance of Oedipus' daughter to Creon's authority, out of loyalty to her brother, seems to have originated with this play. Indeed, Antigone as a character may herself have been Sophocles' invention. (By contrast, Ismene, the other daughter, who is a more cautious and conventionally minded foil to her extraordinary sister in this play, had a more significant role in previous versions of the story.) Likewise, the theme of Haemon's (Creon's son's) betrothal to one of Oedipus' daughters may have been an innovation, together with the concentration on the internal family conflict concerning the burial of the two brothers, rather than on the Argive demand that their soldiers be properly buried. Haemon's suicide, and that of Creon's wife Eurydice, as well as Teiresias' intervention and warnings, are also probably new twists introduced by Sophocles—all of them serving to highlight the shocking downfall and misery of Creon.

In Sophocles' strikingly original play, the collision between the two major characters, Antigone and Creon, and the principles that each of them asserts has captured the imaginations of audiences, critics, and philosophers through the centuries. We may note that it is unusual for Sophocles to have a male chorus when his chief character is female; Antigone's isolation is thereby much enhanced, while the audience's sympathies, like the chorus', end up being divided between them.

The play seems to have been quite frequently performed in the fourth century and later, though direct evidence for this is slim, and it was clearly not as popular as Euripides' *Phoenician Women*, whose plot covered some of the same material (in a very different way). Euripides' *Antigone* (now lost) was also well known, and quite different. Although we know little about its date or contents, it appears that Antigone did not die in Euripides' version, but married Haemon and had a son with him. Representations of scenes from our play in ancient art are few. But *Antigone* eventually became one of the seven Sophoclean plays that were selected for standard school use in antiquity, and thus survived into the Byzantine era. About a dozen medieval manuscripts contain the play.

During the Middle Ages and early Renaissance, it was the Latin *Thebais* by Statius and the (incomplete) *Phoenician Women* by Seneca that were best known; and these are the basis for Boccaccio in his *De claris mulieribus* (*On Famous Women*). Since the eighteenth century, however, it has been above all Sophocles' treatment of Antigone, along with his two *Oedipus* plays, that have come to eclipse all others. Poems, letters, and essays by Shelley, De Quincey, Goethe, and many others were devoted to Antigone, and she was constantly depicted as the embodiment of virginal purity, sisterly love, and self-sacrifice. Especially notable are Hölderlin's translation of the play (1804), the opera by Mendelssohn (1841), and essays by Matthew Arnold (1849), George Eliot (1856), and Søren Kierkegaard (1843, and elsewhere), along with the lectures of G. W. F. Hegel (1818–1835).

In the twentieth and twenty-first centuries, writers, performers, critics, political scientists, and philosophers have continued to turn to Sophocles' heroine as a model of individual resistance to totalitarian rule, and/or as a martyr to the cause of family, or religion, or women's rights: for example, the composers Arthur Honegger (1927) and Carl Orff (1949), and playwright Bertolt Brecht (1947). Jean Anouilh's drama *Antigone* (1944) and Athol Fugard's *The Island* (1973) offer contrasting but equally brilliant variations on Sophocles' original; likewise the psychoanalyst Jacques Lacan (1959) and the philosopher Judith Butler (2000). Meanwhile Sophocles' play itself continues to stand out as one of the three or four most widely performed, read, discussed, and admired of all Greek tragedies.

### *Oedipus the King*

When the play was composed and first performed is unknown. Many scholars have suggested the mid-420s because of the portrayal of the plague, but there is little evidence to support this or any other date. We are informed that Sophocles did not win first prize with *Oedipus the King*, but we do not know which other plays he presented with it, so the failure may not have been the result of the audience's dislike of this play in particular. Certainly we have plenty of evidence that the play did not take long to establish itself as one of Sophocles' best known and most admired.

The title of the play in antiquity was *Oedipus Tyrannos*, a designation signaling that Oedipus' position as ruler of Thebes was not inherited but came to him through some other kind of intervention or invitation: the word *tyrannos* did not necessarily carry pejorative associations (though it often did). We do not know who first attached this label to the play, or why—it may not have occurred until after the composition of *Oedipus at Colonus*, when scholars and commentators would have needed to distinguish the two. In Latin, the play has always been titled *Oedipus Rex*.

As previously noted, the broad outline of the story of Oedipus' fateful birth, unwitting parricide and incest, and ultimate self-discovery, was already well known by the time Sophocles wrote his play. In the modern era, his version has become the standard one, and there is a tendency to see this version as simply the way "the myth" goes. But a number of elements in Sophocles' plot were probably new and perhaps unexpected to the original audience. Certainly such details as the utterances of Apollo's oracle and the involvement of Teiresias, the Corinthian messenger, and the herdsman—all of them crucial to the action—are new.

But Sophocles' most distinctive innovations seem to have consisted—as Aristotle emphasizes in the *Poetics*—in his brilliant organization of the material so as to emphasize the elements of ignorance, irony, and unexpected recognition of the truth. The tragic effect of the play depends heavily on the fact that most of the crucial events occurred in the past, and that the audience knows or suspects much more than any individual character does (except possibly Teiresias). This is most strikingly true of Oedipus' edict stating that he will track down and exile the unknown killer of Laius; but it applies also to the announcement of the death of King Polybus of Corinth, Oedipus' supposed father. Throughout the play, it is the paradoxical—improbable, yet inevitable—process of struggling to recognize (or avoid recognizing) who is really who and what each character has already done, generally with the best of motives but terrible results, that causes Oedipus, Jocasta, and everyone else such intolerable anguish and that triggers in the audience such extraordinarily mixed feelings. This tragic tension is enhanced by the oracles of Apollo and warnings of Teiresias, by the chorus' songs of speculation and (mistaken) joy, by Jocasta's dismissal of the value of oracles, by the reports from the Corinthian messenger and the old herdsman, and above all by Oedipus' own determined pursuit of the city's salvation and the truth about himself.

The play was widely known and read throughout antiquity. Because so many other playwrights, including Aeschylus and Euripides, also composed Oedipus plays that do not survive, it is impossible to judge precisely how much the Sophocles version influenced subsequent writers. But Seneca's *Oedipus*, which had the most impact during the Renaissance, was certainly modeled on Sophocles', even while it also contains several major differences. In Byzantine times, Sophocles' play was frequently copied, so that almost two hundred manuscripts exist, most of them virtual duplicates of one another. Ever since the Renaissance, versions by Corneille (1658), Dryden and Lee (1678), Voltaire (1718), and more recently Stravinsky-Cocteau (1927; spectacularly staged by Julie Taymor in 1993), Gide (1931), and Pasolini (1967) constitute only a few of the most conspicuous examples, out of hundreds of productions and adaptations.

Sigmund Freud's exploration of the "Oedipus complex" as one of the cornerstones of his psychoanalytic theory of course added to the play's popular appeal, and it has remained the best known of all Greek tragedies throughout the twentieth and twenty-first centuries. But other interpretations of the play too, in which a not entirely guilty hero (a scapegoat) suffers so that the community can be saved, or a culture hero dies ("winter") to ensure the rebirth of vegetation and prosperity ("spring"), have also kept *Oedi-*

*pus the King* enduringly in the forefront of theatrical and philosophical attention. So too has the use of Oedipus as a metaphor for every human being's quest for personal identity and self-knowledge in a world full of ignorance and hidden horrors—perhaps even one ruled by divine indifference or malevolent fate. If there is one work that is regarded as most typically reflecting the Greeks' fatalistic or pessimistic outlook, this is probably it. Yet, as Aristotle observed, this is also a play whose astonishingly elegant and intricate construction makes it uniquely satisfying and pleasurable to contemplate.

### *Oedipus at Colonus*

This play was written late in Sophocles' life. It was not performed until after his death, when his son Iophon presented it for the dramatic competition in 401. Ancient and modern critics have observed that a striking analogy exists between ancient anecdotes about the elderly Sophocles being engaged in a bitter dispute with his son and the dramatic scene of furious confrontation between Oedipus and Polyneices. But we cannot tell which may have influenced which.

The plot of this play seems to have been distinctly new with Sophocles. Various Greek authors before him had handled the later years and death of Oedipus in very different ways. In Homer Oedipus remains ruling in Thebes even after his parricide and incest are discovered. In Euripides' *Phoenician Women* (411–409 BC), Oedipus has abdicated but is still living in the palace while his sons take turns ruling Thebes. Even at the end of Sophocles' *Oedipus the King* it is not entirely clear whether or not he will go into exile, though that is his expressed wish and he is shown talking about it with his young daughters. In *Oedipus at Colonus* Sophocles continues along this trajectory, and we learn early in the play that Oedipus, now blind and weak, has been wandering for years from town to town as an outcast, attended only by Antigone. As the play proceeds, we learn that in Thebes his two sons, along with Creon, have refused to offer him shelter or support.

Only near the end of the play is Oedipus informed that an oracle has recently revealed that after his death he and his tomb will provide special protection to the community that harbors him, and that the Theban rulers therefore now wish to bring him back to die close to their borders. Innovations specific to this play include the intense focus on the Attic deme of Colonus (Sophocles' own home) as Oedipus' sanctuary and final resting place, the friendship and long-term alliance between Theseus as king of Athens and Oedipus, and the predictions of future defeats of Theban forces at Colonus thanks to the protection of Oedipus' spirit. Likewise the especially close relationship between Oedipus and his daughters, and the context of his cursing of Polyneices, seem distinctive and new. (In previous versions his curse had preceded and even caused the initial quarrel between the two sons.)

There are fewer signs that this play directly influenced later writers and audiences than there are for *Antigone* and *Oedipus the King*. But the play was included among Sophocles' select seven; and although it has not been extensively performed in the modern era, it has always commanded respect for its harrowing yet inspiring portrait of the long-suffering hero and his devoted daughters, as well as for the beauty of its lyrics. One modern oratorio adaptation, *The Gospel at Colonus* (by Lee Breuer and Bob Telson, 1989), based on Robert Fitzgerald's translation in our series, has been acclaimed by critics and audiences as a high point of twentieth-century adaptation of Greek tragedy.

# ANTIGONE

*Translated by* ELIZABETH WYCKOFF

# ANTIGONE

*Characters* ANTIGONE, daughter of Oedipus
ISMENE, her sister
CHORUS of Theban elders
CREON, king of Thebes
A GUARD
HAEMON, son of Creon
TEIRESIAS
A MESSENGER
EURYDICE, wife of Creon

*Scene: Thebes, before the royal palace.*

*(Antigone and Ismene enter from the palace.)*

ANTIGONE

My sister, my Ismene, do you know
of any suffering from our father sprung
that Zeus does not achieve for us survivors?
There's nothing grievous, nothing full of doom,°
or shameful, or dishonored, I've not seen:
your sufferings and mine.
And now, what of this edict which they say
the commander has proclaimed to the whole people?
Have you heard anything? Or don't you know
that our enemies' trouble comes upon our friends?

ISMENE

I've heard no word, Antigone, of our friends,

not sweet nor bitter, since that single moment
when we two lost two brothers
who died on one day by a double blow.
And since the Argive army went away
this very night, I have no further news
of fortune or disaster for myself.

ANTIGONE

I knew it well, and brought you from the house
for just this reason, that you alone may hear.

ISMENE

What is it? Clearly some news has clouded you.

ANTIGONE

It has indeed. Creon will give the one
of our two brothers honor in the tomb;
the other none. Eteocles, with just observance treated,
as law provides he has hidden under earth
to have full honor with the dead below.
But Polyneices' corpse who died in pain,
they say he has proclaimed to the whole town
that none may bury him and none bewail,
but leave him, unwept, untombed, a rich sweet sight
for the hungry birds' beholding and devouring.
    Such orders they say the worthy Creon gives
to you and me—yes, yes, I say to *me*—
and that he's coming to proclaim it clear
to those who know it not.
Further: he has the matter so at heart
that anyone who dares attempt the act
will die by public stoning in the town.
So there you have it and you soon will show
if you are noble, or worthless, despite your high birth.

ISMENE

If things have reached this stage, what can I do,
poor sister, that will help to make or mend?

ANTIGONE

Think, will you share my labor and my act?

ISMENE

What will you risk? And where is your intent?

ANTIGONE

Will you take up that corpse along with me?

ISMENE

To bury him you mean, when it's forbidden?

ANTIGONE

My brother, and yours, though you may wish he were not.°
I never shall be found to be his traitor.

ISMENE

O reckless one, when Creon spoke against it!

ANTIGONE

It's not for him to keep me from my own.

ISMENE

Alas. Remember, sister, how our father
perished abhorred, ill-famed:
himself with his own hand, through his own curse
destroyed both eyes.
Remember next his mother and his wife
finishing life in the shame of the twisted noose.
And third, two brothers on a single day,
poor creatures, murdering, a common doom
each with his arm accomplished on the other.
And now look at the two of us alone.
We'll perish terribly if we violate law
and try to cross the royal vote and power.
We must remember that we two are women,
so not to fight with men;
and that since we are subject to stronger power
we must hear these orders, or any that may be worse.

So I shall ask of them beneath the earth
forgiveness, for in these things I am forced,
and shall obey the men in power. I know
that wild and futile action makes no sense.

ANTIGONE

I wouldn't urge it. And if now you wished
to act, you wouldn't please me as a partner.
Be what you want to; but that man shall I
bury. For me, the doer, death is best.
Loving, I shall lie with him, yes, with my loved one,
when I have dared the crime of piety.
Longer the time in which to please the dead
than the time with those up here.
There shall I lie forever. You may see fit
to keep from honor what the gods have honored.

ISMENE

I shall do no dishonor. But to act
against the citizens, that's beyond my means.

ANTIGONE

That's your excuse. Now I go, to heap
the burial mound for him, my dearest brother.

ISMENE

Oh my poor sister. How I fear for you!

ANTIGONE

For me, don't worry. You clear your own fate.

ISMENE

At least give no one notice of this act;
you keep it hidden, and I'll do the same.

ANTIGONE

Dear gods! Denounce me. I shall hate you more
if silent, not proclaiming this to all.

ISMENE

You have a hot mind over chilly things.

ANTIGONE

I know I please those whom I most should please.

ISMENE

If but you can. You crave what can't be done.

ANTIGONE

And so, when strength runs out, I shall give over.

ISMENE

Wrong from the start, to chase what cannot be.

ANTIGONE

If that's your saying, I shall hate you first,
and next the dead will hate you in all justice.
But let me and my own ill counseling
suffer this terror. I shall suffer nothing
so great as to stop me dying with honor.

ISMENE

Go, since you want to. But know this: you go
senseless indeed, but loved by those who love you.

*(Exit Ismene into the palace. Exit Antigone to one side. Enter the Chorus from the other side.)*

CHORUS [*singing*]

STROPHE A

*Sun's own radiance, fairest light ever shone on the seven gates of Thebes,*
*then did you shine, O golden day's*
*eye, coming over Dirce's stream,*
*on the man who had come from Argos with all his armor*
*running now in headlong fear as you shook his bridle free.*

[*chanting*]
*He was stirred by the dubious quarrel of Polyneices.*

*So, screaming shrill,*
*like an eagle over the land he flew,*
*covered with white-snow wing,*
*with many weapons,*
*with horse-hair crested helms.*

ANTISTROPHE A [*singing*]

*He who had stood above our halls, gaping about our seven gates,*
*with that circle of blood-thirsting spears:*
*gone, without our blood in his jaws,*
*before the torch took hold on our tower crown.*
*Rattle of war at his back; hard the fight for the dragon's foe.*

[*chanting*]
*The boasts of a proud tongue are for Zeus to hate.*
*So seeing them streaming on*
*in insolent clangor of gold,*
*he struck with hurling fire him who rushed*
*for the high wall's top,*
*hoping to yell out "victory."*

STROPHE B [*singing*]

*Swinging, striking the earth he fell*
*fire in hand, who in mad attack,*
*had raged against us with blasts of hate.*
*He failed. And differently from one to another*
*on both sides great Ares dealt his blows about,*
*first in our war team.*

[*chanting*]
*The captains assigned for seven gates*
*fought with our seven and left behind*
*their brazen arms as an offering*
*to Zeus who is turner of battle.*
*All but those two wretches, sons of one man,*
*one mother's sons, who planted their spears*
*each against each and found the share*
*of a common death together.*

ANTISTROPHE B [*singing*]

*Great-named Victory comes to us*
*answering Thebe's warrior joy.*
*Let us forget the wars just done*
*and visit the shrines of the gods,*
*all, with night-long dance which Bacchus will lead,*
*he who shakes Thebe's acres.*

*(Creon enters from the side.)*

[*chanting*]
*Now here he comes, the king of the land,*
*Creon, Menoeceus' son,*
*newly appointed by the gods' new fate.*
*What plan that beats about his mind*
*has made him call this council session,*
*sending his summons to all?*

CREON

My friends, the very gods who shook the state
with mighty surge have set it straight again.
So now I sent for you, chosen from all,
first, because I knew you constant in respect
to Laius' royal power; and again
when Oedipus had set the state to rights,
and when he perished, you were faithful still
in mind to the descendants of the dead.
When they two perished by a double fate,
on one day struck and striking and defiled
each by each other's hand, now it comes that I
hold all the power and the royal throne
through close connection with the perished men.
You cannot learn of any man the soul,
the mind, and the intent until he shows
his practice of the government and law.
For I believe that he who controls the state
if he holds not to the best plans of all,

but locks his tongue up through some kind of fear,
he is worst of all who are or were.
And he who counts another greater friend
than his own fatherland, I put him nowhere.
So I—may Zeus all-seeing always know it—
could not keep silent as disaster crept
upon the town, destroying hope of safety.
Nor could I count the enemy of the land
friend to myself, not I who know so well
that it's she, the land, who saves us, sailing straight,
and only so can we have friends at all.
With such good rules shall I enlarge our state.
And now I have proclaimed their brother-edict.
In the matter of the sons of Oedipus,
citizens, know: Eteocles who died,
defending this our town with champion spear,
is to be covered in the grave and granted
all holy rites we give the noble dead.
But his brother Polyneices, whom I name
the exile who came back and sought to burn
his fatherland, the gods of his own kin,
who tried to gorge on blood he shared, and lead
the rest of us as slaves—
it is announced that no one in this town
may give him burial or mourn for him.
Leave him unburied, leave his corpse disgraced,
a dinner for the birds and for the dogs.
Such is my mind. Never shall I, myself,
honor the wicked and reject the just.
The man who is well-minded to the state
from me in death and life shall have his honor.

CHORUS LEADER

This resolution, Creon, is your own,
in the matter of the traitor and the true.

For you can make such rulings as you will
about the living and about the dead.

CREON

Now you be sentinels of the decree.

CHORUS LEADER

Order some younger man to take this on.

CREON

Already there are watchers of the corpse.

CHORUS LEADER

What other order would you give us, then?

CREON

Not to take sides with any who disobey.

CHORUS LEADER

No fool is fool to the point of loving death.

CREON

Death is the price. But often we have known
men to be ruined by the hope of profit.

*(Enter, from the side, a Guard.)*

GUARD

My lord, I cannot claim I'm out of breath
from rushing here with light and hasty step,
for I had many haltings in my thought
making me double back upon my road.
My mind kept saying many things to me:
"Why go where you will surely pay the price?"
"Fool, are you halting? And if Creon learns
from someone else, how shall you not be hurt?"
Turning this over, on I dillydallied.
And so a short trip turned itself to long.
Finally, though, my coming here won out.

If what I say is nothing, still I'll say it.
For I come clutching to one single hope
that I can't suffer what is not my fate.

CREON
What is it that brings on this gloom of yours?

GUARD
I want to tell you first about myself.
I didn't do it, didn't see who did it.
It isn't right for me to get in trouble.

CREON
Your aim is good. You fence the facts around.
It's clear you have some shocking news to tell.

GUARD
Terrible tidings make for long delays.

CREON
Speak out the story, and then get away.

GUARD
I'll tell you. Someone left the corpse just now,
burial all accomplished, thirsty dust
strewn on the flesh, the ritual complete.

CREON
What are you saying? What man has dared to do it?

GUARD
I wouldn't know. There were no marks of picks,
no grubbed-out earth. The ground was dry and hard,
no trace of wheels. The doer left no sign.
When the first fellow on the day-shift showed us,
we all were sick with wonder.
For he was hidden, not inside a tomb,
but light dust upon him, enough to avert pollution;
no wild beast's track, nor track of any hound
having been near, nor was the body torn.

We roared bad words about, guard against guard,
almost came to blows. No one was there to stop us.
Each man had done it, nobody had done it
so as to prove it on him—we couldn't tell.
We were prepared to hold to red-hot iron,
to walk through fire, to swear before the gods
we hadn't done it, hadn't shared the plan,
when it was plotted or when it was done.
And last, when all our sleuthing came out nowhere,
one fellow spoke, who made our heads to droop
low toward the ground. We couldn't disagree.
We couldn't see a chance of getting off.
He said we had to tell you all about it.
We couldn't hide the fact.
So he won out. The lot chose poor old me
to win the prize. So here I am unwilling,
quite sure you people hardly want to see me.
Nobody likes the bringer of bad news.

CHORUS LEADER

Lord, while he spoke, my mind kept on debating.
Isn't this action possibly a god's?

CREON

Stop now, before you fill me up with rage,
or you'll prove yourself insane as well as old.
Unbearable, your saying that the gods
take any kindly forethought for this corpse.
Would it be they had hidden him away,
honoring his good service, he who came
to burn their pillared temples and their wealth,
raze their land, and break apart their laws?
Or have you seen them honor wicked men?
It isn't so.
No, from the first there were some men in town
who took the edict hard, and growled against me,
who secretly were shaking their heads, not pulling

honestly in the yoke, no way my friends.
These are the people—oh it's clear to me—
who have bribed these men and brought about the deed.
No current standard among men's as bad
as silver currency. This destroys the state;
this drives men from their homes; this wicked teacher
drives solid citizens to acts of shame.
It shows men how to act as criminals
and know the deeds of utter unholiness.
But every hired hand who helped in this
has brought on himself the sentence he shall have.
And further, as I still revere great Zeus,
understand this, I tell you under oath:
if you don't find the very man whose hands
buried the corpse and bring him for me to see,
not death alone shall be enough for you
till living, strung up, you make clear the crime.
For the future you'll have learned that profiteering
has its rules, and that it doesn't pay
to squeeze a profit out of every source.
For you'll have seen that more men come to doom
through dirty profits than are sustained by them.

GUARD
May I say something? Or just turn and go?

CREON
Aren't you aware your speech is most unwelcome?

GUARD
Does it annoy your ears, or your mind?

CREON
Why are you out to allocate my pain?

GUARD
The doer hurts your mind. I hurt your ears.

CREON

You are a quibbling rascal through and through.

GUARD

But anyhow I never did the deed.

CREON

And you the man who sold your life for money!

GUARD

Oh!
How terrible to guess, and guess at lies!

CREON

Go polish up your guesswork. If you don't
show me the doers you will have to say
that wicked payments work their own revenge.

GUARD

Indeed, I pray he's found, but yes or no,
taken or not as luck may settle it,
you won't see me returning to this place.
Saved when I neither hoped nor thought to be,
I owe the gods a mighty debt of thanks.

*(Exit Creon into the palace. Exit the Guard by the way he came.)*

CHORUS [*singing*]

STROPHE A

*Many the wonders but nothing is stranger than man.*
*This thing crosses the sea in the winter's storm,*
*making his path through the roaring waves.*
*And she, the greatest of gods, the Earth—*
*ageless she is, and unwearied—he wears her away*
*as the ploughs go up and down from year to year*
*and his mules turn up the soil.*

ANTISTROPHE A

*Lighthearted nations of birds he snares and leads,*

*wild beast tribes and the salty brood of the sea,*
*with the twisted mesh of his nets, this clever man.*
*He controls with craft the beasts of the open air,*
*walkers on hills. The horse with his shaggy mane*
*he holds and harnesses, yoked about the neck,*
*and the strong bull of the mountain.*

STROPHE B

*Language, and thought like the wind*
*and the feelings that govern a city,*
*he has taught himself, and shelter against the cold,*
*refuge from rain. He can always help himself.*
*He faces no future helpless. There's only death*
*that he cannot find an escape from. He has contrived*
*refuge from illnesses once beyond all cure.*

ANTISTROPHE B

*Clever beyond all dreams*
*the inventive craft that he has*
*which may drive him one time to good or another to evil.*
*When he honors the laws of the land and the gods' sworn right*
*high indeed is his city; but cityless the man*
*who dares to dwell with dishonor. Not by my fireside,*
*never to share my thoughts, who does these things.*

(*Enter the Guard with Antigone, from the side.*)

[*Chorus now chanting*]
*My mind is split at this awful sight.*
*I know her. I cannot deny*
*Antigone is here.*
*Alas, the unhappy girl,*
*unhappy Oedipus' child.*
*Oh what is the meaning of this?*
*It cannot be you that they bring*
*for breaking the royal law,*
*caught in sheer madness.*

GUARD

This is the woman who has done the deed.
We caught her at the burying. Where's the king?

*(Enter Creon from the palace.)*

CHORUS LEADER

Back from the house again just when he's needed.

CREON

What must I measure up to? What has happened?

GUARD

Lord, one should never swear off anything.
Afterthought makes the first resolve a liar.
I could have vowed I wouldn't come back here
after your threats, after the storm I faced.
But joy that comes beyond the wildest hope
is bigger than all other pleasure known.
I'm here, though I swore not to be, and bring
this girl. We caught her burying the dead.
This time we didn't need to shake the lots;
mine was the luck, all mine.
So now, lord, take her, you, and question her
and prove her as you will. But I am free.
And I deserve full clearance on this charge.

CREON

Explain the circumstance of the arrest.

GUARD

She was burying the man. You have it all.

CREON

Is this the truth? And do you grasp its meaning?

GUARD

I saw her burying the very corpse
you had forbidden. Is this adequate?

CREON

How was she caught and taken in the act?

GUARD

It was like this: when we got back again
struck with those dreadful threatenings of yours,
we swept away the dust that hid the corpse.
We stripped it back to slimy nakedness.
And then we sat to windward on the hill
so as to dodge the smell.
We poked each other up with growling threats
if anyone was careless of his work.
For some time this went on, till it was noon.
The sun was high and hot. Then from the earth
up rose a dusty whirlwind to the sky,
filling the plain, smearing the forest leaves,
clogging the upper air. We shut our eyes,
sat and endured the plague the gods had sent.
Then the storm left us after a long time.
We saw the girl. She cried the sharp and shrill
cry of a bitter bird which sees the nest
bare where the young birds lay.
So this same girl, seeing the body stripped,
cried with great groanings, called out dreadful curses
upon the people who had done the deed.
Soon in her hands she brought the thirsty dust,
and holding high a pitcher of wrought bronze
she poured the three libations for the dead.
We saw this and rushed down. We trapped her fast;
and she was calm. We taxed her with the deeds
both past and present. Nothing was denied.
And I was glad, and yet I took it hard.
One's own escape from trouble makes one glad;
but bringing friends to trouble is hard grief.
Still, I care less for all these second thoughts
than for the fact that I myself am safe.

CREON

You there, whose head is drooping to the ground,
do you admit this, or deny you did it?

ANTIGONE

I say I did it and I don't deny it.

CREON *(To the Guard.)*

Take yourself off wherever you wish to go
free of a heavy charge.

*(To Antigone.)*

You—tell me not at length but in a word.
You knew the order not to do this thing?

ANTIGONE

I knew—of course I knew. The word was plain.

CREON

And still you dared to overstep these laws?

ANTIGONE

For me it was not Zeus who made that order.
Nor did that Justice who lives with the gods below
mark out such laws to hold among mankind.
Nor did I think your orders were so strong
that you, a mortal man, could overrun
the gods' unwritten and unfailing laws.
Not now, nor yesterday's, they always live,
and no one knows their origin in time.
So not through fear of any man's proud spirit
would I be likely to neglect these laws,
and draw on myself the gods' sure punishment.
I knew that I must die—how could I not?—
even without your edict. If I die
before my time, I say it is a gain.
Who lives in sorrows many as are mine
how shall he not be glad to gain his death?

And so, for me to meet this fate's no grief.
But if I left that corpse, my mother's son,
dead and unburied I'd have cause to grieve
as now I grieve not.
And if you think my acts are foolishness
the foolishness may be in a fool's eye.

CHORUS LEADER

The girl is fierce. She's her father's child.
She cannot yield to trouble; nor could he.

CREON

These rigid spirits are the first to fall.
The strongest iron, hardened in the fire,
most often ends in scraps and shatterings.
Small curbs bring raging horses back to terms:
enslaved to his neighbor, who can think of pride?
This girl was expert in her insolence
when she broke bounds beyond established law.
Once she had done it, insolence the second,
to boast her doing, and to laugh in it.
I am no man and she the man instead
if she can have this conquest without pain.
She is my sister's child, but were she child
of closer kin than any at my hearth,
she and her sister should not so escape
a dreadful death. I charge Ismene too.
She shared the planning of this burial.
Call her outside. I saw her in the house,
maddened, no longer mistress of herself.
The sly intent betrays itself sometimes
before the secret plotters work their wrong.
I hate it too when someone caught in crime
then wants to make it seem a lovely thing.

ANTIGONE

Do you want more than my arrest and death?

CREON

No more than that. For that is all I need.

ANTIGONE

Why are you waiting? Nothing that you say
fits with my thought. I pray it never will.
Nor will you ever like to hear my words.
And yet what greater glory could I find
than giving my own brother funeral?
All these would say that they approved my act
did fear not mute them.
A king is fortunate in many ways,
and most, that he can act and speak at will.

CREON

None of these others see the case this way.

ANTIGONE

They see, and do not say. You have them cowed.

CREON

And you are not ashamed to think alone?

ANTIGONE

It is no shame to serve blood relatives.

CREON

Was not he who died on the other side your brother?

ANTIGONE

Full brother, on both sides, my parents' child.

CREON

Your act of grace, in his regard, is crime.

ANTIGONE

The corpse below would never say it was.

CREON

When you honor him and the criminal just alike?

ANTIGONE

It was a brother, not a slave, who died.

CREON

Died to destroy this land the other guarded.

ANTIGONE

Death yearns for equal law for all the dead.

CREON

Not that the good and bad draw equal shares.

ANTIGONE

Who knows but this is holiness below?

CREON

Never is the enemy, even in death, a friend.

ANTIGONE

I cannot share in hatred, but in love.

CREON

Then go down there, if you must love, and love
the dead. No woman rules me while I live.

*(Ismene is brought from the palace under guard.)*

CHORUS [*chanting*]

*Look there! Ismene is coming out.*
*She loves her sister and mourns,*
*with clouded brow and bloodied cheeks,*
*tears on her lovely face.*

CREON

You, lurking like a viper in the house,
who sucked me dry, while I raised unawares
a twin destruction planned against the throne.
Now tell me, do you say you shared this deed?
Or will you swear you didn't even know?

ISMENE

I did the deed if she agrees I did.
I am accessory and share the blame.

ANTIGONE

Justice will not allow this. You did not
wish for a part, nor did I give you one.

ISMENE

You are in trouble, and I'm not ashamed
to sail beside you into suffering.

ANTIGONE

Death and the dead, they know whose act it was.
I cannot love a friend whose love's mere words.

ISMENE

Sister, I pray, don't fence me out from honor,
from death with you, and honor done the dead.

ANTIGONE

Don't die along with me, nor make your own
that which you did not do. My death's enough.

ISMENE

When you are gone what life can I desire?

ANTIGONE

Love Creon. He's your kinsman and your care.

ISMENE

Why hurt me, when it does yourself no good?

ANTIGONE

I also suffer, when I laugh at you.

ISMENE

What further service can I do you now?

ANTIGONE

To save yourself. I shall not envy you.

ISMENE

Alas for me. Am I outside your fate?

ANTIGONE

Yes. For you chose to live when I chose death.

ISMENE

At least I was not silent. You were warned.

ANTIGONE

Some will have thought you wiser. Some will not.

ISMENE

And yet the blame is equal for us both.

ANTIGONE

Take heart. You live. My life died long ago.
And that has made me fit to help the dead.

CREON

One of these girls has shown her lack of sense
just now. The other had it from her birth.

ISMENE

Yes, king. When people fall in deep distress
their native sense departs, and will not stay.

CREON

You chose your mind's distraction when you chose
to work out wickedness with this wicked girl.

ISMENE

What life is there for me to live without her?

CREON

Don't speak of her. For she is here no more.

ISMENE

But will you kill your own son's promised bride?

CREON

Oh, there are other furrows for his plough.

ISMENE

But where the closeness that has bound these two?

CREON

Not for my sons will I choose wicked wives.

ISMENE°

Dear Haemon, your father robs you of your rights.

CREON

You and your marriage trouble me too much.

ISMENE

You will take away his bride from your own son?

CREON

Yes. Death will help me break this marriage off.

CHORUS LEADER

It seems determined that the girl must die.

CREON

You helped determine it. Now, no delay!
Slaves, take them in. They must be women now.
No more free running.
Even the bold will flee when they see Death
drawing in close enough to end their life.

*(Antigone and Ismene are taken inside.)*

CHORUS [*singing*]

STROPHE A

*Fortunate they whose lives have no taste of pain.*
*For those whose house is shaken by the gods*
*escape no kind of doom. It extends to all the kin*
*like the wave that comes when the winds of Thrace*
*run over the dark of the sea.*
*The black sand of the bottom is brought from the depth;*
*the beaten cliffs sound back with a hollow cry.*

ANTISTROPHE A

*Ancient the sorrow of Labdacus' house, I know.*
*Dead men's grief comes back, and falls on grief.*
*No generation can free the next.*
*One of the gods will strike. There is no escape.*
*So now the light goes out*
*for the house of Oedipus, while the bloody knife*
*cuts the remaining root,° in folly and the mind's fury.*

STROPHE B

*What transgression of man, O Zeus, can bind your power?*
*Not sleep can destroy it who governs all,°*
*nor the weariless months the gods have set. Unaged in time*
*monarch you rule in Olympus' gleaming light.*
*Near time, far future, and the past,*
*one law controls them all:*
*any greatness in human life brings doom.*

ANTISTROPHE B

*Wandering hope brings help to many men.*
*But others she tricks with giddy loves,*
*and her quarry knows nothing until he has walked into flame.*
*Word of wisdom it was when someone said,*
*"The bad looks like the good*
*to him a god would doom."*
*Only briefly is that one free from doom.*

*(Haemon enters from the side.)*

[*chanting*]
*Here is Haemon, your one surviving son.*
*Does he come in grief at the fate of his bride,*
*in pain that he's tricked of his wedding?*

CREON

Soon we shall know more than a seer could tell us.
Son, have you heard the vote condemned your bride?
And are you here, maddened against your father,
or are we friends, whatever I may do?

HAEMON

My father, I am yours. You keep me straight
with your good judgment, which I shall ever follow.
Nor shall a marriage count for more with me
than your kind leading.

CREON

There's my good boy. So should you hold at heart
and stand behind your father all the way.
It is for this men pray they may beget
households of dutiful obedient sons,
who share alike in punishing enemies,
and give due honor to their father's friends.
Whoever breeds a child that will not help,
what has he sown but trouble for himself,
and for his enemies laughter full and free?
Son, do not let your lust mislead your mind,
all for a woman's sake, for well you know
how cold the thing he takes into his arms
who has a wicked woman for his wife.
What deeper wound than a loved one who is evil?
Oh spit her forth forever, as your foe.
Let the girl marry somebody in Hades.
Since I have caught her in the open act,
the only one in town who disobeyed,
I shall not now proclaim myself a liar,
but kill her. Let her sing her song of Zeus
the guardian of blood kin.
If I allow disorder in my house
I'd surely have to license it abroad.
A man who deals in fairness with his own,
he can make manifest justice in the state.
But he who crosses law, or forces it,
or hopes to dictate orders to the rulers,
shall never have a word of praise from me.
The man the state has put in place must have

obedient hearing to his least command
when it is right, and even when it's not.
He who accepts this teaching I can trust,
ruler, or ruled, to function in his place,
to stand his ground even in the storm of spears,
a comrade to trust in battle at one's side.
There is no greater wrong than disobedience.
This ruins cities, this tears down our homes,
this breaks the battlefront in panic-rout.
If men live decently it is because
obedience saves their very lives for them.
So I must guard the men who yield to order,
not let myself be beaten by a woman.
Better, if it must happen, that a man
should overset me.
I won't be called weaker than womankind.

CHORUS LEADER

We think—unless our age is cheating us—
that what you say is sensible and right.

HAEMON

Father, the gods have given men good sense,
the highest and best possession that we have.
I couldn't find the words in which to claim
that there was error in your late remarks.
Yet someone else might bring some further light.
Because I am your son I must keep watch
on all men's doing where it touches you,
their speech, and most of all, their discontents.
Your presence frightens any common man
from saying things you would not care to hear.
But in dark corners I have heard them say
how the whole town is grieving for this girl,
unjustly doomed, if ever woman was,
to die in shame for glorious action done.
She would not leave her fallen, slaughtered brother

there, as he lay, unburied, for the birds
and hungry dogs to make an end of him.
Does she not truly deserve a golden prize?
This is the undercover speech in town.
    Father, your welfare is my greatest good.
What precious gift in life for any child
outweighs a father's fortune and good fame?
And so a father feels his children's faring.
So, do not have one mind, and one alone
that only your opinion can be right.
Whoever thinks that he alone is wise,
his eloquence, his mind, above the rest,
come the unfolding, it shows his emptiness.
A man, though wise, should never be ashamed
of learning more, and must not be too rigid.
Have you not seen the trees beside storm torrents—
the ones that bend preserve their limbs and leaves,
while the resistant perish root and branch?
And so the ship that will not slacken sail,
the ropes drawn tight, unyielding, overturns.
She ends the voyage with her keel on top.
No, yield your wrath, allow a change of stand.
Young as I am, if I may give advice,
I'd say it would be best if men were born
perfect in wisdom, but that failing this
(which often fails) it can be no dishonor
to learn from others when they speak good sense.

CHORUS LEADER

Lord, if your son has spoken to the point
you should take his lesson. He should do the same.
Both sides have spoken well.

CREON

At my age I'm to school my mind by his?
This boy instructor is my master, then?

HAEMON

I urge no wrong. I'm young, but you should watch
my actions, not my years, to judge of me.

CREON

A loyal action, to respect disorder?

HAEMON

I wouldn't urge respect for wickedness.

CREON

You don't think she is sick with that disease?

HAEMON

Your fellow citizens maintain she's not.

CREON

Is the town to tell me how I ought to rule?

HAEMON

Now there you speak just like a boy yourself.

CREON

Am I to rule by other mind than mine?

HAEMON

No city is property of a single man.

CREON

But custom gives possession to the ruler.

HAEMON

You'd rule a desert beautifully alone.

CREON *(To the Chorus.)*

It seems he's firmly on the woman's side.

HAEMON

If you're a woman. It is you I care for.

CREON

Wicked, to try conclusions with your father.

HAEMON

When you conclude unjustly, so I must.

CREON

Am I unjust, when I respect my office?

HAEMON

You don't respect it, trampling down the gods' due.

CREON

Your mind is poisoned. Weaker than a woman!

HAEMON

At least you'll never see me yield to shame.

CREON

Your whole long argument is but for her.

HAEMON

And you, and me, and for the gods below.

CREON

As long as she lives, you shall not marry her.

HAEMON

Then she shall die—and her death will bring another.

CREON

Your boldness makes more progress. Threats, indeed!

HAEMON

No threat, to speak against your empty plan.

CREON

Past due, sharp lessons for your empty brain.

HAEMON

If you weren't father, I should call you mad.

CREON

Don't flatter me with "father," you woman's slave.

HAEMON

You wish to speak but never wish to hear.

CREON

You think so? By Olympus, you shall not
revile me with these tauntings and go free.
Bring out the hateful creature; she shall die
full in his sight, close at her bridegroom's side.

HAEMON

Not at my side! Don't think that! She will not
die next to me. And you yourself will not
ever lay eyes upon my face again.
Find other friends to rave with after this.

*(Exit Haemon, to the side.)*

CHORUS LEADER

Lord, he has gone with all the speed of rage.
When such a young man is grieved his mind is hard.

CREON

Oh, let him go, and plan superhuman action.
In any case the girls shall not escape.

CHORUS LEADER

You plan the punishment of death for both?

CREON

Not her who did not do it. You are right.

CHORUS LEADER

And what death have you chosen for the other?

CREON

To take her where the foot of man comes not.
There shall I hide her in a hollowed cave
living, and leave her just so much to eat
as clears the city from the guilt of death.
There, if she prays to Death, the only god

of her respect, she may manage not to die.
Or she may learn at last, though much too late,
how honoring the dead is wasted labor.

*(Exit Creon into the palace.)*°

CHORUS [*singing*]

STROPHE

*Love unconquered in fight, love who falls on our possessions:*°
*You rest at night in the soft bloom of a girl's face.*
*You cross the sea, you are known in the wildest lairs.*
*Not the immortal gods can escape you,*
*nor men of a day. Who has you within him is mad.*

ANTISTROPHE

*You twist the minds of the just. Wrong they pursue and are ruined.*
*You made this quarrel of kindred men before us now.*
*Desire looks clear from the eyes of a lovely bride:*
*power as strong as the founded world.*
*Aphrodite, goddess, is playing, with whom no man can fight.*

*(Antigone is brought from the palace under guard.)*

[*chanting*]
*Now I am carried beyond all bounds.*
*My tears will not be checked.*
*I see Antigone depart*
*to the chamber where all must sleep.*

ANTIGONE [*singing*]

STROPHE A

*Men of my fathers' land, you see me go*
*my last journey. My last sight of the sun,*
*then never again. Death who brings all to sleep*
*takes me alive to the shore*
*of the river underground.*
*Not for me was the marriage hymn, nor will anyone start the song*
*at a wedding of mine. Acheron is my bridegroom.*

CHORUS [*chanting*]

*With praise as your portion you go*
*in fame to the vault of the dead.*
*Untouched by wasting disease,*
*not paying the price of the sword,*
*of your own free will you go.*
*Alone among mortals will you descend*
*in life to the house of Death.*

ANTIGONE [*singing*]

ANTISTROPHE A

*Pitiful was the death that Phrygian stranger died,*
*our queen once, Tantalus' daughter. The rock by Sipylus*
*covered her over, like stubborn ivy it grew.*
*Still, as she wastes, the rain*
*and snow companion her, so men say.*
*Pouring down from her mourning eyes comes the water that*
*soaks the stone.*
*My own putting to sleep a god has arranged like hers.*

CHORUS [*chanting*]

*God's child and god she was:*
*but we are born to death.*
*Yet even in death you will have your fame,*
*to have gone like a god to your fate,*
*in living and dying alike.*

ANTIGONE [*singing*]

STROPHE B

*Laughter against me now. In the name of our fathers' gods,*
*could you not wait till I went? Must affront be thrown in my face?*
*O city of wealthy men.*
*I call upon Dirce's spring,*
*I call upon Thebe's grove in the armored plain,*
*to be my witnesses, how with no friend's mourning,*
*by what decree I go to the fresh-made prison tomb.*
*Alive to the place of corpses, an alien still,*
*never at home with the living nor with the dead.*

CHORUS

*You went to the furthest verge*
*of daring, but there you tripped*
*on the high pedestal of justice, and fell.*
*Perhaps you are paying your father's pain.*

ANTIGONE

ANTISTROPHE B

*You speak of my darkest thought, my pitiful father's fame,*
*spread through all the world, and the doom that haunts our house,*
*the glorious house of Labdacus.*
*My mother's marriage bed.*
*Destruction where she lay with her husband-son,*
*my father. These are my parents and I their child.*
*I go to stay with them. My curse is to die unwed.*
*My brother, you found your fate when you found your bride,*
*you found it for me as well. Dead, you destroy my life.*

CHORUS

*You showed respect for the dead.*
*So we for you: but power*
*is not to be thwarted so.*
*Your self-willed temper has brought you down.*

ANTIGONE

EPODE

*Unwept, no wedding-song, unfriended, now I go*
*down the road made ready for me.*
*No longer am I allowed to see this holy light of the sun.*
*No friend bewails my fate.*

*(Creon enters from the palace.)*°

CREON

When people sing the dirge for their own deaths
ahead of time, no one would ever stop
if they might hope that this would be of use.°
Take her away at once, and open up
the tomb I spoke of. Leave her there alone.

There let her choose: death, or a buried life.
No stain of guilt upon us in this case,
but she is exiled from our life on earth.

ANTIGONE

O tomb, O marriage chamber, hollowed-out
house that will watch forever, where I go—
to my own people, most of whom are there;
Persephone has taken them to her.
Last of them all, beyond the rest ill-fated,
I shall descend, before my course is run.
Still when I get there I may hope to find
I've come as a dear friend to my dear father,
to you, my mother, and my brother too.
All three of you have known my hand in death.
I washed your bodies, dressed them for the grave,
poured out the last libation at the tomb.
And now, Polyneices, you know the price I pay
for doing final service to your corpse.
And yet the wise will know my choice was right.
Were I a mother, with children or husband dead,
I'd let them molder. I should not have chosen
in such a case to cross the state's decree.
What is the law that lies behind these words?
One husband gone, I might have found another,
or a child from a new man in the first child's place;
but with my parents covered up in death,
no brother for me, ever, could be born.
Such was the law by which I honored you.
But Creon thought the doing was a crime,
a dreadful daring, brother of my heart.
So now he takes and leads me out by force.
No marriage bed, no marriage song for me,
and since no wedding, so no child to rear.
I go, without a friend, struck down by fate,
living, to the hollow chambers of the dead.

What divine justice have I disobeyed?
Why, in my misery, look to the gods for help?
Can I call any of them my ally?
I stand convicted of impiety,
the evidence my pious duty done.
If the gods think that this is righteousness,
in suffering I'll see my error clear.
But if it is the others who are wrong
I wish them no greater punishment than mine.

CHORUS [*Chorus, Creon, and Antigone chanting in turn*]
*The same tempest of mind*
*as ever, controls the girl.*

CREON
*Therefore her guards shall regret*
*the slowness with which they move.*

ANTIGONE
*That word comes close to death.*

CREON
*You are perfectly right in that;*
*I offer no grounds for hope.*

ANTIGONE
*O town of my fathers in Thebe's land,*
*O gods of our house!*
*I am led away and must not wait.*
*Look, leaders of Thebes,*
*I am last of your royal line.*
*Look what I suffer, at whose command,*
*because I respected the right.*

*(Antigone is led away, to the side.)*

CHORUS [*singing*]

STROPHE A

*Danaë suffered too.*
*She went from the light to the brass-built room,*

*bedchamber and tomb together. Like you, poor child,*
*she was of great descent, and more, she held and kept*
*the seed of the golden rain which was Zeus.*
*Fate has terrible power.*
*You cannot escape it by wealth or war.*
*No fort will keep it out, no ships outrun it.*

ANTISTROPHE A

*Remember the angry king,*
*son of Dryas, who raged against Dionysus and paid,*
*pent in a rock-walled prison. His bursting wrath*
*slowly went down. As the terror of madness went,*
*he learned of his frenzied attack on the god.*
*Fool, he had tried to stop*
*the dancing women possessed of god,*
*the fire of Bacchic rites, the songs and pipes.*

STROPHE B

*Where the dark rocks divide*
*sea from sea at the Bosporus,*
*is Thracian Salmydessus, where savage Ares*
*beheld the terrible blinding wounds*
*dealt to Phineus' sons by their father's wife.*
*Dark the eyes that looked to avenge their mother.*
*Sharp with her shuttle she struck, and blooded her hands.*°

ANTISTROPHE B

*Wasting they wept their fate,*
*settled when they were born*
*to Cleopatra, unhappy queen.*
*She was a princess too, of the ancient Erechthids,*
*but was reared in the cave of the wild North Wind, her father,*
*swift as a horse over the hills.*
*Half a goddess, still, child, she suffered like you.*

*(Enter, from the side, Teiresias, led by a boy attendant.)*

TEIRESIAS

Elders of Thebes, we two have come one road,
two of us looking through one pair of eyes.
This is the way of walking for the blind.

CREON

Old Teiresias, what news has brought you here?

TEIRESIAS

I'll tell you. You in turn must trust the prophet.

CREON

I've always been attentive to your counsel.

TEIRESIAS

And therefore you have steered this city straight.

CREON

So I can say how helpful you have been.

TEIRESIAS

Again you are balanced on a razor's edge.

CREON

What is it? How I shudder at your words!

TEIRESIAS

You'll know, when you hear the signs that I have marked.
I sat where every bird of heaven comes
in my old place of augury, and heard
bird cries I'd never known. They screeched about
goaded by madness, inarticulate.
I marked that they were tearing one another
with claws of murder. I could hear the wing-beats.
I was afraid, so straightaway I tried
burnt sacrifice upon the flaming altar.
No fire caught my offerings. Slimy ooze
dripped on the ashes, smoked and sputtered there.
Gall burst its bladder, vanished into vapor;

the fat dripped from the bones and would not burn.
These are the omens of the rites that failed,
as this boy here has told me. He's my guide
as I am guide to others.
Why has this sickness struck against the state?
Through your decision.
All of the altars of the town are choked
with leavings of the dogs and birds; their feast
was on that fated, fallen son of Oedipus.
So the gods accept no offering from us,
not prayer, nor flame of sacrifice. The birds
cry out a sound that I cannot distinguish,
gorged with the greasy blood of that dead man.
Think of these things, my son. All men may err,
but error once committed, he's no fool
nor unsuccessful, who can change his mind
and cure the trouble he has fallen in.
Stubbornness and stupidity are twins.
Yield to the dead. Why goad him where he lies?
What use to kill the dead a second time?
I speak for your own good. And I am right.
Learning from a wise counselor is not pain
if what he speaks are profitable words.

CREON

Old man, you all, like bowmen at a mark,
have bent your bows at me. I've had my share
of seers: I've been an item in your accounts.
Make profit, trade in Lydian electrum,
pure gold of India; that's your chief desire.
But you will never cover up that corpse,
not if the very eagles tear their food
from him, and leave it at the throne of Zeus.
I wouldn't give him up for burial
in fear of that pollution. For I know

no mortal being can pollute the gods.
Yes, old Teiresias, human beings fall;
the clever ones the furthest, when they plead
a shameful case so well in hope of profit.

TEIRESIAS

Alas!
What man can tell me, has he thought at all . . .

CREON

What tired cliché's coming from your lips?

TEIRESIAS

How the best of all possessions is good counsel.

CREON

And so is foolishness the worst of all.

TEIRESIAS

But you're infected with that same disease.

CREON

I'm reluctant to be uncivil to a seer . . .

TEIRESIAS

You're that already. You have said I lie.

CREON

Well, the whole crew of seers are money-mad.

TEIRESIAS

And the whole tribe of tyrants grab at gain.

CREON

Do you realize you are talking to a king?

TEIRESIAS

I know. Who helped you save this town you hold?

CREON

You're a wise seer, but you love wickedness.

TEIRESIAS

You'll bring me to speak the unspeakable, very soon.

CREON

Well, speak it out. But do not speak for profit.

TEIRESIAS

Do I seem to have spoken for profit, with regard to you?

CREON

Know this, that you can't buy and sell my policies.

TEIRESIAS

Know well yourself, the sun won't roll its course
many more days, before you come to give
corpse for these corpses, child of your own loins.
For you've confused the upper and lower worlds.
You settled a living person without honor
in a tomb; you keep up here that which belongs
below, a corpse unburied and unholy.
Not you, nor any god on high should have
any business with this. The violation's yours.
So the patient, foul punishers lie in wait
to track you down: the Furies sent by Hades
and by all gods will even you with your victims.
Now say that I am bribed! The time is close
when men and women shall wail within your house,
and all the cities that you fought in war°
whose sons had burial from wild beasts, or dogs,
or birds that brought the stench of your great wrong
back to each hearth, they all will move against you.
A bowman, as you said, I send my shafts,
since you provoked me, straight. You'll feel the wound.
    Boy, take me home now. Let him spend his rage
on younger men, and learn to calm his tongue,
and keep a better mind than now he does.

*(Exit, to the side.)*

CHORUS LEADER

Lord, he has gone. Terrible prophecies!
And since the time my hair turned gray from black,
his sayings to the city have been true.

CREON

I also know this. And my mind is torn.
To yield is dreadful. But to stand against him,
and shatter my spirit in doom is dreadful too.

CHORUS LEADER

Now you must seek good counsel, and take advice.

CREON

What must I do? Speak, and I shall obey.

CHORUS LEADER

Go free the maiden from that rocky house;
and bury the dead who lies in readiness.

CREON

This is your counsel? You would have me yield?

CHORUS LEADER

Quick as you can. The gods move very fast
when they bring ruin on misguided men.

CREON

How hard, abandonment of my desire!
But I can fight necessity no more.

CHORUS LEADER

Do it yourself. Leave it to no one else.

CREON

I'll go at once. Come, followers, to your work.
You that are here round up the other fellows.
Take axes with you, hurry to that place
that overlooks us there.
And I, since my decision's overturned,

the one who bound her will set her free myself.
I've come to fear it's best to hold the laws
of old tradition to the end of life.

*(Exit, to the side.)*

CHORUS [*singing*]

STROPHE A

*God of the many names, Semele's proud delight,*
*child of Olympian thunder, Italy's master,*
*lord of Eleusis, where all men come*
*to Mother Demeter's plain:*
*Bacchus, who dwell in Thebes,*
*by Ismenus' running water,*
*where wild Bacchic women are at home,*
*on the soil of the dragon seed.*

ANTISTROPHE A

*Seen in the glaring flame, high on the double crags,*
*with the nymphs of Parnassus at play on the hill,*
*seen by Castalia's fresh fountain:*
*you come from the ivied heights*
*and the green grape-filled coast of Euboea.*
*In immortal words they cry*
*your name, lord, who watch the roads,*
*the many streets of Thebes.*

STROPHE B

*This is your city, honored beyond the rest,*
*the town of your mother's miracle-death.*
*Now, as we wrestle with grim disease,*
*come with healing step along Parnassus' slope*
*or over the resounding sea.*

ANTISTROPHE B

*Leader in dance of the fire-pulsing stars,*
*overseer of the voices of night,*
*child of Zeus, be manifest,*

*with due companionship of maenads dancing*
*and honoring their lord, Iacchus.*

*(Enter Messenger, from the side.)*

MESSENGER

Neighbors of Cadmus, and Amphion's house,
there is no kind of state in human life
which I would now dare either praise or blame.
Fortune sets straight, and Fortune overturns
the happy or unhappy, day by day.
No prophecy can deal with men's affairs.
Creon was envied once, as I believe,
for having saved this city from its foes
and having got full power in this land.
He steered it well. And he had noble sons.
Now everything is gone.
Yes, when a man has lost all happiness,
he's not alive. Call him a breathing corpse.
Be very rich at home. Live as a king.
But once your joy has gone, though these are left
they are smoke's shadow to lost happiness.

CHORUS LEADER

What is the grief of princes that you bring?

MESSENGER

They're dead. The living are responsible.

CHORUS LEADER

Who died? Who did the murder? Tell us now.

MESSENGER

Haemon is gone. His own flesh and blood did him in.

CHORUS LEADER

But whose arm struck? His father's or his own?

MESSENGER

He killed himself, angry at his father's killing.

CHORUS LEADER

Seer, all too true the prophecy you told!

MESSENGER

This is the state of things. Now make your plans.

*(Enter Eurydice, from the palace.)*

CHORUS LEADER

Eurydice is with us now, I see.
Creon's poor wife. She may have come by chance.
She may have heard something about her son.

EURYDICE

I heard your talk as I was coming out
to greet the goddess Pallas with my prayer.
And as I moved the bolts that held the door
I heard the voice of family disaster.
I fell back fainting in my women's arms.
But say again, just what is the news you bring.
I, whom you speak to, have known grief before.

MESSENGER

Dear lady, I was there, and I shall tell,
leaving out nothing of the true account.
Why should I make it soft for you with tales
to prove myself a liar? Truth is right.
I followed your husband to the plain's far edge,
where Polyneices' corpse was lying still
unpitied. The dogs had torn him all apart.
We prayed the goddess of all journeyings,
and Pluto, that they turn their wrath to kindness;
we gave the final purifying bath,
then burned the poor remains on new-cut boughs,
and heaped a high mound of his native earth.
Then turned we to the maiden's rocky bed,
approaching Hades' hollow marriage chamber.
But, still far off, one of us heard a voice
in keen lament by that unblest abode.

He ran and told the master. As Creon came
he heard confusion crying. He groaned and spoke:
"Am I a prophet now, and do I tread
the saddest of all roads I ever trod?
My son's voice crying! Servants, run up close,
stand by the tomb and look, push through the crevice
where we built the pile of rock, right to the entry.
Find out if that is Haemon's voice I hear
or if the gods are tricking me indeed."
We obeyed the order of our mournful master.
In the far corner of the tomb we saw
her, hanging by the neck, caught in a noose
of her own linen veiling.
Haemon embraced her as she hung, and mourned
his bride's destruction, dead and gone below,
his father's actions, the unfated marriage.
When Creon saw him, he groaned terribly,
and went toward him, and called him with lament:
"What have you done, what did you have in mind,
what happened so as thus to ruin you?
Come out, my child, I do beseech you, come!"
The boy looked at him with his angry eyes,
spat in his face and spoke no further word.
He drew his sword, but as his father ran,
he missed his aim. Then the unhappy boy,
in anger at himself, leant on the blade:
it entered, half its length, into his side.
While he was conscious he embraced the maiden,
holding her gently. Last, he gasped out blood,
red blood on her white cheek.
Corpse on a corpse he lies. He found his marriage,
its celebration in the halls of Hades.
So he has made it very clear to men
that to reject good counsel is a crime.

*(Exit Eurydice, back into the palace.)*

CHORUS LEADER

What do you make of this? The queen has gone
in silence, with no word of evil or of good.

MESSENGER

I wonder at her, too. But we can hope
that she has gone to mourn her son within
with her own women, not before the town.
She knows discretion. She will do no wrong.

CHORUS LEADER

I am not sure. This muteness may portend
as great disaster as a loud lament.

MESSENGER

I will go in and see if some deep plan
hides in her heart's wild pain. You may be right.
There can be heavy danger in mute grief.

*(Exit the Messenger into the palace. Creon enters from the side with his followers. They are carrying Haemon's body on a bier.)*

CHORUS [*chanting*]

*But look, the king draws near.*
*His own hand brings*
*the witness of his crime,*
*the doom he brought on himself.*

CREON [*singing in what follows, while the Chorus and Messenger speak*]

STROPHE A

*O crimes of my wicked heart,*
*harshness bringing death.*
*You see the killer, you see the kin he killed.*
*My planning was all unblest.*
*Son, you have died too soon.*
*Oh, you have gone away*
*through my fault, not your own.*

CHORUS LEADER

You have learned justice, though it comes too late.

CREON

*Yes, I have learned in sorrow. It was a god who struck,*
*who has weighted my head with disaster; he drove me to wild strange ways,*
*his heavy heel on my joy.*
*Oh sorrows, sorrows of men.*

*(Reenter the Messenger, from the palace.)*

MESSENGER

Master, you hold one sorrow in your hands
but you have more, stored up inside the house.

CREON

*What further suffering can come on me?*

MESSENGER

Your wife has died. The dead man's mother indeed,
poor soul, with wounds freshly inflicted.

CREON

ANTISTROPHE A

*Hades, harbor of all,*
*you have destroyed me now.*
*Terrible news to hear, horror the tale you tell.*
*I was dead, and you kill me again.*
*Boy, did I hear you right?*
*Did you say the queen was dead,*
*slaughter on slaughter heaped?*

*(The central doors of the palace open, and the corpse of Eurydice is revealed.)*

CHORUS LEADER

Now you can see. Concealment is all over.

CREON

*My second sorrow is here. Surely no fate remains*
*which can strike me again. Just now, I held my son in my arms.*
*And now I see her dead.*
*Woe for the mother and son.*

MESSENGER

There, by the altar, dying on the sword,°
her eyes fell shut. She wept her older son,
Megareus, who died before, and this one. Finally
she cursed you as the killer of her children.

CREON

STROPHE B

*I am mad with fear. Will no one strike*
*and kill me with cutting sword?*
*Sorrowful, soaked in sorrow to the bone!*

MESSENGER

Yes, for she held you guilty in the death
of him before you, and the elder dead.

CREON

How did she die?

MESSENGER

Struck home at her own heart
when she had heard of Haemon's suffering.

CREON

*This is my guilt, all mine. I killed you, I say it clear.*
*Servants, take me away, out of the sight of men.*
*I who am nothing more than nothing now.*

CHORUS LEADER

Your plan is good—if any good is left.
Best to cut short our sorrow.

CREON

ANTISTROPHE B

*Let me go, let me go. May death come quick,*
*bringing my final day!*
*O let me never see tomorrow's dawn.*

CHORUS LEADER

That is the future's. We must look to now.
What will be is in other hands than ours.

CREON

All my desire was in that prayer of mine.

CHORUS LEADER

Pray not again. No mortal can escape
the doom prepared for him.

CREON [*singing*]

*Take me away at once, the frantic man who killed*
*my son, against my meaning, and you too, my wife.*
*I cannot look at either, I cannot rest.*
*My life is warped past cure. Fate unbearable*
*has leapt down on my head.*

(*Creon and his attendants enter the palace.*)

CHORUS [*chanting*]

*Our happiness depends*
*on wisdom all the way.*
*The gods must have their due.*
*Great words by men of pride*
*bring greater blows upon them.*
*So wisdom comes to the old.*

# OEDIPUS THE KING

*Translated by* DAVID GRENE

# OEDIPUS THE KING

*Characters* OEDIPUS, king of Thebes
A PRIEST
CREON, his brother-in-law (Jocasta's brother)
CHORUS of old men of Thebes
TEIRESIAS, an old blind prophet
JOCASTA, his wife (and mother)
FIRST MESSENGER
A HERDSMAN
SECOND MESSENGER

*Scene: In front of the palace of Oedipus at Thebes. On one side stands the Priest with a crowd of children.*

*(Enter Oedipus, from the palace door.)*

OEDIPUS

Children, young sons and daughters of old Cadmus,
why do you sit here with your suppliant crowns?
The town is heavy with a mingled burden
of sounds and smells, of groans and hymns and incense;
I did not think it fit that I should hear
of this from messengers but came myself—
I, Oedipus whom all men call the Great.

*(To the Priest.)*

You're old and they are young; come, speak for them.
What do you fear or want, that you sit here
suppliant? Indeed I'm willing to give all

that you may need; I would be very hard
should I not pity suppliants like these.

PRIEST

O ruler of my country, Oedipus,
you see our company around the altar;
you see our ages; some of us, like these,
who cannot yet fly far, and some of us
heavy with age; these children are the chosen
among the young, and I the priest of Zeus.
Within the market place sit others crowned
with suppliant garlands, at the double shrine
of Pallas and the temple where Ismenus
gives oracles by fire. King, you yourself
have seen our city reeling like a wreck
already; it can scarcely lift its prow
out of the depths, out of the bloody surf.
A blight is on the fruitful plants of the earth,
a blight is on the cattle in the fields,
a blight is on our women that no children
are born to them; a god that carries fire,
a deadly pestilence, is on our town,
strikes us and spares not, and the house of Cadmus
is emptied of its people while black Death
grows rich in groaning and in lamentation.
We have not come as suppliants to this altar
because we think of you as of a god,
but rather judging you the first of men
in all the chances of this life and when
we mortals have to do with more than man.
You came and by your coming saved our city,
freed us from tribute which we paid of old
to the Sphinx, cruel singer. This you did
in virtue of no knowledge we could give you,
in virtue of no teaching; it was god
that aided you, men say, and you are held

with god's assistance to have saved our lives.
Now Oedipus, greatest in all men's eyes,
here falling at your feet we all entreat you,
find us some strength for rescue.
Perhaps you'll hear a wise word from some god,
perhaps you will learn something from a man
(for I have seen that for those with experience
the outcomes of their counsels live the most).
Noblest of men, go, and raise up our city,
go—and give heed. For now this land of ours
calls you its savior since you saved it once.
So, let us never speak about your reign
as of a time when first our feet were set
secure and straight, but later fell to ruin.
Raise up our city, save it and set it straight.
Once you have brought us luck with happy omen;
be no less now in fortune.
If you will rule this land, as now you rule it,
better to rule it full of men than empty.
For neither tower nor ship is anything
when empty, and none live in it together.

OEDIPUS

I pity you, children. You have come full of longing,
but I have known the story before you told it
only too well. I know you are all sick,
yet there is not one of you, sick though you are,
that is as sick as I myself.
Your several sorrows each have single scope
and touch but one of you. My spirit groans
for city and myself and you at once.
You have not roused me like a man from sleep;
know that I have given many tears to this,
gone many ways wandering in thought.
But as I thought I found only one remedy
and that I took. I sent Menoeceus' son

Creon, Jocasta's brother, to Apollo,
to his Pythian temple,
that he might learn there by what act or word
I could save this city. As I count the days,
it worries me what he's doing; he is gone
far longer than he needed for the journey.
But when he comes, then, may I prove a villain,
if I shall not do all the god commands.

PRIEST

Your words are opportune: for here, your men
signal that Creon is this moment coming.

OEDIPUS

O holy lord Apollo, may his news
be bright for us and bring us light and safety.°

PRIEST

It is happy news, I think, for else his head
would not be crowned with sprigs of fruitful laurel.

*(Enter Creon, from one side.)*

OEDIPUS

We will know soon,
he's within hail. Lord Creon, my good kinsman,
what is the word you bring us from the god?

CREON

A good word—for even things quite hard to bear,
if the final issue turns out well,
I count complete good fortune.

OEDIPUS

What do you mean? What you have said so far
leaves me uncertain whether to trust or fear.

CREON

If you'll hear my news in the presence of these others
I am ready to speak, or else to go within.

OEDIPUS

Speak it to all; the grief I bear, I bear it
more for these people than for my own life.

CREON

I will tell you, then, what I heard from the god.
King Phoebus in plain words commanded us
to drive out a pollution from our land,
pollution grown ingrained within the soil;
drive it out, said the god, not cherish it,
till it's past cure.

OEDIPUS

What is the rite
of purification? How shall it be done?

CREON

By banishing a man, or expiation
of blood by blood, since it is murder guilt
which shakes our city in this destroying storm.

OEDIPUS

Who is this man whose fate the god pronounces?

CREON

My Lord, before you piloted the state
we had a king called Laius.

OEDIPUS

I know of him by hearsay. I never saw him.

CREON

The god commanded clearly: that we must
punish with force this dead man's murderers,
whoever they are.

OEDIPUS

Where are they in the world? Where would a trace
of this old crime be found? It would be hard
to guess where.

CREON

The guilt is in this land;
that which is sought can be found;
the unheeded thing escapes:
so said the god.

OEDIPUS

Was it at home, or in the countryside
that death came to Laius, or traveling abroad?

CREON

He left, he said himself, upon an embassy,
but never returned after he set out from home.

OEDIPUS

Was there no messenger, no fellow traveler
who saw what happened? Such a one might tell
something of use.

CREON

They were all killed save one. He fled in terror
and he could tell us nothing in clear terms
of what he knew, except for one thing only.

OEDIPUS

What was it?
If we could even find a slim beginning
in which to hope, we might discover much.

CREON

This man said that the robbers they encountered
were many and the hands that did the murder
were many; it was no man's single power.

OEDIPUS

How could a robber dare a deed like this
were he not helped with money from the city?

CREON

That indeed was thought. But Laius was dead
and in our trouble there was none to help.

OEDIPUS

What trouble was so great to hinder you
inquiring out the murder of your king?

CREON

The riddling Sphinx induced us to neglect
mysterious crimes and rather seek solution
of troubles at our feet.

OEDIPUS

I'll begin again and bring this all to light.
Fittingly King Phoebus took this care
about the dead, and you too, fittingly.
And justly you will see in me an ally,
a champion of this country and the god.
For when I drive pollution from the land
I will not serve a distant friend's advantage,
but act in my own interest. Whoever
he was that killed the king may readily
wish to dispatch me with his murderous hand;
so helping the dead king I help myself.
Come, children, take your suppliant boughs and go;
up from the altars now. Call the assembly
and let the people of Cadmus meet and know
that I'll do everything. God will decide
whether we shall prosper or shall fail.

PRIEST

Rise, children—it was this we came to seek,
which of himself the king now offers us.
May Phoebus who gave us the oracle
come to our rescue and stop the plague.

*(Exit all. The Chorus enters from the side.)*

CHORUS [*singing*]

STROPHE A

*What is the sweet spoken word of god from the shrine of Pytho*
*rich in gold*

*that has come to glorious Thebes?*
*I am stretched on the rack of doubt, and terror and trembling hold*
*my heart, O Delian Healer, and I worship full of fears*
*for what doom you will bring to pass, new or renewed in the revolving years.*
*Speak to me, immortal voice,*
*child of golden Hope.*

ANTISTROPHE A

*First I call on you, Athena, deathless daughter of Zeus,*
*and Artemis, Earth upholder,*
*who sits in the midst of the marketplace in the throne which men call Fame,*
*and Phoebus, the far-shooter, three averters of Fate,*
*come to us now, if ever before, when ruin rushed upon the state,*
*you drove destruction's flame away*
*out of our land.*

STROPHE B

*Our sorrows defy number;*
*all the ship's timbers are rotten;*
*taking of thought is no spear for the driving away of the plague.*
*There are no growing children in this famous land;*
*there are no women bearing the pangs of childbirth.*
*You may see them one with another, like birds swift on the wing,*
*quicker than fire unmastered,*
*speeding away to the coast of the Western god.*

ANTISTROPHE B

*In the unnumbered deaths*
*of its people the city dies;*
*the children that are born lie dead on the naked earth*
*unpitied, spreading contagion of death; and grey-haired mothers and wives*
*everywhere stand at the altar's edge, suppliant, moaning;*
*the hymn to the healing god rings out, but with it the wailing voices are blended.*

*From these our sufferings grant us, O golden Daughter of Zeus,*
*glad-faced deliverance.*

STROPHE C

*There is no clash of brazen shields but our fight is with the war god,*
*a war god ringed with the cries of men, a savage god who burns us;*
*grant that he turn in racing course backward out of our country's bounds*
*to the great palace of Amphitrite or where the waves of the Thracian sea*
*deny the stranger safe anchorage.*
*Whatsoever escapes the night*
*at last the light of day revisits;°*
*so smite him, Father Zeus,*
*beneath your thunderbolt,*
*for you are the lord of the lightning, the lightning that carries fire.*

ANTISTROPHE C

*And your unconquered arrow shafts, winged by the golden-corded bow,*
*Lycian king, I beg to be at our side for help;*
*and the gleaming torches of Artemis with which she scours the*
*Lycian hills,*
*and I call on the god with the turban of gold, who gave his name*
*to this country of ours,*
*the Bacchic god with the wind-flushed face,*
*you who travel with the maenad company crying Euhoi,*
*come with your torch of pine;*
*for the god that is our enemy is a god unhonored among the gods.*

*(Enter Oedipus.)*

OEDIPUS

For what you ask me—if you will hear my words,
and hearing welcome them and fight the plague,
you will find strength and lightening of your load.
Listen now to me; what I say to you, I say
as one that is a stranger to the story

as stranger to the deed. For I would not
be far upon the track if I alone
were tracing it without a clue or helper.
But since, though late, I also have become
a citizen among you, citizens—
now I proclaim to all the men of Thebes:
who so among you knows the murderer
by whose hand Laius, son of Labdacus,
died—I command him to tell everything
to me—yes, though he fears himself to take the blame
on his own head; for bitter punishment
he shall have none, but leave this land unharmed.
Or if he knows the murderer, another,
maybe a foreigner, still let him speak the truth.
For I will pay him and be grateful, too.
But if you shall keep silence, if perhaps
some one of you, to shield a guilty friend,
or for his own sake shall reject my words—
hear what I shall do then:
I forbid that man, whoever he be, my land,
this land where I hold sovereignty and throne;
and I forbid any to welcome him
or give him greeting or make him a sharer
in sacrifice or offering to the gods,
or give him water for his hands to wash.
I command all to drive him from their homes,
since he is our pollution, as the oracle
of Pytho's god proclaimed him now to me.
So I stand forth a champion of the god
and of the man who died.
Upon the murderer I invoke this curse—°
whether he is one man and all unknown,
or one of many—may he wear out his life
in misery to miserable doom!
If with my knowledge he lives at my hearth
I pray that I myself may feel my curse.

On you I lay my charge to fulfill all this
for me, for the god, and for this land of ours
destroyed and blighted, by the gods forsaken.
Even were this no matter of god's ordinance
it did not fit you so to leave it lie,
unpurified, since a great man is dead,
a king. Indeed, you should have searched it out.
Since I am now the holder of his office,
and have his bed and wife that once was his,
and had his line not been unfortunate
we would have children in common—(but fortune leaped
upon his head)—because of all these things,
I fight in his defense as for my father,
and I shall try all means to take the murderer
of Laius the son of Labdacus
the son of Polydorus and before him
of Cadmus and before him of Agenor.
Those who do not obey me, may the gods
grant no crops springing from the ground they plough
nor children to their women! May a fate
like this, or one still worse than this, consume them!
For you whom these words please, the other Thebans,
may Justice as your ally and all the gods
live with you, blessing you now and for ever!

CHORUS LEADER

As you have held me to my oath, I speak:
I neither killed the king nor can declare
the killer; but since Phoebus set the quest
it is his part to tell us who has done it.

OEDIPUS

Right; but to put compulsion on the gods
against their will—no man can do that.

CHORUS LEADER

May I then say what I think second best?

OEDIPUS

If there's a third best, too, spare not to tell it.

CHORUS LEADER

I know that what the lord Teiresias
sees is most often what the lord Apollo
sees. If you should inquire of this from him
you might find out most clearly.

OEDIPUS

Even in this my actions have not been slow.
On Creon's word I have sent two messengers,
and why the prophet is not here already
I have been wondering.

CHORUS LEADER

His skill apart,
there is besides only an old faint story.

OEDIPUS

What is it? I look at every rumor.

CHORUS LEADER

It was said that he was killed by certain wayfarers.

OEDIPUS

I heard that, too, but no one sees who did it.°

CHORUS LEADER

Yet if he has a share of fear at all,
his courage will not stand firm, hearing your curse.

OEDIPUS

The man who in the doing did not shrink
will fear no word.

CHORUS LEADER

Here comes his prosecutor:
led by these men the godly prophet comes,
in whom alone of humankind the truth
is his by nature.

*(Enter Teiresias from the side, led by a boy.)*

OEDIPUS

Teiresias, you are versed in everything,
things teachable and things not to be spoken,
things of the heaven and earth-creeping things.
You have no eyes but in your mind you know
with what a plague our city is afflicted.
My lord, in you alone we find a champion,
in you alone one that can rescue us.
Perhaps you have not heard the messengers,
but Phoebus sent in answer to our sending
an oracle declaring that our freedom
from this disease would only come when we
should learn the names of those who killed King Laius,
and kill them or expel from our country.
Do not begrudge us messages from birds,
or any other way of prophecy
within your skill; save yourself and the city,
save me; save all of us from this pollution
that lies on us because of that dead man.
We are in your hands; it's a man's most noble labor
to help another when he has the means and power.

TEIRESIAS

Alas, how terrible is wisdom when
it brings no profit to the man that's wise!
This I knew well, but had forgotten it,
else I would not have come here.

OEDIPUS

What is this?
How gloomy you are now you've come!

TEIRESIAS

Let me
go home. It will be easiest for us both

to bear our several destinies to the end
if you will follow my advice.

OEDIPUS

You'd rob us
of this your gift of prophecy? You talk
as one who had no care for law nor love
for Thebes who reared you.

TEIRESIAS

Yes, but I see that even your own words
miss the mark; therefore I must fear for mine.

OEDIPUS

For god's sake if you know of anything,
do not turn from us; all of us kneel to you,
all of us here, your suppliants.

TEIRESIAS

All of you here know nothing. I will not
bring to the light of day my troubles, mine—
rather than call them yours.

OEDIPUS

What do you mean?
You know of something but refuse to speak.
Would you betray us and destroy the city?

TEIRESIAS

I will not bring this pain upon us both,
neither on you nor on myself. Why is it
you question me and waste your labor? I
will tell you nothing.

OEDIPUS

You would provoke a stone! Tell us, you villain,
tell us, and do not stand there quietly
unmoved, unhelpful, set on doing nothing.

TEIRESIAS

You blame my temper but you do not see
your own that lives within you; so you chide
me instead.

OEDIPUS

Who would not feel his temper rise
at words like these with which you shame our city?

TEIRESIAS

Of themselves things will come, although I hide them
and breathe no word of them.

OEDIPUS

Since they will come
tell them to me.

TEIRESIAS

I will say nothing further.
Against this answer let your temper rage
as wildly as you will.

OEDIPUS

Indeed I am
so angry I shall not hold back a jot
of what I think. For I would have you know
I think you were coplotter of the deed
and doer of the deed save insofar
as for the actual killing. Had you had eyes
I would have said alone you murdered him.

TEIRESIAS

Yes? Then I warn you faithfully to keep
the letter of your proclamation and
from this day forth to speak no word of greeting
to these nor me; you are the land's pollution.

OEDIPUS

How shamelessly you started up this taunt!
How do you think you will escape?

TEIRESIAS

I have.
I have escaped; the truth is what I cherish
and that's my strength.

OEDIPUS

And who has taught you truth?
Not your profession surely!

TEIRESIAS

You have taught me,
for you have made me speak against my will.

OEDIPUS

Speak what? Tell me again that I may learn it better.

TEIRESIAS

Did you not understand before or would you
provoke me into speaking?

OEDIPUS

I did not grasp it,
not so to call it known. Say it again.

TEIRESIAS

I say you are the murderer of the king
whose murderer you seek.

OEDIPUS

Not twice you shall
say ghastly things like this and stay unpunished.

TEIRESIAS

Shall I say more to tempt your anger further?

OEDIPUS

As much as you wish; it will be said in vain.

TEIRESIAS

I say that, unknowing, with those you love the best

you live in foulest shame unconsciously
and do not see where you are in calamity.

OEDIPUS

Do you imagine you can always talk
like this, and live to rejoice at it hereafter?

TEIRESIAS

Yes, if the truth has anything of strength.

OEDIPUS

It has, but not for you; it has no strength
for you because you are blind in mind and ears
as well as in your eyes.

TEIRESIAS

You are a poor wretch
to taunt me with the very insults which
everyone soon will heap upon yourself.

OEDIPUS

Your life is one long night so that you cannot
hurt me or any other who sees the light.

TEIRESIAS

It is not fate that I should be your ruin,
Apollo is enough; it is his care
to work this out.

OEDIPUS

Was this your own design
or Creon's?

TEIRESIAS

Creon is no hurt to you.
but you are to yourself.

OEDIPUS

Wealth, kingly rule, and skill outmatching skill

for the contrivance of an envied life!
How great a store of jealousy you are hoarding,
if, for the sake of the office which I hold,
given me by the city, not sought by me,
my friend Creon, friend from the first and loyal,
thus secretly attacks me, secretly
desires to drive me out and secretly
suborns this juggling, trick-devising quack,
this wily beggar who has only eyes
for his own gains, but blindness in his skill.
    For, tell me, where have you seen clear, Teiresias,
with your prophetic mind? When the dark singer,
the Sphinx, was in your country, did you speak
word of deliverance to these citizens?
Yet solving the riddle then was not the province
of a chance comer: it was a prophet's task,
and plainly you had no such gift of prophecy
from birds nor otherwise from any god
to glean a word of knowledge. But I came,
Oedipus, who knew nothing, and I stopped her.
I solved the riddle by my wit alone.
Mine was no knowledge got from birds. And now
you would expel me,
because you think that you will find a place
by Creon's throne. I think you will be sorry,
both you and your accomplice, for your plot
to drive me out. And did I not regard you
as an old man, some suffering would have taught you
that what was in your heart was treason.

CHORUS LEADER

We look at this man's words and yours, my king,
and we find both have spoken them in anger.
We need no angry words but only thought
how we may best hit the god's meaning for us.

TEIRESIAS

If you are king, at least I have the right
no less to speak in my defense against you.
Of that much I am master. I am no slave
of yours, but Loxias', and so I shall not
enroll myself with Creon for my patron.
Since you have taunted me with being blind,
here is my word for you.
You have your eyes but see not where you are
in evil, nor where you live, nor whom you live with.
Do you know who your parents are? Unknowing
you are an enemy to kith and kin
in death, beneath the earth, and in this life.
A deadly footed, double-striking curse,
from father and mother both, shall drive you forth
out of this land, with darkness on your eyes,
that now have such straight vision. Shall there be
a place will not be harbor to your cries,
a corner of Cithaeron will not ring°
in echo to your laments, soon, soon,
when you shall learn the secret of your marriage,
which steered you to a haven in this house,
haven no haven, after lucky voyage?
And of the multitude of other evils
establishing a grim equality°
between you and your children, you know nothing.
So, muddy with contempt my words and Creon's!
Misery shall grind no man as it will you.

OEDIPUS

Is it endurable that I should hear
such words from him? Go and a curse go with you!
Quick, home with you! Away from my house at once!

TEIRESIAS

I would not have come either, had you not called me.

OEDIPUS

I did not know then you would talk like a fool—
or it would have been long before I called you.

TEIRESIAS

I am a fool then, as it seems to you—
but to the parents who begot you, wise.

OEDIPUS

What parents? Stop! Who are they of all the world?

TEIRESIAS

This day will show your birth and will destroy you.

OEDIPUS

How needlessly your riddles darken everything.

TEIRESIAS

But aren't you best at answering such riddles?

OEDIPUS

Yes. Taunt me where you will find me great.

TEIRESIAS

It is this very luck that has destroyed you.

OEDIPUS

I do not care, if it has saved this city.

TEIRESIAS

Well, I will go. Come, boy, lead me away.

OEDIPUS

Yes, lead him off. So long as you are here,
you are a stumbling block and a vexation;
once gone, you will not trouble me again.

TEIRESIAS

I have said
what I came here to say not fearing your
countenance: there is no way you can hurt me.

I tell you, king, this man, this murderer
(whom you have long declared you are in search of,
indicting him in threatening proclamation
as murderer of Laius)—he is here.
In name he is a stranger among citizens
but soon he will be shown to be homegrown,
true native Theban, and he'll have no joy
of the discovery: blindness for sight
and beggary for riches his exchange,
he shall go journeying to a foreign country
tapping his way before him with a stick.
He shall be proved father and brother both
to his own children in his house; to her
that gave him birth, a son and husband both;
a fellow sower in his father's bed
with that same father that he murdered.
Go within, reckon that out, and if you find me
mistaken, say I have no skill in prophecy.

*(Exit separately, Teiresias to the side, Oedipus indoors.)*

CHORUS [*singing*]

STROPHE A

*Who is the man proclaimed*
*by Delphi's prophetic rock*
*as the bloody-handed murderer,*
*the doer of deeds that none dare name?*
*Now is the time for him to run*
*with a stronger foot*
*than wind-swift Pegasus*
*for the child of Zeus leaps in arms upon him*
*with fire and the lightning bolt,*
*and terribly close on his heels*
*are the Fates that never miss.*

ANTISTROPHE A

*Lately from snowy Parnassus*
*clearly the voice flashed forth,*

*bidding everyone track him down,*
*the unknown murderer.*
*In the savage forests he lurks and in*
*the caverns like*
*the mountain bull.*
*He is sad and lonely, and lonely his feet°*
*that carry him far from the navel of earth;*
*but its prophecies, ever living,*
*flutter around his head.*

STROPHE B

*The skilled bird-prophet bewilders me terribly;*
*I do not approve what was said*
*nor can I deny it.*
*I do not know what to say;*
*I am in a flutter of foreboding;*
*I do not see the present*
*nor the past; I never heard of a quarrel between*
*the sons of Labdacus and of Polybus,*
*neither in the past nor now,*
*that I might bring as proof*
*in attacking the popular fame*
*of Oedipus, seeking*
*to take vengeance for undiscovered*
*death in the line of Labdacus.*

ANTISTROPHE B

*Truly Zeus and Apollo are wise*
*and in human things all-knowing;*
*but amongst men there is no*
*distinct judgment, between the prophet*
*and me—which of us is right.*
*One man may pass another in wisdom*
*but I would never agree*
*with those that find fault with the king*
*till I should see the word*
*proved right beyond doubt. For once*

*in visible form the Sphinx*
*came against him, and all of us*
*saw his wisdom and in that test*
*he saved the city. So he will not be condemned by my mind.*

*(Enter Creon, from the side.)*

CREON

Citizens, I have come because I heard
deadly words spread about me, that the king
accuses me. I cannot take that from him.
If he believes that in these present troubles
he has been wronged by me in word or deed
I do not want to live on with the burden
of such a scandal on me. The report
injures me doubly and most vitally—
for I'll be called a traitor to my city
and traitor also to my friends and you.

CHORUS LEADER

Perhaps it was a sudden gust of anger
that forced that insult from him, and no judgment.

CREON

But did he say that it was in compliance
with schemes of mine that the seer told him lies?

CHORUS LEADER

Yes, he said that, but why, I do not know.

CREON

Were his eyes straight in his head? Was his mind right
when he accused me in this fashion?

CHORUS LEADER

I do not know; I have no eyes to see
what princes do. Here comes the king himself.

*(Enter Oedipus, from the palace.)*

OEDIPUS

You, sir, how is it you come here? Have you so much
brazen-faced daring that you venture to
my house although you are proved manifestly
the murderer of that man, and though you tried,
openly, highway robbery of my crown?
For god's sake, tell me what you saw in me,
what cowardice or what stupidity,
that made you lay a plot like this against me?
Did you imagine I should not observe
your crafty scheme that stole upon me or
seeing it, take no means to counter it?
Was it not stupid of you to make the attempt,
to try to hunt down royal power without
the people at your back or friends? For only
with the people at your back and money can
this hunt end in the capture of a crown.

CREON

Do you know what you're doing? Will you listen
to words to answer yours, and then pass judgment?

OEDIPUS

You're quick to speak, but I am slow to grasp you,
for I have found you dangerous—and my foe.

CREON

First of all hear what I shall say to that.

OEDIPUS

At least don't tell me that you are not guilty.

CREON

If you think obstinacy without wisdom
a valuable possession, you are wrong.

OEDIPUS

And you are wrong if you believe that one
can harm a kinsman and then not be punished.

CREON

This is but just—
but tell me, then, of what offense I'm guilty.

OEDIPUS

Did you or did you not urge me to send
to this prophetic mumbler?

CREON

I did indeed,
and I shall stand by what I told you.

OEDIPUS

How long ago is it since Laius . . .

CREON

What about Laius? I don't understand.

OEDIPUS

Vanished—died—was murdered?

CREON

It is long,
a long, long time to reckon.

OEDIPUS

Was this prophet
in the profession then?

CREON

He was, and honored
as highly as he is today.

OEDIPUS

At that time did he say a word about me?

CREON

Never, at least when I was near him.

OEDIPUS

You never made a search for the killer?°

CREON

We searched, indeed, but never learned of anything.

OEDIPUS

Why did our wise old friend not say this then?

CREON

I don't know; and when I know nothing, I
usually hold my tongue.

OEDIPUS

You know this much,
and can declare it if you are truly loyal.

CREON

What is it? If I know, I'll not deny it.

OEDIPUS

That he would not have said that I killed Laius
had he not met with you first.

CREON

You know yourself
whether he said this, but I demand that I
should hear as much from you as you from me.

OEDIPUS

Then hear—I'll not be proved a murderer.

CREON

Well, then. You're married to my sister?

OEDIPUS

Yes,
that I am not disposed to deny.

CREON

You rule
this country giving her an equal share
in the government?

OEDIPUS

Yes, everything she wants
she has from me.

CREON

And I, as third with you,
am rated as the equal of you both?

OEDIPUS

Yes, and it's there you've proved yourself false friend.

CREON

Not if you will reflect on it as I do.
Consider, first, if you think anyone
would choose to rule and fear rather than rule
and sleep peacefully, if the power
were equal in both cases. I, at least,
I was not born with such a frantic yearning
to be a king—but to do what kings do.
And so it is with everyone who has learned
wisdom and self-control. As it stands now,
I get from you all the prizes—and without fear.
But if I were the king myself, I must
do much that went against the grain.
How should despotic rule seem sweeter to me
than painless power and an assured authority?
I am not so deluded yet that I
want other honors than those that come with profit.
Now all men wish me joy; every man greets me;
those who want things from you all fawn on me,
success for them depends upon my favor.
Why should I let all this go to win that?
My mind would not be traitor if it's wise;°
I am no treason lover, by my nature,
nor could I ever bear to join a plot.
Prove what I say. Go to the oracle

at Pytho and inquire about the answers,
if they are as I told you. For the rest,
if you discover I laid any plot
together with the seer, kill me, I say,
not only by your vote but by my own.
But do not charge me on obscure opinion
without some proof to back it. It's not just
lightly to count bad men as honest ones,
nor honest men as bad. To throw away
an honest friend is, as it were, to throw
your life away, which a man loves the best.
In time you'll know all this with certainty;
time is the only test of honest men,
one day is space enough to know who's bad.

CHORUS LEADER

His words are wise, king, for one who fears to fall.
Those who are quick of temper are not safe.

OEDIPUS

When he that plots against me secretly
moves quickly, I must quickly counterplot.
If I wait taking no decisive measure
his business will be done, and mine be spoiled.

CREON

What do you want to do then? Banish me?

OEDIPUS

No, certainly; kill you, not banish you.

CREON

I do not understand why you resent me so.°

. . . . . . . . . . . . . . . . . . .

OEDIPUS

You speak as if you'll not listen nor obey.

CREON

I do not think that you've your wits about you.

OEDIPUS

For my own interests, yes.

CREON

But for mine, too,
you should think equally.

OEDIPUS

You are a traitor.

CREON

Suppose you do not understand?

OEDIPUS

But yet
I must be ruler.

CREON

Not if you rule badly.

OEDIPUS

O, city, city!

CREON

I too have some share
in the city; it is not yours alone.

CHORUS LEADER

Stop, my lords! Here—and in the nick of time
I see Jocasta coming from the house;
with her help settle the quarrel that now stirs you.

*(Enter Jocasta, from the palace.)*

JOCASTA

For shame! Why have you raised this foolish squabbling?
Are you not ashamed to air your private
troubles when the country's sick? Go inside, Oedipus,
and you, too, Creon, go to your house. Don't magnify
your nothing troubles.

CREON

My sister: Oedipus,
your husband, thinks he has the right to do
terrible wrongs to me—he is choosing
between either banishing or killing me.°

OEDIPUS

He's right, Jocasta; for I find him plotting
with evil tricks against my person.

CREON

May never god bless me! May I die
accursed, if I've been guilty in any way
of any of the charges you bring against me!

JOCASTA

I beg you, Oedipus, trust him in this,
spare him for the sake of his oath to god,
for my sake, and the sake of those who stand here.

CHORUS [*singing in what follows, while Oedipus speaks*]

STROPHE

*Think carefully: be gracious, be merciful,*
*we beg of you.*

OEDIPUS

In what would you have me yield?

CHORUS

*He has never been foolish in the past.*
*He is strong in his oath now.*
*Spare him.*

OEDIPUS

Do you know what you ask?

CHORUS

*Yes.*

OEDIPUS

Tell me then.

CHORUS

*He has been your friend, he has sworn an oath; do not cast him away dishonored on an obscure conjecture.*

OEDIPUS

I would have you know that this request of yours
really requests my death or banishment.

CHORUS

*May the sun god, king of gods, forbid!*
*May I die without god's blessing, without friends' help,*
*if I had any such thought.*
*But my spirit is broken by my unhappiness for my wasting country;*
*and this would but add troubles amongst ourselves to the other troubles.*

OEDIPUS

Well, let him go then—if I must die ten times for it,
or be sent out dishonored into exile.
It is your lips praying for him I pitied,
not his; wherever he is, I shall hate him.

CREON

I see you sulk in yielding and you're dangerous
when you are out of temper; natures like yours
are justly hardest for themselves to bear.

OEDIPUS

Leave me alone! Take yourself off, I tell you.

CREON

I'll go. You have not known me, but they have,
and they have known my innocence.

*(Exit Creon, to the side.)*

CHORUS [*singing in what follows, while Jocasta and Oedipus speak*]

ANTISTROPHE

*Won't you take him inside, lady?*

JOCASTA

Yes, when I've found out what was the matter.

CHORUS

*There was some misconceived suspicion*
*of a story, and on the other side*
*the sting of injustice.*

JOCASTA

So, on both sides?

CHORUS

*Yes.*

JOCASTA

What was the story?

CHORUS

*I think it best, in the interests of our country,*
*to leave it where it ended.*

OEDIPUS

You see where you have ended, straight of judgment
although you are, by softening my anger.

CHORUS

*Sir, I have said before and I say again—*
*be sure that I would have been proved a madman,*
*bankrupt in sane council,*
*if I should put you away, you who steered the country I love safely*
*when it was crazed with troubles. God grant that now, too,*
*you may prove a fortunate guide for us.*

JOCASTA

Tell me, my lord, I beg of you, what was it
that roused your anger so?

OEDIPUS

Yes, I will tell you.
I honor you more than I honor them.
It was Creon and the plots he laid against me.

JOCASTA

Tell me—if you can clearly tell the quarrel—

OEDIPUS

Creon says that I'm the murderer of Laius.

JOCASTA

Of his own knowledge or on information?

OEDIPUS

He sent this rascal prophet to me, since
he keeps his own mouth clean of any guilt.

JOCASTA

Do not concern yourself about this matter;
listen to me and learn that human beings
have no part in the craft of prophecy.
Of that I'll show you a short proof.
There was an oracle once that came to Laius—
I will not say that it was Phoebus' own,
but it was from his servants—and it told him
that it was fate that he should die a victim
at the hands of his own son, a son to be born
of Laius and me. But, see now, he,
the king, was killed by foreign highway robbers
at a place where three roads meet—so goes the story;
and for the son—before three days were out
after his birth King Laius pierced his ankles
and by the hands of others cast him forth
upon a pathless hillside. So Apollo
failed to fulfill his oracle to the son,
that he should kill his father, and to Laius
also proved false in that the thing he feared,
death at his son's hands, never came to pass.
So clear in this case were the oracles,
describing the future. Give them no heed, I say;
what the god discovers need of, easily
he will show to us himself.

OEDIPUS

O dear Jocasta,
as I hear this from you, what wandering in my soul
now comes upon me—what turbulence of mind.

JOCASTA

What trouble is it, that you turn again
and speak like this?

OEDIPUS

I thought I heard you say
that Laius was killed at a crossroads.

JOCASTA

Yes, that was how the story went and still
that word goes round.

OEDIPUS

Where is this place, Jocasta,
where he was murdered?

JOCASTA

Phocis is the country
and the road splits there, one of two roads from Delphi,
another comes from Daulia.

OEDIPUS

How long ago was this?

JOCASTA

The news came to the city just before
you became king and all men's eyes looked to you.
What is it, Oedipus, that's in your mind?

OEDIPUS

What have you designed, O Zeus, to do with me?

JOCASTA

What is the thought that troubles your heart?

OEDIPUS

Don't ask me yet—tell me of Laius—
How did he look? How old or young was he?

JOCASTA

He was a tall man and his hair was grizzled
already—partly white—and in his form
not unlike you.

OEDIPUS

O god, I think I have
called curses on myself in ignorance.

JOCASTA

What do you mean? I'm frightened now, my king,
when I look at you.

OEDIPUS

I have a deadly fear
that the old seer had eyes. You'll show me more
if you can tell me one more thing.

JOCASTA

I will.
I'm frightened—but you ask and I will listen,
I'll tell you all I know.

OEDIPUS

How was his company?
Had he few with him when he went this journey,
or many servants, as would suit a prince?

JOCASTA

In all there were but five, and among them
a herald; and one carriage for the king.

OEDIPUS

It's plain—it's plain—who was it told you this?

JOCASTA
The only servant that escaped safe home.

OEDIPUS
Is he at home now?

JOCASTA
No, when he came home again
and saw that you were king and Laius dead,
he came to me and touched my hand and begged
that I should send him to the fields to be
my shepherd and so he might see the city
as far off as he could. So I
sent him away. He was an honest man,
as slaves go, and was worthy of far more
than what he asked of me.

OEDIPUS
So could he quickly now be brought back here?

JOCASTA
It can be done. Why is your heart so set on this?

OEDIPUS
O dear Jocasta, I am full of fears
that I have spoken far too much; and therefore
I wish to see this shepherd.

JOCASTA
He will come;
but, Oedipus, I think I too deserve
to know what is it that disquiets you.

OEDIPUS
It shall not be kept from you, since my mind
has gone so far with its forebodings. Whom
should I confide in rather than you? Who is there
of more importance to me who have passed
through such a fortune?
Polybus was my father, king of Corinth,

and Merope, the Dorian, my mother.
I was held greatest of the citizens
in Corinth till a curious chance befell me,
as I shall tell you—curious, indeed,
but hardly worth the store I set upon it.
There was a dinner and at it was a man,
a drunken man, who accused me in his drink
of being bastard. I was furious
but held my temper under for that day.
Next day I went and taxed my parents with it;
they took the insult ill and came down hard
on the man who had uttered it. So I
was comforted with regard to the two of them;
but still this thing rankled with me, for the story
kept on recurring. And so I went at last
to Pytho, though my parents did not know.
But Phoebus sent me home again unhonored
in what I came to learn, but he foretold
other and desperate horrors to befall me,
that I was fated to lie with my mother,
and show to daylight an accursed breed
which men would not endure, and I was doomed
to be murderer of the father that begot me.
When I heard this I fled, and in the days
that followed I would measure from the stars
the whereabouts of Corinth—yes, I fled
to somewhere where I should not see fulfilled
the infamies told in that dreadful oracle.
And as I journeyed I came to the place
where, as you say, this king met with his death.
Jocasta, I will tell you the whole truth.
When I was near that branching of the crossroads,
going on foot, I was encountered by
a herald and a carriage with a man in it,
just as you tell me. He that led the way
and the old man himself wanted to thrust me

out of the road by force. I became angry
and struck the coachman who was pushing me.
When the old man saw this he waited for his chance,
and as I passed he struck me from his carriage,
full on the head with his two-pointed goad.
He paid for this in full, and more: my stick
quickly struck him backward from the car
and he rolled out of it. And then I killed them
all. If it happens there was any tie
of kinship between this man and Laius,
who is there now more miserable than I,
what man on earth so hated by the gods,
since neither citizen nor foreigner
may welcome me at home or even greet me,
but drive me out of doors? And it is I,
I and no other have so cursed myself.
And I pollute the bed of him I killed
by the hands that killed him. Was I not born evil?
Am I not utterly unclean, if I have to flee
and in my banishment not even see
my kindred nor set foot in my own country,
or otherwise my fate is to be yoked
in marriage with my mother and kill my father,
Polybus who begot me and who reared me?
Would not one rightly judge and say that on me
these things were sent by some malignant god?
O no, no, no—O holy majesty
of god on high, may I not see that day!
May I be gone out of men's sight before
I see the deadly taint of this disaster
come upon me.

CHORUS LEADER

My lord, we fear this too. But till this man
is here and you have heard his story, hope.

OEDIPUS

Yes, I have just this much of hope as well:
to wait until the herdsman comes.

JOCASTA

And what
will you want with him, once he has appeared?

OEDIPUS

I'll tell you; if I find that his story is
the same as yours, I will be clear of guilt.

JOCASTA

What in particular did you learn from my story?

OEDIPUS

You said that he spoke of highway robbers who
killed Laius. Now if he still uses that
same number, I was not the one who killed him.
One man cannot be the same as many.
But if he speaks clearly of one man on his own,
indeed the guilty balance tilts toward me.

JOCASTA

Be sure, at least, that this was how he told the story;
and he cannot unsay this now, for everyone
in the city heard it—not just I alone.
But even if he turns from what he said then,
not ever will he prove, my lord, that rightly
the murder of Laius squares with Apollo's words,
Apollo, who declared that by his son
from me he would be killed. And yet
that poor creature surely did not kill him—
for he himself died first. As far as prophecy
goes, henceforward I won't look to the right
nor to the left hand either.

OEDIPUS

Your opinion's sound. But yet, send someone for
the peasant to bring him here; do not neglect it.

JOCASTA

I will send, and quickly. Now let us go indoors.
I will do nothing except what pleases you.

*(Exit, into the palace.)*

CHORUS [*singing*]

STROPHE A

*May destiny ever find me*
*pious in word and deed*
*prescribed by the laws that live on high:*
*laws begotten in the clear air of heaven,*
*whose only father is Olympus;*
*no mortal nature brought them to birth,*
*no forgetfulness shall lull them to sleep;*
*for god is great in them and grows not old.*

ANTISTROPHE A

*Insolence breeds the tyrant, insolence*
*if it is glutted with a surfeit, unseasonable, unprofitable,*
*climbs to the rooftop and plunges*
*sheer down to the ruin that must be,*
*and there its feet are no service.*
*But I pray that the god may never*
*abolish the eager ambition that profits the state.*
*For I shall never cease to hold the god as our protector.*

STROPHE B

*If a man walks with haughtiness*
*of hand or word and gives no heed*
*to Justice and the shrines of gods*
*despises—may an evil doom*
*smite him for his ill-starred pride of heart!—*
*if he reaps gains without justice*
*and will not hold from impiety*

*and his fingers itch for untouchable things.*
*When such things are done, what man shall contrive*
*to shield his life from the shafts of the god?*
*When such deeds are held in honor,*
*why should I honor the gods in the dance?*

ANTISTROPHE B

*No longer to the holy place,*
*to the navel of earth I'll go*
*to worship, nor to Abae*
*nor to Olympia,*
*unless the oracles are proved to fit,*
*for all men's hands to point at.*
*O Zeus, if you are rightly called*
*the sovereign lord, all-mastering,*
*let this not escape you nor your ever-living power!*
*The oracles concerning Laius*
*are old and dim and men regard them not.*
*Apollo is nowhere clear in honor; the gods' service perishes.*

*(Enter Jocasta from the palace, carrying garlands.)*

JOCASTA

Lords of the land, I have had the thought to go
to the gods' temples, bringing in my hand
garlands and gifts of incense, as you see.
For Oedipus excites himself too much
with all kinds of worries, not conjecturing,
like a man of sense, what will be from what was,
but he is always at the speaker's mercy,
when he speaks terrors. I can do no good
by my advice, and so I come as suppliant
to you, Lycian Apollo, who are nearest.
These are the symbols of my prayer and this
my prayer: grant us escape free of the curse.
Now when we look to him we are all afraid;
he's pilot of our ship and he is frightened.

*(Enter Messenger, from the side.)*

MESSENGER

Might I learn from you, sirs, where is the house of Oedipus?
Or better, if you know, where is the king himself?

CHORUS LEADER

This is his house and he is within; the lady
here is his wife and mother of his children.

MESSENGER

God bless you, lady! God bless your household too!
God bless the noble wife of Oedipus!

JOCASTA

And god bless you, sir, for your kind greeting!
What do you want of us that you have come here?
What have you to tell us?

MESSENGER

Good news, lady.
Good for your house and also for your husband.

JOCASTA

What is your news? And who sent you to us?

MESSENGER

I come from Corinth; the news I bring will give you
pleasure, for sure. Perhaps some pain as well.

JOCASTA

What is it, then, this news of double meaning?

MESSENGER

The people of the Isthmus will choose Oedipus
to be their king. That is the rumor there.

JOCASTA

But isn't their king still aged Polybus?

MESSENGER

No. He is in his grave. Death has got him.

JOCASTA

Is that the truth? Is Oedipus' father dead?

MESSENGER

May I die myself if it be otherwise!

JOCASTA *(To a servant.)*

Be quick and run to tell the king the news!
O oracles of the gods, where are you now?
It was from this man Oedipus fled, long ago,
lest he should be his murderer! And now, by chance,
he is dead, in the course of nature, not killed by him.

*(Enter Oedipus from the palace.)*

OEDIPUS

Dearest Jocasta, why have you sent for me?

JOCASTA

Listen to this man and when you hear, reflect
on what the god's holy oracles have come to.

OEDIPUS

Who is he? What is his message for me?

JOCASTA

He comes from Corinth and tells us that your father
Polybus is no more, but dead and gone.

OEDIPUS

What's this you say, stranger? Tell me yourself.

MESSENGER

If this is what you first want clearly told:
be sure, Polybus has gone down to death.

OEDIPUS

Was it by treachery, or from sickness?

MESSENGER

A small thing will put old bodies asleep.

OEDIPUS

So he died of sickness, it seems—poor old man!

MESSENGER

Yes, and of age—the long years he had measured.

OEDIPUS

Ah! Ah! O dear Jocasta, why should one
look to the Pythian hearth? Why should one look
to the birds screaming overhead? They prophesied
that I should kill my father! But he's dead,
and hidden deep in earth, and I stand here
who never laid a hand on spear against him —
unless perhaps he died of longing for me,
and thus I am his murderer. But they,
the oracles, as they stand—he's taken them
away with him, they're dead as he himself is,
and worthless.

JOCASTA

That I already told you before now.

OEDIPUS

You did, but I was misled by my fear.

JOCASTA

Then lay no more of them to heart, not one.

OEDIPUS

But surely I must fear my mother's bed?

JOCASTA

Why should man fear since chance is all in all
for him, and he can clearly foreknow nothing?
Best to live lightly, as one can, unthinkingly.
As to your mother's marriage bed—do not
feel fear about this: before now, many a man
in his dreams has lain with his own mother.
But he to whom such things are nothing bears
his life most easily.

OEDIPUS

All that you say would be said perfectly
if she were dead; but since she lives I must
still fear, although you talk so well, Jocasta.

JOCASTA

Still in your father's death there's light of comfort?

OEDIPUS

Great light of comfort; but I fear the living.

MESSENGER

Who is the woman that makes you afraid?

OEDIPUS

Merope, old man, Polybus' wife.

MESSENGER

What about her frightens the queen and you?

OEDIPUS

A terrible oracle, stranger, from the gods.

MESSENGER

Can it be told? Or does the sacred law
forbid another to have knowledge of it?

OEDIPUS

O no! Once on a time Loxias said
that I should lie with my own mother and
take on my hands the blood of my own father.
And so for these long years I've lived away
from Corinth; it has been to my good fortune;
but yet it's sweet to see the face of parents.

MESSENGER

This was the fear that drove you out of Corinth?

OEDIPUS

Old man, I did not wish to kill my father.

MESSENGER

Why should I not free you from this fear, sir,
since I have come to you in all goodwill?

OEDIPUS

You would not find me thankless if you did.

MESSENGER

Why, it was just for this I brought the news—
to earn your thanks when you had come safe home.

OEDIPUS

No, I will never come near my parents.

MESSENGER

Son,
it's very plain you don't know what you're doing.

OEDIPUS

What do you mean, old man? For god's sake, tell me.

MESSENGER

If your homecoming is checked by fears like these.

OEDIPUS

Yes, I'm afraid that Phoebus may prove right.

MESSENGER

Pollution from your parents?

OEDIPUS

Yes, old man;
that is my constant terror.

MESSENGER

Do you know
that all your fears are empty?

OEDIPUS

How is that,
if they are father and mother and I their son?

MESSENGER

Because Polybus was no kin to you in blood.

OEDIPUS

What, was not Polybus my father?

MESSENGER

No more than I but just so much.

OEDIPUS

How can
my father be my father as much as one
that's nothing to me?

MESSENGER

Neither he nor I
begot you.

OEDIPUS

Why then did he call me son?

MESSENGER

A gift he took you from these hands of mine.

OEDIPUS

Did he love so much what he took from another's hand?

MESSENGER

His childlessness before persuaded him.

OEDIPUS

Was I a child you bought or found when I
was given to him?

MESSENGER

On Cithaeron's slopes
in the twisting thickets you were found.

OEDIPUS

And why
were you a traveler in those parts?

MESSENGER

I was
in charge of mountain flocks.

OEDIPUS

You were a shepherd?
A hireling vagrant?

MESSENGER

Yes, but at least at that time
the man that saved your life, son.

OEDIPUS

What ailed me when you took me in your arms?

MESSENGER

In that your ankles should be witnesses.

OEDIPUS

Why do you speak of that old pain?

MESSENGER

I loosed you;
the tendons of your feet were pierced and fettered—

OEDIPUS

My swaddling clothes brought me a rare disgrace.

MESSENGER

so that from this you're called your present name.

OEDIPUS

Was this my father's doing or my mother's?
For god's sake, tell me.

MESSENGER

I don't know, but he
who gave you to me has more knowledge than I.

OEDIPUS

You yourself did not find me then? You took me
from someone else?

MESSENGER

Yes, from another shepherd.

OEDIPUS

Who was he? Do you know him well enough
to tell?

MESSENGER

He was called one of Laius' men.

OEDIPUS

You mean the king who reigned here in the old days?

MESSENGER

Yes, he was that man's shepherd.

OEDIPUS

Is he alive
still, so that I could see him?

MESSENGER

You who live here
would know that best.

OEDIPUS

Do any of you here
know of this shepherd whom he speaks about
in town or in the fields? Tell me. It's time
that this was found out once for all.

CHORUS LEADER

I think he is none other than the peasant
whom you have sought to see already; but
Jocasta here can tell us best of that.

OEDIPUS

Jocasta, do you know about this man
whom we have sent for? Is that the man he mentions?

JOCASTA

Why ask of whom he spoke? Don't give it heed;

nor try to keep in mind what has been said.
It will be wasted labor.

OEDIPUS

With such clues
I could not fail to bring my birth to light.

JOCASTA

I beg you—do not hunt this out—I beg you,
if you have any care for your own life.
What I am suffering is enough.

OEDIPUS

Keep up
your heart, Jocasta. Though I'm proved a slave,
thrice slave, and though my mother be thrice slave,
you'll not be shown to be of lowly lineage.

JOCASTA

O be persuaded by me, I entreat you;
do not do this.

OEDIPUS

I will not be persuaded to let be
the chance of finding out the whole thing clearly.

JOCASTA

It is because I wish you well that I
give you this counsel—and it's the best counsel.

OEDIPUS

Then the best counsel vexes me, and has
for some while since.

JOCASTA

O Oedipus, god help you!
God keep you from the knowledge of who you are!

OEDIPUS

Here, someone, go and fetch the shepherd for me;
and let her find her joy in her rich family!

JOCASTA

O Oedipus, unhappy Oedipus!
that is all I can call you, and the last thing
that I shall ever call you.

*(Exit Jocasta into the palace.)*

CHORUS LEADER

Why has the queen gone, Oedipus, in wild
grief rushing from us? I am afraid that trouble
will break out of this silence.

OEDIPUS

Break out what will! I at least shall be
willing to see my ancestry, though humble.
Perhaps she is ashamed of my low birth,
for she has all a woman's high-flown pride.
But I account myself a child of Fortune,
beneficent goddess, and I shall not be
dishonored. Fortune's the mother from whom I spring;
the months, my brothers, marked me, now as small,
and now again as mighty. Such is my breeding,
and I shall never prove so false to it,
as not to find the secret of my birth.

CHORUS [*singing*]

STROPHE

*If I am a prophet and wise of heart*
*you shall not fail, Cithaeron,*
*by the limitless sky, you shall not!—*
*to know that tomorrow's full moon*
*shall honor you as Oedipus' compatriot,*
*his mother and nurse at once;*
*and that you shall be honored in dancing by us,*
*for rendering service to our king.*
*Apollo, to whom we cry, find these things pleasing!*

ANTISTROPHE

*Who was it bore you, child? One of*

*the long-lived nymphs who lay with Pan—*
*the father who treads the hills?*
*Or was your mother a bride of Loxias? The grassy slopes*
*are all of them dear to him. Or perhaps Cyllene's king*
*or the Bacchants' god that lives on the tops*
*of the hills received you, a gift from some*
*one of the dark-eyed Nymphs, with whom he mostly plays?*

*(Enter an old Herdsman from the side, led by Oedipus' servants.)*

OEDIPUS

If someone like myself who never met him
may make a guess—I think this is the herdsman,
whom we were seeking. His old age is consonant
with the other's. And besides, the men who bring him
I recognize as my own servants. But you
perhaps may better me in knowledge since
you've seen the man before.

CHORUS LEADER

You can be sure
I recognize him. For if Laius
had ever an honest shepherd, this was he.

OEDIPUS

You, sir, from Corinth, I must ask you first,
is this the man you spoke of?

MESSENGER

This is he
before your eyes.

OEDIPUS

Old man, look here at me
and tell me what I ask you. Were you ever
a servant of King Laius?

HERDSMAN

I was—
no slave he bought but reared in his own house.

OEDIPUS

What did you do as work? How did you live?

HERDSMAN

Most of my life was spent among the flocks.

OEDIPUS

In what part of the country did you live?

HERDSMAN

Cithaeron and the places near to it.

OEDIPUS

And somewhere there perhaps you knew this man?

HERDSMAN

What was he doing? What man?

OEDIPUS

This man here,
have you had any dealings with him?

HERDSMAN

No—
not such that I can quickly call to mind.

MESSENGER

That is no wonder, master. But I'll help him
remember what he does not know. For I know
that he knows well the country of Cithaeron,
how he with two flocks, I with one, together
kept company for three years—six months each year—
from spring till autumn time. When winter came
I drove my flocks back to our fold, back home,
while this man, he drove his to Laius' steadings.
Am I right or not in what I say we did?

HERDSMAN

You're right—although it's a long time ago.

MESSENGER

Do you remember giving me a baby
to bring up as my foster child?

HERDSMAN

What's this?
Why do you ask this question?

MESSENGER

Look old man,
here he is—here's the man who was that child!

HERDSMAN

Death take you! Won't you hold your tongue?

OEDIPUS

No, no,
do not find fault with him, old man. Your words
are more at fault than his.

HERDSMAN

O best of masters,
how do I give offense?

OEDIPUS

When you refuse
to speak about the child of whom he asks you.

HERDSMAN

He speaks out of his ignorance, without meaning.

OEDIPUS

If you'll not talk to gratify me, you
will talk with pain to urge you.

HERDSMAN

O please, sir,
don't hurt an old man, sir.

OEDIPUS *(To the servants.)*

Here, one of you,
twist his hands behind him.

HERDSMAN

Why, god help me, why?
What do you want to know?

OEDIPUS

You gave a child
to him—the child he asked you of?

HERDSMAN

I did.
I wish I'd died the day I did.

OEDIPUS

You will
unless you tell me truly.

HERDSMAN

And I'll die
far worse if I should tell you.

OEDIPUS

This fellow
is bent on more delays, as it would seem.

HERDSMAN

O no, no! I have told you that I gave it.

OEDIPUS

Where did you get this child from? Was it your own
or did you get it from another?

HERDSMAN

Not
my own at all; I had it from someone.

OEDIPUS

One of these citizens? And from what house?

HERDSMAN

O master, please—I beg you, master, please
don't ask me more.

OEDIPUS

You're a dead man if I ask you again.

HERDSMAN

The child came from the house of Laius.

OEDIPUS

A slave? Or born from himself?

HERDSMAN

O god, I am on the brink of frightful speech.

OEDIPUS

And I of frightful hearing. But I must hear.

HERDSMAN

The child was called his child; but she within,
your wife would tell you best how all this was.

OEDIPUS

She gave it to you?

HERDSMAN

Yes she did, my lord.

OEDIPUS

To do what with it?

HERDSMAN

Make away with it.

OEDIPUS

She was so hard—its mother?

HERDSMAN

Aye, through fear of evil oracles.

OEDIPUS

Which?

HERDSMAN

They said that he
should kill his parents.

OEDIPUS

How was it that you
gave it away to this old man?

HERDSMAN

O master,
I pitied it, and thought that I could send it
off to another country: and this man
was from another country. But he saved it
for the most terrible troubles. If you are
the man he says you are, you're bred to misery.

OEDIPUS

O, O, O, they will all come,
all come out clearly! Light of the sun, let me
look upon you no more after today!
I who first saw the light bred of a coupling
accursed, and accursed in my living
with them I lived with, cursed in my killing.

*(Exit Oedipus into the palace. All but the Chorus depart to the side.)*

CHORUS [*singing*]

STROPHE A

*O generations of men, how I*
*count you as equal with those who live*
*not at all!*
*What man, what man on earth wins more*
*of happiness than a seeming*
*and after that falling away?*
*Oedipus, you are my pattern of this,*
*Oedipus, you and your fate!*
*Luckless Oedipus, as I look at you,*
*I count nothing in human affairs happy.*

ANTISTROPHE A

*Inasmuch as you shot your bolt*
*beyond the others and won the prize*
*of happiness complete—*
*O Zeus—and killed and reduced to naught*
*the hooked taloned maid of the riddling speech,*
*standing a tower against death for my land;*
*hence you are called my king and hence*
*have been honored the highest of all*
*honors; and hence you ruled*
*in the great city of Thebes.*

STROPHE B

*But now whose tale is more miserable?*
*Who is there lives with a savager fate?*°
*Whose troubles so reverse his life as his?*
*O Oedipus, the famous prince*
*for whom the same great harbor*
*the same both for father and son*
*sufficed for bridal bed,*
*how, O how, have the furrows ploughed*
*by your father endured to bear you, poor wretch,*
*and remain silent so long?*

ANTISTROPHE B

*Time who sees all has found you out*
*against your will; judges your marriage accursed,*
*begetter and begotten at one in it.*
*O child of Laius,*
*would I had never seen you.*
*I weep for you and cry*
*a dirge of lamentation.*
*To speak directly, I drew my breath*
*from you at the first and so now I lull*
*my eyes to sleep with your name.*

*(Enter a Second Messenger, from the palace.)*

SECOND MESSENGER

O princes always honored by our country,
what deeds you'll hear of and what horrors see,
what grief you'll feel, if you as trueborn Thebans
care for the house of Labdacus's sons.
No river, not Phasis nor Ister, can purge this house,
I think, with all their streams, such things
it hides, such evils shortly will bring forth
into the light, evils done on purpose;
and troubles hurt the most
when they prove self-inflicted.

CHORUS LEADER

What we had known before did not fall short
of bitter groaning; now what's more to tell?

SECOND MESSENGER

Shortest to hear and say—our glorious queen
Jocasta's dead.

CHORUS LEADER

Unhappy woman! How?

SECOND MESSENGER

By her own hand. You're spared the greatest pain
of what was done—you did not see the sight.
Yet insofar as I remember it
you'll hear the sufferings of our unlucky queen.
When she came raging into the house she went
straight to her marriage bed, tearing her hair
with both her hands, and slammed the bedroom doors
behind her shut, crying upon Laius
long dead—"Do you remember, Laius,
that night long past which bred a child for us
to send you to your death and leave
a mother making children with her son?"
And then she groaned and cursed the bed in which
she brought forth husband by her husband, children

by her own child, an infamous double bond.
How after that she died I do not know—
for Oedipus distracted us from seeing.
He burst upon us shouting and we looked
to him as he paced frantically around,
begging us always: "Give me a sword, I say,
to find this wife no wife, this mother's womb,
this field of double sowing whence I sprang
and where I sowed my children!" As he raved
some god showed him the way—none of us there.
Bellowing terribly and led by some
invisible guide he rushed on the two doors—
wrenching the bending bolts out of their sockets,
he charged inside. There, there, we saw his wife
hanging, the twisted rope around her neck.
When he saw her, he cried out fearfully
and cut the dangling noose. Then, as she lay,
poor woman, on the ground, what happened after,
was terrible to see. He tore the brooches—
the gold chased brooches fastening her robe—
away from her and lifting them up high
dashed them on his own eyeballs, shrieking out
such things as: "You will never see the crime
I have committed or had done upon me!
Dark eyes, now in the days to come look on
forbidden faces, do not recognize
those whom you long for"—with such imprecations
he struck his eyes again and yet again
with the brooches. And the bleeding eyeballs gushed
and stained his cheeks—no sluggish oozing drops
but a black rain and bloody hail poured down.
So it has broken—and not on one head alone°
but troubles mixed for husband and for wife.
The fortune of the days gone by was true
good fortune—but today groans and destruction

and death and shame—of all ills that can be named
not one is missing.

CHORUS LEADER

Is he now in any ease from pain?

SECOND MESSENGER

He shouts
for someone to unbar the doors and show him
to all the men of Thebes, his father's killer,
his mother's—no I cannot say the word,
it is unholy—for he'll cast himself,
out of the land, he says, and not remain
to bring a curse upon his house, the curse
he called upon it in his proclamation. But
he wants for strength, aye, and someone to guide him;
his sickness is too great to bear. You, too,
will be shown that. The bolts are opening.
Soon you will see a sight to waken pity
even in one who feels disgust or hatred.

*(Enter the blinded Oedipus, from the palace.)*

CHORUS [*chanting*]

*This is a terrible sight for men to see!*
*I never encountered a worse horror!*
*Poor wretch, what madness came upon you?*
*What evil spirit leaped upon your life*
*to your ill luck—a leap beyond man's strength!*
*Indeed I pity you, but I cannot*
*look at you, though there's much I want to ask*
*and much to learn and much to see.*
*I shudder at the sight of you.*

OEDIPUS [*singing in what follows, while the Chorus speaks*]

O, O,
*where am I going? Where is my voice*

*borne on the wind to and fro?*
*Spirit, how far have you sprung?*

CHORUS LEADER

To a terrible place which men's ears
may not hear of, nor their eyes see it.

OEDIPUS

STROPHE A

*Darkness!*
*Horror of darkness enfolding, resistless, unspeakable visitant sped*
*by an ill wind in haste!*°
*Madness and stabbing pain and memory*
*of my evils!*

CHORUS LEADER

In such misfortunes it's no wonder
if double weighs the burden of your grief.

OEDIPUS

ANTISTROPHE A

*My friend,*
*you are the only one steadfast, the only one that attends on me;*
*you still stay nursing the blind man.*
*Your care is not unnoticed. I recognize*
*your voice, although this darkness is my world.*

CHORUS LEADER

Doer of dreadful deeds, how did you dare
so far to do despite to your own eyes?
What spirit urged you to it?

OEDIPUS

STROPHE B

*It was Apollo, friends, Apollo,*
*that brought this bitter bitterness, my sorrows to completion.*
*But the hand that struck me*
*was none but my own.*
*Why should I see*
*whose vision showed me nothing sweet to see?*

CHORUS [*now singing*]

*These things are as you say.*

OEDIPUS

*What can I see to love?*
*What greeting can touch my ears with joy?*
*Take me away, and haste—to a place out of the way!*
*Take me away, my friends, the greatly miserable,*
*the most accursed, whom the gods too hate*
*above all men on earth!*

CHORUS LEADER

Unhappy in your mind and your misfortune,
would I had never known you!

OEDIPUS

ANTISTROPHE B

*Curse on the man° who took*
*the cruel bonds from off my legs, as I lay there.*
*He stole me from death and saved me,*
*no kindly service.*
*Had I died then,*
*I would not be so burdensome to friends or to myself.*

CHORUS

*I, too, could have wished it had been so.*

OEDIPUS

*Then I would not have come*
*to kill my father and marry my mother infamously.*
*Now I am godless and child of impurity,*
*begetter in the same seed that created my wretched self.*
*If there is any ill worse than ill,*
*that is the lot of Oedipus.*

CHORUS LEADER

I cannot say your remedy was good;
you would be better dead than blind and living.

OEDIPUS [*now speaking*]

What I have done here was best done—don't tell me
otherwise, do not give me further counsel.
I do not know with what eyes I could look
upon my father when I die and go
under the earth, nor yet my wretched mother—
those two to whom I have done things deserving
worse punishment than hanging. Would the sight
of children, bred as mine are, gladden me?
No, not these eyes, never. And my city,
its towers and sacred places of the gods,
where I was raised as the noblest man in Thebes,
of these I robbed my miserable self
when I commanded all to drive him out,
the criminal since proved by the gods impure
and of the race of Laius.
To this guilt I bore witness against myself—
with what eyes was I to look upon my people?
No. If there were a means to choke the fountain
of hearing I would not have stayed my hand
from locking up my miserable carcass,
seeing and hearing nothing; it is sweet
to keep our thoughts out of the range of hurt.
Cithaeron, why did you receive me? Why
having received me did you not kill me straight?
And so I'd not have shown to men my birth.
O Polybus and Corinth and the house,
the old house that I used to call my father's—
what fairness you were nurse to, and what foulness
festered beneath! Now I am found to be
evil and a son of evil. Crossroads,
and hidden glade, oak and the narrow way
at the crossroads that drank my father's blood—
my own blood—from my hands, do you remember
still what I did as you looked on, and what
I did when I came here? O marriage, marriage!

you bred me and again when you had bred
you produced the same seed again and displayed to men
fathers, brothers, children, an incestuous brood,
brides, wives, and mothers, all the foulest deeds
that can be in this world of ours.
        Come—it's unfit to say what is unfit
to do.—I beg of you in the gods' name hide me
somewhere outside your country, yes, or kill me,
or throw me into the sea, to be forever
out of your sight. Approach and deign to touch me
for all my wretchedness, and do not fear.
No man but I can bear my evil doom.

*(Enter Creon, from the side, with attendants.)*

CHORUS LEADER

Here Creon comes in fit time to perform
or give advice in what you ask of us.
Creon is left sole ruler in your stead.

OEDIPUS

Creon! Creon! What shall I say to him?
How can I justly hope that he will trust me?
In what is past I have been proved toward him
an utter liar.

CREON

                                        Oedipus, I've come
not so that I might laugh at you nor taunt you
with evil of the past.

*(To attendants.)*

                                        But even if you men
have no more shame before the face of men,
reverence at least the flame that gives all life,
our lord the Sun, and do not show unveiled
to him pollution such that neither land
nor holy rain nor light of day can welcome.

Be quick and take him in. It is most decent
that only kin should see and hear the troubles
of kin.

OEDIPUS

I beg you, since you've torn me from
my dreadful expectations and have come
in a most noble spirit to a man
that has used you vilely—do a thing for me.
I shall speak for your own good, not for my own.

CREON

What do you need that you would ask of me?

OEDIPUS

Drive me from here with all the speed you can
to where I may not hear a human voice.

CREON

Be sure, I would have done this had not I
wished first of all to learn from the god the course
of action I should follow.

OEDIPUS

But his word
has been quite clear to let the parricide,
the sinner, die.

CREON

Yes, that indeed was said.
But in the present need we had best discover
what we should do.

OEDIPUS

And will you ask about
a man so wretched?

CREON

Now even you will trust
the god.

OEDIPUS

So. I command you—and will beseech you—
to her that lies inside that house give burial
as you would have it; she is yours and rightly
you will perform the rites for her. For me—
never let this my father's city have me
living a dweller in it. Leave me live
in the mountains where Cithaeron is that's called
my mountain, which my mother and my father
while they were living would have made my tomb.
So I may die by their decree who sought
indeed to kill me. Yet I know this much:
no sickness and no other thing will kill me.
I would not have been saved from death if not
for some strange evil fate. Well, let my fate
go where it will.
Creon, you need not care
about my sons; they're men and so wherever
they are, they will not lack a livelihood.
But my two girls—so sad and pitiful—
whose table never stood apart from mine,
and everything I touched they always shared—
O Creon, have a thought for them! And most
I wish that you might allow me to touch them
and sorrow with them.

*(Enter Antigone and Ismene from the palace.)*

O my lord! O true noble Creon! May I
really touch them, as when I saw?
What shall I say?
Can I hear them sobbing—my two darlings!—
and Creon has had pity and has sent me
what I loved most?
Am I right?

CREON

You're right: it was I gave you this

because I knew from old days how you loved them
as I see now.

OEDIPUS

God bless you for it, Creon,
and may god guard you better on your road
than he did me!
O children,
where are you? Come here, come to my hands,
a brother's hands which turned your father's eyes,
those bright eyes you knew once, to what you see,
a father seeing nothing, knowing nothing,
begetting you from his own source of life.
I weep for you—I cannot see your faces—
I weep when I think of the bitterness
there will be in your lives, how you must live
before the world. At what assemblages
of citizens will you attend? To what
festivals will you go and not come home
in tears instead of sharing in the holiday?
And when you're ripe for marriage, who will he be,
the man who'll risk to take such infamy
as shall cling to my children, to bring hurt
on them and those that marry with them? What
evil is not there? "Your father killed his father
and sowed the seed where he had sprung himself
and begot you out of the womb that held him."
Such insults you will hear. Then who will marry you?
No one, my children; clearly you are doomed
to waste away in barrenness unmarried.
Son of Menoeceus, since you are all the father
left these two girls, and we, their parents, both
are dead to them—do not allow them to wander
like beggars, poor and husbandless.
They are of your own blood.
And do not make them equal with myself

in wretchedness; for you can see them now
so young, so utterly alone, save for you only.
Touch my hand, noble Creon, and say yes.
If you were older, children, and were wiser,
there's much advice I'd give you. But as it is,
let this be what you pray: to find a life
wherever there is opportunity
to live, a better life than was your father's.

CREON

Your tears have had enough of scope; now go within the
house.

OEDIPUS

I must obey, though bitter of heart.

CREON

In season, all is good.

OEDIPUS

Do you know on what conditions I obey?

CREON

You tell me them,
and I shall know them when I hear.

OEDIPUS

That you shall send me out
to live away from Thebes.

CREON

That gift you must ask of the god.

OEDIPUS

But I'm now hated by the gods.

CREON

So quickly you'll obtain your prayer.

OEDIPUS

You consent then?

CREON

What I do not mean, I do not use to say.

OEDIPUS

Now lead me away from here.

CREON

Let go the children, then, and come.

OEDIPUS

Do not take them from me.

CREON

Do not seek to be master in everything,
for the things you mastered did not follow you throughout
your life.

*(Creon and Oedipus depart.)*

CHORUS°

You that live in my ancestral Thebes, behold this Oedipus—
him who knew the famous riddles and was a man most
masterful;
not a citizen who did not look with envy on his lot—
see him now and see the breakers of misfortune swallow him!
Look upon that last day always. Count no mortal happy till
he has passed the final limit of his life secure from pain.

# OEDIPUS AT COLONUS

*Translated by* ROBERT FITZGERALD

# OEDIPUS AT COLONUS

*Characters* OEDIPUS
ANTIGONE, daughter of Oedipus
A STRANGER
CHORUS of old men of Colonus
ISMENE, daughter of Oedipus
THESEUS, king of Athens
CREON, king of Thebes
POLYNICES, son of Oedipus
A MESSENGER

*Scene: A grove in Colonus dedicated to the Furies. A statue or stele of the legendary horseman-hero Colonus can be seen on one side. There is a flat rock, sacred throne of the Furies, in the middle of the orchestra, and another low outcrop of rock to one side.*

*(Enter Oedipus from one side, old, blind, and ragged, led by Antigone.)*

OEDIPUS

My daughter—daughter of the blind old man—
where have we come to now, Antigone?
What lands are these, or holdings of what city?
Who will be kind to Oedipus this evening°
and give alms to the wanderer?
Though he ask little and receive still less,
it is sufficient:
suffering and time,
vast time, have been instructors in contentment,
which kingliness° teaches too.

But now, child,
if you can see a resting place—perhaps
a roadside fountain, or some holy grove,
tell me and let me pause there and sit down:
so we may learn our whereabouts, and take
our cue from what we hear, as strangers should.

ANTIGONE

Father, poor tired Oedipus, the towers
that crown the city still seem far away;
as for this place, it is clearly a holy one,
shady with vines and olive trees and laurel;
a covert for the song and hush of nightingales
in their snug wings.
But rest on this rough stone.
It was a long road for an old man to travel.

OEDIPUS

Help me sit down; take care of the blind man.

ANTIGONE

After so long, you need not tell me, father.

*(Antigone helps Oedipus sit down on the rock, at center.)*

OEDIPUS

What can you say, now, as to where we are?

ANTIGONE

This place I do not know; I know the city
must be Athens.

OEDIPUS

As all the travelers said.

ANTIGONE

Then shall I go and ask what place this is?

OEDIPUS

Do, child, if there is any life nearby.

ANTIGONE

Oh, but indeed there is; I need not leave you;
I see a man, now, not far away from us.

OEDIPUS

Is he coming this way? Has he started toward us?

*(Enter a Stranger, from the side.)*

ANTIGONE

Here he is now.
Say what seems best to you,
father; the man is here.

OEDIPUS

Friend, my daughter's eyes serve for my own.
She tells me we are fortunate enough to meet you;
and no doubt you will inform us—

STRANGER

Do not go on!
First, move from where you sit; the place is holy;
it is forbidden to walk upon that ground.

OEDIPUS

What ground is this? What god is honored here?

STRANGER

It is not to be touched, no one may live upon it;
most dreadful are its divinities, most feared,
Daughters of Darkness and mysterious Earth.

OEDIPUS

Under what solemn name shall I invoke them?

STRANGER

The people here prefer to address them as Gentle
All-Seeing Ones; elsewhere there are other names.

OEDIPUS

Then may they be gentle to the suppliant;
for I shall never leave this resting place.

STRANGER

What is the meaning of this?

OEDIPUS

It was ordained;
I recognize it now.

STRANGER

Without authority
from the city government I dare not move you;
first I must show them what you are doing.

OEDIPUS

Friend, in the name of god, bear with me now!
I turn to you for light; answer the wanderer.°

STRANGER

Speak. You will have no discourtesy from me.

OEDIPUS

What is this region that we two have entered?

STRANGER

As much as I can tell you, I will tell.
This country, all of it, is blessed ground;
the god Poseidon loves it; in it the fire carrier
Prometheus has his influence; in particular
that spot you rest on has been called this earth's
Doorsill of Brass, and buttress of great Athens.
All men of this land claim descent from him
who is sculptured here, Colonus master horseman,
and bear his name in common with their own.
That is this country, stranger: honored less
in histories than in the hearts of the people.

OEDIPUS

Then people live here on their lands?

STRANGER

They do,
the clan of those descended from that hero.

OEDIPUS

Ruled by a prince? Or by the greater number?

STRANGER

The land is governed from Athens, by the king.

OEDIPUS

And who is he whose word has power here?

STRANGER

Theseus, son of Aegeus, the king before him.

OEDIPUS

Ah. Would someone then go to this king for me?

STRANGER

To tell him what? Perhaps to urge his coming?

OEDIPUS

To tell him a small favor will gain him much.

STRANGER

What service can a blind man render him?

OEDIPUS

All I shall say will be clear-sighted indeed.

STRANGER

Friend, listen to me: I wish you no injury;
you seem wellborn, though obviously unlucky;
stay where you are, exactly where I found you.
And I'll inform the people of what you say—
not in the town, but here—it rests with them
to decide if you should stay or must move on.

*(Exit Stranger, to the side.)*

OEDIPUS

Child, has he gone?

ANTIGONE

Yes, father. Now you may speak tranquilly,
for only I am with you.

OEDIPUS (*Praying.*)

Ladies whose eyes
are terrible, Spirits, upon your sacred ground
I have first bent my knees in this new land;
therefore be mindful of me and of Apollo.
For when he gave me oracles of evil,
he also spoke of this: a resting place,
after long years, in the last country, where
I should find home among the sacred Furies:
that I might round out there my bitter life,
conferring benefit on those who received me,
a curse on those who have driven me away.
Portents, he said, would make me sure of this:
earthquake, thunder, or god's smiling lightning.°
But I am sure of it now, sure that you guided me
with feathery certainty° upon this road,
and led me here into your hallowed wood.
How otherwise could I, in my wandering,
have sat down first with you in all this land,
I who drink not, with you who love not wine?
How otherwise had I found this chair of stone?
Grant me then, goddesses, passage from life at last,
and consummation, as the unearthly voice foretold;°
unless indeed I seem not worth your grace,
slave as I am to such unending pain
as no man had before.
O hear my prayer,
sweet children of original Darkness! Hear me,
Athens, city named for great Athena,
honored above all cities in the world!
Pity a man's poor carcass and his ghost,
for Oedipus is not the strength he was.

ANTIGONE

Be still. Some old, old men are coming this way,
looking for the place where you are seated.

OEDIPUS

I shall be still. You get me clear of the path
and hide me in the wood, so I may hear
what they are saying. If we know their temper,
we shall be better able to act with prudence.

*(Oedipus and Antigone move to one side, into the grove. Enter the Chorus, from the other side.)*

CHORUS [*singing*]

STROPHE A

*Look for him. Who could he be? Where*
*is he? Where is the stranger*
*impious, blasphemous, shameless?*
*Use your eyes, search him out!*
*Cover the ground and uncover him!*
*Vagabond!*
*The old man must be a vagabond,*
*not of our land, for he'd never*
*otherwise dare to go in there,*
*in the inviolate thicket*
*of those whom it's futile to fight,°*
*those whom we tremble to name.*
*When we pass we avert our eyes—*
*close our eyes!—*
*in silence, without conversation,*
*shaping our prayers with our lips.*
*But now, if the story is credible,*
*some alien fool has profaned it.*
*Yet I have looked over all the grove and*
*still cannot see him,*
*cannot say where he has hidden.*

*(Oedipus comes forward with Antigone.)*

OEDIPUS [*chanting in turn with the Chorus*]

*That stranger is I. As they say of the blind:*
*sounds are the things I see.*

CHORUS

*Ah!*
*His face is dreadful! His voice is dreadful!*

OEDIPUS

*I beg you not to think of me as a criminal.*

CHORUS

*Zeus defend us, who is this old man?*

OEDIPUS

*One whose fate is not quite to be envied.*
*O my masters, and men of this land;*
*that must be evident: why, otherwise,*
*should I need this girl*
*to lead me, her frailty to put my weight on?*

CHORUS [*now singing*]

ANTISTROPHE A

*Ah! His eyes are blind!*
*And were you brought into the world so?*
*Unhappy life—and so long!*
*Well, not if I can stop it*
*will you have this curse as well.*
*Stranger! You*
*trespass there! But beyond there,*
*in the glade where the grass is still,*
*where the honeyed libations drip*
*in the rill from the brimming spring,*
*you must not step. O stranger,*
*it is well to be careful about it!*
*Most careful!*
*Stand aside and come down then!*
*There is too much space between us!*°
*Say, wanderer, can you hear?*
*If you have a mind to tell us*
*your business, or wish to converse with our council,*

*come away from that place!*
*Only speak where it's proper to do so!*

OEDIPUS [*chanting in turn with Antigone*]
*Now, daughter, what is the way of wisdom?*

ANTIGONE
*We must do just as they do here, father;°*
*we should give in now, and listen to them.*

OEDIPUS
*Stretch out your hand to me.*

ANTIGONE
*There, I am with you.*

OEDIPUS
*Sirs, let there be no injustice done me,*
*once I have trusted you, and left my refuge.*

*(Led by Antigone, he moves forward.)*

CHORUS [*singing in turn with Antigone and Oedipus*]

STROPHE B

*Never, never, will anyone drive you away*
*from rest in this land, old man!*

OEDIPUS
*Shall I come farther?*

CHORUS
*Yes, farther.*

OEDIPUS
*And now?*

CHORUS
*You must guide him, girl;*
*you can see how much further to come.*

ANTIGONE

*Come with your blind step, father;*
*this way; come where I lead you.*

. . . . . . . . . . . . . .

CHORUS°

*Stranger in a strange country,*
*courage, afflicted man!*
*Whatever the state abhors,*
*you too abhor, and honor*
*whatever the state holds dear.*

OEDIPUS [*chanting*]

*Lead me on, then, child,*
*to where we may speak or listen respectfully.*
*Let us not fight necessity.*

CHORUS [*singing*]

ANTISTROPHE B

*Now! Go no further than that platform there,*
*formed of the natural rock.*

OEDIPUS

*This?*

CHORUS

*Far enough; you can hear us.*

OEDIPUS

*Shall I sit down?*

CHORUS

*Yes, sit there to the side,*
*at the edge of the rock.*

ANTIGONE

*Father, this is where I can help you;*
*you must keep step with me; gently now.*

OEDIPUS

*Ah, me!*

ANTIGONE

*Lean your old body on my arm;*
*it is I, who love you; let yourself down.*

OEDIPUS

*How bitter blindness is!*

*(He is seated on the rock, center.)*

CHORUS

*Now that you are at rest, poor man,*
*tell us, what is your name?*
*Who are you, wanderer?*
*What is the land of your ancestors?*

OEDIPUS [*singing in turn with Antigone and the Chorus*]

EPODE

*I am an exile, friends; but do not ask me . . .*

CHORUS

*What is it you fear to say, old man?*

OEDIPUS

*No, no, no! Do not go on*
*questioning me! Do not ask my name!*

CHORUS

*Why not?*

OEDIPUS

*My star was unspeakable.°*

CHORUS

*Speak!*

OEDIPUS

*My child, what can I say to them?*

CHORUS

*Answer us, stranger: what is your family?*
*Who was your father?*

OEDIPUS

*God help me, what will become of me, child?*

ANTIGONE

*Tell them; there is no other way.*

OEDIPUS

*Well, then, I will; I cannot hide it.*

CHORUS

*Between you, you greatly delay. Speak up!*

OEDIPUS

*Have you heard of Laius' family?*

CHORUS

*Ah!*

OEDIPUS

*Of the race of Labdacidae?*

CHORUS

*Ah, Zeus!*

OEDIPUS

*And ruined Oedipus?*

CHORUS

*You are he!*

OEDIPUS

*Do not take fright from what I say—*

CHORUS

*Oh, dreadful!*

OEDIPUS

*I am accursed.*

CHORUS

*Oh, fearful!*

OEDIPUS

*Antigone, what will happen now?*

CHORUS

*Away with you! Out with you! Leave our country!*

OEDIPUS

*And what of the promises you made me?*

CHORUS

*God will not punish the man*
*who makes return for an injury.*
*Deceivers may be deceived:*
*they play a game that ends*
*in grief, and not in pleasure.*
*Leave this grove at once!*
*Our country is not for you!*
*Wind no further*
*your clinging evil upon us!°*

ANTIGONE [*still singing*]

*O men of reverent mind!*
*Since you will not suffer my father,*
*old man though he is*
*and though you know his story—*
*he never knew what he did—*
*take pity still on my unhappiness;*
*and let me intercede with you for him.*
*Not with lost eyes, but looking in your eyes*
*as if I were a child of yours, I beg*
*mercy for him, the beaten man! O hear me!*
*We are thrown upon your mercy as on god's;*
*be kinder than you seem!°*
*By all you have and own that is dear to you,*
*children, wives, possessions, gods, I pray you!*
*For you will never see in all the world*
*a man whom god has led*
*escape his destiny!°*

CHORUS LEADER [*now speaking*]

Child of Oedipus, indeed we pity you,
just as we pity him for his misfortune.
But we tremble to think of what the gods may do;
we dare not speak more generously!

OEDIPUS [*speaking*]

What use is reputation then? What good
comes of a noble name? A noble fiction!
For Athens, so they say, excels in piety;
has power to save the wretched of other lands,
can give them refuge, is unique in this.
Yet, when it comes to me, where is her refuge?
You pluck me from these rocks and cast me out,
all for fear of a name!
Or do you dread
my strength? my actions? I think not, for I
suffered those deeds more than I acted them,
as I might show if it were fitting here
to tell my father's and my mother's story . . .
for which you fear me, as I know too well.
And yet, how was I evil in myself?
I had been wronged, I retaliated; even had I
known what I was doing, was that evil?
Then, knowing nothing, I went on. Went on.
But those who wronged me knew, and ruined me.
Therefore I beg of you before the gods,
for the same cause that made you move me—
in reverence of your gods—give me this shelter,
and thus accord those powers what is theirs.
Think: their eyes are fixed upon the just,
fixed on the unjust too;° no impious man
can twist away from them forever.
Now, in their presence, do not blot your city's
luster by bending to unholy action.
As you would receive an honest petitioner,
give me, too, sanctuary; though my face
be dreadful in its look, yet honor me!
For I come here as one endowed with grace
by those who are over Nature; and I bring
advantage to this race, as you may learn

more fully when some lord of yours is here.°
Meanwhile be careful to be just.

CHORUS LEADER

Old man.
This argument of yours compels our wonder.
It was not feebly worded. I am content
that higher authorities should judge this matter.

OEDIPUS

And where is he who rules the land, strangers?

CHORUS LEADER

In his father's city; but the messenger
who sent us here has gone to fetch him also.

OEDIPUS

Do you think a blind man will so interest him
as to bring him such a distance?

CHORUS LEADER

I do, indeed, when he has heard your name.

OEDIPUS

But who will tell him that?

CHORUS LEADER

It is a long road, and the rumors of travelers
have a way of wandering. He will have word of them.
Take heart—he will be here. Old man, your name
has gone over all the earth; though he may be
at rest when the news comes, he will come quickly.

OEDIPUS

Then may he come with luck for his own city
as well as for me. . . . The good befriend themselves.

ANTIGONE

O Zeus! What shall I say? How interpret this?

OEDIPUS

Antigone, my dear child, what is it?

ANTIGONE

A woman
riding a Sicilian pony and coming toward us;
she is wearing the wide Thessalian sun hat.
I don't know!
Is it or isn't it? Or am I dreaming?
I think so; yes!—no. I can't be sure . . .
Ah, poor child,
it is no one else but she! And she is smiling
now as she comes! It is my dear Ismene!

OEDIPUS

What did you say, child?

*(Ismene enters, with one attendant, from the side.)*

ANTIGONE

That I see your daughter!
My sister! Now you can tell her by her voice.

ISMENE

O father and sister together, dearest voices!°
Now I have found you—how, I scarcely know—
I don't know how I shall see you through my tears!

OEDIPUS

Child, have you come?

ISMENE

Father, how old you seem!°

OEDIPUS

Child, are you here?

ISMENE

And such a time I had!

OEDIPUS

Touch me, little one.

ISMENE

I shall hold you both!

OEDIPUS

My children . . . and sisters.

ISMENE

Oh, unhappy people!

OEDIPUS

She and I?

ISMENE

And I with you, unhappy.

OEDIPUS

Why have you come, child?

ISMENE

Thinking of you, father.

OEDIPUS

You were lonely?

ISMENE

Yes; and I bring news for you.
I came with the one person I could trust.

OEDIPUS

Why, where are your brothers? Could they not do it?

ISMENE

They are—where they are. It is a hard time for them.

OEDIPUS

Ah! They behave as if they were Egyptians,
bred the Egyptian way! Down there, the men
sit indoors all day long, weaving;
the women go out and attend to business.
Just so your brothers, who should have done this work,
sit by the fire like home-loving girls,

and you two, in their place, must bear my hardships.
One, since her childhood ended and her body
gained its strength, has wandered ever with me,
an old man's governess; often in the wild
forest going without shoes, and hungry,
beaten by many rains, tired by the sun;
yet she rejected the sweet life of home
so that her father should have sustenance.
And you, my daughter, once before came out
unknown to Thebes, bringing me news of all
the oracle had said concerning me;
and you remained my faithful outpost there,
when I was driven from that land.
                                        But now,
what news, Ismene, do you bring your father?
Why have you left your house to make this journey?
You came for no light reason, I know that;
it must be something serious for me.

ISMENE

I will pass over the troubles I have had
searching for your whereabouts, father.
They were hard enough to bear; and I will not
go through it all again in telling of them.
In any case, it is your sons' troubles
that I have come to tell you.
First it was their desire, as it was Creon's,
that the throne should pass to him; that thus the city
should be defiled no longer: such was their reasoning
when they considered our people's ancient curse
and how it enthralled your pitiful family.
But then some fury put it in their hearts—°
O pitiful again!—to itch for power,
for seizure of prerogative and throne.
And it was the younger and the less mature
who stripped his elder brother, Polynices,

of place and kingship, and then banished him.
But now the people hear he has gone to Argos,
into the valley land, has joined that nation,°
and is enlisting friends among its warriors:
telling them Argos shall honorably win
Thebes and her plain, or else eternal glory.°
This is not a mere recital, father,
but terrible truth!
How long will it be, I wonder,
before the gods take pity on your distress?

OEDIPUS

You have some hope then that they are concerned
with my deliverance?

ISMENE

I have, father.
The latest sentences of the oracle.

OEDIPUS

How are they worded? What do they prophesy?

ISMENE

That you shall be much solicited by our people
before your death—and after—for their welfare.

OEDIPUS

And what could anyone hope from such as I?

ISMENE

The oracles declare their strength's in you.

OEDIPUS

When I am worn to nothing, strength in me?

ISMENE

For the gods who threw you down sustain you now.

OEDIPUS

Slight favor, now I am old! My doom was early.

ISMENE

The proof of it is that Creon is coming to you
for that same reason, and soon: not by and by.

OEDIPUS

To do what, daughter? Tell me about this.

ISMENE

To settle you near the land of Thebes, and so
have you at hand; but you may not cross the border.

OEDIPUS

What good am I to Thebes outside the country?

ISMENE

It is merely that if your burial were unlucky
that would be perilous for them.

OEDIPUS

Ah, then!
This does not need divine interpretation.

ISMENE

Therefore they want to keep you somewhere near,
just at the border, where you'll not be free.

OEDIPUS

And will they compose my shade with Theban dust?°

ISMENE

Ah, father! No. Your father's blood forbids it.

OEDIPUS

Then they shall never hold me in their power!

ISMENE

If not, some day it will be bitter for them.

OEDIPUS

How will that be, my child?

ISMENE

When they shall stand
where you are buried, and feel your anger there.

OEDIPUS

What you have said—from whom did you hear it, child?

ISMENE

The envoys told me when they returned from Delphi.

OEDIPUS

Then all this about me was spoken there?

ISMENE

According to those men, just come to Thebes.

OEDIPUS

Has either of my sons had word of this?

ISMENE

They both have, and they understand it well.

OEDIPUS

The scoundrels! So they knew all this, and yet
would not give up the throne to have me back?

ISMENE

It hurts me to hear it, but I can't deny it.

OEDIPUS

Gods!
Never quench their fires of ambition!
Let the last word be mine upon this battle
they are about to join, with the spears lifting!
I'd see that he who holds the scepter now
will not have power long, nor would the other,
the banished one, return!
These were the two
who saw me in disgrace and banishment

and never lifted a hand for me. They heard me
howled from the country, heard the thing proclaimed!
And would you say I wanted exile then,
an appropriate clemency, granted by the state?
That is all false! The truth is that at first
my mind was a boiling caldron; nothing so sweet
as death, death by stoning, could have been given me;
yet no one there would grant me that desire.
It was only later, when my madness cooled,
and I had begun to think my rage excessive,
my punishment too great for what I had done;
then it was that the city—in its good time!—
decided to be harsh, and drove me out.
They could have helped me then; they could have
helped him who begot them! Would they do it?
For lack of a little word from that fine pair
out I went, a beggar, to wander forever!
Only by grace of these two girls, unaided,
have I got food or shelter or devotion;
their two brothers held their father of less worth
than sitting on a throne and being king.
Well, they shall never win me in their fight,°
nor will they profit from the rule of Thebes.
I am sure of that; I have heard the prophecies
brought by this girl; I think they fit those others
spoken so long ago, and now fulfilled.
    So let Creon be sent to find me: Creon,
or any other of influence in the state.
If you men here consent—as do those powers
holy and awful, the Spirits of this place—
to give me refuge, then shall this city have
a great savior, and woe to my enemies!

CHORUS LEADER

Oedipus: you are surely worth our pity:
you, and your children, too. And since you claim

also to be a savior of our land,
I'd like to give you counsel for good luck.

OEDIPUS

Dear friend! I'll do whatever you advise.

CHORUS LEADER

Make expiation to these divinities
whose ground you violated when you came.

OEDIPUS

In what way shall I do so? Tell me, friends.

CHORUS LEADER

First you must bring libations from the spring
that runs forever; and bring them with clean hands.

OEDIPUS

And when I have that holy water, then?

CHORUS LEADER

There are some bowls there, by a skillful potter;
put chaplets round the brims, over the handles.

OEDIPUS

Of myrtle sprigs, or woolen stuff, or what?

CHORUS LEADER

Take the fleeces cropped from a young lamb.

OEDIPUS

Just so; then how must I perform the rite?

CHORUS LEADER

Facing the quarter of the morning light
pour your libations out.

OEDIPUS

Am I to pour them from the bowls you speak of?

CHORUS LEADER

In three streams, yes; the last one, empty it.

OEDIPUS

With what should it be filled? Tell me this, too.

CHORUS LEADER

With water and honey; but with no wine added.

OEDIPUS

And when the leaf-dark earth receives it?

CHORUS LEADER

Lay three times nine young shoots of olive on it
with both your hands; meanwhile repeat this prayer:

OEDIPUS

This—I am eager to hear this, for it has great power.

CHORUS LEADER

That as we call them Eumenides,
which means the gentle of heart,
may they accept with gentleness
the suppliant and his wish.
So you, or he who prays for you, address them;
but do not speak aloud or raise a cry;
then come away, and do not turn again.
If you will do all this, I shall take heart
and stand up for you; otherwise, O stranger,
I should be seriously afraid for you.

OEDIPUS

Children, you hear the words of these good people?

ANTIGONE

Yes; now tell us what we ought to do.

OEDIPUS

It need not be performed by me; I'm far
from having the strength or sight for it—I have neither.
Let one of you go and carry out the ritual.
One soul, I think, often can make atonement
for many others, if it be devoted.

Now do it quickly—yet do not leave me alone!
I could not move without the help of someone.

ISMENE

I'll go and do it. But where am I to go?
Where shall I find the holy place, I wonder?

CHORUS LEADER

On the other side of the wood, girl. If you need it,
you may get help from the attendant there.

ISMENE

I am going now. Antigone, you will stay
and care for father. If it were difficult,
I should not think it so, since it is for him.°

*(Exit Ismene to the side.)*

CHORUS [*singing in turn with Oedipus*]

STROPHE A

*What evil things have slept since long ago*
*it is not sweet to waken;*
*and yet I long to be told—*

OEDIPUS

*What?*

CHORUS

*Of that heartbreak for which there was no help,*
*the pain you have had to suffer.*

OEDIPUS

*For kindness' sake, do not open*
*my old wound, and my shame.*

CHORUS

*It is told everywhere, and never dies;*
*I only want to hear it truly told.*

OEDIPUS

*Ah! Ah!*

CHORUS

*Consent I beg you!*
*Give me my wish, and I shall give you yours.*

OEDIPUS

ANTISTROPHE A

*I had to face a thing most terrible,*
*not willed by me, I swear;*
*I would have abhorred it all.*

CHORUS

*So?*

OEDIPUS

*Though I did not know, Thebes married me to evil;*
*Fate and I were joined there.*

CHORUS

*Then it was indeed your mother,*
*with whom the thing was done?°*

OEDIPUS

*Ah! It is worse than death to have to hear it!*
*Strangers! Yes: and these two girls of mine . . .*

CHORUS

*You say—*

OEDIPUS

*These luckless two*
*were given birth by her who gave birth to me.*

CHORUS

STROPHE B

*These then are daughters; they are also—*

OEDIPUS

*Sisters: yes, their father's sisters . . .*

CHORUS

*Ah, pity!*

OEDIPUS

*Pity, indeed. What throngs*
*of pities come into my mind!*

CHORUS

*You suffered—*

OEDIPUS

*Yes, unspeakably.*

CHORUS

*You sinned—*

OEDIPUS

*No, I did not sin!*

CHORUS

*How not?*

OEDIPUS

*I thought*
*of her as my reward. Ah, would that I had never won it!*
*Would that I had never served the state that day!*°

CHORUS

ANTISTROPHE B

*Unhappy man—and you also killed—*

OEDIPUS

*What is it now? What are you after?*

CHORUS

*Killed your father!*

OEDIPUS

*God in heaven!*
*You strike again where I am hurt.*

CHORUS

*You killed him.*

OEDIPUS

*Killed him. Yet, there is—*

CHORUS

*What more?*

OEDIPUS

*A just extenuation.*
*This:*
*I did not know him; and he wished to murder me.*
*Before the law—before god—I am innocent!°*

*(Enter Theseus from the side, with a retinue of soldiers.)*

CHORUS LEADER

The king is coming! Aegeus' eldest son,
Theseus: news of you has brought him here.

THESEUS

In the old time I often heard men tell
of the bloody extinction of your eyes.
Even if on my way I were not informed,
I'd recognize you, son of Laius.
The garments and the tortured face
make plain your identity. I am sorry for you,
and I should like to know what favor here
you hope for from the city and from me:
both you and your unfortunate companion.
Tell me. It would be something dire indeed
to make me leave you comfortless; for I
too was an exile. I grew up abroad;
and in strange lands I fought as few men have
with danger and with death.
Therefore no wanderer shall come, as you do,
and be denied my audience or aid.
I know I am only a man; I have no more
to hope for in the end than you have.

OEDIPUS

Theseus, in those few words your nobility
is plain to me. I need not speak at length.

You have named me and my father accurately,
spoken with knowledge of my land and exile.
There is, then, nothing left for me to tell
but my desire; and then the tale is ended.

THESEUS

Tell me your wish, then; let me hear it now.

OEDIPUS

I come to give you something, and the gift
is my own beaten self: no feast for the eyes;
yet in me is a more lasting grace than beauty.

THESEUS

What grace is this you say you bring to us?°

OEDIPUS

In time you'll learn, but not immediately.

THESEUS

How long, then, must we wait to be enlightened?

OEDIPUS

Until I am dead, and you have buried me.

THESEUS

Your wish is burial? What of your life meanwhile?
Have you forgotten that?—or do you care?

OEDIPUS

It is all implicated in my burial.

THESEUS

But this is a brief favor you ask of me.

OEDIPUS

See to it, nevertheless! It is not simple.°

THESEUS

You mean I shall have trouble with your sons?

OEDIPUS

Those people want to take me back there now.

THESEUS

Will you not go? Is exile admirable?°

OEDIPUS

No. When I wished to go, they would not have it.

THESEUS

What childishness! You are surely in no position—

OEDIPUS

When you know me, admonish me; not now!

THESEUS

Instruct me then. I must not speak in ignorance.

OEDIPUS

Theseus, I have been wounded more than once.

THESEUS

Is it your family's curse that you refer to?

OEDIPUS

Not merely that; all Hellas talks of that.

THESEUS

Then what is the wound that is so pitiless?

OEDIPUS

Think how it is with me. I was expelled
from my own land by my own sons; and now,
as a parricide, my return is not allowed.

THESEUS

How can they summon you, if this is so?

OEDIPUS

The sacred oracle compels them to.

THESEUS

They fear some punishment from his forebodings?

OEDIPUS

They fear they will be struck down in this land!

THESEUS

And how could war arise between these nations?°

OEDIPUS

Most gentle son of Aegeus! The immortal
gods alone have neither age nor death!
All other things almighty Time disquiets.
Earth wastes away; the body wastes away;
faith dies; distrust is born;
and imperceptibly the spirit changes
between a man and his friend, or between two cities.
For some men soon, for others in later time,
their pleasure sickens; or love comes again.
And so with you and Thebes: the sweet season
holds between you now; but time goes on,
unmeasured Time, fathering numberless
nights, unnumbered days: and on one day
they'll break apart with spears this harmony—
all for a trivial word.
And then my sleeping and long-hidden corpse,
cold in the earth, will drink hot blood of theirs,
if Zeus endures; if his son's word is true.
However: there's no felicity in speaking
of hidden things. Let me come back to this:
be careful that you keep your word to me;
for if you do you'll never say of Oedipus
that he was given refuge uselessly—
or if you say it, then the gods have lied.

CHORUS LEADER

My lord: before you came this man gave promise
of having power to make his words come true.

THESEUS

Who would reject his friendship? Is he not

one who would have, in any case, an ally's
right to our hospitality?
Moreover he has asked grace of our deities,
and offers no small favor in return.
As I value that favor, I shall not refuse
this man's desire; I declare him a citizen.
And if it should please our friend to remain here,
I direct you to take care of him;
or else he may come with me.
                    Whatever you choose,
Oedipus, we shall be happy to accord.
You know your own needs best; I accede to them.

OEDIPUS

May god bless men like these!

THESEUS

What do you say then? Shall it be my house?

OEDIPUS

If it were right for me. But the place is here . . .

THESEUS

And what will you do here?—not that I oppose you.

OEDIPUS

Here I shall prevail over those who banished me.

THESEUS

Your presence, as you say, is a great blessing.

OEDIPUS

If you are firm in doing what you promise.

THESEUS

You can be sure of me; I'll not betray you.

OEDIPUS

I'll not ask pledges, as I would of scoundrels.

THESEUS

You'd get no more assurance than by my word.

OEDIPUS

I wonder how you will behave?

THESEUS

You fear?

OEDIPUS

That men will come—

THESEUS

These men will attend to them.

OEDIPUS

Look: when you leave me—

THESEUS

I know what to do!

OEDIPUS

I am oppressed by fear!

THESEUS

I feel no fear.

OEDIPUS

You do not know the menace!

THESEUS

I do know
no man is going to take you against my will.
Angry men are liberal with threats°
and bluster generally. When the mind
is master of itself, threats are no matter.
These people may have dared to talk quite fiercely
of taking you; perhaps, as I rather think,
they'll find a sea of troubles in the way.
Therefore I should advise you to take heart.

Even aside from me and my intentions,
did not Apollo send and guide you here?
However it may be, I can assure you,
while I'm away, my name will be your shield.

*(Exit Theseus and soldiers, to the side.)*

CHORUS [*singing*]

STROPHE A

*The land of running horses, fair*
*Colonus takes a guest;*
*he shall not seek another home.°*
*For this, in all the earth and air,*
*is most secure and loveliest.*

*In the god's untrodden vale*
*where leaves and berries throng,*
*and wine-dark ivy climbs the bough,*
*the sweet, sojourning nightingale*
*murmurs all night long.*

*No sun nor wind may enter there*
*nor the winter's rain;*
*but ever through the shadow goes*
*Dionysus reveler,*
*immortal maenads in his train.*

ANTISTROPHE A

*Here with drops of heaven's dews*
*at daybreak all the year,*
*the clusters of narcissus bloom,*
*time-hallowed garlands for the brows*
*of those great Ladies whom we fear.*

*The crocus like a little sun*
*blooms with its yellow ray;*
*the river's fountains are awake,*
*and his nomadic streams that run*
*unthinned forever, and never stay,°*

*But like perpetual lovers move*
*on the maternal land.*
*And here the choiring Muses come,*
*and the divinity of Love,*
*with the gold reins in her hand.*

STROPHE B

*And our land has a thing unknown*
*on Asia's sounding coast*
*or in the sea-surrounded west*
*where Pelops' kin holds sway:°*
*the olive, fertile and self-sown,*
*the terror of our enemies*
*that no hand tames nor tears away—*
*the blessed tree that never dies!—*
*but it will mock the spearsman in his rage.*

*Ah, how it flourishes in every field,*
*most beautifully here!*
*The gray-leafed tree, the children's nourisher!*
*No young man nor one partnered by his age*
*knows how to root it out nor make*
*barren its yield;*
*for Zeus Protector of the Shoot has sage*
*eyes that forever are awake,*
*and Pallas watches with her sea-gray eyes.*

ANTISTROPHE B

*Last and grandest praise I sing*
*to Athens, nurse of men,*
*for her great pride and for the splendor*
*destiny has conferred on her.*
*Land from which fine horses spring!*
*Land where foals are beautiful!*
*Land of the sea and the seafarer,*
*enthroned on her pure littoral*
*by Cronus' briny son in ancient time.*

*That lord, Poseidon, must I praise again*
*who found our horsemen fit*
*for first bestowal of the curb and bit,*
*to discipline the stallion in his prime;*
*and strokes to which our oarsmen sing,*
*well-fitted, oak and men,*
*whose long sea-oars in wondrous rhyme*
*flash from the salt foam, following*
*the track of winds on waters virginal.*°

ANTIGONE

Land so well spoken of and praised so much!
Now is the time to show those words are true.

OEDIPUS

What now, my child?

ANTIGONE

A man is coming toward us,
and it is Creon—not alone, though, father.

OEDIPUS

Most kindly friends! I hope you may give proof,
and soon, of your ability to protect me!

CHORUS LEADER

No fear: it will be proved. I may be old,
but the nation's strength has not grown old.

*(Enter Creon from the side, with soldiers.)*

CREON

Gentlemen, and citizens of this land:
I can see from your eyes that my arrival
has been a cause of sudden fear to you.
Do not be fearful; and say nothing hostile!
I have not come for any hostile action:
for I am old, and know this city has
power, if any city in Hellas has.

But for this man here: I, despite my age,
am sent to bring him to the land of Thebes.°
This is not one man's mission, but was ordered
by the whole Theban people. I am their emissary,
because it fell to me as a relative
to mourn his troubles more than anyone.
So, now, poor Oedipus, come home.
You know the word I bring. Your countrymen
are right in summoning you—I most of all,
for most of all, unless I am worst of men,
I grieve for your unhappiness, old man.
I see you ravaged as you are, a stranger
everywhere, never at rest,
with only a girl to serve you in your need—
I never thought she'd fall to such indignity,
poor child! And yet she has,
forever tending you, leading a beggar's
life with you; a grown-up girl who knows
nothing of marriage; whoever comes can take her . . .
Is not this a disgrace? I weep to see it!
Disgrace for you, for me, for all our people!
We cannot hide what is so palpable.
But you, if you will listen to me, Oedipus—
and in the name of your father's gods, listen!—
bury the whole thing now;° agree with me
to go back to your city and your home!
Take friendly leave of Athens, as she merits;
but you should have more reverence for Thebes,
since long ago she was your kindly nurse.

OEDIPUS

You brazen rascal! Playing your rascal's tricks
in righteous speeches, as you always would!
Why do you try it? How can you think to take me
into that snare I should so hate if taken?
That time when I was sick with my own life's

evil, when I would gladly have left my land,
you had no mind to give me what I wanted!
But when at long last I had had my fill
of rage and grief, and in my quiet house
began to find some comfort: that was the time
you chose to rout me out.
How precious was this kinship to you then?
It is the same thing now: you see this city
and all its people being kind to me,
so you would draw me away—
a cruel thing, for all your soothing words.
Why is it your pleasure to be amiable
to those who do not want your amiability?
Suppose that when you begged for something desperately
a man should neither grant it you nor give
sympathy even; but later when you were glutted
with all your heart's desire, should give it then,
when charity was no charity at all?
Would you not think the kindness somewhat hollow?
That is the sort of kindness you offer me:
generous in words, but in reality evil.
Now I will tell these men, and prove you evil.
You come to take me, but not to take me home;
rather to settle me outside the city
so that the city may escape my curse,
escape from punishment by Athens.
Yes;
but you'll not have it. What you'll have is this:
my vengeance active in that land forever.
And what my sons will have of my old kingdom
is just so much room as they need to die in!
Now who knows better the destiny of Thebes?
I do, for I have had the best informants:
Apollo, and Zeus himself who is his father.
And yet you come here with your fraudulent speech

all whetted up! The more you talk, the more
harm, not good, you'll get by it!—
however, I know you'll never believe that—
only leave us! Let us live here in peace!
Is this misfortune, if it brings contentment?

CREON

Which of us do you consider is more injured
by talk like this? You hurt only yourself.

OEDIPUS

I am perfectly content, so long as you
can neither wheedle me nor fool these others.

CREON

Unhappy man! Shall it be plain that time
brings you no wisdom? that you shame your age?

OEDIPUS

An agile wit! I know no honest man
able to speak so well under all conditions!

CREON

To speak much is one thing; to speak to the point's another!

OEDIPUS

As if you spoke so little but so fittingly!

CREON

No, not fittingly for a mind like yours!

OEDIPUS

Leave me! I speak for these men, too!
Spare me your wardship, here where I must live!

CREON

I call on these—not you!—as witnesses
of what rejoinder you have made to friends.
If I ever take you—

OEDIPUS

With these men opposing,
who is going to take me by violence?

CREON

You'll suffer without need of that, I promise you!

OEDIPUS

What are you up to? What is behind that brag?

CREON

Your daughters: one of them I have just now
had seized and carried off; now I'll take this one!

OEDIPUS

Ah!

CREON

Soon you shall have more reason to groan about it!

OEDIPUS

You have my child?

CREON

And this one in a moment!

OEDIPUS

Ah, friends! What will you do? Will you betray me?
Expel this man who has profaned your country!

CHORUS LEADER

Go, and go quickly, stranger! You have no right
to do what you are doing, or what you have done!

CREON *(To his soldiers.)*

You there: it would be well to take her now,
whether she wants to go with you or not.

*(Two soldiers approach Antigone.)*

ANTIGONE

Oh, god, where shall I run? What help is there
From gods or men?

CHORUS LEADER

What are you doing, stranger?

CREON

I will not touch this man; but she is mine.

OEDIPUS

O masters of this land!

CHORUS LEADER

This is unjust!

CREON

No, just!

CHORUS LEADER

Why so?

CREON

I take what belongs to me!

OEDIPUS [*now singing*]

STROPHE

*O Athens!*

(*The soldiers seize Antigone.*)

CHORUS [*mostly singing while Creon, Antigone, and Oedipus speak in response*]

*What are you doing, stranger? Will you*
*Let her go? Must we have a test of strength?*

CREON

Hold off!

CHORUS

*Not while you persist in doing this!*

CREON

Your city will have war if you hurt me!

OEDIPUS

Did I not foretell this?

CHORUS LEADER

Take your hands
off the child at once!

CREON

What you cannot enforce,
do not command!

CHORUS LEADER

Release the child, I say!

CREON

And I say—march!

CHORUS

*Help! Here, men of Colonus! Help! Help!*
*The city, my city, is violated!*
*Help, ho!*

ANTIGONE

They drag me away. How wretched! O friends, friends!

OEDIPUS

Where are you, child?

ANTIGONE

They have overpowered me!

OEDIPUS

Give me your hands, little one!

ANTIGONE

I cannot do it!

CREON *(To the soldiers.)*

Will you get on with her?

*(Exit the guards to one side, dragging Antigone.)*

OEDIPUS

God help me now!°

CREON

With these two sticks at any rate you'll never
guide yourself again. But since you wish
to conquer your own people—by whose command,
though I am royal, I have performed this act—
go on and conquer! Later, I think, you'll learn
that now as before you have done yourself no good
by gratifying your temper against your friends!
Anger has always been your greatest sin!

CHORUS LEADER *(To Creon, approaching him.)*

Control yourself, stranger!

CREON

Don't touch me, I say!

CHORUS LEADER

I'll not release you! Those two girls were stolen!

CREON

By god, I'll have more plunder in a moment
to bring my city! I'll not stop with them!

CHORUS LEADER

Now what are you about?

CREON

I'll take him, too!

CHORUS LEADER

A terrible thing to say!

CREON

It will be done!

CHORUS LEADER

Not if the ruler of our land can help it!°

OEDIPUS

Voice of shamelessness! Will you touch me?

CREON

Silence, I say!

OEDIPUS

No! May the powers here
not make me silent until I say this curse:
you scoundrel, who have cruelly taken her
who served my naked eyepits as their eyes!
On you and yours forever may the sun god,
watcher of all the world, confer such days
as I have had, and such an age as mine!

CREON

Do you see this, men of the land of Athens?

OEDIPUS

They see both me and you; and they see also
that when I am hurt I have only words to avenge it!

CREON

I'll not stand for it longer! Alone as I am,
and slow with age, I'll try my strength to take him!

*(Creon advances toward Oedipus.)*

OEDIPUS

ANTISTROPHE

*Ah!*

CHORUS

*You are a bold man, friend,*
*if you think you can do this!*

CREON

I do think so!

CHORUS

If you could, our city would be finished!

CREON

In a just cause the weak will beat the strong!

OEDIPUS

You hear his talk?

CHORUS LEADER

By Zeus, he shall not do it!°

CREON

Zeus may determine that, but you will not.

CHORUS LEADER

Is this not criminal?

CREON *(Laying hold of Oedipus.)*

If so, you'll bear it!

CHORUS [*singing*]

*Ho, everyone! Captains, ho!*
*Come on the run!*
*They are well on their way by now!*

*(Enter Theseus from the side, with armed men.)*

THESEUS

Why do you shout? What is the matter here?
Of what are you afraid?
You have interrupted me as I was sacrificing
to the great sea god, the patron of Colonus.
Tell me, let me know everything;
I do not care to make such haste for nothing.

OEDIPUS

O dearest friend—I recognize your voice—
a fearful thing has just been done to me!

THESEUS

What is it? Who is the man who did it? Tell me.

OEDIPUS

This Creon has had my daughters bound and stolen.

THESEUS

What's this you say?

OEDIPUS

Yes; now you know my loss.

THESEUS *(To his men.)*

One of you go on the double
to the altar place and rouse the people there;
make them leave the sacrifice at once
and run full speed, both foot and cavalry
as hard as they can gallop, for the place
where the two highways come together.
The girls must not be taken past that point,
or I shall be a laughingstock to this fellow,
as if I were a man to be handled roughly!
Go on, do as I tell you! Quick!

*(Exit a soldier, to the side.)*

This man—
if I should act in anger, as he deserves,
I would not let him leave my hands unbloodied;
but he shall be subject to the sort of laws
he has himself imported here.—

*(To Creon.)*

You: you shall never leave this land of Attica
until you produce those girls here in my presence;
for your behavior is an affront to me,
a shame to your own people and your nation.
You come to a city-state that practices justice,
a state that rules by law, and by law only;
and yet you cast aside her authority,
take what you please, and worse, by violence,
as if you thought there were no men among us,
or only slaves; and as if I were nobody.
I doubt that Thebes is responsible for you:
she has no propensity for breeding rascals.
And Thebes would not applaud you if she knew
you tried to trick me and to rob the gods

by dragging helpless people from their sanctuary!
Were I a visitor in your country—
no matter how immaculate my claims—
without consent from him who ruled the land,
whoever he might be, I'd take nothing.
I think I have some notion of the conduct
proper to one who visits a friendly city.
You bring disgrace upon an honorable
land—your own land, too; a long life
seems to have left you witless as you are old.
I said it once and say it now again:
someone had better bring those girls here quickly,
unless you wish to prolong your stay with us
under close guard, and not much liking it.
This is not just a speech; I mean it, friend.

CHORUS LEADER

Now do you see where you stand? Thebes is just;
but you are adjudged to have acted wickedly.

CREON

It was not that I thought this state unmanly,
son of Aegeus; nor ill-governed, either;
rather I did this thing in the opinion
that no one here would love my citizens°
so tenderly as to keep them against my will . . .
And surely, I thought, no one would give welcome
to an unholy man, a parricide,
a man with whom his mother had been found!°
Such at least was my estimate of the wisdom
native to the Areopagus; I thought
Athens was not a home for such exiles.
In that belief I considered him my prize.
Even so, I'd not have touched him had he not
called down curses on my race and me;
that was an injury that deserved reprisal.
There is no old age for a man's anger.

Only death; the dead cannot be hurt.°
You will do as you wish in this affair,
for even though my case is right and just,
I am weak, without support. Nevertheless,
old as I am, I'll try to hold you answerable.

OEDIPUS

O arrogance unashamed! Whose age do you
think you are insulting, mine or yours?
The bloody deaths, the incest, the calamities
you speak so glibly of: I suffered them
by fate, against my will! It was god's pleasure,
and perhaps our family had angered him long ago.°
In me myself you could not find such evil
as would have made me sin against my own.
And tell me this: if there were prophecies
repeated by the oracles of the gods,
that father's death should come through his own son,
how could you justly blame it upon me?
On me, who was yet unborn, yet unconceived,
not yet existent for my father and mother?
If then I came into the world—as I did come—
in wretchedness, and met my father in fight
and knocked him down, not knowing that I killed him
nor whom I killed°—again, how could you find
guilt in that unmeditated act?
As for my mother—damn you, you have no shame,
though you are her own brother, in forcing me
to speak of that unspeakable marriage;
but I shall speak, I'll not be silent now
after you've let your foul talk go so far!
Yes, she gave me birth—incredible fate!—
but neither of us knew the truth; and she
bore my children also—and then her shame.
But one thing I do know: you are content
to slander her as well as me for that;

while I would not have married her willingly
nor willingly would I ever speak of it.
No: I shall not be judged an evil man,
neither in that marriage nor in that death
which you forever charge me with so bitterly.
Just answer me one thing:
if someone tried to kill you here and now,
you righteous gentleman, what would you do,
inquire first if the stranger was your father?
Or would you not first try to defend yourself?
I think that since you like to be alive
you'd treat him as the threat required; not
look around for assurance that you were right.
Well, that was the sort of danger I was in,
forced into it by the gods. My father's soul,
were it on earth, I know would bear me out.
You, however—being a knave, and since you
think it fair to say anything you choose
and speak of what should not be spoken of—
accuse me of all this before these people.
You also think it clever to flatter Theseus,
and Athens—her exemplary government.
But in your flattery you have forgotten this:
if any country comprehends the honors
due to the gods, this country knows them best.
Yet you would steal me from Athens in my age
and in my time of prayer;° indeed, you seized me
and you have seized and carried off my daughters.
Now for that profanation I make my prayer,
calling on the divinities of the grove
that they shall give me aid and fight for me,
so you may know what men defend this town.

CHORUS LEADER

My lord, our friend is worthy; he has had
disastrous fortune; yet he deserves our comfort.

THESEUS

Enough of speeches. While the perpetrators
flee, we who were injured loiter here.

CREON

What will you have me do?—since I am worthless.

THESEUS

You lead us on the way. You can be my escort.
If you are holding the children in this neighborhood,
you yourself will uncover them to me.
If your retainers have taken them in flight,
the chase is not ours; others are after them,
and they will never have cause to thank their gods
for getting free out of this country.
All right. Move on. And remember that the captor
is now the captive; the hunter is in the snare.
What was won by stealth will not be kept.
In this you'll not have others to assist you;
and I know well you had them, for you'd never
dare to go so far in your insolence
were you without sufficient accomplices.
You must have had a reason for your confidence,
and I must reckon with it. The whole city
must not seem overpowered by one man.°
Do you understand at all? Or do you think
that what I say is still without importance?

CREON

To what you say I make no objection here.
At home we, too, shall determine what to do.

THESEUS

If you must threaten, do so on the way.
Oedipus, you stay here, and rest assured
that unless I perish first I'll not draw breath
until I put your children in your hands.

OEDIPUS

Bless you for your noble heart, Theseus,
and you are blessed in what you do for us.°

*(Exit Theseus and Creon to the side, with the soldiers.)*

CHORUS [*singing*]

STROPHE A

*Ah, god, to be where the pillagers make stand!°*
*To hear the shout and brazen sound of war!*
*Or maybe on Apollo's sacred strand,*
*or by that torchlit Eleusinian shore*

*Where pilgrims come, whose lips the golden key*
*of sweet-voiced Ministers has rendered still.*
*To cherish there with grave Persephone*
*consummate rest from death and mortal ill;*

*For even to those shades the warrior king*
*will press the fighting on—until he take*
*the virgin sisters from the foemen's ring,*
*within his country, for his country's sake!*

ANTISTROPHE A

*It may be they will get beyond the plain*
*and reach the snowy mountain's western side.*
*If their light chariots have the racing rein,*
*if they have ponies, and if they can ride;*

*Yet they'll be taken: for the god they fear*
*fights for our land, and Theseus sends forth*
*his breakneck cavalry with all its gear*
*flashing like mountain lightning to the north.*

*These are the riders of Athens, conquered never;°*
*they honor her whose glory all men know,*
*and honor the sea god, who is dear forever*
*to Rhea Mother, who bore him long ago.*

STROPHE B

*Swords out—or has the work of swords begun?*
*My mind leans to a whisper:*
*within the hour they must surrender*
*the woeful children of the blinded one;*
*this day is shaped by Zeus Artificer.*
*I can call up the bright sword play,°*
*but wish the wind would lift me like a dove*
*under the tall cloud cover*
*to look with my own eyes on this affray.*

ANTISTROPHE B

*Zeus, lord of all, and eye of heaven on all,*
*let our home troop's hard riding*
*cut them off, and a charge from hiding*
*carry the combat in one shock and fall.*
*Stand, helmeted Athena, at our side,*
*Apollo, Artemis, come down,*
*hunter and huntress of the flickering deer—*
*pace with each cavalier*
*for honor of our land and Athens town.°*

CHORUS LEADER [*speaking*]
O wanderer! You will not say I lied;
I who kept lookout for you!
I see them now—the two girls—here they come
with our armed men around them.

OEDIPUS
What did you say? Ah, where?

*(Enter Theseus from the side, leading Antigone and Ismene, escorted by soldiers.)*

ANTIGONE
Father, father!
I wish some god would give you eyes to see
the noble prince who brings us back to you!

OEDIPUS

Ah, child! You are really here?

ANTIGONE

Yes, for the might
of Theseus and his kind followers saved us.

OEDIPUS

Come to your father, child, and let me touch you both,
whom I had thought never to touch again!

ANTIGONE

It shall be as you ask; I wish it as much as you.

OEDIPUS

Where are you?

ANTIGONE

We are coming to you together.

OEDIPUS

My sweet children!

ANTIGONE

To our father, sweet indeed.

OEDIPUS

My staff and my support!

ANTIGONE

And partners in sorrow.

OEDIPUS

I have what is dearest to me in the world:
to die, now, would not be so terrible
since you are near me.
Press close to me, child,
be rooted in your father's arms; rest now
from the cruel separation, the going and coming;
and tell me the story as briefly as you can:
a little talk is enough for girls so tired.°

ANTIGONE

Theseus saved us: he is the one to tell you,
and he can put it briefly and make it clear.°

OEDIPUS

Dear friend: don't be offended if I continue
to talk to these two children overlong;
I had scarce thought they would be seen again!
Be sure I understand that you alone
made this joy possible for me.
You are the one that saved them, no one else,
and may the gods give you such destiny
as I desire for you and for your country.
For I have found you truly reverent,
decent, and straight in speech, you only
of all mankind.
I know it, and I thank you with these words.
All that I have I owe to your courtesy.
Now give me your right hand, my lord,
and if it be permitted, let me kiss you . . .
What am I saying? How can a wretch like me
desire to touch a man who has no stain
of evil in him? No, no; I will not do it;
and neither shall you touch me. The only ones
fit to be fellow sufferers of mine
are those with such experience as I have.
Receive my salutation where you are;
and for the rest, be kindly to me still
as you have been up to now.

THESEUS

That you should talk a long time to your children
in joy at seeing them—why, that's no wonder!
Or that you should address them before me—
there's no offense in that. It is not in words
that I should wish my life to be distinguished,
but rather in things done.

Have I not shown that? I was not a liar
in what I swore I'd do for you, old man.
I am here; and I have brought them back
alive and safe, for all they were threatened with.
As to how I found them, how I took them, why
brag of it? You will surely learn from them.
However, there is a matter that just now
came to my attention on my way here—
a trivial thing to speak of, and yet puzzling;
I want your opinion on it.
It is best for a man not to neglect such things.

OEDIPUS

What is it, son of Aegeus? Tell me,
so I may know on what you desire counsel.

THESEUS

They say a man is here claiming to be
a relative of yours, though not of Thebes;
for some reason he has thrown himself in prayer°
before Poseidon's altar, where I was making
sacrifice before I came.

OEDIPUS

What is his country? What is he praying for?

THESEUS

All I know is this: he asks, they tell me,
a brief interview with you, and nothing more.

OEDIPUS

Upon what subject?
If he's in prayer, it cannot be a trifle.

THESEUS

They say he only asks to speak to you
and then to depart safely by the same road.

OEDIPUS

Who could it be that would come here to pray?°

THESEUS

Think: have you any relative in Argos
who might desire this favor of you?

OEDIPUS

Dear friend!
Say no more!

THESEUS

What has alarmed you?

OEDIPUS

No more!

THESEUS

But what is the matter? Tell me.

OEDIPUS

When I heard "Argos" I knew the petitioner.

THESEUS

And who is he whom I must hold at fault?

OEDIPUS

A son of mine, my lord, and a hated one:
nothing could be more painful than to listen to him.

THESEUS

But why? Is it not possible to listen
without doing anything you need not do?
Why should it distress you so to hear him?

OEDIPUS

My lord, even his voice is hateful to me.
Don't overrule me; don't make me yield in this!

THESEUS

But now consider if you are not obliged
to do so by his supplication here:
perhaps you have a duty to the god.

ANTIGONE

Father, listen to me, even if I am young.
Allow this man to satisfy his conscience
and give the gods whatever he thinks their due.
And let our brother come here, for our sake.
Don't be afraid: he will not throw you off
in your resolve, nor speak offensively.
What is the harm in hearing what he says?
If he has ill intentions, he'll betray them.
You sired him; even though he wrongs you, father,
and wrongs you impiously, still you cannot
rightfully wrong him in return!
Do let him come!
Other men have bad sons,
and other men are swift to anger; yet
they will accept advice, they will be swayed
by their friends' pleading, even against their nature.
Reflect, not on the present, but on the past;
think of your mother's and your father's fate
and what you suffered through them! If you do,
I think you'll see how terrible an end
terrible wrath may have.
You have, I think, a permanent reminder
in your lost, irrecoverable eyes.
Ah, yield to us! If our request is just,
we need not, surely, be importunate;
and you, to whom I have not yet been hard,
should not be obdurate with me!°

OEDIPUS

Child, your talk wins you a pleasure
that will be pain for me. If you have set
your heart on it, so be it.
Only, Theseus: if he is to come here,
let no one have power over my life!

THESEUS

That is the sort of thing I need hear only
once, not twice, old man. I do not boast,
but you should know, your life is safe while mine is.°

*(Exit Theseus to the side, with his soldiers, leaving two on guard.)*

CHORUS [*singing*]

STROPHE

*Though he has watched a decent age pass by,*
*a man will sometimes still desire the world.*
*I swear I see no wisdom in that man.*
*The endless hours pile up a drift of pain*
*more unrelieved each day; and as for pleasure,*
*when he is sunken in excessive age*
*you will not see his pleasure anywhere.*
*The last attendant is the same for all,*
*old men and young alike, as in its season*
*man's heritage of underworld appears:*
*there being then no epithalamion,*
*no music and no dance. Death is the finish.*

ANTISTROPHE

*Not to be born surpasses thought and speech.*
*The second best is to have seen the light*
*and then to go back quickly whence we came.*
*The feathery follies of his youth once over,*
*what trouble is beyond the range of man?*
*What heavy burden will he not endure?*
*Jealousy, faction, quarreling, and battle—*
*the bloodiness of war, the grief of war.*
*And in the end he comes to strengthless age,*
*abhorred by all men, without company,*
*unfriended in that uttermost twilight*
*where he must live with every bitter thing.*

EPODE

*This is the truth, not for me only,*

*but for this blind and ruined man.*
*Think of some shore in the north,*
*the concussive waves make stream*
*this way and that in the gales of winter:*
*it is like that with him,*
*the wild wrack breaking over him*
*from head to foot, and coming on forever;*
*now from the plunging down of the sun,*
*now from the sunrise quarter,*
*now from where the noonday gleams,*
*now from the night and the north.*

ANTIGONE

I think I see the stranger near us now,
and no men with him, father; but his eyes
swollen with weeping as he comes.

*(Enter Polynices, from the side.)*

OEDIPUS

Who comes?

ANTIGONE

The one whom we have had so long in mind;
it is he who stands here; it is Polynices.

POLYNICES

Ah, now what shall I do? Sisters, shall I
weep for my misfortunes or for those
I see in the old man, my father,
whom I have found here in an alien land,
with two frail girls, an outcast for so long,
and with such garments! The abominable
filth grown old with him, rotting his sides!
And on his sightless face the ragged hair
streams in the wind. There's the same quality
in the food he carries for his thin old belly.
All this I learn too late.

And I swear now that I have been villainous
in not supporting you! You need not wait
to hear it said by others!
Only, think:
compassion limits even the power of god;°
so may there be a limit with you, father!
For all that has gone wrong may still be healed,
and surely the worst is passed!
Why are you silent?
Speak to me, father! Don't turn away from me!
Will you not answer me at all? Will you
send me away without a word?
Not even
tell me why you are enraged against me?
Daughters of Oedipus, my own sisters,
try to move your so implacable father;
do not let him reject me in such contempt!
Make him reply! I am here on pilgrimage . . .°

ANTIGONE

Poor brother: you yourself must tell him why.
As men speak on they may sometimes give pleasure,
sometimes annoy, or sometimes touch the heart;
and so somehow provide the mute with voices.

POLYNICES

I will speak out then; your advice is fair.
First, however, I must claim the help
of that same god, Poseidon, from whose altar
the governor of this land has lifted me
and sent me here, giving me leave to speak
and to await response, and a safe passage.
These are the favors I desire from you,
strangers, and from my sisters and my father.
And now, father, I will tell you why I came.
I am a fugitive, driven from my country,

because I thought fit, as the eldest born,
to take my seat upon your sovereign throne.
For that, Eteocles, the younger of us,
banished me—but not by a decision
in argument or ability or arms;
merely because he won the city over.
Of this I believe the Furies that pursue you
were indeed the cause: and so I hear
from clairvoyants whom I afterward consulted . . .°
Then, when I went to the Dorian land of Argos,
I took Adrastus as my father-in-law,
and bound to me by oath whatever men
were known as leaders or as fighters there;
my purpose being to form an expedition
of seven troops of spearmen against Thebes,
with which enlistment may I die for justice
or else expel the men who exiled me!

So it is. Then why should I come here now?
Father, my prayers must be made to you,
mine and those of all who fight with me.
Their seven columns under seven captains
even now complete the encirclement of Thebes:
men like Amphiaraus, the hard spear-thrower,
expert in spears and in the ways of eagles;
second is Tydeus, the Aetolian,
son of Oeneus; third is Eteoclus,
born in Argos; fourth is Hippomedon
(his father, Talaus, sent him); Capaneus,
the fifth, has sworn he'll raze the town of Thebes
with fire-brands; and sixth is Parthenopaeus,
an Arcadian who roused himself to war—
son of that virgin famous in the old time
who long years afterward conceived and bore him—
Parthenopaeus, Atalanta's son.
And it is I, your son—or if I am not

truly your son, since evil fathered me,
at least I am called your son—it is I who lead
the fearless troops of Argos against Thebes.
Now in the name of these two children, father,
and for your own soul's sake, we all implore
and beg you to give up your heavy wrath
against me! I go forth to punish him,
the brother who robbed me of my fatherland.
If we can put any trust in oracles,
they say that those you bless shall come to power.
Now by the gods and fountains of our people,
I pray you, listen and comply! Are we not beggars
both of us, and exiles, you and I?
We live by paying court to other men;
the same fate follows us.
But as for him—how insupportable!—
he lords it in our house, luxuriates there,
laughs at us both!
If you will stand by me in my resolve,
I'll waste no time or trouble whipping him;°
and then I'll reestablish you at home,
and settle there myself, and throw him out.
If your will is the same as mine, it's possible
to promise this. If not, I can't be saved.

CHORUS LEADER

For the sake of the one who sent him, Oedipus,
speak to this man before you send him back.

OEDIPUS

Yes, gentlemen: but were it not Theseus,
the sovereign of your land, who sent him here,
thinking it right that he should have an answer,
you never would have heard a sound from me.
Well: he has asked, and he shall hear from me
a kind of answer that will not overjoy him.
You scoundrel! When it was you who held

throne and authority—as your brother now
holds them in Thebes—you drove me into exile:
me, your own father: made me a homeless man,
insuring me these rags you maunder over°
when you behold them—now that you, as well,
have fallen on evil days and are in exile.
Weeping is no good now. However long
my life may last, I have to see it through;
but I regard you as a murderer!
For you reduced me to this misery;
you made me an exile; because of you
I have begged my daily bread from other men.
If I had not these daughters to sustain me,
I might have lived or died for all your interest.
But they have saved me; they are my support,
and are not girls, but men, in faithfulness.
As for you two, you are no sons of mine!
And so it is that there are eyes that watch you°
even now; though not as they shall watch
if those troops are in fact marching on Thebes.
You cannot take that city. You'll go down
all bloody,° and your brother, too. For I
have placed that curse upon you before this,
and now I invoke that curse to fight for me,
that you may see a reason to respect
your parents, though your birth was as it was;
and though I am blind, not to dishonor me.
These girls did not.
And so your supplication and your throne
are overmastered surely—if accepted
Justice still has place in the laws of god.°
Now go! For I abominate and disown you,
wretched scum! Go with the malediction
I here pronounce for you: that you shall never
master your native land by force of arms,
nor ever see your home again in Argos,

the land below the hills; but you shall die
by your own brother's hand, and you shall kill
the brother who banished you. For this I pray.
And I cry out to the hated underworld
that it may take you home; cry out to these
powers indwelling here; and to that power
of furious War that filled your hearts with hate!
Now you have heard me. Go: tell it to Thebes,
tell all the Thebans; tell your faithful fighting
friends what sort of honors
Oedipus has divided among his sons!

CHORUS LEADER

Polynices, I find no matter for sympathy
in your directing yourself here. You may retire.

POLYNICES

Ah, what a journey! What a failure!
My poor companions! See the finish now
of all we marched from Argos for! See me . . .
for I can neither speak of this to anyone
among my friends, nor lead them back again;
I must go silently to meet this doom.
O sisters—daughters of his, sisters of mine!
You heard the hard curse of our father:
for god's sweet sake, if father's curse comes true,
and if you find some way to return home,
do not, at least, dishonor me in death!
But give me a grave and what will quiet me.°
Then you shall have, besides the praise he now
gives you for serving him, an equal praise
for offices you shall have paid my ghost.

ANTIGONE

Polynices, I beseech you, listen to me!

POLYNICES

Dearest—what is it? Tell me, Antigone.

ANTIGONE

Withdraw your troops to Argos as soon as you can.
Do not go to your own death and your city's!

POLYNICES

But that is impossible. How could I command
that army, even backward, once I faltered?

ANTIGONE

Now why, boy, must your anger rise again?
What is the good of laying waste your homeland?

POLYNICES

It is shameful to run; and it is also shameful
to be a laughingstock to a younger brother.

ANTIGONE

But see how you fulfill his prophecies!
Did he not cry that you should kill each other?

POLYNICES

He wishes that. But I cannot give way.

ANTIGONE

Ah, I am desolate! But who will dare
go with you, after hearing the prophecies?

POLYNICES

I'll not report this trifle. A good commander
tells heartening news, or keeps the news to himself.

ANTIGONE

Then you have made up your mind to this, my brother?

POLYNICES

Yes. And do not try to hold me back.
The dark road is before me; I must take it,
doomed by my father and his avenging Furies.
God bless you if you do what I have asked!
It is only in death that you can help me now.°

Now let me go. Good-bye! You will not ever
look in my eyes again.

ANTIGONE

You break my heart!

POLYNICES

Do not grieve for me.

ANTIGONE

Who would not grieve for you,
sweet brother! You go with open eyes to death.

POLYNICES

Death, if that must be.

ANTIGONE

No! Do as I ask!

POLYNICES

You ask the impossible.

ANTIGONE

Then I am lost,
if I must be deprived of you!

POLYNICES

All that
rests with the powers that are over us,
whether it must be so or otherwise.
You two—I pray no evil comes to you;
for all men know you merit no more pain.

*(Exit Polynices to the side.)*

CHORUS [*singing, while Oedipus and Antigone speak in response*]

STROPHE A

*So in this new event we see*
*new forms of terror working through the blind,*
*or else inscrutable destiny.*
*I am not one to say "This is in vain"*

*of anything allotted to mankind.*
*Though some must fall, or fall to rise again,*
*time watches all things steadily*

*(A terrific peal of thunder is heard.)*

*Ah, Zeus! Heaven's height has cracked!*

*(Thunder and lightning.)*

OEDIPUS

O children, children! Could someone here—
could someone bring the hero, Theseus?

ANTIGONE

Father, what is your reason for calling him?

OEDIPUS

Zeus' beating thunder, any moment now,
will clap me underground: send for him quickly!

*(Thunder and lightning.)*

CHORUS

ANTISTROPHE A

*Hear it° cascading down the air!*
*The god-thrown, the gigantic, holy sound!*
*Terror crawls to the tips of my hair!*
*My heart shakes!*
*There the lightning flames again!*
*What heavenly marvel is it bringing 'round?*
*I fear it, for it never comes in vain.*
*But for man's luck or his despair . . .°*

*(Another thunderclap.)*

STROPHE B

*Hear the wild thunder fall!°*
*Towering Nature is transfixed.*
*Be merciful, great spirit, if you run*
*this sword of darkness through our mother land;*

*come not for our confusion,°*
*and deal no blows to me,*
*though your tireless Furies stand*
*by him whom I have looked upon.*
*Great Zeus, I make my prayer to you!*

OEDIPUS

Is the king near by? Will he come in time
to find me still alive, my mind still clear?

ANTIGONE

Tell me what it is you have in mind!

OEDIPUS

To give him now, in return for his great kindness,
the blessing that I promised I would give.

CHORUS

ANTISTROPHE B

*O noble son, return!*
*No matter if you still descend*
*in the deep fastness of the sea god's grove,*
*to make pure offering at his altar fire:*
*receive from this strange man*
*whatever may be his heart's desire*
*that you and I and Athens are worthy of.°*
*My lord, come quickly as you can!*

*(Enter Theseus from the side.)*

THESEUS

Now why do you all together
set up this shout once more?
I see it comes from you, as from our friend.
Is it a lightning bolt from Zeus? a squall
of rattling hail? Those are familiar things
when such a tempest rages over heaven.

OEDIPUS

My lord, I longed for you to come! This is
gods' work, your lucky coming.

THESEUS

Now, what new
circumstance has arisen, son of Laius?

OEDIPUS

My life sinks in the scale: I would not die
without fulfilling what I promised Athens.

THESEUS

What proof have you that your hour has come?°

OEDIPUS

The great, incessant thunder and continuous
flashes of lightning from the hand of Zeus.

THESEUS

I believe you. I have seen you prophesy
many things, none falsely. What must be done?

OEDIPUS

I shall disclose to you, O son of Aegeus,
what is appointed for you and for your city:
a thing that age will never wear away.
Presently now, without a soul to guide me,
I'll lead you to the place where I must die;
but you must never tell it to any man,
not even the neighborhood in which it lies.
If you obey, this will count more for you
than many shields and many neighbors' spears.
These things are mysteries, not to be explained;
but you will understand when you come there
alone. Alone, because I cannot disclose it
to any of your men or to my children,
much as I love and cherish them. But you

keep it secret always, and when you come
to the end of life, then you must hand it on
to your most cherished son, and he in turn
must teach it to his heir, and so forever.°
That way you shall forever hold this city
safe from the men of Thebes, the dragon's sons.
For every nation that lives peaceably,
there will be many others to grow hard
and push their arrogance to extremes. The gods
attend to these things slowly; but they attend
to those who put off god and turn to madness!
You have no mind for that, child of Aegeus.
Indeed, you know already all that I teach.
Let us now proceed to that place
and hesitate no longer; I am driven
by an insistent voice that comes from god.
Children, follow me this way: see, now,
I have become your guide, as you were mine!
Come: do not touch me: let me alone discover
the holy and funereal ground where I
must take this fated earth to be my shroud.
This way, O come! The angel of the dead,
Hermes, and veiled Persephone lead me on!

*(Oedipus begins to walk to the side, leading his daughters.)*

O sunlight of no light! Once you were mine!
This is the last my flesh will feel of you;
for now I go to shade my ending day
in the dark underworld. Most cherished friend!
I pray that you and this your land and all
your people may be blessed: remember me.
Be mindful of my death, and be
fortunate in all the time to come!

*(Exit Oedipus to the side, followed by his daughters
and by Theseus with his soldiers.)*

CHORUS [*singing*]

STROPHE

*If I may dare to adore that lady*
*the living never see,*
*and pray to the master of spirits plunged in night,*
*who of vast Hell has sovereignty:*°
*let not our friend go down in grief and weariness*
*to that all-shrouding fold,*
*the dead man's plain, the house that has no light.*
*Because his sufferings were great, unmerited and untold,*
*let some just god relieve him from distress!*

ANTISTROPHE

*O powers under the earth, and tameless*
*beast in the passageway,*
*rumbler prone at the gate of the strange hosts,*°
*their guard forever, as the legends say:*
*I pray you, even Death, offspring of Earth and Hell,*
*to let the descent be clear*
*as Oedipus goes down among the ghosts*
*on those dim fields of underground that all men living fear.*
*Eternal sleep, let Oedipus sleep well!*

(*Enter a Messenger, from the side.*)

MESSENGER

Citizens, the briefest way to tell you
would be to say that Oedipus is no more;
but what has happened cannot be told so simply—
it was no simple thing.

CHORUS LEADER

He is gone, poor man?

MESSENGER

You may be sure that he has left this world.

CHORUS LEADER

By god's mercy, was his death a painless one?

MESSENGER

That is the thing that seems so marvelous.
You know, for you were witnesses, how he
left this place with no friend leading him,
acting, himself, as guide for all of us.
Well, when he came to the steep place in the road,
the embankment there, secured with steps of brass,
he stopped in one of the many branching paths.
This was not far from the stone bowl that marks
Theseus' and Pirithous' covenant.
Halfway between that place of stone
with its hollow pear tree, and the marble tomb,
he sat down and undid his filthy garments;
then he called his daughters and commanded
that they should bring him water from a fountain
for bathing and libation to the dead.
From there they saw the hillcrest of Demeter,
freshener of all things: they ascended it
and soon came back with water for their father;
then helped him properly to bathe and dress.
When everything was finished to his pleasure
and no command of his remained undone,
then the earth groaned with thunder from the god below;
and as they heard the sound, the girls shuddered
and dropped to their father's knees, and began wailing,
beating their breasts and weeping, as if heartbroken.
And hearing them cry out so bitterly
he put his arms around them, and said to them:
"Children, this day your father is gone from you.
All that was mine is gone. You shall no longer
bear the burden of taking care of me—
I know it was hard, my children. And yet one word
frees us of all the weight and pain of life:°
that word is love. You never shall have more
from anyone than you have had from me.

And now you must spend the rest of life without me."
That was the way of it. They clung together
and wept, all three. But when they finally stopped
and no more sobs were heard, then there was
silence, and in the silence suddenly
a voice cried out to him—of such a kind
it made our hair stand up in panic fear:
again and again the call came from the god:
"Oedipus! Oedipus! Why are we waiting?
You delay too long; you delay too long to go!"
Then, knowing himself summoned by the spirit,
he asked that the lord Theseus come to him;
and when he had come, said: "O my prince and friend,
give your right hand now as a binding pledge
to my two daughters; children, give him your hands.
Promise that you will never willingly
betray them, but will carry out in kindness
whatever is best for them in the days to come."
And Theseus swore to do it for his friend,
with such restraint as fits a noble king.
And when he had done so, Oedipus at once
laid his blind hands upon his daughters, saying:
"Children, you must show your nobility,°
and have the courage now to leave this spot.
You must not wish to see what is forbidden
or hear such voices as may not be heard.
But go—go quickly. Only the lord Theseus
may stay to see the thing that now begins."
This much every one of us heard him say,
and then we came away, sobbing, with the girls.
But after a little while as we withdrew
we turned around—and nowhere saw that man,
but only the king, his hands before his face,
shading his eyes as if from something fearful,
awesome and unendurable to see.

Then very quickly we saw him do reverence
to Earth and to the powers of the air,
with one address to both.
But in what manner
Oedipus perished, no one of mortal men
could tell but Theseus. It was not lightning,
bearing its fire from Zeus, that took him off;
no hurricane was blowing.
But some attendant from the train of heaven°
came for him; or else the underworld
opened in love the unlit door of earth.
For he was taken without lamentation,
illness, or suffering; indeed his end
was wonderful if mortal's ever was.
Should someone think I speak intemperately,
I make no apology to him who thinks so.

CHORUS LEADER

But where are his children and the others with them?

MESSENGER

They are not far away; the sound of weeping
should tell you now that they are coming here.

*(Enter Antigone and Ismene together, from the side.)*

ANTIGONE [*singing in turn with Ismene and the Chorus*]

STROPHE A

*Now we may weep, indeed.*
*Now, if ever, we may cry*
*in bitter grief against our fate,*
*our heritage still unappeased.*
*In other days we stood up under it,*
*endured it for his sake,*
*the unrelenting horror. Now the finish*
*comes, and we know only*
*in all that we have seen and done*
*bewildering mystery.*

CHORUS

*What happened?*

ANTIGONE

*We can only guess, my friends.*

CHORUS

*He has gone?*

ANTIGONE

*He has; as one could wish him to.*
*Why not? It was not war*
*nor the deep sea that overtook him,*
*but something invisible and strange*
*caught him up—or down—*
*into a space unseen.*
*But we are lost, dear sister. A deathly*
*night is ahead of us.*
*For how, in some far country wandering,*
*or on the lifting seas,*
*shall we eke out our lives?*

ISMENE

*I cannot guess. But as for me,*
*I wish that murderous Hades would take me*
*in one death with our father.*
*This is such desolation*
*I cannot go on living.*

CHORUS

*Most admirable sisters:*
*whatever god has brought about*
*is to be borne with courage.*
*You must not feed the flames of grief;*
*no blame can come to you.*

ANTIGONE

ANTISTROPHE A

*One may long for the past*

*though at the time indeed it seemed*
*nothing but wretchedness and evil.*
*Life was not sweet, yet I found it so*
*when I could put my arms around my father.*
*O father! O my dear!*
*Now you are shrouded in eternal darkness.*
*Even in that absence*
*you shall not lack our love,*
*mine and my sister's love.*

CHORUS
*He lived his life . . .*

ANTIGONE
*He did as he had wished!*

CHORUS
*What do you mean?*

ANTIGONE
*In this land among strangers*
*he died where he chose to die.*
*He has his eternal bed well shaded*
*and in his death is not unmourned.*
*My eyes are blind with tears*
*from crying for you, father.*
*The terror and the loss*
*cannot be quieted.*
*I know you wished to die in a strange country,*
*yet your death was so lonely!*
*Why could I not be with you?*

ISMENE
*O pity! What is left for me?*
*What destiny awaits us both*
*now we have lost our father?*°

CHORUS
*Dear children, remember*

*that his last hour was free and blessed.*
*So make an end of grieving!*
*Is anyone in all the world*
*safe from unhappiness?*

ANTIGONE

STROPHE B

*Let us run back there!*

ISMENE

*Why, what shall we do?*

ANTIGONE

*I am carried away with longing—*

ISMENE

*For what—tell me!*

ANTIGONE

*To see the resting place in the earth—*

ISMENE

*Of whom?*

ANTIGONE

*Father's! O, what misery I feel!*

ISMENE

*But that is not permitted. Do you not see?*

ANTIGONE

*Do not rebuke me!*

ISMENE

*And remember, too—*

ANTIGONE

*Oh, what?*

ISMENE

*He had no tomb; there was no one near!*

ANTIGONE

*Take me there and you can kill me, too!*

ISMENE

*Ah! I am truly lost!*
*Helpless and so forsaken!*
*Where shall I go and how shall I live?*

CHORUS

ANTISTROPHE B

*You must not fear, now.*

ANTIGONE

*Yes, but where is a refuge?*

CHORUS

*A refuge has been found—*

ANTIGONE

*Where do you mean?*

CHORUS

*A place where you will be unharmed!*

ANTIGONE

*No . . .*

CHORUS

*What are you thinking?*

ANTIGONE

*I think there is no way*
*for me to get home again.*

CHORUS

*Do not go home!*

ANTIGONE

*My home is in trouble.*

CHORUS

*So it has been before.*

ANTIGONE

*There was no help for it then: but now it is worse.*

CHORUS

*A wide and desolate world it is for you.°*

ANTIGONE

*Great god! What way is there, O Zeus?*
*Do the powers that rule our lives*
*still press me on to hope at all?*

*(Enter Theseus from the side, with attendants.)*

THESEUS° [*chanting in alternation with Antigone and the Chorus until the end of the play*]

*Mourn no more, children. Those to whom*
*the night of earth gives benediction*
*should not be mourned. Retribution comes.*

ANTIGONE

*Theseus: we fall on our knees to you!*

THESEUS

*What is it that you desire, children?*

ANTIGONE

*We wish to see the place ourselves*
*in which our father rests.*

THESEUS

*No, no.*
*It is not permissible to go there.*

ANTIGONE

*My lord and ruler of Athens, why?*

THESEUS

*Because your father told me, children,*
*that no one should go near the spot.*
*No mortal man should tell of it,*
*since it is holy, and is his.*
*And if I kept this pledge, he said,*
*I should preserve my land from its enemies.*

*I swore I would, and the god heard me,*
*the oathkeeper who makes note of all.*°

ANTIGONE

*If this was our father's cherished wish,*
*we must be satisfied.*
*Send us back, then, to ancient Thebes,*
*in hopes we may stop the bloody war*
*from coming between our brothers!*

THESEUS

*I will do that, and whatever else*
*I am able to do for your happiness,*
*for his sake who has gone just now*
*beneath the earth. I must not fail.*

CHORUS

*Now let the weeping cease;*
*let no one mourn again.*
*These things are in the hands of god.*°

# ELECTRA

*Translated by* DAVID GRENE

# ELECTRA: INTRODUCTION

*The Play: Date and Composition*

The date of *Electra*'s first production is not known. Nor do we know which other plays Sophocles presented along with it in the annual competition. On the basis of the play's style and dramatic technique many scholars have come to regard it as one of Sophocles' latest tragedies, probably composed after Euripides' *Electra* (which deals with the same story), perhaps between 420 and 410 BCE. But this assessment is largely subjective, and some scholars prefer to date Sophocles' play earlier than Euripides', in the 430s or 420s BCE.

*The Myth*

The story of the royal dynasty of the Pelopids, legendary rulers of Argos (or Mycenae), provided plots for a large number of Greek tragedies. Many of these focused on the story of Agamemnon and his family. The broad outlines of this story were familiar to all. The brothers Agamemnon and Menelaus, sons of Atreus, led an expedition against the city of Troy to recover Menelaus' wife Helen, who had eloped with the Trojan prince Paris. While Agamemnon was away at Troy, his wife Clytemnestra took another lover, his cousin Aegisthus, and the two of them murdered Agamemnon upon his return home from Troy. Clytemnestra was motivated to kill her husband in part because he had sacrificed their eldest daughter, Iphigenia, to the goddess Artemis in order to procure favorable winds for the expedition to Troy. (As for Aegisthus, he was eager to avenge his father Thyestes, several of whose children had been hideously murdered by his brother

Atreus, who was Agamemnon's and Menelaus' father.) Aegisthus and Clytemnestra then took over the throne of Argos/Mycenae and ruled there for many years.

Agamemnon and Clytemnestra had three children (apart from Iphigenia): two daughters, Electra and Chrysothemis, and a son, Orestes, who was just a baby when his father was murdered. In most versions of the story, Aegisthus and Clytemnestra intended to kill Orestes as well, but he was rescued (largely through Electra's intervention) and was sent off to be raised by a family friend, King Strophius of Phocis, whose own young son Pylades became Orestes' closest friend. During the next several years Orestes was abroad in exile from his native land while Electra was living in misery at home, preserving the memory of her father, hating the usurping murderers, and hoping for her brother's return to exact vengeance. This is the point at which Sophocles' play begins.

The precise means and process by which Orestes and Electra (and Pylades) carry out the act of vengeance varies in important ways from one narrative version to another. In Homer's *Odyssey*, we are told repeatedly that Orestes killed Aegisthus, while the killing of Clytemnestra remains much more vague and Electra is not mentioned. In many subsequent lyric poems (of which only a few small fragments survive), in a wide range of visual representations, and above all in Aeschylus' tragic trilogy the *Oresteia* (458 BCE), which established itself immediately as the classic treatment of the whole saga, Orestes continues to be the main focus. In most versions he is instructed by Apollo's oracle at Delphi to avenge his father's murder by stealth; so he returns home in disguise, accompanied by Pylades, and reveals his identity to Electra only once he has ascertained that she is indeed faithful to their father's cause. Then the brother and sister together plan the killing of the two usurpers, with Orestes (assisted by Pylades) performing the act himself while Electra provides support and encouragement. In most versions the killing of mother by son is the climactic and most shocking moment in the whole drama, and it is usually followed immediately by an onslaught of avenging Furies who seek to punish Orestes for his deed.

Sophocles' *Electra*, Aeschylus' *Libation Bearers* (the second play of the *Oresteia*), and Euripides' *Electra* constitute the only case in which we possess three plays on exactly the same topic written by each of the great Athenian tragedians. The comparison is fascinating, even while we should remember that scores of other plays, now lost, were also doubtless composed on this same theme, with each new version introducing further innovations and modifications. In comparing Sophocles' tragedy to the two others, it is striking that—whereas Euripides' play seems to make a number of obvious references, some of them apparently quite polemical, to the *Oresteia*—Sophocles' version seems to make almost no such direct allusions or revisions and follows quite an independent path. Among Sophocles' innovations are his inclusion of an old tutor who has been Orestes' mentor since childhood and who guides him and Electra through to the final stages of the vengeance, and a third sibling, Chrysothemis, whose rather timid and conventional behavior serves as an effective foil to Electra's boldness in seeking to avenge her father and her unrelenting hatred of her mother and Aegisthus. Sophocles also includes a sensational messenger speech, in which Orestes' fictitious death in a chariot wreck is vividly described, while Electra and Clytemnestra respond to it in opposite ways. Significantly, Sophocles reverses the usual order of the killings, so that Clytemnestra dies first and the play ends with the death of Aegisthus. This makes the matricide seem somewhat less climactic and horrendous than it is in Aeschylus and Euripides. Indeed, the possibility that the Furies will pursue Orestes seems to be almost completely ignored in our play. But scholars debate the significance of these elements for the overall interpretation of the play; and some believe that the ending has suffered damage and truncation, so that we do not have quite all that Sophocles wrote. (See the textual note on lines 1505–10.)

### *Transmission and Reception*

We do not know whether Sophocles' *Electra* won the prize upon its first production. But it seems to have been a popular play throughout antiquity, being performed and read quite widely (more so than Euripides' *Electra*). And of course the whole story of Electra, Orestes, and Pylades continued to be frequently depicted in literature and art. Sophocles' recognition scene between Orestes and Electra was particularly admired, and we are told of famous performances in which the actor playing Electra affected the audience deeply, as he spoke his (her) lines while holding the urn that supposedly contained her brother's ashes. The play was one of the seven Sophoclean plays selected in the first or second century CE for school use. It thus survived into the Byzantine era, and was one of the "triad" of plays most widely copied and distributed between the tenth and fifteenth centuries. We possess over one hundred manuscripts of the play, some of them with quite extensive marginal notes (scholia) that include useful ancient commentary.

The character Electra has remained iconic throughout Western literature and art, from antiquity to the present, as a symbol of a daughter's devotion to her father (and hatred of her mother and stepfather), single-minded loyalty to her brother, and long-suffering determination to punish political and/or familial crimes. In the eighteenth and nineteenth centuries, it was Sophocles' version of her character and her story that was the most influential and inspirational: this lonely but indomitable female figure, ceaselessly voicing her grief, loyalty, and indignation despite every attempt to suppress her, resonated strongly with playwrights, poets, and painters. Since the beginning of the twentieth century, however, playwrights have tended to blend elements from all three Greek tragedians in composing their new versions of her story—as for example Eugene O'Neill does in *Mourning Becomes Electra* (1931), T. S. Eliot in *The Family Reunion* (1939), and more recently Yael Farber in *MoLoRa* (South Africa, 2004). But Jean Giraudoux's brilliant *Electra* (1937) is an exception: Sophocles is his clear inspiration. Films made on this theme have only loosely, though sometimes quite distinctly, picked up on Sophocles' original: for example, the Hungarian film *Electra, My Love*, directed by Miklós Jancsó (1974), or the acerbic comedy *Ellie*, directed by Peter Wittman (1984). But Electra is a household name, almost to the degree that Oedipus is: Sigmund Freud and Carl Jung obviously are partly responsible for this, with the "Electra complex," but Sophocles' play still remains the best-known version of her story. Electra has even reached Marvel Comics, where the character Elektra Natchios has been featured in several episodes, along with her brother Orestez.

The rather free adaptation of Sophocles' play by Hugo von Hofmannsthal (1904) has been especially influential in Germany, and an adaptation of this text was used as a libretto by Richard Strauss for his opera *Elektra* (1909; often since performed all over the world). In earlier periods, there had been numerous operas that more or less freely adapted parts of Electra's story: the most deserving of mention are *Electra* by J. C. F. Haeffner (1787, with libretto by A. F. Ristell) and *Idomeneo* by W. A. Mozart (1781). More definitely based on Sophocles, though still heavily adapted, is the opera by Mikis Theodorakis (1995, with Modern Greek libretto).

Until recently, Sophocles' *Electra* was one of the most frequently performed of all Greek tragedies. Productions of the original play, or adaptations of it, have been numerous ever since the eighteenth century, both on college campuses and in professional theaters: actors and audiences have relished the heroine's role for its emotional range and power, while the scenes of ironic misrecognition around the messenger speech and the urn, and the actual recognition of brother by sister, are among the most intensely theatrical in all of Greek drama. Particularly notable productions include those directed by Jane Addams at Hull-House, Chicago (1880s and 1890s); Max Reinhardt (in Hofmannsthal's adaptation, Berlin 1903); Margaret Anglin in the Hearst Greek Theater, Berkeley, California, 1915, 1918); several by the National Theatre of Greece at Epidaurus, directed by Dimitris Rondiris (1936–78), and later by Lydia Koniordou (1996) and by Peter Stein (2007); Michel Saint-Denis at the Old Vic (1951); Andrei Serban (selected scenes, first produced at La MaMa, New York City, in 1974; available on video); Carolos Koun and the Theatro Technis (1984); Deborah Warner with the Royal Shakespeare Company (1988, 1991); and Suzuki Tadashi (various locations, 1994–2001).

# ELECTRA

*Characters* TUTOR, Orestes' old servant
ORESTES, son of Agamemnon and Clytemnestra
PYLADES (silent character), friend of Orestes from Phocis
ELECTRA, daughter of Agamemnon and Clytemnestra
CHORUS of women of Mycenae
CHRYSOTHEMIS, sister of Electra and Orestes
CLYTEMNESTRA, widow of Agamemnon and wife of Aegisthus
AEGISTHUS, usurping king of Mycenae

*Scene: Before the royal palace in Mycenae.*

*(Enter Orestes, Pylades, and Tutor, from the side.)*

TUTOR

Son of Agamemnon, commander once at Troy,
now you are here, now you can see it all,
all that your heart has always longed for.
This is old Argos of your yearning, the grove
of Inachus' gadfly-haunted daughter, Io.
And here, Orestes, is the Lycian marketplace
of the wolf-killing god. Here on the left
the famous temple of Hera. Where we have come now,
believe your eyes, see golden Mycenae,
and here the death-heavy house of the Pelopids.

Once on a time, from amidst your father's murder,
I took you from this house, received you from the hand
of your sister, the one who shares your blood.
I saved you then. I have raised you from that day
to this moment of your manhood to be the avenger
of that father done to death. Orestes, now,
and you, Pylades, dearest friend, take counsel
quickly on what to do. Already the sunlight,
brightening, stirs dawning birdsong into clearness,
and the black, kindly night of stars is gone.
Before any man leaves the house, you two
must join together in discussion. We are where
we must not shrink. It is high time for action.

ORESTES

Dearest of servants:
very plain are the signs you show of your nobility
toward me. It is so with a well-bred horse:
even in old age, hard conditions
do not break his spirit. His ears are still erect.
So it is with you. You urge me, and yourself
follow among the first. Therefore, I will make plain
all that I have decided. Give keen ear
to what I say, and if I miss the mark
of what I should, correct me.

When I came to Pytho's place of prophecy
to learn how to win revenge
for my father's murder on those that killed him,
Phoebus spoke to me what I tell you now:
to take not help of shields nor host; instead,
by myself perform the slaughter, stealthily,
with just but crafty hand.
Now since this was the oracle we heard,
go you into this house when occasion calls you.
Know all that is done there, and, knowing, report
clear news to us. You are old. It's a long time.

They won't recognize you. They will not suspect you
with this silver hair of yours. Here is your story.
You are a stranger coming from Phanoteus,
their Phocian friend, the greatest of their allies.
Tell them a sudden accident befell
Orestes, and he's dead. Swear it on oath.
Say in the Pythian games he was rolled
out of his chariot at high speed.
Let that be your story.

But we shall go first to my father's grave
and crown it, as the god bade us, with libations
and with luxuriant cuttings from my hair.
And then we shall come back here again
and in our hands a carved bronze-sided urn,
the urn that you know I hid here in the bushes.
By these means we shall bring them the pleasant news
with our tale of lies, that my body is no longer,
but has been burned and reduced to ashes.
What harm does it do me if by dying in word
in deed I come through alive and win my glory?
To my thinking, no word is bad when spoken with profit.
Before now I have seen wise men often
dying empty deaths as far as words reported them,
and then, when they have come to their homes again,
they have been honored more, even to the skies.
So in my case I venture to predict
that I who die according to this rumor
shall, like a blazing star, glare on my foes again.

Land of my father, gods of my country,
welcome me, grant me success in my coming,
and you, too, house of my father;
as your purifier I have come,
in justice sent by the gods.
Do not send me dishonored out of this country,
but ancestrally rich, restorer of my house.

This is all that I have to say. Old man,
let it be yours to go and mind your task.
We two must go away. It is the moment,
and the moment is greatest master of every act.

ELECTRA [*chanting from inside the house*]
*Ah! Ah! What misery!*

TUTOR
Inside the house I thought I heard someone,
one of the servants, crying.

ORESTES
Might it not be
poor suffering Electra? Would you like us
to stay here and to listen to her crying?

TUTOR
No. Nothing must come before our trying
to carry out what Loxias has bidden us.
From there we must make our beginning,
pouring the holy offerings for your father.
For that, I say, will bring us victory,
and mastery in our enterprise.

*(Orestes and the others withdraw to the side.*
*Enter Electra from the palace.)*

ELECTRA [*chanting*]
*O holy light*
*and air, copartner with earth,*
*how many songs of lament,*
*how many plangent strokes*
*beating till my breast was bloody,*
*have you heard from me*
*when the gloomy night has withdrawn?*
*And again in the house of my misery*
*my bed is witness to my all-night sorrowing*
*dirges for my unhappy father.*

*In the land of the foreigner*
*no murderous god of battles entertained him;*
*but my mother and the man who shared her bed,*
*Aegisthus, split his head with a murderous axe,*
*like woodsmen with an oak tree.*
*For all this no pity was given you*
*by any but me, no pity for your death,*
*father, so pitiful, so cruel.*
*But, for my part, I*
*will never cease my dirges and sorrowful laments,*
*as long as I have eyes to see*
*the ever-shining light of the stars and this daylight.*
*So long, like a nightingale who has lost her young,°*
*here before the doors of what was my father's house*
*I shall cry out my sorrow for all the world to hear.*

*House of Hades, house of Persephone,*
*Hermes of the underworld, mighty Curse,*
*and Furies, the Dread Ones, children of gods,*
*who look upon those who die unjustly,*
*who look upon the marriage bed secretly betrayed,*
*come all and help take vengeance for my father,*
*for my father's murder!*
*And send me my brother to my aid.*
*For alone I am no longer strong enough*
*to bear the burden of the grief that weighs against me.*

(*Enter the Chorus of Mycenaean women from one side.*)

CHORUS [*singing*]

STROPHE A

*Electra, child of the wretchedest of mothers,*
*why with ceaseless lament do you waste away*
*sorrowing for one long dead,*
*Agamemnon, godlessly trapped*
*by deceits of your treacherous mother,*
*betrayed by her evil hand?*

*May evil be the end*
*of the one who contrived the deed,*
*if it is allowed for me to utter this!*

ELECTRA [*also singing*]

*Daughters of truehearted families,*
*you have come to console me in my troubles.*
*I know, I understand what you say,*
*nothing of it escapes me.*
*But, all the same, I will not*
*cease my mourning for my poor father.*
*You whose love responds to mine in all ways,*
*allow me thus wildly to grieve,*
*I entreat you.*

CHORUS

ANTISTROPHE A

*But from the all-receptive Lake*
*of Death you shall not raise him,*
*groan and pray as you will.*
*Past the bounds of sense you dwell in grief*
*that is cureless, with sorrow unending,*
*and you are destroying yourself,*
*in a matter where the evil knows no deliverance.*
*Why do you seek*
*such unbearable suffering?*

ELECTRA

*Foolish indeed is the one*
*that forgets parents pitifully dead.*
*Suited rather to my heart*
*is the bird of mourning*
*that always laments "Itys, Itys,"*
*the bird of frenzied sorrow, Zeus's messenger.*
*And Niobe, that suffered all, ah!*
*I count you as a goddess*
*as you weep perpetually*
*in your rocky tomb.*

CHORUS

STROPHE B

*Not alone to you, my child,*
*this burden of grief has come:*
*yet you exceed in your feeling far*
*those of your kin and blood.*
*Consider Chrysothemis and her life,*
*and Iphianassa,*
*and that one who grows up to prosperity in secret,*
*sorrowing, a prince,*
*whom one day this famed land of Mycenae*
*shall welcome home as noble heir,*
*returning here with Zeus' blessing, Orestes.*

ELECTRA

*I await him always*
*sadly, unweariedly,*
*I who am past childbearing,*
*past marriage,*
*always to my own ruin.*
*Wet with tears, I endure*
*an unending doom of misfortune.*
*But he has forgotten*
*what he has suffered, what he has known.*
*What message ever comes from him to me*
*that does not turn out false?*
*Yes, he is always longing to come,*
*but he does not choose to come, for all his longing.*

CHORUS

ANTISTROPHE B

*Take heart, take heart, my child.*
*Still great above is Zeus,*
*who oversees all things in sovereign power.*
*Confide to him your overbitter wrath;*
*do not overburden yourself with hate against*
*your enemies, nor yet forget them quite:*

*for Time is a kindly god.*
*For neither he that lives*
*by Crisa's cattle-grazing shore,*
*the son of Agamemnon, will be neglectful,*
*nor the god that rules by Acheron's waters.*

ELECTRA

*But for me already the most of my life*
*has gone by without hope,*
*and I have no strength anymore.*
*I am one wasted in childlessness,*
*with no loving husband for champion.*
*Like some dishonored foreigner,*
*I serve in my father's house in these ugly rags*
*and stand at empty tables.*

CHORUS

STROPHE C

*Pitiful was the cry at the homecoming,*
*and pitiful, when on your father on his couch*
*the sharp biting stroke of the brazen axe*
*was driven home.*
*Craft was the contriver, lust the killer,*
*dreadfully begetting between them a shape,*
*dreadful, whether divine or human,*
*the one that did this.*

ELECTRA

*That day of all days that have ever been*
*most deeply hateful to me!*
*O night, horrible burden*
*of that unspeakable banquet,*
*shameful death that my father saw*
*dealt him by the hands of the two,*
*hands that took my own life captive,*
*betrayed, destroyed me utterly.*
*For these deeds may god in his greatness,*
*the Olympian one, grant punishment to match them,*

*and may they have no profit of glory,*
*they who accomplished such actions.*

CHORUS

ANTISTROPHE C

*Take heed you do not speak too far.*
*Do you not see from what*
*causes you suffer as you do?*
*Self-inflicted is the ruin*
*that you've fallen into so wretchedly.*
*You have won for yourself*
*superfluity of misfortune,*
*breeding wars in your sullen soul*
*evermore. You cannot fight*
*such conflicts hand to hand, with those who hold power.°*

ELECTRA

*Dreadful things compelled me,*
*to dreadful things I was driven.*
*I know it, I know my own spirit.*
*With dread all around me, I will not hold back*
*from this wild course of ruin, so long as I live.*
*For who, dear friends, who that thinks right*
*could expect there to be suitable comforting*
*words for me?*
*Let me be, let me be—no more comforting!*
*These ills of mine shall be called cureless*
*and never shall I cease my sorrow;*
*the number of my laments will be countless.*

CHORUS

EPODE

*But only in good will to you I speak*
*like a loyal mother, entreating you*
*not to breed ruin from ruin.*

ELECTRA

*What is the natural measure of my sorrow?*

*Come, how when the dead are in question*
*can it be honorable to forget?*
*In what human being is this instinctive?*
*Never may I have honor among such people,*
*nor, if I encounter any good thing,*
*may I live at ease with it, by restraining*
*the wings of shrill lament to my father's dishonor!*
*For if he that is dead*
*is earth and nothing,*
*lying in misery,*
*and they shall never in their turn*
*pay death for murderous death,*
*then shall all shame be dead*
*and all men's piety.*

CHORUS LEADER [*speaking*]
My child, it was with both our interests at heart
I came, both yours and mine. If what I say
is wrong, have your own way. We will obey you.

ELECTRA [*now speaking*]
Women, I am ashamed if I appear
to you too much the mourner with constant dirges.
What I do, I must do. Pardon me. I ask you
how else would any well-bred girl behave
that saw the sufferings of her father's house
as I have seen these, day and night, increasing
and never a check?
First there's my mother, the one who bore me, now
a thing of hate. Then in my own house I live
with those who killed my father. I'm their subject,
and it's their decision whether I get
or go without.
What sort of days do you imagine
I spend, watching Aegisthus sitting
on my father's throne, watching him wear
my father's self-same robes, watching him

at the hearth where he killed him, pouring libations?
Watching the ultimate act of insult,
my father's murderer in my father's bed
with my wretched mother—if mother I should call her,
this woman that sleeps with him.
She is so daring that she cohabits with
this foul, polluted creature and fears no Fury.
No, as though laughing at what was done,
she has picked out the day on which she killed
my father in her treachery, and on that day
has set a dancing festival and sacrifices
sheep, in monthly ritual, "to the gods that saved her."
So within that house I see, to my wretchedness,
the accursed feast named in his honor.
I see it, moan, and waste away, lament—
but only to myself. I may not even cry
as much as my heart would have me.
For this woman, all nobility in words,
abuses me: "You godforsaken, hateful thing,
are you the only one whose father is dead?
Is there no one else of humankind in mourning?
My curse upon you! May the gods below
grant you from your present sorrows no release!"
Such are her insults, unless she hears from someone
that Orestes is coming. Then she grows quite wild
and stands beside me shrieking:
"Aren't you the one responsible for this?
Is not this your doing, you who stole
Orestes from these hands of mine, conveying him
away? But you may be sure you will pay for it
and pay enough." She howls so, and next to her
is her distinguished bridegroom, urging the same,
that utter coward, total piece of mischief,
who makes his wars only with women's help.
But I forever wait for Orestes' coming,
to end our troubles. I wait and wait and die.

For his eternal going-to-do-something
destroys my hopes, both real and absent.

In such a state, my friends, one cannot
be moderate and restrained, nor pious either.
Evil is all around me, evil
is what I am compelled to practice.

CHORUS LEADER

Tell me, as you talk like this, is Aegisthus here,
or is he gone from home?

ELECTRA

Certainly, he's gone.
Do not imagine, if he were near, that I
would wander outside. Now he is on his estate.

CHORUS LEADER

If so, I can talk with you with better confidence.

ELECTRA

For the present, he is away. What is your wish?

CHORUS LEADER

Tell me: what of your brother? Is he really coming
or hesitating? That is what I want to know.

ELECTRA

He says he is—but does nothing of what he says.

CHORUS LEADER

A man often hesitates when he does a big thing.

ELECTRA

I did not hesitate when I rescued him.

CHORUS LEADER

Be easy.
He's a noble man and will surely help his friends.

ELECTRA

I believe in him, or else had not lived so long.

CHORUS LEADER

Say no more now. I see your sister,
blood of your blood, of the same father and mother,
Chrysothemis, carrying grave-gifts in her hands
such as are usually offered to those below.

*(Enter Chrysothemis from the palace.)*

CHRYSOTHEMIS

What have you come to say here out of doors,
sister? Will you never learn, in all this time,
not to give way to your empty anger?
Yet this much I know, and know my own heart, too,
that I am sick at what I see, so that
if I had strength, I would let them know how I feel.
But under threat of punishment, I think,
I must make my voyage with lowered sails,
that I may not seem to be doing something and then
prove ineffectual. I wish you'd do the same.
And yet justice points not where my words are tending,
but where your judgment stands. However, if
I am to live, and not as a prisoner, I must
in all things listen to the ones in power.

ELECTRA

It is strange indeed that you who were born
of our father should forget him
and think only of your mother. All these warnings
of me you have learned from her. Nothing is your own.
Now you must make your choice, one way or the other,
either to be rash and irrational
or to be sensible—but forget your friends.
Here you are saying: "If I had the strength,
I would show my hatred of them!" Yet, when I
try everything to take vengeance for our father,
you do nothing to help—and even discourage my doing.
Doesn't this add cowardice to the list of all our troubles?
Tell me, or let me tell you, what benefit

would I achieve by giving up my mourning?
Do I not live? Yes, I know, badly, but
for me enough. And I hurt them
and so give honor to the dead, if there is, there
in that other world, anything that brings pleasure.
But you who tell me you hate them, hate in words only,
while in fact you are living with our father's murderers.

I tell you: never, not though they brought me all those gifts
in which you now feel pride, would I yield to them.
Have your rich table and your abundant life;
all the food I need is the quiet of my conscience.
I do not want to win your honor.
Nor would you if you were sound of mind. Now, when you
  could
be called the daughter of the best of fathers,
be called instead your mother's. Thus you'll seem to most
a traitor, betraying your friends and your dead father.

CHORUS LEADER

No anger, I entreat you. In the words of both
there is value for both, if you, Electra, can
follow her advice and she take yours.

CHRYSOTHEMIS

Ladies, I am used to her and her words.
I never would have mentioned this, had not
I learned of the greatest of misfortunes coming
her way to put a stop to her long mourning.

ELECTRA

Tell me of your terror. If you can speak to me
of something worse than my present condition,
I'll not keep arguing back.

CHRYSOTHEMIS

Well, I shall tell you
everything I know. They plan, if you don't stop

your present mourning, to send you away, to where
never a gleam of sun shall visit you.
You shall live out your life in an underground cave
outside this country and there bewail your sorrows.
With this in mind, reflect. And do not blame me
later when you are suffering.
Now is a good time to take thought.

ELECTRA

So this is what they have decided to do with me?

CHRYSOTHEMIS

Yes, this exactly, when Aegisthus comes home.

ELECTRA

As far as this goes, let him come home soon.

CHRYSOTHEMIS

Why such a prayer for evil, my poor sister?

ELECTRA

That he may come—if he will do what you say.

CHRYSOTHEMIS

Hoping that *what* may happen to you? Are you crazy?

ELECTRA

That I may get away from you all, as far as I can.

CHRYSOTHEMIS

Have you no care of this, your present life?

ELECTRA

Mine is indeed a fine life, to be envied!

CHRYSOTHEMIS

It might be, if you could learn common sense.

ELECTRA

Do not teach me falseness to those I love.

CHRYSOTHEMIS

That is not what I teach, but to yield to power.

ELECTRA

Keep practicing that flattery. It is not my way.

CHRYSOTHEMIS

It is a good thing, though, not to fall through stupidity.

ELECTRA

I shall fall, if I must, revenging my father.

CHRYSOTHEMIS

Our father does not blame me for this, I know.

ELECTRA

These are the kind of words that cowards praise.

CHRYSOTHEMIS

You will not heed me then? You will not agree?

ELECTRA

No, certainly.
May I not yet be so empty-witted.

CHRYSOTHEMIS

Then I must go on the errand I was sent.

ELECTRA

Where are you going? To whom
bringing those offerings?

CHRYSOTHEMIS

My mother sent me with libations for father's grave.

ELECTRA

What are you saying? To her greatest enemy?

CHRYSOTHEMIS

"Whom she herself killed"—you would add.

ELECTRA

Which of her friends persuaded her? Who thought of this?

CHRYSOTHEMIS

I think it was night terrors drove her to it.

ELECTRA
Gods of my father, now come to help at last!

CHRYSOTHEMIS
Why do "night terrors" make you confident?

ELECTRA
I'll tell you that when you tell me the dream.

CHRYSOTHEMIS
I cannot tell you much, only a little.

ELECTRA
Tell me it, all the same. A little story
has often made or ruined men before now.

CHRYSOTHEMIS
The story goes that she saw my father,
the father that was yours and mine, again
come to life, once more to live with her.
He took and at the hearth planted the scepter
which once he bore and now Aegisthus bears,
and up from out this scepter grew a branch
luxuriant with leaves, and shaded all the land
of this Mycenae. This is what I heard
from someone present when she told the Sun
about her dream.
I know no more beyond this
except that it's for her fear she sends me now.
So, by our family's gods, I pray you: listen
to me and do not fall out of stupidity.
For if you reject me, you'll be back again in distress.°

ELECTRA
My dear one, not one thing that you are holding
allow to touch that grave, no, nothing!
It would not be god's law nor pious that you
should offer to my father libations

and burial offerings from that enemy woman.
Throw them to the winds! Or hide them deep
in the dust, somewhere where no particle of them
may ever reach my father where he lies.
But let them be stored up for her as treasures
below, against the day when *she* shall die.
I tell you, if she were not the most brazen
of all of womankind, would she have dared
to pour these enemy libations
over the body of the man she killed?
Consider if you think that the dead man,
as he lies in his grave, will welcome kindly
these offerings from her by whom he was robbed
of life and honor and foully mutilated?
And to wash her hands clean she wiped the clots of blood
off onto his head? Can you believe
that these offerings will bring absolution for her murder?
No, no. You let them be. You cut a lock
out of your own hair, from the fringe, and mine,
mine, too, his wretched daughter's. Such a small offering,
yet all I have! Give it to him, this rough°
lock of hair, and here, my girdle, unadorned.
Kneel then and pray that from the earth below
he may come himself, a friendly spirit, to help us
against his enemies. Pray that the boy Orestes
may live to fight and win against his enemies,
to set his foot upon them. And if so
in days to come we shall be able to dress
this grave with richer hands than we can now.
I think, oh yes, I think that it was he
that thought to send this evil-boding dream
to her.
    Yet, sister, do yourself this service
and help me, too, and help the dearest of all,
father of us both, that lies dead in the underworld.

CHORUS LEADER

The girl speaks piously. And you, my dear,
if you are wise, will follow her advice.

CHRYSOTHEMIS

I will do it. It is not reasonable for us two
to squabble about what is just. I must haste to do it.
But, my friends, if I attempt this, I must have your silence.
If my mother hears of this, I'm sure I shall regret
indeed the attempt that I'm about to make.

*(Exit Chrysothemis to the side.)*

CHORUS [*singing*]

STROPHE

*If I am not a distracted prophet*
*and lacking in skill of judgment,*
*Justice foreshadowing the event*
*shall come, in her hands a just victory.*
*Yes, she will come, my child, in vengeance*
*and soon:*
*of that I am confident*
*since I lately heard*
*of this dream that blows sweet.*
*Your father, the king of the Greeks,*
*has never forgotten,*
*nor the axe of old,*
*bronze-cast, double-edged,*
*which did him to death*
*in shame and degradation.*

ANTISTROPHE

*There shall come many-footed, many-handed,*
*hidden in dreadful ambush,*
*the bronze-shod Fury.*
*Wicked indeed were they who were seized*
*with a passion for a forbidden bed,*

*for a marriage accursed, stained with murder.*
*In the light of this, I am very sure*
*that never, never shall we see*
*such a portent draw near without hurt*
*to doers and partners in crime.*
*There are indeed no prophecies for mortals*
*in dreadful dreams and soothsayings*
*if this night vision come not*
*well and truly to fulfilment.*

EPODE

*Horsemanship of Pelops long ago,*
*loaded with disaster,*
*how deadly you have proved*
*to this land!*
*For since the day that Myrtilus*
*sank to his rest in the sea,*
*wrecked utterly with the unhappy*
*wreck of his golden chariot,*
*for never a moment since*
*has destruction and ruin*
*ever left this house.*

*(Clytemnestra enters from the palace, with attendants.)*

CLYTEMNESTRA

It seems you are loose again, wandering about.
Aegisthus isn't here, who always restrained you
from going abroad and disgracing your family.
But now that he is away you pay no heed
to me, although you have told a lot of people
at length how brutally and how unjustly
I lord it over you, insulting
you and yours.
There is no insolence in myself,
but being abused by you so constantly
I give abuse in return.

Your father, yes,
always your father. Nothing else is your pretext—
that he was killed by me. By me. I know it,
well. There is no denial in me. Justice,
justice it was that took him, not I alone.
And you too would have served the cause of justice
if you had been right-minded.
For this father of yours whom you always mourn,
alone of all the Greeks, had the brutality
to sacrifice your sister to the gods,
although he had not toiled for her as I did,
the mother that bore her, he the begetter only.
Tell me, now, why he sacrificed her. Was it
for the sake of the Greeks?
But they had no share in my daughter to let them kill her.
Was it for Menelaus' sake, his brother,
that he killed my child? And should he not then pay for it?
Had not this Menelaus two children who
ought to have died rather than mine? It was their parents
for whose sake all the Greeks set sail for Troy.
Or had the god of death some longing to feast
on my children rather than hers? Or had
that accursed father lost his love for my children
while feeling it still for those of Menelaus?
Was not this the act of a father thoughtless
or with bad thoughts? That is how I see it
even if you differ with me. The dead girl,
if she could speak, would bear me out.
I am not dismayed by all that has happened.
If you think me wicked, keep your righteous judgment
and blame your neighbors.

ELECTRA

This is one time you will not be able to say
that the abuse I receive from you was provoked
by something painful on my side.

But if
you will allow me I will speak truthfully
on behalf of the dead man and my dead sister.

CLYTEMNESTRA

Of course, I allow you. If you always began
our conversations so, you would not be
so painful to listen to.

ELECTRA

I will tell you, then.
You say you killed my father. What claim more shameful
than that, whether with justice or without it?
But I'll maintain that it was not with justice
you killed him, but the seduction of that evil man,
with whom you now are living, drew you to it.
Ask Artemis the huntress what made her hold
the many winds in check at Aulis. Or
I'll tell you this, since we may not learn from her.
My father, as I hear, when at his sport,
started from his feet a horned dappled stag
within the goddess' sanctuary. He
let fly and hit the deer and uttered some boast
about his killing of it. The daughter of Leto
was angry at this and so detained the Greeks
in order that my father, to compensate
for the beast killed, would sacrifice his daughter.

Thus was her sacrifice—no other deliverance
for the army either homeward or toward Ilium.
He struggled and fought against it. Finally,
constrained, he killed her—not for Menelaus.
But if—I will plead in your own words—he had done so
for his brother's sake, is that any reason
why he should die at your hands? By what law?
If this is the law you lay down for men, take heed
you do not lay down for yourself pain and repentance.

If we shall kill one in another's requital,
you would be the first to die, if you met with justice.
No. Think if the whole is not a mere excuse.
Please tell me for what cause you now commit
the ugliest of acts—in sleeping with him,
the murderer with whom you first conspired
to kill my father, and breed children to him, and
drive out your former children, honorable ones
born of honorable wedlock. What grounds
for praise shall I find in this? Or will you say
that this, too, is retribution for your daughter?
If you say it, still your saying it is scandalous.
It isn't decent to marry with your enemies
even for a daughter's sake.
                                        But I may not
even rebuke you! What you always say
is that it is my mother I am reviling.
Mother! I do not count you mother of mine,
but slave owner and mistress. My life is wretched
because I live with multitudes of sufferings,
inflicted by yourself and your bedfellow.
But the other, he is away, he has escaped
your hand, though barely: poor Orestes now
wears out his life in misery and exile.
Many a time you have accused me
of rearing him to be your executioner.
I would have done it if I could. Know that.
As far as that goes, you may publicly
proclaim me what you like—traitor, reviler,
a creature full of shamelessness. If I am
naturally skilled at such things, I do no shame
to your nature.

CHORUS LEADER

I see she is angry, but whether it is in justice,
I no longer see if there's concern for that.

CLYTEMNESTRA

What need have I of concern in her regard
who so insults her mother, though old enough
to know better? Don't you think that she will go
to any lengths, so shameless as she is?

ELECTRA

You may be sure I am ashamed of this,
even if you do not think so. I know that
I act improperly, so unlike myself.
But the hate you show for me, and all your actions,
compel me against my will to act this way.
For ugly deeds are taught by ugly deeds.

CLYTEMNESTRA

O shameless creature, I and my words and deeds
give you too much to talk of.

ELECTRA

It is you who talk, not I. It is your deeds,
and it's deeds invent the words.

CLYTEMNESTRA

Now by the Lady Artemis you shall not escape
the results of your behavior, when Aegisthus comes.

ELECTRA

You see? You let me say what I please, and then
you are outraged. You do not know how to listen.

CLYTEMNESTRA

Hold your peace at least. Allow me to sacrifice,
since I have permitted you to say all you will.

ELECTRA

I allow you, yes, I bid you, sacrifice.
Do not blame my tongue; for I will say no more.

CLYTEMNESTRA *(To an attendant.)*

Come, do you lift them up, the offerings
of all the fruits of earth, that to this king here

I may offer prayers for freedom from my fears.
Phoebus Protector, hear me, as I am,
although the word I speak is muted. Not among friends
is it spoken, nor may I unfold the whole
to the light while this girl stands beside me,
lest with her chattering and malicious tongue
she sow in all the city bad reports.
Yet hear me thus, since this is how I will speak.
The dreams of double meaning I have seen
within this night, from them, Lycian king,
grant what is good for me prosperous outcome
but what is ill, turn it back upon
those that do us evil.
And if there are some that from my present wealth
plot to expel me with their stratagems,
do not permit them. Let me live out my life,
just as my life is now, to the end uninjured,
controlling the house of Atreus and the throne,
living with those I love as I do now,
enjoying prosperity, and with such children
as do not hate me nor cause bitter pain.
These are my prayers, Lycian Apollo; hear them
graciously. Grant to all of us what we ask.
For all the rest, although I keep silent,
I know you are a god and know it all.
It is natural that the children of Zeus see all.

*(Enter Tutor, from the side.)*

TUTOR

Excuse me, ladies, how may I know for certain,
is this the palace of the King Aegisthus?

CHORUS LEADER

This is it, sir. Your own guess is correct.

TUTOR

Would I then be right in thinking that this lady
is his wife? She has indeed a royal look.

CHORUS LEADER

Quite right. And here she is for you, herself.

TUTOR

Greetings, Your Majesty. I come with news
from a friend, good news for you and for Aegisthus.

CLYTEMNESTRA

I welcome what you have said. But I would like first
to know who sent you here.

TUTOR

It was Phanoteus
the Phocian, charging me with an important matter.

CLYTEMNESTRA

What is it, sir? Please tell me. I know well
you come from a friend and will speak friendly words.

TUTOR

Orestes is dead. There it is, in one short word.

ELECTRA

O no, O no! This is the day I die.

CLYTEMNESTRA

What's this you say, sir, what? Don't listen to her.

TUTOR

What I said and say again is "Orestes is dead."

ELECTRA

I am ruined, hopeless—I cannot go on living!

CLYTEMNESTRA *(To Electra.)*

Mind your own business!

*(To the Tutor.)*

Sir, tell me the truth:
in what way did he meet his death?

TUTOR

This
I was sent to tell, and I will tell you it all.
He went to the glorious gathering that Greece holds
in honor of the Delphic Games, and when
he heard the herald's loud proclamation
for the first contest—it was a running race—
he entered, looking brilliant, all eyes upon him.
His running was as good as his appearance:
he won the race and came out covered with honor.
There is much I could tell you, but I must tell it briefly.
I have never known a man of such achievement
or prowess. Know this one thing. In all the contests
the marshals announced, he won the prize, was cheered,°
proclaimed the victor as "Argive by birth,
by name Orestes, son of Agamemnon,
who once gathered and led the glorious Greek host."
So far, so good. But when a god sends ruin,
not even the strong man may escape.
Orestes,
when, the next day, at sunrise, there was a race
for chariot teams, entered with many contestants.
There was one Achaean, one from Sparta, two
Libyans, masters in driving racing teams.
Orestes was the fifth among them; he
had as his team Thessalian mares. The sixth
was an Aetolian with young sorrel horses.
The seventh was a Magnesian, and the eighth
an Aenian, by race, with a white team.
The ninth competitor came from god-built Athens,
and then a Boeotian, ten chariots in all.
They stood in their allotted stations where
the appointed judges placed them. At the signal,
a brazen trumpet, they were off. The drivers called
to their horses, and their hands vibrated the reins,
The course was filled with clamor of rattling chariots.

The dust rose up. The drivers, massed together,
applied the goad unsparingly, each one struggling
to advance the nave of his wheel or the snorting mouths
of his horses past his rival, wheels and backs
all slobbered by the breath of the teams behind them.°
So far they all stood upright in their chariots.
But the Aenian's hard-mouthed colts got out of hand
and bolted as they finished the sixth lap
and turned into the seventh; there they crashed
head-on with the Barcaean chariot. After that,
from this one accident, team crashed team
and overturned each other. All the plain
of Crisa was full of wrecks. But the man from Athens,
a clever driver, saw what was happening, pulled
his horses out of the way, and held them in check,
avoiding the disordered mass of teams in the middle.
    Orestes had been driving last and holding
his horses back, putting his trust in the finish.
But when he saw the Athenian left alone,
he sent a shrill cry through his swift horses' ears
and set to catch him. The two drove level,
the poles were even. First one, now the other,
would push his horses' heads in front.
Orestes always drove tight at the corners
barely grazing the edge of the post with his wheel,
loosening the reins of the trace horse on his right
while he checked the near horse.° In his other laps
the young man and his horses had come through safe.
But this time as he slackened the left rein
while the horse was still turning, unaware, he struck
the edge of the pillar and broke the axle box.
He was himself thrown from the rails of the chariot
and tangled in the reins. As he fell, the horses
bolted wildly to the middle of the course.
When the crowd saw him fallen from his chariot,
they cried out with pity for the young man, who'd done

such deeds and now was meeting such misfortune,
thrown earthward first, then with legs pointing
to the sky—until at last the charioteers
with difficulty stopped the runaway team
and freed him, but so covered with blood that no one
of his friends could have recognized the wretched corpse.
They burned him there on a pyre. Men of Phocis
chosen for the task are bringing in a small urn
of bronze the miserable ashes—all that's left
of this great frame, that he may have his grave
here in his father's country.
That is my story,
bitter as stories go, but for us who saw it,
greatest of all misfortunes that I've seen.

CHORUS LEADER

Ah, ah! The ancient family
of our lords has perished, it seems, root and branch.

CLYTEMNESTRA

Zeus, what shall I say? Shall I call it good luck?
Or terrible, yet for the best? Indeed,
my state is painful if I must save
my life by means of my own misfortunes.

TUTOR

My lady, why does this story make you dejected?

CLYTEMNESTRA

Mother and child! It is a strange relation.
A mother cannot hate the child she bore
even when injured by it.

TUTOR

Our coming here, it seems, then is to no purpose.

CLYTEMNESTRA

Not to no purpose. How can you say "no purpose"—
if you have come with certain proofs of death

of one who from my soul was sprung,
but severed himself from my breast, from my nurture, who
became an exile and a foreigner;
who after he quitted this land, never saw me again;
who charged me with his father's murder, threatened
terrors against me. Neither night nor day
could I find solace in sleep: each oncoming moment
kept nagging me like one about to die.
But now, with this one day I am freed from fear
of her and him. She was the greater evil;
she lived with me, constantly draining
the very blood of life—now perhaps I'll have peace
from her threats. The light of day will come again.

ELECTRA
Oh no, no! Now must I mourn indeed
your death, Orestes, when your mother here
pours insults on you, dead. Can this be right?

CLYTEMNESTRA
Not right for you. But he is right as he is.

ELECTRA
Hear, Nemesis, of the man that lately died!

CLYTEMNESTRA
Nemesis has heard what she should, and done things well.

ELECTRA
Insult us now. For now the luck is yours.

CLYTEMNESTRA
Will you not stop this, you and Orestes both?

ELECTRA
We are stopped indeed. We cannot make you stop.

CLYTEMNESTRA *(To the Tutor.)*
Your coming will be worth much, sir, if you
have stopped my daughter's everlasting clamor.

TUTOR

Well, I will go now, if all this is settled.

CLYTEMNESTRA

O no! I should do wrong to myself and to
the friend who sent you if I let you go.
Please go inside. Leave her out here to wail
the misfortunes of herself and those she loves.

*(Exit Clytemnestra and the Tutor into the house.)*

ELECTRA

There's an unhappy mother for you! See
how agonized, how bitter, were the tears,
how terribly she sorrowed for her son
that met the death you heard of! No, I tell you,
she parted from us laughing. O what misery!
Orestes dearest, your death is my death.
By your passing you have torn away from my heart
whatever solitary hope still lingered
that you would live and come some day to avenge
your father and my miserable self.
But now where should I turn? I am alone,
having lost both you and my father. Back again
to be a slave among those I hate most
of all the world, my father's murderers!
Is this what is right for me?
No, this I will not:
live with them any more. Here, at this gate
I will abandon myself to waste away
this life of mine, unloved. If they're displeased,
let someone kill me, someone that lives within.
Death is a favor to me, life an agony.
I have no wish for life.

CHORUS [*singing, with Electra singing in response*]

STROPHE A

*Where are Zeus's thunderbolts,*
*where is the blazing sun,*

*if they see all this and yet keep it hidden,*
*holding their peace?*

ELECTRA

*Oh, oh!*

CHORUS

*Why do you cry, child?*

ELECTRA

*Ah!*

CHORUS

*Speak no great word.*

ELECTRA

*You will destroy me.*

CHORUS

*How?*

ELECTRA

*If you suggest a hope*
*when all is plain, when they are gone*
*to the house of Death, and when I waste*
*my life away, then you are treading me further down.*

CHORUS

ANTISTROPHE A

*King Amphiaraus, as I know,*
*was caught by a woman's golden necklace,*
*and now beneath the earth*
*reigns over all the spirits there.*

ELECTRA

*Oh, woe!*

CHORUS

*Woe indeed, for the murderess . . .*

ELECTRA

*. . . she died!°*

CHORUS

*Yes.*

ELECTRA

*I know, I know. For him in sorrow*
*there came a deliverer.*
*None such for me. For one there was,*
*but he is gone, snatched away by death.*

CHORUS

STROPHE B

*Unhappy girl, unhappiness is yours!*

ELECTRA

*I bear you witness with full knowledge,*
*knowledge too full, bred of a life,*
*the crowded months surging with horrors*
*many and dreadful!*

CHORUS

*We know what you are saying.*

ELECTRA

*So do not then, I pray you, divert my thoughts to where . . .*

CHORUS

*What do you mean?*

ELECTRA

*. . . there is no hope, no brother born*
*of the same noble lineage to help.*

CHORUS

ANTISTROPHE B

*Death comes to all mortal men.*

ELECTRA

*Yes, but to meet it so,*
*as he did, poor man,*
*tangled in the leather reins,*
*among the wild flurry of hoofs!*

CHORUS

*An unwatchable horror!*

ELECTRA

*True indeed, for he's now a stranger*
*that was hidden in earth, by no hand of mine,*
*knew no grave I gave him,*
*knew no weeping from me.*

(*Enter Chrysothemis.*)

CHRYSOTHEMIS

My dearest sister,
I am so glad, I have run here in haste,
regardless of propriety. I bring you
happiness and a relief from all
the troubles you have had and sorrowed for.

ELECTRA [*now speaking*]

Where could you find relief—and who are you
to find it—for my troubles which know no cure?

CHRYSOTHEMIS

We have Orestes here among us—that is
my news for you—as plain as you see myself.

ELECTRA

Are you mad, poor girl, or can it be you laugh
at what are your own troubles as well as mine?

CHRYSOTHEMIS

I swear by our father's hearth. It is not in mockery
I speak. He is here in person with us.

ELECTRA

Ah!
Poor girl! Who told you this that you believed him,
all too credulous?

CHRYSOTHEMIS

My own eyes were the evidence
for what I saw, and no one else.

ELECTRA

Poor thing!
What proof was there to see? What did you look at
that has set your heart incurably afire?

CHRYSOTHEMIS

I pray you, hear me by the gods,
and then, having heard me, call me sane or foolish.

ELECTRA

Tell me, then, if the story gives you pleasure.

CHRYSOTHEMIS

Yes, I will tell you all I saw.
When I came to our father's ancient grave,
I saw that from the very top of the mound
newly poured streams of milk were flowing, and his tomb
was crowned with a wreath of all the flowers
that grow. I saw in wonder, looked about
in case there might be someone near. But when I saw
that all was quiet, I approached the grave.
On top of the pyre I saw a fresh-cut lock of hair;
as soon as I saw that, something jumped within me
at the familiar sight. I knew I saw
the token of my dearest, loved Orestes.
I took it in my hands, never saying a word
for fear of saying what would be ill-omened,
but in pure joy my eyes were filled with tears.
Both then and now I know with certainty
this offering could come from him alone.
Whom else could this concern, save you and me?
I did not do it, I know, and neither did you.
How could you? For you cannot leave this house,

even to worship, but they will punish you for it.
Nor can it be our mother. She is not inclined
to do such things, and if she did, we'd notice it.
These offerings at the grave must be Orestes'.
Dear sister, take heart. It is not always the same
fortune that follows anyone. Till now
our fortune was hateful to us. But now perhaps
this day will seal the promise of much good.

ELECTRA

Oh, how I pity you, long since, for your foolishness!

CHRYSOTHEMIS

What is this? Are you not pleased by what I say?

ELECTRA

You don't know where you are, nor what you're thinking.

CHRYSOTHEMIS

Why, don't I have knowledge of what I saw quite plainly?

ELECTRA

He is dead, my poor dear. And your rescue at his hands
is dead along with him. Look to him no more.

CHRYSOTHEMIS

Alas! From whom on earth did you hear this?

ELECTRA

From one that was near to him, when he was dying.

CHRYSOTHEMIS

Where is that man then? I am lost in wonder.

ELECTRA

He's in the house, as our mother's welcome guest.

CHRYSOTHEMIS

Alas again! But who then would have placed
these many offerings on our father's tomb?

ELECTRA

I think perhaps that someone put them there
as a remembrance of the dead Orestes.

CHRYSOTHEMIS

Unlucky I! I was so happy coming,
hurrying to bring my news to you, not knowing
what misery we were plunged in. Now when I've come,
I find both our old sorrow and the new.

ELECTRA

That is how things are, yes. But now listen to me,
and you can relieve the suffering that weighs on us.

CHRYSOTHEMIS

So can I bring the dead to life again?

ELECTRA

This is not what I mean. I am no such fool.

CHRYSOTHEMIS

What do you bid me do, of which I am capable?

ELECTRA

To have the courage to follow my counsel.

CHRYSOTHEMIS

If I can help at all, I will not refuse.

ELECTRA

Look: there is no success without hardship.

CHRYSOTHEMIS

I know. As far as my strength goes, I will help.

ELECTRA

Hear me tell you, then, the plans that I have laid.
Friends to help—you know that we have none:
death has taken them and robbed us. We alone,
the two of us, are left.
While I still heard my brother lived and flourished,

I had my hopes that he would come again,
some day, to avenge the murder of our father.
But now that he's no more, I look to you,
that you should not draw back from helping me,
your trueborn sister, kill our father's murderer,
Aegisthus.
There is nothing I should now conceal from you.
What are you waiting for, that you are hesitant?
What hope do you look to, that is still standing?
Now you must sorrow that you have been deprived
of our father's wealth; and you must grieve also
that you are growing older, to this point,
without a marriage and a husband. And
don't hope to get them now, for Aegisthus
is not such a fool as to allow children of yours
or mine to grow up, obviously to harm him.
But if you follow my plans,
first, you will win from that dead father, gone
to the underworld, and from our brother with him,
the recognition of your piety.
And, secondly, as you were born to freedom,
so in the days to come you will be called free
and find a marriage worthy of you: everyone
loves to look to the noble.
Do you not see how great a reputation
you will win for yourself and me by doing this?
For who of citizens and foreigners
that sees us will not welcome us with praise:
"These are two sisters. Look, friends, on them well.
They saved their father's house when their enemies
were riding high, and took their stand against murder,
sparing not to risk their lives upon the venture.
Therefore, we all should love them, all revere them,
and all at feasts and public ceremonies
honor these two girls for their bravery."
This is what everyone will say of us,

in life and death, to our undying fame.
My dear one, hear me. Labor to help your father
and help your brother; give me deliverance
from what I suffer, and deliver yourself, knowing this:
living shamefully, for the nobly born, is shameful.

CHORUS LEADER

In matters like this, forethought is an ally
to the one that gives advice and the one that gets it.

CHRYSOTHEMIS

Ladies, before she spoke, if she had good sense,
she would have held to caution; but she has not.

*(To Electra.)*

Where are you looking, that you arm yourself like this
with such audacity and call on me to help?
Can you not see? You are a woman—no man—
and your physical strength is less than is your enemies'!
Their fortune, day by day, grows luckier
while ours declines and comes to nothingness.
Who then, plotting to kill such a man as this,
will escape unharmed and free of all disaster?
We two are now in trouble. Look to it that
we do not get ourselves trouble still worse
if someone hears what you have said.
There is no gain for us, not the slightest help,
to win a noble reputation if
the way to it lies by dishonorable death.
For death is not the worst but when one wants
to die and cannot even have that death.
I beg of you, before you utterly
destroy us and exterminate our family,
check your temper. All that you have said to me
I'll keep, for my part, unspoken and unfulfilled.
Be sensible, you, and, at long last, being weaker,
learn to give in to those that have the strength.

CHORUS LEADER

Follow her advice. There's no greater gain for humans
than prudence and a reasonable mind!

ELECTRA

You have said nothing unexpected. Well
I knew you would reject what I proposed.
The deed must then be done by my own hand
alone. For I won't leave it unattempted.

CHRYSOTHEMIS

Ah!
I would you had felt so when our father died:
you would have carried all before you.

ELECTRA

I was the same in nature then, weaker in judgment.

CHRYSOTHEMIS

Practice to keep that judgment through your life.

ELECTRA

That is advice which means you will not help me.

CHRYSOTHEMIS

Yes—for the attempt most likely brings disaster.

ELECTRA

I envy you your "judgment," but hate your cowardice.

CHRYSOTHEMIS

I will be equally patient when you praise me.

ELECTRA

That you will never experience from me.

CHRYSOTHEMIS

There's a long future to determine that.

ELECTRA

Be gone; for there's no help in you for me.

CHRYSOTHEMIS

There is, but there's no power of learning in you.

ELECTRA

Go and tell all this story to your mother.

CHRYSOTHEMIS

I do not hate you with such a hatred as that.

ELECTRA

Understand, at least, how you dishonor me.

CHRYSOTHEMIS

It is not dishonor, only forethought for you.

ELECTRA

Must I then follow your idea of justice?

CHRYSOTHEMIS

You'll be our leader, once you come to your senses.

ELECTRA

It is terrible to speak well and be wrong.

CHRYSOTHEMIS

A very proper description of yourself.

ELECTRA

What! Don't you think that I say these things with justice?

CHRYSOTHEMIS

There are times when even justice can bring harm.

ELECTRA

These are rules by which I would not wish to live.

CHRYSOTHEMIS

If you make your attempt, you'll find that I am right.

ELECTRA

Yes, I will make it. You will not frighten me.

CHRYSOTHEMIS

Are you sure now? You will not think again?

ELECTRA

No enemy is worse than bad advice.

CHRYSOTHEMIS

You cannot agree with any of what I say?

ELECTRA

I have made my mind up—long ago, in fact.

CHRYSOTHEMIS

I will go away then. You cannot bring yourself°
to approve my words, nor I your disposition.

ELECTRA

Go then. I'll never follow you,
not though you long for it. It is pure folly
to try to pursue vain and empty things.

CHRYSOTHEMIS

Well, if you think that you are right, go on
thinking so. When you are deep in trouble, then
you will agree with what I said.

*(Exit Chrysothemis into the palace.)*

CHORUS [*singing*]

STROPHE A

*Why, when we see above our heads the birds,*
*true in their wisdom,*
*caring for the sustenance*
*of those that gave them life and help,*
*why do we not pay our own debts of gratitude so?*
*But, by Zeus of the lightning bolt,*
*by Themis, dweller in heaven,*
*not for long do we go unpunished.*
*O voice that goes to the dead below,*
*carry the piteous message*
*to the Atridae in the underworld,*
*and tell of wrongs untouched*
*by joy of the dance.*

ANTISTROPHE A

*Tell them that now their house is sick,*
*tell them that their two children*
*fight and struggle, that they cannot*
*any more live in harmony together.*
*Electra, betrayed, alone,*
*is down in the waves of sorrow,*
*constantly bewailing her father's fate,*
*like the nightingale lamenting.*
*She takes no thought of death;*
*she is ready to leave the light*
*if only she can kill the two Furies.*
*Was there ever one so noble*
*born to a father's house?*

STROPHE B

*Nobody truly good will choose to live*
*shamefully, if so living*
*they cloud their renown and die nameless.*
*O my child, my child, even so you°*
*have chosen to share the life of mourning,*
*have rejected dishonor,*
*to win at once two reputations*
*as wise and best of daughters.*

ANTISTROPHE B

*I pray that your life may be lifted high*
*over your foes,*
*in wealth and power as much as now*
*you lie beneath their hand.*
*For I have found you in distress*
*but winning the highest prize*
*by piety toward Zeus*
*for observance of nature's greatest laws.*

*(Enter Orestes and Pylades from the side, disguised as Phocian countrymen and accompanied by attendants who carry an urn.)*

ORESTES

I wonder, ladies, if we were directed right
and have come to the destination that we sought?

CHORUS LEADER

What do you seek? And what do you want here?

ORESTES

I have asked all the way here where Aegisthus lives.

CHORUS LEADER

You have arrived and need not blame your guides.

ORESTES

Would some one of you be so kind to tell
the household we have come, a welcome company?

CHORUS LEADER

This lady, as nearest of kin, could bear the message.

ORESTES

Then, lady, will you please report within
that certain men of Phocis seek Aegisthus.

ELECTRA

O no! Then are you bringing the certain proofs
of those rumors we received before you came?

ORESTES

I do not know about rumor. Old Strophius sent me
here to bring news about Orestes.

ELECTRA

What is it, sir? How fear steals over me!

ORESTES

Within this little urn, as you can see,
we are bringing home his small remains. He is dead.

ELECTRA

Ah, ah! This is it indeed, all clear.
Here is my sorrow visible, before me.

ORESTES

If you are one that sorrows for Orestes
and his troubles, know this urn contains his body.

ELECTRA

Sir, give it to me, by the gods. If he
is hidden in this urn—give it into my hands,
that I may weep and cry lament together
for myself and my whole family with these ashes.

ORESTES [*speaking to his attendants*]

Bring it and give it to her, whoever she is.
It is not in enmity she asks for it.
One of his friends, no doubt, or of his blood.

*(The attendants do as directed.)*

ELECTRA [*speaking*] *(To the urn.)*

Precious memorial of my dearest love,
my most loved in the world, all that remains
of live Orestes, oh, how differently
from the hopes I sent you with do I receive you home!
Now all I hold of you is nothingness;
but you shone brilliantly, child, when from this house
I sent you forth.
Would that I had left life before I sent you
abroad to a foreign country, when I stole you
with these two hands, saved you from being murdered.
Then on that very day you would have died,
and lying there would have found your share,
your common portion of your father's grave.
Now far from home, an exile, on alien soil
without your sister near, you died unhappily.
I did not, to my sorrow, wash you with
these hands that loved you, did not lift you up,
as was my right, a weight of misery,
from the fierce blaze of the pyre. The hands of strangers
gave you your rites, and so you come again,
a tiny weight enclosed in a tiny vessel.

Alas for all my nursing of long ago,
so constant—all for nothing—which I gave you
with such sweet trouble. For you never were
as much your mother's love as you were mine;
none was your nurse but I within that household,
and I was always the one called "sister." Now
in one day all that is gone—for you are dead:
all, all you have snatched with you in your going, like
a hurricane. Our father is dead and gone.
I am dead in you; and you are dead yourself.
Our enemies laugh. Frantic with joy she grows,
mother, no mother, the one you promised me
in secret messages so often you
would come to punish. Now our evil fortune,
yours and mine, has stolen all this away,
and sent you back to me like this—no longer
the form I used to love, only your dust
and idle shade.

[*singing*]
*Ah, ah!!*
*O body pitiable! Ah!*
*O saddest journey that you went, my love,*
*and so have destroyed me! Ah!*
*O brother, loved one, you have destroyed me!*

[*now speaking again*]
Therefore, receive me to your habitation,
nothing to nothing, that with you below
I may dwell from now on. When you were on earth,
I shared all with you equally. Now I claim
in death no less to share a grave with you.
The dead, I see, no longer suffer pain.

CHORUS LEADER

Think, Electra, your father was mortal, and mortal
was Orestes also. Do not sorrow too much.
This is a debt that all of us must pay.

ORESTES

Ah!
What shall I say? What words can I use? It's impossible;
I am no longer master of my tongue.

ELECTRA

What ails you? What is the meaning of your words?

ORESTES

Is this the glorious form of Electra that I see?

ELECTRA

Yes. This is she; and truly miserable.

ORESTES

Alas for this most lamentable event!

ELECTRA

Is it for me, sir, you are sorrowing?

ORESTES

That body, so cruelly and godlessly abused!

ELECTRA

None other than myself must be the subject
of your ill-omened words, sir.

ORESTES

O, alas
for your life without husband or happiness!

ELECTRA

Why do you look at me so, sir? Why lament?

ORESTES

How little then I knew of my own troubles!

ELECTRA

From what that has been said did you learn this?

ORESTES

I see you and your sufferings, so conspicuous.

ELECTRA

It's little of my suffering that you see.

ORESTES

How can there be things worse to see than this?

ELECTRA

Because I live with those that murdered him.

ORESTES

Murderers? Whose? Where is this evil you hint at?

ELECTRA

My father's murderers; and I'm forced to be their slave.

ORESTES

Who is it that forces you to such subjection?

ELECTRA

She is called my mother—but she's like a mother in nothing.

ORESTES

How does she compel you? Hardship or violence?

ELECTRA

With violence and hardship and all ills.

ORESTES

You have no one to help you or prevent her?

ELECTRA

No. There was one. You have shown me his dust.

ORESTES

Poor girl! When I look at you, how I pity you!

ELECTRA

Then you are the only one that ever pitied me.

ORESTES

Yes. I alone came here and felt your pain.

ELECTRA

You haven't perhaps come from somewhere as our kinsman?

ORESTES

I will tell you—if these women here are friends.

ELECTRA

Yes, friends indeed. You may speak quite freely.

ORESTES

Give up this urn then, and you shall know all.

ELECTRA

Don't make me do that, stranger—by the gods!

ORESTES

Do what I bid you. You will not be wrong.

ELECTRA

By your beard! Do not rob me of what I love most!

ORESTES

I will not let you keep it.

ELECTRA

O Orestes!<br>
Alas, if I may not even give you burial!

ORESTES

No words of ill omen! You have no right to mourn.

ELECTRA

Have I no right to mourn for my dead brother?

ORESTES

You have no right to call him by that title.

ELECTRA

Am I then so dishonored in his sight?

ORESTES

No one dishonors you. But this is not for you.

ELECTRA

It is—if it's Orestes' body that I hold here.

ORESTES

But it's not Orestes'—except in make-believe.

ELECTRA

Where is the poor boy buried then?

ORESTES

Nowhere.
There is no grave for living men.

ELECTRA

How, boy,
what do you mean?

ORESTES

Nothing that is untrue.

ELECTRA

Is he alive then?

ORESTES

Yes, if I am living.

ELECTRA

And are you he?

ORESTES

Look at this signet ring
that was our father's, and know if I speak true.

ELECTRA

O happiest light!

ORESTES

Happiest I say, too.

ELECTRA

Voice, have you come?

ORESTES

Hear it from no other source.

ELECTRA

Do my arms hold you?

ORESTES

Never again to part.

ELECTRA

Dearest of women, fellow citizens,
here is Orestes that was dead by contrivance,
and now by contrivance is restored to life again!

CHORUS LEADER

We see, my child, and at your happy fortune
tears of gladness trickle from our eyes.

ELECTRA [*singing, while Orestes speaks*]

STROPHE

*Child of the body that I loved the best,*
*at last you have come,*
*you have come, you have found, you have seen those you yearned for.*

ORESTES

Yes, I have come. But bide your time in silence.

ELECTRA

*Why?*

ORESTES

Silence is better, that none inside may hear.

ELECTRA

*No, by Artemis, ever virgin,*
*this I will never stoop to fear—*
*the women who live inside,*
*a vain burden on the earth.*

ORESTES

Yes, but consider that in women too
there lives a warlike spirit. You have proof of it.

ELECTRA

*Ah, indeed!*
*You have awakened our sorrow*
*the nature of which no cloud can cover,*
*nothing can undo,*
*no forgetfulness overcome,*
*our sorrow in all its evil.*

ORESTES

I know that too. But when the right moment comes,
then will be the time to remember what was done.

ELECTRA

ANTISTROPHE

*Every moment, every moment of all time*
*would justly suit my complaints.*
*For hardly now are my lips free of restraint.*

ORESTES

And I agree. Therefore, hold fast that freedom.

ELECTRA

*By doing what?*

ORESTES

Where there is no occasion,
do not choose to talk too much.

ELECTRA

*Who could find a fit bargain*
*of words for such silence,*
*now you have appeared?*
*Past hope, past calculation,*
*I see you now.*

ORESTES

You see me when the gods moved me to come.°

. . . . . . . . . . . . . . . . . . .

ELECTRA

*You tell me then of a grace surpassing*
*what I knew before, if in very truth*
*the gods have given you to this house.*
*This I do count an action divine.*

ORESTES

Indeed, I hesitate to check your joy;
only I fear your pleasure may be too great.

ELECTRA

EPODE

*Orestes, you have come at last,*
*have made the journey worth all the world to me,*
*have come before me at last.*
*Now that I see you*
*after so much sorrow,*
*do not, I beg you . . .*

ORESTES

What should I not do?

ELECTRA

*. . . do not deprive me*
*of the joy of seeing your face.*

ORESTES

I would be angry if I saw this in anyone else.

ELECTRA

*You agree?*

ORESTES

Of course I do.

ELECTRA

*My dear one, I have heard your voice,*
*the voice I never hoped to hear.*
*Till now I have held my rage speechless;°*

*I did not cry out when I heard bad news.*
*But now I have you. You have come,*
*your dearest face before me*
*that even in suffering I could never forget.*

ORESTES

Spare me all superfluity of speech.
Tell me not how my mother is villainous,
nor how Aegisthus drains my father's wealth
by luxury and waste. Words about this
will shorten time and opportunity.
But tell me what we need for the present moment,
how openly or hidden by our coming now
we can put a stop to our enemies' mockery.
And take care that our mother does not realize
by your radiant face, when we two go inside.
Keep groaning over my destruction, as it was
emptily described in words. For when we have triumphed,
then you may freely show your joy, and laugh.

ELECTRA [*now speaking*]

Brother, your pleasure shall be mine. These joys
I have from you; they are not mine to own.
I would not agree to hurt you in the slightest,
even if this would bring great profit for myself.
If I did so, I would not properly
be serving the god who watches over us.
You know the situation. You have heard
Aegisthus is not at home; our mother is.
And don't be afraid that she will see my face
radiant with smiles: our hatred is too old,
I am too steeped in it. And since I have seen you,
my tears of joy will still run readily.
How can they cease when on the selfsame day
I have seen you dead and then again alive?
For me your coming is a miracle,
so that if my father should come back to life

I would think it no wonder but believe
I saw him. Since your coming is such for me,
lead as you will. Had I been all alone,
I would not have failed to win one of two things,
a noble deliverance or a noble death.

ORESTES

Hush, hush! I hear one of the people within
coming out.

ELECTRA

Please enter our house, dear guests—
more so, since what you are carrying in is that
which no one would refuse—nor be delighted,
if he receives it.

TUTOR *(Entering from the palace.)*

Fools and madmen! No
concern for your own lives at all? No sense
to realize that you are not merely near
the deadliest danger, but in its very midst?
If I had not, this while past, stood guard here
at the door, your plans would now be in the house
before your bodies. I and only I
took the precautions. Have done once and for all
with your long speeches, your insatiable
cries of delight, and in with you at once!
As we are now, delay is ruinous:
it is high time to have done with our task.

ORESTES

How's everything inside, as I go in?

TUTOR

Well. There is no chance of your recognition.

ORESTES

You have announced my death, I understand.

TUTOR

You are down in Hades, as far as they're concerned.

ORESTES

Were they glad of it? Or what did they say?

TUTOR

I will tell you at the end. As things are now,
all on their side is well—even what is not so.

ELECTRA

Brother, who is this man? I beg you, tell me.

ORESTES

Do you not know him?

ELECTRA

I cannot even guess.

ORESTES

Do you not know him to whose hands you gave me?

ELECTRA

What, this man?

ORESTES

By his hands and by your forethought
I was conveyed away to Phocian country.

ELECTRA

Is this the man, alone among so many,
whom I found loyal when our father was murdered?

ORESTES

This is he. There is no need for further questions.

ELECTRA

O light of day most loved! O only rescuer
of Agamemnon's house, how did you come
back here? Are you indeed that man who saved
both Orestes and me from so many dangers?

O most loved hands, service of feet most kind!
To think you were standing beside me for so long,
and I didn't know you, and you gave no sign!
You killed me with your words while in reality
you were bringing sweet joy. Bless you, my father—
for I think I see a father in you. Blessings!
Within a single day, of all mankind
I have most hated and loved you most.

TUTOR

Enough, I think. As for the story
of the happenings in between, there'll be many days
and nights, as time comes round, to tell you all
clearly, Electra.

*(To Orestes and Pylades.)*

But as you two stand here
I say to you: now is your chance to act.
Clytemnestra is alone. No man is within.
If you hold back now, you will have others to fight
more clever and more numerous than these.

ORESTES

Pylades, our need now is not for lengthy speeches,
but to get inside as quick as ever we can,
only first saluting the ancestral gods
whose statues stand beside the forecourt here.

*(Orestes, Pylades, and the Tutor exit into the palace.)*

ELECTRA

Apollo, Lord, give gracious ear to them
and to me, too, that often made you offerings,
out of such store as I had, with prayerful hand.
So now, Lycian Apollo, I kneel before you,
I pray and entreat you, with all the resources
that I possess: please be kind to us,
help us in the fulfilment of our plans

and demonstrate to all mankind the punishment
the gods exact for wickedness.

*(Exit Electra into the palace.)*

CHORUS [*singing*]

STROPHE A

*See how the war god approaches,*
*breathing bloody vengeance, invincible Ares.*
*They have gone under the roof of the house now,*
*those pursuers of evil crimes,*
*hounds that none may escape;*
*so that the dream that hung hauntingly*
*in my mind shall not wait long for fulfilment.*

ANTISTROPHE A

*Stealthy, stealthy-footed, into the house*
*he goes, the champion of dead men,*
*into his father's palace rich from of old,*
*holding the blade of blood,*
*new-whetted, in his hands. Hermes,*
*the child of Maia, hiding the crafty deed in darkness,*
*conducts him to its end, and delays not.*

*(Electra enters from the palace.)*

ELECTRA [*mostly speaking, while Orestes speaks in response*]

STROPHE B

Dear friends, now is the moment that the men
are finishing their work. Wait in silence.

CHORUS LEADER

What do you mean? What are they doing?

ELECTRA

She is preparing
the urn for burial, and they stand beside her.

CHORUS LEADER

Why have you hurried out here?

ELECTRA

To watch
that Aegisthus does not come on them unawares.

CLYTEMNESTRA *(Cries out from within the palace.)*

House, O house
deserted by friends, full of killers!

ELECTRA

Someone cries out, inside. Do you hear?

CHORUS [*singing*]

*What I hear is a terror to the ear.*
*I shudder at it.*

CLYTEMNESTRA *(Cries out again from within.)*

Oh! Oh! Aegisthus, where are you?

ELECTRA

Again, that cry!

CLYTEMNESTRA

My son, my son,
pity your mother!

ELECTRA

You had none for him,
nor for his father that begot him.

CHORUS [*singing*]

*City,*
*and miserable family, now*
*that day-to-day fate of yours is coming to an end.°*

CLYTEMNESTRA

Oh! I am struck!

ELECTRA

If you have strength—again!

CLYTEMNESTRA

Once more! Oh!

ELECTRA

If only Aegisthus were with you!

CHORUS [*singing*]

*The curses are being fulfilled;*
*those under the earth are alive;*
*men long dead draw from their killers*
*blood to answer blood.*

(*Enter Orestes and Pylades from the palace.*)

CHORUS LEADER° [*now speaking*]

ANTISTROPHE B

And here they come. The bloody hand drips
with Ares' sacrifice. I cannot blame them.

ELECTRA

Orestes, how have you fared?

ORESTES

In the house, all
is well, if Apollo prophesied well.

ELECTRA

Is the wretched woman dead?

ORESTES

You need fear no more
that your mother's arrogance will dishonor you.°

CHORUS [*singing*]

*Stop! I can see Aegisthus*
*clearly coming this way.*

ELECTRA

Boys, back to the house!

ORESTES

Where do you see him?

ELECTRA

He's in our power,
walking toward us from the suburb, full of joy.

CHORUS [*singing*]

*Back to the vestibule, quick as you can.*
*You have done one part well; now here is the other.*

ORESTES

Don't worry, we will do it.

ELECTRA

Go
where you will, then.

ORESTES

See, I am gone.

ELECTRA

Leave what is here to me.

*(Exit Orestes into the palace with Pylades.).*

CHORUS [*singing*]

*A few words spoken softly in his ear*
*would be good, that unawares*
*he may rush into his contest against Justice.*

*(Enter Aegisthus from the side.)*

AEGISTHUS

Which of you knows where the Phocian visitors are?
I am told they are come here with news for me
that Orestes met his end in a chariot wreck.
You there, yes, I mean you, who formerly
were so bold and insolent; I should think
it is you this news concerns the most, and therefore
you will know best to tell it to me.

ELECTRA

I know it, of course. Were it not so, I would be
an outsider to what concerns my best beloved.

AEGISTHUS

Where are the strangers then? Tell me that.

ELECTRA

Inside. They have found a very generous hostess.

AEGISTHUS

And do they genuinely report his death?

ELECTRA

Better than that. They have brought himself, not news.

AEGISTHUS

Can I then see the body in plain sight?

ELECTRA

You can indeed. It is an unenviable sight.

AEGISTHUS

What you say delights me—an unusual thing!

ELECTRA

You may delight, if you find these things delightful.

AEGISTHUS *(To the servants.)*

Open the doors, I command you, for all to see,°
all Mycenaeans and Argives, and if there's anyone
who formerly had raised up empty hopes
for Orestes, now he may look on the dead
and so accept my bridle, and thus avoid
a more forcible encounter with myself
and punishment to make him grow some sense.

ELECTRA

I have done everything on my side. At long last
I have learned some sense, agreement with the stronger.

*(The doors of the palace are opened, to reveal a covered body on a bier, with Orestes and Pylades standing in front of it.)*

AEGISTHUS

O Zeus, I see a revelation that has happened
not without the gods' anger. Or if that is something
I should not say, because of Nemesis,
I take it back. Lift all the covers from
that face, so kinship at least may have due mourning.

ORESTES

Handle it yourself. This is not mine,
it's yours—to see and greet with loving words.

AEGISTHUS

True. I accept that. And you, will you call
Clytemnestra, if she is at home?

ORESTES

She is near you.
You need not look elsewhere.

AEGISTHUS *(Lifting the covering.)*

What do I see?

ORESTES

Something you fear? Do you not know the face?

AEGISTHUS

Who are these men that have driven me into their net
to my destruction?

ORESTES

Did you take so long
to find that your names are all astray
and those you call the dead are living?

AEGISTHUS

Ah!
I understand. And you who speak to me
can only be Orestes.

ORESTES

Were you, so good a prophet, so long misled?

AEGISTHUS

This is my end then. But let me say one thing,
one short word.

ELECTRA

I beg you, brother; don't let him draw out the talking.
When men are in the middle of trouble, when one°
is on the point of death, how can time matter?
Kill him as quickly as you can; and when you've killed him,
throw him out to find such burial as suits him,
out of our sights. This is the only thing for me
that can bring release from sufferings long endured.

ORESTES *(To Aegisthus.)*

In with you, then. It is not words that now
are the issue, but your life.

AEGISTHUS

Why into the house?
Why do you need the dark if what you do
is fair? Why is your hand not ready to kill me?

ORESTES

You are not to give orders. Go in, where you killed
my father, so you may die in the same place!

AEGISTHUS

Is it completely necessary that this house
see the evils of the Pelopidae, now and to come?

ORESTES

Yours, at least. Of that I am an excellent prophet.

AEGISTHUS

Your father did not have the skill you boast of.

ORESTES

Too many words! You are slow to take your road.
Go now.

AEGISTHUS

You lead the way.

ORESTES

No, you go first.

AEGISTHUS

Afraid that I'll escape you?

ORESTES

No, but you shall not
die as you choose. I must take care that death
is bitter for you. Justice shall be taken°
directly on all who act above the law—
justice by killing. So we would have less crime.

*(Exit Aegisthus into the palace, followed by Orestes, Pylades, and Electra.)*

CHORUS [*chanting*]

*O family of Atreus, how many sufferings*
*were yours before you came at last so hardly*
*to freedom, by this day's deed perfected.*

# III.

# EURIPIDES

# INTRODUCTION TO EURIPIDES

Little is known about the life of Euripides. He was probably born between 485 and 480 BCE on the island of Salamis near Athens. Of the three great writers of Athenian tragedy of the fifth century he was thus the youngest: Aeschylus was older by about forty years, Sophocles by ten or fifteen. Euripides is not reported to have ever engaged significantly in the political or military life of his city, unlike Aeschylus, who fought against the Persians at Marathon, and Sophocles, who was made a general during the Peloponnesian War. In 408 Euripides left Athens to go to the court of King Archelaus of Macedonia in Pella (we do not know exactly why). He died there in 406.

Ancient scholars knew of about ninety plays attributed to Euripides, and he was given permission to participate in the annual tragedy competition at the festival of Dionysus on twenty-two occasions—strong evidence of popular interest in his work. But he was not particularly successful at winning the first prize. Although he began competing in 455 (the year after Aeschylus died), he did not win first place until 441, and during his lifetime he received that award only four times; a fifth victory was bestowed on him posthumously for his trilogy *Iphigenia in Aulis, The Bacchae, Alcmaeon in Corinth* (this last play is lost), produced by one of his sons who was also named Euripides. By contrast, Aeschylus won thirteen victories and Sophocles eighteen. From various references, especially the frequent parodies of Euripides in the comedies of Aristophanes, we can surmise that many members of contemporary Athenian audiences objected to Euripides' tendency to make the characters of tragedy more modern and less heroic, to represent the passions of women, and to reflect recent developments in philosophy and music.

But in the centuries after his death, Euripides went on to become by far the most popular of the Greek tragedians. When the ancient Greeks use the phrase "the poet" without further specification and do not mean by it Homer, they always mean Euripides. Hundreds of fragments from his plays, mostly quite short, are found in quotations by other authors and in anthologies from the period between the third century BCE and the fourth century CE. Many more fragments of his plays have been preserved on papyrus starting in the fourth century BCE than of those by Aeschylus and Sophocles together, and far more scenes of his plays have been associated with images on ancient pottery starting in the same century and on frescoes in Pompeii and elsewhere and Roman sarcophagi some centuries later than is the case for either of his rivals. Some knowledge of his texts spread far and wide through collections of sententious aphorisms and excerpts of speeches and songs drawn from his plays (or invented in his name).

It was above all in the schools that Euripides became the most important author of tragedies: children throughout the Greek-speaking world learned the rules of language and comportment by studying first and foremost Homer and Euripides. But we know that Euripides' plays also continued to be performed in theaters for centuries, and the transmitted texts of some of the more popular ones (e.g., *Medea, Orestes*) seem to bear the traces of modifications by ancient producers and actors. Both in his specific plays and plots and in his general conception of dramatic action and character, Euripides massively influenced later Greek playwrights, not only tragic poets but also comic ones (especially Menander, the most important dramatist of New Comedy, born about a century and a half after Euripides)—and not only Greek ones, but Latin ones as well, such as Accius and Pacuvius, and later Seneca (who went on to exert a deep influence on Renaissance drama).

A more or less complete collection of his plays was made in Alexandria during the third century BCE. Whereas, out of all the plays of Aeschylus and Sophocles, only seven tragedies each were chosen (no one knows by whom) at some point later in antiquity, probably in the second century CE, to represent their work, Euripides received the distinction of having ten plays selected as canonical: *Alcestis, Andromache, The Bacchae, Hecuba, Hippolytus, Medea, Orestes, The Phoenician Women, Rhesus* (scholars generally think this play was written by someone other than Euripides and was attributed to him in antiquity by mistake), and *The Trojan Women*. Of these ten tragedies, three—*Hecuba, Orestes,* and *The Phoenician Women*—were especially popular in the Middle Ages; they are referred to as the Byzantine triad, after the capital of the eastern Empire, Byzantium, known later as Constantinople and today as Istanbul.

The plays that did not form part of the selection gradually ceased to be copied, and thus most of them eventually were lost to posterity. We would possess only these ten plays and fragments of the others were it not for the lucky chance that a single volume of an ancient complete edition of Euripides' plays, arranged alphabetically, managed to survive into the Middle Ages. Thus we also have another nine tragedies (referred to as the alphabetic plays) whose titles in Greek all begin with the letters *epsilon, êta, iota,* and *kappa*: *Electra, Helen, The Children of Heracles* (*Hêrakleidai*), *Heracles, The Suppliants* (*Hiketides*), *Ion, Iphigenia in Aulis, Iphigenia among the Taurians,* and *The Cyclops* (*Kyklôps*). The Byzantine triad have very full ancient commentaries (scholia) and are transmitted by hundreds of medieval manuscripts; the other seven plays of the canonical selection have much sparser scholia and are transmitted by something more than a dozen manuscripts; the alphabetic plays have no scholia at all and are transmitted only by a single manuscript in rather poor condition and by its copies.

Modern scholars have been able to establish a fairly secure dating for most of Euripides' tragedies thanks to the exact indications provided by ancient scholarship for the first production of some of them and the relative chronology suggested by metrical and other features for the others. Accordingly the five volumes of this third edition have been organized according to the probable chronological sequence:

| | |
|---|---|
| Volume 1: | *Alcestis*: 438 BCE |
| | *Medea*: 431 |
| | *The Children of Heracles*: ca. 430 |
| | *Hippolytus*: 428 |
| Volume 2: | *Andromache*: ca. 425 |
| | *Hecuba*: ca. 424 |
| | *The Suppliant Women*: ca. 423 |
| | *Electra*: ca. 420 |
| Volume 3: | *Heracles*: ca. 415 |
| | *The Trojan Women*: 415 |
| | *Iphigenia among the Taurians*: ca. 414 |
| | *Ion*: ca. 413 |
| Volume 4: | *Helen*: 412 |
| | *The Phoenician Women*: ca. 409 |
| | *Orestes*: 408 |
| Volume 5: | *The Bacchae*: posthumously after 406 |
| | *Iphigenia in Aulis*: posthumously after 406 |
| | *The Cyclops*: date unknown |
| | *Rhesus*: probably spurious, from the fourth century BCE |

In the Renaissance Euripides remained the most popular of the three tragedians. Directly and by the mediation of Seneca he influenced drama from the sixteenth to the eighteenth century far more than Aeschylus or Sophocles did. But toward the end of the eighteenth century and even more in the course of the nineteenth century, he came increasingly under attack yet again, as already in the fifth century BCE, and for much the same reason, as being decadent, tawdry, irreligious, and inharmonious. He was also criticized for his perceived departures from the ideal of "the tragic" (as exemplified by plays such as Sophocles' *Oedipus the*

*King* and *Antigone*), especially in the "romance" plots of *Alcestis, Iphigenia among the Taurians*, *Ion*, and *Helen*. It was left to the twentieth century to discover its own somewhat disturbing affinity to his tragic style and worldview. Nowadays among theatrical audiences, scholars, and nonprofessional readers Euripides is once again at least as popular as his two rivals.

# ALCESTIS

Translated by RICHMOND LATTIMORE

# ALCESTIS: INTRODUCTION

*The Play: Date and Composition*

Euripides' *Alcestis* was produced in 438 BCE at the Great Dionysian Festival in Athens as one of four plays in a tetralogy of which the other three plays have been lost: *The Cretan Women*, *Alcmaeon in Psophis*, and *Telephus*. Euripides took the second prize that year behind Sophocles. Although *Alcestis* is Euripides' earliest securely dated play, he was probably in his forties at the time and had been competing in the dramatic contests for over fifteen years (though he had not won his first victory until 441).

Ancient scholars reported that *Alcestis* was performed fourth in Euripides' tetralogy that year and thus took the place of the satyr-play, the comic play centered on Dionysus and his troop of ribald satyrs that usually followed the three serious and lofty tragedies in any entry in the dramatic competition. Ancient scholars also pointed out the elements of the play that reminded them more of comedy or of satyr-plays than of tragedy—above all, the fact that events turn out happily in the end. They even suggested that *Alcestis* was not to be considered a genuine tragedy. Modern scholars have continued to debate this question. Just what kind of play is *Alcestis*? To which genre or genres, if any, should it be assigned?

*The Myth*

*Alcestis* tells how the god Apollo tries to reward Admetus, king of the town of Pherae in Thessaly, for his hospitality to him by arranging that a substitute die in the king's stead on the fated day of his death. Admetus' parents refuse to sacrifice their lives for him, but his wife, Alcestis, agrees to do so. After she dies, Admetus' friend Heracles shows up; Admetus conceals the news of Alcestis' death and receives him with great hospitality. When Heracles discovers what has happened, he wrestles with Death, defeats him, and leads Alcestis back to Admetus.

The story of the man doomed to die who seeks, and sometimes finds, a substitute willing to die in his place is a widespread motif of folktales from many places and ages. Familiar too from folktales, though less widely attested, is the idea that a hero can wrestle with Death and rescue someone from his clutches. But there are few if any traces of such topics in surviving Greek literature before Euripides. The only important predecessor about whom we have any information is the Greek tragedian Phrynichus, active at the end of the sixth century and the beginning of the fifth century BCE: an *Alcestis* is listed among his works, and the few fragments and references to this lost play that can be gleaned from later authors indicate that it probably included some of the same characters who appear in Euripides' version (especially Apollo, Death, and Heracles) and that Phrynichus may have been the one who invented the fundamental idea of Alcestis being rescued from the dead. Although the main characters of Euripides' play were certainly familiar to his audience, at least as names, it is likely that the specific plot Euripides constructed for them was surprising and fresh.

### *Transmission and Reception*

After Euripides, comic and tragic dramas about Alcestis were occasionally produced by other Greek and Roman authors; at Rome, Alcestis was also a subject for pantomimes. About these later dramatic versions we know too little to be able to say how much Euripides' play influenced them. So too, there are only occasional references to the story of Alcestis among ancient poets and prose writers, who did sometimes mention her briefly as a celebrated example of a loyal wife but generally did not pause to consider in any depth her psychology or her husband's. But there are at least two remarkable instances of the influence of the *Alcestis* in late antiquity: a Latin poem entitled *Alcesta*, which narrates the myth in 162 verses, all recycled entirely from the works of Virgil; and a papyrus of the fourth century CE, recently discovered in Barcelona, which bears 122 lines of a semidramatic poem in Latin about the story of Alcestis and Admetus, demonstrating some knowledge of Euripides' play.

The play survived as a text in the schools and for some private readers, and it belongs to the group of ten plays by Euripides that were most widely diffused during ancient and medieval times. More even than in literature, Alcestis enjoyed remarkable popularity in ancient pictorial art. She appears especially on Roman sarcophagi, presumably as an exemplar of conjugal fidelity and of hopes for the afterlife. Unsurprisingly, the scene that is most often depicted is that of Heracles leading her back from the dead.

In modern times *Alcestis* has never been among Euripides' most popular plays and has not often been staged. But it has provided the inspiration for various successful dramatic and operatic versions, including operas by Philippe Quinault (1674), George Frideric Handel (1727), and especially Christoph Willibald Gluck (1767), and plays by Christoph Martin Wieland (1773; satirized by Johann Wolfgang von Goethe in the same year), Vittorio Alfieri (1806), and Hugo von Hofmannsthal. The Victorian poet Robert Browning interpreted the story of Alcestis in his *Balaustion's Adventure* (1871); other notable lyric versions include those by Rainer Maria Rilke (1904), Erica Jong (ca. 1973), and Donald Justice (1979). In the theater, more or less radical transformation of the Euripidean model has inspired such very different plays as T. S. Eliot's *The Cocktail Party* (1949), Thornton Wilder's *The Alcestiad; or, A Life in the Sun* (1955), Efua Sutherland's Ghanan *Edufa* (ca. 1962), and Marguerite Yourcenar's *Le mystère d'Alceste* (1963), as well as Martha Graham's dance drama *Alcestis* (1960). It has also been depicted in several modern paintings (Jacques-Louis David, 1767; Eugène Delacroix, 1851–52, 1862) and sculptures (Auguste Rodin, 1899).

# ALCESTIS

*Characters* APOLLO
DEATH
CHORUS of citizens of Pherae
MAID, attendant of Alcestis
ALCESTIS, wife of Admetus
ADMETUS of Pherae, king of Thessaly
BOY,° son of Admetus and Alcestis
HERACLES, friend of Admetus
PHERES, father of Admetus
SERVANT of Admetus

*Scene: Pherae, in Thessaly, in front of the house of Admetus*

*(Enter Apollo from the house, armed with a bow.)*

APOLLO

House of Admetus, in which I, god though I am,
had patience to accept the table of the serfs!
Zeus was the cause. Zeus killed my son, Asclepius,
and drove the bolt of the hot lightning through his chest.
I, in my anger for this, killed the Cyclopes,
smiths of Zeus's fire, for which my father made me serve
a mortal man, in penance for what I did.
I came to this country, tended the oxen of this host
and friend, Admetus, son of Pheres, and have kept
his house from danger until this very day.
For I, who know what's right, have found in him
a man who knows what's right, and so I saved him

from dying, tricking the Fates. The goddesses promised me
Admetus would escape the moment of his death
by giving the lower powers someone else to die
instead of him. He tried his loved ones all in turn,
father and aged mother who had given him birth,°
and found not one, except his wife, who would consent
to die for him, and not see daylight any more.
She is in the house now, gathered in his arms and held
at the breaking point of life, because destiny marks
this for her day of death and taking leave of life.
The stain of death in the house must not be on me. I
step therefore from these chambers dearest to my love.
And here is Death himself, I see him coming, Death
who dedicates the dying, who will lead her down
to the house of Hades. He has come on time. He has
been watching for this day on which her death falls due.

*(Enter Death from the side, armed with a sword.)*

DEATH [*chanting*]

*Ah!*
*You at this house, Phoebus? Why do you haunt*
*the place? It is unfair to take for your own*
*and spoil the death-spirits' privileges.*
*Was it not enough, then, that you blocked the death*
*of Admetus, and overthrew the Fates*
*by a shabby wrestler's trick? And now*
*your bow hand is armed to guard her too,*
*Alcestis, Pelias' daughter, though she*
*promised her life for her husband's.*

APOLLO

Never fear. I have nothing but justice and fair words for you.

DEATH [*now speaking*]

If you mean fairly, what are you doing with a bow?

APOLLO

It is my custom to carry it with me all the time.

DEATH

It is your custom to help this house more than you ought.

APOLLO

But he is my friend, and his misfortunes trouble me.

DEATH

You mean to take her corpse, too, away from me?

APOLLO

I never took his body away from you by force.

DEATH

How is it, then, that he is above ground, not below?

APOLLO

He gave his wife instead, and you have come for her now.

DEATH

I have. And I shall take her down where the dead are.

APOLLO

Take her and go. I am not sure you will listen to me.

DEATH

Tell me to kill whom I must kill. Such are my orders.

APOLLO

No, only to put their death off. They must die in the end.

DEATH

I understand what you would say and what you want.

APOLLO

Is there any way, then, for Alcestis to grow old?

DEATH

There is not. I insist on enjoying my rights too.

APOLLO

You would not take more than one life, in any case.

DEATH

My privilege means more to me when they die young.

APOLLO

If she dies old, she will have a lavish burial.

DEATH

What you propose, Phoebus, is to favor the rich.

APOLLO

What is this? Have you unrecognized talents for debate?

DEATH

Those who could afford to buy a late death would buy it then.

APOLLO

I see. Are you determined not to do this favor for me?

DEATH

I will not do it. And you know my character.

APOLLO

I know it: hateful to mankind, loathed by the gods.

DEATH

You cannot always have your way where you should not.

APOLLO

For all your brute ferocity you shall be stopped.
The man to do it is on the way to Pheres' house
now, on an errand from Eurystheus, sent to steal
a team of horses from the wintry lands of Thrace.
He shall be entertained here in Admetus' house
and he shall take the woman away from you by force,
nor will you have our gratitude, but you shall still
be forced to do it, and to have my hate beside.

DEATH

Much talk. Talking will win you nothing. All the same,
the woman will go with me to Hades' house. I go
to her now, to dedicate her with my sword,
for all whose hair is cut in consecration
by this blade's edge are devoted to the gods below.

*(Exit Death into the house, Apollo to the side. Enter the Chorus.)*

CHORUS° [*chanting*]
*It is quiet by the palace. What does it mean?*
*Why is the house of Admetus so still?*
*Is there none here of his family, none*
*who can tell us whether the queen is dead*
*and therefore to be mourned? Or does Pelias'*
*daughter Alcestis live still, still look*
*on daylight, she who in my mind appears*
*noble beyond*
*all women beside in a wife's duty?*
[*singing individually, not as a group*]

FIRST CITIZEN

STROPHE A

*Does someone hear anything?*
*a groan or a hand's stroke or outcry*
*in the house, as if something were done*
*and over?*

SECOND CITIZEN
*No. And there is no servant stationed*
*at the outer gates. O Paean,*
*healer, might you show in light*
*to still the storm of disaster.*

THIRD CITIZEN
*They would not be silent if she were dead.*

FOURTH CITIZEN
*No, she is gone.°*

FIFTH CITIZEN
*They have not taken her yet from the house.*

SIXTH CITIZEN
*So sure? I know nothing. Why are you certain?*
*And how could Admetus have buried his wife*
*with none by, and she so splendid?*

SEVENTH CITIZEN

ANTISTROPHE A

*Here at the gates I do not see*
*the lustral spring water, approved*
*by custom for a house of death.*

EIGHTH CITIZEN

*Nor are there cut locks of hair at the forecourts*
*hanging, such as the stroke of sorrow*
*for the dead makes. I can hear no beating*
*of the hands of young women.*

NINTH CITIZEN

*Yet this is the day appointed.*

TENTH CITIZEN

*What do you mean? Speak.*

NINTH CITIZEN

*On which she must pass to the world below.*

ELEVENTH CITIZEN

*You touch me deep, my heart, my mind.*

TWELFTH CITIZEN

*Yes. He who from the first has claimed to be called*
*a good man himself*
*must grieve when good men are afflicted.*

[*all singing together*]

STROPHE B

*Sailing the long sea, there is*
*not any shrine on earth*
*you could visit, not Lycia,*
*not the unwatered sanctuary of Ammon,*
*to redeem the life*
*of this unhappy woman. Her fate shows*
*steep and near. There is no god's hearth*
*I know you could reach and by sacrifice*
*avail to save.*

ANTISTROPHE B

*There was only one. If the eyes*
*of Phoebus' son Asclepius could have*
*seen this light, if he could have come*
*and left the dark chambers,*
*the gates of Hades.*
*He upraised those who were stricken*
*down, until from Zeus' hand*
*the flown bolt of thunder hit him.*
*Where is there any hope for life*
*left for me any longer?*

[*now chanting*]
*For all has been done that can be done by our kings now,*
*and there on all the gods' altars*
*are blood sacrifices dripping in full,*
*but no healing comes for the evil.*

(*Enter Maid from the house.*)

CHORUS LEADER

But here is a serving woman coming from the house.
The tears break from her. What will she say has taken place?
We must, of course, forgive your sorrow if something
has happened to your masters. We should like to know
whether the queen is dead or if she is still alive.

MAID

I could tell you that she is still alive or that she is dead.

CHORUS LEADER

How could a person both be dead and live and see?

MAID

It has felled her, and the life is breaking from her now.

CHORUS LEADER

Such a husband, to lose such a wife! I pity you.

MAID

The master does not see it and he will not see it
until it happens.

CHORUS LEADER

There is no hope left she will live?

MAID

None. This is the day of destiny. It is too strong.

CHORUS LEADER

Surely, he must be doing all he can for her.

MAID

All is prepared so he can bury her in style.

CHORUS LEADER

Let her be sure, at least, that as she dies, there dies
the noblest woman underneath the sun, by far.

MAID

Noblest? Of course the noblest, who will argue that?
What shall the wife be who surpasses her? And how
could any woman show that she loves her husband more
than herself better than by consent to die for him?
But all the city knows that well. You shall be told
now how she acted in the house, and be amazed
to hear. For when she understood the appointed day
was come, she bathed her white body with water drawn
from running streams, then opened the cedar chest and took
her clothes out, and dressed in all her finery
and stood before the shrine of Hestia, and prayed:
"Mistress, since I am going down beneath the ground,
I kneel before you in this last of all my prayers.
Take good care of my children for me. Give the boy
a loving wife; give the girl a noble husband;
and do not let my children die like me, who gave
them birth, untimely. Let them live a happy life

through to the end and prosper here in their own land."
Afterward she approached the altars, all that stand
in the house of Admetus, made her prayers, and decked them all
with fresh sprays torn from living myrtle. And she wept
not at all, made no outcry. The advancing doom
made no change in the color and beauty of her face.
But then, in their room, she threw herself upon the bed,
and there she did cry, there she spoke: "O marriage bed,
it was here that I undressed my maidenhood and gave
myself up to this husband for whose sake I die.
Good-bye. I hold no grudge. But you have been my death
and mine alone. I could not break my faith with you and him:
I die. Some other woman will possess you now.
She will not be better, but she might be happier."
She fell on the bed and kissed it. All the coverings
were drenched in the unchecked outpouring of her tears;
but after much crying, when all her tears were shed,
she rolled from the couch and walked away with eyes cast down,
began to leave the room, but turned and turned again
to fling herself once more upon the bed. Meanwhile
the children clung upon their mother's dress, and cried,
until she gathered them into her arms, and kissed
first one and then the other, as in death's farewell.
And all the servants in the house were crying now
in sorrow for their mistress. Then she gave her hand
to each, and each one took it, there was none so mean
in station that she did not stop and talk with him.
This is what Admetus and the house are suffering. Had
he died, he would have lost her, but in this escape
he will keep such pain; it will not ever go away.

CHORUS LEADER

Admetus surely must be grieving over this
when such a wife must be taken away from him.

MAID

Oh yes, he is crying. He holds his wife close in his arms,
imploring her not to forsake him. What he wants
is impossible. She is dying. The sickness fades her now.
She has gone slack, just an inert weight on the arm.
Still, though so little breath of life is left in her,
she wants to look once more upon the light of the sun,
since this will be the last time of all, and never again.°
She must see the sun's shining circle yet one more time.
Now I must go announce your presence. It is not
everyone who bears so much good will toward our kings
as to stand by ready to help in their distress.
But you have been my master's friends since long ago.

*(Exit Maid into the house.)*

CHORUS° [*singing*]

STROPHE

*O Zeus, Zeus, what way out of this evil*
*is there, what escape from this*
*which is happening to our princes?*
*A way, any way?° Must I cut short my hair*
*for grief, put upon me the black*
*costume that means mourning?*
*We must, friends, clearly we must; yet still*
*let us pray to the gods. The gods*
*have power beyond all power elsewhere.*

*Paean, my lord,*
*Apollo, make some way of escape for Admetus.*
*Grant it, oh grant it. Once you found*
*rescue in him. Be now*
*in turn his redeemer from death.*
*Oppose bloodthirsty Hades.*

ANTISTROPHE

*Admetus,*
*O son of Pheres, what a loss*

*to suffer, when such a wife goes.*
*A man could cut his throat for this, for this*
*and less he could bind the noose upon his neck*
*and hang himself. For this is*
*not only dear, but dearest of all,*
*this wife you will see dead*
*on this day before you.*

*(Enter Alcestis carried from the house on a litter, supported by Admetus and followed by her children and servants.)*

*But see, see,*
*she is coming out of the house and her husband is with her.*
*Cry out aloud, mourn, you land*
*of Pherae for the bravest*
*of wives fading in sickness and doomed*
*to the Death God of the world below.*

[*now chanting*]
*I will never again say that marriage brings*
*more pleasure than pain. I judge by what*
*I have known in the past, and by seeing now*
*what happens to our king, who is losing a wife*
*brave beyond all others, and must live a life*
*that will be no life for the rest of time.*

ALCESTIS [*singing in the following interchange with Admetus, while he speaks in reply*]

STROPHE A

*Sun, and light of the day,*
*O turning wheel of the sky, clouds that fly.*

ADMETUS

The sun sees you and me, two people suffering,
who never hurt the gods so they should make you die.

ALCESTIS

ANTISTROPHE A

*My land, and palace arching my land,*
*and marriage chambers of Iolcus, my own country.*

ADMETUS

Raise yourself, my Alcestis, do not leave me now.
I implore the gods to pity you. They have the power.

ALCESTIS

STROPHE B

*I see him there at the oars of his little boat in the lake,*
*the ferryman of the dead,*
*Charon, with his hand upon the oar,*
*and he calls me now: "What keeps you?*
*Hurry, you hold us back." He is urging me on*
*in angry impatience.*

ADMETUS

The crossing you speak of is a bitter one for me;
ill starred; it is unfair we should be treated so.

ALCESTIS

ANTISTROPHE B

*Somebody takes me, takes me, somebody takes me,*
*don't you see, to the courts*
*of dead men. He frowns from under dark*
*brows. He has wings. It is Hades.*
*Let me go, what are you doing, let go.*
*Such is the road*
*most wretched I have to walk.*

ADMETUS

Sorrow for all who love you, most of all for me
and for the children. All of us share in this grief.

ALCESTIS

EPODE

*Let me go now, let me down,*
*flat. I have no strength to stand.*
*Hades is close to me.*
*The darkness creeps over my eyes. O children,*
*my children, you have no mother now,*

*not any longer. Daylight is yours, my children.*
*Look on it and be happy.*

ADMETUS [*now chanting*]
*Ah, a bitter word for me to hear,*
*heavier than any death for me.*
*Please by the gods, do not be so harsh*
*as to leave me, please, by your children forlorn.*
*No, up, and fight it.*
*There would be nothing left of me if you died.*
*All rests in you, our life, our not*
*having life. Your love is what we hold sacred.*

ALCESTIS [*speaking*]
Admetus, you can see how it is with me. Therefore,
I wish to have some words with you before I die.
I put you first, and at the price of my own life
made certain you would live and see the daylight. So
I die, who did not have to die, because of you.
I could have taken any man in Thessaly
I wished and lived in queenly state here in this house.
But since I did not wish to live bereft of you
and with our children fatherless, I did not spare
my youth, although I had so much to live for. Yet
your father, and the mother who bore you, betrayed you,
though they had reached an age when it was good to die
and good to save their son and end it honorably.
You were their only one, and they had no more hope
of having other children if you died. That way
I would be living and you would live the rest of our time,
and you would not be alone and mourning for your wife
and tending motherless children. No, but it must be
that some god has so wrought that things shall be this way.
So be it. But swear now to do, in recompense,
what I shall ask you—not enough, oh, never enough,
since nothing is enough to make up for a life,
but fair, and you yourself will say so, since you love

these children as much as I do; or at least you should.
Keep them as masters in my house, and do not marry
again and give our children a stepmother
who will not be so kind as I, who will be jealous
and raise her hand to your children and mine. Oh no,
do not do that, do not. That is my charge to you.
For the new-come stepmother hates the children born
to a first wife; no viper could be deadlier.
The little boy has his father for a tower of strength.°
But you, my darling, what will your girlhood be like,
how will your father's new wife like you? She must not
make shameful stories up about you, and contrive
to spoil your chance of marriage in the blush of youth.
Indeed, your mother will not be there to help you
when you are married, not be there to give you strength
when your babies are born, when only a mother's help will do.
For I must die. It will not be tomorrow, not
the next day, or this month, the horrible thing will come,
but now, at once, I shall be counted among the dead.
Good-bye, be happy, both of you. And you, my husband,
can boast the bride you took made you the bravest wife,
and you, children, can say, too, that your mother was brave.

CHORUS LEADER

Fear nothing; for I dare to speak for him. He will
do all you ask. If he does not, it's his mistake.

ADMETUS

It shall be so, it shall be, do not fear, since you
were mine in life, you still shall be my bride in death
and you alone, no other girl in Thessaly
shall ever be called wife of Admetus in your place.
There is none so marked out in pride of father's birth
nor other form of beauty's brilliant gleam. I have
these children, they are enough; I only pray the gods
grant me the bliss to keep them as we could not keep you.
I shall go into mourning for you, not for just

a year, but all my life while it still lasts, my dear,
and hate the woman who gave me birth always, detest
my father. These were called my own dear ones. They were not.
You gave what was your own and dear to buy my life
and saved me. Am I not to lead a mourning life
when I have lost a wife like you? I shall make an end
of revelry and entertainment in my house,
the flowers and the music that here once held sway.
No, I shall never touch the lute strings ever again
nor have the heart to play music upon the pipe
of Libya, for you took my joy in life with you.
The skillful hands of craftsmen shall be set to work
making me an image of you to set in my room;
I'll pay my devotions to it, hold it in my arms
and speak your name, and clasp it close against my heart,
and think I hold my wife again, though I do not,
cold consolation, I know it, and yet even so
I might drain the weight of sorrow. You would come
to see me in my dreams and comfort me. For they
who love find a time's sweetness in the visions of night.
Had I the lips of Orpheus and his melody
to charm the maiden Daughter of Demeter and
her lord, and by my singing win you back from death,
I would have gone beneath the earth: not Pluto's hound
Cerberus could have stayed me, not the ferryman
of ghosts, Charon at his oar. I would have brought you back
to life. Wait for me, then, in that place, till I die,
and make ready the room where you will live with me,
for I shall have them bury me in the same chest
as you, and lay me at your side, so that my heart
shall be against your heart, and never, even in death
shall I go from you. You alone were true to me.

CHORUS LEADER

And I, because I am your friend and you
are mine, shall help you bear this sorrow, as I should.

ALCESTIS

Children, you now have heard your father promise me
that he will never marry again and not inflict
a new wife on you, but will honor my memory.

ADMETUS

I promise again. I will keep my promise to the end.

ALCESTIS

On this condition, take the children. They are yours.

ADMETUS

I take them, a dear gift from a dear hand.

ALCESTIS

And now
you must be our children's mother, too, instead of me.

ADMETUS

I must be such, since they will no longer have you.

ALCESTIS

O children, this was my time to live, and I must go.

ADMETUS

Ah me, what shall I do without you all alone?

ALCESTIS

Time will soften this. The dead count for nothing at all.

ADMETUS

Oh, take me with you, for god's love, take me down there too.

ALCESTIS

No, I am dying in your place. That is enough.

ADMETUS

O god, what a wife you are taking away from me!

ALCESTIS

It is true. My eyes darken and the heaviness comes.

ADMETUS

But I am lost, dear, if you leave me.

ALCESTIS

There is no use
in talking to me any more. I am not there.

ADMETUS

No, lift your head up, do not leave your children thus.

ALCESTIS

I do not want to, but it is good-bye, children.

ADMETUS

Look at them—oh, look at them!

ALCESTIS

No. There is nothing more.

ADMETUS

Are you really leaving us?

ALCESTIS

Good-bye.

ADMETUS

Oh, I am lost.

CHORUS LEADER

It is over now. Admetus' wife is gone from us.

BOY[u] ⌊*singing*⌋

STROPHE

*O wicked fortune. Mother has gone down there,*
*father; she is not here with us*
*in the sunshine any more.*
*Poor mother, she went away*
*and left me to live all alone.*
*Look at her eyes, look at her hands, so still.*
*Hear me, mother, listen to me, oh please,*

*listen, it is I, mother,*
*I your little one lean and kiss*
*your lips, and cry out to you.*

ADMETUS

She does not see, she does not hear you. You two and I
all have a hard and heavy load to carry now.

BOY

ANTISTROPHE

*Father, I am too small to be left alone*
*by the mother I loved so much. Oh,*
*it is hard for me to bear*
*all this that is happening,*
*and you, little sister, suffer*
*with me too.° Oh, father,*
*your marriage was useless, useless; she did not live*
*to grow old with you.*
*She died too soon. Mother, with you gone away,*
*the whole house is ruined.*

*(Exit Alcestis carried into the house, followed by children and servants.)*

CHORUS LEADER

Admetus, you must stand up to misfortune now.
You are not the first, and not the last of humankind
to lose a good wife. Therefore, you must understand
death is an obligation claimed from all of us.

ADMETUS

I understand it. And this evil which has struck
was no surprise. I knew about it long ago,
and knowledge was hard. But now, since we must bury our dead,
stay with me and stand by me, chant in response the hymn
to the god below who never receives libations.
To all Thessalians over whom my rule extends
I ordain a public mourning for my wife, to be

observed with shaving of the head and with black robes.
The horses that you drive in chariots and those
you ride single shall have their manes cut short with steel,
and there shall be no sound of pipes within the city,
no sound of lyres, until twelve moons have filled and gone;
for I shall never bury any dearer dead
than she, nor any who was better to me. She deserves
my thanks. She died for me, which no one else would do.

*(Exit into the house.)*

CHORUS [*singing*]

STROPHE A

*O daughter of Pelias*
*my wish for you is a happy life*
*in the sunless chambers of Hades.*
*Now let the dark-haired lord of Death himself, and the old man,*
*who sits at the steering oar*
*and ferries the corpses,*
*know that you are the bravest of wives, by far,*
*ever conveyed across the lake*
*of Acheron in the rowboat.*

ANTISTROPHE A

*Much shall be sung of you*
*by the men of music to the seven-strung mountain*
*lyre-shell, and in poems that have no music,*
*in Sparta when the season turns and the month Carneian*
*comes back, and the moon*
*rides all the night;*
*in Athens also, the shining and rich.*
*Such is the theme of song you left*
*in death, for the poets.*

STROPHE B

*Oh, that it were in my power*
*and that I had strength to bring you*
*back to light from the dark of death°*

*with oars on the sunken river.*
*For you, O dearest among women, only you*
*had the hard courage*
*to give your life for your husband's and save*
*him from death. May the dust lie light*
*upon you, my lady. And should he now take*
*a new wife to his bed, he will win my horror and hatred,*
*mine, and your children's hatred too.*

ANTISTROPHE B

*His mother would not endure*
*to have her body hidden in the ground*
*for him, nor the aged father.*°
*He was theirs, but they had not courage to save him.*
*Oh shame, for the gray was upon them.*
*But you, in the pride*
*of youth, died for him and left the daylight.*
*May it only be mine to win*
*such wedded love as hers from a wife; for this*
*is given seldom to mortals; but were my wife such, I would have her*
*with me unhurt through my lifetime.*

*(Enter Heracles from the side.)*

HERACLES

My friends, people of Pherae and the villages
hereby, tell me, shall I find Admetus at home?

CHORUS LEADER

Yes, Heracles, the son of Pheres is in the house.
But tell us, what is the errand that brings you here
to the land of Thessaly and this city of Pherae?

HERACLES

I have some work to do for Eurystheus
of Tiryns.

CHORUS LEADER

Where does it take you? On what far journey?

HERACLES

To Thrace, to take home Diomedes' chariot.

CHORUS LEADER

How can you? Do you know the man you are to meet?

HERACLES

No. I have never been where the Bistones live.

CHORUS LEADER

You cannot master his horses. Not without a fight.

HERACLES

It is my work, and I cannot refuse.

CHORUS LEADER

You must
kill him before you come back; or be killed and stay.

HERACLES

If I must fight, it will not be for the first time.

CHORUS LEADER

What good will it do you if you overpower their master?

HERACLES

I will take the horses home to Tiryns and its king.

CHORUS LEADER

It is not easy to put a bridle on their jaws.

HERACLES

Easy enough, unless their nostrils are snorting fire.

CHORUS LEADER

Not that, but they have teeth that tear a man apart.

HERACLES

Oh no! Mountain beasts, not horses, feed like that.

CHORUS LEADER

But you can see their mangers. They are caked with blood.

HERACLES

And the man who raises them? Whose son does he claim to be?

CHORUS LEADER

Ares'. And he is lord of the golden shield of Thrace.

HERACLES

It sounds like my life and the kind of work I do.
It is a hard and steep way always that I go,
having to fight one after another all the sons
the war god ever got him, with Lycaon first,
again with Cycnus, and now here is a third fight
that I must have with the master of these horses. So—
I am Alcmene's son, and the man does not live
who will see me break before my enemy's attack.

CHORUS LEADER

Here is the monarch of our country coming
from the house himself, Admetus.

*(Enter Admetus from the house.)*

ADMETUS

Welcome and happiness
to you, O scion of Perseus' blood and child of Zeus.

HERACLES

Happiness to you likewise, lord of Thessaly,
Admetus.

ADMETUS

I could wish it. I know you mean well.

HERACLES

What is the matter? Why is there mourning and cut hair?

ADMETUS

There is one dead here whom I must bury today.

HERACLES

Not one of your children! I pray some god shield them from that.

ADMETUS

Not they. My children are well and living in their house.

HERACLES

If it is your father who is gone, his time was ripe.

ADMETUS

No, he is still there, Heracles. My mother, too.

HERACLES

Surely you have not lost your wife, Alcestis.

ADMETUS

Yes
and no. There are two ways that I could answer that.

HERACLES

Did you say that she is dead or that she is still alive?

ADMETUS

She is, and she is no longer. It pains me.

HERACLES

I still do not know what you mean. You are being obscure.

ADMETUS

You know about her and what must happen, do you not?

HERACLES

I know that she has undertaken to die for you.

ADMETUS

How can she still be alive, then, when she has promised that?

HERACLES

Ah, do not mourn her before she dies. Wait for the time.

ADMETUS

The point of death is death, and the dead are lost and gone.

HERACLES

Being and nonbeing are considered different things.

ADMETUS

That is your opinion, Heracles. It is not mine.

HERACLES

Well, but whose is the mourning now? Is it in the family?

ADMETUS

A woman. We were speaking of a woman, were we not?

HERACLES

Was she a blood relative or someone from outside?

ADMETUS

No relation by blood, but she meant much to us.

HERACLES

How does it happen that she died here in your house?

ADMETUS

She lost her father and came here to live with us.

HERACLES

I am sorry,
Admetus. I wish I had found you in a happier state.

ADMETUS

Why do you say that? What do you mean to do?

HERACLES

I mean
to go on, and stay with another of my friends.

ADMETUS

No, my lord, no. The evil must not come to that.

HERACLES

The friend who stays with friends in mourning is in the way.

ADMETUS

The dead are dead. Go on in.

HERACLES

No. It is always wrong
for guests to revel in a house where others mourn.

ADMETUS

There are separate guest chambers. We will take you there.

HERACLES

Let me go, and I will thank you a thousand times.

ADMETUS

You shall not go to stay with any other man.
You there: open the guest rooms which are across the court
from the house, and tell the people who are there to provide
plenty to eat, and make sure that you close the doors
facing the inside court. It is not right for guests
to have their pleasures interrupted by sounds of grief.

*(Heracles is escorted into the house.)*

CHORUS LEADER

Admetus, are you crazy? What are you thinking of
to entertain guests in a situation like this?

ADMETUS

And if I had driven from my city and my house
the guest and friend who came to me, would you have approved
of me more? Wrong. My misery would still have been
as great, and I should be inhospitable too,
and there would be one more misfortune added to those
I have, if my house is called unfriendly to its friends.
For this man is my best friend, and he is my host
whenever I go to Argos, which is a thirsty place.

CHORUS LEADER

Yes, but then why did you hide what is happening here
if this visitor is, as you say, your best friend?

ADMETUS

He would not have been willing to come inside my house
if he had known what trouble I was in. I know.
There are some will think I show no sense in doing this.
They will not like it. But my house does not know how
to push its friends away and not treat them as it should.

*(Exit into the house.)*

CHORUS [*singing*]

STROPHE A

*O liberal and forever free-handed house of this man,*
*the Pythian himself, lyric Apollo,*
*was pleased to live with you*
*and had patience upon your lands*
*to work as a shepherd,*
*and on the hill-folds and the slopes*
*piped to the pasturing of your flocks*
*in their season of mating.*

ANTISTROPHE A

*And even dappled lynxes for delight in his melody*
*joined him as shepherds. From the cleft of Othrys descended*
*a red troop of lions,*
*and there, Phoebus, to your lyre's strain*
*there danced the bright-coated*
*fawn, adventuring from the deep*
*bearded pines, light-footed for joy*
*in your song, in its kindness.*

STROPHE B

*Therefore, your house is beyond*
*all others for wealth of flocks by the sweet waters*
*of Lake Boebias. For spread of cornland*

*and pasturing range its boundary stands*
*only there where the sun*
*stalls his horses in dark air by the Molossians.*
*Eastward he sways all to the harborless*
*Pelian coast on the Aegean main.*

ANTISTROPHE B

*Now he has spread wide his doors*
*and taken the guest in, when his eyes were wet*
*and he wept still for a beloved wife who died*
*in the house so lately. The noble strain*
*comes out, in respect for others.*
*All is there in the noble. I stand*
*in awe at his wisdom,° and good hope has come again to my heart*
*that for this godly man the end will be good.*

*(Enter Admetus from the house, followed by servants with a covered litter.)*

ADMETUS

Gentlemen of Pherae, I am grateful for your company.
My men are bearing to the burning place and grave
our dead, who now has all the state which is her due.
Will you then, as the custom is among us, say
farewell to the dead as she goes forth for the last time?

CHORUS LEADER

Yes, but I see your father coming now. He walks
as old men do, and followers carry in their hands
gifts for your wife, to adorn her in the underworld.

*(Enter Pheres from the side.)*

PHERES

I have come to bear your sorrows with you, son. I know,
nobody will dispute it, you have lost a wife
both good and modest in her ways. Nevertheless,
you have to bear it, even though it is hard to bear.
Accept these gifts to deck her body, bury them

with her. Oh yes, she well deserves honor in death.
She died to save your life, my son. She would not let
me be a childless old man, would not let me waste
away in sorrowful age deprived of you. Thereby,
daring this generous action, she has made the life
of all women become a thing of better repute
than it was.
O you who saved him, you who raised us up
when we were fallen, farewell, even in Hades' house
may good befall you.
I say people ought to marry women
like this. Otherwise, better not to marry at all.

ADMETUS

I never invited you to come and see her buried,
nor do I count your company as that of a friend.
She shall not wear anything that you bring her.
She needs nothing from you to be buried in. Your time
to share my sorrow was when I was about to die.
But you stood out of the way and let youth take my place
in death, though you were old. Will you cry for her now?
It cannot be that my body ever came from you,
nor did the woman who claims she bore me and is called
my mother give me birth. I was got from some slave
and surreptitiously put to your wife to nurse.
You show it. Your nature in the crisis has come out.
I do not count myself as any child of yours.
Oh, you outpass the cowardice of all the world,
you at your age, come to the very last step of life
and would not, dared not, die for your own child. Oh no,
you let this woman, married into our family,
do it instead, and therefore it is right for me
to call her all the father and mother that I have.
And yet you two should honorably have striven for
the right of dying for your child. The time of life
you had left for your living was short, in any case,

and she and I would still be living out our time°
and I should not be hurt and grieving over her.
And yet, all that a man could have to bless his life
you have had. You had your youth in kingship. There was I
your son, ready to take it over, keep your house
in order, so you had no childless death to fear,
with the house left to be torn apart by other claims.
You cannot justify your leaving me to death
on grounds that I disrespected your old age. Always I
showed all consideration. See what thanks I get
from you and from the woman who gave me birth. Go on,
get you other children—you cannot do it too soon—
who will look after your old age, and lay you out
when you are dead, and see you buried properly.
I will not do it. This hand will never bury you.
I am dead as far as you are concerned, and if, because
I found another savior, I still look on the sun,
I count myself that person's child and fond support.
It is meaningless, the way the old men pray for death
and complain of age and the long time they have to live.
Let death only come close, not one of them still wants
to die. Their age is not a burden any more.

CHORUS LEADER

Stop, stop. We have trouble enough already, child.
You will exasperate your father with this talk.

PHERES

Big words, son. Who do you think you are cursing out
like this? Some Lydian slave, some Phrygian that you bought?
I am a free Thessalian noble, nobly born
from a Thessalian. Are you forgetting that? You go
too far with your high-handedness. You volley brash
words at me, and fail to hit me, and then run away.
I gave you life, and made you master of my house,
and raised you. I am not obliged to die for you.
I do not acknowledge any tradition among us

that fathers should die for their sons. That is not Greek either.
Your natural right is to find your own happiness
or unhappiness. All you deserve from me, you have.
You are lord of many. I have wide estates of land
to leave you, just as my father left them to me.
What harm have I done you then? What am I taking away
from you? Do not die for me, I will not die for you.
You like the sunlight. Don't you think your father does?
I count the time I have to spend down there as long,
and the time to live is little, but that little is sweet.
You fought shamelessly for a way to escape death,
and passed your proper moment, and are still alive
because you killed her. Then, you wretch, you dare to call
me coward, when you let your woman outdare you,
and die for her magnificent young man? I see.
You have found a clever scheme by which you *never* will die.
You will always persuade the wife you have at the time
to die for you instead. And you, so low, then dare
blame your own people for not wanting to do this.
Silence. I tell you, as you cherish your own life,
all other people cherish theirs. And if you call
us names, you will be called names, and the names are true.

CHORUS LEADER

Too much evil has been said in this speech and in
that spoken before. Old sir, stop cursing your own son.

ADMETUS

No, speak, as I have spoken.° If it hurts to hear
the truth, you should not have made a mistake with me.

PHERES

I should have made a mistake if I had died for you.

ADMETUS

Is it the same thing to die old and to die young?

PHERES
Yes. We have only one life and not two to live.

ADMETUS
I think you would like to live a longer time than Zeus.

PHERES
Cursing your parents, when they have done you no wrong?

ADMETUS
Yes, for I found you much in love with a long life.

PHERES
Who is it you are burying? Did not someone die?

ADMETUS
And that she died, you foul wretch, proves your cowardice.

PHERES
You cannot say that we were involved in her death.

ADMETUS
Ah.
I hope that some day you will stand in need of me.

PHERES
Go on, and court more women, so they all can die.

ADMETUS
Your fault. You were not willing to die.

PHERES
No, I was not.
It is a sweet thing, this god's sunshine, sweet to see.

ADMETUS
That is an abject spirit, not a man's.

PHERES
You shall
not mock an old man while you carry out your dead.

ADMETUS

You will die in evil memory, when you do die.

PHERES

I do not care what they say of me when I am dead.

ADMETUS

How old age loses all the sense of shame.

PHERES

She was
not shameless, the woman you found; she was only stupid.

ADMETUS

Get out of here now and let me bury my dead.

PHERES

I'll go. You murdered her, and you can bury her.
But you will have her brothers still to face. You'll pay,
for Acastus is no longer counted as a man
unless he sees you punished for his sister's blood.

ADMETUS

Go and be damned, you and that woman who lives with you.
Grow old as you deserve, childless, although your son
still lives. You shall not come again under the same roof
with me. And if I had to proclaim by heralds that I
disown my father's house, I should have so proclaimed.

*(Exit Pheres to the side.)*

Now we, for we must bear the sorrow that is ours,
shall go, and lay her body on the burning place.

CHORUS [*chanting*]

*Ah, cruel the price of your daring,*
*O generous one, O noble and brave,*
*farewell. May Hermes of the world below*
*and Hades welcome you. And if, even there,*
*the good fare best, may you have high honor*
*and sit by the bride of Hades.*

*(Exit all to the side. The stage is empty. Enter a Servant from the house.)*

SERVANT

I have known all sorts of foreigners who have come in
from all over the world here to Admetus' house,
and I have served them dinner, but I never yet
have had a guest as bad as this to entertain.
In the first place, he could see the master was in mourning,
but inconsiderately came in anyway.
Then, he refused to understand the situation
and be content with anything we could provide,
but when we failed to bring him something, demanded it,
and took a cup with ivy on it in both hands
and drank the wine of our dark mother, straight, until
the flame of the wine went all through him, and heated him,
and then he wreathed branches of myrtle on his head
and howled, off-key. There were two kinds of music now
to hear, for while he sang and never gave a thought
to the sorrows of Admetus' house, we servants were
  mourning
our mistress; but we could not show before our guest
with our eyes wet. Admetus had forbidden that.
So now I have to entertain this guest inside,
this ruffian thief, this highwayman, whoever he is,
while she is gone away from the house, and I could not
say good-bye, stretch my hand out to her in my grief
for a mistress who was like a mother to all the house
and me. She gentled her husband's rages, saved us all
from trouble after trouble. Am I not then right
to hate this guest who has come here in our miseries?

*(Enter Heracles from the house, drunk.)*

HERACLES

You there, with the sad and melancholy face, what is
the matter with you? The servant who looks after guests
should be polite and cheerful and not scowl at them.

But look at you. Here comes your master's dearest friend
to visit you, and you receive him with black looks
and frowns, all because of trouble in someone else's family.
Come here, I'll tell you something that will make you wiser.
Do you really know what life is like, the way it is?
I don't think so. How could you? Well then, listen to me.
Death is an obligation that we all must pay.
There is not one man living who can truly say
if he will be alive or dead on the next day.
Fortune is dark; she moves, but we cannot see the way
nor can we pin her down by expertise and study her.
There, I have told you. Now you can understand. Go on,
enjoy yourself, drink, call the life you live today
your own, but only that; the rest belongs to chance.
Then, beyond all gods, pay your best attentions to
Cypris, man's sweetest. There's a god who's kind.
Let everything else go and do as I prescribe
for you, that is, if I seem to talk sense. Do I?
I think so. Well, then, get rid of this too-much grief,
put flowers on your head and drink with us, fight down
these present troubles;° later, I know very well
that the wine splashing in the bowl will shake you loose
from these scowl-faced looks and the tension in your mind.
We are only human. Our thoughts should be human too,
since, for these solemn people and these people who scowl,
the whole parcel of them, if I am any judge,
life is not really life but a catastrophe.

SERVANT

I know all that. But we have troubles on our hands
now that make revelry and laughter out of place.

HERACLES

The dead woman is out of the family. Do not mourn
too hard. Your master and mistress are still alive.

SERVANT

What do you mean, alive? Don't you know what happened
to us?

HERACLES

Certainly, unless your master has lied to me.

SERVANT

He is too hospitable, too much.

HERACLES

Should I not then
have enjoyed myself, because some outside woman was dead?

SERVANT

She was an outsider indeed. That is too true.

HERACLES

Has something happened that he did not tell me about?

SERVANT

Never mind. Go. Our masters' sorrows are our own.

HERACLES

These can be no outsiders' troubles.

SERVANT

If they were,
I should not have minded seeing you enjoy yourself.

HERACLES

Have I been scandalously misled by my own friends?

SERVANT

You came here when we were not prepared to take in guests.
You see, we are in mourning. You can see our robes°
of black, and how our hair is cut short.

HERACLES

Who is dead?
The aged father? Or is one of the children gone?

SERVANT

My lord, Admetus' wife is dead.

HERACLES

What are you saying?
And all this time you were making me comfortable?

SERVANT

He was embarrassed to turn you from this house of his.

HERACLES

My poor Admetus, what a helpmeet you have lost!

SERVANT

We are all dead and done for now, not only she.

HERACLES

I really knew it when I saw the tears in his eyes,
his shorn hair and his face; but he persuaded me
with talk of burying someone who was not by blood
related. So, unwillingly, I came inside
and drank here in the house of this hospitable man
when he was in this trouble! Worse, I wreathed my head
with garlands, and drank freely. But you might have said
something about this great disaster in the house.
Now, where shall I find her? Where is the funeral being held?

SERVANT

Go straight along the Larisa road, and when you clear
the city you will see the monument and the mound.

*(Exit the Servant into the house.)*

HERACLES

O heart of mine and hand of mine, who have endured
so much already, prove what kind of son it was
Alcmene, daughter of Electryon, bore to Zeus
in Tiryns. I must save this woman who has died
so lately, bring Alcestis back to live in this house,
and pay Admetus all the kindness that I owe.

I must go there and watch for Death of the black robes,
master of dead men, and I think I shall find him
drinking the blood of slaughtered beasts beside the grave.
Then, if I can break suddenly from my hiding place,
catch him, and hold him in the circle of these arms,
there is no one who will be able to break my hold
on his bruised ribs, until he gives the woman up
to me. But if I miss my quarry, if he does not come
to the bloody offering, I will go down, I will ask
the Maiden and the Master in the sunless homes
of those below; and I have confidence I shall bring
Alcestis back up, and give her to the arms of my friend
who did not drive me off but took me into his house
and, though he staggered under the stroke of circumstance,
hid it, for he was noble and respected me.
Who in all Thessaly is a truer friend than this?
Who in all Greece? Therefore, he must not ever say
that, being noble, he befriended a worthless man.

*(Exit Heracles to the side. Then enter Admetus from the side, accompanied by the Chorus.)*

ADMETUS [*chanting*]

*Hateful is this*
*return, hateful the sight of this house*
*widowed, empty. Where shall I go?*
*Where shall I stay? What shall I say?*
*How can I die?*
*My mother bore me to a heavy fate.*
*I envy the dead. I long for those*
*who are gone, to live in their houses, with them.*
*There is no pleasure in the sunshine*
*nor the feel of the hard earth under my feet.*
*Such was the hostage Death has taken*
*from me, and given to Hades.*

*(While the Chorus sings, Admetus moans inarticulately.)*

CHORUS

STROPHE A

*Go on, go on. Plunge in the deep of the house.*
*What you have suffered is enough for tears.*
*You have gone through pain, I know,*
*but you do no good to the woman who lies*
*below. Never again to look on the face*
*of the wife you loved hurts you.*

ADMETUS [*now chanting*]

*You have opened the wound torn in my heart.*
*What can be worse for a man than to lose*
*a faithful wife. I envy those*
*without wives, without children. I wish I had not*
*ever married her, lived with her in this house.*
*We have each one life. To grieve for this*
*is burden enough.*
*When we could live single all our days*
*without children, it is not to be endured*
*to see children sicken or married love*
*despoiled by death.*

*(As before: while the Chorus sings, Admetus moans inarticulately.)*

CHORUS

ANTISTROPHE A

*Chance comes. It is hard to wrestle against it.*
*There is no limit to set on your pain.*
*The weight is heavy. Yet still*
*bear up. You are not the first man to lose*
*his wife. Disaster appears, to crush*
*one man now, but afterward another.*

ADMETUS [*chanting*]

*How long my sorrows, the pain for my loves*
*down under the earth.*
*Why did you stop me from throwing myself*

*in the hollow cut of the grave, there to lie*
*dead beside her, who was best on earth?*
*Then Hades would have held fast two lives,*
*not one, and the truest of all, who crossed*
*the lake of the dead together.*

CHORUS [*singing*]

STROPHE B

*There was a man*
*of my people, who lost a boy*
*in his house anyone would mourn for,*
*the only child. But still*
*he bore the evil well enough, though childless,*
*and he stricken with age*
*and the hair gray on him,*
*well on in his lifetime.*

ADMETUS [*chanting*]

*O builded house, how shall I enter you?*
*How dwell in you, with this new turn*
*of my fortune? How different now and then.*
*Then it was with Pelian pine torches,*
*with marriage songs, that I entered my house,*
*with the hand of a sweet bride on my arm,*
*with loud rout of revelers following*
*to bless her who now is dead, and me,*
*for our high birth, for nobilities*
*from either side which were joined in us.*
*Now the bridal chorus has changed for a dirge,*
*and for white robes the costumed black*
*goes with me inside*
*to where our room stands deserted.*

CHORUS [*singing*]

ANTISTROPHE B

*Your luck had been*
*good, so you were inexperienced when*

*this grief came. Still you saved*
*your own life and being.*
*Your wife is dead, your love forsaken.*
*What is new in this? Before*
*now death has parted*
*many from their wives.*

ADMETUS [*now speaking*]

Friends, I believe my wife is happier than I
although I know she does not seem to be. For her,
there will be no more pain to touch her ever again.
She has her glory and is free from much distress.
But I, who should not be alive, who have passed by
my moment, shall lead a sorry life. I see it now.
How can I bear to go inside this house again?
Whom shall I speak to? Who will speak to me, to give
me any pleasure in coming home? Where shall I turn?
The desolation in my house will drive me out
when I see my wife's bed empty, when I see the chairs
she used to sit in, and all about the house the floor
unwashed and dirty, while the children at my knees
huddle and cry for their mother and the servants mourn
their mistress and remember what the house has lost.
So it will be at home, but if I go outside
meeting my married friends in Thessaly, the sight
of their wives will drive me back, for I cannot endure
to look at my wife's age-mates and the friends of her youth.
And anyone who hates me will say this of me:
"Look at the man, disgracefully alive, who dared
not die, but like a coward gave his wife instead
and so escaped death. Do you call him a man at all?
He turns on his own parents, but he would not die
himself." Besides my other troubles, they will speak
about me thus. What have I gained by living, friends,
when reputation, life, and action all are bad?

CHORUS [*singing*]

STROPHE A

*I myself, in the transports*
*of mystic verses, as in study*
*of history and science, have found*
*nothing so strong as Compulsion,*
*nor any means to combat her,*
*not in the Thracian books set down*
*in verse by the voice of Orpheus,*
*not in all the remedies Phoebus has given the heirs*
*of Asclepius to fight the many afflictions of man.*

ANTISTROPHE A

*She alone is a goddess*
*without altar or statue to pray*
*before. She heeds no sacrifice.*
*Majesty, bear no harder*
*on me than you have in my life before!*
*All Zeus himself ordains*
*only with you is accomplished.*
*By strength you fold and crumple the steel of the Chalybes.*
*There is no pity in the sheer barrier of your will.*

STROPHE B

*Now the goddess has caught you in the breakless grip of her hands.*
*Bear up. You will never bring back up, by crying,*
*the dead into the light again.*
*Even the sons of the gods fade*
*and go in death's shadow.*
*She was loved when she was with us.*
*She shall be loved still, now she is dead.*
*It was the best of all women to whom you were joined in marriage.*

ANTISTROPHE B

*The monument of your wife must not be counted among the graves*
*of the dead, but it must be given honors*

*like the gods' worship of wayfarers.*
*And as they turn the bend of the road*
*and see it, men shall say:*
*"She died for the sake of her husband.*
*Now she is a blessed spirit.*
*Hail, majesty, be gracious to us." Thus will men speak in her presence.*

CHORUS LEADER

But here is someone who looks like Alcmene's son, Admetus. He seems on his way to visit you.

*(Enter Heracles from the side, leading a veiled woman.)*

HERACLES

A man, Admetus, should be allowed to speak freely to a friend, instead of keeping his complaints suppressed inside him. Now, I thought I had the right to stand beside you and endure what you endured, so prove my friendship. But you never told me that she, who lay dead, was your wife, but entertained me in your house as if your mourning were for some outsider's death. And so I wreathed my head and poured libations out to the gods, in your house, though your house had suffered so. This was wrong, wrong I tell you, to have treated me thus, though I have no wish to hurt you in your grief. Now, as for the matter of why I have come back again, I will tell you. Take this woman, keep her safe for me, until I have killed the master of the Bistones and come back, bringing with me the horses of Thrace. If I have bad luck—I hope not, I hope to come back home—I give her to the service of your house. It cost a struggle for her to come into my hands. You see, I came on people who were holding games for all comers, with prizes which an athlete might well spend an effort winning.

*(Points to the woman.)*

Here is the prize I won
and bring you. For the winners in the minor events
were given horses to take away, while those who won
the heavier stuff, boxing and wrestling, got oxen,
and a woman was thrown in with them. Since I happened
to be there, it seemed wrong to let this splendid prize
go by. As I said, the woman is for you to keep.
She is not stolen. It cost me hard work to bring
her here. Some day, perhaps, you will say I have done well.

ADMETUS

I did not mean to dishonor nor belittle you
when I concealed the fate of my unhappy wife,
but it would have added pain to pain already there
if you had been driven to shelter with some other host.
This sorrow is mine. It is enough for me to weep.
As for the woman, if it can be done, my lord,
I beg you, have some other Thessalian, who has not
suffered as I have, keep her. You have many friends
in Pherae. Do not bring my sorrows back to me.
I would not have strength to see her in my house and keep
my eyes dry. I suffer now. Do not inflict further
suffering on me. I have sorrow enough to weigh me down.
And where could a young woman live in this house? For
she is young, I can see it in her dress, her style.
Am I to put her in the same quarters with the men?
And how, circulating among young men, shall she be kept
from harm? Not easy, Heracles, to hold in check
a young strong man. I am thinking of your interests.
Or shall I put her in my lost wife's chamber, keep
her there? How can I take her to Alcestis' bed?
I fear blame from two quarters, from my countrymen
who might accuse me of betraying her who helped
me most, by running to the bed of another girl,
and from the dead herself. Her honor has its claim

on me. I must be very careful. You, lady,
whoever you are, I tell you that you have the same
form as my Alcestis; all your body is like hers.
Too much. Oh, by the gods, take this woman away
out of my sight. I am beaten already, do not beat
me again. For as I look on her, I think I see
my wife. It churns my heart to tumult, and the tears
break streaming from my eyes. How much must I endure
the bitter taste of sorrow which is still so fresh?

CHORUS LEADER

I cannot put a good name to your fortune; yet
whoever you are, you must endure what the god gives.

HERACLES

I only wish that my strength had been great enough
for me to bring your wife back from the chambered deep
into the light. I would have done that grace for you.

ADMETUS

I know you would have wanted to. Why speak of it?
There is no way for the dead to come back to the light.

HERACLES

Then do not push your sorrow. Bear it as you must.

ADMETUS

Easier to comfort than to suffer and be strong.

HERACLES

But if you wish to mourn forever, what will you gain?

ADMETUS

Nothing. I know it. But some impulse of my love
makes me.

HERACLES

Why, surely. Love for the dead is cause for tears.

ADMETUS

Her death destroyed me, even more than I can say.

HERACLES

You have lost a fine wife. Who will say you have not?

ADMETUS

So fine

that I, whom you see, never shall enjoy life again.

HERACLES

Time will soften the evil. It still is young and strong.

ADMETUS

You can say time will soften it, if time means death.

HERACLES

A wife, your new marriage will put an end to this desire.

ADMETUS

Silence! I never thought you would say a thing like that.

HERACLES

What? You will not remarry but keep an empty bed?

ADMETUS

No woman ever shall sleep in my arms again.

HERACLES

Do you believe you help the dead by doing this?

ADMETUS

Wherever she may be, she deserves my honors still.

HERACLES

Praiseworthy, yes, praiseworthy. And yet foolish, too.

ADMETUS

Call me so, then, but never call me a bridegroom.

HERACLES

I admire you for your faith and love you bear your wife.

ADMETUS

Let me die if I betray her, though she is gone.

HERACLES

Well then,

receive this woman into your most generous house.

ADMETUS

Please, in the name of Zeus your father, no!

HERACLES

And yet

you will be making a mistake if you do not.

ADMETUS

And I'll be eaten at the heart with anguish if I do.

HERACLES

Obey. The grace of this may come where you need grace.

ADMETUS

Ah.

I wish you had never won her in those games of yours.

HERACLES

Where I am winner, you are winner along with me.

ADMETUS

Honorably said. But let the woman go away.

HERACLES

She will go, if she should. First look. See if she should.

ADMETUS

She should, unless it means you will be angry with me.

HERACLES

Something I know of makes me so insistent with you.

ADMETUS

So, win again. But what you do does not please me.

HERACLES

The time will come when you will thank me. Only obey.

ADMETUS (*To attendants.*)
Escort her in, if she must be taken into this house.

HERACLES
I will not hand this lady over to attendants.

ADMETUS
You yourself lead her into the house then, if you wish.

HERACLES
I will put her into your hands and into yours alone.

ADMETUS
I will not touch her. But she is free to come inside.

HERACLES
No, I have faith in your right hand, and only yours.

ADMETUS
My lord, you are forcing me to act against my wish.

HERACLES
Be brave. Reach out your hand and touch the stranger.

ADMETUS
So.
Here is my hand; I feel like Perseus killing the Gorgon.

HERACLES
You have her?

ADMETUS
Yes, I have her.

HERACLES
Keep her, then. Some day
you will say the son of Zeus came as your generous guest.
But look at her. See if she does not seem most like
your wife. Your grief is over now. Your luck is back.

ADMETUS
Gods, what shall I think! Amazement beyond hope, as I

look on this woman, this wife. Is she really mine,
or some sweet mockery for a god to stun me with?

HERACLES

Not so. This is your own wife you see. She is here.

ADMETUS

Be careful she is not some phantom from the depths.

HERACLES

The guest and friend you took was no necromancer.

ADMETUS

Do I see my wife, whom I was laying in the grave?

HERACLES

Surely. But I do not wonder at your unbelief.

ADMETUS

May I touch her, and speak to her, as my living wife?

HERACLES

Speak to her. All that you desired is yours.

ADMETUS

Oh, eyes
and body of my dearest wife, I have you now
beyond all hope. I never thought I'd see you again.

HERACLES

You have her. May no god begrudge you your happiness.

ADMETUS

O nobly sprung child of all-highest Zeus, may good
fortune go with you. May the father who gave you birth
keep you safe. You alone raised me up when I was down.
How did you bring her back from down there to the light?

HERACLES

I fought a certain deity who had charge of her.

ADMETUS

Where do you say you fought this match with Death?

HERACLES

Beside
the tomb itself. I ambushed him and caught him in my
hands.

ADMETUS

But why is my wife standing here, and does not speak?

HERACLES

You are not allowed to hear her speak to you until
her obligations to the gods who live below
are washed away and the third morning comes. So now
take her and lead her inside, and for the rest of time,
Admetus, be just: treat your guests as they deserve.
And now good-bye. I have my work that I must do,
and go to face the lordly son of Sthenelus.

ADMETUS

No, stay with us and be the guest of our hearth.

HERACLES

There still
will be a time for that, but I must press on now.

ADMETUS

Success go with you. May you find your way back here.

*(Exit Heracles to the side.)*

I proclaim to all the people of my tetrarchy
that, for these blessed happenings, they shall set up
dances, and the altars smoke with sacrifice offered.
For now we shall make our life again, and it will be
a better one.
I was lucky. That I cannot deny.

*(Exit with Alcestis into the house.)*

CHORUS [*chanting*]

*Many are the forms of what is divine.*

*Much that the gods achieve is surprise.*
*What we look for does not come to pass;*
*a god finds a way for what none foresaw.*
*Such was the end of this story.*

*(Exit all.)*

# MEDEA

*Translated by* OLIVER TAPLIN

# MEDEA: INTRODUCTION

*The Play: Date and Composition*

Euripides' *Medea* was produced in 431 BCE as the first of his four plays entered in the annual dramatic competition. The other plays have been lost: *Philoctetes, Dictys,* and the satyr-play *Theristae* (*The Mowers*). Euripides took the third prize. Although *Medea* is one of his earliest securely dated plays to survive, he was probably over fifty years old when he wrote it and had already been competing in the dramatic contests for more than twenty years.

Some ancient scholars report that, according to Aristotle and his student Dicaearchus (fourth century BCE), Euripides revised a play called *Medea* by a certain Neophron (a prolific and successful rival Athenian dramatist) and passed it off as his own; a few even claimed that Euripides' *Medea* was in fact completely the work of Neophron and should be attributed to him. Various ancient commentaries cite passages from Neophron's *Medea* adding up to about twenty-four lines; these do not coincide exactly with Euripides' play, but they are very similar in content. Modern scholars are divided about what to make of all this: some think that Neophron's *Medea* did indeed precede and influence Euripides'; others have maintained instead that Neophron's play came later and that those who thought otherwise in antiquity were mistaken.

*The Myth*

Medea is a well-known figure from archaic Greek epic and legend. Her name is derived from words meaning "counsel, plan, cleverness." Grand-daughter of Helios (god of the sun), she possesses magic powers with which she can help or harm male heroes. In this regard she is similar to her aunt Circe. In some versions of the myth, Medea is a goddess, in others a human. She plays a crucial role in the popular ancient Greek epic stories that told how the Argonauts, led by Jason, sailed to far-off Colchis on the Black Sea and overcame various challenges and obstacles in order to bring back the Golden Fleece with them to Greece—all aided decisively by Medea, who, out of love for Jason, betrayed her own family (the rulers of Colchis and guardians of the Fleece) and chose to put her sorcery at his service. It was through her powers and advice that Jason succeeded in putting a dragon to sleep and killing it, then harnessed fierce oxen with which he plowed furrows to sow the dragon's teeth, killed the armed men who sprang up from the teeth he had sown, and then managed to escape from Colchis and avenge himself on his enemies.

After Jason and Medea escaped they took up residence in Corinth, where they had children together. But Jason subsequently decided instead to marry the daughter of the king of Corinth (Creon). It is here that the action of Euripides' *Medea* begins: we see how Medea kills this new bride and her father and the children she had had with Jason, and then escapes from Corinth to Athens. Various ancient poets and local historians, some of them writing before Euripides, mentioned the death of Jason and Medea's children at Corinth—the local cult in which they were honored there is well attested—but gave different explanations for just how the children had died: that the Corinthians murdered the boys in a temple of Hera out of hatred for Medea; or that, after Medea had killed Creon and fled to Athens, leaving her children at the temple of Hera, Creon's relatives avenged themselves by killing the children; or that Medea tried to make the children immortal but something went wrong and they died. The idea that Medea deliberately killed her own children may or may not have been a new invention by Euripides (or Neophron).

After the events in Corinth, Medea goes on to Athens, where she marries King Aegeus and (in some versions) tries to kill his son Theseus. Years later she returns to her homeland Colchis, where she becomes queen. According to some versions, she ends up marrying Achilles after their deaths and reigning with him over the souls of the dead.

Euripides seems to have been particularly interested in Medea: before he composed this play he had already dramatized two other episodes from the myths involving her, one about earlier events (*The Daughters of Pelias*) and one about later ones (*Aegeus*). But both of these plays are lost.

*Transmission and Reception*

Although *Medea* was not particularly successful when it was first produced, it went on to become enormously popular and influential. It belongs to the group of ten plays by Euripides that were most widely diffused during ancient and medieval times. Its popularity among ancient readers is attested by a dozen papyrus fragments dating from the third century BCE to the sixth century CE. So it is perhaps not surprising that modern scholars have detected what seem to be numerous small interpolations in the text, probably due in some cases to expansion by directors or actors—further evidence for the play's continuing vitality on ancient stages.

Euripides' *Medea* exerted considerable influence upon later Greek and Roman versions of the story. Of Roman tragedies, we possess Seneca's *Medea* and know that Ovid wrote a highly regarded *Medea*, now lost. And the influence of Euripides' play is no less evident in such Greek and Roman narrative epics as Apollonius of Rhodes' *Argonautica*, Ovid's *Metamorphoses*, and Valerius Flaccus' *Argonautica*. Most ancient versions of the Medea story emphasize her magic powers and concentrate on her more terrifying aspects. On south Italian vase paintings of the fourth and third centuries BCE, several of them clearly influenced by theatrical productions, Medea is often displayed killing her children or escaping with their bodies on her winged chariot. Pompeian frescoes show her anguished indecision about whether or not to kill the children. Later Roman sarcophagi frequently depict the terrible death of Creon's daughter and Medea's spectacular escape.

In modern times *Medea* has become one of the very best known of all ancient tragedies. The story of the woman who avenges herself upon her unfaithful husband by killing their children has become part of the popular imagination and has played an important role in such fields as politics (Medea's monologue on the troubles of women was cited regularly in meetings of the British suffragettes), psychoanalysis, and law. Besides the frequent productions of Euripides' play on stages throughout the world in all languages, including ancient Greek—probably no other ancient play has been produced anywhere near as often in the twentieth century—the story has also inspired numerous new versions, including Franz Grillparzer's dramatic trilogy *The Golden Fleece* (1819–21), Christa Wolf's novel *Medea.Voices* (1996), Luigi Cherubini's opera *Medea* (1797), Martha Graham's dance drama *Cave of the Heart* (1946, with music by Samuel Barber), and films by Pier Paolo Pasolini (1969) and Lars von Trier (1988). It has also been depicted in important paintings (Eugène Delacroix, 1862; Gustave Moreau, 1865) and sculptures (Auguste Rodin, 1865–70).

# MEDEA

*Characters* NURSE to Medea
Two SONS of Medea and Jason
TUTOR to the two sons
MEDEA, princess of Colchis, wife of Jason
CREON, king of Corinth
JASON, son of Aeson, king of Iolcus
AEGEUS, king of Athens
SERVANT of Jason as messenger
CHORUS of Corinthian women

*Scene: Corinth, in front of Medea's house.*

*(Enter Nurse from the house.)*

NURSE

If only the swift *Argo* never had swooped in between
the cobalt Clashing Rocks to reach the Colchians' realm;
if only pines had never been chopped down among the woods
of Pelion to put oars in the hands of those heroic men,
who ventured forth to fetch the Golden Fleece for Pelias.
Medea, then, my mistress, never would have sailed
for Iolcus' towers, her heart infatuated with desire for Jason;
nor spurred the daughters of old Pelias to kill their father,
never would have settled here in Corinth
with her husband and her sons.
She managed though an exile° to delight the people of the land

she'd joined, and gave support in every way to Jason—
life's most secure when there is no conflict
to alienate a woman from her man.
But now . . . now hatred rules, and loyal love is sick,
since Jason has betrayed my mistress and their sons,
by mounting the royal bridal bed
beside the daughter of Creon, the monarch of this land.
And so my poor Medea is disdained.
She cries, "What of his oaths?," recalls
the solemn pledge of his right hand, and prays the gods
to witness what poor recompense she has received.
Lying without food, she gives her body up to pain,
and has been wearing down the nights and days with tears,
since she first found she had been wrongly treated by her
man.
Never lifting up her eyes from staring at the ground,
she listens to her friends' advice no more
than if she were a rock or sea-surf—
except for when she turns her pale white neck,
lamenting to herself for her lost father, country, home,
which she betrayed to join the man who now dishonors her.
She's learned from her catastrophe how much
it matters not to lose your homeland.
She hates the children, takes no pleasure in the sight of them.[°]
I fear that she may plan some new mischief;
her temperament is fierce, and she'll not tolerate
mistreatment—I know too well what she is like.
She fills me with alarm,
that she will stab their livers with a sharpened sword,[°]
entering by stealth the palace where the bed is laid,
and kill both monarch and his daughter's new bridegroom,
and so incur some even graver consequence,
for she is fearsome—
and no one who picks a fight with her
will find it easy to descant the victory chant.

*(Enter the two boys and their Tutor from the side.)*

But here the children come, fresh from their exercise,
and unaware of all their mother's sufferings—
young minds are not inclined to cares.

TUTOR

Old servant of my mistress' house,
why are you standing solitary here outside the doors,
bewailing troubles to yourself?
How could Medea want to be left without you near?

NURSE

Old man, you who take care of the young sons of Jason:
when affairs break badly for their masters,
this can affect good slaves as well.
And my distress reached such a pitch I felt compelled
to come out here and tell the problems that beset
my mistress to the earth and sky.

TUTOR

You mean she's still not stopped her grieving cries?

NURSE

You've no idea! Her pain's not even halfway through.

TUTOR

Poor fool—if I may say that of my betters—
how little she knows yet about the latest downward turn.

NURSE

What's that, old man? Don't hold it back from me.

TUTOR

Nothing—I wish I had not said a thing.

NURSE

Do not, I beg you, hide this from your fellow slave.
I shall keep quiet about these matters, if I should.

TUTOR

I overheard a person say—pretending not to hear
as I drew near to where the old men sit
and play their checkers, by the sacred spring of Peirene—
I heard him say that Creon, lord of this land, intends
to drive these children out from Corinth, with their mother.
I do not know whether this rumor's true—I only hope it's not.

NURSE

Will Jason tolerate such treatment of his sons
even if he has this feud against their mother?

TUTOR

Ancient ties become displaced by newer ones;
and he's no friend to this house here.

NURSE

Then we are ruined if we have to add
this new disaster to the one we've not yet drained.

TUTOR

But you at least keep quiet and spread no word of this—
it's not the time to let our mistress find this out.

NURSE

Do you hear how your father's turned against you, children?
I won't say "curse him," since he is my master still.
But he has been exposed as false toward his closest kin.

TUTOR

And who has not? Have you found out so late
that every person loves himself more than those close to him,
some justly, some for profit's sake?°
And so the father of these boys does not feel love for them,
because of his new bride.

NURSE *(To the children.)*

All will be well; now, children, go inside.

*(To the Tutor.)*

And you should keep them well secluded
from their mother for so long as she remains
in such an agitated state; don't let them near.
I've seen her cast a savage look at them,
as though she's contemplating doing something to them.
I know for sure she won't relent her anger
until she's struck some victim to the ground—
but when she does, may it be enemies, not friends.

MEDEA [*singing from inside*]
*Oh, in pain, in pain,*
*I'm so unhappy, I . . .*
*oh for me, for me,*
*if only I could die.*

NURSE [*chanting throughout this scene while Medea continues to sing from inside*]
*As I said, dear children, your mother is stirring*
*her passion, bestirring her fury.*
*Now hurry indoors; don't stray in her sight,*
*don't even go near, keep well away*
*from her violent mood,*
*the wild hate of her passionate will.*
*Hurry along, quickly inside.*
*It is all too clear that she's going to ignite*
*this cloud of complaint now billowing*
*from its beginning to yet hotter resentment.*
*What will she do, now that her heart*
*has been so envenomed,*
*proud to its core, tough to restrain?*

(*Exit the two boys and the Tutor into the house.*)

MEDEA (*Inside.*)
*The suffering I have endured, endured,*
*calling for bitter lament aloud!*
*Accursed children of a hated mother,*

*I wish you were done for along with your father.*
*To hell with the family, all of the house.*

NURSE

*Oh no, terrible! Why should your children*
*share in the guilt of the crimes of their father?*
*Why should you hate them?*
*I'm utterly stricken with fear for your safety,*
*poor children. Rulers have dangerous natures:*
*subjected to little, controlling much,*
*they are not inclined to relent from their passions.*
*Better to live in the ways of fair-sharing:*
*the height of ambition for me is to live out my life*
*without much, but entirely secure.*
*The word "moderation" sounds first*
*in our speaking, and is easily best in enactment.*
*Exaggeration can never provide*
*sound balance for humans.*
*And if ever a god gets angered against*
*some household, the payoff's yet greater disaster.*

*(Enter Chorus of Corinthian women.)*

CHORUS [*singing throughout this scene, while the Nurse continues to chant and Medea sings from inside*]

I heard her call, I heard her cry,
Medea's pain, the Colchian.
So she has still not settled calm?
Old woman, tell. I heard her voice
*from deep inside her mansion gates.*
The sufferings of this household cause
me pain—my friendship's blended close.

NURSE

*No household exists any more—it's all gone.*
*He is possessed by his royal embraces;*
*she is eroding her life away*

*deep in her chamber, my lady,*
*her spirit encouraged not the slightest*
*by any suggestion from any well-wisher.*

MEDEA *(Inside.)*

*May lightning shatter my skull;*
*life no longer brings gain.*
*May I find shelter in death,*
*freed from this hated life.*

CHORUS

STROPHE

*O Zeus, Earth, and shining Sky,*
*do you hear the wailing cry*
*of the inauspicious bride?*
*Why crave for that unwanted bed,*
*poor woman? Death comes with all speed.*
*Don't pray for dying, no.*
*If your husband worships so*
*at his newfound marriage-couch,*
*don't be torn by him so much.*
*Zeus will be your advocate;*
*so don't pine away so much,*
*wasting for your old bedmate.*

MEDEA *(Inside.)*

*Artemis and mighty Themis,*
*see the pain that I'm enduring,*
*I who had my cursed husband*
*tied by strong bonds of his swearing.*
*May I see him and his consort*
*and their palace ripped in pieces,*
*payment for the ways they dared first*
*to mistreat me with injustice.*
*O my father, O my city,*
*after killing my own brother,*

*in disgrace I had to leave you,*
*lost my fatherland forever.*

NURSE

*You hear her calling aloud on Themis*
*and on Zeus, the protector of oaths*
*binding on humans? My mistress will never*
*relent from her anger with some petty gesture.*

CHORUS

ANTISTROPHE

*I wish she would meet with us,*
*and engage us face to face;*
*I wish she would heed our voice*
*to see if she might relent*
*from her heavy-hearted rage*
*and the passion of her heart.*
*May I never stand apart*
*from supporting my own friends.*
*But, you, please return indoors,*
*fetch her, bring her here outside,*
*tell her we are on her side;*
*quick, before she does some harm*
*against those inside her home—*
*because her intense distress*
*comes upon her at a pace.*

NURSE

*I'll do this—although I'm afraid*
*that I'll never prevail on my mistress—*
*I'll try as a favor.*
*Yet she glares like a lioness with new cubs*
*at anyone who comes close and offers her any suggestion.*
*You'd be right to conclude that the people*
*of olden times were stupid and lacking in wisdom*
*when they invented poems*
*to accompany feasts, celebrations, and dinners,*

*sweet ornamentations of life.*
*Still no one has found out the way*
*to abolish our harrowing griefs*
*with poetic powers*
*or with songs and elaborate strings—*
*griefs that result in the deaths and terrible mishaps*
*that overturn households.*
*Yet that would have offered us profit:*
*to medicine these troubles with music.*
*Why bother with loudly voiced singing for nothing,*
*when feasting is garnished with pleasure?*
*All by itself the rich banquet provides*
*full satisfaction for people.*

CHORUS

*I have heard her tearful moans*
*and the piercing words she cries*
*out against that guilty husband*
*who betrayed their marriage ties.*
*She has borne unjust abuse*
*and she calls out aloud on Themis,*
*guardian of the oaths of Zeus,*
*oaths that ferried her to Hellas*
*over ocean's inky dark,*
*opening a salt-sea exit*
*through the daunting Black Sea's lock.*

*(Enter Medea from the house.)*

MEDEA [*speaking*]

Women of Corinth, I have come outside to show
you have no cause to tarnish me with blame.
Understand: I'm all too well aware
that many people are perceived as arrogant—
some privately, others in public life—and there are those
who gather a bad name for idleness by lying low.
Do not suppose there's any justice rests

in people's eyes: they hate on sight,
before they get to know a man's real inner core,
although he's done no wrong to them.
And therefore foreigners should take especial care
to be in tune with the society they join—
nor would I give approval even to a native man°
who foolishly offends his fellow citizens through selfishness.
But in my case, this new and unforeseeable event
has befallen me and crushed my spirit,
so that I've lost delight in life—I long to die, my friends.
I realize the man who was my all in all
has now turned out to be the lowest of the low—my husband.
We women are the most beset by trials
of any species that has breath and power of thought.
Firstly, we are obliged to buy a husband
at excessive cost, and then accept him as
the master of our body—that is even worse.
And here's the throw that carries highest stakes:
is he a good catch or a bad?
For changing husbands is a blot upon
a woman's good repute; and it's not possible
to say no to the things a husband wants.
A bride, when she arrives to join new ways
and customs, needs to be a prophet to predict
the ways to deal best with her new bedmate—
she won't have learned that back at home.
And then . . . then if, when we have spent a deal of trouble
on these things, if then our husband lives with us
bearing the yoke without its being forced,
we have an enviable life.
But if he does not: better death.
But for a man—oh no—if ever he is irked
with those he has at home, he goes elsewhere
to get relief and ease his state of mind.
He turns either to some close friend or to someone his age.°
Meanwhile we women are obliged

to keep our eyes on just one person.
They, men, allege that we enjoy a life
secure from danger safe at home,
while they confront the thrusting spears of war.
That's nonsense: I would rather join
the battle rank of shields three times
than undergo birth-labor once.
In any case, your story's not at all the same as mine:
you have your city here, your father's house,
delight in life, and company of friends,
while I am citiless, deserted,
subjected to humiliation by my husband.
Manhandled from a foreign land like so much pirate loot,
here I have no mother, brother, relative,
no one to offer me a port, a refuge from catastrophe.
So I would like to ask this one small thing of you:
if I can find some means or some device
to make my husband pay the penalty to quit me
for the wrongs he's done, stay silent, please
—also the man who's given him his daughter, and the bride herself.°
Although a woman is so fearful in all other ways—
no good for battle or the sight of weaponry—
when she's been wrongly treated in the field of sex,
there is no other cast of mind more deadly, none.

CHORUS LEADER

I will do this: you're justified inflicting punishment,
Medea, on your husband. I am not surprised you feel such pain.

*(Creon approaches from the side.)*

I see King Creon coming to announce some new decision.

CREON

Grim scowling scourge against your husband—
yes, that's you, Medea:

I proclaim that you must leave this land in banishment,
and take your pair of sons along with you.
And no delay allowed.
I am myself the arbiter of this decree,
and I shall not go home before I have made sure
I've thrown you out beyond the borders of this land.

MEDEA

Aiai!
Utter, complete catastrophe for me!
My enemies are in full sail,
and I have no accessible haven
to land me from this storm of hell.
But I'll still ask, although I am so poorly treated: say,
what reason have you, Creon, for expelling me like this?

CREON

I am afraid of you—no point in mincing words—
I am afraid you'll work incurable mischief
upon my daughter.
And many things combine toward this fear of mine:
you are by nature clever and well versed
in evil practices; and you are feeling bruised
because you've been deprived of the embraces of your man.
And I have heard—so people say—you're threatening
some act against the giver in this marriage
and the taker and the given bride.
Therefore I'm going to move before that happens.
Better to be hated by you, woman, now
than to be soft, and later groan for it.

MEDEA

O misery . . . not for the first time reputation's
done me harm and damaged my whole life.
A man who knows what he's about should never have
his children taught to be more clever than the norm.

They get a name for idleness, and only earn
resentful spite from citizens.
The stupid ones, if you bring new ideas to them,
will view you as not clever but impractical.
And if you are perceived to be superior
to those who are supposed to be the subtle ones,
society will brand you as a troublemaker.
I myself have shared this fate:
because I'm clever, I am resented by some people,
and in some eyes I'm idle and in others opposite to that,°
and for others I'm a nuisance.
Yet, in any case, I'm not so very clever . . .
But still, you say you are afraid of me . . . for what?
Becoming victim of some outrage?
No, don't be scared of me, Creon.
There is no call for me to do offence against the king.
What injury have you done me?
You gave your daughter to the man your heart proposed.
It is my husband; he's the one I hate:
your actions were, I think, quite sensible.
So now I don't begrudge your happy state—
go on, enjoy your wedding, and good luck to you all!
And let me live on in this country here—
since, even though I have been done injustice,
I'll hold my peace, subdued by those who have more power.

CREON

Your words are soothing to the ear;
but I still have a horror that inside your head
you're hatching plans for something bad.
I trust you all the less than I did previously.
A woman acting in hot blood
is easier to guard against—it is the same with men—
than one who's clever and stays secretive.
No—on your way immediately; don't give me speeches.

It's fixed, decided, and you have no art that can contrive
to let you stay among us here as enemy to me.

MEDEA

No, no, I beg you by your knees,
and by your newly married daughter.

CREON

Why waste your breath? You'll never change my mind.

MEDEA

You're going to banish me,
and feel no pang of conscience for my prayers?

CREON

I am. I don't hold you closer than my own family.

MEDEA

My fatherland, how strongly I recall you now . . .

CREON

And mine, after my children, is my closest bond.

MEDEA

Ah, passion is such a deadly ill for humankind!

CREON

Well, that depends upon the luck of those involved.

MEDEA

O Zeus, make no mistake about
who is responsible for all these trials.

CREON

Get out, you crazy woman, and so relieve me of my pains.

MEDEA

Your pains? I have enough of those myself.
I don't need more from you.

CREON

I'm going to get my men to march you off by force.

MEDEA *(Seizing his hand.)*

No, no, please don't resort to that, I beg of you, Creon.

CREON

It's clear you're set upon an ugly squabble, woman.

MEDEA

I shall submit to banishment:
that's not the thing I'm pleading for.

CREON

Then why maintain this grip? Why not release my hand?

MEDEA

Please just allow me to remain today, one day,
and give me time to fix arrangements for
my banishment, and make provisions for my boys,
seeing that their father does not care enough
to organize a thing for his own sons.
Pity them—you're a father after all: it's only natural
that you should feel some kindness for them.
I'm not concerned about myself and exile,
but them—I weep that they're subjected to distress.

CREON

My character is not at all tyrannical;
and often I have suffered harm through my softheartedness.
So now—I'm well aware of my mistake—
you shall obtain this none the less.
I tell you clear, however: if the sun god's coming light
still looks upon you and your boys
within the borders of this land, it means your death.
This word of mine is irreversible.
For now, if you must stay, then stay for one day more.°
You can't do anything I fear.

*(Exit Creon to the side, leaving Medea with the Chorus.)*

CHORUS [*chanting*]

*Unfortunate woman!°*
*Oh, oh, sunk in your misery,*
*where, where on earth can you turn?*
*to what protector, to what home, to what land*
*to save you from your troubles?*
*Some god has cast you adrift, Medea, amidst*
*an unchartable tempest of troubles.*

MEDEA

Everything has turned out badly—no one could deny.
But don't suppose this is the way the course will run.
There are still struggles waiting for the newlyweds,
and for the man who made this match, big troubles still.
Do you suppose I ever would have groveled to him now
except to gain advantage and resource?
I would not have spent words on him, not taken hold of him.
But he has plumbed such depths of foolishness
that, when he could have foiled my plans
by driving me away, he's let me stay for this one day—
the day on which I shall make dead meat of my enemies—
all three: the father and his daughter and my husband.
I have a wealth of ways to post them to their deaths,
and I'm not sure which one to make the first, good friends.
Should I engulf the bridal home in flames,
or stab their livers through with whetted blade,
employing stealth to infiltrate
the chambers where their bed is laid?
But there's this one obstruction: if I get caught
while entering to work my plot, then I'll be put to death,
and hand my enemies the final laugh.
So best to take the straightest route—
my special inborn skill in drugs—
and so by potions send them off.
So be it!
But then what next? Suppose they're dead:

what city then will take me in?
What friend will grant asylum and a home that is secure,
providing safety for my person? There is nobody.
And so I'll bide my time a little while,
and if some stronghold that can keep me safe appears,
deceit and secrecy will be my means to make this kill.
If that turns out to be impossible, and I'm exposed,
then I shall take a sword, although it means my death,
and slaughter them myself.
I'll push my daring to its violent end.
For, by the mistress I revere above all, fellow worker,
Hecate, who has her place in the recesses of my hearth,
not one of them shall rack my heart with pain
and get away with it.
I shall make sure this match of theirs is turned
to bitter anguish; bitter also that man's
marriage arrangements and attempt to exile me.
So down to work, Medea,
don't relax one jot of all your expertise
in schemes and in contrivances.
On to the dreadful test; now's the time to try your mettle.
You see what your position is: you must not become
a laughingstock because of Jason's union with this Sisyphean
dynasty.
You're from a noble father and descended from the Sun.
You have the expertise. What's more, we are born women.
It may be we're unqualified for deeds of virtue:
yet as the architects of every kind of mischief,
we are supremely skilled.

*(Medea stays on stage.)*

CHORUS [*singing*]

STROPHE A

*Pure rivers are running their currents upstream,*
*order and everything's turned upside down,*
*the dogmas of men are exposed as mere sham,*

*oaths by the gods prove no longer firm ground.*
*The stories of women shall be about-turned,*
*so that my life shall achieve proper glory,*
*new value is coming for our female kind,*
*no longer shall slanders pollute our story.*

ANTISTROPHE A

*The poems of long-ago bards shall no more*
*portray us as fickle, untrustworthy friends—*
*bias because lord Apollo forbore*
*to implant his lyrics in feminine minds.*
*Otherwise we could have answered with songs,*
*back to the masculine sex, that long years*
*can easily open up tales of men's wrongs,*
*no less than their narratives all about ours.*

STROPHE B

*You, Medea, sailed off from*
*your father's house,*
*with your heart on fire with love;*
*and cut your course*
*in between the matching rocks*
*of Bosphorus' straits;*
*and you've had to treat as home*
*an alien place,*
*where you've lost your marriage bed—*
*no husband there.*
*Last, you're driven, stripped of rights,*
*far from this shore.*

ANTISTROPHE B

*Dead and gone the bonding charm*
*of oaths men swear;*
*Shame's deserted Greece and flown*
*into the air.*
*You, poor woman, cannot claim*
*a father's roof,*

*place to move your anchorage,*
*sheltered from grief.*
*And another woman rules*
*over your bed,*
*a royal princess, who controls*
*your house instead.*

*(Enter Jason from the side.)*

JASON

This is far from the first time that I have observed
a fiery temper is an uncontrollable disaster.
You could have held on to this place,
even this house, by patiently complying with
the plans of your superiors;
instead, all thanks to your demented rant,
you're getting thrown out from this land.
Not that I care about myself: you can go on abusing Jason,
calling him the worst of men indefinitely.
But after all the things you've said against the ruling family,
count it as profit that your punishment is only exile.
I've constantly been trying to calm down
the enraged ruler; and I wanted you to stay.
But you refuse to curb your stupid tongue,
forever slandering the king.
And so—exile for you.
Yet even after this I've not deserted my own kin:
I've come because I'm looking out for you,
woman, to make quite sure that you do not depart in poverty,
together with our boys, nor under any need.
Exile brings many disadvantages along with it—
and even if you feel the deepest hate for me,
I never could reciprocate ill will for you.

MEDEA

You cheating rat! That's my response to you,
the lowest phrase that I can find to fit your cowardice.
You come to us, you come to us,

when you have proved yourself our most detested enemy.
to gods, to me, and all the human race.°
This is not merely daring or self-confidence,
to treat your kin despicably,
and then to look them in the eye.
It is the worst of all the ills that plague mankind:
sheer deadness to human decency.
Yet you did well to come—since I can speak,
and ease my spirit, by condemning you;
and you will suffer pain through hearing it.
I shall begin our story from the start.
I saved your life—and all the Greeks who went aboard
the *Argo* with you are aware of that—
when you were sent to set the yoke
upon the bulls with breath of fire,
and plant the ploughland with a crop of death.
Meanwhile the serpent which kept sleepless watch
over the Golden Fleece, with implicating coils,
I killed—and raised for you the torchlight of survival.
By my own choice I was a traitor to my home and father,
and accompanied you to Iolcus under Pelion—
from impulse rather than from careful thought.
I killed off Pelias, so that he died most horribly,
at his own daughters' hands—and thus extinguished his
whole line.
And after all these favors you have had from me,
you stinking rat, you have betrayed me,
and found a new wife for your bed—
this even though we have begotten sons.
If you had been still childless, then it might have been
forgivable for you to hanker for this coupling.
The trust that underlies your oaths is lost:
so I'm not sure if you believe the gods of old
no longer wield their power, or else that novel rules
are now established for mankind—

since you must know full well that you
have not made good your oaths to me.
Ah, my right hand, the hand that you so often took,
clasping my knees, how foully you have been
exploited by a cheating coward—
and how mistakenly I aimed my hopes!
Now look, I shall consult you as a friend—
though how can I expect to gain some benefit from you?—
yet all the same, by being asked, you'll be exposed
as even worse. Where shall I turn now?
Maybe my father's house?—the very house and fatherland
that I betrayed for you, to travel here.
Or to the wretched daughters of King Pelias?
yes, they would give me a warm welcome back,
when it was I who killed their father.
For that is how I stand: object of hatred for my kin at home,
I've made the people whom I should have treated well
my enemies—all for your sake.
And as reward you made me, to be sure,
the happy woman in the eyes of many girls in Greece.
O yes, in you I have a husband marvelous and true—
since that is why I am to be expelled from here
to wander as a refugee, devoid of friends,
alone with my poor children, all alone.
That is a fine reproach to grace the new-made groom:
his children beggars wandering
along with her who saved your life.
O Zeus, you've given us the clear criteria to test
if gold is counterfeit: so why is there no stamp of guarantee
marked on the human body to discriminate which ones
among our men are fakes?

CHORUS LEADER

When those who have been close collide in conflict,
their anger is incurable and terrible.

JASON

It seems I'm going to have to prove myself as orator,
and, like a skillful captain, reef my sails
in to the very edge, if I'm to navigate
before your windy and unbridled talk, woman.
For my part, since you emphasize so much my debt to you,
it's my belief that it was Cypris
alone of gods and humans steered my voyage clear of harm.
You may well have a subtle mind,
but modesty forbids me to relate just how Desire
compelled you with unerring shafts to keep my body safe . . .
but I'll not go into too fine detail there.
The benefits you really did for me were well and good.
Yet in return for my survival you've received
far greater profits than you have contributed—
as I'll explain. First you inhabit Greece
instead of some barbarian land;
you've gotten to experience the rule of justice and the law,
without consideration for the threat of force.
The Greeks have all found out about your cleverness;
you're famous for your gifts.
If you inhabited the furthest fringes of the world,
then no one would have heard of you.
I would not ask for vaults of gold, or for the gift to sing
yet more melodiously than Orpheus,
unless my fortune brought me also great celebrity.
So much then for my efforts made on your behalf—
it was you after all embarked on this debate.
I turn now to your condemnations
of the royal match that I have made.
Concerning this I'll demonstrate that I was clever first,
second restrained, and third I've been
a constant friend to you and to my sons.
No, please keep quiet.
When I moved here from Iolcus land, I brought with me

a number of intractable misfortunes.
So what prescription could I have discovered
more fortunate than to win the hand, although an exile,
of the king's daughter, and to marry her?
Not, as gnaws away at you, because I came to hate
sleeping with you, besotted by desire for my new bride.
Nor am I set on rivalry to father many children,
since I've no complaint with those I have—they are enough.
My motive is the highest of priorities:
that is for us to live a prosperous life,
and not go short—remembering that every friend
will run a mile from those who are impoverished.
I wish to raise my children as befits my noble house,
and father brothers for these sons I've had by you;
to put them on a par, to unify the line,
and so achieve a happy life.
For you . . . what need of children do you have?
Whereas for me it cashes in a gain to benefit
my living sons through those as yet unborn.
Not bad, my long-term planning?
You would agree, if you were not so stung by thoughts of sex.
You women go so far as to believe,
as long as your sex life goes well, then everything is fine;
but then if some misfortune strikes the realm of bed,
you count what's best and finest as your deepest hate.
I say it should have been a possibility
for mankind to engender children from some other source,
and for the female sex not to exist.
That way there'd be no troubles spoiling human life.

CHORUS LEADER

Jason, you've laid out a speech all sparkling
with fine embellishments, and yet in my opinion,
although I may be speaking contrary to yours,
you're doing wrong with this betrayal of your wife.

MEDEA

I'm very different from most of humankind,
since, in my book, the clever yet unjust speech maker
should be punished with the heaviest fine.
For, confident that he can dress injustice in fine words,
he is emboldened to stop short of nothing.
Yet he is not so clever as all that—
which goes for you as well.
So don't come all respectable and eloquent with me.
I have one argument to knock you flat:
if you were not a filthy coward, you should
have first persuaded me to give approval
for your knotting these new marriage ties—
not tried to keep it secret from your kin.

JASON

Oh yes, I think it very likely you
would have endorsed my case quite happily,
if I'd but mentioned this new match to you—
considering that even now you cannot bear
to drain away the seething rage that fills your heart.

MEDEA

It was not that that led you to hold back;
it was because a non-Greek wife would not, you thought,
enhance your status in your later years.

JASON

Let me make clear: my motive for espousing the royal bed
I now possess was not the woman in it—
but, as I've said before, the wish to keep you safe,
and to beget royal siblings for my sons, a safeguard for my line.

MEDEA

I would not wish to live a prosperous life
that brings me misery;
nor do I want prosperity that eats away my soul.

JASON

I'll tell you how to change your mind, and to be seen
as far more sensible: don't ever take good things
to be objectionable; and don't regard yourself
as miserable when in fact you are most fortunate.

MEDEA

Humiliate me, go ahead!
You can, since you have somewhere you can turn,
while I'm deserted and must leave this land.

JASON

That's what you chose.
Don't try to pin the blame on anyone except yourself.

MEDEA

What did I do? Did I betray you, then,
by getting into bed with a new wife?

JASON

No, but by calling down unholy curses on the royal house.

MEDEA

I did. I am a curse upon your house as well.

JASON

Well, I'll participate no more in these adjudications.
But if you'd like to draw upon assistance from my means
to help the children and yourself in exile, then say the word.
I am prepared to hand out generously,
and to send tokens to my friends elsewhere
to have them treat you well.
If you refuse this, woman, you're a fool.
Give up your angry fit, and you will be far better off.

MEDEA

I have no wish to beg for favors from your friends,
and I will not accept a penny, so do not offer anything to us.
Donations from a low-life cheat confer no benefit.

JASON

Well, all the same, I call upon the gods
to witness that I am prepared to furnish all I can
to make provision for the boys and you.
Yet in return you spurn these goods,
and willfully you push away your friends.
As a result your hardships will be all the worse.

MEDEA

Just go. So long away from your bedroom,
you must be overcome with yearning
for your freshly bridled bride.
Go on, perform the newlywed. Perhaps—
pray god fulfill this word—perhaps this wedding
will turn out to be a bedding that you mourn.°

*(Exit Jason to the side. Medea stays on stage.)*

CHORUS [*singing*]

STROPHE A

*Desire that overwhelms us*
*with infatuation*
*does not encourage virtue*
*and good reputation.*
*If her approach is gentle,*
*Cypris makes life blissful,*
*sweetest of gods; but never*
*target me, great mistress;*
*don't draw your golden bowstring*
*in my direction, winging*
*me an unerring arrow,*
*tip besmeared with longing.*

ANTISTROPHE A

*May moderation please me—*
*that's the gods' best favor;*
*and may dread Cypris never*
*shake my heart with fervor;*

*nor bring on angry quarrels*
*and unending clashes,*
*by making me inflamed for*
*other men's embraces.*
*May she employ her judgment*
*wisely to encourage*
*concord, by fairly settling*
*women's beds in marriage.*

STROPHE B

*My fatherland, my home place,*
*may I be never homeless,*
*have never the relentless*
*life story of the helpless,*
*most pitiable of all pains.*
*Before that may my death-day*
*dark overcome this life-day.*
*There can be no disaster*
*that is more destructive*
*than to be deprived of*
*your fatherland, your home place.*

ANTISTROPHE B

*I see from my own witness,*
*not secondhand from others:*
*for you there is no city,*
*no friend who will feel pity,*
*not now that you have suffered*
*the worst that can be suffered.*
*The man who is ungracious,*
*may death end his disgraces;*
*who disrespects his dearest,*
*refusing to unfasten*
*the latch of honest thinking.*
*I never shall befriend him.*

*(Enter Aegeus from the side.)*

AEGEUS

Medea, happiness to you:
there is no finer prologue known with which to greet a friend.

MEDEA

May you be happy also, Aegeus, offspring
of wise Pandion. Where have you come from,
to be passing through this country here?

AEGEUS

I've journeyed from Apollo's venerable oracle.

MEDEA

And why did you consult the prophet at earth's navel-stone?

AEGEUS

To find out how I might get children as my heirs.

MEDEA

Good heavens, have you reached your age
still childless?

AEGEUS

Some dispensation of the gods has left me childless, yes.

MEDEA

And do you have a wife,
or have you never known the bond of wedlock?

AEGEUS

I have a wife who shares my marriage bed.

MEDEA

And what did Phoebus say to you about begetting children?

AEGEUS

Words far too subtle for a man to fathom.

MEDEA

Is it permissible for me to hear the oracle?

AEGEUS

It is—it does, indeed, call for a clever mind.

MEDEA

What did it say? Enlighten me if I'm allowed to hear.

AEGEUS

It told me not to tap the wineskin's jutting spout . . .

MEDEA

Before what action, or before you reach what land?

AEGEUS

Before I reach my native hearth.

MEDEA

What motive then has made you sail to this land here?

AEGEUS

There is a man called Pittheus—ruler of Troezen.

MEDEA

The son of Pelops; and most reverend, they say.

AEGEUS

I wish to talk with him about the prophecy.

MEDEA

That's good: the man is wise,
and has experience of matters such as this.

AEGEUS

Of all my allies he's the one I hold most dear.

MEDEA

Then fare you well.
And may you get all that your heart desires.

AEGEUS

But what is this? Why are your cheeks all streaked with tears?

MEDEA

Aegeus, my husband has turned out the lowest of the low.

AEGEUS
What? Tell me clearly all your discontent.

MEDEA
Jason has done me wrong, although I've given him no cause.

AEGEUS
What is it that he's done? Inform me more precisely.

MEDEA
He's made another woman
mistress of his bed instead of me.

AEGEUS
I can't believe he's acted so despicably as that.

MEDEA
It's true. I was his dear, but now I'm disregarded.

AEGEUS
So is he seized by new desire, or does he now detest your bed?

MEDEA
Desire—so great he's not stayed loyal to his family.

AEGEUS
To hell with him, then, if he is as rotten as you say.

MEDEA
This strong desire has led to his alliance with a king.

AEGEUS
So who has made this match with him? Come, tell me all.

MEDEA
It's Creon, ruler of this land of Corinth.

AEGEUS
I see: then, woman, I can understand just why you feel so hurt.

MEDEA

It is disaster for me;
and, what is more, I'm being sent in exile.

AEGEUS

Who by? That's yet another blow you tell me of.

MEDEA

It's Creon who is driving me to banishment from Corinth.

AEGEUS

And Jason goes along with this?
I disapprove of that as well.

MEDEA

He claims he is against . . . but still he's ready to put up
with it.
But I implore you by this beard and by your knees—
I am your suppliant: take pity on me
in my misfortune, take pity.
Don't watch me turned into a refugee:
grant me asylum in your land and in your house.
And then may your desire for children meet success,
thanks to the gods, and may you end your days content.
You may not realize what a find you've found in me:
for I shall end your barrenness,
and I shall make you potent to seed progeny.
Such are the potions that I know.

AEGEUS

There is a host of reasons, woman,
why I am inclined to grant this favor to you.
First, piety to the gods; and then for the fertility
that you assure me of—I'm at my wits' end over that.
This, then, is what I offer you:
if you can once arrive safe in my country,
then I'll do my best to act as your protector there,
as would be only right.

And yet I forewarn you, woman, of this much:°
I am not willing to convey you from this land;
but if you can all by yourself get to my home,
then you may claim asylum.
I shall not surrender you to anyone.
But you must get yourself away
out of this country by yourself;
I wish to stay above reproach with my allies as well.

MEDEA

Yes, I agree. All would be well for me,
if only I could have from you some surety of this.

AEGEUS

Can you distrust me? What is disconcerting you?

MEDEA

I trust you; but the house of Pelias remains my enemy,
and so is Creon. If you are tied by oath,
you would not let them take me from your land,
but if you were agreed with only words,
without an oath sworn by the gods,
you might become on friendly terms with them,
and then comply with their demands for extradition.
For I have no power,
while they are rich, and members of a royal house.

AEGEUS

The things you say show ample foresight.
So if you think it best, I'll not refuse to do this thing,
since for me it's safer if I demonstrate
to your opponents that I have good reasons,
while for you your interests gain more security.
Tell me the gods to be sworn by.

MEDEA

Then swear by Earth and by the Sun,
my father's father, and the whole pantheon together.

AEGEUS

What to do, what not to do? Go on.

MEDEA

That you will never cast me from your land;
and never, if one of my enemies attempts to take me,
never, while you live, abandon me of your free will.

AEGEUS

I swear by Earth and by the pure light of Sun
and all the gods: I shall stay true to all you say.

MEDEA

Enough. But if you fail to keep your oath,
what then should be your fate?

AEGEUS

Those things that are inflicted on the impious.

MEDEA

Then go, and fare you well. For everything's in place.
And as for me, I'll reach your land as quickly as I can,
once I have carried through my plans,
and gained the things I want.

CHORUS LEADER [*chanting*]

*May Hermes, the patron of travelers,*
*usher you safely home;*
*and may you achieve those things*
*which you so strongly desire,*
*because you appear to us, Aegeus,*
*as a man of true nobility.*

*(Exit Aegeus to the side.)*

MEDEA

O Zeus and Justice, child of Zeus, and radiance of the Sun—
now, friends, I'll win the victory against my enemies.
I have set out upon the road; and now I have good hope

that they shall pay the price in full.
For in the very place I was most laboring,
this man has now appeared as a safe haven for my plans.
I'll fix the mooring cable to my prow from him,
once I have reached Athena's citadel.
And now I'll tell you all my plans:
attend my words, although they are not pleasant words to hear.
I'll send one of my servants asking Jason
to come and meet me face to face.
And when he's here, I'll reassure him with smooth words
and tell him I agree: that he is marrying well
the royal match he has contracted by betraying us°
and that this brings advantages, and is well planned.
And I'll request my children may stay here—
not that I wish to leave them in a hostile land
for enemies to foully treat my children°
no, but so that I can kill the princess by deception.
I'll send them carrying presents for her in their hands,
to take them to the bride so as not to have to leave this land:°
a finespun dress and plaited wreath of beaten gold.
If she accepts and puts the finery next to her skin,
she will die horribly, and so will anyone
who even comes in contact with the girl—
such are the poisons that I'll smear upon the gifts.
But now I'll leave that part of the story.
I grieve for the deed that I must do then:
that I must kill my sons—
there is no one can spirit them away.
And after I have utterly wrecked Jason's house,
I'll depart this land, escaping from the slaughter
of my beloved children, once I've steeled myself
to do this most abominable of deeds.
Because, my friends, to be derided
by one's enemies is not to be endured.
So let it be. What profit have I from my life?°

I have no fatherland, no home, no way to turn from my
misfortunes.
My first mistake was when I deserted my ancestral home,
seduced by sweet talk from a man, a Greek—
with a god's help he will pay me dearly.
Nevermore shall he behold his sons from me alive;
nor shall he have a child with his new-wedded bride,
since she must die a horrid death by my strong poisons.
No one should think of me as slight and weak,
or as compliant—quite the contrary:
I'm deadly to my enemies, supportive to my friends.
It's people of this sort whose lives are crowned with glory.

CHORUS LEADER

Since you have shared this plan with us,
and since we'd like to help you, and promote the human law,
we tell you: do not do this thing.

MEDEA

There's no alternative.
It's understandable you talk like this
when you have not been made to suffer wrong like me.

CHORUS LEADER

But, woman, can you steel yourself to kill your body's fruit?

MEDEA

Yes, that's the way my husband can be deepest pierced.

CHORUS LEADER

You would become the wretchedest of women.

MEDEA

Then let it be. Meanwhile all words are mere excess.

*(To a maid.)*

You, go and summon Jason here
—you are the one I use for all my tasks of closest trust.
And tell him nothing of the things I have decided,

not if you are true to your mistress,
and if you are a woman born.

*(Exit maid to the side; Medea stays on stage.)*

CHORUS [*singing*]

STROPHE A

*Through their forefather Erechtheus,*
*derived from gods by birth,*
*long have Athenians prospered,*
*bred from unconquered earth.*
*There they nourish their spirits*
*with arts famous and fine,*
*ever pacing with light steps*
*the luminous air's shine;*
*and the Muses, as they report,*
*the Pierian nine,*
*at one time gathered there to fill*
*fair Harmony with breath.*

ANTISTROPHE A

*And legend says that Aphrodite*
*scoops water with her hand*
*from the pure river Cephisus,*
*as all about the land*
*she blows breezes of sweet breath.*
*And ever plaiting round*
*a rose garland for her hair,*
*a sweetly scented crown,*
*she sends the pleasures of Desire*
*to sit beside wise Thought—*
*who work together to create*
*the best of every sort.*

STROPHE B

*This city of pure waters,*
*this land of friendly guidance,*
*how could it give asylum*

*to you, the children-killer?*
*hold you, impure, inside it?*
*Just think about the stabbing,*
*think of the actual murder.*
*Do not—they are your children—*
*we utterly implore you,*
*do not kill your own children.*

ANTISTROPHE B

*Where can you find the will-power,°*
*where find the heart and vigor*
*to drive this gruesome daring?*
*Once you see your own darlings,*
*how can you then stay tearless,*
*as you stare at their slaughter?*
*No, you'll not have the power to,*
*not when they fall and beg you,*
*no, not to drench all gory*
*your hands, with heart remorseless.*

*(Enter Jason from the side.)*

JASON

Well, here I am at your command.
Although you are so ill disposed, you should not be
deprived of this: I shall pay due attention. Woman,
what new is there that you might want from me?

MEDEA

Jason, I ask you to forgive the things I said.
It's only fair for you to tolerate
my angry moods, since there has been
much friendship between us in the past.
I came to words within myself, and scolded in these terms:
"Stubborn, why am I raging and resenting
those who show good foresight?
Why pit myself in conflict with the royal powers
of the land, and my own husband?

He's only taking the most advantageous course,
by marrying the princess, and producing siblings for my sons.
So should I not relent from anger?
—what is wrong with me?—
the gods are taking helpful care of me.
I must confront the truth: that I have children,
and that we are exiles, much in need of friends."
And thinking through these things,
I recognized that I have been extremely stupid,
and mistakenly felt outraged.
So now I give approval; I believe you've shown good sense
in forging this new kinship tie on our behalf—
it's I have been the fool.
I should have been there sharing in your plans,
advancing them: I should be waiting on your bed,
and gladly taking care of your new bride.
We . . . I do not say we're evil,
but we are just what we are . . . we women.
So you should not yourself
behave like us, and bandy trivial disputes.
I'm sorry, I admit I had it wrong back then;
but now I've thought things through more sensibly.
Children, my children, leave the house,
come here outside.

*(The two boys and the Tutor come out from the house.)*

Embrace your father, talk to him along with me,
and with your mother now be reconciled from enmity
against those who should be near and dear.
We have made peace, and all our anger is dissolved.
Take his right hand.
Ah me! That makes me think of hidden wrongs.
Will you live many years, my children,
to reach out your loving arms like this?

Poor fool, how close to tears I am, how racked by fear.
Here am I making up my quarrel with your father at long last,
and yet my tender sight's all blurring full of tears.

CHORUS LEADER

A glistening tear has brimmed out from my eyes as well.
I hope this present wrong may not advance yet further.

JASON

I like this thinking, and I don't blame those things,
because it's only natural for females to be jealous,
if some alien partner° gets imported to her bed.
But now your feelings have been altered for the better,
and you've recognized, eventually, the winning plan.
These are the actions of a woman who is sensible.
For you, my boys, your father has, with careful forethought,
arranged, thanks to the gods, complete security.
It's my belief that you, with your new brothers,
shall enjoy the foremost standing in this land of Corinth.
Your simple task is to grow up; the rest your father manages;
and with some favorable god, I hope to see you thrive,
and come to full maturity, superior to my enemies.

*(To Medea.)*

But you . . . why are your eyes engulfed with glistening tears?
Why turn your pallid cheek away?
Why not be glad to hear these words from me?

MEDEA

It's nothing. I was only thinking of the children . . .

JASON

Don't worry. I'll ensure that all goes well for them.

MEDEA

I shall do as you say, and take your good advice.
But woman is a tender creature and inclined to tears.°

JASON

But why on earth such grieving for the children here?

MEDEA

I gave them birth. And when you prayed
for life for them, a pang came over me
in fear for whether this would come to be.
But of the things you came to talk with me about:
some we have discussed, and there are others I have yet to mention.
Since the ruler has decided he will banish me,
I shall depart this land, an exile—
this is best for me, I know full well, and not to stay
and live where I might trouble you and the royal family,
since I'm considered hostile to this house.
But for the boys: if they're to be brought up by you,
you must beg Creon not to make them leave this land.

JASON

I'm not so sure I can persuade him, but I have to try.

MEDEA

At least then get your wife to beg her father
not to make the children leave this land in exile.

JASON

A good idea. And I believe I can persuade her—
if she is a woman like the rest of them.

MEDEA

I shall myself take part in this attempt as well:
I'll send her gifts, by far the most exquisite
known to humans of our times—
a finespun robe, and plaited wreath of beaten gold.°
And I'll have the children carry them.
One of you servants, bring the finery
out here as quickly as you can.

*(She sends a maid into the house.)*

She'll win good fortune in innumerable ways,
not only one: she'll get in you the best of husbands
as her bedmate, and acquire the finery
that Helios, my father's father,
handed down to his descendants.

*(The maid enters from the house, bringing out to Medea gifts which she hands to the two boys.)*

Here, boys, take hold of these fine wedding gifts;
go and present them to the blessed royal bride.
She'll have no reason to complain at these.

JASON

You're being foolish: why deplete your own resources?
Do you believe the royal house is short
of dresses—short of gold, do you think?
Preserve these things; don't hand them out.
For if my wife holds me of any value, she'll estimate
my wish above material possessions, I am sure of that.

MEDEA

No, not your way. They say that gifts persuade the gods, even;
and gold means more to humans than a million words.
She has the divine touch; for now
the gods are raising her; she is the young empress.
And I would trade my life, not merely gold,
to get my boys reprieved from exile.
Now, boys, proceed inside the splendid palace,
and implore your father's newfound wife, my mistress;
beg her not to make you leave this land—
and give this finery to her. This is what matters most:
she must receive these gifts with her own hands.
Now quickly, off you go.
May you succeed and bring your mother
good reports about the things she longs to get.

*(Exit the two boys to the side, with Jason and the Tutor.)*

CHORUS [*singing*]

STROPHE A

*Now I've no hope for them, no longer,*
*the children cannot live, no longer;*
*they are already gone to slaughter.*
*The bride, unhappy girl, will take it,*
*the golden diadem, will take it;*
*and she shall set the crown of Hades*
*around her head—her hand will place it.*

ANTISTROPHE A

*The charm and the unearthly glitter*
*will lure her to enfold around her*
*the robe and gold-entwined tiara.*
*She's dressing up to hold her wedding*
*down with the dead. Now she is heading*
*for such a trap, a fate so lethal,*
*she can't escape from disaster.*

STROPHE B

*As for you, sad man, you've tied*
*a fatal knot with kings,*
*not knowing that it brings*
*the end of your boys' life,*
*and cruel death for your bride.*
*You were, unfortunate,*
*so wrong about your fate.*

ANTISTROPHE B

*And I feel pain with you,*
*sad mother of the two,*
*you'll strike your children dead,*
*all for the marriage bed*
*your husband has betrayed—*
*now he holds in your stead*
*another as his wife.*

(*The Tutor and the two boys enter again from the side.*)

TUTOR

Mistress, here are your sons, reprieved from banishment.
Also the princess has received the wedding gifts
delightedly with her own hands.
So all's plain sailing for your boys in that direction.
What's this?
why rooted there confounded when you've done so well?
Why turn your pallid cheek away?°
Why not be glad to hear these words from me?

MEDEA

Ah me!

TUTOR

This tune is not in harmony with my report.

MEDEA

Ah me, again!

TUTOR

Can I be bringing news
of some misfortune I don't know about,
mistaken in believing my report is good?

MEDEA

The news you've given is the news that you have given.
I don't hold that against you.

TUTOR

Then why cast down your eyes and shed these tears?

MEDEA

There's no avoiding it, old man:
the gods and I, with my bad thoughts,
have engineered this outcome.

TUTOR

Take comfort. You shall yet come back,
thanks to your children's influence.

MEDEA

I shall myself fetch others back before that day,
to my own pain.

TUTOR

You're not the only woman to be sundered from her children.
You are a mortal, and must endure misfortunes.

MEDEA

Agreed. But go inside and make provision
for the children's daily needs.

*(Exit the Tutor into the house; the two boys stay on stage.)*

O children, O my children,
you two have a city and a home,
and you shall leave me in my misery
to live for always there, cut off from your mother.
Meanwhile I'm heading for another country as an exile—
too soon to have enjoyed you, to have seen
you happily grown up, too soon to decorate
your wedding bath, your wife, your marriage bed,
and raise up high the ceremonial torch—
unhappy in my willfulness.
For nothing, children, have I nurtured you,
for nothing gone through labor, and been raked with pain,
enduring the sharp agonies of giving birth.
I used, poor fool, to pin all sorts of hopes on you:
that you would care for me when I was old,
and lay me out with your own hands when I was dead—
that's something people value highly.
But now . . . this lovely kind of thought is finished now.
Deprived of you I shall drag through my bitter, painful days.
And you shall never see your mother more
with those dear eyes of yours, once you're transported
to another kind of life.
Ah, ah
why look at me like that, my little ones?

why smile what is to be your latest smile of all?
Ah, ah,
what shall I do? My passion has all melted, women,
now that I see my children's shining looks.
I cannot, no.
Good-bye to all my former resolutions:
I shall convey my children from this land.
Why should I use what's bad for them
to pierce their father's heart,
and so inflict upon myself double the pain as well?
No, I shall not. So good-bye, my resolutions.
But stop, what's wrong with me?
Do I want to be a laughing-stock,
and let my enemies get off scot-free?
I must endure. It is mere cowardice
to even let such feeble words into my mind.
So, children, go inside.

*(The two boys stay on stage.)*

Let anyone who thinks it wrong to stay
near to my sacrifice look after matters for themselves;
I'll not unnerve my hand.
No, no, my heart, do not enact these things, I beg of you,°
just let them be, show mercy for the children.
They can live there with us, and bring you gladness.
No, by the avenging demons of the world below,
I swear, there is no way that I shall leave
my boys among my enemies so they
can treat them with atrocity.
Now they are bound to die in any case, and since they must,
it will be me, the one who gave them birth,
who'll be the one to deal them death.
In any case these things are fixed and inescapable.
She has the garland on her head already;
the princess-bride is in her death throes
in the gown, I'm sure of it.

But now, because I am about to tread
the most unhappy of all roads,
and I am sending these two down a track more wretched yet,
I want to say some parting words to them.
Come here, my children, reach out
your arms and hold your mother tight.
O dearest arms, and dearest mouth,
and shapeliness, and children's noble looks!
May you fare well, but over there:
your father has despoiled what there is here.
Your lovely touch, your silken skin,
and such sweet children's breath!
Away, go, go. I can no longer bear to look at you,
I'm overwhelmed by pain.
I realize what evil things I am about to do,
but it's my anger dominates my resolution—anger,
the cause of all the greatest troubles for humanity.

*(Exit the two boys into the house; Medea stays on stage.)*

CHORUS [*chanting*]
*Repeatedly I have explored*
*ideas of intricacy*
*and entered on deeper disputes*
*than usually womankind does.*
*We have inspiration as well*
*that prompts dialogue leading truly*
*to wisdom (not everyone,*
*you'll only discover a few,*
*one woman among many more,*
*with true inspirational thought).*

*My conclusion is this:*
*that people who've never had children,*
*and have no experience of them,*
*are certainly happier far*

*than those under parenthood's yoke.*
*With no opportunity to*
*experience children as joy,*
*nor as causes of pain—*
*they steer clear of many ordeals.*

*And those with that sweetness of growth,*
*with children as plants in their house—*
*I notice how all of the time*
*they are worn down to shadows with cares.*
*Struggling with how to nurture good health,*
*then how they can leave them well off . . .*
*and, after that, it's still unsure*
*just whether this labor is spent*
*to raise them as bad or as good.*

*And lastly I have to include*
*one final disaster of all*
*for humans. Supposing all's well—*
*they've put aside plentiful means,*
*their children have grown to the full,*
*their character makeup is good—*
*still, if destiny has it this way,*
*then Death takes their bodies below,*
*abducting your child's lovely life.*
*Yet how can it profit the gods*
*to pile upon humans this worst*
*and most agonizing of blows—*
*a fine for the bearing of children.*

MEDEA

I have been waiting for some time, my friends,
to see how things develop over there.
At last I see this man of Jason's coming;
his labored breathing shows he brings grave news.

*(Enter Servant from the side.)*

SERVANT

Oh, you have done a terrible, atrocious crime,°
Medea. Run, run fast away—by sea-borne craft
or earth-borne chariot—take what you can.

MEDEA

And what has happened that demands escape like this?

SERVANT

They're dead—your poisons
have just destroyed the princess and her father Creon.

MEDEA

That's excellent news—
I'll always number you among my friends and benefactors.

SERVANT

What's that? Can you be sane? Or are you mad?
To devastate the royal house, and then be pleased,
and not afraid to hear of things like this?

MEDEA

I too have things I could reply.
But take your time, my friend, and tell me all:
how did they die? You'll give me twice
the pleasure if they met their end most horribly.

SERVANT

When your two children and their father had arrived
inside the palace of the bride, we servants
who were anxious for your troubles were well pleased—
a lively rumor had just reached our ears
that you and your spouse had laid your former strife to rest.
One of us kissed your children's hands, another kissed
their shining hair, and I myself accompanied
the youngsters to the women's chambers with a joyful heart.
The mistress we now wait upon instead of you,
before she saw your pair of boys,
was glancing with excited looks toward Jason.

But then she covered up her eyes and turned away
her pallid cheek to show how much she loathed
the children's access there.
Your husband then set out to mollify
the woman's angry mood by saying this:
"You should not be unfriendly to your own;
give up this anger and turn back your face.
Consider as your own, your dear ones, those your husband
does.
Why not accept these presents, and entreat
your father to release the children from their banishment?—
please, for my sake."
Once she had looked close at the finery, she was unable to
resist;
she went along with everything her husband wanted.
And before he and your boys had gone
far from the palace, she unwrapped
the ornamented gown, and draped it round herself;
and placed the golden wreath about her curls;
holding a burnished mirror to arrange her hair,
she smiled to see the lifeless image of her body there.
Then rising from her throne, she moved around the room,
stepping lightly on her snow white feet.
She was enraptured by the gifts, and kept on looking down
to check the dress was straight against her ankle.
But then there came a horrifying sight to see:
her color altered, and, with limbs convulsing,
she lunged sideways, collapsing on her throne,
and only just avoided falling on the floor.
And some old serving woman, thinking that the fit
must be inspired by Pan, or through some god,
raised up the ritual glory cry—
until, that is, she saw white flecks of foam
discharging from her mouth,
her eyes contorting in their sockets,
her skin all drained of blood.

Then she let out a piercing scream,
in answering discord to her earlier cry.
Immediately one maid set off toward
her father's chambers, and another to report
the bride's collapse to her new husband.
The building echoed through with hectic footsteps.
After about the time that it would take a sprinting runner
to arrive at the finish of a two-hundred-meter racing track,
the wretched girl awakened from her silenced voice
and tight-shut eyes, and moaned a dreadful cry of pain.
Two pincer torments were invading her:
first the golden band around her head spat
an astounding fountain of incendiary fire;
and then the clinging fabric, given by your boys,
began to eat into the poor girl's milky flesh.
Engulfed in flames she rose up from her throne,
and bolted, shaking hair and head this way and that,
attempting to throw off the wreath.
But still the gold clung tightly by its fastenings;
and when she shook her hair,
instead the blazing doubled in intensity.
Then, overcome by agony,
she crumpled to the ground, unrecognizable
to anyone except her parents' view.
The position of her eyes was not distinct,
nor any feature of her pretty face;
and blood was trickling from her crown, mixed sputtering
with fire.
Her flesh was dripping from her bones like tears of resin,
melted by the hidden action of your poison's jaws.
It was a fearsome sight, and all of us
were scared to touch her corpse—
forewarned by what had happened.
Her father, ignorant, poor man, of the disaster,
ran into the room and came upon her body.
He cried aloud and flung his arms about her,

kissing her, and said: "O my poor child,
which of the gods has cut you down
so undeservedly like this? Which has bereaved me
of your life, an old man at death's door?
If only I could die with you, my child."
When he had finished his lament,
and tried to stand his aged body back upright,
he found that, as with ivy gripping laurel branches,
he was held tightly by the finespun robe.
The struggle then was terrible.
While he did all he could to straighten up his limbs,
she tugged him down again.
And if he tried to pull by force,
she wrenched the old man's flesh from off his bones.
And in the end he was exhausted and gave up the ghost,
poor man, no longer strong enough to fight the dreadful end.
And so they lie there corpses, daughter and old father, dead,°
beside each other, a disaster that cries out for tears.
For me, your fate must lie beyond my scope;
you will discover for yourself
the payback of your punishment.
But as for human life, I think of it—
not for the first time as a flitting shade.
I'm not afraid to say that those who seem to be so clever
and who take such trouble over making speeches, those are
the very people who are guilty of the worst stupidity.
No human is a truly happy man:
it might be some are luckier than others
when prosperity flows with the tide . . .
but truly happy—no.

*(Exit Servant to the side.)*

CHORUS LEADER

It would appear that on this day the god
is rightly loading many evils onto Jason's back.
O wretched daughter born of Creon, how much we pity you°

for your misfortunes. You've had to go away
to Hades' house, thanks to your union with Jason.

MEDEA

My deed has been decided, friends—
as quickly as I can I'll end the children's lives,
and move on from this land.
I must make no delay, and give no time
for someone else's crueler hand to slaughter them.
Now they are bound to die in any case;
and since they must, it will be me, who gave them birth,
who'll be the one to deal them death.
Come, come, my heart, it's time to put your armor on.
What use postponing now the evil deed,
inevitable acts that must be done?
Advance, my wretched hand, and grip the sword,
grip hard, and make toward life's painful finish line.
No cowardice, and no remembering your children,
how they were your dears, or how you gave them birth.
Instead for this one fleeting day forget that they are yours,
and afterward take time to grieve.
Although it's you who's killing them,
they were your lovely babes.
And I'm a woman made of sorrow.

*(Exit Medea into the house.)*

CHORUS [*singing*]

STROPHE A

*I call on Earth and you, Sun, full*
*illumination,*
*look down and see this woman's foul*
*abomination,*
*before she strikes her deadly blow,*
*infanticidal.*
*Since they're descended from your glow,*
*celestial, golden—*

*a fearsome thing for divine blood*
*in desecration*
*to fall to earth by human deed.*
*Fire transcendental,*
*great god of light, restrain, detain*
*her, exorcising*
*out from the house this deadly bane,*
*avenging demon.*

ANTISTROPHE A

*In vain your toil for children, void,*
*evaporated;*
*in vain you bore the pair you loved,*
*obliterated,*
*you who escaped those narrow crags,*
*the most forbidding,*
*between the cobalt Clashing Rocks,*
*the never yielding.*
*Why does such heavy anger load*
*you, soul-destroying?*
*Why does blood demand more blood?*
*For internecine*
*kin-murder brings for us humans*
*extreme pollution,*
*kin-killers bring down on their homes*
*concordant anguish.*

ONE BOY *(Inside.)*

No! help, help!

CHORUS [*singing*]

STROPHE B

*You hear the children? You hear their shout?°*
*O wretched woman, your cursed fate!*

ONE BOY

What can I do to get free from my mother's grip?

THE OTHER BOY *(Inside.)*

I see no way, dear brother—we are lost.

CHORUS [*singing*]

*So should I enter? Yes, I choose*
*to fend off murder from these poor boys.*

ONE BOY *(Inside.)*

Yes, for god's sake, help—now is our hour of need.

THE OTHER BOY *(Inside.)*

The net, the sword are closing in on us.

CHORUS [*singing*]

*So you are really made out of iron,*
*or out of granite. You will cut down*
*the lives you nurtured from your womb's field,*
*doom them to slaughter at your own hand.*

ANTISTROPHE B

*I've heard of only one woman past,*
*who killed the nurslings of her own nest.*
*And that was Ino, sent mad by the gods,*
*when Hera drove her wandering away from home.*
*She leapt down into the salty waves,*
*wickedly drowning her clutch of babes.*
*She pressed her steps from land into the sea,*
*and died herself, along with her two sons.*
*Can there be any event so foul*
*that it remains still impossible?*
*The bed of women, love-bed of night—*
*how many troubles are caused by your might.*

*(Enter Jason from the side, alone and sword in hand.)*

JASON

You women standing by this building here,
is the perpetrator of these dreadful things inside—Medea—

or has she run away in flight?
She's going to have to hide herself deep underground,
or lift herself on wings high in the air above,
if she is to avoid due punishment from this royal dynasty.
Or does she think that she can kill the rulers,
and escape from this house here scot-free?
But it's not her I came about:
much more my children.
Those that she has done damage to will do the same to her:
I've come to save the lives of my two sons,
and stop the kinsmen from inflicting harm
on them in retribution for the awful murder
that their mother has committed.

CHORUS LEADER

O Jason, you unhappy man, you've no idea
how far you are advanced in troubles,
or you never would have said those words you did.

JASON

What's this? I don't suppose she wants to murder me as well?

CHORUS LEADER

Your boys are dead, dead by their mother's hand.

JASON

What are you saying, women? You have shattered me.

CHORUS LEADER

Your children live no more—of that be sure.

JASON

Where did she kill them? Indoors, or outside the house?

CHORUS LEADER

Open the doors, and you will see your murdered sons.

*(Jason tries to force open the doors.)*

JASON

Quickly, undo the bars; quick, servants,
release the bolts, so I may see this double havoc
both those who are dead, and her—so I may punish her.°

*(Medea appears above, in a flying chariot,*
*with the bodies of their two sons.)*

MEDEA

Why rattle at these doors, and try to force them open?
Searching for the bodies
and for me the one who did it?
Then abandon all this effort.
And if you have some need of me,
then speak up if you wish.
But you shall never lay your hands on me—
you see what kind of vehicle the Sun,
my father's father, has bestowed upon me,
as protection from unfriendly hands.

JASON

You thing of hate, woman most loathsome
to the gods, and me, and all humanity.
You who could steel yourself to drive your sword
into the children you yourself had borne;
and you have ruined me with childlessness.
Now you have done these things,
how can you dare to look upon the sun and earth,
when you've committed this abominable act?
To hell with you. Now I see straight: back then I was not
thinking,
when I conveyed you from your home
in a barbarian land to my household in Greece—
already then a powerful evil,
traitor to your father and the country that had nurtured you.
The gods have sprung on me the demon of revenge
that came with you, because you killed

your brother at the hearth, and then embarked
upon the *Argo*'s glorious deck.
You started out from things like that;
and then, when you had married me
and borne my children, you murdered them—
all for the sake of sexual pride, the bed.
No woman born a Greek would ever have gone through
with such a crime; yet I saw fit to marry you,
in preference to one of them—a loathsome
and destructive union it has proved to be for me.
A lioness not woman, you,
more cruel in nature than the Etruscan Scylla.
But not even with a thousand insults
could I pierce your skin, so toughened is your callousness;
so go to hell, foul creature, and defiled with children's blood.
All I can do is grieve for my own destiny.
I never shall enjoy my new-laid marriage bed;
I never shall share words again
with these two children that I sowed and bred,
not in this life—no, they are lost to me.

MEDEA

I might have contradicted you at length,
if it were not that father Zeus knows well
how you have fared by me,
and how you have behaved to me.
You can't have thought that you could spurn my marriage bed
and then proceed to live a life of pleasure,
reveling in mockery of me?—
nor could the princess, nor could Creon who set up
this match, and wanted to eject me from this land,
and thought to get away with it.
So go ahead, and call me lioness
and Scylla, occupant of the Etruscan cave.°
I do not mind, since now I've fairly clawed into your heart.

JASON

Yet you yourself must also suffer grief,
and be joint sharer in the sorrow.

MEDEA

Yes, surely, but the anguish is well worth it,
as long as you can't mock at me.

JASON

O my poor children, what a vicious mother
yours has proved to be.

MEDEA

O my poor boys, what a sad end you've met,
thanks to your father's failing.

JASON

It was not by my hand they died.

MEDEA

It was, though, because of your own arrogance
and your new-saddled marriage.

JASON

And you believe it justified
to kill them for the sake of sex?

MEDEA

Do you suppose such troubles to be trivial for a woman?

JASON

It is for one who's sensible:
but everything is bad for you.

MEDEA

These children live no more, and that will pierce you through.

JASON

They are still here to bring down vengeance
on your guilt-stained head.

MEDEA

The gods know which one started this catastrophe.

JASON

For sure they know your mind and its full loathsomeness.

MEDEA

Yes, hate away.
The very timbre of your voice fills me with loathing.

JASON

And so does yours with me.
Our terms of parting will be easy.

MEDEA

Then tell me—what am I to do?
I too am keen to bring this to an end.

JASON

Just let me bury and lament for these poor corpses.

MEDEA

Never—because I'll bury them with these my hands.
I'll take them to the shrine of Hera on the Peak
to make sure no one of my enemies
can triumph over them by ripping up their graves.
I shall impose upon this land of Sisyphus
a solemn cult and festival for all of future time,
atonement for this heinous murder.
Then I shall make my way to Athens, country of Erechtheus,
where I shall cohabit with King Aegeus, son of Pandion.
And you . . . you shall, appropriately enough,
meet a rotten end,
cracked on the head by a disintegrating piece
from off the *Argo*'s hulk,
and see the bitter outcome of your union with me.°

JASON [*chanting henceforth*]

*I pray that the children's Avenging Spirit*
*and Justice for murder may hound you to death.*

MEDEA [*chanting henceforth*]

*What god or spirit is going to hear you,*
*who perjured your oaths, and deceived your hosts?*

JASON

*Child-killer, pollution!*

MEDEA

*Back to your home and bury your wife.*

JASON

*I go, bereft of both my sons.*

MEDEA

*It's early to lament: wait for your old age.*

JASON

*My children, my darlings . . .*

MEDEA

*Not your darlings—but their mother's!*

JASON

*And that is why you murdered them?*

MEDEA

*For you, to torture you with pain.*

JASON

*I ache to enfold my sons,*
*to touch their dearest lips!*

MEDEA

*Now you address them with love,*
*now you desire to embrace,*
*but then you pushed them away.*

JASON

*Just allow me a touch*
*of the delicate skin of my sons.*

MEDEA

*Unthinkable. Your words are wasted in air.*

*(Medea flies away in the chariot with the bodies of their sons.)*

JASON

*Pay attention to this, great Zeus:*
*how I am driven away;*
*what I have suffered at the hands*
*of this polluted, this children-devouring she-lion.*
*With my every morsel of strength*
*I cry in my grief, and I call on the gods*
*to be witnesses,*
*how you prevent me from touching*
*the children you killed,*
*deny me the burial rites for their bodies.*
*Would that I'd never begotten them,*
*only to see them lie butchered by you.*

CHORUS [*chanting*]

*Zeus stores many things on Olympus;°*
*gods do many things that surprise us.*
*The endings expected do not come to pass:*
*those unexpected—the god finds a way.*
*That sort of story has happened today.*

*(Exit all.)*

# HIPPOLYTUS

*Translated by* DAVID GRENE

# HIPPOLYTUS: INTRODUCTION

*The Play: Date and Composition*

Euripides' *Hippolytus* was produced in Athens in 428 BCE. In the dramatic competition that year, Euripides took first prize, Iophon second, Ion third. It is not known what other three plays Euripides produced together with *Hippolytus*.

Ancient scholars report that this was the second play Euripides wrote about Hippolytus and Phaedra. They called this one *Hippolytus Bearing a Garland* (cf. lines 73ff. of the play) and the earlier one *Hippolytus Veiled*. The earlier version (its date is unknown) seems to have scandalized its audience by depicting Phaedra shamelessly yielding to her passion for Hippolytus and approaching the young man directly in order to seduce him; the title probably derived from his horrified reaction. Ancient authors cite about twenty small fragments or paraphrases from the earlier version and suggest that in the surviving version of the story Euripides "corrected . . . what was unseemly and worth condemning" in the earlier play; most modern scholars have followed their lead. If this is correct, it is the only case we know of in which an Athenian tragedian rewrote a play and staged the revised version in Athens. The ancient scholars also say that this tragedy is one of Euripides' best ones, and most readers, both ancient and modern, agree.

*The Myth*

Euripides' play begins with Aphrodite, the goddess of sexual desire, describing her resentment of Hippolytus, the son of the great Athenian hero Theseus by an Amazon, for his rejection of her and his devotion to Artemis instead. To punish Hippolytus, Aphrodite inflames Phaedra, Theseus' lawful wife, with an unwilling passion for her stepson. Phaedra attempts to suppress her desires and keep them secret, but her nurse conveys them to Hippolytus. When he reacts with horror and outrage, Phaedra fears that he will denounce her, and so she writes a letter accusing him of having raped her and then hangs herself. Theseus discovers her corpse and the letter, and in a rage he uses one of the three curses his father Poseidon had granted him to have Hippolytus killed.

Theseus was originally a hero associated with the small town of Troezen near Athens but was later incorporated into Athenian local mythology. Hippolytus likewise was worshipped in a cult in Troezen—girls who were about to marry sacrificed some of their hair to him—and also in Athens. There may well have been some links in myths and cult between Hippolytus and Aphrodite, since in both cases the sanctuary of Hippolytus also contained a temple of Aphrodite. Although there is no direct evidence for the story of Hippolytus, Phaedra, and Theseus before the fifth century BCE, it is likely to have been ancient even then. It is also worth noting that the basic plot pattern of the wife who fails to seduce her stepson and then accuses him of raping her (best known as the story of Potiphar's wife, from the biblical story of Joseph in the book of Genesis) seems to be part of the fundamental stock of folktales throughout the world and is found in different forms in many cultures and ages. In the fifth century BCE it was the subject not only of Euripides' two versions but also of a *Phaedra* by Sophocles of which very little is preserved (its date is also unknown, and there is no proof that it influenced or even preceded Euripides' second *Hippolytus*).

### *Transmission and Reception*

*Hippolytus* was unusually successful when it was first produced—it supplied Euripides with one of the few victories he received in the dramatic competitions during his life—and it went on to become enormously popular and influential throughout antiquity and thereafter. As late as the second century CE, the travel writer Pausanias remarked that even barbarians who had learned the Greek language knew the story. It belongs to the group of ten plays by Euripides that were most widely diffused during ancient and medieval times. Its popularity among ancient readers is attested by eight papyrus fragments and clay sherds bearing small portions of texts of the play and dating from the third century BCE to the second century CE.

So it is not surprising that *Hippolytus* seems from our scanty evidence to have exerted considerable influence upon later Greek versions of the story, and it certainly influenced the two most important extant Roman versions: a poetic epistle from Phaedra to Hippolytus composed by Ovid in his *Heroides* and Seneca's tragedy *Phaedra*. In both of these, as in most of the later tradition (and perhaps already in Sophocles' lost *Phaedra*), the attention shifts markedly from Hippolytus to Phaedra. In the ancient visual arts, too, the story was extremely popular: in the fourth century BCE, south Italic vases depict Hippolytus' death; later, other artistic media, such as mosaics, paintings, sarcophagi, mirrors, coins, and gems, often depict Phaedra sitting sadly holding the letter and accompanied by the Nurse. Many Roman funerary sarcophagi represent on adjacent panels a whole sequence of episodes from the story, usually emphasizing Hippolytus hunting or dying, and often showing him with Phaedra or Theseus.

In modern times *Hippolytus* remains well known. Besides the frequent productions of Euripides' play on stages throughout the world in all languages (including ancient Greek), the story has offered material for numerous new versions. Jean Racine's *Phèdre* (1677) was only one of many dramatic versions of the story written in Renaissance France, but its genius has overshadowed them all—and has made Phaedra a classic figure of the modern stage. The challenge of turning Racine's French poetry into English verse has attracted numerous American and British poets, including Robert Lowell (1961), Richard Wilbur (1962), C. H. Sisson (1989), Derek Mahon (1999), and Ted Hughes (2000). At the end of the nineteenth century, Phaedra's passion inspired various poets (Algernon Charles Swinburne, *Phaedra*, 1866; Gabriele d'Annunzio, *Fedra*, 1908) and artists (Aubrey Beardsley, "Phèdre," 1898); and more recently it has especially drawn a number of women writers, such as H. D. (*Hippolytus Temporizes*, 1927), Marina Tsvetaeva (*Fedra*, 1928), Marguerite Yourcenar ("Phaedra, or Despair," 1936; *Who Doesn't Have His Minotaur?*, 1963), and Sarah Kane (*Phaedra's Love*, 1996).

Euripides' own play still appears on stages and in films, but less often than Racine's, and it continues to inspire modern dramatic versions, such as those by Eugene O'Neill (*Desire under the Elms*, 1924), Robinson Jeffers (*The Cretan Woman*, 1964), Tony Harrison (*Phaedra Britannica*, 1975), and Brian Friel (*Living Quarters*, 1977), as well as cinematic ones such as Jules Dassin's *Phaedra* (1962). Phaedra and to a lesser extent Hippolytus have also been the subject of a number of dance dramas (Martha Graham, *Phaedra*, 1962; *Phaedra's Dream*, 1983) and musical compositions (Christoph Willibald Gluck, *Ippolito*, 1745; Franz Schubert, "Hippolits Lied," 1826; Benjamin Britten, *Phaedra*, 1975), and have also been represented in several paintings (Peter Paul Rubens, ca. 1610; Théodore Géricault; Lawrence Alma-Tadema, 1860; Giorgio de Chirico, 1951ff.) and sculptures (J.-B. Lemoyne, 1715; Leonard Baskin, 1969).

# HIPPOLYTUS

*Characters*

THESEUS, king of Athens
HIPPOLYTUS, his son by the queen of the Amazons
PHAEDRA, Theseus' wife, stepmother to Hippolytus
A SERVANT
A MESSENGER°
THE NURSE
CHORUS OF WOMEN of Troezen
A CHORUS OF HUNTSMEN, in attendance on Hippolytus
APHRODITE
ARTEMIS

*Scene: Troezen, in front of the house of Theseus. In front of the house there are two statues, one of Artemis and one of Aphrodite.*

*(Enter Aphrodite.)*

APHRODITE

I am called the Goddess Cypris:
I am mighty among men and they honor me by many names.
Of all who live and see the light of sun
from Atlas' pillars to the tide of Pontus,
those who worship my power in all humility
I exalt in honor.
But those whose pride is stiff-necked against me
I lay by the heels.

There is joy in the heart of a god also
when honored by men.
Now I will quickly tell you the truth of this story.
Hippolytus, son of Theseus by the Amazon,
pupil of holy Pittheus,
alone among the folk of this land of Troezen has blasphemed me
counting me vilest of the gods in heaven.
He will none of the bed of love nor marriage,
but honors Apollo's sister, Artemis, Zeus' daughter,
counting her greatest of all divinities.
He is with her continually, this maiden goddess, in the greenwood.
He hunts with swift hounds and clears the land of wild beasts,
sharing in greater than mortal companionship.
I do not grudge him such privileges: why should I?
But for the wrongs that he has done to me
I shall punish Hippolytus this day.
I have no need to toil to win my end:
much of the task has been already done.
He came once from Pittheus' house to the country of Pandion
that he might see and be initiate in the holy mysteries.
Phaedra, his father's noble wife, saw him
and her heart was filled with the longings of dreadful love.
This was my work.
So before ever she came to this land of Troezen
close to the rock of Pallas that looks across to it,
she dedicated a temple to Cypris,
for her love dwells in a foreign land.
Ages to come will call this temple after him,
the temple of the Goddess Near Hippolytus.
When Theseus left the land of Cecrops,
flying from the guilty stain of the murder of the Pallantids,
condemning himself to a year's exile
he sailed with his wife to this land.
Here she groans in bitterness of heart

and the goads of love prick her cruelly,
and she is like to die—in silence,
and none of the servants know of her sickness.
But her love is not to end up that way.
I will reveal the matter to Theseus and all shall come out.
Father shall slay son with curses—
this son that is hateful to me.
For once lord Poseidon, the ruler of the sea,
granted this favor to Theseus,
that three of his prayers to the god would find answer.
Renowned shall Phaedra be in her death, but none the less
die she must.
Her suffering shall not weigh in the scale so much
that I should let my enemies go untouched
escaping payment of a retribution
sufficient to satisfy me.
Look, here is the son of Theseus, Hippolytus!
He has just left the toils of his hunting.
I will leave this place.
See the great crowd of servants that throngs upon his heels
and sings the praise of Artemis in hymns!
He does not know
that the doors of death are open for him,
that he is looking on his last sun.

*(Exit Aphrodite. Enter Hippolytus from the side, attended by a Chorus of friends and servants carrying hunting implements.)*

HIPPOLYTUS [*singing*]
*Follow me, follow me singing*
*of Artemis,*
*heavenly one, child of Zeus,*
*Artemis!*
*We are the wards of your care.*

CHORUS OF HUNTSMEN [*singing*]
*Hail, mistress and queen, holiest one!*

*Hail, daughter of Zeus!*
*Hail, Artemis, maiden Daughter of Zeus and Leto!*
*Most beautiful of virgins by far!*
*Dweller in the spacious sky,*
*in the palace of your noble father,*
*in Zeus' golden glistening house!*
*Hail!*
*Maiden goddess most beautiful, most beautiful of all those who live in Olympus!*

*(Hippolytus lays a garland on the statue of Artemis.)*

HIPPOLYTUS

My sovereign lady, I bring you ready woven
this garland. It was I that plucked and wove it,
plucked it for you in your inviolate meadow.
No shepherd dares to feed his flock within it;
no reaper plies a busy scythe within it:
only the bees in springtime haunt the inviolate meadow.
Its gardener is the spirit Reverence who
refreshes it with water from the river.
Not those who by instruction have profited
to learn, but in whose very soul the seed
of purity and self-control toward
all things alike Nature has deeply rooted,
they alone may gather flowers there! The others,
the impure, may not.
Loved Mistress, here I offer you this coronal;
it is a true worshipper's hand that gives it you
to crown the golden glory of your hair.
With no man else I share this privilege
that I am with you and to your words
can answer words. True, I may only hear:
I may not see you face to face.
So may I turn the post set at life's end
even as I began the race.

SERVANT

King—for I will not call you "Master," that belongs
to the gods only—will you take good advice?

HIPPOLYTUS

Certainly I will. I would not want to seem a fool.

SERVANT

In men's communities one rule holds good,
do you know it, King?

HIPPOLYTUS

Not I. What is this rule?

SERVANT

Men hate the haughty of heart who will not be
the friend of every man.

HIPPOLYTUS

And rightly too:
For a haughty heart breeds odium among men.

SERVANT

And affability wins favor, then?

HIPPOLYTUS

Abundant favor Yes, and profit, too,
at little cost of inconvenience.

SERVANT

Do you think that it's the same among the gods?

HIPPOLYTUS

If we in our world and the gods in theirs
know the same usages—yes.

SERVANT

Then, King, how comes it
that for a venerable goddess you have not even
a word of salutation?

HIPPOLYTUS

Which goddess?
Be careful, or you will find that tongue of yours
may make a serious mistake.

SERVANT

This goddess here
who stands before your gates, the goddess Cypris.°

HIPPOLYTUS

I worship her—but from a long way off,
for I am pure.

SERVANT

Yet she's a venerable goddess,
and great is her renown throughout the world.

HIPPOLYTUS

Men make their choice: one man honors one god,°
and one another.

SERVANT

Well, good fortune guard you,
if you have as much good sense as you should have.

HIPPOLYTUS

A god of nocturnal prowess is not my god.

SERVANT

The honors of the gods you must not scant, my son.

HIPPOLYTUS

Go, men, into the house and look to supper.
A plentiful table is an excellent thing
after the hunt. And you

*(Singling some out.)*

rub down my horses.
When I have eaten I shall set them in the yoke and exercise
them as is suitable.
As for your Cypris here—a long good-bye to her!

*(Exit Hippolytus into the house accompanied by the Chorus, except for the old Servant.)*

SERVANT

O sovereign Cypris, we must not imitate
the young men when they have such thoughts as these.
As fits a slave to speak, here at your image
I pray and worship. You should be forgiving
when one that has a young tempestuous heart
speaks foolish words. Seem not to hear them.
You should be wiser than mortals, being gods.

*(Exit the Servant. Enter Chorus of women of Troezen.)*

CHORUS [*singing*]

STROPHE A

*There is a rock streaming with water,*
*whose source, men say, is Ocean,*
*and it pours from the heart of its stone a spring*
*where pitchers may dip and be filled.*
*My friend was there and in the river water*
*she dipped and washed the royal purple robes,*
*and spread them on the rock's warm back*
*where the sunbeams played.*
*It was from her I heard at first*
*of the news of my mistress' sorrow.*

ANTISTROPHE A

*She lies on her bed within the house*
*and fever wracks her,*
*and she hides her golden head in finespun robes.*
*This is the third day*
*she has eaten no bread*
*and her body is pure and fasting.*
*For she would willingly bring her life to anchor*
*at the end of its voyage*
*in the gloomy harbor of death.*

STROPHE B

*Is it Pan's frenzy that possesses you*
*or is Hecate's madness upon you, maid?*
*Can it be the holy Corybants,*
*or the Mighty Mother who rules the mountains?*
*Are you wasted in suffering thus*
*for a sin against Dictynna, queen of hunters?*
*Are you perhaps unhallowed, having offered*
*no sacrifice to her from taken victims?*
*For she goes through the waters of Limnae*
*and can travel on dry land beyond the sea,*
*the eddying salt sea.*

ANTISTROPHE B

*Can it be that some other woman's love,*
*a secret love that hides itself from you,*
*has beguiled your husband,*
*the sovereign lord of Erechtheus'*
*people, that prince of noble birth?*
*Or has some sailor from the shores of Crete*
*put in at this harbor hospitable to sailors,*
*bearing a message for our queen,*
*and so because he told her some calamity*
*her spirit is bound in chains of grief*
*and she lies on her bed in sorrow?*

EPODE

*Unhappy is the compound of woman's nature;*
*the torturing misery of helplessness,*
*the helplessness of childbirth and its madness,*
*are linked to it forever.*
*My body, too, has felt this thrill of pain,*
*and I called on Artemis, queen of the bow;*
*she has my reverence always*
*as she goes in the company of the gods.*

[*chanting*]

*But here is the old woman, the queen's nurse,*
*here at the door. She is bringing her mistress out.*
*There is a gathering cloud upon her face.*
*What is the matter? My soul is eager to know.*
*What can have made the queen so pale?*
*What can have wasted her body so?*

*(Enter the Nurse from the house, supporting Phaedra.)*

NURSE [*chanting, while Phaedra sings*]
*A weary thing is sickness and its pains!*
*What must I do now? What should I leave undone?*
*Here is light and air, the brightness of the sky.*
*I have brought out the couch on which you tossed*
*in fever—here, clear of the house.*
*Your every word has been to bring you out,*
*but when you're here, you hurry in again.*
*You find no constant pleasure anywhere*
*for when your joy is upon you, suddenly*
*you're foiled and cheated.*
*There's no content for you in what you have*
*for you're forever finding something dearer,*
*some other thing—because you have it not.*
*It's better to be sick than nurse the sick.*
*Sickness is single trouble for the sufferer:*
*but nursing means vexation of the mind,*
*and hard work for the hands besides.*
*The life of humankind is complete misery:*
*we find no resting place from calamity.*
*But something other dearer still than life°*
*the darkness hides and mist encompasses;*
*we are proved luckless lovers of this thing*
*that glitters in our world: no man*
*can tell us of that other life, expounding*
*what is under the earth: we know nothing of it.*
*Idly we drift, on idle stories carried.*

PHAEDRA *(To the servants.)*

*Lift me up! Lift my head up! All the muscles*
*are slack and useless. Here, you, take my hands.*
*They're beautiful, my hands and arms!*
*Take away this headdress! It is too heavy to wear.*
*Take it away! Let my hair fall free on my shoulders.*

NURSE

*Quiet, child, quiet! Do not so restlessly*
*keep tossing to and fro! It's easier*
*to bear an illness if you have some patience*
*and the spirit of good breeding.*
*We all must suffer sometimes: we are mortal.*

PHAEDRA

*Oh,*
*if I could only draw from the dewy spring*
*a draught of fresh pure water!*
*If I could only lie beneath the poplars,*
*in the tufted meadow and find my rest there!*

NURSE

*Child, why do you rave so? There are others here.*
*Cease tossing out these wild demented words*
*whose driver is madness.*

PHAEDRA

*Bring me to the mountains! I will go to the mountains,*
*among the pine trees where the huntsmen's pack*
*trails spotted stags and hangs upon their heels.*
*By the gods, how I long to set the hounds on, shouting,*
*and poise the Thessalian javelin drawing it back—*
*here where my fair hair hangs above the ear—*
*I would hold in my hand a spear with a steel point.*

NURSE

*What ails you, child? What is this love of hunting,*
*and you a lady! Draught of fresh spring water?*

*Here, beside the tower there is a sloping ridge*
*with springs enough to satisfy your thirst.*

PHAEDRA

*Artemis, mistress of the Salty Lake,*
*mistress of the ring echoing to the racers' hoofs,*
*if only I could gallop your level stretches,*
*and break Venetian colts!*

NURSE

*This is sheer madness again,*
*that prompts such whirling, frenzied, senseless words.*
*Here at one moment you're afire with longing*
*to hunt wild beasts and you'd go to the hills,*
*and then again all your desire is horses,*
*horses on the sands beyond the reach of the breakers.*
*Indeed, it would need a mighty prophet, my child,*
*to tell which of the gods it is that*
*jerks you from your true course and thwarts your wits!*

PHAEDRA [*chanting*]

*O, I am miserable! What is this I've done?*
*Where have I strayed from the highway of good sense?*
*I was mad. It was the madness sent from some god*
*that made me fall.*
*I am unhappy, so unhappy! Nurse,*
*cover my face again. I am ashamed*
*of what I said. Cover me up. The tears*
*are flowing, and my face is turned to shame.*
*Having my mind straight is bitterness to my heart;*
*yet madness is terrible. It is better then*
*that I should die and know no more of anything.*

NURSE [*chanting*]

*There, now, you are covered up. But my own body:*
*when will death cover that? I have learned much*
*from my long life. The mixing bowl of friendship,*

*the love of one for the other, must be tempered.*
*Fondness must not touch the marrow of the soul.*
*Our affections must be breakable chains, that we*
*can cast them off or tighten them.*
*That one soul so for two should be in travail*
*as I for her, that is a heavy burden.*
*The ways of life that are most unbending*
*trip us up more, they say, than bring us joy.*
*They're enemies to health. So I praise less*
*the extreme than temperance in everything.*
*The wise will agree with me.*

CHORUS LEADER

Old woman, you are Phaedra's faithful nurse.
We can see that the queen is in trouble, but the cause
that ails her is black mystery to us.
We would like to hear you tell us what is the matter.

NURSE [*speaking*]

I have asked and know no more. She will not tell me.

CHORUS LEADER

Not even what began it?

NURSE

And my answer
is still the same: of all this she will not speak.

CHORUS LEADER

But see how ill she is, and how her body
is wracked and wasted!

NURSE

Yes, she has eaten nothing
for two days now.

CHORUS LEADER

Is this the scourge of madness?
Or can it be . . . that dying is what she seeks?

NURSE

Dying? Well, she is starving herself to death.

CHORUS LEADER

I wonder that her husband allows this.

NURSE

She hides her troubles, says that she isn't sick.

CHORUS LEADER

But does he not look into her face and see
a witness that disproves her?

NURSE

No, he is gone.
He is away from home, in foreign lands.

CHORUS LEADER

Why, you must force her then, to find the cause
of this mind-wandering sickness!

NURSE

Every means
I have tried and still have won no foot of ground.
But I'll not give up trying, even now.
You are here and can in person bear me witness
that I am loyal to my masters always,
even in misfortune's hour.
Dear child, let us both forget our former words.
Be kinder, you: unknit that ugly frown
and track of thought. And as for me, I'll leave
that point I could not follow you at: I'll take
another and a better argument.
If you are sick and it is some unmentionable malady,
here are women standing at your side to help.
But if your troubles may be told to men,
speak, that a doctor may pronounce upon it.
So, not a word! Oh, why will you not speak?
There is no remedy in silence, child.

Either I am wrong and then you should correct me;
or right, and you should yield to what I say.
Say something! Look at me!
  Women, I have tried and tried and all for nothing.
We are as far as ever from our goal.
It was the same before—she was not melted
by anything I said, and now she still won't listen.
  But this you shall know, though to my reasoning
you are more dumbly obstinate than the sea:
If you die, you will be a traitor to your children.
They will never know their share in a father's palace.
No, by the Amazon queen, the mighty rider
who bore a master for your children,
one bastard in birth but trueborn son in mind,
you know him well—Hippolytus . . .

PHAEDRA

Ah!

NURSE

So that has touched you?

PHAEDRA

You have killed me, nurse. For the gods' sake, I entreat you,
never again speak about that man to me.

NURSE

You see? You have come to your senses, yet despite that,
you will not make your children happy nor
save your own life besides.

PHAEDRA

I love my children.
It's another storm of fortune that batters me.

NURSE

There is no stain of blood upon your hands?

PHAEDRA
My hands are clean: the stain is in my heart.

NURSE
The hurt comes from outside? Some enemy?

PHAEDRA
One I love destroys me. Neither of us wills it.

NURSE
Has Theseus done some wrong against you then?

PHAEDRA
May I be equally guiltless in his sight!

NURSE
What is this terror urging you to death?

PHAEDRA
Leave me to do wrong. My wrongs are not against you.

NURSE
Not of my will, but yours, you'll cast me off.

PHAEDRA
Are you trying to force me, clasping my hand as suppliant?

NURSE
Your knees too—and I never will let you go.

PHAEDRA
Sorrow, nurse, sorrow for you, if you find out.

NURSE
Can I know greater sorrow than losing you?

PHAEDRA
It will kill you. But for me, honor lies in silence.

NURSE
And yet you hide it, though I plead for what's good?

PHAEDRA
Yes, for I seek to win good out of shame.

NURSE
But won't you earn more honor if you speak?

PHAEDRA
By the gods, let go my hand and go away!

NURSE
No, for you have not given me what you must.

PHAEDRA
I yield. Your suppliant hand compels my reverence.

NURSE
I will say no more. Yours is the word from now.

PHAEDRA
Unhappy mother, what a love was yours!

NURSE
It is her love for the bull you mean, dear child?

PHAEDRA
Unhappy sister, bride of Dionysus!

NURSE
Why these ill-boding words about your kin?

PHAEDRA
And I the unlucky third, see how I end!

NURSE
Your words are wounds. Where will your tale conclude?

PHAEDRA
Mine is an inherited curse. It is not new.

NURSE
I have not yet heard what I most want to know.

PHAEDRA

Ah!
If you could say for me what I must say myself.

NURSE

I am no prophet to know your hidden secrets.

PHAEDRA

What does it mean to say someone's in love?

NURSE

Sweetest and bitterest, both in one, at once.

PHAEDRA

One of those two, I've known, and all too well.

NURSE

Are you in love, my child? And who is he?

PHAEDRA

There is a man . . . his mother was an Amazon . . .

NURSE

You mean Hippolytus?

PHAEDRA

You
have spoken it, not I.

NURSE

What do you mean? This is my death.
Women, this is past bearing. I'll not bear
life after this. A curse upon the daylight!
A curse upon this shining sun above us!
I'll throw myself from a cliff, throw myself headlong!
I'll be rid of life somehow, I'll die somehow!
Farewell to all of you! This is the end for me.
Chaste and temperate people—not of their own will—
fall in love, badly. Cypris, you are no god.

You are something stronger than a god if that can be.
You have ruined her and me and all this house.

(*Exit the Nurse.*)

CHORUS [*singing*]

STROPHE

*Did you hear, did you hear*
*the queen crying aloud,*
*telling of a calamity*
*which no ear should hear?*
*I would rather die*
*than think such thoughts as yours.*
*I am sorry for your trouble.*
*Alas for troubles, man-besetting.*
*You are dead, you yourself*
*have dragged your ruin to the light.*
*What can happen now in the long*
*dragging stretch of the rest of your days?*
*Some new thing will befall the house.*
*We know now, we know now*
*how your love will end,*
*poor unhappy Cretan girl!*

PHAEDRA

Hear me, you women of Troezen who live
in this extremity of land, this anteroom to Argos.
Many a time in night's long empty spaces
I have pondered on the causes of a life's shipwreck.
I think that our lives are worse than the mind's quality
would warrant. There are many who know good sense.
But look. We know the good, we see it clear.
But we can't bring it to achievement. Some
are betrayed by their own laziness, and others
value some other pleasure above virtue.
There are so many pleasures in this life—
long gossiping talks and leisure, that sweet curse.

Then there is shame that thwarts us. Shame is of two kinds.
The one is harmless, but the other's a plague.
For clarity's sake, we should not talk of "shame,"
a single word for two quite different things.
These then are my views. Nothing can now seduce me
to the opposite opinion. I will tell you
in my own case the track which my mind followed.
At first when love had struck me, I reflected
how best to bear it. Silence was my first plan:
to conceal that illness. For I knew the tongue
is not to be trusted: it can criticize
another's faulty thoughts, but on its owner
it brings a thousand troubles.
Next, I believed that I could conquer love,
conquer it with discretion and good sense.
And when that too failed me, I resolved to die.
And death is the best plan. No one will dispute that.
I want to have my virtues known and honored—
not many witnesses when I do something wrong!
I know what is involved: I know the scandal;
and all too well I know that I am a woman,
object of hate to all. Destruction light
upon the wife who first did shame her bed
by dalliance with strangers. In the wives
of noble houses first this taint began:
when wickedness approves itself to those
of noble birth, it will surely be approved
by their inferiors. Truly, too, I hate
lip-worshippers of purity and temperance, who
own lecherous daring when they have privacy.
O Cypris, sea-born goddess, how can they
look frankly in the faces of their husbands
and never shiver with fear lest their accomplice,
the darkness and the rafters of the house,
take voice and cry aloud?
This then, my friends, is my destruction:

I cannot bear that I should be discovered
a traitor to my husband and my children.
God grant them rich and glorious life in Athens—
famous Athens—freedom in word and deed,
and from their mother an honorable name.
It makes the stoutest-hearted man a slave
if in his soul he knows his parents' shame.
The proverb runs: "There is one thing alone
that stands comparison with life in value,
a quiet conscience," . . . a just and quiet conscience
for whoever can attain it.
Time holds a mirror, as for a young girl,
and sometimes as occasion falls, it shows us
the evildoers of the world. I would not wish
that I should be seen among them.

CHORUS LEADER

How virtue is held lovely everywhere,
and harvests a good name among mankind!

*(Enter the Nurse again.)*

NURSE

Mistress, the trouble you told me just now,
coming on me so suddenly, frightened me;
but now I realize that I was foolish.
In this world second thoughts, it seems, are best.
Your case is not so extraordinary,
beyond thought or reason. The goddess in her anger
has smitten you, and you are in love. What wonder
is this? There are many thousands suffer with you.
So, you will die for love? And all the others,
who love, and who will love, must they die, too?
How will that profit them? The tide of Cypris,
at its full surge, is not withstandable.
Upon the yielding spirit she comes gently,

but if she finds one arrogant and superior
she seizes him and abuses him completely.
Cypris wings her way through the air; she is in the sea,
in its foaming billows; from her everything
that is, is born. For she engenders us
and sows the seed of desire whereof we're born,
all we her children, living on the earth.
He who has read the writings of the ancients
and has spent much time with poetry, knows well
that Zeus once loved the lovely Semele;
he knows that Dawn, the bright light of the world,
once ravished Cephalus hence to the gods' company
for love's sake. Yet they still dwell in heaven
and do not flee in exile from the gods—
they are content, I am sure, to be subdued
by the stroke of love.
But you, you won't submit? Why, you should certainly
have had your father beget you on fixed terms
or with other gods for masters, if you don't like
the laws that rule this world. Tell me, how many
men of good enough sense do you suppose
turn a blind eye to the sickness of their marriage;
how many fathers have helped their erring sons
procure a lover? It is the wise man's part
to leave in darkness everything that is ugly.
We should not in the conduct of our lives
be too exacting. Look, see this roof here—
these overarching beams that span your house—
could builders with all their skill lay them dead straight?
You've fallen into the great sea of love
and with your puny swimming would escape!
If in the sum you have more good than bad,
count yourself fortunate—for you are mortal.
Come on, dear child, give up your wicked thoughts.
Give up your insolence. It's only insolent pride

to wish to be superior to the gods.
Endure your love. A god has willed it so.
Indeed, you are sick. So try to find some means
to turn your sickness into health again.
There are magic love charms, spells of enchantment;
we'll find some remedy for your lovesickness.
Men would take long to hunt devices out,
if we the women did not find them first.

CHORUS LEADER

Phaedra, indeed she speaks more usefully
for this present trouble. But it is you I praise.
And yet my praise brings with it more discomfort
than do her words: it is bitterer to the ear.

PHAEDRA

This is the deadly thing that devastates
well-ordered cities and the homes of men—
this art of all-too-attractive-sounding words.
It's not the words ringing delight in the ear
that one should speak, but those that have the power
to save their hearer's honorable name.

NURSE

This is high moralizing! What you need
is not fine words, but the man! Come, let's be done,
and tell your story frankly and directly.
For if there were not such danger to your life,
or if you were a pure and temperate woman,
I never would have led you on so far,
merely to please your fancy or your lust.
But now a great prize hangs on our endeavors,
and that's the saving of a life—yours, Phaedra!
There's none can blame us for our actions now.

PHAEDRA

What you say is wicked, wicked! Hold your tongue!
I will not hear such shameful words again.

NURSE

Oh, they are shameful! But for you they're better
than noble-sounding moral sentiments.
The deed is better if it saves your life
than your good name in which you die exulting.

PHAEDRA

For the gods' sake, do not proceed any further!
What you say sounds good, but is terrible!
My very soul is subdued by my love
and if you plead the cause of wrong so well
I'll fall into the ruin that now I flee.

NURSE

If that is what you think, ideally, you'd be virtuous;
But if not, you should obey me: that's next best.
It has just come to my mind, I have in the house
some magic love charms. They will end your trouble;
they'll neither harm your honor nor your mind.
They'll end your trouble . . . only you must be brave.
But first we need from him you desire some token—
a lock of his hair or some piece of his clothes—
we'll take this and make one joy out of two.

PHAEDRA

This charm: is it an ointment or a drink?

NURSE

I don't know. Don't be overanxious, child,
to find out what it is. Accept its benefits.

PHAEDRA

I fear you will be too clever for my good.

NURSE

You are afraid of everything. What is it you fear?

PHAEDRA

You surely will not tell this to Theseus' son?

NURSE

Come, let that be: I will arrange all well.
Only, my lady Cypris of the Sea,
be my helper you. The other thoughts I have
I'll tell to those we love within the house;
that will suffice.

*(Exit the Nurse into the house.)*

CHORUS [*singing*]

STROPHE A

*Eros, Eros that distills desire upon the eyes,*
*that brings bewitching grace into the heart*
*of those you would destroy:*
*I pray that you may never come to me*
*with murderous intent,*
*in rhythms measureless and wild.*
*Not fire nor stars have stronger bolts*
*than those of Aphrodite sent*
*by the hand of Eros, Zeus's child.*

ANTISTROPHE A

*In vain, in vain by Alpheus' stream,*
*in the halls of Phoebus' Pythian shrine*
*the land of Greece increases sacrifice.*
*But Eros the king of men we honor not,*
*although he keeps the keys*
*of the temple of desire,*
*although he goes destroying through the world,*
*author of dread calamities*
*and ruin when he enters human hearts.*

STROPHE B

*The untamed Oechalian filly who had never known*
*the bed of love, known neither man nor marriage,*
*the goddess Cypris gave her to Heracles.*
*She took her from the home of Eurytus,*

*maiden unhappy in her marriage song,*
*wild as a Naiad or a Bacchant,*
*with blood and fire, a murderous wedding song!*

ANTISTROPHE B

*O holy walls of Thebes and Dirce's fountain*
*bear witness you, to Cypris' grim journeying:*
*once you saw her bring Semele to bed,*
*lull her to sleep, clasped in the arms of Death,*
*pregnant with Dionysus by the thunder king.*
*Love is like a flitting bee in the world's garden,*
*and for its flowers destruction is in its breath.*

PHAEDRA *(Listening at the door.)*

Women, be silent!
Oh, I am destroyed forever.

CHORUS LEADER

What is there terrible within the house?

PHAEDRA

Hush, let me hear the voices within!

CHORUS LEADER

And I obey. But this is sorrow's prelude.

PHAEDRA

Oh no!
Oh, I am the most miserable of women!

CHORUS [*singing, while Phaedra speaks*]

*What does she mean by her cries?*
*Why does she scream?*
*Tell us the fear-winged word, mistress,*
*rushing upon the heart.*

PHAEDRA

I am lost. Go, women, stand and listen there yourselves
and hear the tumult that falls on the house.

CHORUS

*Mistress, you stand at the door.*
*It is you who can tell us best*
*what happens within the house.*
*Tell me, tell me, what evil has befallen.*

PHAEDRA

It is the son of the horse-loving Amazon,
Hippolytus, cursing my servant maid.

CHORUS

*My ears can catch a sound,*
*but I can hear nothing clear.*
*I can only hear a voice that has come,*
*that has come through the door.*

PHAEDRA

It is plain enough. He cries aloud against
the mischievous bawd who betrays her master's bed.

CHORUS

*Lady, you are betrayed!*
*How can I help you?*
*What was hidden is revealed.*
*You are destroyed.*
*Those you love have betrayed you.*

PHAEDRA

She loved me and she told him of my troubles,
and so has ruined me. She was my doctor,
but her cure has made my illness fatal now.

CHORUS LEADER

What will you do? There is no cure any more.

PHAEDRA

I know of one, and only one—quick death.
That is the only cure for my disease.

*(Enter Hippolytus and the Nurse from the house.)*°

HIPPOLYTUS

O Mother Earth! O Sun and open sky!
What words I have heard from this accursed tongue!

NURSE

Hush, son! Someone may hear you shouting.

HIPPOLYTUS

You cannot expect that I'll hear horror in silence!

NURSE

I beg you, by your strong right hand, don't speak!

HIPPOLYTUS

Don't lay your hand on me! Let go my cloak!

NURSE

By your knees then . . . don't destroy me!

HIPPOLYTUS

What is this?
Don't you declare that you have done nothing wrong?

NURSE

Yes, but the story, son, is not for everyone.

HIPPOLYTUS

Why not? A pleasant tale makes pleasanter telling,
when there are many listeners.

NURSE

You will not break your oath to me, surely you will not?

HIPPOLYTUS

My tongue swore, but my mind was quite unpledged.

NURSE

Son, what would you do? You'll not destroy your friends?

HIPPOLYTUS

"Friends"!
I spit the word away. None of the wicked
are friends of mine.

NURSE

Then pardon, son. It's natural
that we should make mistakes, since we are human.

HIPPOLYTUS

Women! This coin which men find counterfeit!
Why, why, Lord Zeus, did you put them in the world,
in the light of the sun? If you were so determined
to breed the race of man, the source of it
should not have been women. Men might have dedicated
in your own temples images of gold,
iron, or weight of bronze, and thus have bought
the seed of progeny . . . to each been given
his worth in sons according to the assessment
of his gift's value. So we might have lived
in houses free of the taint of women's presence.
But now, to bring this plague into our houses
we destroy° the fortunes of our homes. In this
we have a proof how great a curse is woman.
For the father who begets her, rears her up,
must add a dowry gift to pack her off
to another's house and thus be rid of the load.
And he again that takes the cursed creature
rejoices and enriches his heart's jewel
with dear adornment, beauty heaped on vileness.
With lovely clothes the poor wretch tricks her out
spending the wealth that underprops his house.
For of necessity either one weds well,°
rejoicing in his in-laws, but must keep
a bitter bed; or else his marriage works
but his in-laws are useless, so that benefit
is all he has to counteract misfortune.

That husband has the easiest life whose wife
is a mere nothingness, a simple fool,
uselessly sitting by the fireside.
I hate a clever woman—yes, I pray
that I may never have a wife at home
with more than woman's wits! Lust breeds mischief
in the clever ones. The limits of their minds
deny the stupid ones lecherous delights.
We should not suffer servants to approach them,
but give them as companions voiceless beasts,
dumb—but with teeth, that they might not converse,
and hear another voice in answer.
But now at home the mistress plots the mischief,
and the maid carries it abroad.
So you, vile woman,
came here to me to bargain and to traffic
in the sanctity of my father's marriage bed.
I'll go to a running stream and pour its waters
into my ear to purge away the filth.
Shall I who cannot even hear such impurity,
and feel myself untouched—shall I turn wicked?
Woman, know this. It is my piety saves you.
Had you not caught me off guard and bound
my lips with an oath, by heaven I would not refrain
from telling this to my father.
Now I will go and leave this house until
Theseus returns from his foreign wanderings,
and I'll be silent. But I'll watch you close.
I'll walk with my father step by step and see
how you look at him . . . you and your mistress both.
I have tasted of the daring of your infamy.
I'll know it for the future.° Curses on you!
I'll hate you women, hate and hate and hate you,
and never have enough of hating . . .
Some
say that I talk of this eternally,

yes, but eternal, too, is woman's wickedness.
Either let someone teach them to be temperate,
or allow me to trample on them forever.

*(Exit Hippolytus to the side.)*

PHAEDRA° [*singing*]

ANTISTROPHE

*Bitter indeed is woman's destiny!*
*I have failed. What trick is there now, what cunning plea*
*to loose the knot around my neck?*
*I have had justice. Oh, earth and the sunlight!*
*Where shall I escape from my fate?*
*How shall I hide my trouble, dear friends?*
*What God or man would appear*
*to bear hand or part in my crime?*
*There is a limit to all suffering and I have reached it.*
*I am the unhappiest of women.*

NURSE°

Alas, mistress, all is over now.
your servant's schemes have failed and you are ruined.

PHAEDRA

This is fine service you have rendered me,
corrupted, damned seducer of your friends!
May Zeus, the father of my father's line,
blot you out utterly, raze you from the world
with thunderbolts! Did I not see your purpose,
did I not say to you, "Breathe not a word of this"
which now overwhelms me with shame? But you,
you did not hold back. And so it's without honor
that I will die.
Enough of this. We need a new scheme now.
The anger of Hippolytus is whetted.
He will tell his father all the wrongs you did,
to my disparagement. He will tell old Pittheus, too.
He will fill all the land with my dishonor.

May my curse
light upon you, on you and all the others
who eagerly help unwilling friends to ruin.

NURSE

Mistress, you may well blame my ill success,
for sorrow's bite is master of your judgment.
But I have an answer to make if you will listen.
I reared you up. I am your loyal servant.
I sought a remedy for your love's sickness,
and found . . . not what I sought.
Had I succeeded, I'd have been a wise one.
Our wisdom varies in proportion to
our failure or achievement.

PHAEDRA

So, that's enough
for me? Do I have justice if you deal me
my deathblow and then say "I was wrong: I grant it"?

NURSE

We talk too long. True, I was not wise then.
But even from this desperate plight, my child,
you can escape.

PHAEDRA

You, speak no more to me.
You gave me then dishonorable advice.
And what you tried has brought dishonor too.
Away with you!
Think of yourself. For me and my concerns
I will arrange all well.

*(Exit Nurse into the house.)*

You noble ladies of Troezen, grant me this,
this one request, that what you have heard here
you wrap in silence.

CHORUS LEADER

I swear by holy Artemis, child of Zeus,
never to bring your troubles to the daylight.

PHAEDRA

I thank you. I have found one sole device
in this unhappy business, one alone,
so that I can pass on to my children after me
life with an uncontaminated name,
and myself profit by the present throw
of Fortune's dice. For I will never shame you,
my Cretan home, nor will I go to face
Theseus, defendant on an ugly charge,
never—for one life's sake.

CHORUS LEADER

What is the desperate deed you mean to do,
the deed past cure?

PHAEDRA

To die. But the way of it, that
is what I now must plan.

CHORUS LEADER

Oh, do not speak of it!

PHAEDRA

No, I'll not speak of it. But on this day
when I shake off the burden of this life
I shall delight the goddess who destroys me,
the goddess Cypris.
Bitter will have been the love that conquers me,
but in my death I shall at least bring sorrow
upon another, too, that his high heart
may know no arrogant joy at my life's shipwreck;
he will have his share in this my mortal sickness
and learn to be more temperate himself.

*(Exit Phaedra into the house.)*

CHORUS *[singing]*

STROPHE A

*Would that I were under the cliffs, in the secret hiding places of*
*the rocks,*
*that a god might change me to a wingèd bird*
*and set me among the feathered flocks.*
*I would rise and fly to where the sea*
*washes the Adriatic coast,*
*and to the waters of Eridanus.*
*Into that deep-blue tide,*
*where their father, the Sun, goes down,*
*the unhappy maidens weep*
*tears from their amber-gleaming eyes*
*in pity for Phaethon.*

ANTISTROPHE A

*I would win my way to the coast,*
*apple-bearing Hesperian coast,*
*of which the minstrels sing,*
*where the lord of the ocean*
*denies the voyager further sailing,*
*and fixes the solemn limit of heaven*
*which giant Atlas upholds.*
*There the streams flow with ambrosia*
*by Zeus's bed of love,*
*and holy Earth the giver of life,*
*yields to the gods rich blessedness.*

STROPHE B

*O Cretan ship with the white sails,*
*from a happy home you brought her,*
*my mistress over the tossing foam, over the salty sea*
*to bless her with a marriage unblessed.*
*Black was the omen that sped her here,*

*black was the omen for both her lands,*
*for glorious Athens and her Cretan home,*
*as they bound to Munychia's beach*
*the cables' ends with their twisted strands*
*and stepped ashore on the continent.*

ANTISTROPHE B

*The presage of the omen was true;*
*Aphrodite has broken her spirit*
*with the terrible sickness of impious love.*
*The waves of destruction are over her head,*
*from the roof of her room with its marriage bed,*
*she will tie the twisted noose.*
*And it will go around her fair white neck!*
*She felt shame at her cruel fate.*
*She has chosen good name rather than life:*
*she is easing her heart of its bitter load of love.*

NURSE *(Within.)*

Ho, there, help!
You who are near the palace, help!
My mistress, Theseus' wife, has hanged herself.

CHORUS LEADER

It is done, she is hanged in the dangling rope.
Our queen is dead.

NURSE *(Within.)*

Quick! Someone bring a knife!
Help me cut the knot around her neck.

*(Individual members of the Chorus speak.)*

FIRST WOMAN

What shall we do, friends? Shall we cross the threshold,
and take the queen from the grip of the tight-drawn cords?

SECOND WOMAN

Why should we? There are servants enough within

for that. Where outsiders intervene,
there is no safety.

NURSE (*Within.*)

Lay her out straight, poor lady.
Bitter shall my lord find this housekeeping.

THIRD WOMAN

From what I hear, the queen is dead.
They are already laying out the corpse.

(*Theseus enters from the side.*)

THESEUS

Women, what is this crying in the house?
I heard heavy wailing on the wind,
as it were servants, mourning. And my house
deigns me, a returning envoy, no warm welcome.
The doors are shut against me. Can it be
something has happened to my father? He is old.
His life has traveled a great journey,
but bitter would be his passing from our house.

CHORUS LEADER

Theseus, it's not the old that trouble has struck.
Young is the dead one, and bitterly you'll grieve.

THESEUS

My children . . . has death snatched a life away?

CHORUS LEADER

Your children live—but sorrowfully, King.
Their mother is dead.

THESEUS

It cannot be true, it cannot.
My wife! How could she be dead?

CHORUS LEADER

She herself tied a rope around her neck.

THESEUS

Was it grief and numbing loneliness drove her to it,
or has some misadventure been at work?

CHORUS LEADER

I know no more than this. I, too, came lately
to mourn for you and yours, King Theseus.

THESEUS

Oh,
why did I plait this coronal of leaves,
and crown my head with garlands, I the envoy
who find my journey end in misery?
Servants! Open the doors! Unbar the fastenings,
that I may see this bitter sight, my wife
who killed me in her own death.

*(The door is opened, revealing Phaedra's corpse.)*

CHORUS [*in the following exchange, the Chorus sings, the Chorus Leader speaks, and Theseus sings the lines in italics and speaks the others*]

*Woman unhappy, tortured,*
*your suffering, your death,*
*has shaken this house to its foundations.*
*You were daring, you who died*
*in violence and guilt.*
*Here was a wrestling: your own hand against your life.*
*Who can have cast a shadow on your life?*

THESEUS

STROPHE

*Bitterness of sorrow!*
*Extremest sorrow that a man can suffer!*
Fate, you have ground me and my house to dust,
fate in the form of some ineffable
pollution, some grim spirit of revenge.
*The file has whittled away my life until*
*it is a life no more.*

I am like a swimmer that falls into a great sea:
I cannot cross this towering wave I see before me.
*My wife! I cannot think*
*of anything said or done to drive you to this horrible death.*
You are like a bird that has vanished out of my hand.
You have made a quick leap out of my arms
into the land of Death.
*It must be the sin of one of my ancestors in the dim past*
*gods in their vengeance make me pay now.*

CHORUS LEADER

You are not the only one, King.
Many another as well as you
has lost a noble wife.

THESEUS

ANTISTROPHE

*Darkness beneath the earth, darkness beneath the earth!*
*How good to lie there and be dead,*
now that I have lost you, my dearest companion.
Your death is no less mine.
*Where did this deadly misfortune come from,*
*poor woman, upon your heart?*
Will any of you
tell me what happened?
Or does the palace keep a flock of you for nothing?
*Oh,° the pain I saw in the house!*
I cannot speak of it, I cannot bear it. I am a dead man.
My house is empty and my children orphaned.
*You have left them, left them, you*
*my darling wife—*
*the best of wives*
*of all the sun looks down on or the blazing stars of the night.*

CHORUS

*Woe for the house! Such storms of ill assail it.*
*My eyes are wells of tears and overrun,*
*and still I fear the evil that shall come.*

THESEUS

But wait a moment!
What is this tablet fastened to her dear hand?
Does it want to tell me some news?
Has the poor woman written begging me to care
for our marriage and children?
Sad one, rest confident.
There is no woman in the world who shall come to this house
and sleep by my side.
Look, the familiar golden signet ring,
hers who was once my wife, beckons me!
Come, I will break the seals,
and see what this letter wants to tell me.

CHORUS

*Surely some god*
*brings sorrow upon sorrow in succession.°*
*The house of our lords is destroyed: it is no more.*

CHORUS LEADER

God, if it so may be, hear my prayer.°
Do not destroy this house utterly. I am a prophet:
I can see the omen of coming trouble.

THESEUS

Alas, here is endless sorrow upon sorrow.
It passes speech, passes endurance.

CHORUS LEADER

What is it? Tell us if we may share the story.

THESEUS

*It cries aloud, this tablet, cries aloud,*
*and Death is its song!*
*How shall I escape this weight of evils? I am ruined, destroyed.*
*What a song I have seen, sung in this writing!*

CHORUS LEADER

Ah! Your speech shows a prelude of ruin!

THESEUS

*I shall no longer hold this secret prisoner*
*in the gates of my mouth. It is horrible,*
*yet I will speak.*
*Citizens!*
Hippolytus has dared to rape my wife.
He has dishonored Zeus's holy sunlight.
Father Poseidon, once you gave to me
three curses. . . . Now with one of these, I pray,
kill my son. Suffer him not to escape
this very day, if you have promised truly.

CHORUS LEADER

Call back your curses, King, call back your curses.
Else you will realize that you were wrong
another day, too late. I pray you, trust me.

THESEUS

I will not. And I now make this addition:
I banish him from this land's boundaries.
So fate shall strike him, one way or the other,
either Poseidon will respect my curse,
and send him dead into the house of Hades,
or exiled from this land, a beggar wandering,
on foreign soil, his life shall suck the dregs
of sorrow's cup.

CHORUS LEADER

Here comes your son, at the right moment, King Theseus.
Give over your deadly anger, you will best
determine for the welfare of your house.

*(Enter Hippolytus with cosmpanions from the side.)*

HIPPOLYTUS

I heard you crying, father, and came quickly.
I know no cause why you should mourn.
Tell me.

*(He sees the body of Phaedra.)*

O father, father—I see your wife! She's dead!
I cannot believe it. But a few moments since
I left her. . . . And just now she was still alive.
But what could it be? How did she die, father?
I must hear the truth from you. You say nothing to me?
When you are in trouble is no time for silence.
The heart that would hear everything
is proved most greedy in misfortune's hour.
You should not hide your troubles from your friends,
and, father, those who are closer than your friends.

THESEUS

What fools men are! You work and work for nothing,
you teach ten thousand skills to one another,
invent, discover everything. One thing only
you do not know: one thing you never hunted for—
a way to teach intelligence to fools.

HIPPOLYTUS

Clever indeed
would be the teacher able to compel
the stupid to be wise! But this is no time
for such fine logic chopping.
I am afraid
your tongue runs wild through sorrow.

THESEUS

If there were
some token now, some mark to make the division
clear between friend and friend, the true and the false!
All men should have two voices, one the just voice,
and one as chance would have it. In this way
the treacherous scheming voice would be confuted
by the just, and we should never be deceived.

HIPPOLYTUS

Has some friend poisoned your ear and slandered me?
Am I suspected despite my innocencc?
I am amazed. I am amazed to hear
your words. They are distraught. They go indeed
far wide of the mark!

THESEUS

The mind of man—how far will it advance?
Where will its daring impudence find limits?
If human villainy and human life
shall grow in due proportion during a man's life,
if the one who's later shall always grow in wickedness
past the earlier, the gods must add another
world to this one, to hold all the villains.
   Look at this man! He is my son and he
dishonored my wife's bed! By the dead's testimony
he's clearly proved the vilest, falsest wretch.
Come—since you have already reached depravity—
show me your face; show it to me, your father.
   So you are the veritable holy man?
You walked with gods in purity immaculate?
I'll not believe your arrogant boasts: the gods
are not at all so stupid as you think.
Go, boast that you eat no meat, that you have Orpheus
for your king. Read until you are demented
your great thick books whosc substance is as smoke.
For I have found you out. I tell you all,
avoid such men as he. They hunt their prey
with holy-seeming words, but their designs
are black and ugly. She is dead. You thought
that this would save you? Wretch, it is chiefly that
which proves your guilt. What oath that you can swear,
what speech that you can make for your acquittal,
outweighs her body here? You'll say, to be sure,

she was your enemy and that the bastard son
is always hateful to the legitimate line.
Your words would argue her a foolish merchant
whose stock of merchandise was her own life,
if she should throw away what she held dearest
to gratify her enmity for you.
    Or will you tell me that this frantic folly
is part of woman's nature but a man
is different? Yet I know that young men
are no more to be trusted than are women
when Cypris disturbs the youthful blood in them.
But the very male in them helps and protects them.
But why should I debate against you in words?
Here is the woman dead, the surest witness.
Get from this land with all the speed you can
to exile—may you rot there! Never again
come to our city, god-built Athens, nor
to any land over which my spear is king.
    If I should take this injury at your hands
and pardon you, then Sinis of the Isthmus,
whom once I killed, would vow I never killed him,
but only bragged of the deed. And Sciron's rocks
washed by the sea would call me liar when
I swore I was a terror to ill-doers.

CHORUS LEADER

I cannot say of any man: he is happy.
See here how former happiness lies uprooted!

HIPPOLYTUS

Your furious spirit is terrifying, father:
but this subject, though it's dressed in eloquence,
if you will lay the matter bare of words,
you'll find it is not eloquent. I am
no man to speak with vapid, precious skill
before a mob, although among my equals

and in a narrow circle I am held
not unaccomplished as a speaker.
That is as it should be. The demagogue
who charms a crowd is scorned by wiser judges.
But here in this necessity I must speak.
First I shall take the argument you first
urged as so irrefutable and deadly.
You see the earth and air about you, father?
In all of that there lives no man more pure
or temperate than I, though you deny it.

It is my rule to honor the gods first
and then to have as friends only such men
as try to do no wrong, men who feel shame
at ordering evil or treating others meanly
in return for kindness. I am no mocker
of my companions. Those who are my friends
find me as much their friend when they are absent
as when we are together.

There is one thing that I have never done, the thing
of which you think that you convict me, father.
I am a virgin to this very day.
Save what I have heard or what I have seen in pictures,
I'm ignorant of the deed. Nor do I wish
to see such things, for I've a maiden soul.
But say you disbelieve my temperance.
Then tell me how I came to be corrupted:
was it because she was more beautiful
than all the other women in the world?
Or did I think that by taking her,
I'd win your place and kingdom for a dowry
and live in your own house? I would have been
a fool, a senseless fool, if I had dreamed it.
Was monarchy so sweet? Never, I tell you,
for the wise. A man whom power has so enchanted
must be demented. I would wish to be

first in the athletic contests of the Greeks,
but in the city I'd take second place
and an enduring happy life among
the best society who are my friends.
So one can do what he wants, and danger's absence
has charms above the royal diadem.
But one word more and my defense is finished.
If I possessed a witness to my character,
if I were tried when she still saw the light,
deeds would have helped you as you scanned your friends
to know the true from the false. But now I swear,
I swear to you by Zeus, the god of oaths,
by this deep-rooted fundament of earth,
I never did you wrong with your own wife
nor would have wished or even thought of it.
If I have been a villain, may I die
unfamed, unknown, a homeless stateless beggar,
an exile! May the earth and sea refuse
to take my body in when I am dead!
Out of what fear your wife took her own life
I do not know. More I may not say.
Pure she was in deed, although not pure:
I that have purity have used it to my ruin.

CHORUS LEADER

You have rebutted the charge enough by your oath:
it is a great pledge you took in the gods' name.

THESEUS

Why, here's a spell-binding magician for you!
He wrongs his father and then trusts his craft,
his smooth beguiling craft to lull my anger.

HIPPOLYTUS

Father, I must wonder at this in you.
If I were your father now, and you my son,

I would not have banished you to exile! I
would have killed you if I thought you touched my wife.

THESEUS

This speech is worthy of you: but you'll not die so,
by this rule that you have laid down for yourself.
A quick death is the easiest of ends
for a miserable man. No, you'll go wandering
far from your fatherland and beg your way
in foreign lands, draining dry a bitter life.
This is the payment of the impious man.°

HIPPOLYTUS

What will you do? You will not wait until
time's pointing finger proves me innocent?
Must I then go at once to banishment?

THESEUS

Yes, and had I the power, your place of exile
would be beyond Pontus and Atlas' pillars.
That is the measure of my hate, my son.

HIPPOLYTUS

Pledges, oaths, and oracles—you will not test them?
You will banish me from the kingdom without trial?

THESEUS

This letter here is proof without lot-casting.
As for the birds that fly above my head:
a long good-bye to them.

HIPPOLYTUS

Eternal gods!
Why don't I speak, since I am ruined now
through loyalty to the oath I took by you?
No, he would not believe who should believe,
and I should be false to my oath for nothing.

THESEUS

Here's more of that holy and haughty manner of yours!
I cannot stomach it. Away with you!
Get from this country—and go quickly!

HIPPOLYTUS

Where shall I turn? What friend will take me in,
when I am banished on a charge like this?

THESEUS

Doubtless some man who loves to entertain
a wife's seducer, a housemate in wickedness.

HIPPOLYTUS

That blow went home.
I am near crying when I think that I
am judged to be wicked and that it is you who are judge.

THESEUS

You should have sobbed and thought of that before,
when you resolved to rape your father's wife.

HIPPOLYTUS

My house, if only you could speak for me!
Take voice and testify if I am wicked.

THESEUS

You have a clever trick of citing witnesses
whose testimony is mute. Here is your handiwork.

*(He points to the body.)*

It, too, can't speak—but it convicts you.

HIPPOLYTUS

Ah!
If I could only find
another me to look me in the face
and see my tears and all that I am suffering!

THESEUS

Yes, in self-worship you are certainly practiced.
You are more at home there than in the other virtues,
justice, for instance, and duty toward a father.

HIPPOLYTUS

Unhappy mother mine, and bitter birth pangs,
when you gave me to the world! I would not wish
on any of my friends a bastard's birth.

THESEUS *(To the servants.)*

Drag him away!
Did you not hear me, men, a long time since
proclaiming his decree of banishment?

HIPPOLYTUS

Let one of them touch me at his peril! But you,
you drive me out yourself—if you have the heart!

THESEUS

I'll do it, too, unless you obey my orders.
No pity for your exile will change my heart.

*(Exit Theseus into the house.)*

HIPPOLYTUS

So, I'm condemned and there is no escape.
I know the truth but cannot tell the truth.

*(To the statue of Artemis.)*

Daughter of Leto, dearest of the gods to me,
comrade and partner in the hunt, behold me,
banished from famous Athens.
Farewell, city! Farewell, Erechtheus' land!
Troezen, farewell! So many happy times
you knew to give a young man, growing up.
This is the last time I shall look upon you,
the last time I shall greet you.

*(To his companions.)*

Come friends, you are of my age and of this country,
say your farewells and set me on my way.
You'll never see a man more pure and temperate—
even if my father thinks that I am not.

*(Exit Hippolytus to the side.)*

CHORUS OF HUNTSMEN° [*singing*]

STROPHE A

*The care of the gods for us is a great thing,*
*whenever it comes to my mind:*
*it plucks the burden of sorrow from me.*
*So I have a secret hope of knowledge;*
*but my hopes grow dim when I see*
*the deeds of men and their destinies.*
*For fortune is ever veering, and the currents of men's lives are shifting,*
*wandering forever.*

CHORUS OF WOMEN [*singing*]

ANTISTROPHE A

*This is the lot in life I seek*
*and I pray that the gods may grant it me,*
*luck and prosperity*
*and a heart untroubled by anguish;*
*and a mind that is neither inflexible*
*nor false clipped coin,*
*that I may easily change my ways,*
*my ways of today when tomorrow comes,*
*and so be happy all my life long.*

CHORUS OF HUNTSMEN°

STROPHE B

*My heart is no longer clear:*
*I have seen what I never dreamed.*

*I have seen the brightest star of Athens,°*
*stricken by a father's wrath,*
*banished to an alien land.*
*Sands of the seashore!*
*Thicket of the mountain!*
*Where with his pacing hounds*
*he hunted wild beasts and killed*
*to the honor of holy Dictynna.*

CHORUS OF WOMEN

ANTISTROPHE B

*He will never again mount his car*
*with its span of Venetian mares,*
*nor fill the ring of Limnae with the sound of horses' hoofs.*
*The music that never slept*
*on the strings of his lyre, shall be mute,*
*shall be mute in his father's house.*
*The haunts of the maiden goddess*
*in the deep, rich meadow shall lack their crowns.*
*You are banished: there's an end*
*of the rivalry of maids for your love.*

EPODE

*But my sorrow shall not die;*
*still my eyes shall be wet with tears*
*for your dreadful doom.*
*Sad mother, you bore him in vain;*
*I am angry against the gods.*
*Sister Graces, why did you let him go,*
*guiltless, out of his native land,*
*out of his father's house?*

CHORUS LEADER

But here I see Hippolytus' servant,
in haste making for the house, his face sorrowful.

*(Enter a Messenger° from the side.)*

MESSENGER

Where shall I go to find King Theseus, women?
If you know, tell me. Is he within doors?

CHORUS

Here he is coming out.

MESSENGER

Theseus, I bring you news worthy of distress
for you and all the citizens who live
in Athens' walls and boundaries of Troezen.

THESEUS

What is it? Has some still newer disaster
seized my two neighboring cities?

MESSENGER

Hippolytus is dead: I may almost say dead:
he sees the light of day still, though the balance
that holds him in this world is slight indeed.

THESEUS

Who killed him? I can guess that someone hated him,
whose wife he raped, as he did mine, his father's.

MESSENGER

It was the horses of his own car that killed him,
they, and the curses of your lips,
the curses you invoked against your son,
and prayed the lord of ocean to fulfill them.

THESEUS

O gods—Poseidon, you are then truly
my father! You have heard my prayers!
How did he die? Tell me. How did the beam
of Justice's deadfall strike him, my dishonorer?

MESSENGER

We were combing our horses' coats beside the sea,

where the waves came crashing to the shore. And we were
crying,
for one had come and told us that our master,
Hippolytus, should walk this land no more,
since you had laid hard banishment upon him.
Then he came himself down to the shore to us,
with the same refrain of tears,
and with him walked a countless company
of friends and young men his own age.
But at last he gave over crying and said:
"Why do I rave like this? It is my father
who has commanded and I must obey him.
Prepare my horses, men, and harness them.
For this no longer is a city of mine."
Then every man made haste. Before you could say the words,
we had made the horses ready before our master.
He put his feet into the driver's rings,
and took the reins from the rail into his hands.
But first he folded his hands and prayed the gods:
"Zeus, let me die now, if I have been wicked!
Let my father perceive that he has done me wrong,
whether I live to see the day or not."
With that, he took the goad and touched the horses.
And we his servants followed our master's car,
close by the horses' heads, on the straight road
that leads to Argos and to Epidaurus.
When we were entering the lonely country
the other side of the border, where the shore
goes down to the Saronic Gulf, a rumbling
deep down in the earth, terrible to hear,
roared loudly like the thunder of Father Zeus.
The horses raised their heads, pricked up their ears,
and mighty fear was on us all to know
whence came the sound. As we looked toward the shore,
where the waves were beating, we saw a wave appear,

a miracle wave, lifting its crest to the sky,
so high that Sciron's coast was blotted out
from my eye's vision. And it hid the Isthmus
and the Asclepius Rock. To the shore it came,
swelling, boiling, crashing, casting its surf around,
to where the chariot stood.
But at the very moment when it broke,
the wave threw up a monstrous savage bull.
Its bellowing filled the land, and the land echoed it,
with shuddering emphasis. And for those who saw it
the sight was too great to bear. Then sudden panic
fell on the horses in the car. But the master—
he was used to horses' ways—all his life long
he had been with horses—took firm grip of the reins
and lashed the ends behind his back and pulled
like a sailor at the oar. The horses bolted:
their teeth were clenched upon the fire-forged bit.
They heeded neither the driver's hand nor harness
nor the jointed car. As often as he would turn them
with guiding hand to the soft sand of the shore,
the bull appeared in front to head them off,
maddening the team with terror.
But when in frenzy they charged toward the cliffs,
the bull came galloping beside the rail,
silently following—until he brought disaster,
capsizing the car, striking the wheel on a rock.
Then all was in confusion. The naves of wheels
and axle pins flew up into the air,
and he the unlucky driver, tangled in the reins,
was dragged along in an inextricable
knot, and his dear head pounded on the rocks,
his body bruised. He cried aloud and terrible
his voice rang in our ears: "Stand, horses, stand!
You were fed in my stables. Do not kill me!
My father's curse! His curse! Will none of you
save me? I am a good, true man. Save me!"

Many of us had will enough, but all
were left behind. Cut somehow free of the reins,
he fell. There was still a little life in him.
But the horses vanished and that ill-omened monster,
somewhere, I know not where, in the rough cliffs.
I am only a slave in your household, your majesty,
but I shall never be able to believe
that your son was wicked, not though the race of women
were all hanged for it, not though they filled with writing
the whole of the pine forest on Mount Ida—
for I know that he's a good and noble man.

CHORUS LEADER

It has been fulfilled, this bitter, new disaster:
from what is doomed and fated there's no escape.

THESEUS

For hatred of the sufferer I was glad
at what you told me. Still, he was my son.
As such I have reverence for him and for the gods:
I neither rejoice nor sorrow at these evils.

MESSENGER

What is your pleasure that we do with him?
Would you have him brought to you? If I might counsel,
do not be harsh with your son—now that he's ruined.

THESEUS

Bring him to me that I may see his face.
He swore that he had never wronged my bed.
I'll refute him with the gods' own punishing stroke.

*(Exit Messenger to the side.)*

CHORUS [*singing*]

*Cypris, you guide the inflexible hearts of gods*
*and of men,*
*and with you*
*comes Eros with the flashing wings,*

*with the swiftest of wings.*
*Over the earth he flies*
*and the loud-echoing salt sea.*
*Winged, golden, he bewitches and maddens the heart*
*of the victim he swoops upon.*
*He bewitches the whelps of the mountains*
*and of the sea,*
*and all the creatures that earth feeds,*
*and the blazing sun sees—*
*and men, too—*
*over all you hold royal dominion,*
*Cypris, you are only ruler*
*over all these.*

*(Artemis appears on the roof of the house.)*

ARTEMIS [*chanting*]

*I call on you, noble son of Aegeus,*
*to hear me! It is I,*
*Artemis, child of Leto.*
*Theseus, poor man, what joy have you here?*
*You have murdered your son most impiously.*
*Dark indeed was the conclusion*
*you drew from your wife's lying stories,*
*but plain to see is the destruction*
*to which they led you.*
*There's a hell underground: haste to it,*
*and hide your head there! Or will you take wings,*
*choose the life of a bird instead of a man,*
*keep your feet from treading destruction's path?*
*Among good men, at least, you have no share in life.*

[*speaking*]

Hear, Theseus, how these evils came to pass.
I shall gain nothing, but I'll give you pain.
I've come for this—to show that your son's heart
was always just, so that in his death

his good name may live on. I will show you, too,
the frenzied love that seized your wife, or I may call it
a noble innocence. For that most hated goddess,
hated by all of us whose joy is virginity,
drove her with love's sharp prickings to desire
your son. She tried her best to vanquish Cypris
with the mind's power, but at last against her will
she was destroyed by the nurse's stratagems,
who told your son under oath her mistress loved him.
But he, just man, did not fall in with her
counsels, and even when reviled by you
refused to break the oath that he had pledged.
Such was his piety. But your wife feared
lest she be put to the proof and wrote a letter,
a letter full of lies; and so she killed
your son by treachery; but she convinced you.

THESEUS

Alas!

ARTEMIS

This is a bitter story, Theseus. Stay,
hear further, that you may sorrow all the more.
You know you had three curses from your father,
three, clear for you to use? One you have launched,
vile wretch, at your own son, when you might have
spent it upon an enemy. Your father,
king of the sea, in loving kindness to you
gave you, as he had promised, all he ought.
But you've been proven wicked both in his eyes
and mine in that you did not stay for oaths
nor voice of oracles, nor put to proof,
nor let long time investigate—too quickly
you hurled the curses at your son and killed him.

THESEUS

Mistress, I am destroyed.

ARTEMIS

What you have done indeed is dreadful—but
you still might gain forgiveness for these things.
For it was Cypris managed the thing this way
to gratify her anger against Hippolytus.
This is the settled custom of the gods:
No one may fly in the face of another's wish:
we remain aloof and neutral. Else, I assure you,
had I not feared Zeus, I never would have endured
such shame as this—my best friend among men
killed, and I could do nothing.
As for you, in the first place ignorance acquits you,
and then your wife, by dying, destroyed the chance
to test her words, and thus convinced your mind.
You, Theseus, are the one who suffers most—
misfortune for you, but also grief for me.
The gods do not rejoice when the pious die;
the wicked we destroy, children, house and all.

*(Enter Hippolytus from the side, supported by attendants.)*

CHORUS [*chanting*]

*Here comes the suffering Hippolytus,*
*his fair young body and his golden head*
*a battered wreck. O trouble of the house,*
*what double sorrow from the hand of a god*
*has been fulfilled for this our royal palace!*

HIPPOLYTUS [*chanting*]

*A battered wreck of body! Unjust father,*
*and oracle unjust—this is your work.*
*Woe for my fate!*
*My head is filled with shooting agony,*
*and in my brain there is a leaping fire.*
*Let me be!*
*For I would rest my weary frame awhile.*
*Ah, ah!*

*Curse on my team! How often have I fed you*
*from my own hand—you've killed, you've murdered me!*
*Oh, oh!*
*By the gods, gently! Servants, lay hands*
*lightly on my wounded body.*
*Who is this standing on the right of me?*
*Come lift me carefully, bear me easily,*
*a man unlucky, by my own father cursed*
*in bitter error. Zeus, do you see this,*
*see me that worshipped the gods in piety,*
*me that outdid all men in purity,*
*see me now go to death that gapes before me;*
*all my life lost, and all for nothing,*
*labors of piety in the face of men?*

[*singing*]

*Ah, ah!*
*Oh, the pain, the pain that comes upon me!*
*Let me be, let me be, wretched as I am!*
*May death the healer come for me at last!*
*You kill me ten times over with this pain.*
*O for a spear with a keen cutting edge*
*to shear me apart—and give me my last sleep!*
*Father, your deadly curse!*
*This evil comes from some manslaying of old,*
*some ancient tale of murder among kin.*
*But why should it strike me, who am clear of guilt?*
*Alas!*
*What is there to say? How can I painlessly shake*
*from my life this agony? O death, black night of death,*
*resistless death, come to me now the miserable,*
*and give me sleep!*

ARTEMIS

Unhappy boy! You are yoked to a cruel fate.
The nobility of your mind has proved your ruin.

HIPPOLYTUS [*now speaking*]

Wait!
O divine fragrance! Even in my pain
I sense it, and the suffering is lightened.
The goddess Artemis is in this place.

ARTEMIS

She is, poor man, the dearest god to you.

HIPPOLYTUS

You see my suffering, mistress?

ARTEMIS

I see it. But the law forbids my tears.

HIPPOLYTUS

Gone is your huntsman, gone your servant now.

ARTEMIS

Yes, truly: but you die beloved by me.

HIPPOLYTUS

Gone is your groom, gone your shrine's guardian.

ARTEMIS

Cypris, the worker of mischief, so contrived.

HIPPOLYTUS

Alas, I know now the goddess who destroyed me!

ARTEMIS

She blamed your disrespect, hated your temperance.

HIPPOLYTUS

She is but one—yet ruined all three of us.

ARTEMIS

Yes, you, your father, and his wife, all three.

HIPPOLYTUS

Indeed I'm sorry for my father's suffering.

ARTEMIS

He was deceived by a goddess' cunning snares.

HIPPOLYTUS

O father, this is great sorrow for you!

THESEUS

I am done for; I have no joy left in life.

HIPPOLYTUS

I sorrow for you in this more than for me.

THESEUS

Would that it was I who was dying instead of you!

HIPPOLYTUS

How bitter your father Poseidon's gifts, how bitter!

THESEUS

Would that they had never come into my mouth.

HIPPOLYTUS

Even without them, you would still have killed me—
you were so angry.

THESEUS

Gods tripped up my judgment.

HIPPOLYTUS

O, if only men might be a curse to gods!

ARTEMIS

Enough! Though dead, you'll not be unavenged,
Cypris shall find the angry shafts she hurled
against you shall cost her dear, and this will be
your recompense for piety and goodness.
Another mortal, whichever one she loves
the most, I'll punish with these unerring arrows
shot from my own hand.
To you, unfortunate Hippolytus,
by way of compensation for these ills,

I will give the greatest honors of Troezen.
Unwedded maids before the day of marriage
will cut their hair in your honor. You will reap
through the long cycle of time a rich reward in tears.
And when young girls sing songs, they will not forget you,
your name will not be left unmentioned,
nor Phaedra's love for you remain unsung.

*(To Theseus.)*

Son of old Aegeus, take your son
to your embrace. Draw him to you. Unknowing
you killed him. It is natural for men
to err when they are blinded by the gods.

*(To Hippolytus.)*

And you, don't bear a grudge against your father.
It was your fate that you should die this way.
Farewell, I must not look upon the dead.
My eye must not be polluted by the last
gaspings for breath. I see you are near this.

*(Exit Artemis.)*

HIPPOLYTUS

Farewell to you, too, holy maiden! Go in peace.
You lightly leave a long companionship.
You bid me end my quarrel with my father,
and I obey. In the past, too, I obeyed you.
Ah!
The darkness is upon my eyes already.
Father, lay hold on me and lift me up.

THESEUS

Alas, what are you doing to me, my son?

HIPPOLYTUS

I am dying. I can see the gates of death.

THESEUS

And so you leave me, my hands stained with murder.

HIPPOLYTUS

No, for I free you from all guilt in this.

THESEUS

You will acquit me of blood guiltiness?

HIPPOLYTUS

So help me Artemis of the conquering bow!

THESEUS

Dear son, how noble you have proved to me!

HIPPOLYTUS

Farewell to you, too, father, a long farewell!

THESEUS

Alas for your goodness and your piety.

HIPPOLYTUS

Yes, pray that your trueborn sons will prove as good!

THESEUS

Dear son, bear up. Do not forsake me.

HIPPOLYTUS

This is the end of what I have to bear.
I'm gone, father. Cover my face up quickly.

THESEUS

Pallas Athena's famous city,
what a man you will have lost! Alas for me!
Cypris, your evils I shall long remember.

CHORUS [*chanting*]

*This common grief for all the city,°*
*it came unlooked for. A constant stream*
*of manifold tears will beat down on us;*
*for lamentable stories about the great*
*affect us all the more.*

(*Exit all.*)

# HECUBA

*Translated by* WILLIAM ARROWSMITH

# HECUBA: INTRODUCTION

### *The Play: Date and Composition*

It is not certain when Euripides' *Hecuba* was first produced, but metrical considerations suggest a date of around 424 BCE. Presumably Euripides wrote it for the annual competition at the Great Dionysian Festival in Athens. What the other three plays were in Euripides' tetralogy of that year, and how they fared in the dramatic competition, are unknown.

### *The Myth*

Euripides' *Hecuba* combines two stories from the fall of Troy, both involving the sufferings of its last queen, Hecuba. First her daughter Polyxena is sacrificed by the Greeks to the dead Achilles. Then she learns that her youngest son Polydorus, who had been entrusted for safekeeping to the Thracian king Polymestor, has instead been treacherously murdered by him. Hecuba avenges herself upon Polymestor by blinding him and killing his children; at the end it is foretold that she will be transformed into a dog.

The bloody aftermath of the Trojan War—including the Greeks' sacrifice of Polyxena—was recounted in ancient Greek legend in gruesome detail and was often depicted in ancient Greek art. Euripides himself dramatized these events repeatedly, for example in *Andromache* (written only a year or two before *Hecuba*) and *The Trojan Women* (written less than ten years after *Hecuba*). Of the two stories that make up this play, the one involving Polyxena is likely to have been well known to Euripides' audience from heroic myth and epic poetry, though her willingness to be put to death is a characteristically Euripidean motif and may well have been a surprising innovation. By contrast, there is no trace of anything like Euripides' version of the Polydorus story before this play. In Homer, Polydorus is the youngest son of Priam; however, his mother is not Hecuba but Laothoe, another wife of Priam, and the boy is killed in battle by Achilles. Polymestor does not appear anywhere in Greek legend or art before this play, and his etymologically transparent name ("much-planning") suggests that Euripides may well have invented his character and the whole story that centers on him and Polydorus.

Ancient scholars noted that the story of Polyxena was to be found also in a tragedy by Sophocles titled *Polyxena*. While we do not know the date of this play and only very few fragments of it have survived, it seems to have borne a certain degree of resemblance to Euripides' *Hecuba*. Modern scholars disagree about which play came first and whether, if Sophocles' play preceded Euripides', the older playwright might have influenced Euripides' version of the Polyxena story.

### *Transmission and Reception*

There is plenty of evidence that *Hecuba* was quite popular throughout antiquity, including quotations and allusions by later authors and the survival of at least ten papyri containing fragments of the play. It not only was selected as one of the ten canonical plays most studied and read in antiquity, but together with *Orestes* and *The Phoenician Women* it was included in the so-called Byzantine triad. As a result, it is transmitted by hundreds of medieval manuscripts and is equipped with very full ancient and medieval commentaries. Greek and Latin authors who portrayed Hecuba's sufferings after the fall of Troy inevitably drew upon this play and upon Euripides' *Trojan Women*. Narrative poets like Virgil, Ovid, and Quintus of Smyrna (the Greek author of an epic about the events in the Trojan War that occurred after the end of the *Iliad*; probably late fourth century CE) followed the outlines of Euripides' plot at least in part and presumed their readers' familiarity with his text. The Latin dramatists Ennius, in his tragedy *Hecuba*, and Pacuvius, in his tragedy *Ilione* (both plays are lost), seem to have taken Euripides' play as their model; so too Seneca, in his *Trojan Women*, which has been preserved; and Hecuba eventually became a widely recognized figure of the vicissitudes of fortune. In ancient art, the sacrifice of Polyxena is often represented, other scenes that can be connected with Euripides' *Hecuba* much less so.

The popularity of *Hecuba* in the Greek Middle Ages and the fact that its title is alphabetically the first in the Byzantine triad meant that it was usually the first play of Euripides to be read in medieval Byzantium as well as in the West during the Renaissance. As early as the fourteenth century, the first part of the Greek play was accompanied by an interlinear Latin translation, intended to make the play more accessible, that scholars attribute to Leonzio Pilato, who taught Greek to Petrarch and Boccaccio; and a number of other Latin translations survive, starting in the fifteenth century and culminating in Erasmus' successful metrical version. In the same century, Latin and then vernacular translations began to proliferate; and by the sixteenth century *Hecuba* was the most translated and imitated Greek play of all. Euripides' play was especially admired for its demonstration of the mutability of human circumstances, for its careful dramatic construction, for the polished eloquence of its speeches, and for its excessive violence. For the authors and audiences of Elizabethan and Jacobean revenge tragedies, *Hecuba* was a particularly compelling study of the nature and limits of vengeance. So too, the sacrifice of Polyxena fascinated many European painters starting in the seventeenth century (Pietro da Cortona, before 1625; Nicolas Poussin, ca. 1645–50; Giovanni Francesco Romanelli; Luca Giordano; Giovanni Battista Pittoni).

But by the beginning of the nineteenth century *Hecuba* had entered a period of prolonged disparagement and neglect. August Wilhelm Schlegel's influential Vienna lectures *On Dramatic Art and Literature* (1808) established a view of the play as the worst tragedy by the worst Greek tragedian—indeed as the worst surviving Greek tragedy of all—that dominated for more than a century. The play's portrayal of unrelieved suffering, its lyric excesses, the balanced rhetoric of its speeches, and its claustrophobic focus on Hecuba were regarded as intolerable weaknesses. It required considerable changes in classical scholarship, in modern drama, and not least in our sense of the world as a whole, changes characteristic of the second half of the twentieth century, before *Hecuba* could come back into its own. Only recently has this tragedy begun to recover its prominence, both in the estimation of scholars and as a dramatic force in the theater—and largely because of the very same features that nineteenth-century readers had scorned.

# HECUBA

*Characters*

GHOST OF POLYDORUS, son of Hecuba
HECUBA, queen of Troy
CHORUS of captive Trojan women
POLYXENA, daughter of Hecuba
ODYSSEUS, a Greek leader
TALTHYBIUS, herald of the Greeks
HANDMAID of Hecuba
AGAMEMNON, commander in chief of the Greeks at Troy
POLYMESTOR, king of Thracian Chersonese
SONS of Polymestor (silent characters)

*Scene: The shore of the Thracian Chersonese in front of a tent housing the captive Trojan women. The time is just before dawn.*

*(Enter the Ghost of Polydorus.)*

GHOST OF POLYDORUS

Back from the pit of the dead, from the somber door
that opens into hell, where no god goes,
I have come,
the ghost of Polydorus,
last son of Cisseus' daughter Hecuba
and Priam, king of Troy.
My father, fearing
that Troy might fall to the assembled arms of Hellas,
had me conveyed in secret out of danger
sending me here to Thrace, to Polymestor,

his friend, who rules this plain of Chersonese
and curbs with harsh power a nation of horsemen.
With me my father secretly sent much gold,
intending that, if Troy should someday fall,
his living sons might be provided for.
Being the youngest, I was chosen, still too small
and slight to carry arms or throw a spear.
As long as Troy's fixed border stones stood proud
and unbreached, so long as our towers held intact
and Hector, my brother, prospered in the fighting,
I flourished like a green shoot under the care
of my father's Thracian friend—doomed as I was.
But when Troy fell and Hector died,
and picks and shovels rooted up our hearth,
and there, by the altar that a god once built,
Priam fell, butchered by Achilles' son,
then my father's friend killed me heartlessly
for the gold and threw my body to the sea,
so that he'd have the gold himself at home.
Here, pounded by the surf, my corpse still lies,
carried up and down on the heaving swell of the sea,
unburied and unmourned.
                                        Disembodied now,
I hover as a wraith over my mother's head,
riding for three long days upon the air,
since she left Troy and came here to Chersonese.
Here on the shore of Thrace, in sullen idleness
beside its ships, the whole Greek army sits
and cannot sail. For Achilles' ghost appeared
above his tomb and stopped the Achaean fleet
as they stood out for sea on the journey home.
He demanded my sister Polyxena as prize,
the blood of the living to sweeten a dead man's grave.
And he shall have her, a prize of honor and a gift
bestowed upon him by his friends. On this day
destiny shall take my sister down to death.

And you, poor mother, you must see two corpses,
your two last children, each one dead this day,
my unhappy sister and me—I shall appear,
so that at last my body can be buried,
washed up on shore at the feet of a slave.
These were the favors I asked of the gods below—
to find my mother and be buried by her hands—
and they have granted my request.
Now I go,
for there I see my aged mother coming,
stumbling from Agamemnon's tent, still shaken
by that dream in which she saw my ghost.

*(Enter Hecuba from the tent, accompanied by some Trojan serving women.)*

—O Mother,
fallen from a royal palace to a slave's life,
as wretched now as formerly you were blessed!
It must be that some god destroys you now,
making you pay for having once been happy.

*(Exit Ghost of Polydorus.)*

HECUBA [*chanting*]
*O helplessness of age!*
*Too old, too weak, to stand—*
*Help me, women of Troy.*
*Give this slave those hands*
*you offered to her once*
*when she was queen of Troy.*
*Prop me with your arms*
*and help these useless*
*stumbling legs to walk.*

[*singing*]
*O star of morning,*
*light of Zeus*

*shining in the night!*
*What apparition rose,*
*what shape of terror stalking the darkness?*
*O goddess Earth,*
*womb of dreams*
*with dusky wings!*

*I repel that dream I dreamed!*
*that horror that rose in the night, those phantoms of children,°*
*my son Polydorus in Thrace, Polyxena, my daughter!*
*Call back that vision of horror!*

*O gods of the underworld,*
*preserve my son, save him,*
*the last surviving anchor of my house,*
*still dwelling in the snows of Thrace,*
*still warded by his father's friend!*

*Disaster I dreamed,*
*terror on terror!*
*Never has my heart*
*so shivered with fear!*

*O Helenus, I need you now,*
*interpreter of dreams!*
*Help me, Cassandra,*
*help me read my dreams!*
*I saw a little doe, a dappled doe, torn from between my knees,°*
*cruelly ripped away, mangled by a wolf with blood-red claw!*
*And then fresh terror rose:*
*I saw Achilles' ghost*
*stalk upon his tomb,*
*demanding a prize,*
*one of the wretched women of Troy.*

*O gods, I implore you,*
*beat back this dream,*
*preserve my daughter!*

*(Enter Chorus of captive Trojan women.)*

CHORUS [*chanting*]
*I come to you in haste,*
*Hecuba.*
*I left the tent*
*where the lot assigned us.*
*Slaves, torn from home*
*when Troy was burnt and sacked*
*by the conquering Greeks!*
*I bring you painful news.*
*I cannot lighten your load.*
*I bring you worse to bear.*
*Just now, in full assembly,*
*the Greek decree came down.*
*They voted your daughter must die . . .*
*to be slaughtered alive for Achilles!*
*The sails had been unfurled,*
*and the fleet stood out to sea,*
*when from his tomb Achilles rose,*
*armor blazing, and held them back,*
*crying:*
*"Ho, Argives, where do you sail,*
*leaving my grave unhonored?"*
*Waves of argument broke loose,*
*dividing Greek from Greek.*
*If one man spoke for death,*
*another spoke against it.*
*On your behalf spoke Agamemnon,*
*lover of your daughter,*
*poor, mad Cassandra.*
*Then the two sons of Theseus,*
*twin shoots of Athens, rose and spoke,*
*two speeches with one intent—*
*to crown Achilles' grave*
*with living blood, asking*

*if Cassandra's love meant more*
*than the spear of Achilles.*
*And so the struggle swayed,*
*equally poised—*
*Until he spoke—*
*that hypocrite with honeyed tongue,*
*that demagogue Odysseus.*
*And in the end he won,*
*asking what any slave was worth*
*when laid in the balance*
*with the honor of Achilles.*
*He wouldn't have the dead*
*descending down to Hades*
*telling tales of Greeks,*
*leaving the field of Troy,*
*ungrateful to Greeks*
*who fell for Hellas.*
*Now Odysseus is coming here*
*to tear your daughter from your breast*
*and wrench her from your old arms.*
*Go to the temples!*
*Go to the shrines!*
*Fall at Agamemnon's knees!°*
*Call on heaven's gods!*
*Invoke the gods below!*
*Unless your prayers prevent her death,*
*unless your pleas can keep her safe,*
*then you shall see your child,*
*face downward before the tomb,*
*as the red blood spreads black*
*from her gold-jeweled throat.*

HECUBA [*singing*]

STROPHE

*O grief!*

*What can I say?*
*What are the words for loss?*
*O bitterness of age,*
*slavery not to be borne,*
*unendurable!*
*To whom can I turn?*
*Childless and homeless,*
*my husband murdered,*
*my city stained with fire . . .*
*Where can I go?*
*Where shall I find safety?*
*What god, what power*
*will help me now?*
*O women of Troy,*
*heralds of evil,*
*bringers of loss,*
*this news you bring is my sentence of death.*
*Why should I live? How live in the light*
*when its goodness is gone,*
*when all I have is grief?*
*Bear me up,*
*poor stumbling feet,*
*and take me to the tent.*
*O my child!*
*Polyxena,*
*step from the tent!*
*Come and hear the news*
*your wretched mother brings,*
*this news of horror°*
*that touches your life!*

*(Enter Polyxena from the tent.)*

POLYXENA [*chanting throughout the following interchange with Hecuba, who also chants*]
*That terror in your voice!*

*That cry of fear*
*flushing me forth*
*like a bird in terror!*

HECUBA
*O my child! My baby . . .*

POLYXENA
*Again that ill-omened cry! Why this evil prelude?*

HECUBA
*I am afraid for you—*

POLYXENA
*Tell me the truth now, Mother.*
*I am afraid, I am afraid.*
*Why are you groaning?*

HECUBA
*O my child! My child—*

POLYXENA
*You must tell me, Mother.*

HECUBA
*The Greeks,*
*in full assembly,*
*have decreed your death,*
*a living sacrifice*
*upon Achilles' tomb.*

POLYXENA
*Oh no, Mother, what are you saying?*
*Tell me this horrible evil,*
*tell me, Mother.*

HECUBA
*I tell you, child, ill-omened news,*
*the Argives have voted about your fate.*

POLYXENA [*now singing*]

ANTISTROPHE

*O my poor mother!*
*How I pity you,*
*this brokenhearted life*
*of pain!*
*What god*
*could make you suffer so,*
*impose such pain,*
*such grief in one poor life?*
*Alive, at least*
*I might have shared*
*your slavery with you,*
*my unhappy youth*
*with your miserable age.*
*But now I die,*
*and you must see my death—*
*butchered like a calf,*
*like a wild mountain beast's young,*
*ripped from your arms,°*
*throat cut, and sinking*
*downward into dark*
*with the unconsolable dead.*
[*now chanting again*]
*It is you I pity,°*
*Mother.*
*For you I cry.*
*Not for myself,*
*not for this life*
*whose suffering is such*
*I do not care to live,*
*but call it happiness to die.*

CHORUS LEADER [*speaking*]

Look, Hecuba. Odysseus is coming here
quickly. There must be news.

*(Enter Odysseus from the side, attended by several soldiers.)*

ODYSSEUS

By now, woman,
I think you know what decision the army has taken
and how we voted.
But let me review the facts.
The Greeks have decreed to sacrifice your daughter
Polyxena at the mound of Achilles' tomb.
The army has delegated me to act as escort.
Achilles' son will supervise the rite
and officiate as priest.
There matters rest.
You understand your position? You must not attempt
to hold your daughter here by force, nor,
I might add, presume to match your strength with mine.
Remember your weakness and accept this tragic loss
as best you can.
Under the circumstances,
the logical course is resignation.

HECUBA

O gods,
it seems a great ordeal of suffering is here,
one full of groans and tears.
Why do I live?
I should have died, I now see, long ago.
But Zeus kept me alive instead, poor wretch,
only to suffer, each time to suffer worse
than all the grief that went before.
Odysseus,
if a slave may make inquiries of the free—
without intent to hurt or give offense—
then let me ask some questions of you now
and hear your answers.

ODYSSEUS

Ask me your questions.
I can spare you the time.

HECUBA

Do you remember once
how you came to Troy, a spy, in beggar's disguise,
smeared with filth, in rags, and blood was streaming
from your brows down to your chin?

ODYSSEUS

I remember
the incident. It left its mark on me.

HECUBA

But Helen penetrated your disguise
and told me who you were? Told me alone?

ODYSSEUS

I stood, I remember, in danger of death.

HECUBA

And how humble you were? How you fell at my knees
and begged for life?

ODYSSEUS

And my hand almost froze on your dress.

HECUBA

And you were at my mercy, my slave then.
Do you remember what you said?

ODYSSEUS

Said?
Anything I could. Anything to live.

HECUBA

And I let you have your life? I let you go?

ODYSSEUS

Because of what you did, I live today.

HECUBA

Then can you say that all these plans of yours
are not contemptible? To take from me
what you confess you took, and in return
do everything you can to do me wrong
and ruin me?
O gods, spare me the sight
of this thankless breed, these politicians
who do not care what harm they do their friends,
providing they can please a crowd!
Tell me,
what cleverness can justify their vote
to kill this girl?
Necessity of fate?
But how? What kind of necessity requires
the shedding of human blood upon a grave,
where custom calls for cattle?
Or is it vengeance
that Achilles' ghost demands, death for his death,
and exacts of her? But what has she to do
with his revenge? Who ever hurt him less
than this poor girl? If death is what he wants,
let Helen die. He went to Troy for her;
for her he died.
Or is it merely looks
that you require, some surpassing beauty in a girl
for this fastidious ghost? Then do not look
for loveliness from us. Look to Helen,
loveliest of lovely women on this earth
by far—lovely Helen, who did him harm
far more than we.
So much by way of answer
to the justice of your case.
Now, Odysseus,
I present my claim for your consideration,

my just demand for payment of your debt
of life.
   You admit yourself you took my hand;
you grasped my cheek and begged for life.
                                        But see—

*(Hecuba kneels at the feet of Odysseus and takes his hand.)*

now I touch you in turn as you touched me.
I kneel before you on the ground and beg
for mercy back:
                    Let her stay with me.
Let her live.
Surely there are dead enough
without her death. And everything I lost
lives on in her. This one life
redeems the rest. She is my comfort, my Troy,
my staff, my nurse; she guides me on my way.
She is all I have.
                    And you have power,
Odysseus, greatness and power. But clutch them gently,
use them kindly, and don't suppose, because
you're lucky now, that it will last. It won't.
All greatness goes.
                    I know. I too was great
but I am nothing now. One day
cut down my greatness and my joy.
                                        But I implore you,
Odysseus, be merciful, take pity on me!
Go to the Greeks. Argue, coax them, convince them
that what they do is wrong. Accuse them of murder!
Tell them we are helpless, we are women,
the same women whom they tore from sanctuary
at the altars. But they pitied us, they spared us then.
Plead with them.
                    Read them your law of murder. Tell them how

it applies to slave and free without distinction.
But go.
Even if your arguments were weak,
if you faltered or forgot your words, it would not matter.
That prestige you have will guarantee success.
The same speech has a different effect
spoken by a famous man or by a cipher.

CHORUS LEADER

No man could be so callous or so hard of heart
that he could hear your heartbreak and not weep.

ODYSSEUS

Allow me to give you, Hecuba, some good advice,
and don't in anger think me your enemy.

I readily admit how much I owe you,
and in return I stand ready and willing
to honor my debt by saving your life. Indeed,
I have never suggested otherwise.
But note:
I gave my word that when we captured Troy
your daughter should be given to our best soldier
as a prize upon request. That was my promise,
a solemn public commitment which I intend to keep.
Besides, there is a principle at stake
in whose neglect cities have come to grief,
because their keenest, their most exceptional men
received no greater honor than the common run.
And Achilles deserves our honor far more than most,
a great man and a great soldier who died greatly
for his country.
Tell me, what conduct could be worse
than to give your friend a lifetime of honor and respect
but neglect him when he dies?
And what then,

if war should come again and we enlist our citizens
to serve? Would we fight or would we save our skins,
seeing that dead men get no honor?
No:
for my lifetime give me nothing more than what I need;
I ask no more. But as regards my grave,
I hope for honor, since that gratitude
lasts for a lengthy time.
You speak of pity,
but I can talk of pity too. Pity us,
pity our old people, those men and women in Greece
no less miserable than you, the brides and parents
of all those brave young men who found a grave
in the dust of Troy.
Endure; bear your losses,
and if you think me wrong to honor courage
in a man, then call me callous.
But what of you,
barbarians who refuse your dead their rights
and break your faith with friends? And then you wonder
that Hellas should prosper while your countries suffer
the fate they deserve!

CHORUS LEADER

This is what it means
to be a slave: to be abused and bear it,
compelled by violence to suffer wrong.

HECUBA

O my child,
all my prayers are lost, thrown away
on the empty air!
So try your powers now.
Implore him, use every skill that pity has,
every voice. Be like the nightingale,
touch him, move him! Fall at his knees,

beg him for life!
For he has children too
and may pity them in you.

POLYXENA

I see your hand,
Odysseus, hidden in the folds of your robes and your face
averted, lest I try to touch your chin
and beg for life.
Have no fear. You are safe
from me.
I shall not call on Zeus who helps
the helpless.
I shall not beg for life.
No:
I go with you because I must, but most
because I wish to die. If I refuse,
I prove myself a coward, in love with life.
But why should I live?
I had a father once,
king of all Phrygia. And so I started life,
a princess of the blood, nourished on lovely hopes
to be a bride for kings—that suitors would come
competing for my hand, while over the maidens
and women of Troy, I stood acknowledged mistress,
among the girls equal to a goddess,
though bound by death.
And now I am a slave.
It is that name of slave, so ugly, so strange,
that makes me want to die. Or should I live
to be sold to some pitiless new master
for cash? Sister of Hector, sister of princes,
at work in the kitchen, standing by the loom,
and scrubbing the floors, compelled to drag out
endless weary days? And the bride of kings,
forced by some low slave from god knows where

to share his filthy bed?
Never.
With eyes still free, I now renounce the light
and dedicate myself to death.
Odysseus,
lead me off. For I see nothing in this life
to give me hope, and nothing here at all
worth living for.
As for you, Mother,
do nothing, say nothing now to hinder me.
Help me instead; help me to die, now,
before I live disgraced.
I am a novice
to miseries, whose yoke I might endure,
but with such pain that I prefer to die
than go on living badly.

CHORUS LEADER

Noble birth
is a stamp, conspicuous, awesome, among mortals.
And nobility's name grows greater with worthy actions.

HECUBA

I am proud of you, my child, but anguish sticks
in these fine words.
If your Achilles
must have his victim, Odysseus, if you
have any care for your own honor left,
then let her live. Let me take her place
upon the tomb; kill me; be merciless
to me, not her. For I gave birth to Paris
whose arrows brought Achilles down.

ODYSSEUS

The ghost
demanded this girl's blood, not yours,
old woman.

HECUBA

Then let me die with her at least,
and we shall be a double drink of blood
for earth and this demanding ghost below.

ODYSSEUS

Your daughter's death will do. We should not pile
one on another. If only we did not need
this one!

HECUBA

But I must die with her! I must!

ODYSSEUS

Must? A strong word, Hecuba. It was my impression
I was the master here.

HECUBA

I shall stick to her
like ivy to the oak.

ODYSSEUS

Take my advice, Hecuba.
For your own good, do not.

HECUBA

Never, never
will I let her go.

ODYSSEUS

While I, for my part,
refuse to leave her here.

POLYXENA

Mother, listen.
And you, Odysseus, be gentle with a mother's love.
She has reasons for her anger.

Poor Mother,
do not struggle with those stronger than you.
Is this what you want—to be thrown down in the dust,

this poor old body torn away from me,
humiliated by younger and stronger arms?
They will do it. No, this is not for you.
O Mother, Mother,
give me your hand,
and put your cheek to mine for one last time
and then no more. For the last, last time
I look upon this gleaming circle of the sun
and speak the last words I shall ever say.
O Mother, Mother,
now I go below!

HECUBA

Leaving me to live, a slave in the light!°

POLYXENA

Unmarried to my death, no wedding songs for me!

HECUBA

Pity for you, and wretchedness for me!

POLYXENA

To lie in the dark in Hades, far from you!

HECUBA

O gods, where can I go? Where shall I die?

POLYXENA

I was born to freedom and I die a slave.

HECUBA

Fifty children I once had, and all are dead.

POLYXENA

What message shall I take to Hector and old Priam?

HECUBA

Tell them this: I am the queen of sorrow.

POLYXENA

O sweet breasts that nourished me!

HECUBA

So wrong, so wrong! So young to die!

POLYXENA

Farewell, Cassandra! Mother, farewell!

HECUBA

Let others fare well. I never shall.

POLYXENA

Goodbye, Polydorus, my brother in Thrace!

HECUBA

If he lives at all—for all I have is loss.

POLYXENA

He lives. He will close your dying eyes.

HECUBA

I have died of sorrow while I was still alive.

POLYXENA

Shroud my head, Odysseus, and lead me out.
Even before I die, my cries have broken
my mother's heart, and she has broken mine.
O light of day!
I still can cry the light
in that little space of life I have to live
before I die upon Achilles' tomb!

*(Exit Odysseus and Polyxena to the side.)*

HECUBA

I am faint—my legs give way beneath me—
Polyxena!
Touch your mother, give me your hand,
reach me! Do not leave me childless!
My friends,
I've been destroyed. If only I could see
Helen of Sparta, sister of Zeus' sons,

destroyed like me. For she with her fair eyes
made ashes of the happiness of Troy!

CHORUS [*singing*]

STROPHE A

*O wind of ocean,*
*wind that blows on the sea*
*and drives the scudding ships,*
*where are you blowing me?*
*Where shall I be slave?*
*Where is there home for me?*
*There in distant Doris,*
*or in Phthia far away*
*where men say Apidanus runs,*
*father of waters, river whose lovely flowing*
*fattens the fields?*

ANTISTROPHE A

*Or there in the islands?*
*The salt sea churning, borne on by oars,*
*to days of mourning in the house,*
*there where the primal palm*
*and the bay broke out their leaves*
*for lovely Leto*
*in honor of her son?*
*There shall I sing*
*with the maidens of Delos,*
*praising Artemis'*
*bow and fillets of gold?*

STROPHE B

*Or in the city of Pallas,*
*in Athens, shall I yoke*
*the horses on the goddess' robe,*
*stitching cloth of saffron*
*with threads of every color,*
*sewing the Titans there,*

*who were killed by stabbing fire,*
*the thunderbolts of Zeus?*

ANTISTROPHE B

*O my children!*
*O my forefathers!*
*O city, ruined land,*
*ashes and smoke, wasted*
*by the spear of the Argives!*
*I live, but live a slave,*
*forced to a foreign land,*
*torn westward out of Asia,*
*exchanging the chambers of death*
*for a home in Europe!*

*(Enter Talthybius from the side.)*

TALTHYBIUS

Women of Troy, where can I find Hecuba,
your onetime queen?

CHORUS LEADER

There she lies, Talthybius,
in the dust at your feet, her head buried in her robes.

TALTHYBIUS

O Zeus, what can I say?
That you look on mankind
and care?
Or do we, holding that the gods exist,
deceive ourselves with unsubstantial lies
while chance controls the world?
Is this the queen
of Troy once rich in gold? Is this the wife
of Priam the great?
And now, childless, old,
enslaved, her home and city wrecked by war,
she lies there on the ground, her wretched head
fouled in the dust.

Oh horror! I am old,
but I would rather die than sink as low
as this poor woman has fallen now.
Rise,
unhappy lady. Lift your body up,
and raise your white-haired head.

HECUBA

Who are you
who will not let me lie? Who disturbs
my wretchedness? Why?

TALTHYBIUS

I am Talthybius,
servant of the Greeks, lady. I bring you a message
from Agamemnon.

HECUBA

Have the Greeks decreed my death?
Tell me that, and you are welcome, dearest man.
No other news could please me better now.
Let's go in haste. You lead the way, old man.

TALTHYBIUS

No, not that.
I come on behalf of the army and the sons of Atreus
to bid you bury your daughter. She is dead.

HECUBA

Is that your news, herald?
So I cannot die?
You came to tell me this?
O gods, my child!
My poor child! Torn from my arms! Dead!
Dead. Without you, I now am childless.
So how did you all put her to death? With honor
and respect, or did you kill her savagely,
as an enemy? Tell me, old man. Let me hear it all,
no matter how it hurts.

TALTHYBIUS

There is a cost
in telling too, a double price of tears,
for I was crying when your daughter died,
and I will cry again while telling you,
lady. But listen.
The whole army of the Greeks
was present for your daughter's sacrifice,
and Achilles' son took Polyxena's hand
and led her up the tomb. I stood nearby;
with them, a troop of soldiers purposely appointed
to prevent her struggles.
Then Achilles' son
lifted a golden beaker to pour the offering
of wine to his dead father and nodded to me
to call for silence.
"Quiet, Achaeans!" I shouted,
"Silence in the ranks! Keep quiet!" A hush
fell upon the army and he began to pray:
"Father Achilles, Peleus' son, receive
this offering I pour to summon your spirit up.
Rise and drink this gift we give to you,
this virgin's dark blood. Be gracious to us:
set free our ships and loose our mooring ropes.
Grant to us all our day of coming home,
grant us all to come home safe from Troy!"
So he prayed, and the army with him.
Then,
grasping the hilt of his gilded sword, he drew it
from the sheath, and nodded to the chosen youths
to seize her. But she spoke first:
"Wait, you Greeks
who sacked my city! Of my own free will I die.
Let no man touch me. I offer my throat
bravely to the sword. But by the gods,
let me be free for now. Let me die free.

I am of royal blood, and I scorn to be called
a slave among the dead."
"Yes!" the army roared,
and Agamemnon told the young men to let her go.
And they, when they had heard the final decree°
of the man with highest authority, let go.
When she heard the rulers' words she grasped her robes
and ripped them open from the shoulder down
as far as the waist, exposing her naked breasts,
bare and lovely like a sculptured goddess.
Then she sank, kneeling on the ground, and gave
this most heroic speech:
"Strike, captain.
Here is my breast. Will you stab me there?
Or in the neck? Here is my throat, ready
for your blow."
Torn between pity and duty,
Achilles' son stood hesitating, and then
slashed her throat with the edge of his sword. The blood
gushed out, and she fell, dying, to the ground,
but even as she dropped, managed to fall somehow
with grace, modestly hiding what should be hidden
from men's eyes.
The execution finished,
the soldiers set to work. Some scattered leaves
upon her corpse, while others brought big logs
of pine and heaped her pyre. Those who shirked
found themselves abused by the rest.
"You loafers,"
they shouted, "how can you stand there empty-handed,
doing nothing? Where's your present for the girl?
When did you ever see greater courage
than that?"
And now you know it all.
For my part,
having seen your daughter die, I count you

of all women the one most blessed in her children
and also the unhappiest.

CHORUS LEADER

Blow after blow
disaster drops from heaven; suffering shakes
my city and the house of Priam.

HECUBA

O my child,
how shall I deal with this thronging crowd of blows,
these sufferings, each with its petition, clamoring
for attention? If I lay my hand on one,
another shoulders in, and then a third
comes on, distracting, each fresh sorrow
breeding new successors in its turn.
But now,
although I can't forget your death, can't stop
crying—
yet a kind of comfort comes in knowing
how nobly you died.
And yet how strange it seems.
Even worthless ground, given a gentle push
from heaven, will harvest well, while fertile soil,
starved of what it needs, bears badly.
But human nature never seems to change;
ignoble stays itself, bad to the end;
and nobility good, its nature uncorrupted
by any shock or blow, always the same,
enduring excellence.
Is it in our blood°
or something we acquire? But goodness can be taught,
and any man who knows what goodness is
knows evil too, because he judges
from the good.
But all this is the rambling nonsense
of despair.

Talthybius, go to the Greeks
and tell them this from me: that not a hand
is to be laid on my child; make them keep
the crowd away.
For in armies the size of this,
men are prone to violence, sailors undisciplined
worse than a fire, while the man who stands apart
is called a coward.

*(Exit Talthybius to the side.)*

—Take your pitcher, old servant,
fill it with water from the sea and then return.
I must give my daughter's body its last bath
before her burial, this wedding which is death.
For she marries Achilles, and I must bathe the bride
and lay her out—not as she deserves, but as well
as I can.
But how? I've nothing precious left.
What then?
I'll gather from my women in the tent
whatever poor trinkets they managed to pilfer
from their own homes.

*(Exit Handmaid to the side.)*

Where is greatness gone?
Where is it now, that stately house, the home
that was so happy once? King Priam,
blessed with children once, in your pride of wealth?
And what am I of all I used to be,
mother of sons, mother of princes?
Gone,
all gone, and nothing left.
Now who
will boast, be proud, or plume his confidence—
the rich man in his insolence of wealth,
the public man's conceit of office or success?

For we are nothing; our ambition, greatness, pride,
all vanity.
That man is happiest
who lives from day to day and asks no more,
garnering no evil in his simple life.

*(Exit Hecuba into the tent.)*

CHORUS [*singing*]

STROPHE

*That morning was my fate,*
*that hour doom was done,*
*when Paris felled the tree*
*that grew on Ida's height*
*and made a ship for sea*
*and sailed to Helen's bed—*
*loveliest of women*
*the golden sun has seen.*

ANTISTROPHE

*Grief, and worse than grief,*
*necessity surrounds us.*
*One man's folly made*
*a doom shared by all,*
*ruin over Simois.*
*Paris sat as judge*
*upon three goddesses.*
*His verdict was war.*

EPODE

*War, slaughter, and the ruin of my house,*
*while in her house the Spartan girl mourns too,*
*grieving by the wide Eurotas,*
*and mothers mourn for their sons,*
*and tear out their snowy hair*
*and dredge their cheeks with bloody nails.*

*(Enter the Handmaid from the side.)*

HANDMAID

Where is the queen, women?
Where is Hecuba
whose sufferings outstrip all rival runners?
No one shall take that crown away.

CHORUS LEADER

Speak.
What new sorrow do you bring her? Will all this news
of anguish never sleep?

*(Enter other women, carrying on a bier a shrouded corpse.)*

HANDMAID

This is the grief
I bring to Hecuba. Gentle words are hard
to find: the burden I bring is disaster.

*(Enter Hecuba from the tent.)*

CHORUS LEADER

Look: here she's coming now from out the tent,
she's just in time to hear your news.

HANDMAID

My queen,
more wretched, more miserable than I can say.
Now you live no more, the light is gone!
No child, no husband, no city—utterly ruined!

HECUBA

This is mockery, not news. I know it all.
But why have you brought Polyxena's body here?
I heard the Greeks were busied with her funeral.

HANDMAID

Poor woman, she thinks it is Polyxena.
She does not know the worst.

HECUBA

O gods, no!

Not my poor mad daughter, Cassandra?

HANDMAID

Cassandra is alive. Mourn for this dead boy.

*(She strips the shroud from the corpse, revealing the dead Polydorus.)*

Look at this corpse that I uncover now,
this unexpected horror.

HECUBA

It is my son!

Polydorus, warded by my friend in Thrace!
No!
O gods in heaven, let me die!
[*singing; the Handmaid and the Chorus Leader speak in reply*]
*O my son, my son,*
*now the awful dirge begins,*
*the fiend, the fury,*
*singing, wailing in me now,*
*shrieking madness!*

HANDMAID

So now, poor woman, you've seen your child is dead?

HECUBA

*Horror too sudden to be believed,*
*unbelievable loss,*
*blow after blow!*
*And this is all my life:*
*the mourning endless,*
*the anguish unending.*

CHORUS LEADER

Dreadful, poor woman, the evils that we suffer.

HECUBA

*O my son, my child,*

*how were you killed?*
*What fate, what hand*
*could take your life?*

HANDMAID

I do not know. I found him on the shore.

HECUBA

*Drowned, his body washed on the sand?*
*Or was he murdered?*

HANDMAID

The surf had washed his body up.

HECUBA

*O gods, my dream!*
*I see it now,*
*those black wings beating the dark,*
*its message has not missed me,*
*you live no longer in Zeus' light!*

CHORUS LEADER

Who murdered him? Did your dream show you that?

HECUBA

*Who but my friend, horseman in Thrace,*
*where his father hid him away from harm?*

CHORUS LEADER

Murdered? Murdered by a friend? Killed for gold?

HECUBA

*Unspeakable, unimaginable crime,*
*unbearable!*
*Where is friendship now?*
*O fiend, monster, so pitiless,*
*to mangle him so, to hack*
*his sweet flesh with the sword!*

CHORUS LEADER

Unhappy Hecuba, most miserable of mortals

upon this earth, how heavily some god
falls on you.
—But look: I see your master,
Agamemnon, coming here. So we'll be silent.

*(Enter Agamemnon from the side with attendants.)*

AGAMEMNON

Why this delay of yours, Hecuba,
in burying your daughter? I received your message
from Talthybius that none of our men should touch her,
and I gave strict orders to that effect.
Hence I found your delay all the more surprising
and came to fetch you myself. In any case,
I can report that matters there are well in hand
and proceeding nicely—if a word like "nicely"
has any meaning in this connection.

*(He sees the corpse of Polydorus.)*

Here,
what's that Trojan corpse beside the tents?
I can see from his clothes that he's not a Greek.

*(Hecuba turns away from him.)*

HECUBA *(Aside.)*

Poor Hecuba—it's I that I mean now,
saying "you"—what shall I do?
Throw myself
at his knees and beg for mercy or hold my tongue
and suffer in silence?

AGAMEMNON

Why do you turn away
in silence? And what's the meaning of these tears?
What happened here? Who is this man?

HECUBA (*Aside.*)

But suppose he treats me like an enemy slave,
and pushes me away? I could not bear it.

AGAMEMNON

I am not a prophet, Hecuba. Unless you speak,
you make it quite impossible for me to help you.

HECUBA (*Aside.*)

And yet I could be wrong. Am I imagining?
He may mean well.

AGAMEMNON

If you have nothing to say,
Hecuba, very well. I have no wish to hear.

HECUBA (*Aside.*)

But without his help I lose my only chance
of revenging my children. So why should I hesitate?
Win or lose, he is my only hope.

(*She turns to Agamemnon and falls at his knees.*)

Agamemnon, I implore you, I beg you
by your chin, your knees, by this conquering hand, help me!

AGAMEMNON

What can I do to help you, Hecuba? Your freedom
is yours for the asking.

HECUBA

No, not freedom.
Revenge. Only give me my revenge
and I'll gladly stay a slave the rest of my life.

AGAMEMNON

Well, what's the help you're asking me for?

HECUBA

My lord,
not the revenge you think, not that at all.
Do you see this body here for which I mourn?

AGAMEMNON

I see him—but I don't see what this means.

HECUBA

This was my son. I gave him birth.

AGAMEMNON

Which son,
poor woman?

HECUBA

Not one of Priam's sons who died
in Troy.

AGAMEMNON

You mean you had another son?

HECUBA

Another son, in vain. This was he.

AGAMEMNON

But where was he living when Troy was taken?

HECUBA

His father sent him away to save his life.

AGAMEMNON

This was the only son he sent away?
Where did he send him?

HECUBA

Here. To this country
where his body was found.

AGAMEMNON

He sent him to Polymestor,
the king of Thrace?

HECUBA

And with his son he also sent
a sum of fatal gold.

AGAMEMNON

But how did he die? Who killed him?

HECUBA

Who else
could it have been? His host, our Thracian friend.

AGAMEMNON

Then his motive, you think, was the gold?

HECUBA

Yes.
The instant he heard that Troy had fallen, he killed.

AGAMEMNON

But where was the body found? Who brought him here?

HECUBA

This woman servant here. She found his body
lying on the beach.

AGAMEMNON

What was she doing there?
Searching for him?

HECUBA

No. She went for water
for Polyxena's burial.

AGAMEMNON

He must have killed him first,
then thrown his body in the sea.

HECUBA

Hacked him, tossed him
to the pounding surf.

AGAMEMNON

I pity you, Hecuba.
Your suffering has no end.

HECUBA

I died
long ago. Nothing can touch me now.

AGAMEMNON

What woman on this earth was ever cursed
like this?

HECUBA

There is none but goddess Fortune
herself.
But let me tell you why I kneel
at your feet. And if my sufferings seem just,
then I must be content. But if otherwise,
give me my revenge on that treacherous friend
who flouted every god in heaven and in hell
to do this impious murder.
At our table°
he was our frequent guest; was counted first
among our friends, respected, honored by me,
receiving every kindness that a man could meet—
and then, in cold deliberation, killed
my son.
Murder may have its reasons, its motives,
but he even refused my son a grave and threw him
to the sea, unburied!
I am a slave, I know,
and slaves are weak. But the gods are strong, and over them
there stands the law that governs all. It is
by virtue of this law that we believe
the gods exist, and by this law we live,
distinguishing good from evil.

Apply that law
now. For if you flout it, so that those
who murder their own guests or defy the gods
go unpunished, then human justice withers,
corrupted at its source.
Honor my request,
Agamemnon.
Punish this murder.
Pity me.
Be like a painter. Stand back, see me
in perspective,
see me whole, observe
my wretchedness—
once a queen, and now
a slave; blessed with children, happy once,
now old, no children, no city, utterly alone,
unhappiest of mortals . . .

*(Agamemnon turns away.)*

O no! You turn away—
what can I do? My only hope is lost.
O this helplessness!
Why, why
do we make so much of knowledge, struggle so hard
to get some skill, quite rightly, at many things,
but persuasion, the only art whose power
is absolute, worth any price we pay,
the sole ruler over human minds, by which
we persuade others and gain what we want—persuasion
we totally neglect. And so we fail;
we lose our hopes.
I have seen my children die,
and bound to shame I walk this homeless earth,
a slave, and see the smoke that leaps up
over Troy.

It may be futile now
to urge the claims of love, but let me urge them
anyway. At your side sleeps my daughter
Cassandra, once the priestess of Apollo.
What will you give, my lord, for those nights of love?
What thanks for all her tenderness in bed
does she receive from you, and I, in turn,
for her?°
Look now at this dead boy,
Cassandra's brother. Help him, and you help
your brother-in-law. Revenge him.
One word more.
If by some magic, some gift of the gods,
I could become all speech—tongues in my arms,
hands that talked, voices from my hair and feet—
then, all together, I'd fall and touch your knees,
crying, begging, imploring with a thousand tongues—
O master, greatest light of Hellas, hear me,
help an old woman, though she's worth nothing, avenge her!
You must do your duty as a man of honor:
see justice done. Punish the murderer.

CHORUS LEADER

How strange in their reversals are our lives!
The laws of harsh necessity° decide,
joining enemies in common cause
and alienating friends.

AGAMEMNON

I pity you deeply,
Hecuba, for the terrible death of this poor boy.
And I am moved by your fortunes and suppliant hand.
So far as justice is concerned, the gods know well,
nothing would please me more than to bring
this murderer to book.
But my position
here is delicate. If I give you your revenge,

the army is sure to charge that I connived
at the death of the king of Thrace because of my love
for Cassandra. This is my dilemma. The army
thinks of Polymestor as its friend,
this boy as its enemy—if to me° he's precious,
that's irrelevant and no matter to the Greeks.
Put yourself in my position.
Believe me,
Hecuba, I should like to act on your behalf
and would come instantly to your defense.
But if the army complains, then I must
be slow.

HECUBA

Then no man on earth is truly free.
All are slaves of money or necessity.
Or public opinion or fear of prosecution
prevents each one from doing what he thinks
is right.
But since your fears make you defer
to the mob, let me, a slave, set you free
from what you fear.
Be my confidant,
the silent partner of my plot to kill my son's
murderer. Give me your passive support.
Then if some uproar breaks out or the Greeks
attempt a rescue, obstruct them covertly
without appearing to act for me.
For the rest,
have no fear. I shall manage.

AGAMEMNON

How?
Poison? Or do you think your agèd hand
could lift a sword and kill? Who would help you?
On whom could you count?

HECUBA

Remember: Trojan women
are hidden in these tents.

AGAMEMNON

You mean our prisoners?

HECUBA

They will help me get revenge.

AGAMEMNON

But women?
Women overpower men?

HECUBA

There's dreadful power
in numbers, when they are combined with cunning.

AGAMEMNON

True,
though I admit to being skeptical of women
in a matter like this.

HECUBA

Why?

Women killed
Aegyptus' sons. Women emptied Lemnos
of its males: they murdered every one. And so
it shall be here. Let's bandy no more words,
and let this woman here have your safe-conduct
through the army.

*(Agamemnon nods. Hecuba turns to the Handmaid.)*

Go to our Thracian friend
and give him this message:
"Hecuba, once queen of Troy,
summons you on business that concerns you both
and requests you bring your sons. They also share
in what she has to say."

*(Exit Handmaid with one or more of Agamemnon's attendants to the side.)*

One more favor,
Agamemnon.
Defer my daughter's funeral
until my son's corpse can be placed beside her
on the pyre. Let them burn together,
brother and sister joined in a single flame,
their mother's double grief.

AGAMEMNON

As you wish.
If we could sail, I could not grant this. But now,
until the god sends us a favoring wind,
we must ride at anchor here and wait to sail.
May things turn out well! The common interests
of states and individuals alike demand
that good men prosper and evil men be punished.

*(Exit Agamemnon to the side, followed by attendants. Exit Hecuba and her women into the tent with the body of Polydorus.)*

CHORUS [*singing*]

STROPHE A

*O Ilium! O my country,*
*whose name men speak no more*
*among unfallen cities!*
*So dense a cloud of Greeks*
*came, spear on spear, destroying!*
*Your crown of towers shorn away,*
*and everywhere the staining smoke,*
*most pitiful. O Ilium,*
*whose streets I shall not walk again!*

ANTISTROPHE A

*At midnight came my doom,*
*midnight when the feast is done*

*and sleep falls sweetly on the eyes.*
*The songs and sacrifice,*
*the dances, all were done.*
*My husband lay asleep,*
*his spear upon the wall,*
*on Ilium's peak,*
*no longer seeing the ships*
*massed on Ilium's shore.*

STROPHE B

*I was setting my hair*
*in the soft folds of the net,*
*gazing at the endless light*
*deep in the golden mirror,*
*preparing myself for bed,*
*when tumult broke the air*
*and shouts and cries*
*shattered the empty streets—*
*"Onward, onward, you Greeks!*
*Sack the city of Troy*
*and see your homes once more!"*

ANTISTROPHE B

*Dressed only in one gown*
*like a girl of Sparta,*
*I left the bed of love*
*and prayed to Artemis.*
*But the answer was, "No."*
*I saw my husband lying dead,*
*and they took me away to the sea.*
*Backward I looked at Troy,*
*as the ship sped on*
*and Ilium slipped away,*
*and I was dumb with grief.*

EPODE

*A curse on Helen,*
*sister of the sons of Zeus,*

*and my curse on him,*
*disastrous Paris,*
*whose wedding wasted my Troy*
*and banished me from my home!*
*No marriage but a curse, the curse of some demon!*
*Let the salty sea*
*never bring her home!*
*Let there be no return*
*for Helen of Troy!*

*(Enter Polymestor from the side, followed by his two young sons, the Handmaid, and several attendants. Hecuba keeps her eyes fixed on the ground.)*

POLYMESTOR

Dearest Hecuba, wife of my dear friend,
poor unhappy Priam!°
How I pity you,
you and your ruined Troy. And now this latest blow,
your daughter's death . . .
What can we take on trust
in this uncertain life? Happiness, greatness,
fame—nothing is secure, nothing keeps.
The inconsistent gods make chaos of our lives,
pitching us about with such savagery of change
that we, out of our anguish and uncertainty,
may turn to them.
But how does my sorrow help?
Your loss remains.
But perhaps you are angry with me, Hecuba,
for not coming to you earlier. If so, forgive me.
It just so happened that I was inland, in the middle
of Thrace, at the time when you arrived. In fact,
I was on the point of coming here myself
when your servant arrived and gave me your message.
Needless to say, I lost no time.

HECUBA

Polymestor,
I am so embarrassed by the state in which you see me,
fallen so low since when you saw me last,
I cannot look you in the face.
Forgive it,
and do not think me rude, Polymestor.
In any case, habit and custom excuse me,°
forbidding that a woman look directly at a man.

POLYMESTOR

I quite understand.
Now, how can I help you?
You sent for me on some business, I believe?

HECUBA

I have a matter to discuss with you and your sons.
But privately, if possible.
Could you ask your men
to withdraw?

POLYMESTOR *(To his attendants.)*

You may leave. There is no danger here.
This woman is my friend and the army of the Greeks
is well disposed.

*(Exit his attendants to the side.)*

Now, Hecuba, to business.
How can I, your prosperous friend, help you now
in your time of troubles? I am ready.

HECUBA

First
one question. How's my son Polydorus, your ward?
Is he alive?
Anything else can wait.

POLYMESTOR

Alive and well. In this respect at least,
you may put your mind at rest.

HECUBA

My dearest friend,
how like you your kindness is!

POLYMESTOR

What else
would give you comfort?

HECUBA

Does he still remember his mother?

POLYMESTOR

So much that he wanted to run away
and visit you in secret.

HECUBA

And the gold from Troy?
Is it safe?

POLYMESTOR

Quite safe. Locked in my palace
under strong guard.

HECUBA

Guard it well, my friend.
Do not let it tempt you.

POLYMESTOR

Have no fears.
I hope that what I have myself will stand
me in good stead.

HECUBA

Do you know why I sent for you
and your sons?

POLYMESTOR

Not yet. We are waiting to hear.

HECUBA

You are my friend, a friend for whom I feel
no less love than you have shown to me.
And my business concerns . . .

POLYMESTOR

Yes? Yes? Go on.

HECUBA

. . . the ancient vaults, the gold of Priam's house.

POLYMESTOR

I am to pass this information to your son?

HECUBA

In person. I know you for a man of honor.

POLYMESTOR

But why did you ask that my sons be present?

HECUBA

I thought they should know. Something, for instance,
might happen to you.

POLYMESTOR

A prudent precaution.
I quite agree.

HECUBA

Do you know where Athena's temple
once stood in Troy?

POLYMESTOR

The gold is there?
Is there a marker?

HECUBA

A black rock jutting up
above the ground.

POLYMESTOR

Is that all?

HECUBA

No:
my money. I smuggled some money away from Troy.
Could you keep it for me?

POLYMESTOR

You have it on you?
Where is it hidden?

HECUBA

There, inside the tent,
beneath a heap of spoils.

POLYMESTOR

Inside the tent?
Here, in the Greek camp?

HECUBA

The women's quarters
are separate from the main camp.

POLYMESTOR

Is it safe?
Are there men around?

HECUBA

No Greeks; only women.
But come inside. We have no time to lose.
Quick.
The Greek army is waiting and eager
to raise their anchors and sail for home.
Then,
when our business here is done, you may go
and take your children where you left my son.

*(Exit Polymestor and his sons, accompanied by Hecuba, into the tent.)*

CHORUS LEADER

Death is life's debt. Perhaps now yours falls due.

CHORUS [*singing*]

*As though you stumbled in the surf*
*hurled from high ambition down*
*trapped, thrashing with terror*
*in the swirling tow*
*and the water*
*closing overhead*
*until*
*you drown.*
*And now you know:*
*Those who take a life—*
*repay it with their own.*
*Justice and the gods*
*exact the loan at last.*
*Your hopes for this road misled you.*
*You took the final turn*
*where the bitter road veers off*
*and runs downhill*
*to death!*
*Hands which never held a sword*
*shall wrench your twisted life away!*

*(Screams and commotion are heard from inside the tent.)*

POLYMESTOR *(From within.)*

Blind! Blind!
O light!
Light of my eyes!

CHORUS LEADER

That scream of anguish! Did you hear, my friends?

POLYMESTOR *(From within.)*

Help!
Look out, children!

Murder!

Run! Murder!

CHORUS LEADER

New murder, fresh horror in the tent!

POLYMESTOR *(From within.)*

Run! Will you run?
But I'll get you yet!
I'll batter down this tent with my bare fists!
See there, a heavy fist has launched its blow!°

CHORUS LEADER

What should we do?
Break down the door?
Hurry!
Hecuba needs our help!

*(Enter Hecuba from the tent.)*

HECUBA

Pound away!
Go on, batter down the door!
Nothing can ever give you back the light
of your eyes.
Never shall you see your sons
alive again. For I have killed them both!

CHORUS LEADER

Have you done it? Have you felled your Thracian host
and rule him now? Have you done this thing you say?

HECUBA

Be patient a moment, and then see for yourself.
Watch him as he stumbles and staggers out of the tent—
stone-blind.
See the bodies of his two sons,
killed by my women and me.
His debt is paid

and I have my revenge.

But hush: here he comes,

raging from the tent. Let me keep out of his reach.
In his Thracian fury he will stop at nothing.

*(Enter Polymestor blinded from the tent on all fours. His sons' bodies are visible in the doorway of the tent.)*

POLYMESTOR [*singing*]

*Where?*
*Where shall I run?*
*Where shall I stop?*
*Where?*
*Like a raging beast I go,*
*running on all fours*
*on my hands on the track!*
*Where?*
*Where?*
*Here?*
*Where?*
*Where can I pounce*
*on those murderous hags of Troy?*
*Where are you, women?*
*Where are they hiding,*
*those bitches of Troy?*

*O god of the sun,*
*heal these bleeding eyes!*
*Give me back the light of my eyes!*
*Shh.*
*The sound of footsteps.*
*But where?*
*Where can I leap?*
*To gorge their blood,*
*to rip the living flesh,*
*feed like a starving beast,*

*blood for blood, outrage for outrage!*
*No, no.*
*Where am I running now?*
*My children abandoned,*
*for Bacchants of hell to claw,*
*for savage bitches to gorge,*
*their mangled bodies thrown*
*pitilessly on the hill!*
*But where?*
*Where shall I run?*
*Where can I stand at bay?*
*Run, run, run,*
*gather robes and run!*
*Let me run for my lair,*
*race like a ship,*
*sails furled, for the shore!*
*I'll run for my lair*
*and stand at bay*
*where my children lie!*

CHORUS LEADER
Tormented man! Tortured past enduring.
You suffer now as you made others suffer.°

POLYMESTOR [*singing*]
*Help me, you men of Thrace!*
*Help!*
*Soldiers, horsemen,*
*help! Come with spears!*
*Achaeans, help! Help me,*
*sons of Atreus!*
*Help!*
*Help!*
*Hear me, help me, help!*
*Where are you?*
*Help me!*

*Women have destroyed me.*
*Dreadful sufferings!*
*Butchery! Horror!*
*Help me!*
*Help!*
*Where can I go?*
*Where can I run?*
*You gods in heaven,*
*give me wings to fly!*
*Let me leap to heaven*
*where the vaulted stars,*
*Sirius and Orion,*
*flare out their fire,*
*or plunge to Hades*
*on the blackened flood!*

CHORUS LEADER

Who could reproach this man for wanting to die?
Death is what men want when the anguish of living
is more than they can bear.

*(Enter Agamemnon from the side, attended by soldiers.)*

AGAMEMNON

Shouting and screams
of terror brought me here. Ringing Echo,
born of the mountain crags, resounded the cries
throughout the camp. Unless we knew for a fact
that Troy had fallen to our arms, this uproar
could have caused no little terror or disturbance.

POLYMESTOR

That voice! I know it.
My friend, Agamemnon!
Look, look at me now!

AGAMEMNON

Oh. Awful sight!
Poor Polymestor! Those blind bleeding eyes,

those dead children . . . Who did this, Polymestor?
Whoever it was must have hated you and your sons
with savage anger.

POLYMESTOR

Hecuba. She did it,
she and the other women. They destroyed me,
they worse than destroyed me.

AGAMEMNON

You, Hecuba?
Do you admit this hideous, inhuman crime?
Is this atrocity your work?

POLYMESTOR

Hecuba?
Is she near?
Where? Tell me where she is,
and I'll claw her to pieces with these bare hands!

AGAMEMNON

What? Have you lost your mind?

POLYMESTOR

For the gods' sake,
let me at her! Let me rip her limb from limb!

AGAMEMNON

Stop.
No more of this barbarian savagery now.
Each of you will give his version of the case
and I shall try to judge you both impartially.

POLYMESTOR

Then listen, Agamemnon.
Hecuba had a son
called Polydorus, her youngest. His father Priam,
apprehensive that Troy would one day be taken,
sent the boy to me to be raised in my own house.

I killed him, and I admit it.
My action, however,
was dictated, as you shall see, by a policy
of wise precaution.
My primary motive was fear,
fear that if this boy, your enemy, survived,
he might someday found a second and resurgent Troy.
Further, when the Greeks heard that Priam's son
was still alive, I feared that they would raise
a second expedition against this new Troy,
in which case these fertile plains of Thrace
would once again be ravaged by war; once again
Troy and her troubles would work her neighbors harm,
as they have done just now.
Hecuba, however,
somehow hearing that her son was dead,
lured me here on the pretext of revealing
the secret hiding place of Priam's gold
in Troy. Then, alleging that we might be overheard,
she led my sons and me, all unattended,
into the tent.
Surrounded by Trojan women
on every side, I sat down on a couch.
The atmosphere seemed one of friendliness.
The women fingered my robes, then lifted the cloth
to inspect it better under the light, exclaiming
over the quality of our Thracian weaving.
Still others stood admiring my two lances
and before I knew it I was stripped of all
my weaponry.
Meanwhile the young mothers
were fussing over my children, jouncing them in their arms
with hugs and kisses and passing them from hand to hand
until they were out of reach.
Then, incredibly,
out of that scene of domestic peace,

they suddenly pulled daggers from their robes
and butchered both my sons, while troops of women
rushed to tackle me, seizing my arms and legs
and holding me down. I tried to leap up
but they caught me by the hair and pulled me down.
I fought to free my arms, but I was swamped
beneath a flood of women. I could not move.
And then they crowned their hideous work with worse,
the most inhuman brutal crime of all.
They took their brooches and stabbed my hapless eyes
till they poured out blood! Then they ran for cover,
scattering through the tent. I leaped to my feet,
like a wounded animal chasing a pack of hounds,
tracking along every wall, like a hunter
beating and striking everywhere.
                    This is my reward, Agamemnon,
for my efforts in disposing of your enemy.
One word more.
                    On behalf of all those dead
who learned their hatred of women long ago,
for those who hate them now, for those unborn
who shall live to hate them yet, I now declare
my firm conviction:
                    neither earth nor ocean
produces a creature as savage and as monstrous
as woman. Any man who has ever met one
will know that this is true.

CHORUS LEADER

                    Do not presume,
Polymestor, whatever your provocation,
to include all women in this sweeping curse
without distinction.°

HECUBA

                    The clear actions of a man,
Agamemnon, should speak louder than any words.

Good words should get their goodness from our lives;
the evil that we do should show in speech
and never make injustice sound attractive.
Some men, I know, make a science of such persuasion,
but in the end their speciousness will show.
The impostors are punished; not one escapes
his downfall.
So much by way of beginning.
Now for him.

*(To Polymestor.)*

You claim you killed my son
on behalf of Agamemnon, and to spare
the Greeks the horrors of a second war.
You liar!
First, what possible friendship could there be
between civilized Greeks and barbarians
like you?
Clearly none.
Then why this zeal
to serve their cause?
Are you related to them?
Or would you be by marriage?
Then what's your motive?
Fear, you say, that they would sail for Troy
and ravage the harvest of your land again.
Who could believe that preposterous lie?
No,
if you'd speak the truth, it was gold and your greed
that killed my son.
For tell me: why, when Troy
still flourished and its ramparts ringed the city,
when Priam was alive and Hector had his day—
why, if you wanted to be Agamemnon's friend,
did you not then kill my son or hand him over
alive to the Greeks? It would have been so easy—

you were keeping and raising him in your house.
But no.
You waited, biding your time, until our sun
had set, and the smoke announced the sack of Troy.
Then you moved, killing your guest and friend
who sat at your hearth.
And what of this,
which shows your crime for what it was?
Why,
if you loved the Greeks as much as you assert,
did you miss your chance to present them with the gold—
that gold you claim does not belong to you
but to Agamemnon? For they were desperate then,
long years away from home.
But no. Even now
you cannot bear the thought of giving up
the gold, but hoard it for yourself at home.
Another point.
If you had done your duty
by my son, raised him and kept him safe,
men would honor and respect you as a noble friend.
For real friendship is shown in times of trouble;
prosperity has friends galore.
And then,
if someday you had stood in need of help
and if my son had prospered he'd have been
a mighty treasury for you. Instead,
you've killed your friend, your gold is worthless now,
your sons are dead, and you are as you are.

*(To Agamemnon.)*

Agamemnon, this is what I say to you:
if you assist this man, you prove yourself
unjust.
This is a man who betrayed his trust,
who killed against the laws of man and god,

faithless, evil, corrupt.
Assist him now
and we shall say the same is true of you.
But you are my master: I criticize no further.

CHORUS LEADER

Ah, true it is: for mortals, a good cause
will always find good arguments to back it.

AGAMEMNON

It does not give me any satisfaction
to sit as judge on the miseries of others.
But I should cut a sorry figure in the world
if I took on this case and then refused
to give a verdict.
Know then, Polymestor,
I find you guilty of murder as charged.
You murdered your ward, killed him in cold blood,
and not, as you assert, for the Greeks or me,
but out of simple greed, to get his gold.
You then construed the facts to fit your case.
Perhaps you think it but a trifling matter
to kill a guest.
Well, we Greeks call it murder.
How, therefore, could I acquit you now
without incurring blame among men?
I could not.
You committed a brutal crime; therefore accept
the consequences of your act.

POLYMESTOR

Oh no!
Defeated by a slave woman! I shall be
punished by my inferiors, it seems.

HECUBA

But justly so, since you committed evil.

POLYMESTOR

O my children!
And O light of my eyes!

HECUBA

It hurts, does it? And what of me? I mourn
my child too.

POLYMESTOR

Does it give you pleasure
to mock at me?

HECUBA

I rejoice in my revenge.

POLYMESTOR

Enjoy it now. You shall not enjoy it long.
Hear my prediction.
I foretell the seawaters . . .

HECUBA

Shall carry me on ship across to Greece?

POLYMESTOR

. . . shall drown you, after you fall from the masthead.

HECUBA

Who will force me to jump?

POLYMESTOR

You shall climb the mast
of your own free will . . .

HECUBA

Climb the mast? With wings?

POLYMESTOR

. . . changed to a dog, a bitch with blazing eyes.

HECUBA

How do you know of this transformation?

POLYMESTOR

Because our Thracian prophet, Dionysus,
told me so.

HECUBA

He neglected, I see, to foretell
your own woes.

POLYMESTOR

True: had he told my future then,
I never would have fallen into your trap.

HECUBA

Does the prophecy say I'll live or die?

POLYMESTOR

You'll die.
And when you die your tomb shall then be called . . .

HECUBA

In memory of my change, perhaps? Please tell me!

POLYMESTOR

. . . Cynossema, "the bitch's grave," a landmark
to sailors.

HECUBA

What do I care how I die?
I have my revenge.

POLYMESTOR

And your daughter Cassandra
must also die . . .

HECUBA

I spit your prophecies back.
Use them on yourself.

POLYMESTOR

. . . killed by this man's wife,
cut down by the bitter keeper of his house.

HECUBA

Clytemnestra? May she never be so crazed!

POLYMESTOR

Yes, she will lift the deadly axe on high
and kill this man, her husband, too.

AGAMEMNON

You're mad!
Are you asking for more trouble?

POLYMESTOR

Kill me,
but a bath of blood waits for you in Argos.

AGAMEMNON

Slaves, carry him off! Drag him away!

POLYMESTOR

Have I touched you now?

AGAMEMNON

Stop him. Gag his mouth.

POLYMESTOR

Gag me. I have spoken.

AGAMEMNON

Take him away
this instant.
Then throw him on some desert island
since his tongue cannot stop its impudence.

*(Exit Polymestor to the side escorted by attendants.)*

As for you, Hecuba, go now and bury
your two dead children.
You other Trojan women,
go to your masters' tents. For now I see
the sudden wind sits freshly in our sails.
May heaven grant that our ordeal is done

at last!
May all be well at home in Argos!

*(Exit Agamemnon with remaining attendants to the side, Hecuba and her women with the corpse of Polydorus into the tent.)*

CHORUS [*chanting*]
*File to the tents,*
*file to the harbor.*
*There we embark*
*on life as slaves.*
*Necessity is harsh.*
*Fate has no reprieve.*

# ELECTRA

Translated by EMILY TOWNSEND VERMEULE

# ELECTRA: INTRODUCTION

*The Play: Date and Composition*

There is no external evidence available for determining when Euripides' *Electra* was first produced. The play used to be dated to 413 BCE on the basis of a presumed allusion near its end to an episode in Athens' expedition against Sicily in that year, but more recently scholars have grown wary of this kind of argument and prefer to use the play's meter to date it, which would place it around 420 BCE. Presumably Euripides wrote it for the annual competition at the Great Dionysian Festival in Athens. What the other three plays were in Euripides' tetralogy of that year, and how they fared in the competition, are unknown.

*The Myth*

*Electra* presents an episode from the tragic vicissitudes of the house of the Pelopids, the royal dynasty of Argos (or Mycenae): Agamemnon, his wife Clytemnestra, her lover Aegisthus, and her children Iphigenia, Electra, and Orestes. After Agamemnon returned from Troy, Clytemnestra and Aegisthus murdered him. The action of Euripides' play begins some years later. Aegisthus and Clytemnestra are still in power; Orestes has been hiding in exile; in what is surely a surprising Euripidean innovation, Electra has been married off to a local farmer to ensure that she will not bear children of high enough status to avenge her father's murder. After the beginning of the play introduces us to Electra and the farmer, Orestes returns from exile with his companion Pylades and is recognized by Electra. By the play's end, with the help of his sister, Orestes has succeeded in killing first Aegisthus, then their mother, Clytemnestra.

Euripides' *Electra* dramatizes one of the most popular stories in all of Greek tragedy. Euripides himself returned repeatedly to this mythic complex to treat other episodes from it, in *Iphigenia among the Taurians* (written ca. 414 BCE), *Orestes* (produced 408 BCE), and *Iphigenia in Aulis* (produced posthumously after 406 BCE). The same events that serve as the basis for Euripides' play also formed the subject of Aeschylus' surviving trilogy the *Oresteia*—it is its second play, *The Libation Bearers*, that bears closest comparison to Euripides' *Electra*—and Euripides' tragedy seems to make a number of obvious references, some of them apparently quite polemical, to Aeschylus' version. Furthermore, Sophocles dealt with exactly the same material in his *Electra*, which has also survived but cannot be dated precisely. There are evident similarities and no less evident differences between Sophocles' and Euripides' plays, and for centuries scholars have argued inconclusively about which play preceded—and may have influenced—the other. But only internal evidence is available, and it is slight and slippery. The question remains open.

### *Transmission and Reception*

*Electra* was not one of Euripides' most popular plays in antiquity, in contrast to his enormously popular *Orestes*, but it has become increasingly influential in recent years, especially because of its obvious allusions and contrasts to Aeschylus' *Oresteia*. It survived antiquity only by the accident of being among the so-called "alphabetic plays" (see "Introduction to Euripides" in this volume, p. 571). Like the others in this group, it comes down to us only by a single manuscript in rather poor condition (and by its copies) and it is not accompanied by the ancient commentaries (scholia) that explain various kinds of interpretative difficulties. Further evidence that it was not very popular in antiquity is that only two papyri bearing parts of its text have been discovered. The play has left little or no trace in ancient pictorial art.

While the story of Orestes' vengeance on Clytemnestra and Aegisthus has never ceased to fascinate authors and audiences in all literary genres and other media, it is hard to find clear cases in which it is specifically Euripides' tragedy—rather than Aeschylus' or Sophocles'—that has influenced a later version. Since the Renaissance it has tended to be Sophocles' tragedy, or, especially since the nineteenth century, Aeschylus' trilogy, that has been preferred. Some of the few twentieth-century texts that display the direct influence of Euripides' tragedy are Maurice Baring's play *After Euripides' "Electra"* (1911), Robinson Jeffers' dramatic poem *The Tower beyond Tragedy* (1926, adapted for the stage 1950), Richard Aldington's poem "Troy's Down" (1943), Michael Cacoyannis' film *Elektra* with Irene Papas and music by Mikis Theodorakis (1962), Hugo Claus' tragedy *Orestes* (1976), and Suzuki Tadashi's Japanese adaptation *Clytemnestra* (1980).

# ELECTRA

*Characters*

FARMER, married to Electra
ELECTRA, daughter of Agamemnon and Clytemnestra
ORESTES, son of Agamemnon and Clytemnestra
PYLADES, a friend of Orestes (nonspeaking)
CHORUS of Argive peasant women
OLD MAN
MESSENGER, a servant of Orestes
CLYTEMNESTRA, widow of Agamemnon, mother of Electra and Orestes
CASTOR and POLYDEUCES (the Dioscuri), Clytemnestra's brothers

*Scene: In front of the Farmer's cottage in the countryside near Argos; before the house stands an altar to Apollo.*

FARMER

Argos, old bright floor of the world,° Inachus' pouring
tides—King Agamemnon once on a thousand ships
hoisted the war god here and sailed across to Troy.
He killed the monarch of the land of Ilium,
Priam; he sacked the glorious city of Dardanus;
he came home to Argos here and high on the towering
  shrines
nailed up the massive loot of Barbary for the gods.
So, over there he did well. But in his own house

he died in ambush planned for him by his own wife
Clytemnestra and by her lover Aegisthus' hand.
He lost the ancient scepter of Tantalus; he is dead.
Thyestes' son Aegisthus walks king in the land
and keeps the dead man's wife for himself, Tyndareus' child.
As for the children he left home when he sailed to Troy,
his son Orestes and his flowering girl Electra,
Orestes almost died under Aegisthus' fist,
but his father's ancient servant snatched the boy away,
gave him to Strophius to bring up in the land of Phocis.
Electra kept on waiting within her father's house.
But when the burning season of young ripeness took her,
then the great princes of the land of Greece came begging
her bridal. Aegisthus was afraid—afraid her son
if noble in blood would punish Agamemnon's death.
He held her in the house sundered from every love.
Yet, even guarded so, she filled his nights with fear
lest she in secret to some prince might still bear sons;
he laid his plans to kill her. But her mother, though
savage in soul, then saved her from Aegisthus' hand.
The lady had excuse for murdering her husband
but flinched from killing a child, afraid of the world's ill will.
So then Aegisthus framed a new design. He swore
to any man who captured Agamemnon's son
running in exile and murdered him, a price of gold.
Electra—he gave her to me as a gift, to hold
her as my wife.
Now, I was born of Mycenaean
family, on this ground I have nothing to be ashamed of,
in breeding I shine bright enough. But in my fortune
I rank as a pauper, which blots out all decent blood.
He gave her to me, a weak man, to weaken his own fear,
for if a man of high position had taken her
he might have roused awake the sleeping Agamemnon's
blood—justice might have knocked at Aegisthus' door.
I have not touched her and the love god Cypris knows it:

I never shamed the girl in bed, she is still virgin.
I would feel ugly taking the daughter of a wealthy man
and violating her. I was not bred to such an honor.
And poor laboring Orestes, my brother-in-law in name—
I suffer his grief, I think his thoughts, if he came home
to Argos and saw his sister so unlucky in her wedding.
   Whoever says that I am a born fool to keep
a young girl in my house and never touch her body,
I say he measures wisdom by a crooked line
of morals. He should know he's as great a fool as I.

*(Enter Electra from the house, carrying a water jar on her head.)*

ELECTRA

O night, black night, whose breast nurses the golden stars,
I wander through your darkness, head lifted to bear
this pot I carry to the sources of the river—
I do not need to, I chose this slavery myself
to demonstrate to the gods Aegisthus' outrageousness—
and cry my pain to Father in the great bright air.
For my own mother, she, Tyndareus' deadly daughter,
has thrown me out like dirt from the house, to her husband's
   joy,
and while she breeds new children in Aegisthus' bed
has made me and Orestes mere appendages to the house.

FARMER

Now why, unhappy girl, must you for my sake wrestle
such heavy work though you were raised in comfort?
Although I tell you often to stop, you just refuse.

ELECTRA

I think you equal to the gods in kindliness:
for you've never taken advantage of me though I'm in
   trouble.
It's great fortune for people to find a kind physician
of suffering, which I have found in finding you.
Indeed without your bidding I should make your labor

as light as I have strength for; you will bear it better
if I claim some share with you in the work. Outdoors
you have enough to do; my place is in the house,
to keep it tidy. When a man comes in from work
it is nice to find his hearthplace looking swept and clean.

FARMER

Well, if your heart is set on helping, go. The spring
is not so distant from the house. At light of dawn
I will put the cows to pasture and start planting the fields.
A lazy man may rustle gods upon his tongue
but never makes a living if he will not work.

*(Exit Farmer and Electra to the side. Enter Orestes and Pylades from the other side, with attendants.)*

ORESTES

Pylades, I consider you the first of men
in loyalty and love to me, my host and friend.
You only of my friends gave honor and respect
to me, Orestes, suffering as I suffer from Aegisthus.
He killed my father—he and my destructive mother.
I come from secret converse with the holy god
to this outpost of Argos—no one knows I am here—
to counterchange my father's death for death to his killers.
During the night just passed I found my father's tomb,
gave him my tears in gift and sheared my hair in mourning,
and sprinkled ceremonial sheep's blood on the fire,
holding these rites concealed from the tyrants who rule here.
  I will not set my foot inside the city walls.
I chose this gatepost of the land deliberately,
compacting a double purpose. First, if any lookout
should recognize me I can run for foreign soil;
second, to find my sister. For they say she married
and, tamed to domestic love, lives here no longer virgin.
I want to be with her and take her as my partner
in killing, and learn more about things inside the city.

And now, since lady dawn is lifting her white face,
let's come away from the path on which we have been
treading.
Perhaps a field-bound farmer or some serving woman
will meet us on the road, and we can ask discreetly
whether my sister lives anywhere in this place.
Quick now! I see some sort of serving girl approach
with a jar of fountain water on her close-cropped head—
it looks heavy for her. Let's sit here, let us listen
to the slave girl. Pylades, perhaps at last we shall hear
the news we hoped for when we crossed into this land.

*(They hide behind the altar. Enter Electra from the side.)*

ELECTRA [*singing*]

STROPHE A

*Quicken the foot's rush—time has struck—O*
*walk now, walk now weeping aloud,*
*O for my grief!*
*I was bred Agamemnon's child,*
*formed in the flesh of Clytemnestra,*
*Tyndareus' hellish daughter,*
*Argos' people have named me true:*
*wretched Electra.*
*Cry, cry for my toil and pain,*
*cry for the hatred of living.*
*Father who in the halls of death*
*lie hacked by your wife and Aegisthus, O*
*Agamemnon!*

MESODE A

*Come, waken the mourning again,*
*rouse up for me the sweetness of tears.*

ANTISTROPHE A

*Quicken the foot's rush—time has struck—*
*walk now, walk now weeping aloud,*
*O for my grief!*

*In what city and in what house, O*
*brother of grief, do you wander in exile?°*
*You left me locked in the cursed*
*palace chambers for doom to strike*
*your sister in sorrow.*
*Come, loose me from miseries, come*
*save me, pitiful me—O Zeus,*
*Zeus!—to help avenge our father's hate-spilled blood,*
*steering your exiled foot to land*
*in Argos.*

STROPHE B

*Set this vessel down from my head, O*
*take it, while I lift music of mourning*
*by night to my father.*
*Father, the maenad song of death°*
*I cry you among the dead*
*beneath the earth, the words I pour*
*day after day unending*
*as I move, ripping my throat with sharp*
*nails, fists pounding my shorn*
*head for your dying.*

MESODE B

*Ai, ai, strike my head!*
*I, like the swan of echoing song*
*in descant note at the water's edge*
*who calls to its father so dearly loved*
*but dead now in the hidden net*
*of twisted meshes, mourn you thus*
*in agony dying, father,*

ANTISTROPHE B

*body steeped in the final bath,*
*rest most pitiful, sleep of death.*
*O for my grief!*
*Bitter the axe and bitter the gash,*

*bitter the road you walked°*
*from Troy straight to their plotted net—*
*your lady did not receive you*
*with victor's ribbons or flowers to crown you,*
*but with double-edged steel she made you*
*savage sport for Aegisthus, and won*
*herself a shifty lover.*

*(Enter the Chorus of Argive peasant women from the side.)*

CHORUS [*singing in a lyric interchange with Electra, who continues to sing*]

STROPHE

*Princess, daughter of Agamemnon,*
*we have come to your country dwelling,*
*Electra, to see you.*
*There came, came a man*
*bred on the milk of the hills,*
*a Mycenaean mountaineer*
*who gave me word that two days from now*
*the Argives proclaim at large*
*a holy feast, when all the maidens*
*will pass in procession up to the temple of Hera.*

ELECTRA

*Dear friends, not for festivities,*
*not for twisted bracelets of gold*
*does my heart take wing in delight.*
*I am too sad, I cannot stand*
*in choral joy with the maidens of Argos*
*or beat the tune with my whirling foot;*
*rather with tears by night*
*and tears by day I fill my soul*
*shaking in grief and fear.*
*Look! Think! Would my filthy hair*
*and robe all torn into slavish rags*
*do public honor to Agamemnon's*

*daughter, the princess?*
*Honor to Troy which will never forget*
*my conquering father?*

CHORUS

ANTISTROPHE

*Great, great is the goddess. Come,*
*I will lend you a dress to wear,*
*thick-woven of wool,*
*and gold—be gracious, accept—*
*gold for holiday glitter.*
*Do you think your tears and refusing*
*honor to the gods will ever hurt*
*your haters? Not by sounding lament*
*but only by prayer and reverent love*
*for the gods, my child, will you have gentler days.*

ELECTRA

*Gods? Not one god has heard*
*my helpless cry or watched of old*
*over my murdered father.*
*Mourn again for the wasted dead,*
*mourn for the living outlaw*
*somewhere prisoned in foreign lands*
*passing from one laborer's hearth to the next*
*though born of a glorious sire.*
*And I! I in a peasant's hut*
*waste my life like melting wax,*
*exiled and barred from my father's home*
*to a scarred mountain field,*
*while my mother rolls in her bloody bed*
*and plays at love with another man.*

CHORUS LEADER [*speaking*]

Yes, like Helen, your mother's sister—charged and found
guilty of massive pain by Greece and by your house.

*(Orestes and Pylades appear from behind the altar.)*

ELECTRA [*now speaking*]

Oh, oh! women, I break off my death-bound cry.
Look! there are strangers here close to the house who crouch
huddled beside the altar and rise up in ambush.
Run, you take the path, and I into the house
with one swift rush can still escape these criminals.

ORESTES

Poor girl, stand still, and fear not. I would never hurt you.

ELECTRA

Phoebus Apollo, help! I kneel to you. Do not kill me.

ORESTES

I hope I shall kill others hated more than you.

ELECTRA

Go away; don't touch. You have no right to touch my body.

ORESTES

There is no person I could touch with greater right.

ELECTRA

Why were you hiding, sword in hand, so near my house?

ORESTES

Stand still and listen. You will agree I have rights here.

ELECTRA

I stand here utterly in your power. You are stronger.

ORESTES

I have come to bring you a spoken message from your brother.

ELECTRA

Dearest of strangers, is he alive or is he dead?

ORESTES

Alive. I wish to give you all the good news first.

ELECTRA

God bless your days, as you deserve for such sweet words.

ORESTES

I share your gift with you that we may both be blessed.

ELECTRA

Where is he now, attempting to bear unbearable exile?

ORESTES

He is wrecked, and is included in no city's laws.

ELECTRA

Tell me, he is not poor? not hungry for daily bread?

ORESTES

He has bread, yet he has the exile's constant hunger.

ELECTRA

You came to bring a message—what are his words for me?

ORESTES

"Are you alive? And if you are, what is your life?"

ELECTRA

I think you see me. First, my body wasted and dry.

ORESTES

Yes, sadness has wasted you so greatly I could weep.

ELECTRA

Next, my head razor-cropped like a victim of the Scythians.

ORESTES

Your brother's life and father's death both bite at your heart.

ELECTRA

Alas, there's nothing else that I love more than them.

ORESTES

You grieve me. Whom do you think your brother loves
but you?

ELECTRA

He is not here. He loves me, but he is not here.

ORESTES
Why do you live in a place like this, so far from town?

ELECTRA
Because I married, stranger—a wedding much like death.

ORESTES
Bad news for your brother. Your husband is a Mycenaean?

ELECTRA
But not the man my father would have wished me to marry.

ORESTES
Tell me. I am listening, I can say it to your brother.

ELECTRA
This is his house. I live quite isolated here.

ORESTES
A ditchdigger, a cowherd would look well living here.

ELECTRA
He is a poor man but well born, and he respects me.

ORESTES
Respects? What does your husband understand by "respect"?

ELECTRA
He has never been violent or touched me in my bed.

ORESTES
A vow of chastity? or he finds you unattractive?

ELECTRA
He finds it attractive not to insult my royal blood.

ORESTES
How could he not be pleased at marrying so well?

ELECTRA
He judges the man who gave me had no right to, stranger.

ORESTES
I see—afraid Orestes might avenge your honor.

ELECTRA

Afraid of that, yes—he is also decent by nature.

ORESTES

Ah.
You paint one of nature's gentlemen. We must treat him well.

ELECTRA

We will, if my absent brother ever gets home again.

ORESTES

Your mother took the wedding calmly, I suppose?

ELECTRA

Women save all their love for their men, not for their children.

ORESTES

What was in Aegisthus' mind, to insult you so?

ELECTRA

He hoped that I, so wedded, would have worthless sons.

ORESTES

Too weak for undertaking blood-revenge on him?

ELECTRA

That was his hope. I hope to make him pay for it.

ORESTES

This husband of your mother's—does he know you are virgin?

ELECTRA

No, he knows nothing. We have played our parts in silence.

ORESTES

These women listening as we talk are friends of yours?

ELECTRA

Good enough friends to keep what we say well concealed.

ORESTES

How should Orestes play his part, if he comes to Argos?

ELECTRA

If he comes? Ugly talk. The time has long been ripe.

ORESTES

Say he comes; still how could he kill his father's killers?

ELECTRA

By being just as daring as once his enemies were.°

ORESTES

To kill your mother with his help—could you do that?

ELECTRA

Yes, with the very same axe that cut Father to ruin.

ORESTES

May I tell him what you say and how determined you are?

ELECTRA

Tell him how gladly I would die in Mother's blood.

ORESTES

O, I wish Orestes could stand here and listen.

ELECTRA

Yet if I saw him I should hardly know him, sir.

ORESTES

No wonder. You were both very young when you were parted.

ELECTRA

I have only one friend who might still know his face.

ORESTES

The man who saved him once from death, as the story goes?

ELECTRA

Yes, very old now—he was my father's tutor.

ORESTES

When your father died did his body find some burial?

ELECTRA

He found what he found. He was thrown on the dirt
outdoors.

ORESTES

I cannot bear it. What have you said? Even a stranger's
pain bites strangely deep and hurts us when we hear it.
Tell me the rest, and with new knowledge I will bring
Orestes your tale, so harsh to hear but so imperative
to be heard. Uneducated men are pitiless,
but we who are educated pity much. And we pay
a high price for being intelligent. Wisdom hurts.

CHORUS LEADER

The same excitement stirs my mind in this as his—
I live far from the city and I know its troubles
hardly at all. Now I would like to learn them too.

ELECTRA

I will tell if I must—and must tell you as my friend—
how my luck, and my father's, is too heavy to lift.
Since you have moved me to speak so, stranger, I must beg
that you will tell Orestes all my distress, and his.
First tell him how I am kept like a beast in stable rags,
my skin heavy with grease and dirt. Describe to him
this hut—my home, who used to live in the king's palace.
I weave my clothes myself and slavelike at the loom
must work or else walk naked through the world in nothing.
I fetch and carry water from the riverside,
I am deprived of holy festivals and dances,
I can't spend time with women since I am a girl,°
I can't spend time with Castor, who is close in blood
and was my suitor, before he rose to join the gods.
My mother in the glory of her Phrygian loot

sits on the throne, while circled at her feet the girls
of Asia stoop, whom Father won at the sack of Troy,
their clothes woven in snowy wool from Ida, pinned
with golden brooches, while the walls and floor are stained
still with my father's black and rotting blood. The man
who murdered him goes riding grand in Father's chariot,
with bloody hands and high delight lifting the staff
of office by which Father marshaled the Greek army.
The tomb of Agamemnon finds no honor yet,
never yet drenched with holy liquids or made green
in myrtle branches, barren of bright sacrifice.
But in his drunken fits, my mother's lover, brilliant
man, triumphant leaps and dances on the mound
and pelts my father's stone memorial with rocks
and dares to shout against us with his boldened tongue:
"Where is your son Orestes? When will that noble youth
come to protect your tomb?" Insults to an absent man.
  Kind stranger, as I ask you, tell him all these things.
For many call him home again— and I speak for them,
all of them, with my hands and tongue and grieving mind
and head, shaven in mourning; and his father calls too.
All will be shamed if he whose father captured Troy
cannot in single courage kill a single man,
although his strength is younger and his birth more noble.

CHORUS LEADER

Electra! I can see your husband on the road.
He has finished his field work and is coming home.

*(The Farmer enters from the side.)*

FARMER

Hey there! Who are these strangers standing at our gates?
What is the errand that could bring them to our distant
courtyard? Are they demanding something from me? A nice
woman should never stand in gossip with young men.

ELECTRA

My dearest husband, do not come suspecting me.
You shall hear their story, the whole truth. They come
as messengers to me with tidings of Orestes.
Strangers, I ask you to forgive him what he said.

FARMER

What news? Is Orestes still alive in the bright light?

ELECTRA

So they have told me, and I do not doubt their words.

FARMER

Does he still remember his father's troubles, and yours?

ELECTRA

We hope so. But an exile is a helpless man.

FARMER

Then what is this message of his? What have they come to tell?

ELECTRA

He sent them simply to see my troubles for themselves.

FARMER

What they don't see themselves I imagine you have told them.

ELECTRA

They know it all. I took good care that they missed nothing.

FARMER

Why were our doors not opened to them long ago?
Come into the house, you will find entertainment
to answer your good news, such as my roof can offer.
Servants, pick up their baggage, bring it all indoors.
Come, no polite refusals. You are here as friends
most dear to me who meet you now. Though I am poor
in money, I think you will not find our manners poor.

ORESTES

By the gods! Is this the man who helps you fake a marriage,
the one who does not wish to cast shame on Orestes?

ELECTRA

This is the man they know as poor Electra's husband.

ORESTES

Alas,
we try to find good men and cannot recognize them
when met, since all our human heritage runs mongrel.
At times I have seen descendants of the noblest family
quite worthless, while poor fathers had outstanding sons;
inside the souls of wealthy men bleak famine lives
while minds of stature struggle trapped in starving bodies.
How then can man distinguish man, what test can he use?°
The test of wealth? That measure means poverty of mind.
Of poverty? The pauper owns one thing, the sickness
of his condition, a compelling teacher of evil.
By nerve in war? Yet who, when a spear is aimed right at
his face, will stand to witness his companion's courage?
We might as well just toss these matters to the winds.
This fellow here is no great man among the Argives,
not dignified by family in the eyes of the world—
he is a face in the crowd, and yet I choose him champion.
Can you not come to understand, you empty-minded,
opinion-stuffed people, to judge a man by how
he lives with others: manners are nobility's touchstone?
Such men of manners can control our cities best,°
and homes, but the wellborn sportsman, long on muscle, short
on brains, is only good for a statue in the park—
not even sterner in the shocks of war than weaker
men, for courage is the gift of character.
Now let us take whatever rest this house can give;
this man here, Agamemnon's child, the absent man
for whom I've come, deserves no less. We should go now

indoors, servants, inside the house, since a poor host
who's eager to entertain is better than a rich one.
I do praise and accept his most kind reception
but would have been more pleased if your brother on the crest
of fortune could have brought me into a fortunate house.
Perhaps he may still come; Apollo's oracles
are strong, though human prophecy is best ignored.

*(Exit Orestes and Pylades into the house with their attendants.)*

CHORUS LEADER

Now more than ever in our lives, Electra, joy
makes our hearts light and warm. Perhaps now fortune, first
running such painful steps, will stand on firmer footing.

ELECTRA *(To the farmer.)*

You thoughtless man! You know quite well the house is bare;
why take these strangers in? They are better born than you.

FARMER

Why? Because if they are the gentlemen they seem,
will they not be content with small things as with great?

ELECTRA

Small is the word for you. Now the mistake is made,
go quickly to my father's loved and ancient servant
who by Tanaus river, where it cuts the land
of Argos off from Spartan country, goes his rounds
watching his flocks in distant exile from the town.
Tell him these strangers have descended on me;° ask
him to come and bring some food fit for distinguished guests.
He will surely be happy; he will bless the gods
when he hears the child he saved so long ago still lives.
Besides, we cannot get help from the family house,
from Mother—our news would fly to her on bitter wings,
cruel as she is, if she should hear Orestes lives.

FARMER

Well, if you wish it, I can pass your message on
to the old man. But you get quick into the house
and ready up what's there. A woman when she has to
can always find some food to set a decent table.
The house holds little, yet it is enough, I know,
to keep these strangers full of food at least one day.

*(Exit Electra into the house.)*

When things like this occur, my intellect reflects.
I contemplate the mighty power found in money:
money you can spend on guests; money you can pay the
doctor
when you get sick. But little difference does money make
for our daily bread, and when a man has eaten that,
the rich man and the poor one hold just the same amount.

*(Exit the Farmer to the side.)*

CHORUS [*singing*]

STROPHE A

*O glorious ships that sailed across to Troy once*
*moving on infinite wooden oars*
*attending the circling chorus of Nereid dancers*
*where the dolphin delighting in the pipe-*
*melody all about the sea-*
*blue prows went plunging;*
*you led the goddess Thetis' son,*
*light-striding Achilles, on his way*
*with Agamemnon to Ilium's cliffs*
*where Simois pours into the sea.*

ANTISTROPHE A

*The Nereids passed Euboea's headlands*
*bringing the heavy shield of gold,*
*forged on Hephaestus' anvil, and golden armor.*
*Up Mount Pelion, up the jut*

*of Ossa's holy slopes on high,*
*up the nymphs' spy-rocks*
*they hunted the aged horseman's hill*
*where he trained the boy as a dawn for Greece,*
*the son of Thetis, sea-bred and swift-*
*footed for the sons of Atreus.*

STROPHE B

*Once I heard from a man out of Troy, known to the port*
*in Nauplia close to Argos,*
*of your brilliant shield, O goddess'*
*child, how in its circled space*
*these signs, scenes, were in blazon warning,*
*terrors for Phrygia:*
*running in frieze on its massive rim,*
*Perseus lifting the severed head*
*of the Gorgon, cut at the neck;°*
*he walks on wings over the sea;*
*Hermes is with him, messenger of Zeus,*
*great Maia's*
*child of the flocks and forests.*

ANTISTROPHE B

*Out of the shield's curved center glittered afar the high*
*shining round of the sun*
*driving with wingèd horses,*
*and the chorused stars of upper air—*
*Pleiades, Hyades—Hector eyed them,*
*and swerved to flight.*
*Over the helmet of beaten gold*
*Sphinxes snatch in hooking nails*
*their prey trapped with song. On the hollow*
*greave, the lioness' fire breath*
*flares in her clawed track as she runs,*
*staring*
*at the wind-borne foal of Peirene.*

EPODE

*All along the blade of the deadly sword, hooves pounding,*
*horses leapt; black above their backs the dust blew.*
*But the lord of such spearmen*
*you killed by lust of sex and sin*
*of mind, daughter of Tyndareus.*
*For this the sons of heaven will send*
*you a judgment of death;° some far*
*day I shall still see your blood fall*
*red from your neck by the iron sword.*

*(Enter the Old Man from the side, carrying provisions for a feast.)*

OLD MAN

Where is my young mistress and my lady queen,
the child of Agamemnon, whom I raised and loved?
How steep this house seems set to me, with rough approach,
as I grow old for climbing on these withered legs.
But when your friends call, you must come and drag along
and hump your spine till it snaps and bend your knees like pins.

*(Enter Electra from the house.)*

Why there she is my daughter, look at you by the door!
I am here. I have brought you from my cropping sheep
a newborn lamb, a tender one, just pulled from the teat,
and flowers looped in garlands, cheese white from the churn,
and this stored treasure of the wine god, aged and fragrant—
not much of it, I know, but sweet, and very good
to pour into the cup with other, weaker wine.
Let someone take this all in to the guests indoors,
for I have cried a little and would like to dry
my face and eyes out here on my cloak—more holes than wool.

*(A servant does as instructed.)*

ELECTRA

Old man, please tell me, why is your face so stained with tears?
After so long has my grief stirred your thoughts again,
or is it poor Orestes in his cheerless exile
you mourn for, or my father, whom your two old hands
once raised and helped without reward for self or loved ones?

OLD MAN

Reward, no. Yet I could not stop myself, in this:
for I came past his tomb, circling from the road,
and fell to the earth there, weeping for him, alone,
and opening this winesack intended for your guests
I poured libation, and I wreathed the stone in myrtle.
And there I saw on the burning-altar a black-fleeced
sheep, throat cut and blood still warm in its dark stream,
and curling locks of bright blond hair cut off in gift.
I stopped, quiet, to wonder, child, what man had courage
to visit at that tomb. It could not be an Argive.
Is there a chance your brother has arrived in secret
and paused to wonder at his father's shabby tomb?
Look at the lock of hair, match it to your own head,
see if it is not exactly twin to yours in color.
Often a father's blood, running in separate veins,
makes siblings' bodies almost mirrors in their form.

ELECTRA

Old man, I always thought you were wiser than you sound
if you really think my brother, who is brave and bold,
would come to our land in hiding, frightened by Aegisthus!
Besides, how could a lock of his hair match with mine?
one from a man with rugged training in the ring
and games, one combed and girlish? It is not possible.
Besides, you could find many matching curls of many people
not bred in the same house, old man, nor matched in blood.

OLD MAN

At least go set your foot in the print of his hunting boot
and see if it is not the same as yours, my child.

ELECTRA

But how could rocky ground possibly receive
the imprint of a foot? And if it could be traced,
it would not be the same for brother and for sister,
a man's foot and a girl's—of course his would be bigger.

OLD MAN

Is there no piece then, if your brother should come home,°
of weaving, that loom pattern by which you would know the cloth
you wove and I wrapped him in, to rescue him from death?

ELECTRA

You know quite well that when Orestes left for exile
I was still very small. And even if a child's hand
could weave, how could a grown man still wear those boy's clothes
unless his shirt and tunic lengthened with his body?
Some pitying stranger must have passed the tomb and cut
a mourning lock, or townsmen slipping past the lookouts.°

OLD MAN

Where are the strangers now? I want to look them over
and draw them out with conversation of your brother.

*(Enter Orestes and Pylades from the house.)*

ELECTRA

Here they come striding lightly from the cottage now.

OLD MAN

Well. They look highborn enough, but the coin may prove
false. Often a noble face hides filthy ways.
Nevertheless—
Greetings, strangers, I wish you well.

ORESTES

And greetings in return, old sir.
Electra, tell me,
to what friends of yours does this human antique belong?

ELECTRA

This is the man who raised and loved my father, sir.

ORESTES

What! the one who saved your brother once from death?

ELECTRA

Indeed he saved him—if indeed he still is safe.

ORESTES

Ah, so!
Why does he stare upon me like a man who squints
at the bright stamp on silver? Do I look like somebody?

ELECTRA

Perhaps he's just happy seeing someone of Orestes' age.

ORESTES

Dear Orestes. Why does he walk round me in circles?

ELECTRA

Stranger, I am astonished too as I look at him.

OLD MAN

Mistress, now pray. Daughter Electra, pray to the gods.

ELECTRA

For which of the things I have, or which that I don't have?

OLD MAN

For a treasure of love within your grasp, which god reveals.

ELECTRA

As you please; I pray the gods. Now, what was in your mind?

OLD MAN

Look now upon this man, my child—your dearest love.

ELECTRA

I have been looking long already; are you crazy?

OLD MAN

And am I crazy if my eyes have seen your brother?

ELECTRA

What have you said, old man? What hopeless impossible
word?

OLD MAN

I said I see Orestes—here—Agamemnon's son.

ELECTRA

How? What sign do you see? What can I know and trust?

OLD MAN

The scar above his eye where once he slipped and drew
blood as he helped you chase a fawn in your father's court.

ELECTRA

I see the mark of a fall, but I cannot believe you.

OLD MAN

How long will you stand, hold back from his arms and love?

ELECTRA

I will not any longer, for my heart has trust
in the token you show.
O Brother so delayed by time,
I hold you against hope . . .

ORESTES

And I hold you at last.

ELECTRA

. . . and never thought I'd see you.

ORESTES

I too abandoned hope.

ELECTRA

And are you he?

ORESTES

I am, your sole defender and friend.
Now if I catch the prey for which I cast my net!°
I'm confident. Or never believe in the gods' power
again if evil can still triumph over good.

CHORUS [*singing*]

*You have come, you have come, our slow, bright day,*
*you have shone, you have shown a beacon-*
*lit hope for the state, who fled of old*
*your father's palace, doomed and pained,*
*drifting in exile.*
*Now god, some god restores us strong*
*to triumph, my dear.*
*Lift high your hands, lift high your voice, raise*
*prayers to the gods, that in fortune, fortune*
*your brother may march straight to the city's heart.*

ORESTES

Enough. I find sweet pleasure in embrace and welcome,
but let us give ourselves over to pleasure later.
Old man, you came on the crest of opportunity—
tell me what I must do to punish Father's killer
and Mother too who lives in foul adultery.
Have I in Argos any strong measure of friends
or am I bankrupt in backing as I am in fortune?
Whom shall I look to? Shall it be by day or night?
What hunting track will lead me toward my enemies?

OLD MAN

My son, you lost your friends when luck deserted you.
That would indeed be luck met on the road for you,
someone to share both good and evil without change.
But you from root to leaf-top have been robbed of friends
while, leaving, you left them without all hope. Hear me:
in your own hand and in your fortune you hold all,
to capture back your city, home, and patrimony.

ORESTES

But what should we be doing now to reach our goal?

OLD MAN

Kill him. Kill Thyestes' son. And kill your mother.

ORESTES

Such the triumphal crown I came for, yet—how reach it?

OLD MAN

Not inside the city even if you were willing.

ORESTES

Is he so strongly fenced by bodyguards and spears?

OLD MAN

You know it. The man's afraid of you and cannot sleep.

ORESTES

Let that go, then. Tell me another way, old man.

OLD MAN

Yes—you shall hear, for something came to me just now.

ORESTES

I hope your plan and my reaction are equally good.

OLD MAN

I saw Aegisthus as I hauled my way up here.

ORESTES

Good, that sounds hopeful. Where did you happen on him?

OLD MAN

Close, down in the meadows where his horses graze.

ORESTES

What was he doing? Out of despair I see new light.

OLD MAN

Offering a banquet to the goddess nymphs, I think.

ORESTES

To keep his children safe? Or for one not yet born?

OLD MAN
I know only that he was preparing to kill a bull.

ORESTES
How many men were with him? Simply alone with servants?

OLD MAN
No citizens were there; a handful of household servants.

ORESTES
No one who might still recognize my face, old man?

OLD MAN
They are his private servants and they have never seen you.°

ORESTES
And would they, if we conquered, be, ah—kindly disposed?

OLD MAN
That is characteristic of slaves, and luck for you.

ORESTES
How would you suggest my getting close to him?

OLD MAN
Walk past where he will see you as he sacrifices.

ORESTES
He has his fields, I gather, right beside the road?

OLD MAN
And when he sees you he will ask you to join the feast.

ORESTES
He shall find a bitter banquet-fellow, if god wills.

OLD MAN
What happens next—you play it as the dice may fall.

ORESTES
Well spoken. The woman who gave me birth is—where?

OLD MAN
In Argos. She will join him for the feast tonight.

ORESTES
But why did she—my mother—not start out with him?

OLD MAN
The gossip of the crowd disturbs her. She held back.

ORESTES
Of course. She feels the city's disapproving looks.

OLD MAN
That's how it is. Everyone hates a promiscuous wife.

ORESTES
Then how can I kill them both at the same time and place?

ELECTRA
I will be the one to manage my mother's killing.

ORESTES
Good—then fortune will arrange that business well.

ELECTRA
Let our single friend here help the two of us.

OLD MAN
It shall be done. What death have you decided for her?

ELECTRA
Old uncle, you must go to Clytemnestra; tell her°
that I am kept in bed after bearing a son.

OLD MAN
Some time ago? Or has your baby just arrived?

ELECTRA
Ten days ago, which days I have kept ritually clean.

OLD MAN
And how will this achieve the murder of your mother?

ELECTRA
She will come, of course, when she hears about the birth.

OLD MAN

Why? Do you think she cares so deeply for you, child?

ELECTRA

Yes—and she will weep about the boy's low breeding.

OLD MAN

Perhaps. Return now to the goal of your design.

ELECTRA

She will come; she will be killed. All that is clear.

OLD MAN

I see—she comes and walks directly in your door.

ELECTRA

From there she need go only a short way down to Hades.

OLD MAN

I will gladly die too, when I have seen her die.

ELECTRA

But first, old man, you ought to guide Orestes now.

OLD MAN

Where Aegisthus holds his sacrifices to the gods?

ELECTRA

Then go see my mother, tell her all about me.

OLD MAN

I'll speak so well she'll think it is Electra speaking.

ELECTRA *(To Orestes.)*

Your task is ready. You have drawn first chance at killing.

ORESTES

Well, I will go if anyone will show me where.

OLD MAN

I will escort you on your way with greatest joy.

ORESTES°

O Zeus of our Fathers, now be Router of Foes,
have pity on us, for our days are piteous.

OLD MAN

Pity them truly—children sprung of your own blood.

ELECTRA

O Hera, holy mistress of Mycenae's altars,
grant us the victory if our claim to victory is just.

OLD MAN

Grant them at last avenging justice for their father.

ORESTES

And you, O Father, dwelling wronged beneath the earth . . .

ELECTRA

. . . and Earth, ruler below, to whom I stretch my hands . . .

OLD MAN

. . . protect, protect these children here, so dearly loved.

ORESTES

Come now and bring as army all the dead below . . .

ELECTRA

. . . who stood beside you at Troy with the havoc of their
spears . . .

OLD MAN

. . . all who hate the godless guilty criminals.

ORESTES

Did you hear us, wretched victim of our mother?°

OLD MAN

All, your father hears all, I know. Time now to march.

ELECTRA

I call to you again and say: "Aegisthus dies!"°
And if, Orestes, in your struggle you should die,

I too am dead, let them no longer say I live,
for I will stab myself with a two-edged sword.
I will go in and make our dwelling fit for the outcome:
then if a message of good fortune comes from you
the whole house shall ring out in triumph. If you die
triumph will shift to desolation. This is my word.

ORESTES

I understand you.

ELECTRA

Make yourself fit man for the hour.
You, my women, with your voices scream a fire-
signal of shouting in this trial. I shall stand guard,
a sword raised ready for the issue in my hand.
If I'm defeated, I shall never grant to those
I hate the right to violate my living flesh.

*(Exit Orestes, the Old Man, and Pylades to the side, Electra into the house.)*

CHORUS [*singing*]

STROPHE A

*The ancient tale is told*
*in Argos*
*still—how a magic lamb*
*from its gentle mother on the hills*
*Pan stole, Pan of the wild*
*beasts, kind watcher, Pan*
*who breathes sweet music to his jointed reed.*
*He brought it to show the gold*
*curls of its wool. On the stone*
*steps a standing herald called:*
*"To the square, to the square, you men*
*of Mycenae! Come, run, behold*
*a strange and lovely thing*
*for our blessed kings." Swiftly the chorus in dance*
*beat out honor to Atreus' house.*

ANTISTROPHE A

*The altars spread their wings*
*of hammered*
*gold, fire gleamed in the town*
*like the moon on Argos' stones*
*of sacrifice, lotus pipes*
*tended the Muses, lilting*
*ripples of tune. The dance swelled in desire*
*tense for the lamb of gold—*
*whose? Quick, Thyestes' trick:*
*seducing in the dark of sleep*
*Atreus' wife, he brought*
*the strange lamb home, his own.*
*Back to the square he calls*
*all to know how he holds the golden creature,*
*fleece and horn, in his own house.*

STROPHE B

*That hour—that hour Zeus*
*changed the stars on their blazing course,*
*utterly turned the splendid sun,*
*turned the white face of the dawn*
*so the sun drives west over heaven's spine*
*in glowing god-lit fire.*
*The watery weight of cloud moved north,*
*the cracked waste of Egyptian Ammon*
*dried up, died, never knowing dew,*
*robbed of the beautiful rain that drops from Zeus.*

ANTISTROPHE B

*Thus it is always told.*
*I myself am won only to slight belief*
*that the sun would swerve or change his gold*
*countenance of fire, moved in pain*
*and sorrow at sin in the mortal world,*
*to judge or punish humans.*
*Yet terrible myths are useful,*

*they call men to the worship of the gods—*
*whom you forgot when you killed your husband,*
*sister of glorious brothers.*

*(A cry is heard from offstage.)*

Listen, listen.
Friends, did you hear a shout? Or did anxiety
trick me? A shout deep-rolling like the thunder of Zeus?

*(Another cry.)*

Again it comes! The rising wind is charged with news.
Mistress, come out! Electra, leave the house!

*(Enter Electra from the house.)*

ELECTRA
Dear friends, what is it? How do we stand now in our trial?

CHORUS
I only know one thing: I heard a voice of death.

ELECTRA
I heard it too. It was far off. But I too heard it.

CHORUS
It comes from a great distance, yet it is quite clear.

ELECTRA
Is it an Argive groaning there—or is it our friends?

CHORUS
I cannot tell; the note of clamoring is slurred.

ELECTRA
So you announce my death by sword. Why am I slow?

CHORUS
Lady, hold back until you learn the outcome clearly.

ELECTRA
Not possible. We are beaten. Where are the messengers?

CHORUS

They will come soon. To kill a king is not quick or light.

*(Enter a Messenger, one of Orestes' servants, from the side.)*

MESSENGER

Hail maidens of Mycenae, glorious in triumph!
Orestes is victor! I proclaim it to all who love him.
The murderer of Agamemnon lies on the earth
crumpled in blood, Aegisthus. Let us thank the gods.

ELECTRA

Who are you? Why should I think your message is the truth?

MESSENGER

You do not know you're looking on your brother's servant?

ELECTRA

Dearest of servants! Out of fear I held my eyes
shaded from recognition. Now indeed I know you.
What is your news? My father's hated murderer dead?

MESSENGER

Dead, dead. I say it twice if that is what you wish.

ELECTRA

O gods! O Justice watching the world, you have come at last.
How did he die? What style of death did Orestes choose,
to kill Thyestes' son? Give me the details.

MESSENGER

When we rose from your cottage and walked down the hill
we came across a beaten double wagon-track,
and there we found the new commander of Mycenae.
He happened to be walking in the water-meadow,
picking young green shoots of myrtle for his hair.
He saw us and called out: "You are most welcome, strangers.
Who are you? Have you traveled far? Where is your home?"
Orestes answered, "We are Thessalians on our way
toward Alpheus' valley where we shall sacrifice to Zeus

of Olympia." When Aegisthus heard, he called again,
"Now you must stop among us as our guests and share
our feast. I am at the moment slaughtering a bull
for the nymphs. Tomorrow morning you shall rise at dawn
and get there just as soon. Come with me to the house"—
while he was still talking he took us by the hand
and led us off the road—"I will take no refusal."
When we were in the house he gave his men commands:
"Quick, someone fill a bowl of water for the strangers
so their hands will be clean near the lustrations at the altar."
But Orestes interrupted: "We are clean enough.
We washed ourselves just now in the clear river water.
If strangers may join citizens in sacrifice,
we are here, Aegisthus. We shall not refuse you, prince."
So this is what they said in public conversation.
Now the king's bodyguard laid down their spears
and sprang all hands to working.
Some brought the lustral bowl, and others baskets of grain,
some laid and lit the fire or around the hearth
set up the sacred ewers—the whole roof rang with sound.
Your mother's lover took the barley in his hands
and cast it on the altar as he said these words:
"Nymphs of the Rocks, may I kill many bulls for you,
and my wife, Tyndareus' child, who is at home.
Guard us in present fortune, ruin our enemies."
(Meaning you and Orestes.) But my master prayed
the utter reverse, keeping his words below his breath,
to take his dynastic place again. Aegisthus raised
the narrow knife from the basket, cut the calf's front lock,
with his right hand dedicated it to the holy fire,
and, as his servants hoisted the beast upon their shoulders,
slashed its throat.
Now he turns to your brother and says,
"One of your great Thessalian talents, as you boast,
is to be a man of two skills: disjointing bulls

and taming horses. Stranger, take the iron knife,
show us how true Thessalian reputation runs."
Orestes seized the beautifully tempered Dorian blade,
loosened his brooch, flung his fine cloak back from his
shoulders,
chose Pylades as his assistant in the work,
and made the men stand off. Holding the calf by its foot,
he laid the white flesh bare by pulling with his hand.
He stripped the hide off whole, more quickly than a runner
racing could double down and back the hippodrome course,
and opened the soft belly. Aegisthus scooped the prophetic
portions up in his hands and looked.
The liver lobe
was missing. But the portal vein and gall sac showed
disaster coming at him even as he looked.
His face darkened, drew down. My master watched and
asked,
"What puts you out of heart?" "Stranger, I am afraid.
Some ambush is at my door.° There is a man I hate,
the son of Agamemnon, an enemy to my house."
He answered, "You can scarcely fear a fugitive's
tricks when you control the state? So we can feast
on sacrificial flesh, will someone bring a chopper—
Phthian, not Dorian—and let me split this breastbone?"
He took it and struck. Aegisthus heaped the soft parts, then
sorted them out. But while his head was bent above them,
your brother stretched up, balanced on the balls of his feet,
and smashed a blow to his spine. The vertebrae of his back
broke. Head down, his whole body convulsed, he gasped
to breathe, writhed with a high scream, and died in his blood.
The servingmen who saw it leaped straight to their spears,
an army for two men to face. And yet with courage
they stood, faced them, shook their javelins, engaged—
Pylades and Orestes, who cried, "I have not come
in wrath against this city nor against my servants.

I have only paid my father's killer back in blood.
I am the much-suffering Orestes—do not kill me, men
who helped my father's house of old."
They, when they heard
his words, lowered their spears, and he was recognized
by some old man who used to serve the family.
Swiftly they crowned your brother's head with flower
wreaths,
shouting aloud in joy and triumph. He comes to you
bringing something to show you—not the Gorgon's head,
only Aegisthus whom you loathe, who was in debt
for blood and found the paying bitter at his death.

*(Exit to the side.)*

CHORUS [*singing*]

STROPHE

*Come, lift your foot, lady, to dance*
*now like a fawn who in flying*
*arcs leaps for joy, light, almost brushing the sky.*
*He wins a garland of glory*
*greater than any Olympic victory,*
*your own brother; now, in the hymn strain,*
*praise the fair victor, chant to my step.*

ELECTRA

O flame of day and sun's great chariot charged with light,
O earth below and dark of night where I watched before,
my eyes are clear now, I can unfold my sight to freedom,
now that Aegisthus, who had killed my father, falls.
Bring me my few belongings, what my house keeps treasured
as ornaments of splendor for the hair, dear friends,
for I will crown my brother as a conqueror.

CHORUS [*singing*]

ANTISTROPHE

*Lay now the bright signs of success*
*over his brow, as we circle*

*our chorused step, dancing to the Muses' delight.*
*Now again in our country*
*our old and loved kings of the blood capture the power,*
*in high justice routing the unjust.*
*Raise to the pipe's tune shouts of our joy.*

*(Enter Orestes, Pylades, and servants with a corpse from the side.)*

ELECTRA

O man of triumph sprung of our triumphant father
who fought and won below the walls of Troy—Orestes!
Take from my hands these woven bindings for your hair.
You come, a runner in no trifling race, but long
and challenging, to your home goal, killing Aegisthus
who was your enemy, who once destroyed our father.
And you, companion of the shield, Pylades, son
of a most pious father, please receive your crown
from my hand, for you have won an equal share of glory
in this trial. May I see your fortune always high!

ORESTES

You must believe, Electra, that the gods have been
first founders of our fortune; then you may turn to praise
me as the simple servant of both god and fortune.
I come to you the killer of Aegisthus, not
in words but action. You know this, but more than this°
I have here in my hands the man himself, quite dead.
You may want to display him for the beasts to eat
or stick him on a stake as a toy for carrion birds
born of bright air. He's yours—once master, now slave.

ELECTRA

I am ashamed to speak and yet I wish to speak.

ORESTES

What is it? Speak your mind, for now you're free from fear.

ELECTRA

I am ashamed to insult the dead; some hate may strike me.

ORESTES

There is no man on earth, nor will be, who could blame you.

ELECTRA

Our city is harsh to please and takes delight in slander.

ORESTES

Speak as you need to, sister. We were joined to him
in bonds of hatred which could know no gentle truce.

ELECTRA

So be it.
Which words of hatred shall I speak in prelude;
which shall I make finale, or marshal in the center?
And yet dawn after dawn I never once have missed
calling aloud what I wished to tell you to your face
if only I were liberated from my fears
now past. We are at that point now. I'll give you the full
torrent of abuse I hoped to tell you living.
You ruined me, orphaned me, and him too, of a father
we loved dearly, though we had done no harm to you.
You bedded my mother in shame, and killed her husband
who captained the Greeks abroad while you skulked far from Phrygia.
You climbed such heights of stupidness that you imagined
your marriage to my mother would not marry you
to cuckoldry, though she had stained our father's bed
adulterously. Know this: when a man seduces another's°
wife in secret sex and then is forced to keep her,
he must be stupid if he thinks that she, unchaste
to her first husband, will suddenly turn chaste for him.
Your household life was painful though you could not see it;
you knew in your heart that you had made a godless marriage,
and Mother knew she had acquired a godless husband,
so each in working evil shouldered the other's load
in mutual pain: she got your evil, you got hers.

Every time you walked outdoors in Argos, you heard
these words: "He's hers." And never: "She belongs to him."
O what perversion, when the woman in the house
stands out as master, not the man. I shake in hate
to see those children whom the city knows and names
not by their father's name but only by their mother's.
It marks the bridegroom who has climbed to a nobler bed;
when no one mentions the husband, everyone knows the
wife.
Where you were most deceived in your grand
unawareness
was your boast to be a man of power since you had money.
Wealth stays with us a little moment if at all;
only our characters are steadfast, not our possessions,°
for character stays with us to the end and faces
trouble, but unjust wealth dwells with poor fools but then
wings swiftly from their house after brief blossoming.
The women in your life I will not mention—a maiden
ought not—but only hint that I know all about them.
You took liberties since you lived in a grand palace
and were handsome enough. But let me have a husband
not girlish-faced like you but virile and well built,
whose sons would cling bold to the craggy heights of war;
good looks are only ornamental at the dance.
To hell with you! You know not what you did, but time
has found you out. You've paid the price. So should no
criminal
who starts his race without a stumble vainly believe
that he has outrun Justice, till in the closing stretch
he nears the finish line and gains life's final goal.

CHORUS LEADER

He wrought horrors, and has paid in horror to you
and your brother. Justice has enormous power.

ELECTRA

Enough now. Servants, take his corpse into the house;

conceal it well in darkness so that when she comes
my mother sees no dead man till her throat is cut.

*(The corpse is carried into the house.)*

ORESTES°

Hold off a little; let us speak of something else.

ELECTRA

What's there? You see his men from Mycenae coming to help?

ORESTES

Not his men. What I'm seeing is my mother who bore me.

ELECTRA

How beautifully she marches straight into our net!°
See how grandly she rides with chariot and finery.

ORESTES

What—what is our action now toward Mother? Do we kill her?

ELECTRA

Don't tell me pity catches you at the sight of her.

ORESTES

O god!
How can I kill her when she bore me and brought me up?

ELECTRA

Kill her just the way she killed your father and mine.

ORESTES

O Phoebus, your holy word was brute and ignorant . . .

ELECTRA

Where Apollo is ignorant shall men be wise?

ORESTES

. . . that said to kill my mother, whom I must not kill.

ELECTRA

Nothing will hurt you. You are only avenging Father.

ORESTES

As matricide I'll be exiled. But I was clean before.

ELECTRA

Not clean before the gods, if you neglect your father.

ORESTES

I know—but will I not be punished for killing Mother?

ELECTRA

And will you not be punished for not avenging Father?

ORESTES

Did a polluted demon speak in the shape of god?

ELECTRA

Throned on the holy tripod? I shall not believe so.

ORESTES

And I shall not believe those oracles were pure.

ELECTRA

You must not play the coward now and fall to weakness.
Go in. I will bait her a trap as she once baited one°
which sprang at Aegisthus' touch and killed her lawful husband.

ORESTES

I am going in. I walk a cliff edge in a sea°
of evil, and evil I will do. If the gods approve,
let it be so. This game of death is bitter, not° sweet.

*(Exit Orestes and Pylades into the house. Enter Clytemnestra from the side in a chariot, attended by Trojan slaves.)*

CHORUS [*chanting*]

*Hail! hail!*
*Queen and mistress of Argos, hail,*

*Tyndareus' child,*
*sister in blood to the lordly sons*
*of Zeus who dwell in starred and flaming*
*air, saviors adored by men*
*in the roar of the salt sea.*
*Hail! I honor you like the gods*
*for your wealth and brilliant life.*
*The time to serve° your fortunes*
*is now, O Queen. Hail!°*

CLYTEMNESTRA

Get out of the carriage, Trojan maids; hold my hand
tight, so I can step down safely to the ground.

*(They do as instructed.)*

Mostly we gave the temples of our gods the spoils
from Phrygia, but these girls, the best in Troy, I chose
to ornament my own house and replace the child
I lost, my loved daughter. The compensation is small.

ELECTRA

Then may not I, who am a slave and also tossed
far from my father's home to live in misery,
may I not, Mother, take your most distinguished hand?

CLYTEMNESTRA

These slaves are here to help me. Do not trouble yourself.

ELECTRA

Why not? You threw me out of home like a war captive;
and with my home destroyed, then I too was destroyed,
as they are too—left dark, lonely, and fatherless.

CLYTEMNESTRA

And dark and lonely were your father's plots against
those he should most have loved and least conspired to kill.
I can tell you—no. When a woman gets an evil
reputation she finds a bitter twist to her words.

This is my case now, but it is not rightly so.
If you have something truly to hate, you ought to learn
the facts first; then hate is more decent. But not in the dark.
My father Tyndareus gave me to your father's care,
not to kill me, not to kill what I bore and loved.
And yet he tempted my daughter, slyly whispering
of marriage with Achilles, took her from home to Aulis
where the ships were stuck, stretched her high above the altar
and, like pale field grass, slashed Iphigenia's throat.
If this had been to save the state from siege and ruin,
if it had helped our home and spared our other children,
to rack one girl for many lives—I could have forgiven.
But now for the sake of Helen's lust and for the man
who took a wife and could not punish her seducer—
for their lives' sake he took the life of my dear child.
I was unfairly wronged in this, yet not for this
would I have gone so savage, nor murdered my own husband,
but he came home to me with a mad, god-filled girl
and introduced her to his bed. So there we were,
two brides being stabled in a single stall.
Oh, women are fools for sex, deny it I shall not.
Since this is in our nature, when our husbands choose
to despise the bed they have, a woman is quite willing
to imitate her man and find another lover.
But then the dirty gossip puts us in the spotlight;
the guilty ones, the men, are never blamed at all.
If Menelaus had been abducted from home on the sly,
should I have had to kill Orestes so my sister's
husband could be rescued? You think your father would
have borne it? Then was it fair for him to kill my child
and not be killed, while he could make me suffer so?
I killed. I turned and walked the only path still open,
straight to his enemies. Would any of his friends
have helped me in the task of murder I had to do?
Speak if you have need or reason. Refute me freely;
demonstrate how your father died without full justice.

CHORUS LEADER

Justice is in your words but your justice is shameful.
A wife should give way to her husband in all things
if her mind is sound; if she refuses to see this truth
she cannot be fully counted in my reckoning.

ELECTRA

Keep in mind, Mother, those last words you spoke,
giving me license to speak out freely against you.

CLYTEMNESTRA

I say them once again, child; I will not deny them.

ELECTRA

But when you hear me, Mother, will you then treat me badly?

CLYTEMNESTRA

Not so at all. I shall be glad to humor you.°

ELECTRA

Then I shall speak—and here is the keynote of my song:
Mother, you who bore me, if only your mind were healthier!
Although for beauty you deserve tremendous praise,
both you and Helen, flowering from a single stalk,
you both grew foolish and have been a disgrace to Castor.
When she was abducted she walked of her own will to ruin,
while you brought ruin on the finest man in Greece
and screened it with the argument that for your child
you killed your husband. The world knows you less well
than I.
You, long before your daughter came near sacrifice,
the very hour your husband marched away from home,
were setting your blond curls by the bronze mirror's light.
Now any woman who works on her beauty when her man
is gone from home indicts herself as being a whore.
She has no decent cause to show her painted face
outside the door unless she wants to look for trouble.
Of all Greek women, you were the only one I know

to hug yourself with pleasure when Troy's fortunes rose,
but when they sank, to cloud your face in sympathy.
You wanted Agamemnon never to come home.
And yet life gave you every chance to be wise and fine.
You had a husband not at all worse than Aegisthus,
whom Greece herself had chosen as her king and captain;
and when your sister Helen did the things she did,
that was your time to capture glory. For black evil
is outlined clearest to our sight by the blaze of virtue.
Next. If, as you say, our father killed your daughter,
did I do any harm to you, or did my brother?
When you killed your husband, why did you not bestow
the ancestral home on us, but took to bed the gold
which never belonged to you to buy yourself a lover?
And why has he not gone in exile in exchange
for your son's exile, or not have died to pay for me
who still alive have died my sister's death twice over?
If murder judges and calls for murder, I will kill
you—and your son Orestes will kill you—for Father.
If the first death was just, the second too is just.
Whoever has a view to money or to birth°
and marries a bad woman is stupid: better to have
a low-born wife who's chaste than one of noble birth.

CHORUS LEADER

It's luck determines marriage. Some seem to turn out well,
but I have seen that others have been the opposite.

CLYTEMNESTRA

My child, from birth you always have adored your father.
This is part of life. Some children always love
the male; some turn more closely to their mother than to him.
I know you and forgive you. I am not so happy
either, child, with what I have done or with myself.
How poorly you look. Have you not washed? Your clothes are bad.°

I suppose you just got up from bed and giving birth?
O god, how miserably my plans have all turned out.
Perhaps I drove my hate too hard against my husband.

ELECTRA

Your mourning comes a little late. There is no cure.
Father is dead now. If you grieve, why not
bring back the son you sent to wander in foreign lands?

CLYTEMNESTRA

I am afraid. I have to watch my life, not his.
They say his father's death has made him very angry.

ELECTRA

Why do you let your husband act like a beast against us?

CLYTEMNESTRA

That is his nature. Yours is wild and stubborn too.

ELECTRA

I was hurt. But I am going to bury my anger soon.

CLYTEMNESTRA

Good; then he never will be harsh to you again.

ELECTRA

He has been haughty; now he is staying in my house.

CLYTEMNESTRA

You see? You want to blow the quarrel to new flames.

ELECTRA

I will be quiet; I fear him—the way I fear him.

CLYTEMNESTRA

Stop this talk. You called me here for something, girl.

ELECTRA

I think that you have heard that I have given birth.
Make me the proper sacrifice—I don't know how—

as the law runs for children at the tenth night moon.
I have no knowledge; I have never had a child.

CLYTEMNESTRA

This is work for the woman who acted as your midwife.

ELECTRA

I acted for myself. I was alone at birth.

CLYTEMNESTRA

Your house is set so desolate of friends and neighbors?

ELECTRA

No one is willing to make friends with poverty.

CLYTEMNESTRA

Then I will go and make the gods full sacrifice
as law prescribes for a child. I give you so much
grace and then pass to the meadow where my husband is,
sacrificing to the nymphs. Servants, take the wagon,
set it in the stables. When you think this rite
of god draws to an end, come back to stand beside me,
for I have debts of grace to pay my husband too.

ELECTRA

Enter our poor house. And, Mother, take good care
the smoky walls put no dark stain upon your robes.
Pay sacrifice to heaven as you ought to pay.

*(Exit Clytemnestra into the house, her slaves to the side with the chariot.)*

The basket of grain is ready and the knife is sharp
which killed the bull, and close beside him you shall fall
stricken, to keep your bridal rites in the house of death
with him you slept beside in life. I give you so
much grace and you shall give my father grace of justice.

*(Exit Electra into the house.)*

CHORUS [*singing*]

STROPHE

*Evils are interchanging. The winds of this house*
*shift now to a new track. Of old in the bath*
*my leader, mine, fell to his death;*
*the roof rang, the stone heights of the hall echoed loud*
*to his cry: "O terrible lady, will you kill me now*
*newly come to my dear land at the tenth cycle of seed?"°*

ANTISTROPHE

*Justice circles back and brings her to judgment,*
*she pays grief for love errant. She, when her lord*
*came safe home, after dragging years,*
*where his stone Cyclopes' walls rose straight*
*to the sky, there with steel*
*freshly honed to an edge killed him, hand on the axe. O wretched*
*husband, whatever*
*suffering gripped that cruel woman:*
*a lioness mountain-bred, ranging out*
*from her oak-sheltered home, she sprang. It was done.*

CLYTEMNESTRA [*singing in this brief lyrical interchange from inside the house while the Chorus sings in reply*]

*O children—by the gods—do not kill your mother—no!*

CHORUS

*Do you hear a cry within the walls?*

CLYTEMNESTRA

*O, O, I am hurt—*

CHORUS

*I moan aloud too, to hear her in her children's hands.*
*Justice is given down by god soon or late;*
*you suffer terribly now, you acted terribly then,*
*cruel woman, against your husband.*

(*Enter Orestes, Electra, and Pylades from the house, and the corpses of Aegisthus and Clytemnestra are revealed.*)

CHORUS LEADER

Behold them coming from the house in robes of blood
newly stained by a murdered mother, walking straight,°
living signs of triumph over her frightful cries.
There is no house, nor has there been, more suffering
or pitiable than this, the house of Tantalus.

ORESTES [*singing this lyric ode in alternation with Electra and the Chorus*]

STROPHE A

*O Earth and Zeus who watch all work*
*men do, look at this work of blood*
*and corruption, two bodies in death*
*lying battered along the dirt°*
*under my hands, payment*
*for my pain.*

ELECTRA

*Weep greatly, my brother, but I am to blame.*
*A girl burning in hatred I turned against*
*the mother who bore me.*

CHORUS

*Weep for destiny; destiny yours°*
*to mother unforgettable wrath,*
*to suffer unforgettable pain*
*beyond pain at your children's hands.*
*You paid for their father's death as justice asks.*

ORESTES

ANTISTROPHE A

*Phoebus, you hymned justice in obscure*
*melody, but the deed has shone*
*white as a scar. You granted me rest*
*as murderers rest—to leave the land*
*of Greece. But where else can I go?*
*What state, host, god-fearing man*

*will look steady upon my face,*
*who killed my mother?*

ELECTRA

*O weep for me. Where am I now? What dance—*
*what marriage may I come to? What man will take*
*me as bride to his bed?*

CHORUS

*Circling, circling, your uncertain mind*
*veers in the blowing wind and turns;*
*you think piously now, but then*
*thoughtless you did an impious thing,*
*dear girl, to your brother, whose will was not with you.*

ORESTES

STROPHE B

*You saw her agony, how she threw aside her dress,*
*how she was showing her breast there in the midst of death?*
*My god, how she bent to earth*
*the limbs which I was born through? and I melted!°*

CHORUS

*I know, I understand; you have come*
*through grinding torment hearing her cry*
*so hurt, your own mother.*

ORESTES

ANTISTROPHE B

*She broke into a scream then, she stretched up her hand*
*toward my face: "My son! Oh, be pitiful, my son!"*
*She clung to my face,*
*suspended, hanging; my arm dropped with the sword.*

CHORUS

*Unhappy woman—how could your eyes*
*bear to watch her blood as your own mother*
*fought for her breath and died there?*

ORESTES

STROPHE C

*I snatched a fold of my cloak to hood my eyes, and, blind,*
*took the sword and sacrificed*
*my mother—sank steel into her neck.*

ELECTRA

*I urged you on, I urged you on,*
*I touched the sword beside your hand,*
*I worked a terrible pain and ruin.°*

ORESTES°

ANTISTROPHE C

*Take it! shroud my mother's dead flesh in a cloak;*
*clean and close the sucking wounds.*
*Your own murderers were the children you bore.*

ELECTRA

*Behold! I wrap her close in this robe,*
*her whom I loved and could not love,*
*ending our family's great disasters.*

*(Enter the Dioscuri above the house.)*

CHORUS [*now chanting*]

*Whom do I see high over your house*
*shining in radiance? Are they hero spirits*
*or gods of the heavens? They are more than men*
*in their moving. Why do they come so bright*
*into the eyes of mortals?*

CASTOR [*speaking for both Dioscuri*]

O son of Agamemnon, hear us: we call to you,
the Twins, born with your mother, named the sons of Zeus,
I Castor, and my brother Polydeuces here.
We come to Argos having turned the rolling storm
of a sea-tossed ship to quiet, when we saw the death
of this our murdered sister, your murdered mother.

Justice has claimed her, but you have not worked in justice.
As for Phoebus, Phoebus—yet he is my lord,
silence. He knows what is wise, but his oracles were not wise.
Compulsion is on us all to accept this, and in future
to go complete those things which fate and Zeus assigned you.
Give Pylades Electra as a wife in his house,
and leave Argos yourself. The city is not yours
to walk in any longer, since you killed your mother.
The dreadful beast-faced goddesses of destiny
will roll you like a wheel through maddened wandering.
But when you come to Athens, fold the holy wood
of Pallas' statue to your breast—then she will check
the fluttering horror of their snakes, they cannot touch you
as she holds her Gorgon-circled shield above your head.
In Athens is the Hill of Ares, where the gods
first took their seats to judge murder by public vote,
the time raw-minded Ares killed Halirrhothius
in anger at his daughter's godless wedding night,
in anger at the sea lord's son. Since then this court
has been holy and trusted by both men and gods.
There you too must run the risk of trial for murder.
But the voting pebbles will be cast equal and save you;
you shall not die by the verdict: Loxias will take
all blame on himself for having required your mother's death,
and so for the rest of time this law shall be established:
"When votes are equal the accused must have acquittal."
The dreadful goddesses, shaken in grief for this,
shall go down in a crack of earth beside the Hill
to keep a dark and august oracle for men.
Then you must found a city near Arcadian
Alpheus' stream, beside the wolf god's sanctuary.
and by your name that city shall be known to men.
So much I say to you. Aegisthus' corpse the men
of Argos will hide, buried in an earth-heaped tomb.

Menelaus will bury your mother. He has come just now
to Nauplia for the first time since he captured Troy.
Helen will help him. She is home from Proteus' halls,
leaving Egypt behind. She never went to Troy.
Instead, Zeus made and sent a Helen-image there
to Ilium so men might die in hate and blood.
So. Let Pylades take Electra, girl and wife,
and start his journey homeward, leaving Achaea's lands;
let him also to his Phocian estates escort
her "husband," as they call him—set him deep in wealth.
Turn your feet toward Isthmus' narrow neck of earth;
make your way to the blessed hill where Cecrops dwelt.
When you have drained the fullness of this murder's doom
you will again be happy, released from these distresses.

CHORUS [*chanting from now until the end of the play, like all the other characters*]
*Sons of Zeus, does the law allow us*
*to draw any closer toward your voice?*

CASTOR
*The law allows; you are clean of this blood.*

ELECTRA
*Will you speak to me too, Tyndarids?*[26]

CASTOR
*Also to you. On Phoebus I place all*
*guilt for this death.*

CHORUS
*Why could you, who are gods and brothers*
*of the dead woman here,*
*not turn her Furies away from our halls?*

CASTOR
*Fate is compelling; it leads and we follow—*
*fate and the unwise song of Apollo.*

ELECTRA

*And I? What Apollo, what oracle's voice*
*ordained I be marked in my mother's blood?*

CASTOR

*You shared in the act, you share in the fate:*
*both children a single*
*curse on your house has ground into dust.*

ORESTES

*O sister, I found you so late, and so soon*
*I lose you, robbed of your healing love,*
*and leave you behind as you leave me.*

CASTOR

*She has a husband, she has a home, she*
*needs no pity, she suffers nothing*
*but exile from Argos.*

ELECTRA

*Are there more poignant sorrows or greater*
*than leaving the soil of a fatherland?*

ORESTES

*But I go too; I am forced from my father's*
*home; I must suffer foreigners' judgment*
*for the blood of my mother.*

CASTOR

*Courage. You go*
*to the holy city of Pallas. Endure.*

ELECTRA

*Hold me now closely breast against breast,*
*dear brother. I love you.*
*But the curses bred in a mother's blood*
*dissolve our bonds and drive us from home.*

ORESTES

*Come to me, clasp my body, lament*
*as if at the tomb of a man now dead.*

CASTOR

*Alas, your despair rings terribly, even*
*to listening gods;*
*pity at mortal labor and pain still*
*lives in us and the lords of heaven.*

ORESTES

*I shall not see you again.*

ELECTRA

*I shall never more walk in the light of your eye.*

ORESTES

*Now is the last I can hear your voice.*

ELECTRA

*Farewell, my city.*
*Many times farewell, women of my city.*

ORESTES

*O loyal love, do you go so soon?*

ELECTRA

*I go. These tears are harsh for my eyes.*

ORESTES

*Pylades, go, farewell; and be kind to*
*Electra in marriage.*

CASTOR

*Marriage shall be their care. But the hounds*
*are here. Quick, to Athens! Run to escape,*
*for they hurl their ghostly tracking against you,*
*serpent-fisted and blackened of flesh,*
*offering the fruit of terrible pain.*

*We two must hurry to Sicilian seas,*
*rescue the salt-smashed prows of the fleet.*
*As we move through the open valleys of air*
*we champion none who are stained in sin,*
*but those who have held the holy and just*
*dear in their lives we will loose from harsh*
  *toils and save them.*
*So let no man be desirous of evil*
*nor sail with those who have broken their oaths—*
  *as god to men I command you.*

(*Exit with Polydeuces.*)

CHORUS

*Farewell. The mortal who can fare well,°*
*not broken by trouble met on the road,*
  *leads a most blessed life.*

(*Exit all.*)

# THE TROJAN WOMEN

*Translated by* RICHMOND LATTIMORE

# THE TROJAN WOMEN: INTRODUCTION

*The Play: Date and Composition*

External evidence indicates that *The Trojan Women* was most likely produced in 415 BCE, as the third play of a tetralogy with *Alexander*, *Palamedes*, and the satyr-play *Sisyphus* (all lost). Unusually for Euripides, all three tragedies were thus drawn from the same body of mythic material involving the Trojan War: *Alexander* (of which quite substantial fragments survive) dealt with the rediscovery of Paris as an adult after he had been exposed as an infant, *Palamedes* with Odysseus' treachery by which he tricked the Greeks into killing their fellow soldier Palamedes. Though the three plays did not form a single coherently connected narrative of the sort Aeschylus seems to have favored in his trilogies, they did present the three episodes in chronological order and were linked with one another by various shared themes. In the competition that year, Euripides came in second to the obscure playwright Xenocles' tetralogy of *Oedipus*, *Lycaon*, *The Bacchae*, and the satyr-play *Athamas* (all lost).

A few months before the date on which, according to most scholars, the play was produced, the Athenians had captured the small Greek island of Melos and slaughtered all the adult men and enslaved all the women and children. Under the circumstances, it is difficult not to see Euripides' play, with its extended reflection on the piteous fate of a defeated city and its people, as being colored by that recent event.

## *The Myth*

Euripides' *Trojan Women* portrays the fall of Troy from the point of view of the defeated: given that all the Trojan men have been slain by the Greek victors, it is their women—mothers, daughters, wives—who give voice to the suffering of the city. The play begins with the two gods Poseidon and Athena setting aside their previous opposition during the Trojan War and amicably negotiating the destruction of the victorious Greeks for their sacrilege during the sack of the city. But then it moves to a purely human level of unrelieved distress focused above all on Hecuba, the aged former queen of the city, and her family. In contrast to the play *Hecuba*, here the woman who had ruled Troy and, with her, all the defeated Trojan women and children are deprived not only of the act of vengeance, but even of the bare hope for it. Amid the laments of the chorus of anonymous Trojan captives, the various members of Hecuba's family are assigned as slaves or concubines to their future Greek masters; the prophetess Cassandra exults over the death of Agamemnon, which she can foresee; Hector's widow Andromache announces that Polyxena has been sacrificed to the dead Achilles (in contrast to *Hecuba*, Polyxena's death is much less prominent here); and Andromache's young son Astyanax is carried off to be hurled down from the city's walls. Then Helen, Menelaus' wife, whose elopement with the Trojan prince Paris (a son of Hecuba and Priam) had caused the war, debates with Menelaus and Hecuba about how much she should be blamed for what has happened and whether or not she ought to be punished; Menelaus promises to have her killed when they arrive home in Sparta (but we know he will not do so). Finally the corpse of little Astyanax is brought on stage and mourned, and Hecuba and the remaining Trojan women leave to sail off with Odysseus, to whom she has been assigned.

The bloody and heart-rending aftermath of the Trojan War—including all the episodes dramatized here—was extensively depicted in ancient Greek epic, lyric poetry, and art. Euripides himself chose to base a number of different tragedies upon these stories. For example, about ten years before he wrote *The Trojan Women*, he had dramatized later events in *Andromache*. In *Hecuba*, written about nine years before *The Trojan Women*, he portrayed many of the same incidents as he does here. So the main events of this play are likely to have been well known to Euripides' audience already, though the formal and rather legalistic debate between Helen and Hecuba seems characteristically Euripidean and in this form is probably his invention. The play seeks to create an effect upon its audience less by surprise and original plot inventions than by its exploration of the traumatic consequences of war and its almost unrelieved, yet lyrical, portrayal of loss and displacement.

### *Transmission and Reception*

*The Trojan Women* was not especially popular in antiquity, certainly much less so than *Hecuba*, which treats much of the same legendary material. For example, only a couple of papyri of the play have survived, containing fragments of a plot summary and of some lines. But it did end up being selected as one of the ten canonical plays most studied and read in antiquity. As a result, it is transmitted by three medieval manuscripts and is equipped with ancient and medieval commentaries.

Greek and Latin authors who portrayed Hecuba's sufferings after the fall of Troy inevitably drew upon this play and upon *Hecuba*. Roman tragedies by Ennius (*Andromache*) and Accius (*Astyanax*) are lost; but Seneca's *Troades* (*Trojan Women*) does survive, containing many close echoes of this play of Euripides along with others from his *Hecuba*, and was widely read during the Renaissance. Epic poets like Virgil, Ovid, and Quintus of Smyrna also followed the outlines of Euripides' plot at least in part and presumed their readers' familiarity with his text; and Hecuba eventually became a standard example for the vicissitudes of fortune.

Although during the Middle Ages and Renaissance *The Trojan Women* was largely overshadowed by *Hecuba* (and Seneca), things have been very different in modern times. Already in the middle of the nineteenth century, Hector Berlioz based the first two acts of his opera *Les Troyennes* (1856–59) not only, unsurprisingly, upon Virgil's *Aeneid* but also, innovatively, upon *The Trojan Women*. Since the mid-twentieth century, the experience of the horrors of war, along with changes in dramatic taste, have led to a remarkable resurgence in the play's popularity, and in recent decades it has been one of the most frequently staged of all Greek tragedies. The play has been successfully adapted by such authors as Jean-Paul Sartre (*The Trojan Women*, 1965), Suzuki Tadashi (1974), Hanoch Levin (*The Lost Women of Troy*, 1984), Andrei Serban (1974/1996; with music by Elizabeth Swados), Charles Mee (n.d.), and Ellen McLaughlin (2008). It has also been the subject of notable films by such directors as the Mexican Sergio Véjar (*Las Troyanas*, 1963) and the Greek Michael Cacoyannis (*The Trojan Women*, 1971, starring Katharine Hepburn, Vanessa Redgrave, and Irene Papas).

# THE TROJAN WOMEN

*Characters*
POSEIDON
ATHENA
HECUBA, former queen of Troy
TALTHYBIUS, herald of the Greeks
CASSANDRA, daughter of Priam and Hecuba
ANDROMACHE, widow of Hector
ASTYANAX, young son of Hector and Andromache (silent character)
MENELAUS, co-leader of the Greek army
HELEN, wife of Menelaus
CHORUS of Trojan women

*Scene: An open space before the walls of the ruined city of Troy, with a tent that temporarily houses the captive women. As the play opens, Hecuba is lying on the ground in front of the tent.*

*(Enter Poseidon above the scene.)*

POSEIDON

I am Poseidon. I come from the Aegean depths
of the sea beneath whose waters Nereid choirs evolve
the intricate bright circle of their dancing feet.
For since that day when Phoebus Apollo and I laid down
on Trojan soil the close of these stone walls, drawn true
and straight, there has always been affection in my heart
unfading for these Phrygians and for their city,
which smolders now, fallen before the Argive spears,

ruined, sacked, gutted. Such is Athena's work, and his,
the Parnassian, Epeius of Phocis, architect
and builder of the horse that swarmed with inward steel,
that fatal bulk which passed within the battlements,
whose fame hereafter shall be loud among men unborn,°
the wooden horse, which hid the secret spears within.
Now the gods' groves are desolate, their thrones of power
blood-spattered where beside the lift of the altar steps
of Zeus Defender, Priam was cut down and died.
The ships of the Achaeans load with spoils of Troy
now, the piled gold of Phrygia. And the men of Greece
who made this expedition and took the city stay
only for the favoring stern-wind now to greet their wives
and children after ten years' harvests wasted here.

The will of Argive Hera and Athena won
its way against my will. Between them they broke Troy.
So I must leave my altars and great Ilium,
since once a city sinks into sad desolation
the gods' state sickens also, and their worship fades.
Scamander's valley echoes to the wail of slaves,
the captive women given to their masters now,
some to Arcadia or the men of Thessaly
assigned, or to the lords of Athens, Theseus' strain;
while all the women of Troy yet unassigned are here
beneath the shelter of these walls, chosen to wait
the will of princes, and among them Tyndareus' child
Helen of Sparta, treated—rightly—as a captive slave.

Nearby, beside the gates, for any to look upon
who has the heart, she lies face upward, Hecuba,
weeping for multitudes her multitude of tears.
Polyxena, one daughter, even now was killed
in secrecy and pain beside Achilles' tomb.
Priam is gone, their children dead; one girl is left,
the maiden Cassandra, crazed by Lord Apollo's stroke,

whom Agamemnon, in despite of the gods' will
and all religion, will lead by force to his secret bed.

O city, long ago a happy place, good-bye;
good-bye, hewn bastions. Pallas, child of Zeus, did this.
But for her hatred, you might stand strong-founded still.

*(Enter Athena above the scene.)*

ATHENA

August among the gods, O vast divinity,
closest in kinship to Zeus the father of all, may one
who quarreled with you in the past make peace, and speak?

POSEIDON

You may, lady Athena; for the strands of kinship,
close drawn, work no small magic to enchant the mind.

ATHENA

I thank you for your gentleness, and bring you now
questions whose issue touches you and me, my lord.

POSEIDON

Is this the annunciation of some new word spoken
by Zeus, or any other of the divinities?

ATHENA

No; but for Troy's sake, on whose ground we stand, I come
to win the favor of your power, as my ally.

POSEIDON

You hated Troy once; did you throw your hate away
and change to pity, now its walls are black with fire?

ATHENA

Come back to the question. Will you take counsel with me
and help me gladly in all that I would bring to pass?

POSEIDON

I will indeed; but tell me what you wish to do.
Are you here for the Achaeans' or the Phrygians' sake?

ATHENA

For the Trojans, whom I hated this short time since,
to make the Achaeans' homecoming a thing of sorrow.

POSEIDON

This is a springing change of character. Why must
you hate too hard, and love too hard, your loves and hates?

ATHENA

Did you not know they outraged my temple, and shamed me?

POSEIDON

I know that Ajax dragged Cassandra thence by force.

ATHENA

And the Achaeans did nothing. They did not even speak.

POSEIDON

Yet they captured Ilium by your strength alone.

ATHENA

True; therefore help me. I would do some evil to them.

POSEIDON

I am ready for anything you ask. What will you do?

ATHENA

Make their home voyage a most unhappy coming home.

POSEIDON

While they stay here ashore, or out on the deep sea?

ATHENA

When they take ship from Ilium and set sail for home
Zeus will shower down his rainstorms and the weariless beat
of hail, to make black the bright air with roaring winds.
He has promised my hand the gift of the blazing thunderbolt
to dash and overwhelm with fire the Achaean ships.
Yours is your own domain, the Aegean crossing. Make
the sea thunder to the tripled wave and spinning surf,
cram thick the hollow Euboean fold with floating dead;

so after this Greeks may learn how to use with fear
my sacred places, and respect all gods beside.

POSEIDON

This shall be done, and joyfully. It needs no long
discourse to tell you. I will shake the Aegean Sea.
Myconos' headlands and the swine-back reefs of Delos,
the Capherean promontories, Scyros, Lemnos
shall take the washed-up bodies of men drowned at sea.
Back to Olympus now; gather the thunderbolts
from your father's hands, then take your watcher's post, to wait
the chance, when the Achaean fleet puts out to sea.
That mortal who sacks fallen cities is a fool
if he gives the temples and the tombs, the hallowed places
of the dead, to desolation. His own turn must come.

*(Exit Poseidon and Athena. Hecuba rises slowly to her feet.)*

HECUBA [*chanting*]

*Rise, stricken head, from the dust;*
*lift up the throat. This is Troy, but Troy*
*and we, Troy's kings, are perished.*
*Stoop to the changing fortune.*
*Steer for the crossing and your fortune,*
*hold not life's prow on the course against*
*wave beat and accident.*
*Ah me,*
*what need I further for tears' occasion,*
*state perished, my sons, and my husband?*
*O massive pride that my fathers heaped*
*to magnificence, you meant nothing.*
*Must I be hushed? Were it better thus?*
*Should I cry a lament?*
*Unhappy, accursed,*
*limbs cramped, I lie*
*backed on this stiff bed.*
*O head, O temples*

*and sides; sweet, to shift,*
*let the tired spine rest,*
*weight eased by the sides alternate,*
*against the strain of the tears' song*
*where stricken people find music yet*
*in the song undanced of their wretchedness.*

[*singing*]
*You ships' prows, that the rapid*
*oars swept here to blessed Ilium*
*over the sea's blue water*
*and the placid harbors of Hellas*
*to the pipes' grim beat*
*and the swing of the shrill boat whistles;*
*you made the crossing, made fast ashore*
*the Egyptians' skill, the sea cables,*
*alas, by the coasts of Troy;*
*it was you, ships, that carried the fatal bride*
*of Menelaus, her brother Castor's shame,*
*the stain on the Eurotas.*
*Now she has killed*
*the sire of the fifty sons,*
*Priam; me, unhappy Hecuba,*
*she drove on this reef of ruin.*
*Such state I keep*
*to sit by the tents of Agamemnon.*
*I am led captive*
*from my house, an old, unhappy woman,*
*like my city ruined and pitiful.*
*Come then, sad wives of the Trojans*
*whose spears were bronze,*
*their daughters, brides of disaster,*
*let us mourn the smoke of Ilium.*
*And I, as among winged birds*
*the mother, lead out*
*the clashing cry, the song; not that song*

*wherein once long ago,*
*when Priam leaned on his scepter,*
*my feet were queens of the choir and led*
*the proud dance to the gods of Phrygia.*

(*Enter the First Half-Chorus from the tent.*)

FIRST HALF-CHORUS [*singing this lyric interchange with Hecuba, who continues to sing in reply*]

STROPHE A

*Hecuba, what are these cries?*
*What news now? Through the tent walls*
*I heard your pitiful weeping,*
*and fear shivered in the breasts*
*of the Trojan women, who within*
*sob out the day of their slavery.*

HECUBA

*My children, the ships of the Argives*
*will move today. The hand is at the oar.*

FIRST HALF-CHORUS

*They will? Why? Must I take ship*
*so soon from the land of my fathers?*

HECUBA

*I know nothing. I look for disaster.*

FIRST HALF-CHORUS

*Alas!*
*Poor women of Troy, torn from your homes,*
*come, hear of miseries.*
*The Argives push for home.*

HECUBA

*Oh,*
*let her not come forth,*
*not now, my child*
*Cassandra, driven delirious*
*to shame us before the Argives;*
*not the mad one, to bring fresh pain to my pain.*

*Ah no.*
*Troy, ill-starred Troy, this is the end;*
*your last sad people leave you now,*
*both living and broken.*

*(Enter the Second Half-Chorus from the tent.)*

SECOND HALF-CHORUS [*singing, while Hecuba continues to sing in reply*]

ANTISTROPHE A

*Ah me. Trembling, I left the tents*
*of Agamemnon to listen.*
*Tell us, our queen. Did the Argive council*
*decree my death?*
*Or are the seamen manning the ships now,*
*oars ready for action?*

HECUBA

*My child, I have come stunned with terror in my soul,*
*awake ever since the dawn.*

SECOND HALF-CHORUS

*Has a herald come from the Danaans yet?*
*Whose wretched slave shall I be ordained?*

HECUBA

*You are near the lots now.*

SECOND HALF-CHORUS

*Alas!*
*Who will lead me away? An Argive?*
*To an island home? To Phthiotis?*
*Unhappy, surely, and far from Troy.*

HECUBA

*And I,*
*whose wretched slave*
*shall I be? Where, in my gray age,*
*a faint drone,*
*poor image of a corpse,*

*weak shining among dead men? Shall*
*I stand and keep guard at their doors,*
*shall I nurse their children, I who in Troy*
*held state as a princess?*

*(The two Half-Choruses now unite to form a single Chorus.)*

CHORUS [*all singing together*]

STROPHE B

*So pitiful, so pitiful*
*your shame and your lamentation.*
*No longer shall I move the shifting pace*
*of the shuttle at the looms of Ida.*
*I shall look no more on the houses of my parents.°*
*No more. I shall have worse troubles.*
*Shall I be forced to the bed of Greek masters?*
*I curse that night and my fortune.*
*Must I draw the water of Peirene,*
*a servant at sacred springs?*
*Might I only be taken to Athens, domain*
*of Theseus, the bright, the blessed!*
*Never to the whirl of Eurotas, not Sparta*
*detested, who gave us Helen,*
*not look with slave's eyes on the scourge*
*of Troy, Menelaus.*

ANTISTROPHE B

*I have heard the rumor*
*of the hallowed ground by Peneus,*
*bright doorstone of Olympus,*
*deep burdened in beauty of wealth and harvest.*
*There would I be next after the blessed,*
*the sacrosanct land of Theseus.*
*And they say that the land of Aetna,*
*the keep against Punic men,*
*mother of Sicilian mountains, sounds*
*in the herald's cry for games' garlands;*

*and the land washed*
*by the streaming Ionian Sea,*
*that land watered by the loveliest*
*of rivers, Crathis, that turns hair red-gold*
*and draws from the depths of sacred wells*
*blessings on a strong people.*
[*chanting*]
*See now, from the host of the Danaans*
*the herald, charged with new orders, takes*
*the speed of his way toward us.*
*What message? What command? Since we count as slaves*
*even now in the Dorian kingdom.*

(*Talthybius enters from the side, accompanied by some soldiers.*)

TALTHYBIUS

Hecuba, incessantly my ways have led me to Troy
as the messenger of all the Achaean armament.
You know me from the old days, my lady; I am sent,
Talthybius, with new messages for you to hear.

HECUBA [*singing in this interchange with Talthybius, who speaks in reply*]

*It comes, beloved daughters of Troy; the thing I feared.*

TALTHYBIUS

You are all given your masters now. Was this your dread?

HECUBA

*Ah, yes. Is it Phthia, then? A city of Thessaly?*
*Tell me. The land of Cadmus?*

TALTHYBIUS

All are allotted separately, each to a man.

HECUBA

*Who is given to whom? Oh, is there any hope*
*left for the women of Troy?*

TALTHYBIUS

I understand. Yet ask not for all, but for each apart.

HECUBA

*Who was given my child? Tell me, who shall be lord*
*of my poor abused Cassandra?*

TALTHYBIUS

King Agamemnon chose her. She was given to him.

HECUBA

*Slave woman to that Lacedaemonian wife?*
*My unhappy child!*

TALTHYBIUS

No. Rather to be joined with him in a dark bed of love.

HECUBA

*She, Apollo's virgin, blessed in the privilege*
*the gold-haired god gave her, a life forever unwed?*

TALTHYBIUS

Love's archery and the prophetic maiden struck him hard.

HECUBA

*Dash down, my daughter,*
*the twigs of your consecration,*
*break the god's garlands to your throat gathered.*

TALTHYBIUS

Is it not high favor to be brought to a king's bed?

HECUBA

*And my poor youngest whom you took away,*
*where is she?°*

TALTHYBIUS

You spoke now of Polyxena. Is it not so?

HECUBA

*To whose arms did the lot force her?*

TALTHYBIUS

She is given a guardianship, to serve Achilles' tomb.

HECUBA

*To serve, my child? Over a tomb?*
*Tell me, is this their way,*
*some law, friend, established among the Greeks?*

TALTHYBIUS

Speak of your child in words of blessing. She feels no pain.

HECUBA

*What did that mean? Does she live in the sunlight still?*

TALTHYBIUS

She lives her destiny, and her cares are over now.

HECUBA

*And the wife of bronze-embattled Hector: tell me of her,*
*Andromache the forlorn. What shall she suffer now?*

TALTHYBIUS

The son of Achilles chose her. She was given to him.

HECUBA

*And I, my aged frailty crutched for support on staves,*
*whom shall I serve?*

TALTHYBIUS

You shall be slave to Odysseus, lord of Ithaca.

HECUBA

*Oh no, no!*
*Tear the shorn head,*
*rip nails through both cheeks.*
*Must I?*
*To be given as slave to serve that vile, that slippery man,*
*right's enemy, brute, murderous beast,*
*that mouth of lies and treachery, that makes void*
*faith in things promised*

*and turns to hate what was beloved! Oh, mourn,*
*daughters of Ilium, weep as one for me.*
*I am gone, doomed, undone,*
*O wretched, given*
*the worst lot of all.*

CHORUS LEADER

You know your destiny now, Queen Hecuba. But mine?
What Hellene, what Achaean is my master now?

TALTHYBIUS

Men-at-arms, do your duty. Bring Cassandra forth
without delay. Our orders are to deliver her
to the general at once. And afterward we can bring
to the rest of the princes their allotted captive women.
But see! What is that burst of a torch flame inside?
What can it mean? Are the Trojan women setting fire
to their chambers, at point of being torn from their land
to sail for Argos? Have they set themselves aflame
in longing for death? I know it is the way of freedom
in times like these to stiffen the neck against disaster.
Open, there, open; let not the fate desired by these,
dreaded by the Achaeans, hurl their wrath on me.

*(Enter Cassandra from the tent, carrying a flaming torch.)*

HECUBA [*now speaking*]

You are wrong, they're not setting fires. It is my Cassandra
whirled out on running feet in the passion of her frenzy.

CASSANDRA [*singing*]

STROPHE

*Lift up, heave up; carry the flame; I bring fire of worship,*
*torches to the temple.*
*Io, Hymen, my lord! Hymenaeus!*
*Blessed the bridegroom.*
*Blessed am I indeed to lie at a king's side,*
*blessed the bride of Argos.*

*Hymen, my lord, Hymenaeus!*
*Yours were the tears, my mother,*
*yours was the lamentation for my father fallen,*
*for your city so dear beloved,*
*but mine this marriage, my marriage,*
*and I shake out the torch flare,*
*brightness, dazzle,*
*light for you, Hymenaeus,*
*Hecate, light for you,*
*for the bed of virginity as man's custom ordains.*

ANTISTROPHE

*Let your feet dance, rippling the air; let the chorus go,*
*as when my father's fate went in blessedness.*
*O sacred circle of dance.*
*Lead now, Phoebus Apollo; I wear your laurel,*
*I tend your temple,*
*Hymen, O Hymenaeus!*
*Dance, Mother, dance, laugh; lead; let your feet*
*wind in the shifting pattern and follow mine,*
*keep the sweet step with me,*
*cry out the name Hymenaeus*
*and the bride's name in the shrill*
*and the blessed incantation.*
*O you daughters of Phrygia robed in splendor,*
*dance for my wedding,*
*for the husband fate appointed to lie beside me.*

CHORUS LEADER

Can you not, Queen Hecuba, stop this bacchanal before
her light feet whirl her away into the Argive camp?

HECUBA

Fire God, in mortal marriages you lift up your torch,
but here you throw a melancholy light, not seen
through my hopes that went so high in days gone past.
O child,

there never was a time I dreamed you'd wed like this,
like this, at spear's edge, under force of Argive arms.
Let me take the light; crazed, passionate, you cannot carry
it straight enough, poor child. Your fate is intemperate
as you are, always. There is no relief for you.

*(Hecuba takes the torch from Cassandra and gives it to some Trojan women.)*

You Trojan women, take the torch inside, and change
to songs of tears this poor girl's marriage melodies.

*(Exit these women with the torch into the tent.)*

CASSANDRA

O Mother, star my hair with flowers of victory.
This is a king I marry; then be glad; escort
the bride—and if she falters, thrust her strongly on.
If Loxias lives, the Achaeans' pride, great Agamemnon
has won a wife more fatal than ever Helen was.
Since I will kill him, and avenge my brothers' blood
and my father's in the desolation of his house.
But I leave this in silence and sing not now the axe
to drop against my throat and other throats than mine,
the agony of the mother murdered, brought to pass
from our marriage rites, and Atreus' house made desolate.
I am ridden by god's curse still, yet I will step so far
out of my frenzy as to show our city's fate
is blessed beyond the Achaeans'. For one woman's sake,
one act of love, these hunted Helen down and threw
thousands of lives away. Their general—clever man—
in the name of a vile woman cut his darling down,
gave up for a brother the sweetness of children in his house,
all to bring back that brother's wife, a woman who went
of her free will, not caught in constraint of violence.
The Achaeans came beside Scamander's banks, and died
day after day, though none sought to wrench their land from
them

nor their own towering cities. Those the war god caught
never saw their sons again, nor were they laid to rest
decently in winding sheets by their wives' hands, but lie
buried in alien ground; while all went wrong at home
as the widows perished, and couples who had raised in vain
their children were left childless, no one left to tend
their tombs and give to them the sacrificial blood.
For such success as this congratulate the Greeks.°
No, but the shame is better left in silence, for fear
my singing voice become the voice of wretchedness.
The Trojans have that glory which is loveliest:
they died for their own country. So the bodies of all
who took the spears were carried home in loving hands,
brought, in the land of their fathers, to the embrace of earth
and buried becomingly as the rite fell due. The rest,
those Phrygians who escaped death in battle, day by day
came home to happiness the Achaeans could not know;
their wives, their children. Then was Hector's fate so sad?
You think so. Listen to the truth. He is dead and gone
surely, but with reputation, as a valiant man.
How could this be, except for the Achaeans' coming?
Had they held back, none might have known how great he
was.
The bride of Paris was the daughter of Zeus. Had he
not married her, his wife's name would sleep in endless
silence.
Though surely the wise man will forever shrink from war,
yet if war come, the hero's death will lay a wreath
not lusterless on the city. The coward alone brings shame.
Let no more tears fall, Mother, for our land, nor for
this marriage I make; it is by marriage that I bring
to destruction those whom you and I have hated most.

CHORUS LEADER

You smile on your disasters. Can it be that you
some day will invalidate the darkness of this song?

TALTHYBIUS

Were it not that Apollo has driven wild your wits
I would make you sorry for sending the princes of our host
on their way home in augury of foul speech like this.
Now pride of majesty and wisdom's outward show
have fallen to stature less than what was nothing worth
since he, almighty prince of the assembled Hellenes,
Atreus' son beloved, has stooped—by his own will—
to find his love in a crazed girl. I, a plain man,
would not marry this woman or keep her as my lover.
You then, with your wits unhinged by idiocy,
your scolding of Argos and your Trojans glorified
I throw to the winds to scatter them. Come now with me
to the ships, a bride—and such a bride—for Agamemnon.

Hecuba, when Laertes' son calls you, be sure
you follow; if what all say who came to Ilium
is true, at the worst you will be a virtuous woman's slave.

CASSANDRA

That servant is a vile thing. Oh, how can heralds keep
their name of honor? Lackeys for despots be they, or
lackeys to the people, all men must despise them still.
You tell me that my mother must be slave in the house
of Odysseus? Where are all Apollo's promises
uttered to me, to my own ears, that Hecuba
would die in Troy? What else awaits her—but enough!
Poor wretch, he little dreams of what he must go through,
when he will think Troy's pain and mine were golden grace
beside his own luck. Ten years he spent here, and ten
more years will follow before he at last comes home, forlorn°
after the terror of the rock and the thin strait,
Charybdis; and the mountain-striding Cyclops, who eats
men's flesh; the Ligyan witch who changes men to swine,
Circe; the wreck of all his ships on the salt sea,
the lotus passion, the sacred oxen of the sun
slaughtered, their dead flesh moaning into speech, to make

Odysseus listening shiver. Cut the story short:
he will go down to the water of death, and return alive
to reach his home and thousand sorrows waiting there.

Why must I hurl forth each of Odysseus' labors one by one?
Lead the way quick to the house of death where I shall take my mate.
Lord of all the sons of Danaus, haughty in your mind of pride,
not by day, but evil in the evil night you shall find your grave
when I lie corpse-cold and naked next my husband's sepulcher,
piled in the ditch for animals to rip and feed on, beaten by
streaming storms of winter, I who wore Apollo's sacraments.
Garlands of the god I loved so well, prophetic spirit's dress,
leave me, as I leave those festivals where once I was so proud.
See, I tear your adornments from my skin not yet defiled by touch,
throw them to the running winds to carry off, O lord of prophecy.
Where is this general's ship, then? Lead me where I must set my feet on board.
Wait the wind of favor in the sails; yet when the ship goes out
from this shore, she carries one of the three Furies in my shape.
Land of my ancestors, good-bye; O Mother, weep no more for me.
You beneath the ground, my brothers, Priam, father of us all,
I will be with you soon and come triumphant to the dead below,
leaving behind me, wrecked, the house of Atreus, which destroyed our house.

*(Exit Cassandra escorted by Talthybius and his soldiers to the side. Hecuba collapses.)*

CHORUS LEADER

Handmaids of aged Hecuba, can you not see
how your mistress, powerless to cry out, lies prone? Oh, take
her hand and help her to her feet, you wretched maids.
Will you let an aged helpless woman lie so long?

HECUBA

No. Let me lie where I have fallen. Kind acts, my maids,
must be unkind, unwanted. All that I endure
and have endured and shall, deserves to strike me down.
O gods! What wretched things to call on—gods!—for help
although the decorous action is to invoke their aid
when all our hands lay hold on is unhappiness.
No. It is my pleasure first to tell good fortune's tale,
to cast its count more sadly against disasters now.
I was a princess, who was once a prince's bride,
mother by him of sons preeminent, not just
mere empty numbers of them, but the lords of the Phrygian
domain,
such sons for pride to point to as not one woman ever,
no Hellene, none in the wide barbarian world might match.
And then I saw them fall before the spears of Greece,
and cut my hair for them, and laid it on their graves.
I mourned their father, Priam. None told me the tale
of his death. I saw it, with these eyes. I stood to watch
his throat cut, at the altar of the protecting god.
I saw my city taken. And the girls I nursed,
choice flowers to wear the pride of any husband's eyes,
matured to be dragged by hands of strangers from my arms.
There is no hope left that they will ever see me more,
no hope that I shall ever look on them again.
There is one more stone to key this arch of wretchedness:
I must be carried away to Hellas now, an old
slave woman, where all those tasks that wrack old age shall be
given me by my masters. I must work the bolt

that bars their doorway, I whose son was Hector once;
or bake their bread; lay down these withered limbs to sleep
on the bare ground, whose bed was royal once; abuse
this skin once delicate the slattern's way, exposed
through robes whose rags will mock my luxury of long since.
Unhappy, O unhappy! And all this came to pass
and shall be, for the way one woman chose a man.
Cassandra, O Daughter, whose inspiration was god-shared,
you have paid for your consecration now; at what a price!
And you, my poor Polyxena, where are you now?
Not here, nor any boy or girl of mine, who were
so many once, is near me in my unhappiness.
And you would lift me from the ground? What hope? What
use?

*(Hecuba rises painfully.)*

Guide these feet long ago so delicate in Troy,
a slave's feet now, to the straw sacks laid on the ground
and the piled stones; let me lay down my head and die
in an exhaustion of tears. Of all who walk in bliss
call not one happy yet, until the man is dead.

*(Hecuba is led to the back of the stage, and then falls to the ground once more.)*

CHORUS [*singing*]

STROPHE

*Voice of singing, stay*
*with me now, for Ilium's sake;*
*take up the burden of tears,*
*new song of sorrow;*
*the dirge for Troy's death*
*must be chanted;*
*the tale of my enslavement*
*by the wheeled stride of the four-foot beast of the Argives,*
*the horse they left in the gates,*
*thin gold at its cheeks,*
*inward, the spears' high thunder.*

*Our people thronging*
*the rock of Troy roared out the great cry:*
*"The war is over! Go down,*
*bring this sacred wood idol*
*to the Maiden of Ilium, Zeus' daughter."*
*Who stayed then? Not one girl, not one*
*old man, in their houses,*
*but singing for happiness*
*let the lurking death in.*

ANTISTROPHE

*And the generation of Troy*
*swept solid to the gates*
*to give the goddess*
*her pleasure: the horse immortal, unbroken,*
*the nest of Argive spears,*
*death for the children of Dardanus*
*sealed in the sleek hill pine chamber.*
*In the sling of the flax twist, shipwise,*
*they berthed the black hull*
*in the shrine of Pallas Athena,*
*stone paved, washed now in the blood of our people.*
*Strong, joyful work*
*deep into black night*
*to the stroke of the Libyan lute*
*and all Troy singing, and girls'*
*light feet pulsing the air*
*in joyous dance measures;*
*indoors, lights everywhere,*
*torchflares on black*
*to forbid sleep's onset.*

EPODE

*I was there also: in the great room*
*I danced for the maiden of the mountains,*
*Artemis, Zeus' daughter.*
*Then the cry went up, sudden,*

*bloodshot, up and down the city, to stun*
*the keep of the citadel. Children*
*reached shivering hands to clutch*
*at their mother's dress.*
*War stalked from his hiding place.*
*Pallas did this.*
*Beside their altars the Trojans*
*died in their blood. Desolate now,*
*men murdered, our sleeping rooms gave up*
*their brides' beauty*
*to breed sons for Greek men,*
*sorrow for our own country.*

*(Enter Andromache holding Astyanax and sitting in a wagon that comes from the side accompanied by Greek soldiers and heaped with spoils of war.)*

[*chanting*]
*Hecuba look, I see her, rapt*
*to the enemy wagon, Andromache,*
*close to whose beating breast clings*
*the boy Astyanax, Hector's sweet child.*
*O carried away—to what land?—unhappy woman,*
*on the wagon floor, with the brazen arms*
*of Hector, of Troy*
*captive and heaped beside you,*
*torn now from Troy, for Achilles' son*
*to hang in the shrines of Phthia.*

ANDROMACHE [*singing in this lyric interchange together with Hecuba, who sings in reply*]

STROPHE A

*I go at the hands of Greek masters.*

HECUBA

*Alas!*

ANDROMACHE

*Must the incantation . . .*

HECUBA

*(Ah me!)*

ANDROMACHE

*... of my own grief win tears from you?*

HECUBA

*It must—O Zeus!*

ANDROMACHE

*My own distress?*

HECUBA

*O my children ...*

ANDROMACHE

*... once. No longer.*

HECUBA

ANTISTROPHE A

*Lost, lost, Troy our dominion ...*

ANDROMACHE

*... unhappy ...*

HECUBA

*... and my lordly children.*

ANDROMACHE

*Gone, alas!*

HECUBA

*They were mine.*

ANDROMACHE

*Sorrows only.*

HECUBA

*Sad destiny ...*

ANDROMACHE

*... of our city ...*

HECUBA

*... a wreck, and burning.*

ANDROMACHE

STROPHE B

*Come back, O my husband.°*

HECUBA

*Poor child, you invoke*
*a dead man; my son once ...*

ANDROMACHE

*... my defender.*

ANDROMACHE

ANTISTROPHE B

*You, who once killed the Greeks ...*

HECUBA

*... oldest of the sons*
*I bore to Priam ...*

ANDROMACHE

*... take me to my death now.*

ANDROMACHE

STROPHE C

*Longing for death drives deep ...*

HECUBA

*... O sorrowful, such is our fortune ...*

ANDROMACHE

*... lost our city ...*

HECUBA

*... and our pain lies deep under pain piled over.*

ANDROMACHE

*We are the hated of the gods, since once your youngest, escaping*
*death, brought down Troy's towers in the arms of a worthless woman;*

*piled at the feet of Pallas the bleeding bodies of our young men*
*sprawled, kites' food, while Troy takes up the yoke of captivity.*

HECUBA

ANTISTROPHE C

*O my city, my city forlorn . . .*

ANDROMACHE

*. . . abandoned, I weep this . . .*

HECUBA

*. . . miserable last hour . . .*

ANDROMACHE

*. . . of the house where I bore my children.*

HECUBA

*O my sons, this city and your mother are desolate of you.*
*Sound of lamentation and sorrow,°*
*tears on tears shed. Home, farewell.*
*The dead have forgotten all sorrows.*

CHORUS LEADER

They who are sad find somehow sweetness in tears, the song
of lamentation and the melancholy Muse.

ANDROMACHE [*now speaking*]

Hecuba, mother of the man whose spear was death
to the Argives, Hector: do you see what they have done to us?

HECUBA [*now speaking*]

I see the work of gods who pile tower-high the pride
of those who were nothing, and dash present grandeur down.

ANDROMACHE

We are carried away, sad spoils, my boy and I; our life
transformed, we who were noble have now become mere
slaves.

HECUBA

Such is the terror of necessity. I lost
Cassandra, roughly torn from my arms before you came.

ANDROMACHE

Another Ajax to haunt your daughter? Some such thing
it must be. Yet you have lost still more than you yet know.

HECUBA

There is no numbering my losses. Infinitely
misfortune comes to outrace misfortune known before.

ANDROMACHE

Polyxena is dead. They cut your daughter's throat
to pleasure dead Achilles' corpse, above his grave.

HECUBA

O wretched. This was what Talthybius meant, that speech
cryptic, incomprehensible, yet now so clear.

ANDROMACHE

I saw her die, and left this wagon seat to lay
a robe upon her body and sing the threnody.

HECUBA

Poor child, poor wretched, wretched darling, sacrificed,
in pain, to a dead man. What monstrous sacrilege!

ANDROMACHE

She is dead, and this was death indeed; and yet to die
as she did was happier than to live as I live now.

HECUBA

Child, no. No life, no light is any kind of death,
since death is nothing, and in life the hopes live still.

ANDROMACHE

O Mother, our mother, hear me while I reason through°
this matter fairly—might it even hush your grief!
Death, I am sure, is like never being born, but death
is better thus by far than to live a life of pain,
since the dead, with no perception of evil, feel no grief,°
while he who was happy once and then unfortunate
finds his heart driven far from the old lost happiness.

She died; it is as if she never saw the light
of day, for she knows nothing now of what she suffered.
But I, who aimed the arrows of ambition high
at honor, and made them good, see now how far I fall,
I, who in Hector's house worked out all custom that brings
discretion's name to women. Blame them or blame them not,
there is one act that swings the scandalous speech their way
beyond all else: to leave the house and walk abroad.
I longed to do it, but put the longing aside, and stayed
always within the enclosure of my own house and court.
The witty speech some women cultivate I would
not practice, but kept my honest inward thought, and made
my mind my only and sufficient teacher. I gave
my lord's presence the tribute of hushed lips, and eyes
quietly downcast. I knew when my will must have its way
over his, knew also how to give way to him in turn.
Men learned of this; I was talked of in the Achaean camp,
and reputation has destroyed me now. At the choice
of women, Achilles' son picked me from the rest, to be
his wife: a murderer's house, and I shall be his slave.
If I dash back the beloved memory of Hector
and open wide my heart to my new lord, I shall be
a traitor to the dead love, and know it; if I cling
faithful to the past, I win my master's hatred. Yet
they say one night of love suffices to dissolve
a woman's aversion to share the bed of any man.
I hate and loathe that woman who casts away the once
beloved, and takes another in her arms of love.
Even the young mare torn from her running mate and
    teamed
with another will not easily wear the yoke. And yet
this is a brute and speechless beast of burden, not
like us intelligent, lower far in nature's scale.
    Dear Hector, when I had you I had a husband, great
in understanding, rank, wealth, courage: all my wish.
I was a virgin when you took me from the house

of my father; I gave you all my maiden love, my first,
and now you are dead, and I must cross the sea, to serve,
prisoner of war, the slave's yoke on my neck, in Greece.
No, Hecuba; can you not see my fate is worse
than hers you mourn, Polyxena's? That one thing left
always while life lasts, hope, is not for me. I keep
no secret deception in my heart—sweet though it be
to dream—that I shall ever be happy any more.

CHORUS LEADER

You stand where I do in misfortune, and while you mourn
your life, you tell me what I, too, am suffering.

HECUBA

I have never been inside the hull of a ship, but know
what I know only by hearsay and from painted scenes,
yet think that seamen, while the gale blows moderately,
take pains to spare unnecessary work, and send
one man to the steering oar, another aloft, and one
to pump the bilge from the hold. But when the tempest comes
and seas wash over the decks, they lose their nerve, and let
her go by the run at the waves' will, leaving all to chance.
So I, in this succession of disasters, swamped,
battered by this storm immortally inspired, have lost
my voice. I hold my tongue and let misfortune go
as it will. Yet still, beloved child, you must forget
what happened with Hector. Tears will never save you now.
Give your obedience to the new master; let your ways
entice his heart to make him love you. If you do
it will be better for all who are close to you. This boy,
my own son's child, might grow to manhood and bring back—
he alone could do it—something of our city's strength.
On some far day the children of your children might
come home, and build. There still may be another Troy.
But *we* say this, and others will speak also. See,

here is some runner of the Achaeans coming now.
Who is he? What news? What counsel have they taken now?

*(Enter Talthybius again from the side with his escort.)*

TALTHYBIUS

O wife of Hector, once the bravest man in Troy,
do not hate me. This is the will of the Danaans and
the kings. I wish I did not have to give this message.

ANDROMACHE

What can this mean, this hint of hateful things to come?

TALTHYBIUS

The council has decreed that your son—how can I say this?

ANDROMACHE

That he shall serve some other master than I serve?

TALTHYBIUS

No man of Achaea shall ever make this boy his slave.

ANDROMACHE

Must he be left behind in Phrygia, all alone?

TALTHYBIUS

Worse; horrible. There is no easy way to tell it.

ANDROMACHE

I thank your courtesy—unless your news be really good.

TALTHYBIUS

They will kill your son. It is monstrous. Now you know the truth.

ANDROMACHE

Oh, this is worse than anything I heard before.

TALTHYBIUS

Odysseus. He urged it before the Greeks, and got his way.

ANDROMACHE

This is too much grief, and more than anyone could bear.

TALTHYBIUS

He said a hero's son could not be allowed to live.

ANDROMACHE

Even thus may his own sons some day find no mercy.

TALTHYBIUS

He must be hurled down from the battlements of Troy.
Let it happen this way. It will be wiser in the end.
Do not fight it. Take your grief nobly, as you were born;
give up the struggle where your strength is feebleness
with no force anywhere to help. Listen to me!
Your city is gone, your husband. You are in our power.
How can one woman hope to struggle against the arms
of Greece? Think, then. Give up the passionate contest.
Don't
do any shameful thing, or any deed of hatred.
And please—I request you—hurl no curse at the Achaeans
for fear the army, savage over some reckless word,
forbid the child his burial and the dirge of honor.
Be brave, be silent; out of such patience you'll be sure
the child you leave behind will not lie unburied here,
and that to you the Achaeans will be less unkind.

ANDROMACHE

O darling child I loved too well for happiness,
your enemies will kill you and leave your mother forlorn.
Your own father's nobility, where others found
protection, means your murder now. The memory
of his valor comes luckless for you. O bridal bed,
O marriage rites that brought me home to Hector's house
a bride, you were unhappy in the end. I lived
never thinking the baby I had was born for butchery
by Greeks, but for lordship over all Asia's pride of earth.
Poor child, are you crying too? Do you know what they
will do to you? Your fingers clutch my dress. What use,

to nestle like a young bird under the mother's wing?
Hector cannot come back, not burst from underground
to save you, that spear of glory caught in the quick hand,
nor Hector's kin, nor any strength of Phrygian arms.
Yours the sick leap head downward from the height, the fall
where none have pity, and the spirit smashed out in death.
O last and loveliest embrace of all, O child's
sweet fragrant body. Vanity in the end. I nursed
for nothing the swaddled baby at this mother's breast;
in vain the wrack of the labor pains and the long weakness.
Now once again, and never after this, come close
to your mother, lean against my breast and wind your arms
around my neck, and put your lips against my lips.
Greeks! Your Greek cleverness is simple barbarity.
Why kill this child, who never did you any harm?
O flower of the house of Tyndareus! Not his,
not Zeus' daughter, never that, but child of many fathers
I say; the daughter of Vindictiveness, of Hate,
of Blood, Death; of all wickedness that swarms on earth.
I cry it aloud: Zeus never was your father, but you
were born a pestilence to all Greeks and the world beside.
Accursed, who from those lovely and accursed eyes
brought down to shame and ruin the bright plains of Troy.
Oh, seize him, take him, dash him to death if it must be done;
feed on his flesh if it is your will. These are the gods
who damn us to this death, and I have no strength to save
my boy from execution. Cover my wretched face
and throw me into the ship and that sweet bridal bed
I walk to now across the death of my own child.

*(Talthybius lifts the child out of the wagon, which exits to the side carrying Andromache.)*

CHORUS LEADER

Unhappy Troy! For the sweetness in one woman's arms,
embrace unspeakable, you lost these thousands slain.

TALTHYBIUS [*chanting*]

*Come, boy, taken from the embrace beloved*
*of your mourning mother. Climb the high circle*
*of the walls your fathers built. There*
*end life. This was the order.*
*Take him.*

*(He hands Astyanax to the guards, who carry him out to the side.)*

*I am not the man*
*to do this. Some other*
*without pity, not as I ashamed,*
*should be herald of messages like this.*

*(Exit to the side.)*

HECUBA [*chanting*]

*O child of my own unhappy son,*
*shall your life be torn from your mother*
*and from me? Wicked! Can I help,*
*dear child, not only suffer? What help?*
*Tear face, beat bosom. This is all*
*my power now. O city,*
*O child, what have we left to suffer?*
*Are we not hurled*
*down the whole length of disaster?*

CHORUS [*singing*]

STROPHE A

*Telamon, O king in the land where the bees swarm,*
*Salamis the surf-pounded isle where you founded your city*
*to front that hallowed coast where Athena broke*
*forth the primeval pale branch of olive,*
*wreath of the bright air and a glory on Athens the shining:*
*O Telamon, you came in your pride of arms*
*with Alcmene's archer from Greece*
*to Ilium, our city, to sack and destroy it*
*on that age-old venture.*

ANTISTROPHE A

*This was the first flower of Hellenic strength Heracles brought in anger*
*for the horses promised; and by Simois' fair waters*
*checked his surf-wandering oars and made fast the ships' stern cables.*
*From those vessels came out the deadly bow hand,*
*death to Laomedon, as the scarlet wind of the flames swept over*
*masonry straight-hewn by the hands of Apollo.*
*This was a desolation of Troy*
*twice taken; twice in the welter of blood the walls Dardanian*
*went down before the red spear.*

STROPHE B

*In vain, then, Laomedon's child,*
*you walk in delicate pride*
*by the golden pitchers*
*in loveliest servitude*
*to fill Zeus' wine cups;*
*while Troy your mother is given to the flame to eat,*
*and the lonely beaches*
*mourn, as sad birds sing*
*for the young lost,*
*for the wives and the children*
*and the aged mothers.*
*Gone now the shining pools where you bathed,*
*the fields where you ran*
*all desolate. And you,*
*Ganymede, go in grace by the throne of Zeus*
*with your young, calm smile even now*
*as Priam's kingdom*
*falls to the Greek spear.*

ANTISTROPHE B

*O Love, Love, it was you*
*in the high halls of Dardanus,*
*the gods were thinking of you,*

*who greatly glorified Troy*
*on that day, binding her in marriage*
*with the gods. I speak no more*
*against Zeus' name.*
*But the light men love, that shines*
*through the pale wings of morning,*
*baleful star for this earth,*
*watched the collapse of Pergamum:*
*Dawn. Her lord was of this land;*
*she bore his children,*
*Tithonus, caught away by the golden car*
*and the starry horses,*
*who made our hopes so high.*
*For the gods loved Troy once.*
*Now they have forgotten.*

*(Enter Menelaus from the side, attended by soldiers.)*

MENELAUS

O splendor of sunburst breaking forth this day, whereon
I lay my hands once more on Helen, my wife.° And yet
it is not, so much as men think, for a woman's sake
I came to Troy, but against that guest proved treacherous,
who like a robber carried the woman from my house.
Since the gods have seen to it that *he* paid the penalty,
fallen before the Hellenic spear, his kingdom wrecked,
I come for *her* now, the Spartan once my own, whose name
I can no longer speak with any happiness,
to take her away. In this house of captivity
she is numbered among the other women of Troy, a slave.
And those men whose work with the spear has won her back
gave her to me, to kill, or not to kill, but lead
alive to the land of Argos, if such be my pleasure.
And such it is; the death of Helen in Troy I will let
pass, have the oars take her by seaways back to Greek
soil, and there give her over to execution;

blood penalty for friends who are dead in Ilium here.
Go to the house, my followers, and take her out;
no, drag her out; lay hands upon that hair so stained
with men's destruction. When the winds blow fair astern
we will take ship again and bring her back to Hellas.

*(Exit several soldiers into the tent.)*

HECUBA

O power, who mount the world, wheel where the world rides,
O mystery of man's knowledge, whosoever you be,
named Zeus, nature's necessity or mortal mind,
I call upon you; for you walk the path none hears
yet bring all human action back to right at last.

MENELAUS

What can this mean? How strange a way to call on gods.

HECUBA

Kill your wife, Menelaus, and I will bless your name.
But keep your eyes away from her. Desire will win.
She looks enchantment, and where she looks homes are set fire;
she captures cities as she captures the eyes of men.
We have had experience, you and I. We know the truth.

*(Enter Helen from the tent escorted by soldiers.)*

HELEN

Menelaus, your first acts are argument of terror
to come. Your lackeys put their hands on me. I am dragged
out of my chambers by brute force. I know you hate
me; I am almost sure. And still there is one question
I would ask you, if I may. What have the Greeks decided
to do with me? Or shall I be allowed to live?

MENELAUS

You are not strictly condemned, but all the army gave
you into my hands, to kill you for the wrong you did me.

HELEN

Is it permitted that I argue this, and prove
that my death, if I am put to death, will be unjust?

MENELAUS

I did not come to talk with you. I came to kill.

HECUBA

No, Menelaus, listen to her. She should not die
unheard. But give me leave to make the opposite case;
the prosecution. There are things that happened in Troy
which you know nothing of, and the long-drawn argument
will mean her death. She never can escape us now.

MENELAUS

This is a gift of leisure. Yet if she wants to speak
she may. But it is for your sake, understand, that I give
this privilege I never would have given for her.

HELEN *(To Menelaus.)*

Perhaps it will make no difference if I speak
well or badly, and your hate will not let you answer me.
All I can do is to foresee the arguments
you will use in accusation of me, and set against
the force of your charges, charges of my own.
First, then!

*(Pointing to Hecuba.)*

*She* mothered the beginning of all this wickedness.
For Paris was her child. And next to her the old king,
who would not destroy the infant Alexander, that dream
of the firebrand's agony, has ruined Troy and me.
This is not all; listen to the rest I have to say.
Alexander was the judge of the goddess trinity.
Pallas Athena would have given him power, to lead
the Phrygian arms on Hellas and make it desolate.
All Asia was Hera's promise, and the uttermost zones

of Europe for his lordship, if her way prevailed.
But Aphrodite, marveling at my loveliness,
promised it to him, if he would say her beauty surpassed
all others. Think what this means, and all the consequence.
Cypris prevailed, and I was won in marriage: all
for Greek advantage. You are not ruled by barbarians,
you have not been defeated in war nor serve a tyrant.
Yet Hellas' fortune was my own misfortune. I,
sold once for my body's beauty, stand accused, who should
for what has been done wear garlands on my head.
I know.
You will say all this is nothing to the immediate charge:
I did run away; I did go secretly from your house.
But when he came to me—call him any name you will:
Paris? or Alexander? that ruinous spirit sent
to haunt this woman—he came with a goddess at his side,
no weak one. And you—it was criminal—took ship for Crete
and left me there in Sparta in the house, alone.
You see?
I wonder—and I ask this of myself, not you—
why *did* I do it? What made me run away from home
with the stranger, and betray my country and my hearth?
Challenge the goddess then; show your strength greater than
Zeus'
who has the other gods in his power, and still is slave
to Aphrodite alone! Shall I not be forgiven?
Still you might have some show of argument against me.
When Paris was gone to the deep places of death, below
ground, and my marriage given by the gods was gone,
I should have come back to the Argive ships, left Troy.
I did try to do it, and I have witnesses,
the towers' gatekeepers and the sentinels on the wall,
who caught me again and again as I let down the rope
from the battlements and tried to slip away to the ground.
As for Deiphobus, my second husband: he took me away°
by force and kept me his wife against the Phrygians' will.

O my husband, can you kill me now and think you kill
in righteousness?° I was the bride of force. Besides,
my natural beauty brought me the sorrow of slavery
instead of victory. Would you be stronger than the gods?
Try, then. But any such ambition is absurd.

CHORUS LEADER

O Queen of Troy, stand by your children and your country!
Break down the beguilement of this woman, since she speaks
well, but has done wickedly. This is dangerous.

HECUBA

First, to defend the honor of the gods, and show
that the woman is a scandalous liar. I will not
believe it! Hera and the virgin Pallas Athena
could never be so silly and empty-headed
that Hera would sell Argos to the barbarians,
or Pallas let Athenians be the slaves of Troy.
They went to Ida in girlish emulation, vain
of their own loveliness? Why? Tell me the reason Hera
should fall so much in love with the idea of beauty.
To win some other lord more powerful than Zeus?
Or had Athena marked some god to be her mate,
she, whose virginity is a privilege won from Zeus,
she who abjures marriage? Do not trick out your own sins
by calling the gods stupid. No wise man will believe you.
You claim, and I must laugh to hear it, that Aphrodite
came at my son's side to the house of Menelaus?
She could have caught up you and your city of Amyclae
and set you in Ilium, moving not from the quiet of heaven!
Nonsense. My son was handsome beyond all other men.
You looked at him, and sense went Cyprian at the sight,
since Aphrodite is nothing but the human lust,
named rightly, since the word of lust begins the god's name.°
You saw him in the barbaric splendor of his robes,
gorgeous with gold. It made your senses itch. You thought,
being queen only in Argos, in little luxury,

that once you got rid of Sparta for the Phrygian city
where gold streamed everywhere, you could let extravagance
run wild. No longer were Menelaus and his house
sufficient for your spoiled luxurious appetites.
So much for that. You say my son took you away
by force. What Spartan heard you cry for help? You did
cry out? Or did you? Castor, your brother, was there, a young
man, and his twin not yet caught up among the stars.
Then when you had reached Troy, and the Argives at your
  heels
came, and the agony of the murderous spears began,
when the reports came in that Menelaus' side
was winning, you would praise him, simply to make my son
unhappy at the strength of his love's challenger,
forgetting your husband when the luck went back to Troy.
You worked hard: not to make yourself a better woman,
but to make sure always to be on the winning side.
You claim you tried to slip away with ropes let down
from the ramparts, and this proves you stayed against your
  will?
Perhaps. But when were you ever caught in the strangling
  noose,
or sharpening a dagger? Which any noble wife
would do, desperate with longing for her lord's return.
Yet over and over again I gave you good advice:
"Make your escape, my daughter; there are other girls
for my sons to marry. I will help you get away
to the ships of the Achaeans. Let the Greeks, and us,
stop fighting." So I argued, but you were not pleased.
Spoiled in the luxury of Alexander's house
you liked foreigners to kiss the ground before your feet.
All that impressed you.
                    And now you dare to come outside,
figure fastidiously arranged, to look upon
the same sky as your husband, O abominable
heart, who should walk submissively in rags of robes,

shivering with anxiety, head Scythian-cropped,
your old impudence gone and modesty gained at last
with reference to your sinful life.
O Menelaus,
mark this, the end of my argument. Be true to your
high reputation and to Hellas. Grace both, and kill
Helen. Thus make it the custom toward all womankind
hereafter, that the price of adultery is death.

CHORUS LEADER

Menelaus, keep the ancestral honor of your house.
Punish your wife, and clear your name of the accusation
of cowardice. You shall seem great even to your enemies.

MENELAUS

All you have said falls into line with my own thought.
This woman left my household for a stranger's bed
of her own free will, and all this talk of Aphrodite
is for pure show. Away, and face the stones of the mob.
Atone for the long labors of the Achaeans in
the brief act of dying, and know your penance for my shame.

*(Helen falls before him and embraces his knees.)*

HELEN

No, by your knees! I am not guilty of the mind's
infection, which the gods sent. Do not kill! Have pity!

HECUBA

Be true to the memory of all your friends she murdered.
It is for them and for their children that I plead.

*(Menelaus pushes Helen away.)*

MENELAUS

Enough, Hecuba. I am not listening to her now.
I speak to my servants: see that she is taken away
to where the ships are beached. She will make the voyage
home.

HECUBA

But let her not be put in the same ship with you.

MENELAUS

What can you mean? That she is heavier than she was?

HECUBA

A man in love once never is out of love again.

MENELAUS

Sometimes; when the beloved's heart turns false to him.
Yet it shall be as you wish. She shall not be allowed
in the same ship I sail in. This was well advised.
And once in Argos she must die the vile death earned
by her vile life, and be an example to all women
to live temperately. This is not the easier way;
and yet her execution will tincture with fear
the lust of women even more depraved than she.

*(Exit Menelaus and Helen to the side escorted by soldiers.)*

CHORUS [*singing*]

STROPHE A

*Thus, O Zeus, you betrayed all*
*to the Achaeans: your temple*
*in Ilium, your misted altar,*
*the flame of the clotted sacraments,*
*the smoke of the skying incense,*
*Pergamum the hallowed,*
*the ivied ravines of Ida, washed*
*by the running snow, the utter*
*peaks that surprise the sun bolts,*
*shining and primeval place of divinity.*

ANTISTROPHE A

*Gone are your sacrifices, the choirs'*
*glad voices singing, for the gods*
*night long festivals in the dark;*
*gone the images, gold on wood*

*laid, the twelves of the sacred moons,*
*the magic Phrygian number.*
*Can it be, can it be, my lord, you have forgotten,*
*from your throne high in heaven's*
*bright air, my city which is ruined*
*and the flame storm that broke it?*

STROPHE B

*O my dear, my husband, O wandering ghost*
*unwashed, unburied; the sea hull must carry me*
*in the flash of its wings' speed*
*to Argos, city of horses, where*
*the stone walls built by giants invade the sky.*
*The multitudes of our children stand*
*clinging to the gates and cry through their tears.*
*And one girl weeps:°*
*"O Mother, the Achaeans take me away*
*lonely from your eyes*
*to the black ship*
*where the oars dip surf*
*toward Salamis the blessed,*
*or the peak between two seas*
*where Pelops' castle*
*keeps the gates at the Isthmus."*

ANTISTROPHE B

*Oh that as Menelaus' ship*
*makes way through the mid-sea*
*the bright pronged spear immortal of thunder might smash it*
*far out in the Aegean,*
*as in tears, in bondage to Hellas,*
*I am cut from my country;*
*as she holds the golden mirror*
*in her hands, girls' grace,*
*she, Zeus' daughter.*
*Let him never come home again, to a room in Laconia*
*and the hearth of his fathers;*

*never more to Pitana's streets*
*and the bronze gates of Athena;*
*since he possesses his shame*
*and the vile marriage, the sorrows*
*of great Hellas and the land*
*watered by Simois.*

*(Enter Talthybius again from the side, accompanied by soldiers who carry the body of Astyanax, laid on the shield of Hector.)*

[*chanting*]
*But see!*
*New evils multiply in our land.*
*Behold, O pitiful wives*
*of the Trojans. This is Astyanax,*
*dead, dashed without pity from the walls, and borne*
*by the Danaans, who murdered him.*

TALTHYBIUS

Hecuba, one last ship, that of Achilles' son,
remains, manned at the oar sweeps now, to carry back
to the shores of Phthiotis his last spoils of war.
Neoptolemus himself has put to sea. He heard
news of old Peleus in difficulty and his land
invaded by Acastus, son of Pelias.
Such news put speed above all pleasure of delay.
So he is gone, and took with him Andromache,
whose lamentations for her country and farewells
to Hector's tomb as she departed brought these tears
crowding into my eyes. And she implored that we
bury this dead child, your own Hector's son, who died
flung from the battlements of Troy. She asked as well
that the bronze-backed shield, terror of the Achaeans once,
when the boy's father slung its defense across his side,
be not taken to the hearth of Peleus, nor the room
where the slain child's Andromache must be a bride
once more, to waken memories by its sight, but used°

in place of the cedar coffin and stone-chambered tomb
for the boy's burial. He shall be laid in your arms
to wrap the body about with winding sheets, and flowers,
as well as you can, out of that which is left to you.
For she is gone. Her master's speed prevented her
from giving the rites of burial to her little child.

The rest of us, once the corpse is laid out, and earth
is piled above it, must raise the mast tree, and go.
Do therefore quickly everything that you must do.
There is one labor I myself have spared you. As
we forded on our way here Scamander's running water,
I washed the body and made clean the wounds. I go
now, to break ground and dig the grave for him, that my
work be made brief, as yours must be, and our tasks end
together, and the ships be put to sea, for home.

HECUBA

Lay down the circled shield of Hector on the ground:
a hateful thing to look at; it means no love to me.

*(Exit Talthybius and his escort to the side.)*

Achaeans! All your strength is in your spears, not in
the mind. What were you afraid of, that it made you kill
this child so savagely? That Troy, which fell, might be
raised from the ground once more? Your strength meant
 nothing, then.
When Hector's spear was fortunate, and numberless
strong hands were there to help him, we were still destroyed.
Now when the city is fallen and the Phrygians slain,
this baby terrified you? I despise the fear
which is pure terror in a mind unreasoning.

O darling child, how wretched was this death! You might
have fallen fighting for your city, grown to man's
age, and married, and with the king's power like a god's,

and died happy, if there is any happiness here.
But no. You grew to where you could see and learn, my child,
yet your life was not old enough to win advantage
of fortune. How wickedly, poor boy, your fathers' walls,
Apollo's handiwork, have shorn your pitiful curls
tended and trimmed to ringlets by your mother's hand,
and the face she kissed once, where the brightness now is
blood
shining through the torn bones—too horrible to say more.
O little hands, sweet likenesses of Hector's once,
now you lie broken at the wrists before my feet;
and mouth beloved whose words were once so confident,
you are dead; and all was false, when you would jump into
my bed, and say: "Grandmother, when you die I will cut
my long hair in your memory, and at your grave
bring companies of boys my age, to sing farewell."
It did not happen; now I, a homeless, childless, old
woman must bury your poor corpse, which is so young.
Alas for all the tendernesses, my nursing care,
and our shared slumbers gone. What would the poet say,
what words might he inscribe upon your monument?
"Here lies a little child the Argives killed, because
they were afraid of him." That? The epitaph of Greek shame.
You will not win your father's heritage, except
for this, which is your coffin now: the brazen shield.

O shield, that guarded the strong shape of Hector's arm:
the bravest man of all, who wore you once, is dead.
How sweet the impression of his body on your sling,
and at the true circle of your rim the stain of sweat
where in the grind of his many combats Hector leaned
his chin against you, and the drops fell from his brow!

Take up your work now; bring from what is left some fair
coverings to wrap this poor dead child. The gods will not
allow us much. But let him have what we can give.

That mortal is a fool who, prospering, thinks his life
has any strong foundation; since our fortune's course
of action is the reeling way a madman takes,
and no one person is ever happy all the time.

*(Hecuba's handmaidens bring out a robe and ornaments from the tent and help Hecuba prepare the body of Astyanax for burial.)*

CHORUS LEADER

Here are your women, who bring you from the Trojan spoils
what is left, to deck the corpse for burial.

HECUBA

O child, it is not for victory in riding, won
from boys your age, not archery—in which acts our people
take pride, without driving competition to excess°—
that your sire's mother lays upon you now these treasures
from what was yours before; though now the god-accursed,
Helen, has robbed you, she who has destroyed as well
the life in you, and brought to ruin all our house.

CHORUS [*singing in this interchange with Hecuba, who for the most part replies speaking*]

*My heart,*
*you touched my heart, you who were once*
*a great lord in my city.°*

HECUBA [*speaking*]

These Phrygian robes' magnificence you should have worn
at your marriage to some princess uttermost in pride
in all the East. I lay them on your body now.
And you, once so victorious and mother of
a thousand conquests, Hector's huge beloved shield:
here is a wreath for you, who die not, yet are dead
with this body; since it is better far to honor you
than the armor of Odysseus the wicked and clever.

CHORUS

*Ah me.*

*Earth takes you, child;*
*our tears of sorrow.*
*Cry aloud, our mother.*

HECUBA [*singing*]
*Yes.*

CHORUS
*The dirge of the dead.*

HECUBA [*singing*]
*Ah me.*

CHORUS
*Evils never to be forgotten.*

HECUBA [*speaking*]
I'll bind some of your wounds with bandages, and be
your healer: a wretched one, in name alone, no use.
Among the dead your father will take care of the others.

CHORUS
*Rip, tear your faces with hands*
*that beat like oars.*
*Alas.*

HECUBA
Dear women....

CHORUS
*Hecuba, speak to us. We are yours.° What did you cry aloud?*

HECUBA
The gods meant nothing° except to make life hard for me,
and of all cities they chose Troy to hate. In vain
we sacrificed. And yet had not the very hand
of a god gripped and crushed this city deep in the ground,
we should have disappeared in darkness, and not given
a theme for music, and the songs of men to come.
You may go now, and hide the dead in his poor tomb;
he has those flowers that are the right of the underworld.

I think it makes small difference to the dead, if they
are buried in the tokens of luxury. All that
is an empty glorification left for those who live.

*(The body of Astyanax is carried off to the side.)*

CHORUS [*singing*]

*Sad mother, whose hopes were so huge*
*for your life. They are broken now.*
*Born to high blessedness*
*and a lordly line, child,*
*your death was horror.*

*But see, see*
*on the high places of Ilium*
*the torchflares whirling in the hands*
*of men. For Troy*
*some other new agony.*

*(Enter Talthybius with soldiers from the side.)*

TALTHYBIUS

I call to the captains who have orders to set fire
to the city of Priam: keep no longer in the hand
the shining flame. Let loose the fire upon it. So
with the citadel of Ilium broken to the ground
we can take leave of Troy, in gladness, and go home.

I speak to you, too, for my orders include this,
daughters of Troy. When the lords of the armament sound
the high echoing crash of the trumpet call, then go
to the ships of the Achaeans, to be taken away
from this land. And you, unhappiest and aged woman,
go with them. For Odysseus' men are here, to whom
enslaved the lot exiles you from your native land.

HECUBA

Ah, wretched me. So this is the unhappy end
and goal of all the sorrows I have lived. I go

forth from my country and a city lit with flames.
Come, aged feet; make one last weary struggle, that I
may hail my city in its affliction. O Troy, once
so huge over all Asia in the drawn wind of pride,
your very name of glory shall be stripped away.
They are burning you, and us they drag forth from our land
enslaved. O gods! Do I call upon the gods for help?
We cried to them before now, and they would not hear.
Come then, hurl ourselves into the pyre. Best now
to die in the flaming ruins of our fathers' house!

TALTHYBIUS

Unhappy creature, ecstatic in your sorrows! Men,
take her, don't wait. She is Odysseus' property.
You have orders to deliver her into his hands.

HECUBA [*singing, with the Chorus also singing in reply*]

STROPHE A

*O sorrow.*
*Cronion, Zeus, lord of Phrygia,*
*prince of our house, have you seen*
*the dishonor done to the seed of Dardanus?*°

CHORUS

*He has seen, but the great city*
*is a city no more, it is gone. There is no Troy.*

HECUBA

ANTISTROPHE A

*O sorrow.*
*Ilium flares.*
*The chambers of Pergamum take fire,*
*the citadel and the wall's high places.*

CHORUS

*Our city fallen to the spear*
*fades as smoke winged in the sky,*

*halls hot in the swept fire°*
*and the fierce lances.*

HECUBA

STROPHE B

*O soil where my children grew.*

CHORUS

*Alas.*

HECUBA

*O children, hear me; it is your mother who calls.*

CHORUS

*They are dead you cry to. This is a dirge.*

HECUBA

*I lean my old body against the earth*
*and both hands beat the ground.*

CHORUS

*I kneel to the earth, take up*
*the cry to my own dead,*
*poor buried husband.*

HECUBA

*We are taken, dragged away . . .*

CHORUS

*. . . a cry of pain, pain . . .*

HECUBA

*. . . under the slave's roof . . .*

CHORUS

*. . . away from my country.*

HECUBA

*Priam, my Priam. Dead,*
*graveless, forlorn,*
*you know not what they have done to me.*

CHORUS

*Now dark, holy death*
*in the brutal butchery closed his eyes.*

HECUBA

ANTISTROPHE B

*O gods' house, city beloved . . .*

CHORUS

*. . . alas . . .*

HECUBA

*. . . you are given the red flame and the spear's iron.*

CHORUS

*You will collapse to the dear ground and be nameless.*

HECUBA

*Ash as the skyward smoke wing*
*piled will blot from my sight the house where I lived once.*

CHORUS

*Lost shall be the name of the land,*
*all gone, perished. Troy, city of sorrow,*
*is there no longer.*

*(A loud crash is heard.)*

HECUBA

*Did you see, did you hear?*

CHORUS

*The crash of the citadel.*

HECUBA

*The earth shook, riven . . .*

CHORUS

*. . . to engulf the city.*

HECUBA

*O*
*shaking, tremulous limbs,*
*this is the way. Forward:*
*into the slave's life.*

CHORUS

*Mourn for the ruined city, then go away*
*to the ships of the Achaeans.*

*(Exit all.)*

# IPHIGENIA AMONG THE TAURIANS

*Translated by* ANNE CARSON

# IPHIGENIA AMONG THE TAURIANS: INTRODUCTION

*The Play: Date and Composition*

There is no external evidence available for determining when Euripides' *Iphigenia among the Taurians* was first produced. Scholars date it to 414–13 BCE on the basis of various metrical features. The play is strikingly similar to *Helen*, which is known to have been produced in 412 BCE, and it seems unlikely that Euripides would have staged two such similar plays in the very same year. Presumably Euripides wrote *Iphigenia* for the annual competition at the Great Dionysian Festival in Athens. What the other three plays were in Euripides' tetralogy of that year, and how they fared in the competition, are unknown.

The play is often called *Iphigenia in Tauris*, but there was never any country or physical region called Tauris; the Taurians or Tauri were a primitive, warlike people who lived on the Crimean peninsula on the northern coast of the Black Sea, and the Greek title of the play designates Iphigenia as being "among" these people (as does the Latin title *Iphigenia in Tauris*). Euripides probably originally titled his play simply *Iphigenia*, and the further specification was added when it was included in a complete edition of his works (perhaps around the third century BCE) in order to distinguish it from his *Iphigenia in Aulis*.

*The Myth*

*Iphigenia among the Taurians* presents one of the final episodes of the tragic vicissitudes of the house of Atreus, the royal dynasty of Argos (or Mycenae): Agamemnon, his wife Clytemnestra, her lover Aegisthus, and her children Iphigenia, Electra, and Orestes. According to the version of the myth that Euripides presupposes, Iphigenia, who all the Greeks thought had been sacrificed by her father at Aulis at the beginning of the Trojan War, was in fact rescued by Artemis and transported to the land of the Taurians. There she has become a priestess of Artemis and participates in the local ritual whereby any foreigners who arrive, especially Greeks, are sacrificed to the goddess. Meanwhile, her brother Orestes, who was just a child at the time of the events at Aulis, has grown up and killed his mother to avenge her murder of his father, and is consequently being pursued by Furies (some of whom have continued to torment him even after he was acquitted at a trial in Athens). Now Apollo has prophesied to Orestes that, if he brings back to Greece the cult statue of Artemis from the land of the Taurians, he will finally be cleansed of his guilt and cured of his sufferings.

It is at this point that the action of Euripides' play begins. Orestes and his comrade Pylades arrive by ship in the land of the Taurians but are captured and brought to the temple to be killed. Not knowing who they are, Iphigenia is just about to sacrifice one or both of them—both Orestes and Pylades demonstrate extraordinary nobility and generosity by each offering to die so that the other can be saved—but a complex and suspenseful scene leads surprisingly to the brother's and sister's recognition of each other. In the second half of the play, Iphigenia devises an escape for all three of them: she pretends that the cult statue has been polluted by contact with matricides and must be cleansed in the sea, and the three Greeks manage to flee with it but become embroiled in a battle with the Taurians on the beach. At the end, Athena appears so that she can placate Thoas, the king of the Taurians, and foretell the future: Orestes must bring the statue to Halae in Attica, founding a ritual in which a man's throat will merely be scratched by a sword to draw a little blood; and Iphigenia will become a priestess at the Greek cult center of Artemis at Brauron, also in Attica.

The episode dramatized in Euripides' *Iphigenia among the Taurians* belongs to one of the most popular sets of stories in all of Greek tragedy. Euripides himself returned repeatedly to this mythic complex to treat other tales from it, in such plays as *Electra* (written ca. 420 BCE), *Orestes* (408 BCE), and *Iphigenia in Aulis* (produced posthumously after 406 BCE). But while the other episodes of the history of the sons of Atreus were dramatized by many other tragedians, including Aeschylus (in the *Oresteia*) and Sophocles (in his *Electra*), Euripides' selection of this particular story and his treatment of it seem to have been entirely unprecedented.

Euripides drew upon three different kinds of material in creating this play: regional religious cults, poetic narratives, and historiography.

- The cult of the goddess Artemis and her priestess Iphigenia at Brauron celebrated fertility and protected reproduction and the young, especially among women. By contrast, the cult of Artemis Tauropolos at Halae seems to have focused somewhat more upon male coming-of-age. Both cults were well established and certainly familiar to most members of the original audience, but the link between the cults and the legendary stories about the children of Agamemnon was presumably much less clear.
- In Greek legend and early poetry, Iphigenia was either killed at Aulis or else (the usual version) she was rescued by Artemis and made immortal. In this play she is indeed saved and conveyed to the Taurians, but she remains fully mortal, a human counterpart to the goddess Artemis: each of them is out of place among this savage race and needs to be rescued by her brother and brought back to the civilization of Greece. So too, Orestes' pollution from killing his mother and his persecution by the Furies were familiar elements of Greek myth, lyric poetry, and tragedy (most notably in Aeschylus' *Oresteia*), but Euripides has innovated boldly in the myth so as to bring Orestes to the land of the Taurians and have him meet Iphigenia there.

- Besides these religious and mythical dimensions, Euripides' tragedy also makes use of recent ethnographic field reporting. Only a couple of decades before this play was composed, the historian Herodotus had provided a detailed description of the Taurians as a savage and bloodthirsty race who sacrificed Greeks and shipwrecked mariners to a goddess they identified as Iphigenia. The general characteristics and many details of the Taurians described by Herodotus recur emphatically in Euripides' play.

Out of all these disparate elements, with characteristic panache and pathos, Euripides has contrived one of his most brilliant and gripping dramas. In particular, the elements of pathetic misunderstanding, mistaken identities, and last-minute recognition, clever Greeks escaping from stupid barbarians, miraculous guidance and intervention by the gods, and an unexpected "happy ending" after a seemingly interminable series of disasters for this long-suffering family, mark this play as a perfect example (along with *Ion*, *Helen*, and other plays now lost) of the "romantic" type of tragedy, in contrast to the more common plot structure that ends in disaster and death for the main characters.

### *Transmission and Reception*

*Iphigenia among the Taurians* seems to have been one of Euripides' more popular plays in antiquity. Aristophanes parodies it in at least two of his comedies; Aristotle discusses it repeatedly in the *Poetics* to illustrate how a recognition scene should be constructed; and later Greek and Latin authors frequently refer to the play, alluding particularly to its portrayal of the exemplary friendship between Orestes and Pylades. We know from an inscription that the play was performed at the Great Dionysian Festival in 341 BCE and won a prize. Further testimony to its ancient popularity comes from a dozen Attic and south Italic vases of the fourth century BCE (all focus on the first half of the play) and from Pompeian wall frescoes of the first century CE and Roman sarcophagi of the second century CE—these show later scenes as well. Finally, at least four papyri with parts of the play have been discovered; they range from the third century BCE to the fourth century CE.

But for some reason we do not know, *Iphigenia among the Taurians* was not one of the canonical ten plays selected for more intense study and wider diffusion. It survived antiquity only by the accident of being among the so-called alphabetic plays (see "Introduction to Euripides," p. 571), and it is transmitted by a single manuscript (and its copies) and is not accompanied by the ancient commentaries (scholia) that explain various kinds of interpretative difficulties.

The standard story of Iphigenia's sacrifice at Aulis has always fascinated authors and artists and has tended to be even more popular than Euripides' innovative account of her survival and of her and Orestes' adventures among the Taurians. But in the world of Renaissance colonialism the adventures of brave young Europeans among exotic savages acquired new topicality, while the noble self-sacrifice of the two friends Orestes and Pylades displayed virtues that were not only pagan. Both themes inspired tragedians as early as Giovanni Rucellai (*L'Oreste*, 1525) and painters as late as Anselm Feuerbach (1862). Jean Racine planned an *Iphigénie en Tauride* (1673–76?) but never wrote it; only an outline of the first act survives. But the high point of the reception of Euripides' play was the eighteenth century, among painters like Giovanni Battista Tiepolo (1736), Benjamin West (1766), and Henry Fuseli; tragedians like John Dennis (*Iphigenia*, 1699), Johann Elias Schlegel (*Die Geschwister in Taurien*, 1739; revised as *Orest und Pylades*, 1742), and Claude Guimond de La Touche (*Iphigénie en Tauride*, 1757); and composers of operas like Domenico Scarlatti (*Ifigenia in Tauri*, 1713). The two greatest adaptations both date from 1779: Christoph Willibald Gluck's opera *Iphigénie en Tauride* and Johann Wolfgang Goethe's drama *Iphigenie auf Tauris* (revised 1787). Both these Enlightenment texts humanize and ennoble the Euripidean original, transforming a suspenseful and rather racy stage play into an exploration of universal human emotions and a document of philanthropy. They have also dominated the subsequent reception of the play, even in music (Franz Schubert, "Orest auf Tauris" and "Iphigenia," 1817) and comic opera (Eugène Scribe, *Oreste et Pylade,* 1844). Noteworthy interpretations in the twentieth century include dance dramas by Isadora Duncan (1916) and Pina Bausch (1974), a poem by Randall Jarrell ("Orestes at Tauris," 1936), and a drama by the German author Egon Fritz (*Iphigenie in Amerika,* 1948).

# IPHIGENIA AMONG THE TAURIANS

*Characters*

IPHIGENIA, daughter of Agamemnon and Clytemnestra; priestess of Artemis
ORESTES, son of Agamemnon and Clytemnestra
PYLADES, friend of Orestes
CHORUS of captive Greek women
TAURIAN HERDSMAN
THOAS, king of the Taurians
MESSENGER, a servant of Thoas
ATHENA

*Scene: The entrance to the temple of Artemis in the land of the Taurians, with a large, bloodstained altar in front of it.*

*(Enter Iphigenia from the temple.)*

IPHIGENIA

Pelops son of Tantalus came to Pisa on swift horses
and married Oenomaus' daughter
who begot Atreus.
Atreus begot Menelaus and Agamemnon.
Agamemnon begot me.
I am Iphigenia, daughter of the daughter of Tyndareus.
My father killed me—
at Euripus where stiff breezes
spin the salt-blue sea in spirals,
for Helen's sake

a sacrifice to Artemis in famous Aulis—
or so people think.

For at Aulis Agamemnon
had assembled a thousand ships,
a Greek expedition to take the crown of Troy.
He wanted the Greeks to avenge Helen's rape
and gratify Menelaus.
What befell him was the disaster of windlessness.
He resorted to divination
and Calchas said this:
"Agamemnon, commander of this Greek army,
not one ship will cast off from this shore
until Artemis receives your own girl
Iphigenia
as a sacrifice.
You made a vow once
to Artemis Lightbringer to offer up
the finest fruit of that year
and that year
your wife bore a child in the house—"
that "finest fruit" was me!
"Her you must kill."

So Odysseus planned it:
they got me from my mother on pretext of marrying Achilles.
And I came to Aulis—sad day for me!
Lifted high above the altar I was right on the verge of death
when Artemis snatched me,
put a deer in my place.
Sent me clear through the air to the land of the Taurians: here!
The land is barbarian, so is the king—Thoas
(his name means "swift" and he is).
The goddess put me here in her temple as priestess.
And there's a ritual°
beautiful in name only,
that Artemis finds pleasing—well,

I won't say more. She terrifies me.
The fact is, by a law of the city older than me
I sacrifice any Greek man who comes here.
That is, I start things off. Others do the killing.
Inside the temple.
We don't talk about this.

New strange dreams came in the night.
I shall tell them—it might bring relief.
In my dream it seemed I'd gone from this land to live in
Argos.
I was lying asleep in a room of girls
when the earth gave a jolt.
I fled, stood outside, saw the cornice falling
and the whole roof collapse to the ground in a heap.
One pillar remained of our ancestral home:
I saw it grow blonde hair and speak a human voice.
Then putting my stranger-killing skills to use
I began sprinkling water
as on one about to die.
And I was weeping.
Here's how I read this dream:
Orestes is dead, it was him I sprinkled with water.
Boys are the pillars of a house, are they not,
and anyone I consecrate does die.°
So I want to offer libations to my brother.
He and I are far apart
but this at least I can do.
I'll go with my women—Greeks given me by the king.
For some reason they're not here yet.
I shall go into the temple—that's where I live.

*(Exit Iphigenia into the temple.*
*Enter Orestes and Pylades from the side.)*

ORESTES

Look, be careful. Might be someone on the path.

PYLADES

Yes, I'm peering in every direction.

ORESTES

Pylades, does this look to you like the goddess' temple,
the one we sailed here from Argos to find?

PYLADES

Yes it does, Orestes.

ORESTES

And this is the altar, wet with Greek blood?

PYLADES

The top of it anyway is bloodstained red.

ORESTES

And do you see spoils hanging from the top?

PYLADES

Spoils from foreigners who died here.
But I think I should take a good look around.

ORESTES

O Phoebus, what is this net you have led me into?
Your oracle bid me avenge my father's blood
by killing my mother
but relays of Furies
came hounding me from my land
and after I'd run lap after lap on their turning track
I came to you, asked how to find my way out
of wheeling madness and pain.°
You told me to go to the Taurian land
where your sister Artemis has her altars
and steal a statue of the goddess
that (people say) fell from the sky to this temple here.
Take it by cunning or take it by luck, no matter the risk,
and give it to Athens.
That's all you said.

If I do this, I breathe free.
So
I obeyed you, I came here.
To a land unknown and inhospitable.
But, Pylades, tell me, what should we do?
You're my partner in this.
You see those high encircling walls?
Should we mount ladders?
But won't we be seen? Or force the bolts with crowbars?°
But we know of no crowbars.
And if we're caught opening the gates
or devising a way in, we're dead.
Let's just run for it, before we get killed—
we can use the same boat we came on.

PYLADES
To run is unacceptable. We're not like that.
And the oracle of god must be respected.
Let's quit this temple and go hide in the caves
where the dark seawater washes in.
We'll keep our distance from the ship
in case someone sees it, reports us and has us arrested.
And as soon as the eye of night darkens
we must nerve ourselves to steal that statue from the temple
any way we can.°
Good men find the nerve for ordeals, cowards are nothing.°

ORESTES
You're right, yes, we should hide out somewhere.
It won't be my fault if the god's oracle goes unfulfilled.
We will find the nerve!
Young men have no excuse shirking hard work!

*(Exit Orestes and Pylades to one side. Enter the Chorus of captive Greek women from the other side.)*

CHORUS° *[singing]*
*Silence!*

*O you who dwell by the Clashing Rocks and the Hostile Sea!*
*O Dictynna,*
*child of Leto, wild as mountains,*
*to your court, to your gold columns I come,*
*a pure holy girl on pure holy feet,*
*serving the one who holds your holy key,*
*I who have lost the towers and walls of Greece rich in horses,*
*lost the groves and grasslands of Europe,*
*lost the halls of my father,*
*here I am.*
*Tell me your news, tell me your troubles.*
*Why have you brought me, brought me to the temple,*
*O child of the man*
*who came against the towers of Troy*
*with a glorious fleet of a thousand ships*
*and ten thousand glorious men?°*

*(Enter Iphigenia from the temple.)*

IPHIGENIA [*singing in this lyric interchange with the Chorus, who continue to sing in reply*]
*My ladies!*
*I'm oppressed by the pain of lament,*
*by lyreless unmusical music,*
*by keening.*
*Ruin comes at me.*
*I grieve for my brother—*
*such a vision I saw in the night just past.°*
*I am lost.*
*Am lost.*
*Our house is no more.*
*Our family gone.*
*What sorrows swept Argos!*
*O god, you god,*
*who rob me of my only brother*
*by sending him down to death.*
*For him I pour out these libations*

*and a mixing bowl to wet the earth—*
*milk of mountain cows,*
*wine of Bacchus,*
*honey of yellow bees,*
*these I pour.*
*They comfort the dead.*

*Now hand me that vessel of gold,*
*libation for the god of death.*

*O child of Agamemnon under the ground,*
*these are for you.*
*Receive them.*
*I'll not be bringing bright locks of hair to crown your tomb,*
*I'll not be bringing tears.*
*I am far far away from our homeland, yours and mine,*
*and the people there think I am butchered and dead.*

CHORUS

*Mistress,*
*I'll sing you antiphonies,*
*the rough raw noise of Asian songs,*
*dirges for the dead*
*what Hades sings—the opposite of paeans.*
*Pity the house of Atreus!*
*Gone is its light, its scepter.*
*Gone is the pomp of all those brilliant kings.°*
*Trouble rushes on trouble.*
*One day in a whirl of winged horses*
*the Sun changed course*
*and turned his holy face away.*
*Then sorrow upon sorrow came to the house of the golden lamb,*
*killing on killing, grief on grief:*
*from all that ancient Tantalid wrong*
*punishment unfolds now.*
*And the god is zealous against you.*

IPHIGENIA

*From the beginning my luck was unlucky.°*
*Right from my mother's womb, that first night,*
*the Fates wove an absolute education for me.*
*I was the firstborn of Leda's poor daughter,*
*victim of a father's atrocity,*
*an offering that brought no joy.°*
*They rode me in chariots over Aulis' sands—*
*a bride!*
*Pity me—I was no bride! Bride of Achilles,*
*alas!*
*Now I live as a stranger in a barren house by the Hostile Sea.*
*I've no marriage, no children, no city, no loved ones.*
*Once the Greeks wooed me.°*
*I no longer sing songs for Hera at Argos,*
*I no longer weave Athenas and Titans*
*to the hum of the loom.*
*No, I work in blood—making death for strangers°*
*who cry out for pity, who shed tears for pity.*
*I give not a thought to them now.*
*It's my brother I weep, killed in Argos.*
*Him I left a mere infant,*
*a baby, a young thing, a tendril in his mother's hands,*
*at his mother's breast:*
*the rightful scepter-bearing king of Argos, Orestes.*

*(Enter Herdsman from the side.)*

CHORUS LEADER

But look, here comes a herdsman
heading up from the shore with news for you.

HERDSMAN

Child of Agamemnon and Clytemnestra,
listen to my strange report.

IPHIGENIA [*now speaking*]

What strange report?

HERDSMAN

New arrivals—two young men—have come to our land.
Their boat escaped the dark-blue Clashing Rocks.
What a welcome contribution to our goddess!
Get your holy water ready and your consecrations.

IPHIGENIA

Where are they from? What do they look like?

HERDSMAN

Greeks. That's all I know.

IPHIGENIA

You heard no names?

HERDSMAN

One called the other Pylades.

IPHIGENIA

What about his companion?

HERDSMAN

Didn't hear, don't know.

IPHIGENIA

Where did you catch them?

HERDSMAN

Down by the edge of the Hostile Sea.

IPHIGENIA

What are herdsmen doing down by the sea?

HERDSMAN

Bathing our oxen in salt water.

IPHIGENIA

Go back to the question
where you caught them and how.
This I want to know.
It's been a long time since the goddess' altar ran red with
Greek blood.°

HERDSMAN

Well, we were driving our oxen into the water that flows
out through the Clashing Rocks.
There was a cleft drilled through by the beat of the sea
where purplefishers shelter.
Here one of us caught sight of two young men.
He came back on tiptoe and said
"Look—gods sitting there!"
Another (a pious fellow) lifted his hands to pray:
"Son of sea goddess Leucothea, protector of ships,
lord Palaemon, be gracious—
whether those are the twin sons of Zeus there
or some sweet offspring of Nereus
who bore the fifty dancing daughters!"
Then a bold skeptical fellow laughed at the prayers
and said it was two shipwrecked sailors
sitting terrified in the cleft—"no doubt they've heard we
  slaughter strangers."
This made sense to most of us.
We decided to take them for the goddess to sacrifice
as per usual.
Meanwhile
one of the strangers came out of the cave. He stood.
He tossed his head up and down, howling aloud,
trembling to the tips of his fingers
and staggering in fits.
He cried out like a hunter, "See that one, Pylades?
And there, that snake of hell—look, she's itching to kill me,
her horrible snakes are mouthing out at me.
And this one's belching fire and death and thrashing her
  wings,°
she's got a stone shaped like my mother in her arms—
she's going to hurl it!
Help, she'll kill me! Where can I run?"

Yet those shapes were not visible.

Only voices of cows and dogs were answering him.°
And we for our part, expecting him to die any minute,
sat crouched in silence.
But he drew his sword, leapt among the cattle like a lion
and began laying about him, his blade striking flank and rib,
fantasizing he was driving off the Furies.°
The sea bloomed red with blood.
And now
seeing the slaughter of the cows
everyone began to arm himself
and we blew conches to summon the locals
(figuring cowherds were no match for these strong young
  foreigners).
We soon had a crowd.
But the stranger let go the pulse of his frenzy
and dropped to the ground.
Foam dripped off his chin.
We all set to work on him, pelting and pounding,
while the other man kept trying to wipe off the foam
and shield his friend's body with his cloak,
warding off wounds
and ministering to his friend every way he could.

Now the stranger
all of a sudden sane
jumped up.
Saw the tide of foes falling on them° and groaned.
But we did not slack off, kept pitching rocks from this side
  and that.
Then we heard this awful exhortation:
"Pylades, we're about to die. Let's die brilliantly!
Draw your sword and follow me!"
At sight of their swords we fled back to the ravines
and as each one fled, others pressed forward
bombarding the strangers.
And if these were pressed back

the ones retreating pelted them with stones.
Yet here was the amazing thing:
so many hands throwing—not one hit the victims!
Anyway, in the end, however unheroically, we won the day.
Surrounded them and knocked° the swords from their hands
with rocks.
They sank to their knees exhausted.
We brought them to our king,
who took one look and dispatched them here
for you to wash and sacrifice.

Lady, these strangers are exactly the sort of victims
you should pray for.
Execute them and Greece will really be paying you back
for your own murder,
paying the price for that slaughter at Aulis.

CHORUS LEADER

Amazing story!—whoever this man is
who's come from Hellas to the Hostile Sea.

IPHIGENIA

Okay, off you go.
Bring the strangers back with you
and we'll attend to sacred duties here.

*(Exit Herdsman to the side.)*

O my poor breaking heart,
once you were kind and compassionate to strangers;
you always spared them a kindred tear when they were
Greeks.
But dreams have ensavaged me.
Whoever you are, you'll find me ill-disposed.
This is the truth, it's clear to me, ladies:
our own bad luck does not make us benevolent
toward those who are worse off.
And the thing is,
no breeze of Zeus has ever come here,

no ship brought Helen through the Clashing Rocks
with her Menelaus
to pay back what they did to me—
they murdered me!—
to make an Aulis here for that Aulis there
where the Danaans laid their hands on me
as if I were a sacrificial calf
and my own father was the sacrificing priest!
I cannot forget those evils!
How many times did I fling my hands at his face crying,
"Father, you marry me to degradation!
While you're killing me here
my mother and her women in Argos
are singing wedding songs!
Our house fills with music of pipes
as I die at your hands!
Achilles, it seems, was Hades' son, not Peleus'—
you gave me him as a husband
and steered me into a wedding of blood.
It was just a filthy trick!"

And I did not lift my little brother in my arms—
who now is dead!
I did not kiss my sister; no, I
kept my face in veils for I was blushing—
I believed I was going to Peleus' house
and put off many an embrace till later,
thinking I'd come back to Argos again.
Poor Orestes—
if you are dead, what a fine patrimony you forfeit!
As for the sophistry of the goddess, I condemn it.
She who drives from her altar
anyone who touches blood or childbirth or corpses,
who calls them polluted,
this same goddess revels in human sacrifice!
Impossible the wife of Zeus is mother to such folly!

Nor do I credit that story of Tantalus' banquet—
how the gods happily digested a meal of his son.
The people here are murderous themselves,
this is my opinion,
so they ascribe base behavior to their deity.
No god is evil, I do not believe it.

CHORUS [*singing*]

STROPHE A

*Deep deep blue roads of ocean*
*where the gadfly out of Argos*
*crossed the Hostile Sea°*
*from Asia to Europe,*
*who are these men who left behind the clear Eurotas*
*green with reeds*
*or the holy streams of Dirce*
*to come to this implacable country*
*where the altars and temples of Zeus' daughter*
*are doused with human blood?*

ANTISTROPHE A

*Did they sail to the double beat of pinewood oars*
*with ocean billows beneath them°*
*and an ocean breeze at their back*
*all for greed, for riches to bring home?*
*Don't fall in love with hope—it can be insatiable.°*
*Men lug rich cargo with them*
*as they roam strange cities and seas,*
*all suffering the same delusion.*
*Some people understand measure;*
*others can't think straight about wealth.*

STROPHE B

*How did they pass the Clashing Rocks*
*or the restless shores of Phineus*
*or the sea-swept coast of Amphitrite*
*where the fifty daughters of Nereus° dance in a circle and sing?*
*How did they go*

*racing the waves*
*with swelling sail*
*and hissing oar,*
*under southerly breeze*
*or western wind,*
*to the land where birds throng the White Shore*
*and Achilles*
*has his fair running ground*
*by the edge of the Hostile Sea?*

ANTISTROPHE B

*I pray along with my lady's prayers*
*that Helen might leave Troy and come here*
*to die at my lady's hands*
*with her throat cut*
*and a circle of bloody dew on her hair.*
*Helen ought to pay!*
*And how glad I would be*
*to hear some Greek traveler say*
*my miserable slavery is at an end.*
*Even in dreams°*
*how I long to go to my homeland*
*and share in the happiness there.*

*(Enter Orestes and Pylades from the side escorted by Taurian guards.)*

*[chanting]*
*But look, here come the two of them with their hands tied,*
*fresh victims for the goddess.*
*That herdsman wasn't lying.*
*Silence, women.*
*Choice Greek offerings are at hand.*
*Lady, if you are pleased with these civic rituals,*
*accept the sacrifice*
*which our own law calls unholy.*

IPHIGENIA

So be it.

First I must take care that all arrangements for the goddess are correct.
Untie the strangers' hands.
They are sacred and should not be bound.
Now go in and prepare what is needed and proper for our task.

*(Exit the Taurian guards into the temple.)*

Ah pity.
Who is the mother who bore you,
the father, the sister—have you a sister?
Robbed of two young men like you
she will be brotherless now.
Who can know if his luck will lead in this direction?
Gods' plans are all invisible,
no one knows anything clear.
And luck seduces us sideways to stupidity.

Where did you come from, you poor strangers?
Surely you sailed a long way to get here.
And you'll stay a long time underground,
far from home.

ORESTES

Why do you lament these things and vex yourself
over troubles of ours—woman, whoever you are?
It doesn't make sense to me that someone bent on killing
wants to cancel the dread of death with pity.
Nor for a man near death with no hope of escape
to pity himself:
he makes one evil into two—
shows himself foolish and dies anyhow.
Let luck go its way.
Sing no dirges for us.
We know about the sacrifices here; we understand this.

IPHIGENIA

My first question is, which of you is Pylades?

ORESTES

If it please you, this man is Pylades.

IPHIGENIA

From what city of Greece?

ORESTES

What good will it do you to know this, woman?

IPHIGENIA

Are you two brothers, from one mother?

ORESTES

Brothers in love. We are not related.

IPHIGENIA

What sort of name did your father give you?

ORESTES

By rights I should be called Unlucky.

IPHIGENIA

Tell that to Fortune, it wasn't my question.

ORESTES

My body, not my name, is what you plan to sacrifice.

IPHIGENIA

Why begrudge this? You think you're so important?

ORESTES

If I die nameless I am spared mockery.

IPHIGENIA

You won't tell me your city either?

ORESTES

How will it profit me? I'm about to die.

IPHIGENIA

Then what prevents you granting it as a favor?

ORESTES

Glorious Argos is the home I claim.

IPHIGENIA

By the gods! Stranger, were you really born there?

ORESTES

In Mycenae, once a splendid city. 510

IPHIGENIA

You are surely welcome here if you've come from Argos.° 515

ORESTES

Not by my reckoning! Maybe yours. 516

IPHIGENIA

Did you leave your home as an exile, or why? 511

ORESTES

A kind of exile. Willing and unwilling at once.

IPHIGENIA

Will you tell me something I want to know?

ORESTES

Well, it might distract me from my problems. 514

IPHIGENIA

You've heard of Troy, whose fame is everywhere? 517

ORESTES

How I wish I never had, even in dreams!

IPHIGENIA

They say it is gone, wiped out by war.

ORESTES

That is the case, no idle rumor. 520

IPHIGENIA

And Helen's gone home to Menelaus' house?

ORESTES

She has. And her going brought harm to one of mine.

IPHIGENIA

Where is she now? She owes a debt to me as well.

ORESTES

She lives in Sparta with her former husband.

IPHIGENIA

O object of hatred—for the Greeks, not just me!

ORESTES

Yes, I've felt the effect of her marriages too.

IPHIGENIA

And the homecoming of the Achaeans was as reported?

ORESTES

Your questions certainly encompass everything!

IPHIGENIA

I want to make the most of you before you die.

ORESTES

Ask away then, I'll answer your pleasure.

IPHIGENIA

Did a prophet named Calchas come back from Troy?

ORESTES

He's dead according to the story at Mycenae.

IPHIGENIA

Excellent! What of Laertes' son, Odysseus?

ORESTES

Not reached home yet, but he lives, they say.

IPHIGENIA

May he perish and never reach home!

ORESTES

Don't bother cursing him: his whole life has gone wrong.

IPHIGENIA
And Achilles is alive?

ORESTES
No he is not. A futile marriage he made at Aulis.

IPHIGENIA
A travesty of marriage, so people say who suffered it.

ORESTES
Who are you? Your questions about Greece are strangely apt.

IPHIGENIA
I came from there. Was lost as a child.

ORESTES
Naturally you long for news of it, woman.

IPHIGENIA
And what of the general, the one they called "blessedly
happy"?

ORESTES
I'm not aware of one I'd call "blessedly happy."

IPHIGENIA
A son of Atreus, King Agamemnon, was so called.

ORESTES
I don't know. Change the subject.

IPHIGENIA
By the gods, no! Answer my question, stranger!

ORESTES
The poor man is dead. And took another with him.

IPHIGENIA
Dead? How? Oh no! Oh no!

ORESTES
Why do you groan? What's he to you?

IPHIGENIA
I groan for the great good fortune he once had.

ORESTES
Hideously he perished, murdered by his wife.

IPHIGENIA
Oh there are tears in this—for the killer and the killed!

ORESTES
Stop now. No more questions.

IPHIGENIA
Just this one: is the poor man's wife alive?

ORESTES
No, she is not. Her own son killed her.

IPHIGENIA
O house confounded! What did he want?

ORESTES
To avenge his father dead at her hands.

IPHIGENIA
Pity! He did well then, to carry out so righteous a wrong.

ORESTES
Righteous or not, he wins no grace from gods.

IPHIGENIA
And Agamemnon left another child at home?

ORESTES
One daughter, Electra.

IPHIGENIA
Is there not some tale of another daughter, sacrificed?

ORESTES
None except she's dead and looks no more upon the daylight.

IPHIGENIA
Pity that girl, pity the father who slew her.

ORESTES

Her death: a thankless gift to an evil woman.

IPHIGENIA

And the dead king's son, he lives in Argos?

ORESTES

He lives in misery, nowhere and everywhere.

IPHIGENIA

False dream, farewell, you were nothing after all!

ORESTES

Nor are the so-called wise gods
any more reliable than winged dreams.°

CHORUS LEADER

I feel a sudden sorrow! What of my mother and father—
are they alive? Dead? Who can say?

IPHIGENIA

Listen:
I've got a plan, beneficial for you, beneficial for me as well.
And things tend to succeed, do they not,
when one plan is pleasing to all.°
Would you be willing, if I saved your life,
to take a message to my loved ones at Argos—
a writing tablet inscribed for me by a captive
who took pity on me once?
(He didn't blame me for his murder,
but rather the law of the gods.)°
I've had no one to send the letter with till now.
But you are not ill-disposed to me, it seems,
and you know Mycenae, you know the people I mean.
So keep your life and go there—you'll win no mean reward—
salvation in return for a little letter.
And this man here, since the city requires it,
can be the goddess' victim, apart from you.

ORESTES

Fine plan, strange lady, except one thing.
This man's death would be a terrible weight on me.
I am captain of this ship of catastrophes;
he sails with me as friend to my need.
How unjust for me to win favor myself,
to slip out of harm's way and let him die.
So how about this.
Give the letter to him
(he'll take it to Argos, your purpose is served)
and let whoever wants to kill me kill me.
It is utterly base to save oneself
by sabotaging one's friends.
This man is my friend and that's that.
No less than myself I want him to look upon the daylight.

IPHIGENIA

O excellent spirit! What nobility you were born from,
what a true friend you are.
I wish my one surviving brother were a man such as you—
yes I do have a brother,
though I never see him.
But since it is your wish, we'll send this fellow
off with the letter
and you shall die.
A profound desire for this seems to possess you.

ORESTES

Who will sacrifice me and bear the horror?

IPHIGENIA

I have this duty from the goddess.

ORESTES

Not an enviable duty, girl, nor a lucky one.

IPHIGENIA

But necessary and I must honor it.

ORESTES

You, a female, kill men with a sword?

IPHIGENIA

No, but I'll sprinkle sacred water around your head.

ORESTES

Who does the actual slaughtering if I may ask?

IPHIGENIA

Inside this temple are men who have that function.

ORESTES

And what sort of grave will receive me?

IPHIGENIA

Sacred fire inside then a wide chasm in the rock.

ORESTES

Ah! How I wish my sister's hand could lay me out!

IPHIGENIA

That is a pointless prayer, you poor man, whoever you are.
She lives far from this barbarian country.
But still, since you're Argive
I'll not stint from giving you all I can possibly give.
I shall lay much ornament on your grave,
anoint° your body with yellow oil,
and throw on your fire
the flowery brightness of yellow bees.

Well, I go. I shall bring you the letter from the temple.
And so you won't hate me—

*(To the servants.)*

no fetters.
Guard them here unbound.

I wonder if my news will come as a shock at Argos—
whomever I send to—

a shock of incredible joy—
to hear that the one they thought dead is alive!

*(Exit into the temple.).*

CHORUS [*singing*] *(To Orestes.)*
*I cry for you,*
*for your end marked out,*
*the bloody rain of lustral water.*

ORESTES [*speaking*]
This needs no pity, strangers, be joyful.

CHORUS [*singing*] *(To Pylades.)*
*But you, young man blessed in fortune,*
*we honor you, soon to set foot on your native land.*

PYLADES [*speaking*]
There is nothing blessed about friends going to their death.

CHORUS [*singing*]
*O grim journey!*
*O death near at hand!*
*What sorrow! My heart hesitates*
*which to lament.*

ORESTES
Pylades, by the gods, do you have the same feeling as I?

PYLADES
I can't say.

ORESTES
Who is this young girl?
How very Greek her questions
about the troubles at Troy, the Achaean returns,
wise Calchas and his birds, the name of Achilles!
What pity she showed when she asked after poor
Agamemnon,
his wife, his children.

She comes from there, this strange woman, she is Argive by birth
or she would not be sending this letter;
she'd not be probing these matters in general
as if she had some share in the fortunes of Argos.

PYLADES

You're a little ahead of me—still, I agree
except for one thing:
this royal family's woes are familiar
to any reasonably alert person.
Still I have another worry.

ORESTES

Share it. You'll think better.

PYLADES

It would be shameful for me to go on living
while you do not.
I sailed with you and I must die with you.
Coward and criminal they'll call me in Argos
and in the folded hills of Phocis
if I come home alone.
Most men (most men are malicious) will assume
I betrayed you to get home safely.
Or even murdered you,
plotted your death to get your power,
now that your kingship is tottering
and I'm married to your sister who stands to inherit it.
I feel both fear and shame.
For me to breathe my last with you is absolutely the right thing.
To be killed and set on a pyre with you, yes.
I am your friend. I dread the blame.

ORESTES

Don't say that. My hardships are mine to bear.

Where trouble is single I won't make it double.
You say base and shameful—it's the same for me
if I make you share in my suffering and cause your death.
In fact for me personally it's no catastrophe,
faring as I do at the hands of gods,
to cease from life.
But you, you're successful and your house is sound,
not sick. Mine is defiled, unlucky.
Now if you live on and get sons from my sister
whom I gave you to wife,
my name will survive,
my ancestral house will not vanish childless.

No, you go. Live your life. Keep my father's house.
And when you reach Greece and horse-breeding Argos,
by your right hand I lay this charge upon you:
build me a burial mound and set a monument on it.
Have my sister give tears to the tomb and locks of her hair.
Report how I perished by the hand of some Argive woman
at an altar, consecrated to death.
Do not forsake my sister ever,
though you see the marriage, the house, desolate.

And now, farewell. You are the dearest friend I found.
You hunted with me, you shared my upbringing,
you bore with my pains and despairs.
Prophetic Apollo betrayed me and lied to me.
He used a trick to drive me as far away from Greece as I
could go
because he was ashamed of his own former prophecies.
I gave myself to him—trusting his words
I murdered my mother. Now I die in turn!

PYLADES

Yes, you will have your burial.
And your sister's bed I'll not betray, O my poor comrade,

for I shall hold you a more beloved friend
dead than living.
Still, the oracle of god has not yet destroyed you
though you stand right next to death.
And it is the case, you know it is the case,
that extraordinary misfortune
can call forth extraordinary reversals:
all it takes is luck.

*(Enter Iphigenia from the temple.)*

ORESTES
Silence! The word of Phoebus is no help to me at all.
And here comes the woman from the house.

IPHIGENIA *(To servants.)*
Go, go in, get everything ready
for the men in charge of the sacrifice.

*(To Orestes and Pylades.)*

Here is the letter, strangers, folded up tight.
And here's what I want in addition:
no man is the same when he's under stress
as when he regains confidence.
My fear is, no sooner he quits this land—
the one who takes my news to Argos—
than he consigns the letter to oblivion.

ORESTES
So what do you want?

IPHIGENIA
Let him swear an oath he will carry this letter
to my people in Argos, the ones I choose.

ORESTES
And you'll give such an oath in return?

IPHIGENIA

To do or say what?

ORESTES

To let him go alive from this barbarous land.

IPHIGENIA

That sounds fair. How else could he carry the message?

ORESTES

And the king will go along with this?

IPHIGENIA

Yes, I'll persuade him. And put the man on board a boat myself.

ORESTES *(To Pylades.)*

Go ahead, swear.

*(To Iphigenia.)*

And you dictate an oath that's properly pious.

IPHIGENIA

Say "I will give this letter to your loved ones."

PYLADES

I will give this letter to your loved ones.

IPHIGENIA

And I will send you safe past the dark-blue rocks.

PYLADES

To which god will you swear this oath?

IPHIGENIA

Artemis, in whose house I hold office.

PYLADES

And I by the king of heaven, sublime Zeus.

IPHIGENIA

And if you forsake your oath and do me wrong?

PYLADES

May I never reach home. And you, if you do not save me?

IPHIGENIA

May I never set foot in Argos so long as I live.

PYLADES

Oh but listen, here's a point we've overlooked.

IPHIGENIA

Share it.

PYLADES

Grant me this exception: should something happen to the ship
so the letter is lost in the waves along with the cargo
and I can save only my skin,
the oath is off.

IPHIGENIA

Here's what I'll do (let's maximize our options):
I'll tell you everything written in the folds of the letter.
You can repeat it to my loved ones.
That way we're safe. If you get the letter there intact
it can tell its own tale silently.
But if the writing disappears in the sea
you'll save my words by saving yourself.

PYLADES

A good plan for both of us.
Tell me who is to receive the letter
and what to say from you.

IPHIGENIA

Give the message to Orestes, son of Agamemnon:
"The one slaughtered at Aulis sends you word—

Iphigenia, who is alive
although at Argos they think otherwise."

ORESTES

Where is she? Come back from the dead?

IPHIGENIA *(To Orestes.)*

You're looking at her.
Now stop interrupting.

*(To Pylades.)*

Say "Bring me to Argos before I die, brother,
out of this barbarous land!
Free me from my official task
of slaughtering strangers for a goddess!"

ORESTES

What shall I say, Pylades? Where in the world are we?

IPHIGENIA

"Or I'll become a curse on your house, Orestes!"
(That name you'll learn from hearing it twice.)

ORESTES°

O gods!

IPHIGENIA

Why are you invoking gods amid my instructions?

ORESTES

No reason. Go on. My mind wandered.
I'm on the verge of some miracle—no more questions.

IPHIGENIA

Tell them Artemis rescued me
by putting a deer in my place,
which my father sacrificed
thinking his sharp knife was slicing into me.

The goddess settled me in this land.
That is my message
as written in the letter.

PYLADES

Oh these oaths are easy to swear
and what you swore was beautiful too!
I won't take long to fulfill my vow.

*(To Orestes.)*

Behold, I bring you this letter from your sister,
your sister, Orestes, right here.

ORESTES

And I do welcome it!
But I shall lay the writing aside
and take hold of a joy that is not just words!
O dearest beloved sister, I am stunned
but I embrace you with my disbelieving arms
in open joy! This news astounds me!

IPHIGENIA°

Stranger, you transgress! It defiles the servant of a goddess
to touch her inviolable robes.

ORESTES

O my sister, born like me from Agamemnon,
don't turn away! You're holding the brother you never
thought to hold again.

IPHIGENIA

You my brother? Stop this talk! Argos is his territory, and
Nauplia.

ORESTES

Poor woman, that's not where your brother is.

IPHIGENIA

But who is your mother—Tyndareus' daughter from Sparta?

ORESTES
Yes, and my father is grandson of Pelops.

IPHIGENIA
What are you saying? Have you any proof?

ORESTES
Yes. Ask me anything about our father's house.

IPHIGENIA
Shouldn't you go first?

ORESTES
Yes. First this, I heard it from Electra:
you know there was strife between Atreus and Thyestes?

IPHIGENIA
Yes, some quarrel about a golden lamb.

ORESTES
So you know you wove it into a fine piece of cloth?

IPHIGENIA
Oh dear one, you come very close to my own heart.

ORESTES
And you also wove one showing the sun turned back in its course?

IPHIGENIA
I did, I wove this too, into a fine, fine cloth.

ORESTES
And the ritual bath you got from your mother at Aulis?

IPHIGENIA
Yes! There was no happy marriage to cancel that memory.

ORESTES
And what about sending your mother locks of your hair?

IPHIGENIA
They belonged on my grave, not my body.

ORESTES

Now I'll give you the proofs I've seen myself:
that ancient spear in our father's house—
the one Pelops wielded
the day he won Hippodameia at Pisa
and killed Oenomaus—
it's hidden in your old bedroom.

IPHIGENIA [*singing in this interchange with Orestes, who speaks in reply*]

*O most beloved! Nothing else—you are my most beloved!*
*Far from our fatherland, far from Argos,°*
*but I have you, O my love.*

ORESTES

And I have you,
though you were dead. So people thought.

IPHIGENIA

*Tears and lamentation mixed with joy,*
*make your eyes wet, and mine.*
*That day I left you, left you behind, just an infant,*
*just a babe in the house.*
*O happiness greater than words!*
*O my soul, what can I say?*
*These things have gone far beyond amazement,*
*beyond language.*

ORESTES

From now on I pray we are happy side by side.

IPHIGENIA

*I cannot place the joy I feel, O my friends, O ladies,*
*yet I fear it'll take wing and fly from my hands to the sky!*
*O Cyclopean hearth, O fatherland,*
*O dear Mycenae,*
*I thank you for his life,*

*I thank you for his cherishing:*
*you've raised a light of salvation for our house,*
*this brother of mine.*

ORESTES

We are blest in our birth
but not in our contingencies, O my sister.
Ours is no lucky life.

IPHIGENIA

*I realized that*
*the day my poor father laid his sword on my throat.*

ORESTES

O poor love, I was not there but I can see it.

IPHIGENIA

*There was no wedding song, brother,*
*when I was so treacherously led to the bed of Achilles.*
*By the altar instead were tears and lamentations.*
*Alas! I say alas, for the ritual waters poured out there.*

ORESTES

Alas! I say it too, for the deed my father dared.

IPHIGENIA

*He was no father to me.*
*Still, things do look different now*
*through some godsent stroke of luck.°* 867

ORESTES

Pitiful woman, suppose you had murdered your brother! 866

IPHIGENIA

*Pitiful indeed, and I did have it in me to do that!*
*Dread things I dared, dread things, brother.*
*You barely escaped an unholy death at my hands.*
*And how will it end?°*
*What chance will arise?*

*What means will I find to send you away*
*from violent death in a foreign land*
*to our home in Argos*
*before the bloody sword descends on you?*
*O my soul, this is your task: find the way.*
*Should it be on land, not by sea but on foot?*
*But death is nearby in the form of savage tribes*
*and impassable roads.*
*Yet surely that narrow passage through the dark-blue rocks*
*makes a long journey.*
*Ah, I feel desperate.*
*What god or mortal or miracle°*
*will find a way where there is no way*
*and show two lone offspring of Atreus*
*their exit from evils?*

CHORUS LEADER

This is all quite astounding, beyond words—
and I saw it with my own eyes!

PYLADES

When loved ones meet, Orestes, it's natural for them
to fall into one another's arms
but now you must leave off emotion and confront the issue:
how shall we win the glorious name of salvation
and escape this barbaric land?
It's the mark of a wise man to accept his luck for what it is,°
seize the moment, maximize his happiness.

ORESTES

Well said. And I think we have luck on our side here.
If someone acts resolute, the divine force is more effective
  too.

IPHIGENIA

You'll not restrain or silence me until I learn
what fate befell Electra.
This matters a great deal to me.°

ORESTES
She is happily married to Pylades here.

IPHIGENIA
And where is he from? Whose son is he?

ORESTES
Strophius of Phocis is his father.

IPHIGENIA
So he's born of a daughter of Atreus—he is my kinsman?

ORESTES
Yes, cousin to you and sole true friend to me.

IPHIGENIA
He was not yet born when my father killed me?

ORESTES
No, Strophius was childless a long time.

IPHIGENIA
I greet you, husband of my sister.

ORESTES
And my savior too, not just our kinsman.

IPHIGENIA
But how did you nerve yourself for those horrific deeds
against our mother?

ORESTES
Let's not talk of it. I was avenging my father.

IPHIGENIA
What cause had she to kill her husband?

ORESTES
Let our mother be! It's an evil thing for you to hear.

IPHIGENIA
I am silent. But does Argos look to you now as its leader?

ORESTES

Menelaus rules there. I am exiled from my land.

IPHIGENIA

Surely our uncle did not take advantage of our faltering house?° 930

ORESTES

No, fear of the Furies drove me away. 931

IPHIGENIA

I understand: the goddesses haunted you for our mother's sake. 934

ORESTES

To force their bloody bit onto my mouth. 935

IPHIGENIA

Your fit of madness on the shore—was that their doing? 932

ORESTES

Not the first time I've been a spectacle of suffering. 933

IPHIGENIA

But why did you make your way here? 936

ORESTES

On orders from Phoebus.

IPHIGENIA

To do what? Are you permitted to say?

ORESTES

Yes, I can say. Here's how my troubles began:
after I undertook those dread deeds against our mother,
which I pass over in silence, 940
I was driven into exile with the Furies at my heels,
first Delphi,
then Athens, where Apollo sent me°
to render justice to the goddesses whose names we do not name.

For there is a holy court there established once by Zeus
to cleanse Ares' hands of blood pollution.
At first when I arrived
none of my guest-friends was willing to receive me,
a man despised by gods as I am.
But some felt ashamed and gave me a table off by myself
although under the same roof.
They addressed no word to me so that
I might enjoy my food and drink apart from them.
Each filled his own jug with equal measure of wine
and took his pleasure.
Pretending not to notice, I challenged no one,
suffering in silence
and groaning deep in myself that I was a mother-killer.
(I hear the Athenians made a ritual of my misfortune
and still keep the custom of the Three-Quart Jug.)

Then I came to the Hill of Ares and stood trial,
I on one platform, the eldest Fury on the other.
We each said our piece about my mother's murder
and Phoebus saved me with his testimony.
Athena counted out the votes: half for me.
I left my own murder trial a victor.
So all the Furies who acceded to the judgment
settled in a holy shrine right near the court.
But the Furies who dissented from the law
began to drive me in an endless restless chase
until I came again to Phoebus' holy ground
and laid myself before his sanctuary.
I was starving myself
and I swore I would cut my life off and die there on the spot
if Phoebus did not save me—he had ruined me!
Then Phoebus shrieked out from his golden tripod
and sent me here to get the statue that fell from the sky.
I am to set it up in Athens.
Come,

help me accomplish the salvation set out for us.
If we can seize the statue of the goddess
my mad fits will end
and I'll sail you back to Mycenae on our well-oared boat.
O dearest beloved, O dear sister's head,
save your father's house, save me!
All is lost for me,
all is lost for the race of Pelops,
unless we get our hands on that heaven-dropped statue.

CHORUS LEADER

Some dread wrath of a god has boiled up
against the seed of Tantalus and drives it on through woes.

IPHIGENIA

Since before you came here, brother, I've had an intense desire
to be in Argos and set my eyes on you.
I want what you want: to release you from troubles
and restore our ailing ancestral home—
for I've no anger left for my killer.
That way I could withdraw my hand from your slaughter
and save our house.
But how to elude the goddess
and also the king (when he finds that empty base robbed of its statue)
this gives me pause.
How shall I escape death? What story can I come up with?
On the other hand, if our plan works,
you'll take the statue and me on board your fine ship
and the risk dissolves.
Apart from this, I perish,
though you may accomplish your task and get away home.
Well, I do not shrink. Not even if I die to save you.
Because you know, when a man is lost from home
they long for him. But a woman doesn't signify.

ORESTES

I will not be the murderer of you as well as my mother!
Her blood is enough. I'm your partner—I want
to share life and death with you equally.
I shall bring you home, provided I get there,
or stay here and die by your side.
But listen—I wonder, if this were displeasing to Artemis
why would Loxias give me an oracle
to take her statue away to Athena's city
and look upon your face?
On that calculation, I'm hopeful of achieving our return.

IPHIGENIA

Yes, how can we both avoid death and get what we want?
This is the weak point in our homecoming plan,
though the will is there.

ORESTES

Could we kill the king?

IPHIGENIA

Horrific suggestion, for strangers to murder their host.

ORESTES

But if it will save you and me, worth risking.

IPHIGENIA

I couldn't do it, but I admire your energy.

ORESTES

What if you hid me in the temple here?

IPHIGENIA

Thinking to escape under cover of darkness?

ORESTES

Yes—night belongs to thieves, daylight to truth.

IPHIGENIA

There are guards in the temple, we could not elude them.

ORESTES

Oh I give up, we're ruined. What way out is there?

IPHIGENIA

I think I have a new idea.

ORESTES

What? Share it, teach me.

IPHIGENIA

I'll turn your troubles to use in a cunning way.

ORESTES

Women are awfully good at scheming.

IPHIGENIA

I'll declare you came from Argos a murderer of your mother.

ORESTES

Use my misery, if it profits you.

IPHIGENIA

We'll say it isn't permitted to sacrifice you to the goddess.

ORESTES

On what grounds? Or can I guess?

IPHIGENIA

On the grounds you're impure. I'll be keeping the sacrifice
holy.

ORESTES

So how is this better for capturing the statue?

IPHIGENIA

I shall propose to purify you in seawater.

ORESTES

But the statue we need is still in the temple.

IPHIGENIA

And to wash that too. Because you touched it, I'll say.

ORESTES

Where will you go on the sea's wet shore?

IPHIGENIA

To where your ship is moored by its flaxen ropes.

ORESTES

Will you or someone else bring the statue in your hands?

IPHIGENIA

I myself. To touch it is holy for me alone.

ORESTES

And Pylades here, what task will he have?

IPHIGENIA

He'll be said to share the same pollution as you.

ORESTES

You'll do this in secret from the king or not?

IPHIGENIA

I'll win him with words—no way to prevent him noticing. 1049
So you must take care, take very great care, of everything else. 1051

ORESTES

Well, our fine oared ship is standing ready.° 1050

IPHIGENIA

And one last thing: these women must join in our deception.° 1052

ORESTES

Exhort them, then; find convincing arguments.
A woman has the power to stir pity.
And everything else might just work out perfectly!

IPHIGENIA *(To the Chorus.)*

Dearest friends, I look to you.
My fate is in your hands, whether it turn out well
or come to naught with me bereft of my homeland,
my beloved brother, my own dear sister.

Let this be the substance of my appeal:
we are women, as a species devoted to one another,
staunch in defending our common interests.
Keep silence for us and support our attempt to escape.
A loyal tongue is a fine thing.
Look how one turn of fate encircles the three of us
joined in love—to reach home or die.
And besides, if I survive you'll share my good luck,
I'll get you back safe to Greece. Come, I entreat you,
and you, by your right hand, your dear cheek,
your loved ones at home,
by your mother, your father, your child if you have one°—
what do you say? Who says yes, who says no?
Speak out:
if you reject me I perish and my poor brother too.

CHORUS LEADER

Take heart, dear lady. Do but save yourself.
All is silence on my side, as you request,
let great Zeus be witness!

IPHIGENIA

Bless your words and bless your fortunes!

*(To Orestes and Pylades.)*

Your task now is to enter the temple.
The king will be here any minute
to investigate whether the strangers' sacrifice is done.
O goddess who saved me in the folds of Aulis
from a terrible murdering father's hand,
save me now too along with these men—
or else by your fault is the word of Loxias
discredited among mortals.
Be gracious, depart this barbarous land,
go to Athens.
It is not right for you to dwell here
when you could have a city blessed and happy.

*(Exit Iphigenia, Orestes, and Pylades into the temple.)*

CHORUS [*singing*]

STROPHE A

*Halcyon bird who*
*all along the rocky sea ridges*
*sings that song of sorrow*
*understood by those who know*
*you always mourn your husband,*
*how like you I am!—*
*in my lament*
*a bird without wings,*
*longing for Greek marketplaces,*
*for Artemis goddess of childbirth*
*who dwells on the Cynthian hill,*
*for the delicate palm*
*and the flourishing bay*
*and the sacred silver olive shoot*
*so dear to Leto in her travail,*
*for the lake of circling waters*
*where a melodious swan*
*pays service to the Muses.*

ANTISTROPHE A

*O streams of tears*
*that fell down my cheeks*
*the day the towers were toppled,*
*the day I was shipped off*
*by enemy oar and enemy spear.*
*I was trafficked for gold*
*and got a barbarian home.*
*Here I serve the girl*
*who serves deer-killer Artemis—*
*Agamemnon's daughter,*
*at an altar where no sheep die.*
*And I envy the man whose life is solid misery—*
*amid necessity*

*he does not grow exhausted*
*because he lives with it every day.*
*But happiness keeps shifting.*
*To fall into evils after good fortune*
*makes a heavy life for a mortal.*

STROPHE B

*Now you, lady—an Argive ship*
*will carry you home*
*and the waxbound reed of mountain Pan*
*will call out to the beat of the oars*
*while prophetic Apollo*
*singing along with his seven-stringed lyre*
*brings you safe*
*to the bright shore of Athens.*
*But I,°*
*I will be left behind here*
*when you go your way on dashing oars*
*and the sails*
*of your swift-running ship*
*are spread to the air.*

ANTISTROPHE B

*If only I could travel those blazing roads*
*that fiery Helios travels,*
*then right above my own chambers at home*
*I would stop*
*my wings in midair.*
*If only I could take my place in the dances°*
*where once as a girl at fancy weddings*
*I made my feet whirl*
*alongside my girlfriends—*
*we were rivals in grace,*
*in delicate ornaments*
*and eager to win the contest.*
*I decked myself in robes of rich design*
*and let my hair hang down to shadow my cheeks.*

*(Enter Thoas from the side.)*

THOAS

Where is the woman who keeps these gates,
the Greek? Has she consecrated the strangers already?
Are their bodies ablaze inside the shrine?

*(Enter Iphigenia from the temple bearing a statue.)*

CHORUS

Here she is, king, she will answer you plainly.

THOAS

Ho there! daughter of Agamemnon!
Why are you hoisting this statue of the goddess off its base?

IPHIGENIA

Stop right there in the doorway, king.

THOAS

Is there something unusual happening in the temple,
    Iphigenia?

IPHIGENIA

I spit that away (a word to keep things holy).

THOAS

What are you hinting? Speak out plainly.

IPHIGENIA

The victims you've caught for me are not pure, king.

THOAS

What evidence do you have—or is this your own notion?

IPHIGENIA

The goddess' image turned its back.

THOAS

All on its own or did an earthquake turn it?

IPHIGENIA

All on its own. It closed its own eyes too.

THOAS

For what reason? The pollution of the strangers?

IPHIGENIA

Exactly, yes. Dread deeds were done by them.

THOAS

They murdered some barbarian on the shore?

IPHIGENIA

They were carrying bloodstains from home when they came here.

THOAS

What bloodstains? I'm very curious.

IPHIGENIA

They cut down their mother with a common sword.

THOAS

Apollo! Not even a barbarian would dare that.

IPHIGENIA

They were pursued all through Greece.

THOAS

So that's why you're bringing the statue out?

IPHIGENIA

Yes, out to the holy open air, away from bloodstains.

THOAS

And how did you discover the strangers' pollution?

IPHIGENIA

I interrogated them when the statue turned around.

THOAS

How perceptive! Greece raised you to be clever.

IPHIGENIA
Besides, they set out a sweet bait for me.

THOAS
Tried to charm you with some news from Argos?

IPHIGENIA
That my only brother, Orestes, is faring well.

THOAS
So you would spare them, I guess, in joy at their news.

IPHIGENIA
And that my father is alive and prospering too.

THOAS
Naturally you remained loyal to the goddess.

IPHIGENIA
Oh yes, I hate Greece utterly. Greece ruined me!

THOAS
Then what should we do about the strangers, tell me.

IPHIGENIA
We must honor the existing law.

THOAS
But aren't your lustrations and sword already at work?

IPHIGENIA
I want to cleanse them first with purifying rituals.

THOAS
In fresh-flowing streams or water of the sea?

IPHIGENIA
The sea washes away all human evil.

THOAS
Yes, they'll be purer victims for your goddess surely.

IPHIGENIA

And that might improve my lot too.

THOAS

Doesn't the sea wash up right here by the temple?

IPHIGENIA

We need a deserted spot—we have other tasks to do.

THOAS

Take them wherever you want. I've no desire to see forbidden things.

IPHIGENIA

I must purify the goddess' statue as well.

THOAS

Yes you must, if the matricides' pollution touched her.

IPHIGENIA

Why else would I have lifted her from her pedestal?

THOAS

Your piety and forethought are impeccable.

IPHIGENIA

Do you know what I'd like you to do?

THOAS

Tell me.

IPHIGENIA

Tie the strangers up.

THOAS

But where could they escape to?

IPHIGENIA

You can't trust anything Greek.

THOAS

Servants, fetch ropes.

IPHIGENIA

Let them bring the strangers out here . . .

THOAS

So be it.

IPHIGENIA

. . . Covering their heads with robes.

THOAS

To keep off the gaze of the sun.

IPHIGENIA

Send some of your servants with me.

THOAS

These will attend you.

IPHIGENIA

And send someone to announce to the city . . .

THOAS

What?

IPHIGENIA

. . . that they should all stay indoors.

THOAS

To avoid contact with blood?

IPHIGENIA

Yes, such things do pollute.

THOAS

*(To servant.)*

You, go, make the announcement . . .

IPHIGENIA

. . . that no one come into their sight.

THOAS

How well you care for our city!

IPHIGENIA

And for the friends I have to protect.

THOAS

You mean me!

IPHIGENIA°

THOAS

No wonder our whole community admires you.

IPHIGENIA

You yourself stay here before the temple and . . .

THOAS

What shall I do?

IPHIGENIA

. . . cleanse the chamber of the goddess with sulfur.

THOAS

So it's pure for your return.

IPHIGENIA

And when the strangers emerge . . .

THOAS

What should I do?

IPHIGENIA

. . . pull your robe in front of your eyes.

THOAS

So as not to look on a guilty man.°

IPHIGENIA

And if I seem to take too long . . .

THOAS

What limit do I set for this?

IPHIGENIA

. . . don't be surprised.

THOAS

Take your time, do the work
of the goddess properly.

IPHIGENIA

May this purification go according to plan!

THOAS

I second this prayer!

*(Enter Orestes and Pylades from the temple escorted by Taurian guards.)*

IPHIGENIA

Here come the strangers now out from the temple.
I see ornaments for the goddess and newborn lambs too—
I shall wash blood with blood to get rid of the defilement—
and blaze of torches and all the other purifications
I ordered for the men and the goddess.
I call upon you citizens to keep your distance from this pollution—
anyone who keeps his hands pure as doorkeeper of a temple,
anyone about to enter a marriage,
anyone heavy with child:
keep back, step away, lest this uncleanness fall upon you.
O virgin queen, child of Zeus and Leto,
if I succeed in washing the blood from these men
and performing the requisite sacrifice,
your dwelling will be purified
and we shall prosper.
As for the rest,
I do not say it but I make a sign
to the gods who know more
and to you, goddess.

*(Exit Iphigenia, Orestes, and Pylades to the side, escorted. Exit Thoas into the temple.)*

CHORUS [*singing*]

STROPHE

*A fine son is Leto's:*
*she bore him in the fruitful fields of Delos*
*a god with golden hair.*
*He is a master of the lyre and loves*
*to sight an arrow straight along the bow.*
*She left the place of her travail and carried her child*
*from the sheer sea cliffs*
*to the mother of rushing waters*
*who dances for Dionysus*
*on top of Mount Parnassus*
*where a wine-dark speckle-backed snake,*
*monster of earth,*
*glittered from the shade of a laurel tree,*
*guarding the oracle.°*
*You were still an infant*
*bouncing in your mother's arms,*
*O Phoebus,*
*when you killed it*
*and mounted your holy oracle:*
*now you sit on the golden tripod,*
*in the place that tells no lies,*
*dispensing to mortals god-spoken oracles*
*from your sanctuary*
*in the middle room of the world*
*beside Castalia's streams.*

ANTISTROPHE

*But when he had removed Themis, child of Gaia,°*
*from her holy oracle,*
*Earth concocted dream phantoms of night*
*who revealed things to the cities of men—*
*how it all began, what came next, the future—*
*as they slept in their beds wrapped in dark.*
*So Gaia, jealous for her daughter,*

*robbed Phoebus of his oracular office.*
*He went straight to Olympus*
*on his swift feet,*
*wrapped his child hands around Zeus' throne*
*and begged*
*that the earth goddess' anger be banished*
*from his Pythian home.*
*Zeus laughed*
*to see his son so quick and greedy*
*for solid gold oblations.*
*With a shake of his head he stopped the night voices—*
*stole from mortals those truths that take shape in the night—*
*gave back his honors to Loxias*
*and upon those mortals*
*who throng his throne*
*he bestowed*
*trust*
*in the singing of the god's word.*

*(Enter Messenger from the side.)*

MESSENGER

O temple guards and keepers of the altars,
where is Thoas, king of this land, to be found?
Throw open these bolted doors and call him out.

CHORUS LEADER

Why, if I may ask?

MESSENGER

The two young men are clean gone.
By the schemes of Agamemnon's daughter
they're fleeing this land and taking
the holy image on board their Greek ship.

CHORUS LEADER

That's incredible. But the king you want is not here,
he rushed out of the temple.

MESSENGER

Where to? He needs to know what's happening.

CHORUS LEADER

No idea. Run after him, find him
and tell him your news.

MESSENGER

See how treacherous is the female species!
You too have some share in these goings-on, don't you?

CHORUS LEADER

You're mad. What would escaping foreigners have to do with us?
And shouldn't you be hastening off to the palace gates?

MESSENGER

Not until an interpreter tells me
whether the king is inside or not.
Hey, you inside, undo these bolts!
And tell your master I'm here at the door
with a boatload of bad news.

*(Enter Thoas from the temple.)*

THOAS

Who's making this racket at the house of the goddess,
banging doors, interrupting us inside?

MESSENGER

These women lied to me,° kept trying to drive me away,
said you were out. But you were here all the time!

THOAS

Why? What did they think to gain?

MESSENGER

I'll explain that later. Listen to what's happening right now.
The young girl who was in charge of the altar here, Iphigenia,
has fled the land along with the strangers
and the holy statue. The purification was a trick.

THOAS

What do you mean? What lucky breeze did she catch?

MESSENGER

She is saving Orestes. Surprise for you!

THOAS

Who? You mean the boy who is son of Tyndareus' daughter?

MESSENGER

Yes, and the one who'd been dedicated by the goddess for this altar.

THOAS

That's amazing! What more can I say?

MESSENGER

Don't fuss about it, just hear me out:
when you've thoroughly listened and pondered,
plan a way to track those foreigners down.

THOAS

You're right, go ahead. They have no short voyage
ahead of them if they think to escape my spear.

MESSENGER

Well, when we came to the shore of the sea
where Orestes' ship was secretly anchored,
holding on to those strangers' ropes as you bid us,
Agamemnon's daughter signaled us to stand back
saying she was kindling forbidden fire
and performing special purificatory rites.
Then she took their ropes in her own hands
and walked behind them.
Now this was suspicious
but your servants went along with it, my lord.
After a while, to give the impression she was doing something,
she let out an ululation and started chanting

barbarian songs, as if she were
some kind of priest cleansing blood pollution.

And when we'd been sitting a long time on the ground
it struck us that once they were set free
the strangers might kill her and make their escape.
We sat in silence, afraid to look at things forbidden.
But finally the same conclusion came to us all,
to go where they were, forbidden or not.
There we saw the Greek ship
fitted with oars that spread out like wings
and fifty sailors holding their oars on the pins
and the young men—loose from their bonds—
standing on the stern.
Some sailors were holding the bow with poles,
some were fastening the anchor to its supports,
others hastened to lower ladders from the stern
into the sea for the foreign woman.

Well, we lost restraint now that we'd seen her treachery.
Laying hold of the foreign woman and the stern ropes
we began pulling the steering oars out of their sockets.
Words went back and forth:
"What's your explanation—making off from our land
with statues and priestesses?
Who are you, whose son are you, trafficking this woman
away?"
The other replied:
"I am Orestes, for your information,
brother of this woman, son of Agamemnon.
And the woman I'm transporting is my own sister, lost from
home."
Still we held on to her,
trying to force her to come along with us to you.
That's how I got these terrible knocks on the jaw!
They had no iron to hand, nor had we,
but fists were pummeling

and kicks were landing from both young men at once
onto our ribs and livers—
the pain was intense, our limbs grew exhausted.
Covered in awful marks we fled to the cliff,
bloody and wounded on heads and faces.
Then taking a stand on the hill we fought more cautiously
and pelted with rocks.
But archers stationed on the ship's stern
were hindering us with arrows and keeping us back.
Meanwhile
a monstrous wave had run the ship aground
and the girl° was afraid to wet her foot
so Orestes took her on his left shoulder,
stepped into the sea and leapt onto the ladder,
setting his sister down on the well-benched ship
along with that thing that fell from the sky—
the image of Zeus' daughter.
And from midship there came a shout:
"You band of sailors from the land of Greece,
take your oars, make the sea white with foam.
We have the prize for which we sailed through
the hostile passage of the Clashing Rocks."

They roared out a glad shout
and struck the salt sea. And so long as the ship
was within the harbor it kept advancing
but as it crossed the mouth
it went under
the deluge of a violent wave.
For a terrible wind came up suddenly
and was thrusting the ship backward.
They persevered, kicking against the wave,
but a back-rushing surf was driving the ship to land.
Then Agamemnon's daughter stood up and prayed:
"O daughter of Leto,
send me, your priestess, safe

back to Greece from this barbarian land
and forgive my thievery.
You surely love your brother, goddess.
Know that I too love my kin."

The sailors seconded the girl's prayer with a paean
and at a command put their bare shoulders to the oars.
But the boat was coming more and more toward the rocks.
Then one of our men leapt into the sea on foot,
another tried to catch the woven ropes,
and I was sent straight here to you
to let you know what's happening over there, king.
Go then, bring bonds and ropes with you.
For unless the rising sea turns quiet again
there is no hope of salvation for these strangers.
Reverend Poseidon, ruler of the ocean and
watcher over Troy, is hostile to Pelops' family.
And now it seems he will deliver Agamemnon's son
into your hands—yours and your citizens'—
along with his guilty sister—she who forgot
the sacrifice at Aulis and betrayed her own goddess.

CHORUS LEADER

O poor Iphigenia, you will die with your brother
now you've fallen again into the tyrant's hands.

THOAS

I address you all, people of this barbarian land.
Come, throw reins on your horses and race along the shore
to welcome the wreck of the Greek ship,
and while some of you hurry to hunt down these impious
 men
with the help of the goddess,
others will drag swift vessels into the water
so we can take them by sea and ride them down on land,
then throw them off a steep rock
or skewer their bodies on stakes!

And you women who collaborated in these plots,
I'll punish you later at my leisure.
Right now I'm busy, can't linger.

*(Enter Athena above the temple.)*

ATHENA

Where oh where are you off to on this hot pursuit, King
  Thoas?
Hear what I, Athena, have to say!
Stop your hunting; don't launch the full flood of your men.
It was fated by Loxias' oracles for Orestes to come here
fleeing the anger of Furies,
to transport his sister back home to Argos
and bring the holy image to my land,
so to find rest from his toils.
This is the word I have for you.
As for Orestes,
whom you expect to catch and kill on the tossing sea,
Poseidon is even now, as a favor to me,
smoothing the waves for his oar to traverse.
Orestes (you do hear my divine voice
though you are not present),
heed my instructions.
Take the image and your sister and go.
When you reach god-built Athens,
there is a place near the far edge of Attica,
close by the hills of Carystus,
a holy place called Halae by my people.
There build a temple and set down the statue.
Call it "Tauric" after the Taurian land
and the ordeals you survived,
roaming up and down Greece goaded by Furies.
People in future will hymn her as Artemis Tauropolus.
And you must establish this custom:
when they celebrate her festival
let them hold a sword at a man's throat and draw blood,

in payment for your sacrifice—so to mark its sanctity
and let the goddess keep her honors.
Now you, Iphigenia,
must continue to hold the keys of this goddess
in the holy meadows of Brauron.
There you will die and be buried
and they will make an offering to you
of finewoven robes left behind in their homes
by women who die in childbirth.
As for these women of Greece—I command you
to send them from this country
as reward for their righteousness.°
I rescued you once already, Orestes,
on the Hill of Ares when I judged the votes equal.
This too shall become customary:
whoever gets equal votes will win his case.
Go then, child of Agamemnon,
bring your sister out of this land.
And you, Thoas, calm your rage.

THOAS

Queen Athena, that man is not in his right mind
who hears gods' words and disobeys.
I harbor no rage against Orestes for departing with the
   image,
nor against his sister.
Is there any good in fighting powerful gods?
Let them go to your land and take the goddess' statue,
let them enshrine it there with all success.
I will also send these women to blessed Greece
as you enjoin me.
And I will no longer raise my spear,
nor my ship's oars,
against the strangers,
since this is your will, goddess.

ATHENA

I commend you.
Necessity governs both you and the gods.
Go, winds, convey the son of Agamemnon to Athens.
I shall accompany the voyage
to keep my sister's sacred image safe.

*(Exit Athena.)*

THOAS [*chanting*]

*Go on your way rejoicing in good fortune,°*
*blessed by salvation.*

CHORUS [*chanting*]

*O holy among immortals and mortals,*
*Pallas Athena,*
*we will do as you bid.*
*Surely delightful and unexpected*
*is this utterance I hear.*
*O great holy Victory,°*
*may you uphold my life*
*and not cease to crown me with crowns.*

*(Exit all.)*

# THE BACCHAE

*Translated by* WILLIAM ARROWSMITH

# THE BACCHAE: INTRODUCTION

*The Play: Date and Composition*

Euripides' *Bacchae* was first produced posthumously at the Great Dionysian festival in 405 BCE. Euripides had left Athens for Macedonia three years earlier and had died there in 406. *The Bacchae* was staged in his absence by one of his sons (also named Euripides), together with *Iphigenia in Aulis* (preserved) and *Alcmaeon in Corinth* (lost); this tetralogy won first prize for Euripides after his death, an award that he had won only four times during his lifetime.

*The Myth*

Euripides' *Bacchae* is the only surviving Greek tragedy to focus on a myth concerning Dionysus himself (otherwise known as Bacchus, or Bromius), the god of wine and theater in whose honor all these tragedies were performed. This play dramatizes Dionysus' establishment of his first cult in Greece, in the city of Thebes; it quickly became the classic version of the story. Dionysus had been conceived in Thebes as the son of Zeus by Cadmus' daughter, the mortal woman Semele, but she had been blasted by the god's thunderbolt before she could give birth to the child. The unborn infant Dionysus was rescued by Zeus, and in due course was born from Zeus' thigh; then after growing up he proceeded triumphantly throughout much of Asia, introducing his rites among the various peoples there. Now, accompanied by Asian bacchants, he has returned to Thebes, where the original ruler, Cadmus, has abdicated in favor of his grandson Pentheus. Semele's sisters, including Pentheus' mother, Agave, are denying her claim that Dionysus was the fruit of her union with a god, and Dionysus has punished them by driving all the women of Thebes mad and sending them in a frenzy out from the city onto the nearby mountain Cithaeron.

It is at this point that the action of the play begins. Dionysus, disguised as a mortal priest of his cult, sets the scene and introduces the action; only the audience knows his true identity. First the Asian bacchants (the chorus) arrive, and then Cadmus and Teiresias, all of them dedicated in different ways to celebrating this new god's worship. Pentheus rushes in, agitated at the news of the foreigner's arrival, and proceeds to do all he can to suppress the new cult and its representatives, even attempting to lock up the stranger (the disguised Dionysus) in prison and to capture the Theban bacchants on the mountainside. His efforts fail humiliatingly, yet he still cannot recognize the reality of Dionysus' power, despite being fascinated with the women's activities on Cithaeron. Eventually, at Dionysus' suggestion, Pentheus agrees to disguise himself as a bacchant himself and to go spy upon them. There he ends up being torn to pieces by Agave and the others, who in their crazed state mistake him for a lion. As the play comes to a close, Agave comes to realize what she has done. She and her father, Cadmus, go into exile, in misery, and Dionysus proclaims his future worship throughout Greece.

As early as Homer's *Iliad*, various myths told of the establishment of cults of Dionysus despite bitter human resistance, and of the god's bloody vengeance upon such unbelievers as Pentheus and the Thracian king Lycurgus. Scholars disagree about whether, and if so to what extent, the very earliest Athenian tragedies represented legends involving Dionysus himself. But it is certain that such myths had sometimes been presented in tragedies, now lost, by a number of playwrights before Euripides. Aeschylus composed two tetralogies on Dionysiac themes, a *Lycurgeia* (comprising *Edonians*, *Bassarai* [a term for Thracian bacchants], *Youths*, and the satyr-play *Lycurgus*) and a Theban tetralogy (including probably *Semele*, *Wool-Carders*, *Pentheus*, and the satyr-play *Nurses*). Lesser known tragedians wrote other plays on the subject: Polyphrasmon a tetralogy on Lycurgus, Xenocles a *Bacchae*, Sophocles' son Iophon a *Bacchae* or *Pentheus*, Spintharos a *Lightning-Struck Semele*, Cleophon a *Bacchae*; and, probably later than Euripides, Chaeremon wrote a *Dionysus*, Carcinus a *Semele*, and Diogenes too a *Semele*. Little or nothing is known about most of these plays, but when fragments or reports have survived, they usually indicate striking affinities with Euripides' play. In particular, the fragments of Aeschylus' *Lycurgeia* show an effeminate Dionysus being captured and interrogated, the bacchants being imprisoned and miraculously escaping, and the house shaking in a bacchic frenzy. So at least in its general outline and in some of its incidents Euripides' play will not have seemed entirely unusual to its first audience, though some scenes—perhaps especially Teiresias' sophistic lecture on Dionysian religion and the whole gruesome episode of Agave—are likely to have been surprising Euripidean innovations.

What is Euripides' own attitude to the story and characters he has dramatized in *The Bacchae*? Is this play his final declaration of faith in traditional Greek religion, a recantation of the notorious expressions of doubt made by some of the characters in his earlier plays? Or is it a denunciation of the catastrophes to which religious fanaticism can lead? To what extent may we imagine that elements of actual Dionysian ritual are being represented in the scenes of dance, cross-dressing, and collective dismemberment of a victim? Certainly the benefits that Dionysus provides—wine, music, and dance, as well as temporary release from toil and worry, especially for women, laborers, and the socially marginalized—are vividly and eloquently presented, both by the chorus and by several characters in the play. At the same time, the violence and wild behavior of some of the god's crazed worshippers are shocking and disturbing. In the end, the play leaves the audience in no doubt as to the disastrous consequences of rejecting Dionysus, even as it also reminds us of the ambiguous delights—and dangers—of the altered states, disguises, and transgressions of norms that his worship traditionally brings and that theater especially thrives on. To what extent does the play explore the crucial but ambiguous relation of Dionysian drama to politics and the dangers to which a city exposes itself if it refuses to accept tragedy within its walls? In any case, Euripides' decision, in self-imposed exile at the Macedonian court (where tragedy appears by this date to have become almost as popular as in Athens), to compose this play—perhaps his last completed one—for production at the Great Dionysian festival back home in Athens raises questions that have always fascinated not only scholars but also ordinary readers and theatergoers.

*Transmission and Reception*

The evidence of quotations and allusions among later authors and the survival of at least eight papyri containing fragments of the play indicate that *The Bacchae* was quite popular throughout antiquity. The tragedy is frequently referred to by pagan and Christian writers, and it deeply influenced a number of later works of Greek literature, especially the *Dionysiaca*, a forty-eight-book epic on Dionysus (the longest surviving poem from antiquity) by the early fifth-century CE poet Nonnus, and *The Passion of Christ*, an anonymous Byzantine Christian cento (a poem made up entirely of recycled verses from earlier poetry) which uses many lines from Euripides' tragedy about the experiences of Dionysus (as well as verses from other plays, especially by Aeschylus and Euripides) to tell of Jesus' sufferings and resurrection. So too, in Latin literature Euripides' play seems to have been a model for the Roman tragedians Pacuvius for his *Pentheus* and Accius for his *Bacchae* (whereas Naevius seems in his *Lycurgus* to have gone back to Aeschylus); but unfortunately none of these plays survive.

Directly and indirectly, Euripides' *Bacchae* remained a vital presence not only in ancient schoolrooms but also on ancient stages—one bizarre but striking piece of evidence is an incident at the Parthian court in 53 BCE when an actor dressed as Agave sang her lines "*We bring this branch to the palace, / this fresh-cut tendril from the mountains. / Happy was the hunting*" (1169–71) to general applause while holding the severed head of the defeated

Roman general Crassus. And somewhat over a century later the emperor Nero may have sung excerpts from the play while accompanying himself on the kithara. But scholars disagree about whether this tragedy left substantial traces in ancient pictorial art: a number of vases and frescoes depict the death of Pentheus, and scenes of Dionysiac revelry are frequent in all forms of ancient art, including sarcophagi, but it is unclear to what extent these are related directly to Euripides' play.

*The Bacchae* seems to have been selected as one of the ten canonical plays most studied and read in antiquity, but it was probably the very last play in that edition and as a result was more liable to damage, particularly at its ending. In fact, it is transmitted to us only by one manuscript and its copy; the former breaks off about halfway through, at line 755, so for the rest of the play we are dependent upon a single manuscript—and that one has at least one large gap near the end and a couple of smaller ones. Editors use a combination of different sources—summaries, citations, and allusions from other authors, verses from *The Passion of Christ*, and papyri—to try to fill out that large gap, at least speculatively. Unlike the other plays in the collection of ten, *The Bacchae* does not have any ancient or medieval commentaries.

In modern times, it was not until the end of the eighteenth century that *The Bacchae* began to be regarded as one of the supreme achievements of Greek tragedy, and also as crucial evidence for the religious significance of Dionysus in antiquity. This development began in Germany, with the poets Friedrich Hölderlin (who began, but did not complete, a translation of the play in 1799 and composed a number of poems about Dionysus and Jesus) and Johann Wolfgang von Goethe (who translated the whole play starting in 1821); and it culminated there in the philosopher Friedrich Nietzsche, whose *Birth of Tragedy* (1872) conceived of the Dionysian element as a vital counter to the Apollinian one in ancient Greek and also in contemporary European culture. Thereafter, it is difficult to separate the influence of Euripides from that of Nietzsche, among such authors as Hugo von Hofmannsthal ("Pentheus," 1904: a dramatic sketch), Robinson Jeffers ("The

Women on Cythaeron," 1928, a poem, later retitled "The Humanist's Tragedy"), Egon Wellesz (*The Bacchants*, 1931, an opera), Martha Graham (*Three Choric Dances for an Antique Greek Tragedy*, 1933), W. H. Auden (with Chester Kallman, the libretto for Hans Werner Henze's opera *The Bassarids*, 1966), and Donna Tartt (*The Secret History*, 1992, a novel). Starting in the late 1960s, the play was staged ever more frequently as a celebration of erotic, musical, and hippy vitality, a questioning of traditional masculinity and gender roles, and a condemnation of prudish censoriousness: the production by Richard Schechner and the Living Theater, *Dionysus in '69*, was a controversial milestone. Other recent notable dramatic versions include Joe Orton's *The Erpingham Camp* (1966), Nigerian author Wole Soyinka's *The Bacchae of Euripides: A Communion Rite* (first staged 1973), and Brad Mays' staging at the Complex in Los Angeles (1997, filmed 2000). Euripides' *Bacchae* continues to be one of the most frequently produced and read of all Greek tragedies, one of the most popular—and one of the most perplexing.

# THE BACCHAE

*Characters* DIONYSUS (also called Bacchus, Bromius, Dithyrambus, Euhius, and Iacchus)
CHORUS of Asian Bacchae (female followers of Dionysus, also called Bacchants and maenads)
TEIRESIAS, Theban seer
CADMUS, father of Semele (Dionysus' mother) and of Agave
PENTHEUS, king of Thebes
ATTENDANT of Pentheus
FIRST MESSENGER, a shepherd
SECOND MESSENGER, a servant of Pentheus
AGAVE, daughter of Cadmus, mother of Pentheus

*Scene: Pentheus' palace at Thebes. In front of it stands the tomb of Semele.*

*(Enter Dionysus from the side.)*

DIONYSUS

I am Dionysus, the son of Zeus,
come back to Thebes, this land where I was born.
My mother was Cadmus' daughter, Semele by name,
midwived by fire, delivered by the lightning's
blast.
And here I stand, a god incognito,
disguised as man, beside the stream of Dirce
and the waters of Ismenus. There before the palace

I see my lightning-blasted mother's grave,
and there upon the ruins of her shattered house
the living fire of Zeus still smolders on
in deathless witness of Hera's violence and rage
against my mother. But Cadmus wins my praise:
he has made this tomb a shrine, sacred to his daughter.
It was I who screened her grave with the green
of the clustering vine.
                                        Far behind me lie
the gold-rich lands of Lydia and Phrygia,
where my journeying began. Overland I went,
across the steppes of Persia where the sun strikes hotly
down, through Bactrian fastness and the grim waste
of Media. Thence to blessed Arabia I came;
and so, along all Asia's swarming littoral
of towered cities where barbarians and Greeks,
mingling, live, my progress made. There
I taught my dances to the feet of living men,
establishing my mysteries and rites
that I might be revealed to mortals for what I am:
a god.
    And thence to Thebes.
                                        This city, first
in Hellas, now shrills and echoes to my women's cries,
their ecstasy of joy. Here in Thebes
I bound the fawnskin to the women's flesh and armed
their hands with shafts of ivy. For I have come
to refute that slander spoken by my mother's sisters—
those who least had right to slander her.
They said that Dionysus was no son of Zeus,
but Semele had slept beside a man in love
and foisted off her shame on Zeus—a fraud, they sneered,
contrived by Cadmus to protect his daughter's name.
They said she lied, and Zeus in anger at that lie
blasted her with lightning.

Because of that offense
I have stung them with frenzy, hounded them from home
up to the mountains where they wander, crazed of mind,
and compelled them to wear my ritual uniform.
Every woman in Thebes—but the women only—
I drove from home, mad. There they sit,
all of them, together with the daughters of Cadmus,
beneath the silver firs on the roofless rocks.
Like it or not, this city must learn its lesson:
it lacks initiation in my mysteries;
so I shall vindicate my mother Semele
and stand revealed to mortal eyes as the god
she bore to Zeus.
Cadmus the king has abdicated,
leaving his throne and power to his grandson Pentheus,
who revolts against divinity, in me;
thrusts me from his offerings; omits my name
from his prayers. Therefore I shall prove to him
and everyone in Thebes that I am god
indeed. And when my worship is established here,
and all is well, then I shall go my way
and be revealed to other men in other lands.
But if the town of Thebes attempts to force
my Bacchae from the mountainside with weapons,
I shall marshal my maenads and take the field.
To these ends I have laid divinity aside
and go disguised as man.

*(Calling toward the side.)*

On, my women,
women who worship me, women whom I led
out of Asia where Tmolus heaves its rampart
over Lydia!
On, comrades of my progress here!
Come, and with your native Phrygian drum—

Rhea's invention and mine—pound at the doors
of Pentheus' palace! Let the city of Thebes behold you,
while I myself go to Cithaeron's glens
where my Bacchae wait, and join their whirling dances.

*(Exit Dionysus to one side. Enter the Chorus of Asian Bacchae from the other.)*

CHORUS [*singing*]

*Out of the land of Asia,*
*down from holy Tmolus,*
*speeding the god's service,*
*for Bromius we come!*
*Hard are the labors of god;*
*hard, but his service is sweet.*
*Sweet to serve, sweet to cry:*
*Bacchus! Euhoi!*
*You on the streets! You on the roads!*
*You in the palace! Come out!*
*Let every mouth be hushed.*
*Let no ill-omened words*
*profane your tongues.*
*For now I shall raise the old, old hymn to Dionysus.*

STROPHE A

*Blessed, those who know the god's mysteries,°*
*happy those who sanctify their lives,*
*whose souls are initiated into the holy company,*
*dancing on the mountains the holy dance of the god,*
*and those who keep the rites of Cybele the Mother,*
*and who shake the thyrsus,*
*who wear the crown of ivy.*
*Dionysus is their god!*
*On, Bacchae, on, you Bacchae,*
*bring the god, son of god,*
*bring Bromius home,*
*from Phrygian mountains,*
*to the broad streets of Hellas—Bromius!*

ANTISTROPHE A

*His mother bore him once in labor bitter;*
*lightning-struck, forced by fire that flared from Zeus,*
*consumed, she died, untimely torn,*
*in childbed dead by blow of light!*
*Zeus it was who saved his son,*
*swiftly bore him to a private place,*
*concealed his son from Hera's eyes*
*in his thigh as in a womb,*
*binding it with clasps of gold.*
*And when the weaving Fates fulfilled the time,*
*the bull-horned god was born of Zeus.*
*He crowned his son with garlands,*
*wherefrom descends to us the maenad's writhing crown,*
*wild creatures in our hair.*

STROPHE B

*O Thebes, nurse of Semele,*
*crown your head with ivy!*
*Grow green with bryony!*
*Redden with berries! O city,*
*with boughs of oak and fir,*
*come dance the dance of god!*
*Fringe your skins of dappled fawn*
*with tufts of twisted wool!*
*Handle with holy care*
*the violent wand of god!*
*And at once the whole land shall dance*
*when Bromius leads the holy company*
*to the mountain!*
*to the mountain!*
*where the throng of women waits,*
*driven from shuttle and loom,*
*possessed by Dionysus!*

ANTISTROPHE B

*And I praise the holies of Crete,*

*the caves of the dancing Curetes,*
*there where Zeus was born,*
*where helmed in triple tier*
*the Corybantes invented this leather drum.*
*They were the first of all*
*whose whirling feet kept time*
*to the strict beat of the taut hide*
*and the sweet cry of the Phrygian pipes.*
*Then from them to Rhea's hands*
*the holy drum was handed down,*
*to give the beat for maenads' dances;*
*and, taken up by the raving satyrs,*
*it now accompanies the dance*
*which every other year*
*celebrates your name:*
*Dionysus!*

EPODE

*He is sweet upon the mountains, when he drops to the earth*
*from the running packs.*
*He wears the holy fawnskin. He hunts the wild goat*
*and kills it.*
*He delights in raw flesh.*
*He runs to the mountains of Phrygia, of Lydia,*
*Bromius, who leads us! Euhoi!*
*With milk the earth flows! It flows with wine!*
*It runs with the nectar of bees!*
*Like frankincense in its fragrance*
*is the blaze of the torch he bears,*
*flaming from his trailing fennel wand*
*as he runs, as he dances,*
*kindling the stragglers,*
*spurring with cries,*
*and his long curls stream to the wind!*
*And he cries, as they cry,°*
*"On, Bacchae!*

*On, Bacchae!*
*Follow, glory of golden Tmolus,*
*hymning Dionysus*
*with a rumble of drums,*
*with the cry, Euhoi! to the Euhoian god,*
*with cries in Phrygian melodies,*
*when the holy pipe like honey plays*
*the sacred song for those who go*
*to the mountain!*
*to the mountain!"*
*Then, in ecstasy, like a colt by its grazing mother,*
*the bacchant runs with flying feet, she leaps!*

*(Enter Teiresias from the side, dressed in the bacchant's fawnskin and ivy crown, and carrying a thyrsus.)*

TEIRESIAS

Ho there, who keeps the gates?
Summon Cadmus—
Cadmus, Agenor's son, who came from Sidon
and built the towers of our Thebes.
Go, someone.
Say Teiresias wants him. He will know what errand
brings me, that agreement, age with age, we made
to deck our wands, to dress in skins of fawn
and crown our heads with ivy.

*(Enter Cadmus from the palace, dressed like Teiresias.)*

CADMUS

My old friend,
I knew it must be you when I heard your summons.
For there's a wisdom in his voice that makes
the man of wisdom known.
So here I am,
dressed in the costume of the god, prepared to go.
Insofar as we are able, Teiresias, we must
do honor to this god, for he was born

my daughter's son, who has been revealed to men,°
the god, Dionysus.
Where shall we go, where
shall we tread the dance, tossing our white-haired heads
in the dances of the god?
Expound to me, Teiresias,
age to age: for you are wise.
Surely
I could dance night and day, untiringly
beating the earth with my thyrsus! And how sweet it is
to forget my old age.

TEIRESIAS

It is the same with me.
I too feel young, young enough to dance.

CADMUS

Good. Shall we not take our chariots to the mountain?

TEIRESIAS

Walking would be better. It shows more honor
to the god.

CADMUS

So be it. I shall lead, my old age
conducting yours.

TEIRESIAS

The god will guide us there
with no effort on our part.

CADMUS

Are we the only men
who will dance for Bacchus?

TEIRESIAS

The others are all blind.
Only we can see.

CADMUS

But we delay too long.
Here, take my arm.

TEIRESIAS

Link my hand in yours.

CADMUS

I am a man, nothing more. I do not scoff
at gods.

TEIRESIAS

We do not trifle with divinity.°
No, we are the heirs of customs and traditions
hallowed by age and handed down to us
by our fathers. No quibbling logic can topple them,
whatever subtleties this clever age invents.
People may say: "Aren't you ashamed? At your age,
going dancing, wreathing your head with ivy?"
Well, I am not ashamed. Did the god declare
that just the young or just the old should dance?
No, he desires his honor from all mankind.
He wants no one excluded from his worship.

CADMUS

Because you cannot see, Teiresias, let me be
interpreter for you this time. Here comes
the man to whom I left my throne, Echion's son,
Pentheus, hastening toward the palace. He seems
excited and disturbed. What is his news?

*(Enter Pentheus from the side.)*

PENTHEUS

I happened to be away, out of this land,
but I've heard of some strange mischief in the town,
stories of our women leaving home to frisk
in mock ecstasies among the thickets on the mountain,

dancing in honor of the latest divinity,
a certain Dionysus, whoever he may be!
In their midst stand bowls brimming with wine.
And then, one by one, the women wander off
to hidden nooks where they serve the lusts of men.
Priestesses of Bacchus they claim they are,
but it's really Aphrodite they adore.
I have captured some of them; my jailers
have bound their hands and locked them in our prison.
Those who run at large shall be hunted down
out of the mountains like the animals they are—
yes, my own mother Agave, and Ino
and Autonoë, the mother of Actaeon.
In no time at all I shall have them trapped
in iron nets and stop this obscene disorder.
        I am also told a foreigner has come to Thebes
from Lydia, one of those charlatan magicians,
with long yellow curls smelling of perfumes,
with flushed cheeks and the spells of Aphrodite
in his eyes. His days and nights he spends
with women and girls, dangling before them the joys
of initiation in his mysteries.
But let me catch him in this land of mine
and I'll stop his pounding with his wand and tossing
his head. I'll have his head cut off his body!
And *this* is the man who claims that Dionysus
is a god and was sewn into the thigh of Zeus,
when, in point of fact, that same blast of lightning
consumed him and his mother both, for her lie
that she had lain with Zeus in love. Whoever
this stranger is, aren't such impostures,
such unruliness, worthy of hanging?

*(He catches sight of Teiresias and Cadmus.)*

What!
But this is incredible! Teiresias the seer

tricked out in a dappled fawnskin!
And you,
you, my grandfather, playing the bacchant—what a laugh!—
with a fennel wand!
Sir, I shrink to see your old age
so foolish. Shake that ivy off, grandfather!
Now drop that wand. Drop it, I say.
Aha,
I see: this is your doing, Teiresias.
Yes, you want still another god revealed to men
so you can pocket the profits from burnt offerings
and bird-watching. By heaven, only your age
restrains me now from sending you to prison
with those Bacchic women for importing here to Thebes
these filthy mysteries. When once you see
the glint of wine shining at the feasts of women,
then you may be sure the festival is rotten.

CHORUS LEADER

What blasphemy! Stranger, have you no respect
for the gods? For Cadmus who sowed the dragon teeth?
Will the son of Echion disgrace his house?

TEIRESIAS

Give a wise man an honest brief to plead
and his eloquence is no remarkable achievement.
But you are glib; your phrases come rolling out
smoothly on the tongue, as though your words were wise
instead of foolish. The man whose glibness flows
from his conceit of speech declares the thing he is:
a worthless and a stupid citizen.
I tell you,
this god whom you ridicule shall someday have
enormous power and prestige throughout Hellas.
Mankind, young man, possesses two supreme blessings.
First of these is the goddess Demeter, or Earth—
whichever name you choose to call her by.

It was she who gave to man his nourishment of dry food.
But after her there came the son of Semele,
who matched her present by inventing liquid wine
from grapes as his gift to man. For filled with juice from
    vines,
suffering mankind forgets its grief; from it
comes sleep; with it oblivion of the troubles
of the day. There is no other medicine
for misery. And when we pour libations
to the gods, we pour the god of wine himself
that through his intercession man may win
the good things of life.
                    You sneer, do you, at that story
that Dionysus was sewn into the thigh of Zeus?
Let me teach you what that really means. When Zeus
rescued from the thunderbolt his infant son,
he brought him to Olympus. Hera, however,
plotted at heart to hurl the child from heaven.
Like the god he is, Zeus countered her. Breaking off
a tiny fragment of that ether which surrounds the earth,
he molded from it a substitute Dionysus.
This piece of "sky" he gave to Hera as a hostage,
and thereby saved Dionysus from Hera's hate. With time,
men garbled the word and said that he'd been sewn
into the "thigh" of Zeus. This was their story,
whereas, in fact, Zeus made a fake for Hera
and gave it as a hostage for his son.
                              Moreover,
this is a god of prophecy. His worshippers,
like maniacs, are endowed with mantic powers.
For when the god goes greatly into a man,
he drives him mad and makes him tell the future.
                              Besides,
he has usurped even some functions of warlike Ares.
Thus, at times, you see an army mustered under arms
stricken with panic before it lifts a spear.

This panic comes from Dionysus.
Someday
you shall even see him bounding with his torches
among the crags at Delphi, leaping the pastures
that stretch between the peaks, whirling and waving
his thyrsus: great throughout Hellas.
Mark my words,
Pentheus. Don't be so sure that domination
is what matters in the life of man; do not mistake
for wisdom the fantasies of a sick mind.
Welcome the god to Thebes; crown your head;
pour him libations and join his revels.
Dionysus does not, I admit, compel a woman
to be chaste.° Always and in every case
it is her character and nature that keep°
a woman chaste. But even in the rites of Dionysus,
the chaste woman will not be corrupted.
Think:
you are pleased when men stand outside your doors
and the city glorifies the name of Pentheus.
And so the god: he too delights in honor.
So Cadmus, whom you ridicule, and I will crown
our heads with ivy and join the dances of the god—
an ancient gray-haired pair perhaps, but dance
we must. Nothing you have said would make me
change my mind or fight against a god.
You are mad, grievously mad, beyond the power
of any drugs to cure, for you are drugged
with madness.

CHORUS LEADER

Apollo would approve your words.
Wisely you honor Bromius: a great god.

CADMUS

My boy,
Teiresias advises well. Your home is here

with us, with our customs and traditions, not
outside, alone. You flit about, and though
you may be smart, your smartness is all nothing.
Even if this Dionysus is no god,
as you assert, persuade yourself that he is.
The falsehood is a noble one, for Semele will seem
to be the mother of a god, and this confers
no small distinction on our family.
You see
that dreadful death your cousin Actaeon died
when those man-eating hounds he had raised himself
savaged him and tore his body limb from limb
because he boasted that his prowess in the hunt surpassed
the skill of Artemis.
Do not let his fate be yours.
Here, let me wreathe your head with leaves of ivy.
Then come with us and glorify the god.

PENTHEUS

Take your hands off me! Go worship your Bacchus,
but do not wipe your madness off on me.
By god, I'll make him pay, the man who taught you
this folly of yours.

*(To his attendants.)*

Go, someone, this instant,
to the place where this prophet prophesies.
Pry it up with crowbars, heave it over,
upside down; demolish everything you see.
Throw his fillets out to wind and weather.
That will provoke him more than anything.

*(Exit an attendant to one side.)*

As for you others, go and scour the city
for that effeminate stranger, the man who infects our women
with this new disease and pollutes their beds.

And if you catch him, clap him in chains
and march him here. He shall die as he deserves—
by being stoned to death. He shall come to rue
his merrymaking here in Thebes.

*(Exit other attendants to the other side.)*

TEIRESIAS

Reckless fool,
you do not know the meaning of what you say.
You were out of your mind before, but this is raving
lunacy!
Cadmus, let us go and pray
for this crazed fool and for this city too,
pray to the god that he take no vengeance
upon us.
Take your staff and follow me.
Support me with your hands, and I shall help you too
lest we stumble and fall, a sight of shame,
two old men together.
But go we must,
acknowledging the service that we owe to god,
Bacchus, the son of Zeus.
And yet take care
lest someday your house repent of Pentheus
for its sufferings. I speak not prophecy
but fact. The words of fools finish in folly.

*(Exit Teiresias and Cadmus to the side.)*

CHORUS [*singing*]

STROPHE A

*Holiness, queen of heaven,*
*Holiness on golden wing*
*who fly over the earth,*
*do you hear what Pentheus says?*
*Do you hear his blasphemy*
*against the prince of the blessèd,*

*the god of garlands and banquets,*
*Bromius, Semele's son?*
*These blessings he gave:*
*the sacred company's dance and song,*
*laughter to the pipe*
*and the loosing of cares*
*when the shining wine is poured*
*at the feast for the gods,*
*and the wine bowl casts its sleep*
*on feasters crowned with ivy.*

ANTISTROPHE A

*A tongue without reins,*
*defiance, unwisdom—*
*their end is disaster.*
*But the life of quiet good,*
*the wisdom that accepts—*
*these abide unshaken,*
*preserving, sustaining*
*the houses of men.*
*Far in the air of heaven,*
*the sons of heaven live.*
*But they watch the lives of men.*
*And what passes for wisdom is not;*
*unwise those who outrange mortal limits.*
*Briefly, we live. Wherefore*
*he who hunts great things*
*may lose his harvest here and now.*
*I say: such men are mad,*
*their counsels evil.*

STROPHE B

*O let me go to Cyprus,*
*island of Aphrodite,*
*home of the Loves that cast*
*their spells on the hearts of men!*

*Or Paphos where the hundred-*
*mouthed barbarian river*
*brings ripeness without rain!*
*To loveliest Pieria, haunt of the Muses,*
*the holy hill of Olympus!*
*O Bromius, leader, god of joy,*
*Bromius, take me there!*
*There the lovely Graces are,*
*and there Desire, and there*
*the bacchants have the right to worship.*

ANTISTROPHE B

*The deity, the son of Zeus,*
*in feast, in festival, delights.*
*He loves the goddess Peace,*
*generous of good,*
*preserver of the young.*
*To rich and poor he gives*
*the painless delight of wine.*
*But him he hates who scoffs*
*at the happiness of those*
*for whom the day is blessed*
*and blessed the night;*
*whose simple wisdom shuns the thoughts°*
*of proud, uncommon men.*
*What the common people*
*believe and do,*
*I too believe and do.*

*(Enter Dionysus from the side, led captive by several attendants.)*

ATTENDANT

Pentheus, here we are; not empty-handed either.
We captured the quarry you sent us out to catch.
Our prey here was quite tame: refused to run,
but just held out his hands as willing as you please,

completely unafraid. His wine-red cheeks were flushed
and did not pale at all. He stood there smiling,
telling us to rope his hands and march him here.
That made things easy—and it made me feel ashamed.
"Listen, stranger," I said, "I am not to blame.
We act under orders from Pentheus. He ordered
your arrest."

As for those bacchants you clapped in chains
and sent to the prison, they're gone, clean away,
went skipping off to the fields crying on their god
Bromius. The chains on their legs snapped apart
by themselves. Untouched by any human hand,
the doors swung wide, opening of their own accord.
Sir, this stranger who has come to Thebes is full
of many miracles. I know no more than that.
The rest is your affair.

PENTHEUS

Untie his hands.
We have him in our net. He may be quick,
but he cannot escape us now, I think.

*(The attendants do as instructed.)*

So,
you are attractive, stranger, at least to women—
which explains, I think, your presence here in Thebes.
Your curls are long; they fall along your cheeks.
You do not wrestle, I take it. And what fair skin!
You must take care of it—not in the sun, by night
when you hunt Aphrodite with your beauty.

Now then,
what country do you come from?

DIONYSUS

It is nothing
to boast of and easily told. You have heard, I suppose,
of Mount Tmolus and her flowers?

PENTHEUS

I know of the place.
It rings the city of Sardis.

DIONYSUS

I come from there.
My country is Lydia.

PENTHEUS

And from where comes this cult
you have imported into Hellas?

DIONYSUS

Dionysus, the son of Zeus.
He initiated me.

PENTHEUS

You have some local Zeus there
who spawns new gods?

DIONYSUS

He is the same as yours:
the Zeus who married Semele.

PENTHEUS

How did you see him?
In a dream or face to face?

DIONYSUS

Face to face.
He gave me his rites.

PENTHEUS

What form do they take,
these rituals of yours?

DIONYSUS

It is forbidden
to tell the uninitiate.

PENTHEUS
Tell me the benefits
that those who know your mysteries enjoy.

DIONYSUS
You're not allowed to hear. But they are worth knowing.

PENTHEUS
Your answers are designed to make me curious.

DIONYSUS
No:
our mysteries abhor an unbelieving man.

PENTHEUS
You say you saw the god. What form did he assume?

DIONYSUS
Whatever form he wished. The choice was his,
not mine.

PENTHEUS
You evade the question.

DIONYSUS
Talk sense to a fool
and he calls you foolish.

PENTHEUS
Have you introduced your rites
in other cities too? Or is Thebes the first?

DIONYSUS
Barbarians everywhere now dance for Dionysus.

PENTHEUS
They are more ignorant than Greeks.

DIONYSUS
In this matter
they are not. Customs differ.

PENTHEUS

Do you hold your rites
during the day or night?

DIONYSUS

Mostly by night.
The darkness is well suited to devotion.

PENTHEUS

Better suited to lechery and seducing women.

DIONYSUS

You can find debauchery by daylight too.

PENTHEUS

You shall regret these clever answers.

DIONYSUS

And you,
your stupid blasphemies.

PENTHEUS

What a bold bacchant!
You wrestle well—when it comes to words.

DIONYSUS

Tell me,
what punishment do you propose?

PENTHEUS

First of all,
I shall cut off your girlish curls.

DIONYSUS

My hair is holy.
My curls belong to god.

*(Pentheus shears away some of the god's curls.)*

PENTHEUS

Second, you will surrender
your wand.

DIONYSUS

*You* take it. It belongs to Dionysus.

*(Pentheus takes the thyrsus.)*

PENTHEUS

Last, I shall place you under guard and confine you
in the palace.

DIONYSUS

The god himself will set me free
whenever I wish.

PENTHEUS

You will be with your women in prison
when you call on him for help.

DIONYSUS

He is here now
and sees what I endure from you.

PENTHEUS

Where is he?
My eyes don't see him.

DIONYSUS

With me. Your blasphemies
have made you blind.

PENTHEUS

*(To attendants.)*

Seize him. He is mocking me
and Thebes.

DIONYSUS

And I say, Don't chain me up! I am sane
but you are not.

PENTHEUS

But I say: chain him.
And I'm the ruler here.

DIONYSUS

You do not know
what is the life you live.° You do not know
what you do. You do not know who you are.

PENTHEUS

I am Pentheus, the son of Echion and Agave.

DIONYSUS

Pentheus: you shall repent that name.

PENTHEUS

Off with him.
Chain his hands; lock him in the stables by the palace.
Since he desires the darkness, give him what he wants.
Let him dance down there in the dark.
As for these women,
your accomplices in making trouble here,
I shall have them sold as slaves or put to work
at my looms. That will silence their drums.

DIONYSUS

I go,
for I won't suffer what I'm not meant to suffer.
But Dionysus whom you outrage by your acts,
who you deny is god, will call you to account.
You mistreat me—but it's he you drag to prison.

*(Exit Pentheus, Dionysus, and attendants into the palace.)*

CHORUS [*singing*]

STROPHE

*O Dirce, holy river,*
*child of Achelous' water,*
*yours the springs that welcomed once*
*divinity, the son of Zeus!*
*For Zeus his father snatched him in his thigh*
*from deathless flame, crying:*

*Dithyrambus, come!*
*Enter my male womb.*
*I name you, Bacchius, and to Thebes*
*proclaim you by that name.*
*But now, O blessed Dirce,*
*you spurn me when to your banks I come,*
*crowned with ivy, bringing revels.*
*O Dirce, why do you reject me? Why do you flee me?*
*By the clustered grapes I swear,*
*by Dionysus' wine,*
*someday you shall come to know*
*the worship of Bromius!*

ANTISTROPHE

*Pentheus, son of Echion,*°
*shows he was born of the breed of Earth,*
*spawned by the dragon, whelped by Earth,*
*inhuman, a rabid beast,*
*a Giant in wildness,*
*defying the children of heaven.*
*He will fetter me soon,*
*me, who belong to Bromius!*
*He cages my comrades with chains;*
*he has cast them in prison darkness.*
*O lord, son of Zeus, do you see?*
*O Dionysus, do you see*
*how your spokesmen are wrestling with compulsion?*
*Descend from Olympus, lord!*
*Come, whirl your wand of gold*
*and quell the violence of this murderous man!*

EPODE

*O lord, where do you brandish your wand*
*among the holy companies?*
*There on Nysa, mother of beasts?*
*There on the ridges of Corycia?*
*Or there among the forests of Olympus*

*where Orpheus fingered his lyre*
*and mustered with music the trees,*
*mustered the wilderness beasts?*
*O Pieria, you are blessed!*
*Euhius honors you. He will come to dance,*
*bringing his Bacchae, crossing the swift rivers*
*Axios and Lydias,*
*generous father of wealth*
*and famed, I hear, for his lovely waters*
*that fatten a land of good horses.*

*(In the following scene, sounds of thunder, lightning, and earthquake are heard from offstage.)*

DIONYSUS [*singing from within in this lyric interchange with the Chorus, who sing in reply*]
*Ho!*
*Hear me! Ho, Bacchae!*
*Ho, Bacchae! Hear my cry!*

CHORUS
*Who cries?*
*Who calls me with that cry*
*of Euhius?*

DIONYSUS
*Ho! Again I cry—*
*I, the son of Zeus and Semele!*

CHORUS
*O lord, lord Bromius!*
*Bromius, come to our holy company now!*

DIONYSUS
*Let the earthquake come! Shatter° the floor of the world!*

CHORUS
*Look there, soon the palace of Pentheus will totter.*
*Dionysus is within. Adore him!*

*We adore him!*
*Look there!*
*Above the pillars, how the great stones*
*gape and crack!*
*Listen. Bromius cries his victory!*

DIONYSUS
*Launch the blazing thunderbolt of god!*
*Consume with flame the palace of Pentheus!*

CHORUS
*Ah,*
*look how the fire leaps up*
*on the holy tomb of Semele,*
*the flame of Zeus of Thunders,*
*his lightnings, still alive!*
*Down, maenads,*
*throw to the ground your trembling bodies!*
*Our lord attacks this palace,*
*turns it upside down,*
*the son of Zeus!*

*(The Chorus falls to the ground in terror and veneration. Enter Dionysus from the palace.)*

DIONYSUS [*speaking*]
What's this, women of Asia? So overcome with fright
that you fell to the ground? I think you must have heard
how Bacchius jostled the palace of Pentheus. But come, rise.°
Do not be afraid.

CHORUS LEADER
O greatest light of our holy revels,
how glad I am to see your face! Without you I was lost.

DIONYSUS
Did you despair when they led me away to cast me down
in the darkness of Pentheus' prison?

CHORUS LEADER

What else could I do?
Where would I turn for help if something happened to you?
But how did you escape that godless man?

DIONYSUS

No problem.
I saved myself with ease.

CHORUS LEADER

But the manacles on your wrists?

DIONYSUS

There I, in turn, humiliated him, outrage for outrage.
He seemed to think that he was chaining me but never once
so much as touched my hands. He fed upon his hopes.
Inside the stable he intended as my jail, instead of me,
he found a bull and tried to rope its knees and hooves.
He was panting desperately, biting his lips with his teeth,
his whole body drenched with sweat, while I sat nearby,
quietly watching. But at that moment Bacchus came,
shook the palace and lit his mother's grave with tongues
of fire. Imagining the palace was in flames,
Pentheus went rushing here and there, shouting to his slaves
to bring him water. Every hand was put to work: in vain.
Then, afraid I had escaped, he suddenly stopped short,
drew his sword and rushed to the palace. There, it seems,
Bromius had made a phantom—at least it seemed to me—
within the court. Pursuing, Pentheus thrust and stabbed
at that thing of gleaming air° as though he were killing me.
And then, once again, Bacchius humiliated him.
He razed the palace to the ground where it lies, shattered
in utter ruin—his reward for my imprisonment.
At that bitter sight, Pentheus dropped his sword, exhausted
by the struggle. A man, a man, and nothing more,
yet he presumed to wage a war with god.

For my part,
I left the palace quietly and made my way outside.
For Pentheus I care nothing.
But judging from the sound
of tramping feet inside the court, I think our man
will soon come out. What, I wonder, will he have to say?
But let him bluster. I shall not be touched to rage.
Wise men know constraint: our passions are controlled.

*(Enter Pentheus from the palace.)*

PENTHEUS

What has happened to me is monstrous! That stranger, that man
I clapped in irons, has escaped.

*(He catches sight of Dionysus.)*

What! You?
Well, what do you have to say for yourself?
How did you escape? Answer me.

DIONYSUS

Your anger
walks too heavily. Tread lightly here.

PENTHEUS

How did you escape?

DIONYSUS

Don't you remember?
Someone, I said, would set me free.

PENTHEUS

Someone?
But who? The things you say are always strange.

DIONYSUS

He who makes the grape grow its clusters
for mankind.

PENTHEUS

His chiefest glory is his reproach.°

DIONYSUS

The god himself will come to teach you wisdom.

PENTHEUS

I hereby order every gate in every tower
to be bolted tight.

*(Exit some attendants to the sides.)*

DIONYSUS

And so? Could not a god
hurdle your city walls?

PENTHEUS

You are clever—very—
but not where it counts.

DIONYSUS

Where it counts the most,
there I am clever.

*(Enter a herdsman as Messenger from the side.)*

But hear this messenger
who brings you news from the mountain of Cithaeron.
I shall remain where we are. Do not fear:
I will not run away.

MESSENGER

Pentheus, king of Thebes,
I come from Cithaeron where the gleaming flakes of snow
fall on and on forever.

PENTHEUS

Get to the point.
What is your message, man?

MESSENGER

Sir, I have seen

the holy maenads, the women who ran barefoot
and crazy from the city, and I wanted to report
to you and Thebes what strange fantastic things,
what miracles and more than miracles,
these women do. But may I speak freely
of what happened there, or should I trim my words?
I fear the harsh impatience of your nature, sire,
too kingly and too quick to anger.

PENTHEUS

Speak freely.
You have my promise: I shall not punish you.
Displeasure with a man of justice is not right.°
However, the more terrible this tale of yours,
that much more terrible will be the punishment
I impose upon this man who taught our womenfolk
these strange new skills.

MESSENGER

About that hour
when the sun sends forth its light to warm the earth,
our grazing herds of cows had just begun to climb
the path along the mountain ridge. Suddenly
I saw three companies of women dancers,
one led by Autonoë, the second captained
by your mother Agave, while Ino led the third.
There they lay in the deep sleep of exhaustion,
some resting on boughs of fir, others sleeping
where they fell, here and there among the oak leaves—
but all modestly and soberly, not, as you think,
drunk with wine, nor wandering, led astray
by the music of the pipe, to hunt their Aphrodite
through the woods.

But your mother heard the lowing
of our hornèd herds, and springing to her feet,
gave a great cry to waken them from sleep.
And they too, rubbing the bloom of deep sleep

from their eyes, rose up lightly and straight—
a lovely sight to see: all together in fine order,
the old women and the young and the unmarried girls.
First they let their hair fall loose, down
over their shoulders, and those whose fastenings had slipped
closed up their skins of fawn with writhing snakes
that licked their cheeks. Breasts swollen with milk,
new mothers who had left their babies behind at home
nestled gazelles and young wolves in their arms,
suckling them. Then they crowned their hair with leaves,
ivy and oak and flowering bryony. One woman
struck her thyrsus against a rock and a fountain
of cool water came bubbling up. Another drove
her fennel in the ground, and where it struck the earth,
at the god's touch, a spring of wine poured out.
Those who wanted milk scratched at the soil
with bare fingers and the white milk came welling up.
Pure honey spurted, streaming, from their wands.
If you had been there and seen these wonders for yourself,
you'd surely yourself have approached with fervent prayers
the god you now deny.
                    We cowherds and shepherds
gathered together, wondering and arguing
among ourselves at these fantastic things,
the awesome miracles those women did.°
But then a city fellow with the knack of words
rose to his feet and said: "All you who live
upon the pastures of the mountain, what do you say?
Shall we earn a little favor with King Pentheus
by hunting his mother Agave out of the revels?"
Falling in with his suggestion, we withdrew
and set ourselves in ambush, hidden by the leaves
among the undergrowth. At the appointed time
the bacchants began to shake their wands in worship
of Bacchus. With one voice they cried aloud:
"O Iacchus! Son of Zeus!" "O Bromius!" they cried

until the beasts and all the mountain were
wild with divinity. And when they ran,
everything ran with them.
It happened, however,
that Agave ran near the ambush where I lay
concealed. Leaping up, I tried to seize her,
but she gave a cry: "Hounds who run with me,
men are hunting us down! Follow, follow me!
Use your wands for weapons."
At this we fled
and barely escaped being torn to pieces by the women.
Unarmed, they swooped down upon the herds of cattle
grazing there on the green of the meadow. And then
you could have seen a single woman with bare hands
tear a fat calf, still bellowing with fright,
in two, while others clawed the heifers to pieces.
There were ribs and cloven hooves scattered everywhere,
and scraps smeared with blood hung from the fir trees.
And bulls, their raging fury gathered in their horns,
lowered their heads to charge, then fell, stumbling
to the earth, pulled down by hordes of women
and stripped of flesh and skin more quickly, sire,
than you could blink your royal eyes. Then,
carried up by their own speed, they flew like birds
across the spreading fields along Asopus' stream
where the rich soil yields plentiful grain for Thebes.
Like invaders they swooped on Hysiae
and on Erythrae in the foothills of Cithaeron.
Everything in sight they pillaged and destroyed.
They snatched the children from their homes. And see—whatever
they piled as plunder on their shoulders stayed in place,
untied. Nothing, neither bronze nor iron,
fell to the dark earth.° They were carrying fire
in their hair—it did not burn them. Then the villagers,
furious at what the Bacchae did, took to arms.

And there, sire, was something terrible to see.
For the men's spears were pointed and sharp, and yet
drew no blood, whereas the wands the women threw
inflicted wounds. And then the men ran,
routed by women! Some god, I say, was with them.
The women then returned where they had started,
by the springs the god had made, and washed their hands
while the snakes licked away the drops of blood
that dabbled their cheeks.
Whoever this god may be,
sire, welcome him to Thebes. For he is great
in many ways, but above all it was he,
or so they say, who gave to mortal men
the gift of lovely wine by which our suffering
is stopped. And if there is no god of wine,
there is no love, no Aphrodite either,
nor other pleasure left to men.

*(Exit Messenger to the side.)*

CHORUS LEADER

I tremble
to speak my words in freedom before a tyrant.
But nonetheless I'll say: there is no god
greater than Dionysus.

PENTHEUS

Like a blazing fire
this Bacchic violence spreads. It comes too close.
We are disgraced, humiliated in the eyes
of Hellas. This is no time for hesitation.

*(To an attendant.)*

You there. Go down quickly to the Electran gates
and order out all heavy-armored infantry;
call up the fastest troops among our cavalry,
the mobile squadrons and the archers. We'll march

against the Bacchae! Affairs are out of hand
if we tamely endure such conduct in our women.

*(Exit attendant to the side.)*

DIONYSUS

Pentheus, you seem to hear, and yet you disregard
my words of warning. You have done me wrong,
and yet, in spite of that, I warn you once
again: do not take arms against a god.
Stay quiet here. Bromius will not let you
drive his women from their worship on the mountains.

PENTHEUS

Don't you lecture me. You escaped from prison.
Or shall I punish you again?

DIONYSUS

If I were you,
I would offer him a sacrifice, not rage
and kick against necessity, a man defying
god.

PENTHEUS

I shall give your god the sacrifice
that he deserves: the blood of those same women.
I shall make a great slaughter in the woods of Cithaeron.

DIONYSUS

You will all be routed, shamefully defeated,
when their wands of ivy turn back your shields
of bronze.

PENTHEUS

Impossible to wrestle with this foreigner!
Whether he's victim or culprit, he won't hold his tongue.

DIONYSUS

Friend,
you can still save the situation.

PENTHEUS

How?

By accepting orders from my own slaves?

DIONYSUS

No.

I undertake to lead the women back to Thebes.
Without weapons.

PENTHEUS

This is some trap.

DIONYSUS

A trap?

How so, if I save you by my own devices?

PENTHEUS

I know.

You and they have agreed to establish your rites
forever.

DIONYSUS

True, I've agreed to this—with the god.

PENTHEUS

Bring my armor, someone. And you—stop talking!

DIONYSUS

Wait!
Would you like to see them sitting on the mountains?

PENTHEUS

I would pay a lot of gold to see that sight.

DIONYSUS

What? Are you so passionately curious?

PENTHEUS

Of course

I'd be sorry to see them drunk.

DIONYSUS

But for all your pain,
you'd be very glad to see it?

PENTHEUS

Yes, very much.
I could crouch beneath the fir trees, quietly.

DIONYSUS

But if you try to hide, they will track you down.

PENTHEUS

Your point is well taken. I will go openly.

DIONYSUS

Shall I lead you there now? Are you ready to go?

PENTHEUS

The sooner the better. I want no delay!

DIONYSUS

Then you must dress yourself in women's clothes.

PENTHEUS

Why?
I'm a man. You want me to become a woman?

DIONYSUS

If they see that you're a man, they'll kill you instantly.

PENTHEUS

True. You are an old hand at cunning, I see.

DIONYSUS

Dionysus taught me everything I know.

PENTHEUS

How can we arrange to follow your advice?

DIONYSUS

I'll go inside with you and help you dress.

PENTHEUS

In a woman's dress, you mean? I'd be ashamed.

DIONYSUS

Then you no longer hanker to see the maenads?

PENTHEUS

What is this costume I must wear?

DIONYSUS

On your head
I shall make your hair long and luxuriant.

PENTHEUS

And then?

DIONYSUS

Next, robes to your feet and a headband for your hair.

PENTHEUS

Yes? Go on.

DIONYSUS

Then a thyrsus for your hand
and a skin of dappled fawn.

PENTHEUS

I could not bear it.
I cannot bring myself to dress in women's clothes.

DIONYSUS

Then you must fight the Bacchae. That means bloodshed.

PENTHEUS

Right. First we must go and reconnoiter.

DIONYSUS

Surely a wiser course than that of hunting bad
with worse.

PENTHEUS

But how can I pass through the city
without being seen?

DIONYSUS

We shall take deserted streets.
I will lead the way.

PENTHEUS

It's all fine with me,
provided those women of Bacchus don't jeer at me.
First, however, I shall ponder your advice,°
whether to go or not.

DIONYSUS

Do as you please.
I am ready, whatever you decide.

PENTHEUS

I'll go in.
Either I shall march with my army to the mountain
or act on your advice.

*(Exit Pentheus into the palace.)*

DIONYSUS

Women, our prey is walking
into the net we threw. He shall see the Bacchae
and pay the price with death.
O Dionysus,
now action rests with you. And you are near.
Punish this man. But first distract his wits;
bewilder him with madness. For sane of mind
this man would never wear a woman's dress;
but obsess his soul and he will not refuse.
After those threats with which he was so fierce,
I want him made the laughingstock of Thebes,
led through the town in woman's form.
But now
I shall go and costume Pentheus in the clothes
which he will wear to Hades when he dies, butchered
by the hands of his mother. He shall come to know

Dionysus, son of Zeus, consummate god,
most terrible, and yet most gentle, to humankind.

*(Exit Dionysus into the palace.)*

CHORUS [*singing*]

STROPHE

*When shall I dance once more*
*with bare feet the all-night dances,*
*tossing my head for joy*
*in the damp air, in the dew,*
*as a running fawn would frisk*
*for the green joy of the wide fields,*
*freed from fear of the hunt,*
*freed from the circling beaters*
*and the nets of woven mesh*
*and the hunters hallooing on*
*their yelping packs? And then, hard pressed,*
*she sprints with the quickness of wind,*
*bounding over the marsh,*
*leaping for joy by the river,*
*joyous at the green of the leaves,*
*where no man is.*
*What is wisdom? What gift of the gods°*
*is held in honor like this:*
*to hold your hand victorious*
*over the heads of those you hate?*
*Honor is cherished forever.*

ANTISTROPHE

*Slow but unmistakable*
*the might of the gods moves.*
*It punishes that man*
*who honors folly*
*and with mad conceit*
*disregards the gods.*
*The gods are crafty:*

*they lie in ambush*
*a long step of time*
*to hunt the unholy.*
*Beyond the old beliefs,*
*no thought, no act shall go.*
*Small, small is the cost*
*to believe in this:*
*whatever is god is strong,*
*whatever long time has sanctioned,*
*and the law of nature.*
*What is wisdom? What gift of the gods°*
*is held in honor like this:*
*to hold your hand victorious*
*over the heads of those you hate?*
*Honor is cherished forever.*

EPODE

*Blessed is he who escapes a storm at sea,*
*who comes home to his harbor.*
*Blessed is he who emerges from under affliction.*
*In various ways one man outraces another in the*
*race for wealth and power.*
*Ten thousand men possess ten thousand hopes.*
*A few bear fruit in happiness; the others go awry.*
*But he who garners day by day a happy life,*
*him I call truly blessed.*

*(Enter Dionysus from the palace.)*

DIONYSUS

Pentheus! If you are still so curious to see
and do forbidden sights, forbidden things,
come out. Let us see you in your woman's dress,
disguised in maenad clothes so you may go and spy
upon your mother and her company.

*(Enter Pentheus from the palace, dressed as a bacchant and carrying a thyrsus.)*

Why,
you look exactly like one of the daughters of Cadmus.

PENTHEUS

I seem to see two suns blazing in the heavens.
And now two Thebes, two cities, and each
with seven gates. And you—you are a bull
who walks before me there. Horns have sprouted
from your head. Have you always been a beast?
Well, now you have become a bull.

DIONYSUS

The god
was hostile formerly, but now declares a truce
and goes with us. You now see what you should.

PENTHEUS *(Coyly primping.)*

How do I look in my getup? Don't I move like Ino?
Or like my mother Agave?

DIONYSUS

So much alike
I think I might be seeing one of them. But look:
one of your curls has come loose from under the band
where I tucked it.

PENTHEUS

It must have worked loose
when I was dancing for joy and tossing my head.

DIONYSUS

Then let me assist you now and tuck it back.
Hold still.

PENTHEUS

Arrange it. I am in your hands
completely.

*(Dionysus rearranges Pentheus' hair.)*

DIONYSUS

And your strap has slipped. Yes,
and your robe hangs askew at the ankles.

PENTHEUS *(Bending backward to look.)*

I think so.
At least on my right leg. But on the left the hem
lies straight.

DIONYSUS

You will think me the best of friends
when you see to your surprise how chaste the Bacchae are.

PENTHEUS

But to be a real bacchant, should I hold
the wand in my right hand? Or this way?

DIONYSUS

No.
In your right hand. And raise it as you raise
your right foot. I commend your change of heart.

PENTHEUS

Could I lift Cithaeron up, do you think?
Shoulder the cliffs, Bacchae and all?

DIONYSUS

If you wanted.
Your mind was once unsound, but now you think
as sane men do.

PENTHEUS

Should we take crowbars with us?
Or should I put my shoulder to the cliffs
and heave them up?

DIONYSUS

What? And destroy the haunts
of the nymphs, the holy groves where Pan plays
his woodland pipes?

PENTHEUS

You are right. In any case,
women should not be mastered by brute strength.
I will hide myself among the firs instead.

DIONYSUS

You will find all the ambush you deserve,
creeping up to spy on the maenads.

PENTHEUS

Think.
I can see them already, there among the bushes,
mating like birds, caught in the toils of love.

DIONYSUS

Exactly. This is your mission: you go to watch.
You may surprise them—or they may surprise you.

PENTHEUS

Then lead me through the very heart of Thebes,
since I'm the only one who's man enough to go.

DIONYSUS

You and you alone will labor for your city.
A great ordeal awaits you, the one that you're allotted
as your fate. I shall lead you safely there;
someone else shall bring you back . . .

PENTHEUS

Yes, my mother.

DIONYSUS

. . . conspicuous to all men.

PENTHEUS

It is for that I go.

DIONYSUS

You will be carried home . . .

PENTHEUS

O luxury!

DIONYSUS

. . . cradled in your mother's arms.

PENTHEUS

You will spoil me!

DIONYSUS

Yes, in a certain way.

PENTHEUS

I go to my reward.

DIONYSUS

You are an extraordinary young man, and you go
to an extraordinary experience. You shall win
fame high as heaven.
Agave, Cadmus' daughters,°
reach out your hands! I bring this young man
to a great contest, where I shall be the victor,
I—and Bromius. The rest the event shall show.

*(Exit Dionysus to the side, followed by Pentheus.)*

CHORUS [*singing*]

STROPHE

*Run to the mountain, fleet hounds of madness!*
*Run, run to the holy company of Cadmus' daughters!*
*Sting them against the man in women's clothes,*
*the madman who spies on the maenads!*
*From behind the rocks, keen-sighted,*
*his mother shall see him spying first.*
*She will cry to the maenads:*
*"Who is this who has come*
*to the mountains to peer at the mountain revels*
*of the women of Thebes?*
*Who bore him, Bacchae?*

*This man was born of no woman. Some lioness*
*gave him birth, some Libyan Gorgon!"*
*O Justice,*
*come! Be manifest; reveal yourself with a sword!*
*Stab through the throat that godless, lawless, unjust man,*
*the earth-born spawn of Echion!*

ANTISTROPHE

*Uncontrollable, the unbeliever goes,°*
*in spitting rage, rebellious and amok,*
*madly assaulting Bacchus' mysteries and his mother's.*
*Against the unassailable he runs, with rage*
*obsessed. But death will chastise his ideas.°*
*To accept the gods, to act as a mortal—*
*that is a life free from pain.*
*I do not resent wisdom and I rejoice to hunt it.*
*But other things are great and clear*
*and make life beautiful:*
*purity, piety, day into night,*
*honoring the gods,*
*rejecting customs outside justice.*
*O Justice,*
*come! Be manifest; reveal yourself with a sword!*
*Stab through the throat that godless, lawless, unjust man,*
*the earth-born spawn of Echion!*

EPODE

*O Dionysus, reveal yourself a bull! Be manifest,*
*a snake with darting heads, a lion breathing fire!*
*O Bacchus, go! Go with your smile!*
*Cast your deadly noose about this man who hunts*
*your Bacchae! Make him fall*
*to your maenad throng!*

*(Enter from the side a servant of Pentheus as a second Messenger.)*

MESSENGER

How prosperous in Hellas these halls once were,

this house founded by Cadmus, the old man from Sidon°
who sowed the earth-born crop of the dragon snake!
I am a slave and nothing more, yet even so
I mourn the fortunes of this fallen house.°

CHORUS LEADER

What is it?
Is there news from the Bacchae?

MESSENGER

This is my news:
Pentheus, the son of Echion, is dead.

CHORUS [*singing and continuing to sing in the following*]
*All hail to Bromius! Our god is a great god!*

MESSENGER
What is this you say, woman? You dare to rejoice
at these disasters which destroy this house?

CHORUS
*I am no Greek. I hail my god*
*in barbarian song. No longer need I*
*shrink with fear of prison.*

MESSENGER
If you suppose this city is so short of men . . .°

CHORUS
*Dionysus, Dionysus, not Thebes,*
*has power over me.*

MESSENGER
Your feelings might be forgiven, then. But this,
your exultation in disaster—it is not right.

CHORUS
*Tell us how that lawless man died.*
*How was he killed?*

MESSENGER

There were three of us in all: Pentheus and I,
attending my master, and that stranger who volunteered
to guide us to the show. Leaving behind us
the last outlying farms of Thebes, we forded
the Asopus and struck into the barren scrubland
of Cithaeron.
                    There in a grassy glen we halted,
unmoving, silent, without a word,
so we might see but not be seen. From that vantage,
in a steep meadow along the sheer rock of the cliffs,
a place where water ran and the pines grew dense
with shade, we saw the maenads sitting, their hands
busily moving at their happy tasks. Some
wound the stalks of their tattered wands with tendrils
of fresh ivy; others, frisking like fillies
newly freed from the painted bridles, chanted
in Bacchic songs, responsively.
                    But Pentheus—
unhappy man—could not quite see the companies
of women. "Stranger," he said, "from where we stand,
I cannot see these counterfeited maenads.°
But if I climbed that towering fir that overhangs
the banks, then I could see their shameless orgies
better."
                    And now the stranger worked a miracle.
Reaching for the highest branch of the great fir,
he bent it down, down, down to the dark earth,
till it was curved the way a taut bow bends
or like a rim of wood when forced about the circle
of a wheel. Like that he forced that mountain fir
down to the ground. No mortal could have done it.
Then he seated Pentheus at the highest tip
and with his hands let the trunk rise straightly up,
slowly and gently, lest it throw its rider.
And the tree rose, towering to heaven, with my master

seated at the top. And now the maenads saw him
more clearly than he saw them. But barely had they seen,
when the stranger vanished and there came a great voice
out of heaven—Dionysus', it must have been—
crying: "Women, I bring you the man who mocks
at you and me and at our holy mysteries.
Take vengeance upon him." And as he spoke
a flash of awful fire bound earth and heaven.
The high air hushed, and along the forest glen
the leaves hung still; you could hear no cry of beasts.
The Bacchae heard that voice but missed its words,
and leaping up, they stared, peering everywhere.
Again that voice. And now they knew his cry,
the clear command of Bacchius. Breaking loose
like startled doves,° through grove and torrent,
over rocks, the Bacchae flew, their feet maddened
by the god's breath. And when they saw my master
perching on his tree, they climbed a great rock
that towered opposite his perch and showered him
with stones and branches of fir, while the others
hurled their wands. What grim target practice!
But they didn't hit Pentheus, barely out of reach
of their eager hands, treed, unable to escape.
Finally they splintered branches from the oaks
and with those bars of wood tried to lever up the tree
by prying at the roots. But every effort failed.
Then Agave cried out: "Maenads, make a circle
about the trunk and grip it with your hands.
Unless we take this climbing beast, he will reveal
the secrets of the god." With that, thousands of hands
tore the fir tree from the earth, and down, down
from his high perch fell Pentheus, tumbling
to the ground, sobbing and screaming as he fell,
for he knew his end was near.
His own mother,
like a priestess with her victim, fell upon him

first. But snatching from his hair the headband
so poor Agave would recognize and spare him, he said,
touching her cheeks, "No, Mother! I am Pentheus,
your own son, the child you bore to Echion!
Pity me, spare me, Mother! I have done a wrong,
but do not kill your own son for that offense."
But she was foaming at the mouth, and her crazed eyes
rolled with frenzy. She was mad, stark mad,
possessed by Bacchus. Ignoring his cries of pity,
she seized his left arm at the wrist; then, planting
her foot upon his chest, she pulled, wrenching away
the arm at the shoulder—not by her own strength,
for the god had put inhuman power in her hands.
Ino, meanwhile, on the other side, was scratching off
his flesh. Then Autonoë and the whole horde
of Bacchae swarmed upon him. Shouts everywhere—
him groaning with what little breath was left,
them shrieking in triumph. One bore off an arm,
another a foot still warm in its shoe. His ribs
were clawed clean of flesh and every hand
was smeared with blood as they played ball with scraps
of Pentheus' body.
The pitiful remains lie scattered,
one piece among the sharp rocks, others
among the leaves in the deep woods—not easy
to search for. His mother, picking up his head,
impaled it on her wand. She seems to think it is
some mountain lion's head which she carries in triumph
through the thick of Cithaeron. Leaving her sisters
at the maenad dances, she is coming here, gloating
over her grisly prize. She calls upon Bacchius:
he is her "fellow huntsman," "comrade of the chase,"
"crowned with victory." But all the victory
she carries home is her own grief.
Now,
before Agave returns, I shall leave

this scene of sorrow. Humility,
a sense of reverence before the sons of heaven—
of all the prizes that a mortal man might win,
these, I say, are wisest; these are best.

*(Exit Messenger to the side.)*

CHORUS [*singing*]

*Let us dance to the glory of Bacchius,*
*dance to the death of Pentheus,*
*the death of the spawn of the dragon!*
*He dressed in woman's dress;*
*he took the lovely thyrsus;*
*it waved him down to death,*°
*led by a bull to Hades.*
*Hail, Bacchae of Thebes!*
*Your victory is fair, fair the prize,*
*this famous prize of grief, of tears!*
*Glorious the game, to fold your child*
*in your arms, streaming with his blood!*

*(Enter Agave from the side carrying the head of Pentheus impaled upon her thyrsus.)*

CHORUS LEADER

But look: here comes Pentheus' mother, Agave,
running wild-eyed toward the palace.
Welcome,
welcome to the reveling band of the god of joy!

AGAVE [*singing in this lyric interchange with the Chorus, who sing in reply*]

STROPHE

*Bacchae of Asia . . .*

CHORUS

*Tell me.*

AGAVE

*. . . we bring this branch to the palace,*

*this fresh-cut tendril from the mountains.*
*Happy was the hunting.*

CHORUS

*I see.*

*I welcome our fellow-reveler.*

AGAVE

*The cub of a wild mountain lion,°*
*and snared by me without a noose—*
*look, look!*

CHORUS

*Where was he caught?*

AGAVE

*Cithaeron . . .*

CHORUS

*Cithaeron?*

AGAVE

*. . . killed him.*

CHORUS

*Who struck him?*

AGAVE

*The first honor is mine.*
*The maenads call me "Agave the blest."*

CHORUS

*And then who?*

AGAVE

*Cadmus' . . .*

CHORUS

*Cadmus'?*

AGAVE

*. . . daughters.*

*After me, they hit the prey.*
*After me. Happy was their hunting.*

ANTISTROPHE

*Share the feast!*

CHORUS

*Share, unhappy woman?*

AGAVE

*See, the cub is young and tender.*
*Beneath the soft mane of hair,*
*the down is blooming on the cheeks.*

CHORUS

*Yes, that mane does look like a wild beast's.*

AGAVE

*Our god is wise. Cunningly, cleverly,*
*Bacchius the hunter lashed the maenads*
*against his prey.*

CHORUS

*Our king is a hunter.*

AGAVE

*Do you praise?*

CHORUS

*Yes, I praise.*

AGAVE

*The men of Thebes soon . . .*

CHORUS

*. . . and Pentheus, your son . . .*

AGAVE

*. . . will praise his mother. She caught*
*a great quarry, this lion's cub.*

CHORUS

*Extraordinary catch.*

AGAVE

*Extraordinary skill.*

CHORUS

*You are proud?*

AGAVE

*Proud and happy.*
*I have won the trophy of the chase,*
*a great prize, manifest to all.*

CHORUS LEADER [*speaking*]

Then, poor woman, show the citizens of Thebes
this great prize, this trophy you have won
in the hunt.

AGAVE [*speaking*]

You citizens of this towered city,
men of Thebes, behold the trophy of your women's
hunting! This is the quarry of our chase, taken
not with nets nor Thessalian spears but by
the dainty hands of women. What are they worth,
your javelins now and all that uselessness
your armor is, since we, with our bare hands,
captured this quarry and tore its bleeding body
limb from limb?
But where is my old father, Cadmus?
He should come. And my son. Where is Pentheus?
Fetch him. I will have him set his ladder up
against the wall and, there upon the beam,
nail the head of this wild lion I have killed
as a trophy of my hunt.

*(Enter Cadmus from the side, with attendants bearing a covered bier.)*

CADMUS

Follow me, attendants.
Bear your dreadful burden of Pentheus and set it down
there before the palace.

*(The attendants do as instructed.)*

Now I bring it,
this body—after long and weary searchings
I painfully gathered it from Cithaeron's glens
where it lay, scattered in shreds, dismembered
throughout the forest, no two pieces
in a single place.°
Old Teiresias and I
had returned to Thebes from the Bacchae on the mountain
before I learned of this atrocious crime
my daughters did. And so I hurried back
to the mountain to recover the body of this boy
murdered by the maenads. There among the oaks
I found Aristaeus' wife, the mother of Actaeon,
Autonoë, and with her Ino, both
still stung with madness. But Agave, they said,
was on her way to Thebes, still possessed.
And what they said was true, for there she is,
and not a happy sight.

AGAVE

Now, Father,
yours can be the proudest boast of living men,
because you are the father of the bravest daughters
in the world. All of your daughters are brave,
but I above the rest. I have left my shuttle
at the loom; I raised my sight to higher things—
to hunting animals with my bare hands.
You see?
Here in my hands I hold the quarry of my chase,
a trophy for our house, to be nailed up high

upon its walls. Come Father, take it in your hands.
Glory in my kill and invite your friends to share
the feast of triumph. For you are blest, Father,
by this great deed we have done.

CADMUS

This is a grief°
so great it knows no size. I cannot look.
This is the awful murder your hands have done.
This, this is the noble victim you have slaughtered
to the gods. And to share a feast like this
you now invite all Thebes and me?
O gods,
how terribly I pity you and then myself.
Justly—yes, but excessively has lord Bromius,
this god of our own blood, destroyed us all,
every one.

AGAVE

How scowling and crabbed is old age
in mortals. I hope my son takes after his mother
and wins, as she has done, the laurels of the chase
when he goes hunting with the younger men of Thebes.
But all my son can do is quarrel with god.
He should be scolded, Father, and you are the one
who should scold him. Yes, someone call him here
so he can see his mother's triumph.

CADMUS

Enough. No more.
If you realize the horror you have done,
you shall suffer terribly. But if instead
your present madness lasts until you die,
you'll not seem unhappy, but you won't be happy.

AGAVE

Why do you reproach me? Is there something wrong?

CADMUS

First raise your eyes to the heavens.

AGAVE

There.
But why?

CADMUS

Does it look the same as it did before?
Or has it changed?

AGAVE

It seems—somehow—clearer,
brighter than it was before.

CADMUS

Do you still feel
the same flurry inside you?

AGAVE

The same—flurry?
No, I feel—somehow—calmer. I feel as though—
my mind were somehow—changing.

CADMUS

Can you still hear me?
Can you answer clearly?

AGAVE

Yes. I have forgotten
what we said before, Father.

CADMUS

Who was your husband?

AGAVE

Echion—a man, they said, born of the dragon seed.

CADMUS

What was the name of the child you bore your husband?

AGAVE
Pentheus.

CADMUS
And whose head do you hold in your hands?

AGAVE
A lion's head—or so the hunters told me.

CADMUS
Look directly at it. That's quickly done.

AGAVE
Aah! What is it? What am I holding in my hands?

CADMUS
Look more closely still. Study it carefully.

AGAVE
No! O gods, I see the greatest grief there is.

CADMUS
Does it look like a lion now?

AGAVE
No, no. It is—
Pentheus' head—I hold.

CADMUS
And mourned by me
before you ever knew.

AGAVE
But who killed him?
Why am I holding him?

CADMUS
O savage truth,
what a time to come!

AGAVE

For god's sake, speak.
My heart is beating with terror.

CADMUS

You killed him.
You and your sisters.

AGAVE

But where was he killed?
Here at home? Where?

CADMUS

He was killed on Cithaeron,
there where the hounds tore Actaeon to pieces.

AGAVE

But why? Why had Pentheus gone to Cithaeron?

CADMUS

He went to your revels to mock the god.

AGAVE

But we—
what were we doing on the mountain?

CADMUS

You were mad.
The whole city was possessed.

AGAVE

Now, now I see:
Dionysus has destroyed us all.

CADMUS

You outraged him.
You denied that he was truly god.

AGAVE

Father,
where is my poor boy's body now?

CADMUS

There it is.
I gathered the pieces with great difficulty.

AGAVE

Is his body entire? Has he been laid out well?

CADMUS

. . . . . . . . . . . . . . . . . . . . . .°

AGAVE

But how did Pentheus share in my own folly?

CADMUS

He, like you, blasphemed the god. And so
the god has brought us all to ruin at one blow,
you, your sisters, and this boy. All our house
the god has utterly destroyed and, with it,
me. For I have no sons, have no male heir;
and I have lived only to see this boy,
this fruit of your own body, most horribly
and foully killed.

*(To the corpse.)*

To you my house looked up.
Child, you were the stay of my house; you were
my daughter's son. Of you this city stood in awe.
No one who once had seen your face dared outrage
the old man, for if he did, you punished him.
Now I must go, a banished and dishonored man—
I, Cadmus the great, who sowed the soldiery
of Thebes and harvested a great harvest. My son,
dearest to me of all men—for even dead,
I count you still the man I love the most—
never again will your hand touch my chin;
no more, child, will you hug me and call me
"Grandfather" and say, "Who is wronging you?
Does anyone trouble you or vex your heart, old man?

Tell me, Grandfather, and I will punish him."
No, now there is grief for me; the mourning
for you; pity for your mother; and for her sisters,
sorrow.
        If there is still any mortal man
who despises or defies divinity, let him look
on this boy's death and believe in the gods.

CHORUS LEADER

Cadmus, I pity you. Your daughter's son
has died as he deserved, and yet his death
bears hard on you.

AGAVE

        O Father, now you can see
how all my life has changed.

. . . . . . . . . . . . . . . . . . *°

DIONYSUS *(Addressing Cadmus.)*

        You, Cadmus, shall be changed
to a serpent, and your wife, the child of Ares,

*At this point there is a break in the manuscript of at least fifty lines. The general outlines of the missing section can be reconstructed as follows: Agave, aware that she is now polluted, asks if she may nonetheless lay her son's corpse out so that she can say farewell to him and he can be buried. Cadmus agrees but warns her of its pitiful state. Leaning over the body, she voices piteous accusations against herself, embracing Pentheus' limbs one by one and mourning over them. Suddenly Dionysus appears above the palace, probably no longer in his human disguise but in his divine splendor, and addresses all those present: He accuses the Thebans, who had denied his divinity and rejected his gift of wine, and especially Pentheus for his many outrages against him. He then foretells the future of each survivor in turn: the descendants of Cadmus will someday be banished from Thebes; Agave and her sisters must immediately be exiled as murderers. Finally the god addresses Cadmus; it is at this point that the manuscript resumes. For the sources used by scholars to reconstruct the missing section, see the textual note on line 1329; see also the introduction to this play. Arrowsmith's own hypothetical version of the missing section is provided in the appendix.

immortal Harmonia, shall undergo your doom,
a serpent too. With her, it is your fate
to make a journey in a cart drawn on by oxen,
leading behind you a huge barbarian host.
For thus decrees the oracle of Zeus.
You shall ravage many cities; but when your army
plunders the shrine of Apollo, its homecoming
shall be wretched and hard. Yet in the end
the god Ares shall save Harmonia and you
and settle you both in the Land of the Blessed.
So say I, born of no mortal father,
Dionysus, true son of Zeus. If then,
when you would not, you had muzzled your madness
and been self-controlled, you'd all be happy now,
and would have the son of Zeus as your ally.

CADMUS°

We implore you, Dionysus. We have done wrong.

DIONYSUS

Too late. You did not know me when you should have.

CADMUS

We have learned. But you punish us too harshly.

DIONYSUS

I am a god. I was blasphemed by you.

CADMUS

Gods should be exempt from human passions.

DIONYSUS

Long ago my father Zeus ordained these things.

AGAVE

It is fated, Father. We must go.

DIONYSUS

Why then delay?
For you must go.

*(Exit Dionysus.)°*

CADMUS

Child, to what a dreadful end
have we all° come, poor you, your wretched sisters,
and my unhappy self. An old man, I must go
to live a stranger among barbarian peoples, doomed
to lead against Hellas a motley barbarian army.
Transformed to serpents, I and my wife,
Harmonia, the child of Ares, we must captain
spearmen against the tombs and shrines of Hellas.
Never shall my sufferings end; not even
in Hades shall I ever have peace.

AGAVE

O Father,
to be banished, to live without you!

CADMUS

Poor child,
like a swan embracing its hoary, worn-out father,
why do you clasp your arms about my neck?

AGAVE

But banished! Where shall I go?

CADMUS

I do not know,
my child. Your father can no longer help you.

AGAVE *[chanting]*

*Farewell, my home! City, farewell.*
*O bedchamber, banished I go,*
*in misery, I leave you now.*

CADMUS *[chanting henceforth]*

*Go, poor child, to the burial place°*
*of Aristaeus' son on Cithaeron.*

AGAVE *[chanting]*

*I pity you, Father.*

CADMUS

*And I pity you, my child,*
*and I grieve for your poor sisters. I pity them.*

AGAVE [*singing*]

*Terribly has Dionysus brought°*
*disaster down upon this house.*

CADMUS°

*He was terribly blasphemed by us,*
*his name dishonored in Thebes.*

AGAVE [*chanting henceforth*]

*Farewell, Father.*

CADMUS

*Farewell to you, unhappy child.*
*Fare well. But you shall find your faring hard.*

AGAVE

*Lead me, guides, to where my sisters wait,*
*poor sisters of my exile. Let me go*
*where I shall never see Cithaeron more,*
*where that accursed hill may not see me,°*
*where I shall find no trace of thyrsus!*
*All that I leave to other Bacchae.*

*(Exit Cadmus and Agave to the side with the bier and attendants.)*

CHORUS [*chanting*]

*The gods have many shapes.°*
*The gods bring many things*
*to accomplishment unhoped.*
*And what was most expected*
*has not been accomplished.*
*But god has found his way*
*for what no man expected.*
*So ends this story.*

# APPENDIX TO THE BACCHAE

This appendix provides Arrowsmith's hypothetical version of the section missing after line 1329.

AGAVE

I am in anguish now,
tormented, who walked in triumph minutes past,
exulting in my kill. And that prize I carried home
with such pride was my own curse. Upon these hands
I bear the curse of my son's blood. How then
with these accursed hands may I touch his body?
How can I, accursed with such a curse, hold him
to my breast? O gods, what dirge can I sing
[that there might be] a dirge [for every]
broken limb?

. . . . . . . . . . . . . . . . . . . . . . .

Where is a shroud to cover up his corpse?
O my child, what hands will give you proper care
unless with my own hands I lift my curse?

*(She lifts up one of Pentheus' limbs and asks the help of Cadmus in piecing the body together. She mourns each piece separately before replacing it on the bier.)*

Come, Father. We must restore his head
to this unhappy boy. As best we can, we shall make
him whole again.
—O dearest, dearest face!
Pretty boyish mouth! Now with this veil

I shroud your head, gathering with loving care
these mangled bloody limbs, this flesh I brought
to birth

. . . . . . . . . . . . . . . . . . . . .

CHORUS LEADER

Let this scene teach those [who see these things:
Dionysus is the son] of Zeus.

*(Above the palace Dionysus appears in epiphany.)*

DIONYSUS

[I am Dionysus,
the son of Zeus, returned to Thebes, revealed,
a god to men.] But the men [of Thebes] blasphemed me.
They slandered me; they said I came of mortal man,
and not content with speaking blasphemies,
[they dared to threaten my person with violence.]
These crimes this people whom I cherished well
did from malice to their benefactor. Therefore,
I now disclose the sufferings in store for them.
Like [enemies], they shall be driven from this city
to other lands; there, submitting to the yoke
of slavery, they shall wear out wretched lives,
captives of war, enduring much indignity.

*(He turns to the corpse of Pentheus.)*

This man has found the death which he deserved,
torn to pieces among the jagged rocks.
You are my witnesses: he came with outrage;
he attempted to chain my hands, abusing me
[and doing what he should least of all have done.]
And therefore he has rightly perished by the hands
of those who should the least of all have murdered him.
What he suffers, he suffers justly.
Upon you,
Agave, and on your sisters I pronounce this doom:

you shall leave this city in expiation
of the murder you have done. You are unclean,
and it would be a sacrilege that murderers
should remain at peace beside the graves [of those
whom they have killed].

*(He turns to Cadmus.)*

# TEXTUAL NOTES

*(Line numbers are in some cases only approximate.)*

## THE PERSIANS

13: Some words are missing, but the general sense is not in doubt.

93–114: The order of stanzas is uncertain: strophe and antistrophe C are written in the manuscripts as lines 102–13, but many modern editors transpose them here (to follow line 92) because of the sense.

237: The order of lines here is uncertain.

675–80: The text here is uncertain, but the general sense is not in doubt.

732: Text uncertain.

767: Some editors transpose this line to follow "brought peace to all he cared for," so as to refer to Cyrus.

859–60: Text uncertain.

922–1074: The rest of the play consists of a sustained lament (*thrênos*) sung antiphonally by Xerxes and the chorus. The language is heavily repetitive and includes many onomatopoeic exclamations of misery, here translated simply as "Oh" or "Ah." The words were obviously subsidiary to the music, choreography, and gestures. Furthermore, the text is not well preserved. In some cases the assignment of the sung phrases to Xerxes, to the chorus, or to both together is unclear or disputed. The translation in what follows should therefore be understood as being quite sketchy as a record of the scene's overall meaning and impact.

935: Text uncertain.

944–45: Text uncertain.

980: Text uncertain.

981–82: A name is missing here.

1008: Text very uncertain.

1072: Two lines appear to be missing here.

## PROMETHEUS BOUND

128: The text seems to indicate that the chorus enters flying, presumably either onto the roof of the stage building or by means of some kind of "machine" (*mêchanê*) that allows them to hover in the air. Modern scholars have disagreed whether or not to take these indications literally, and if so, where and how to envisage the staging of this unparalleled aerial entry of twelve or fifteen chorus members.

283: If the chorus were hovering in the air during the opening scene, they probably depart now, to reappear at ground level at 397. It is notable that they make no contact at all with Ocean (their father) in the scene that follows now, so they are probably not present.

354: Text uncertain.

397: Presumably the chorus reenters at this point into the orchestra, from the side. See note to line 283.

410: A word or two has dropped out here; "your fall" is a modern supplement.

430: A line may be missing here.

463: "Pack saddles" is an emendation accepted by most scholars for the manuscript reading "with their bodies."

541: Text uncertain.

543: Text uncertain.

558: The phrase "with your gifts" is deleted by many editors, for the meter.

760: Text uncertain. Some editors emend to read, "Since things are truly thus, you may rejoice."

792: Some editors read instead, "crossing the waves of the sea." The "waveless sea" means the dry steppes.

848: Some editors think a line has dropped out here, in which the impregnation of Io by Zeus is mentioned as well.

860: Text uncertain. Some editors think a line has dropped out here too.

880: Text uncertain.

895: There are several textual uncertainties in this stanza, but the general sense is not in doubt.

970: A line spoken by Prometheus seems to be missing before this one.

1079: How the ending was staged—whether or not the chorus departed before Prometheus' final words and whether and how Prometheus exited—is unclear.

## AGAMEMNON

70. Text uncertain.

84. Perhaps Clytaemestra has entered silently at this point: scholars disagree.

144. Text and interpretation uncertain.

216. Text uncertain: some editors emend to read, "it is right for them to yearn furiously for the maiden's blood."

256–57. It is unclear whether the chorus mean Clytaemestra, or themselves. When exactly Clytaemestra enters is uncertain. Some scholars think that she enters silently as early as line 84.

287. Perhaps one or more lines are missing at this point.

470. Text uncertain: possibly "crash on the towering mountains."

489–500. The manuscripts (and a few editors) assign these lines to Clytaemestra, not the chorus.

570–75. Some scholars suggest that these lines must be put into a different order and that several lines are missing here.

804. Text very uncertain; some words may be missing.

934. Text uncertain. Possibly, "I, if anyone, would have known and spoken this duty."

985. Text uncertain.

1001–7. Some words seem to be missing here, and the text is very uncertain.

1090–92. Text very uncertain.

1284. This line is transposed here (from its position between 1289 and 1290 in the manuscripts) by almost all modern editors.

1359. Text uncertain.

1447. Exact reading uncertain, but the reference to a "spicy side dish" is definite.

1474. The text is defective here.

1499. Exact text and interpretation are disputed.

1527. Exact text uncertain, but the general sense is clear.

1650–54. The assignment of speakers for each of these lines is disputed.

1657. Text uncertain.

1662. Text uncertain.

## THE LIBATION BEARERS

1–9. These lines are supplied from references in other Greek authors, including Aristophanes' *Frogs*, as separate quotations (1–3, 4–5a, 5b, 6–7, 8–9). The first page of the only existing manuscript of our play is missing, and it is unknown exactly how many lines have been lost or how many lines may intervene between these separate quotations.

92. The ordering of lines 92–99 is disputed. The translation here follows the order in the manuscript.

123. This line is transmitted by the manuscript as line 165 and is transposed here by modern scholars.

197. Text uncertain: possibly, "but I could know for sure to throw this strand . . ."

227–30. Scholars disagree on the proper sequence of these lines, and one line may be missing.

245. "Your" is an emendation; the manuscript reading is "be on my side"; some editors write "on our side." Some scholars assign lines 244–45 to Orestes rather than Electra.

255–263. Some editors assign these lines to Electra rather than Orestes.

285–90. The text of these lines is very uncertain.

314–509. In this long ritualized invocation of Agamemnon's spirit, the distribution of stanzas or individual verses between the chorus, Orestes, and Electra is not reliably recorded in the manuscript, and sometimes the correct assignment remains uncertain.

360. A possible alternative reading is, “you were king on earth when you lived.”

375–79. Reading and interpretation very uncertain; a phrase may have dropped out.

386. Text uncertain.

415–18. Reading and sense extremely uncertain.

482. Text very uncertain, and some syllables are missing in the manuscript. Different supplements have been proposed by various editors. Some scholars have restored the text to read, “to bring death on Aegisthus and find myself a husband.”

503–9. Distribution of speakers uncertain (see note on 314–509): some editors give 503–4 to Orestes, 505–7 to Electra, 508–9 to Orestes. Others delete 505–7 completely and assign 508–9 to Electra.

517. Reading uncertain.

534. Reading and sense very uncertain; some editors emend to read, “This vision would not be empty.”

628. Text uncertain.

727. Reading and sense very uncertain.

785–86. Text very uncertain.

803. Two or three words are missing in the manuscript at this point.

831–36. The precise reading is uncertain in several places here, but the general sense is not in doubt.

929. The manuscript seems to assign this line (“indeed, this terror . . . clearly”) to Orestes; some modern scholars prefer to attribute it to Clytaemestra.

## THE EUMENIDES

85–87. Some scholars transpose these lines to before line 64.

104–5. Most editors delete line 104 (“Eyes . . . brain”); some delete 105 as well.

188. The exact reading and translation are uncertain; but the general sense is not in doubt.

352. One line appears to be missing after this.

360–61. The text and meaning of these two lines are very uncertain.

381. Some editors adopt here the emendation, "For we alone" (*monai*), instead of the manuscript's "all holds" (*menei*).

404. After this line, the manuscripts contain a line that says, "after yoking this chariot of mine to speedy horses." Editors delete this as it contradicts the previous two lines. Presumably the line was inserted for an alternative mode of entry to the stage for Athena in a later production.

435. The precise reading here is uncertain.

491. The manuscripts here read "overthrow of new laws." Most editors have adopted some kind of emendation, since "new" appears to mean the opposite of what is required by the context. In the first edition, Lattimore translated as "overthrow of all the young laws."

565. Scholars disagree as to whether Athena appoints eleven or twelve human jurors. Since in the end her vote is counted along with theirs and the total of votes is then equal (711–53), it appears that they should be an odd number.

632–33. Some scholars have suggested that a line may be missing here.

775–77. Some scholars assign these lines to Apollo rather than to Orestes.

932. Text uncertain.

1027. Some lines may be missing here. Perhaps in them the Erinyes were called "Eumenides" (the name, which gives this play its title, does not occur anywhere in the extant text).

## ANTIGONE

5. Text uncertain.

45. Exact text and interpretation uncertain.

572–76. The assignment of speakers in lines 572, 574, and 576 varies among the manuscripts, early printed editions, and modern editors. Some assign 572 and 574 to Antigone; some assign all three lines (572, 574, 576) to Ismene.

602. Text uncertain: "knife" (*kopis*) is a modern emendation; the manuscripts have "dust" (*konis*).

606. The exact text and sense are uncertain.

781. Possibly Creon does not go inside now but remains onstage for the chorus's song, which would be unusual but not unprecedented in Greek tragedy.

782. Text and interpretation uncertain.

882. Possibly Creon has been present onstage throughout the lyric scene that preceded: see note on 781.

882–84. Text and precise meaning uncertain.

978. Exact text and interpretation not certain.

1080–83. Some editors delete these lines, in the belief that they were added (by someone other than Sophocles) so as to remind the audience of the story of the "Successors of the Seven" (*Epigoni*). Other editors retain the lines, but suggest that a few additional lines of explanation may have dropped out between 1080 and 1081.

1301. Text and interpretation uncertain; it appears that a line is missing here as well.

## OEDIPUS THE KING

81. Text uncertain: possibly "be happy like his eyes, and bring us safety."

198. Text uncertain.

246–51. Some editors reject these lines, regarding them as redundant after 236–43.

293. This emendation is widely accepted for the manuscript reading "No one sees who saw it."

420–21. The precise reading and interpretation are uncertain.

425. This is the reading of the manuscripts. Some editors emend the text to read, "other evils / annihilating you together with your children."

479. Or possibly "limping on his feet."

566. This is a widely accepted emendation of the manuscript reading, which has "search for the dead man."

600. This line is deleted by some scholars as an interpolation.

623–27. Two or three lines appear to have dropped out here, as the sequence of dialogue is unsatisfactory and the sense unclear.

641. The precise reading is uncertain here.

1205. The reading and interpretation here are quite uncertain, though the general sense is clear.

1280. The precise reading here is uncertain.

1316. Text and translation uncertain.

1349–50. Some editors adopt an emendation which gives, "Curse on the shepherd who . . ."

1522–30. Some editors have rejected all these final lines, arguing that they are not written in proper Sophoclean style.

## OEDIPUS AT COLONUS

3. More exactly, "this day."

8. More accurately, "nobility."

49–50. Or more literally, "By the gods, stranger, do not dishonor a wanderer such as I am, by refusing to tell me what I ask."

95. More exactly, "the bright flash of Zeus."

97. Or, "with trustworthy omens."

103. More exactly, "according to the sacred utterances of Apollo."

127–28. More literally, "into the inviolate grove of these dreadful Maidens," that is, the Furies.

164. Some editors emend to read "Let there be a greater distance from there."

171. More exactly, "Father, we should pay attention to the townsmen."

183. About four lyric lines appear to be missing before this, since the corresponding antistrophe has several more phrases than the strophe here.

212. More exactly, "My birth and nature are dreadful."

235–37. Or more exactly, "Depart quickly from my land, lest you bring some further trouble to my city!"

248. More literally, "Grant your unexpected approval!"

253. More accurately, "You will never see a mortal man who, if a god leads, can escape."

279–80. More exactly, "upon the mortal who is reverent, and upon the irreverent too."

287–90. More accurately, "I come here sacred and reverent, and I bring advantage to this race, as you may learn more fully when the man with authority comes, whoever is your leader."

325. Or "sweetest names to utter!"

327. Text uncertain: the manuscripts have "unfortunate," but the emendation "old and worn" is preferred by many editors.

371. More exactly, "some god" and "their own evil/sinful mind."

378. More exactly, "has gone to Argos . . . as an exile."

380–81. The text is uncertain here. Many editors adopt a simple emendation, so that instead of "Argos shall . . . win . . . ," Polynices is telling them that "he himself shall . . . win Thebes . . . or else go up to heaven."

406. More exactly, "Will they cover my body with Theban dust?"

450. More exactly, "They will never win me as their ally."

508–9. More literally, "For parents, not even if one labors should it be thought of as labor."

527–28. More exactly, "Was it with your mother, as I hear, that you shared your ill-famed bed?"

539–40. More literally, "I received a gift, which I wish I had never accepted, for having given help."

547. Text uncertain. Some editors emend to read "I was captured by doom; I killed . . ."

579. More accurately, "What profit do you claim to bring?"

587. More exactly, "The contest is no small one."

590. More accurately, "But if you wish that, it is not good for you to remain in exile."

606. More literally, "And how would my affairs and theirs become bitter?"

658–60. Many scholars have rejected these lines as a post-Sophoclean interpolation.

669–71. More exactly, "*you have come, guest, to Colonus . . . and you shall not seek another home.*"

685–87. More literally, "*the river's fountains are awake, Cephisus' nomadic streams that run unthinned forever, and never stay . . .*"

695–98. More precisely, "*And our land has a thing unknown in Asia's vast terrain or in the Dorian isle to our west where Pelops' race holds sway.*"

718–19. Or, a little more exactly, "*following the hundred-footed Nereids and their dance.*"

735–36. More exactly, "I, despite my age, am sent to persuade him to follow me back to Thebes."

756–57. Text uncertain.

848. Literally, "Oh wretched, wretched am I!"

861–62. In the manuscripts, both these lines are spoken by Creon, and the reading is "It will be done, unless the ruler of this land prevents me!" Several modern editors have emended the second line so as to read "you," as here, and have assigned this line to the chorus.

882. A few words in the chorus' reply seem to be missing here.

942. More literally, "my relatives."

945. The reading is uncertain. The text in the manuscripts seems to refer to "someone with whom children from an unholy marriage are living."

954–55. Some editors regard these two lines as an interpolation.

964–65. More exactly, "It was the gods' pleasure, and perhaps our family had angered them long ago."

975–76. More exactly, "and killed him, not knowing what I was doing, nor whom I was doing it to."

1007–8. More literally, "me, an old man and a suppliant . . ."

1033. Some editors transpose lines 1028–33 to follow 1019.

1043. More literally, "and may you benefit from your righteous concern for us!"

1044–95. Robert Fitzgerald's version of this choral song is composed as a sequence of rhyming stanzas and refrains, and it is somewhat freer as a translation of Sophocles' Greek than his rendering of the other choral songs of the play. A less poetic, but more exact, version of the first strophe and antistrophe might be the following:

STROPHE A

*Oh, to be where the enemies wheel about,*
*to hear the shout and brazen sound of war!*
*Or maybe on Apollo's sacred shore,*
*or by that torchlit Eleusinian plain*
*where pilgrims come, so that*
*the Great Ladies may provide solemn rites*
*for those mortals on whose tongues the golden key*
*of the sweet-voiced Ministers rests.*
*For even to those regions the warrior king Theseus*
*will press the fighting on—as he brings*
*help to the two maiden sisters,*
*self-sufficient in his battle-strength!*

ANTISTROPHE A

*Perhaps they are approaching now the plain*
*west of snowy mount Oea,*
*if they are fleeing on horses*
*or on swift-racing chariots;*
*yet they'll be taken: for fearsome is the spirit*
*of the local people, and fearsome Theseus's army;*
*the harnesses flash like mountain lightning.*
*These are the riders of Athens, conquered never;*
*they honor her whose glory all men know,*
*and honor Poseidon too, son of Rhea and god of the sea,*
*the one who holds the earth firm.*

1067–69. Text uncertain.

1080. More exactly, "I can prophesy a good outcome to this contest!"

1094–95. More exactly, "so that both of you come to lend your help to this land and its citizens."

1116. More accurately, "for girls so young."

1118. The precise text is uncertain here, but the general sense seems clear.

1158. More literally, "sitting as a suppliant at Poseidon's altar."

1166. More exactly, "would come here to make this supplication?"

1202–3. Or, more exactly, "and you, who are yourself being well treated, should know how to pay proper return for such treatment."

1210. More exactly, "you are safe, if one of the gods will keep my life safe too."

1268. More exactly, "of Zeus."

1278. More literally, "I am a suppliant of the god."

1300. This line is rejected by some editors as an interpolation.

1341. More literally, "scattering him."

1357. More exactly, "clad in these rags that now you are weeping about."

1370. More exactly, "And so it is that a god is watching you."

1373. Literally, "polluted by blood."

1382. More accurately, "of Zeus."

1410. More literally, "proper funeral rites."

1436. Some editors reject this line as an interpolation.

1463. More exactly, "Look there!"

1470. After this line, the manuscripts contain several more lines, which Robert Fitzgerald originally translated as follows:

CHORUS [*singing*]
*Ah, Zeus! Majestic heaven!*

OEDIPUS
My children, the appointed end has come;
I can no longer turn away from it.

ANTIGONE
How do you know? What is the sign that tells you?

OEDIPUS
I know it clearly now. Let someone quickly
send for the king and bring him here to me!

(*Thunder and lightning.*)

1477. In the manuscripts, this choral stanza begins, "*Ah, ah, see once more!*"

1482–84. Or more exactly:

*May I find you favorably disposed,*
*and though I have looked on an accursed man,*
*may I not be paid back to my loss!*

1498. More exactly, "*as just repayment to you and the city and his dear ones for what he has endured.*"

1511–13. The manuscripts here contain three lines which Robert Fitzgerald does not translate:

OEDIPUS

The gods themselves as heralds proclaim to me
with no deception; the signs are plain and true.

THESEUS

What do you mean? How are these things revealed?

1531–32. More literally:

then you must tell it
only to the foremost citizen, and he in turn
must teach it to his successor, and so forever.

1559–60. More literally, "*pray to you, Aidoneus, king of the regions of night.*"

1570. More exactly, "*the invincible beast Cerberus, growling at the gate of the all-welcoming hosts.*"

1615. More literally, "And yet one word dissolves all those hardships."

1640. The exact text is uncertain but the meaning is clear.

1661. More exactly, "But either some escort sent from the gods . . ."

1717. Some words have apparently dropped out here, since the antistrophe is two lines shorter than the corresponding strophe.

1746. More literally, "*A wide sea of troubles it is for you.*" This line is followed in the manuscripts by Antigone singing "Yes, yes" and the chorus "I agree too." Some scholars reject these phrases as an interpolation.

1751–53. The manuscripts attribute these lines to the Chorus Leader, but modern scholars assign them to Theseus.

1767. More exactly, "*and the god heard me, and so did Oath, the son of Zeus, who hears everything.*"

1779. More literally, "*Altogether, these things have their appointed end.*"

## ELECTRA

106: Another possible translation would be, "like the nightingale who has killed her child."

220: The text here is uncertain.

428–30: Some editors reject these lines as an interpolation.

451: Text and interpretation are uncertain: the manuscripts' reading means literally "nonshining."

691: An unmetrical and ungrammatical line in the manuscripts here, "the double-track race and pentathlon, as are customary," is omitted by modern editors.

720: After this the medieval manuscripts have three lines that many (but by no means all) modern editors transpose to follow line 740 instead: see the note on lines 741–43.

741–43: These three lines have been transposed here from 720–22 by several modern editors.

841–43: Text very uncertain.

1050–54: Some editors delete these lines, regarding them as interpolated.

1085–87: Text uncertain: perhaps "you have chosen a glorious life."

1264: One line is missing after this.

1283: Two or three words are missing here in the manuscripts, but the general sense is not in doubt.

1413: Text and interpretation uncertain.

1422–23: Modern editors mostly assign these lines to the chorus; the manuscripts assign them to Electra. "Blame" is also a modern conjecture, accepted by almost all editors, for the manuscripts' "speak."

1428: Two lines may be missing here, alternated between Electra and Orestes.

1458: This emendation is accepted by almost all editors, for the manuscripts' "I bid you be silent, and to reveal the doors."

1485–86: One manuscript omits these two lines, and some editors delete them.

1505–10: Some editors think these final lines have suffered damage in transmission, and that several more lines have also dropped out, leaving the ending incomplete.

## ALCESTIS

Characters: The list of characters prefixed to the play in the manuscripts identifies the boy's name as Eumelus, but there is nothing to support this in the play itself and it is probably just an ancient scholarly guess. In Homer's *Iliad* Eumelus is the son of Admetus and Alcestis.

16: Many scholars reject this line as an interpolation.

77: The manuscripts indicate that different members of the chorus chant or sing the various sections of the following entrance song; editors differ on the exact distribution.

93–94: Text uncertain.

207–8: These two lines are identical to *Hecuba* 411–12 and are probably an interpolation here.

211: Many editors divide the chorus here into groups and distribute the various sections of this song to different groups.

215: Text uncertain.

312: The manuscripts add here the line, "He can talk with him and be spoken to in turn." This is rejected by most scholars as an interpolation (cf. 195).

393: See note on Characters above.

411: About a line of text is missing here.

458: This line is rejected by some scholars; if it is retained, then a line must be missing before 469 (in the antistrophe).

469: See on line 458 (in the strophe).

603: The manuscripts are punctuated to read, "*All of wisdom is there in the noble. I stand in awe, and good hope . . .*" The translation reflects a modern repunctuation.

651–52: These two lines are almost identical to 295–96 and are rejected here by most scholars as an interpolation.

708: Some manuscripts read not "have spoken" but "am speaking."

795–96: The words "put flowers on your head" and "fight down these present troubles" are repeated in the Greek text in lines 829 and 832, and are probably an interpolation here.

818–19: These two lines are said by ancient commentators to have been missing in some manuscripts, and are rejected by most modern scholars.

## MEDEA

12: Text uncertain.

36: This line is rejected by some scholars as an interpolation.

40–43: Some or all of these lines are rejected by most scholars as interpolations.

87: This line is probably an interpolation.

223–24: These lines are rejected by some scholars as an interpolation.

246: This line is rejected by many scholars as an interpolation.

262: Rejected by many scholars as an interpolation.

304: This line is probably an interpolation.

355–56: Some scholars reject these lines as an interpolation.

357: This line is placed by some scholars after the following one and is rejected by other scholars as an interpolation.

468: This line is probably an interpolation.

626: Text uncertain.

725–29: The order of these lines is uncertain, and some or all of them are rejected by many scholars as an interpolation.

778–79: The first of these two lines, or both of them, are rejected by some scholars as an interpolation.

782: This line is probably an interpolation.

785: Probably an interpolation.

798–99: These lines are rejected by many scholars as an interpolation.

856–57: Text uncertain.

910: Text uncertain.

928: This line is rejected by some scholars as an interpolation.

949: Probably an interpolation.

1006–7: These lines are probably an interpolation.

1056–80: Some or all of these lines are rejected by some scholars as an interpolation.

1121: Rejected by most scholars as an interpolation.

1220–21: Some scholars reject the second of these two lines, or both of them, as an interpolation; in addition, the text of the second one is uncertain.

1233–35: These lines are rejected by most scholars as an interpolation.

1273–74: The order and location of these lines are uncertain.

1316: Rejected by some scholars as an interpolation.

1359: Rejected by some scholars as an interpolation.

1388: Rejected by some scholars as an interpolation.

1415–19: These lines are rejected by most scholars as an interpolation.

## HIPPOLYTUS

Characters: See textual note on line 1153.

101: An ancient papyrus reads not "before your gates, the goddess Cypris," but rather "before your gates, nearby."

103–8: The translation follows the order of these lines in the manuscripts; many editors have proposed various transpositions of them.

191–97: These lines are suspected by some scholars of being an interpolation.

601: Scholars disagree about the staging of the following scene and especially about exactly where Phaedra is during the following interchange between Hippolytus and the Nurse—they take no notice of her, but she evidently hears most or all of what they say.

626: Text uncertain. Some scholars excise lines 626–27 as an interpolation.

634–37: These lines are suspected by some scholars of being an interpolation.

663: This line is suspected by many scholars of being an interpolation.

668–79: Most medieval manuscripts assign the following short song (the antistrophe to the strophe in lines 361–72) to the Nurse, but most modern scholars prefer, as do a few manuscripts, to give it to Phaedra.

680–81: The manuscripts assign these lines to the Chorus Leader, but it is probably better to give them to the Nurse.

844: A few words are missing here.

867–68: In the manuscripts there follow two lines of which the text and meaning are quite uncertain.

871–73: The ancient commentators report that these lines were missing in some manuscripts; they are rejected by many modern scholars as an interpolation.

1050: Ancient commentators report that this line was missing in many manuscripts; it is rejected by most modern scholars as an interpolation.

1102–50: In this ode, the chorus refers to itself with the masculine gender in the first strophe and with the feminine in the first antistrophe. Scholars disagree about whom to assign the ode to: the chorus of women (to whom the manuscripts attribute it), Hippolytus' hunting companions, or both in alternation (as we have printed it here).

1123: Text uncertain.

1153: This messenger may be identical with the old servant who spoke with Hippolytus at lines 88–120.

1462–66: Some scholars suspect these final lines of being due to a later author.

## HECUBA

74–76: These lines are rejected as interpolations by many scholars; the text of the last one is uncertain.

90–97: Some or all of these lines are rejected as interpolations by many scholars.

145: This line is rejected as an interpolation by some scholars.

175–76: These lines are rejected as interpolations by many scholars.

206: Some words seem to be missing after this line.

211–15: These lines are rejected as interpolations by some scholars.

415–20: Different scholars have proposed various rearrangements of these lines.

555–56: These lines are rejected as interpolations by many scholars.

599–602: These lines are rejected as interpolations by many scholars.

793–97: These lines are rejected as interpolations by most scholars.

830: After this line the manuscripts transmit two lines, "From darkness and the delights of night comes the greatest pleasure for mortals" (831–32); these are rejected as interpolations by most scholars.

847: Text uncertain.

859: The manuscripts read "to you"; the translation reflects a widely accepted modern scholarly emendation.

953: This line is rejected as an interpolation by many scholars.

973–75: These lines are rejected as an interpolation by many scholars.

1041: Some manuscripts assign this line to Polymestor, some to the Chorus Leader, some to a half chorus; most modern scholars give it to Polymestor.

1086: After this line the manuscripts transmit a line: "Some divinity has given this who is heavy upon you" (1087); it is almost identical with line 723 and is rejected as an interpolation here by most scholars.

1184: After this line the manuscripts transmit two lines, "For there are many of us: some are odious, others have been born into the ranks of the evil " (1185–86); these are rejected as interpolations by most scholars.

## ELECTRA

1: Text uncertain.

131: The manuscript reads "are you a slave"; the translation reflects a plausible modern emendation.

143–44: The text of these lines is corrupt, but their meaning is clear.

161–62: The text of these lines is very uncertain.

277: The text is corrupt but the general meaning is clear.

311: Text and meaning uncertain.

373–79: These lines are rejected by many scholars as an interpolation.

386–90: These lines are rejected by many scholars as an interpolation.

413: This phrase seems corrupt but its general sense is not in doubt.

460: Text and meaning uncertain.

484: The manuscript is corrupt here; the translation reflects a plausible modern emendation.

538: Many scholars suggest that a line has been lost in the text after this verse.

546: Text uncertain, and many scholars suggest that another line is missing after this one.

582: A line has probably been lost after this verse.

631: The manuscript reads "and I have never seen them"; the translation reflects a plausible modern emendation.

651–52: Some scholars suggest that line 651 should be rejected as an interpolation, while others suggest that it be kept but that another line has been lost in the text after it.

671–84: The assignment of verses to the individual speakers in this passage is uncertain.

682–92: The sequence, authenticity, and meaning of these lines are very uncertain.

685–89: Many scholars reject these lines as an interpolation.

832: Or "some ambush comes from abroad."

894: The text and meaning of these words are uncertain.

921–37: Some scholars suspect some of these lines of being interpolated.

941–44: Some scholars suspect these lines of being interpolated.

962–65: The manuscript assigns line 962 to Electra, 963 to Orestes, 964 to Electra, and 965 to Orestes; the translation reflects the consensus of modern scholars.

965: Many scholars suggest that a line spoken by Orestes has been lost in the text after this verse.

983–84: Text very uncertain.

985–86: Some editors emend to "I am beginning to step forward, and evil I will do."

987: The Greek manuscript reads "bitter and sweet"; the translation reflects a widely accepted modern scholarly emendation.

996: The Greek verb can mean "serve, worship, flatter, cure medically"; all these meanings are pertinent here.

997: The last words of the chorus' anapests here are corrupt.

1059: The text is uncertain but its meaning is clear.

1097–1101: These lines are rejected by most scholars as an interpolation.

1107–8: Some scholars transpose these two lines to follow line 1131.

1153: After these words, the last two lines of this strophe are missing in the manuscript.

1173: Many scholars suggest that a line has been lost in the text after this verse.

1180–82: The first of these lines is corrupt and a couple of lines have been lost after it.

1185–86: The text of these lines is uncertain.

1209: The manuscript reads "and her hair!"; the translation reflects a widely accepted modern scholarly emendation.

1226: This line is assigned to the chorus in the manuscript, but most modern scholars give it instead to Electra.

1227–29: These lines are assigned to the chorus in the manuscript, but most modern scholars give them instead to Orestes.

1295–97: Some scholars transpose these lines to follow line 1302.

1357–59: Some scholars reject these lines as an interpolation.

## THE TROJAN WOMEN

13–14: These two lines are rejected by most scholars as an interpolation.

201: The manuscripts read "the bodies of my sons"; the translation reflects an emendation accepted by most scholars.

261: A word or two seem to be missing here.

383–85: Some or all of these lines are rejected as interpolations by many scholars.

434: After this line, one or more verses seem to be missing; line 435 gives the probable sense.

587–94: Scholars disagree on which of these lines to assign to Hecuba, which to Andromache.

604–5: A word or two seem to be missing from each of these two lines.

634–35: These two lines are rejected by most scholars as interpolations.

638: Text uncertain.

861: After this line, the manuscripts transmit two lines, "For I am Menelaus, I who indeed have toiled much, and the Greek army" (862–63); they are rejected by most scholars as an interpolation.

959–60: These two lines are rejected by some scholars as an interpolation.

961: After this verse many scholars suggest that one or more lines have been lost.

990: The beginning of the name "Aphrodite" sounds like various Greek words for folly or lust.

1090: Text uncertain.

1140: This line is rejected by many scholars as an interpolation.

1211: Text uncertain.

1217: Astyanax's name means etymologically "lord of the city."

1239: Text uncertain.

1240: Text uncertain.

1290: Text uncertain.

1299–1300: Text uncertain.

## IPHIGENIA AMONG THE TAURIANS

35–41: Text uncertain.

58: After this line the manuscript transmits two lines (59–60) that are rejected by most modern scholars as an interpolation: "Nor can I apply this dream to my dear ones: for Strophius did not have a son when I was being killed."

83: After this line the manuscript transmits one line (84): "which I suffered wandering throughout Greece." This line is similar to line 1455 and is deleted here by some scholars as an interpolation.

98–100: Text uncertain.

112: After this line the manuscript transmits one and a half lines (113–14) of which the text and translation are uncertain.

115: After this line the manuscript transmits two lines (116–17) which it assigns to Orestes: "We certainly did not come by ship on such a long voyage only to set out again from its limits for home." Scholars are divided whether to maintain that attribution, assign them to Pylades instead, transpose them elsewhere, or delete them.

123–25: Scholars disagree on whether to assign these first three verses to Iphigenia, to the chorus, or to both.

140: After this line the manuscript transmits one metrically defective line (141): "of the famous sons of Atreus." The correct text of these words is uncertain.

150: Text uncertain.

190–97: Text uncertain.

203: Two half-lines may be missing here.

212: After this line the manuscript transmits one line (213): "she bore, she raised, invoked by prayer." The text and meaning of this line are uncertain.

208: This line is transposed here by many scholars.

225: Text and translation uncertain.

258–59: Some scholars transpose these lines so that they come after line 245 or 335, in either case assigning them to the Herdsman.

288–90: Text uncertain.

293: After this line the manuscript transmits one line (294): "which they say the Erinyes emit as imitations." The text and meaning of this line are uncertain and many scholars reject it as an interpolation.

299: Rejected by some scholars as an interpolation.

316: After this line the manuscript transmits one line (317): "and the present disaster near to them." This line is rejected by some scholars as an interpolation.

331: The manuscript reads "stole"; the translation reflects a widely adopted modern emendation.

395: One or two words are probably missing here.

409: Text uncertain.

415: Text uncertain.

427: One word is probably missing here.

451–55: Text and translation uncertain.

515–16: These two lines are transmitted in the manuscript after line 514 and are transposed to after line 510 by many modern scholars.

571: After this line the manuscript transmits three lines (572–74): "There is much turmoil in divine affairs and in those of mortals. He feels grief in one regard only, when, although he is not stupid, he has been convinced by the words of seers and is destroyed as he is destroyed for those who know." The text and meaning of these lines is uncertain.

580: Text uncertain.

587: Text uncertain.

633: Text uncertain.

780–81: The assignment of the speakers for these lines is confused in the manuscript; the translation reflects a plausible modern scholarly correction.

798–99: These lines are assigned by the manuscript to the chorus, but most modern scholars give them to Iphigenia instead.

829: Text uncertain.

867: This line is transmitted after line 866 in the manuscript, where it is attributed to Orestes; it is transposed to after 865 and attributed to Iphigenia by modern scholars.

874: Text uncertain.

895–97: Text and translation uncertain.

907–8: Rejected by some scholars as an interpolation.

914: Text and translation uncertain.

930–36: The manuscript transmits the lines in the order indicated by the numbering; the order in which they are translated here reflects a transposition accepted by most modern scholars.

942–43: Text uncertain.

1050: This line is transmitted in the manuscript between lines 1049 and 1051 and is transposed to after line 1051 by modern scholars.

1052: This line is attributed in the manuscript to Orestes; some modern scholars assign it instead to Iphigenia.

1071: Rejected by some scholars as an interpolation.

1132–36: Text uncertain.

1143–52: Text uncertain.

1214: Iphigenia's words are missing in the manuscript.

1218: Text and translation uncertain.

1249: Text and translation uncertain.

1260: One word is probably missing in the manuscript here.

1309: Text uncertain.

1380: This word is missing in the manuscript and is supplied by modern scholars.

1469: Probably one or more lines are missing here.

1490–91: These lines are assigned to Athena by the manuscript; some scholars give them to the chorus, but it would probably be better to give them to Thoas instead. Lines 1490–96 are suspected by some scholars of being an interpolation.

1497–99: These lines are identical to *The Phoenician Women* lines 1764–66, *Orestes* 1691–93, and *Hippolytus* lines 1466a–c; most scholars reject them here as an interpolation.

## THE BACCHAE

72–82: Euripides' language here employs some traditional elements of ceremonial Greek "blessing" (*makarismos*), and William Arrowsmith's original translation of these lines used Christian language, especially from the Beatitudes in the (King James) Authorized Version of the New Testament, to convey something of the sacral fervor of the chorus:

—Blessèd, blessèd are those who know the mysteries of god.
—Blessèd is he who hallows his life in the worship of god,
  he whom the spirit of god possesseth, who is one
  with those who belong to the holy body of god.
—Blessèd are the dancers and those who are purified,
  who dance on the hill in the holy dance of god.
—Blessèd are they who keep the rite of Cybele the Mother.
—Blessèd are the thyrsus-bearers, those who wield in their hands
  the holy wand of god.
—Blessèd are those who wear the crown of the ivy of god.
—Blessèd, blessèd are they: Dionysus is their god!

151: The text of this line is uncertain.

182: This line is similar to line 860 and is rejected by some scholars as an interpolation here.

200: Some scholars assign this line to Cadmus. Possibly one line may have dropped out after it.

315: Text uncertain.

316: This line is identical to *Hippolytus* 80 and is rejected by many scholars here as an interpolation.

428–29: The text of these lines is uncertain, though their sense is clear.

506: The text of these words is suspect.

540: Before this line the manuscripts transmit the words "What fury, what fury!"; they are rejected by most modern scholars as an ungrammatical interpolation.

585: This word is missing in the manuscripts and is supplied by modern scholars.

606: The text of the last part of this line is uncertain.

631: This word is missing in the manuscripts and is supplied by modern scholars.

652: A line has almost certainly been lost in the manuscript, most likely containing Dionysus' reply to Pentheus' disparagement of the god in line 652; on this assumption, the words "The god himself will come to teach you wisdom" give one possible indication of what might have been lost. But some scholars instead assign line 652 to Dionysus and suggest that the line that has been lost was the previous one, containing Pentheus' retort in response to Dionysus' praise of the god in line 651.

673: This line is similar to one transmitted as part of a quotation from a lost play of Euripides and is rejected here by some scholars as an interpolation.

716: This line is similar to line 667 and is rejected here by many scholars as an interpolation.

757: This sentence seems out of place here and is transposed by many scholars, with some changes, to follow after line 761.

842: Two half lines seem to have been lost here.

877: Text and meaning of this line are uncertain.

896: Text and meaning of this line are uncertain.

973–76: Either Pentheus exits before these lines and does not hear them; or else he is still on stage but is so dazed that he does not seem to hear or understand them. Given that Dionysus leads him throughout this whole episode, the latter alternative seems likelier.

996–1010: Arrowsmith's original translation of this antistrophe elaborates freely upon the themes suggested by the very uncertain and difficult Greek text:

—Uncontrollable, the unbeliever goes,
in spitting rage, rebellious and amok,
madly assaulting the mysteries of god,
profaning the rites of the mother of god.
Against the unassailable he runs, with rage
obsessed. Headlong he runs to death.
For death the gods exact, curbing by that bit
the mouths of men. They humble us with death
that we remember what we are who are not god,
but men. We run to death. Wherefore, I say,
accept, accept:
humility is wise; humility is blest.
But what the world calls wise I do not want.
Elsewhere the chase. I hunt another game,
those great, those manifest, those certain goals,
achieving which, our mortal lives are blest
Let these things be the quarry of my chase:
purity; humility; an unrebellious soul,
accepting all. Let me go the customary way,
the timeless, honored, beaten path of those who walk
with reverence and awe beneath the sons of heaven.

1002–7: The meter and meaning of these lines are very uncertain.

1025–26: These lines are rejected by some scholars as an interpolation.

1028: This line is similar to *Medea* 54 and is rejected by many scholars here as an interpolation.

1036: The rest of this line and probably one more following line are missing in the manuscript.

1060: The translation reflects the text of the manuscript; many editors accept a modern scholarly emendation that yields the sense, "I cannot see their frantic illnesses."

1090: After this line the medieval manuscript has two lines that are missing in an ancient papyrus and that are rejected by modern scholars: "running with intense runnings of the feet, mother Agave and her kindred sisters."

1158: The text of these last words is uncertain.

1174: Most of a line is missing here.

1221: After this line the manuscript transmits a line that has been omitted here: "having picked them up where they were lying in a forest difficult to search."

1244–45: One or both of these lines are rejected by many scholars as an interpolation.

1301: At least one line containing Cadmus' reply to Agave, and probably rather more, has been lost here.

1329: Scholars use the following sources to reconstruct the missing section of the play: (1) one of the hypotheses (ancient scholarly summaries) of the play, according to which "Dionysus appeared and then addressed all of them and revealed to each one what would happen to him or her" (there follow some corrupt words); (2) Apsines, a third-century CE rhetorician, who writes, "In Euripides, Pentheus' mother Agave is freed from her madness and recognizes her son who has been torn apart; then she accuses herself and arouses pity. . . . Euripides deploys this rhetorical device because he wishes to arouse commiseration for Pentheus: the mother takes up each of his limbs in her hands and laments each one in turn"; (3) *Christus Patiens* (*The Passion of Christ*), an anonymous Byzantine cento (a poetic text consisting entirely of citations from famous works by earlier poets) which is probably to be dated to the twelfth century, and containing a number of lines that have been attributed with more or less probability to this play (especially lines 1011, 1120–23, 1256–57, 1312–13, 1449, and 1466–72 for Agave's speech; and 300, 1360–62, 1639–40, 1663–1679, 1690, and 1756 for Dionysus'); (4) a line quoted from the scholia (ancient commentary) on line 907 of Aristophanes' *Wealth* as coming from this play; and (5) a few very scrappy papyrus fragments.

1344, 1346, 1348: Some scholars assign these lines to Agave.

1351: It is not certain, but most likely, that Dionysus exits at this point. But see note on lines 1377–78.

1353: This word is missing in the manuscript and has been restored by modern scholars.

1372: After this line a line is missing containing the rest of Cadmus' reply to Agave; the words "burial place . . . son on Cithaeron" give one possible indication of what has been lost.

1374–76: Text uncertain.

1377–78: The manuscript assigns these lines to Dionysus (who in that case did not exit after line 1351) and reads, "I was terribly blasphemed by you, / my name dishonored in Thebes"; the translation reflects a widely accepted modern scholarly emendation.

1385: Text uncertain.

1388–92: These lines are rejected by many scholars as non-Euripidean.